OCEANS ODYSSEY 2

This book is dedicated to the parents of all the Odyssey team members who have provided so much support during the course of our mission to bring the great secrets of the deep ocean to the light of day.

In particular, the editors would like to recognize Bob and Norma Stemm and Madeleine and Andrew Kingsley, who taught us to follow our dreams – no matter where they lead.

OCEANS ODYSSEY 2

Underwater Heritage Management & Deep-Sea Shipwrecks in the English Channel & Atlantic Ocean

Edited by
Greg Stemm & Sean Kingsley

Odyssey Marine Exploration
Reports 2

Oxbow Books
Oxford and Oakville

Published by
Oxbow Books, Oxford, UK

ISBN 978-1-84217-442-5

This book is available direct from:

Oxbow Books, Oxford, UK
(Phone: 01865-241249; Fax: 01865-794449)

and

The David Brown Book Company
PO Box 511, Oakville, CT 06779, USA
(Phone: 860-945-9329; Fax: 860-945-9468)

or from our website

www.oxbowbooks.com

A CIP record for this book is available from the British library

Library of Congress Cataloging-in-Publication Data

Oceans Odyssey 2 : underwater heritage management & deep-sea shipwrecks in the English Channel & Atlantic Ocean / edited by Greg Stemm & Sean Kingsley.
p. cm. -- (Odyssey marine exploration reports ; 2)
Includes bibliographical references and index.
ISBN 978-1-84217-442-5 (hbk. : alk. paper)
1. Underwater archaeology--English Channel. 2. Underwater archaeology--Atlantic Ocean. 3. Shipwrecks--English Channel. 4. Shipwrecks--Atlantic Ocean. 5. Historic preservation--English Channel. 6. Historic preservation--Atlantic Ocean. 7. English Channel--Antiquities. 8. Atlantic Ocean--Antiquities. I. Stemm, Greg. II. Kingsley, Sean A.
CC77.U5O23 2011
930.1028'04--dc22
2011010640

Printed and bound in
Wales by Gomer Press

Contents

Preface

For thousands of years the salvage of lost property from the sea was considered a noble and beneficial service to society. It was seen as such an important endeavor that salvage law, one of the oldest recorded legal regimes, evolved to reward salvors promptly for the services they provided. A significant reward for the swift return of valuables and property to the stream of commerce was meant to encourage entrepreneurs and seamen to risk their own lives, money, ships and resources to return materials to where they would be most useful – on land.

Society's almost universal endorsement and appreciation for the purely economic benefit of this service ran unchallenged until the dawn of underwater archaeology in the 1960s. At that time, a handful of archaeological and shipwreck exploration pioneers – George Bass, Peter Throckmorton, Margaret Rule and Mendel Peterson, among others – began to promote the idea that underwater sites contained a trove of archaeological information waiting to be unlocked.

In the early heady days of the aqualung, other undersea pioneers like Jacques Cousteau, Kip Wagner, Mel Fisher, Henri Delauze, Teddy Tucker and Robert Marx went in another direction, focusing less on archaeology than on the amazing treasures that could be found and returned to the public eye. During the 1970s and 1980s, the pendulum swung – and swung hard. Archaeologists began to successfully promote the concept that many archaeological sites were in danger from the depredations of treasure hunters, who they claimed did not use proper archaeological protocols, did not record and conserve their finds properly and did not publish their data.

The lines were drawn. On the one side stood the treasure hunters, who were primarily concerned with the treasures from wrecks and to some degree the stories they told, especially where the tales enhanced the value and interest in the treasure. On the other were the archaeologists, who focused on the knowledge that could be gleaned from sites and adherence to newly evolving archaeological protocols.

In the early days of the debate the relationship between the camps was relatively cordial and had not yet fallen prey to the prejudices and dogma that characterize the issue today. Battles over public funding, allocation of economic value and academic jealousies have created an ugly turf war over shipwrecks. A collegial sharing of knowledge was abandoned in favor of attempts to discredit the other camp. The most obvious victim of this evolution was cooperation in developing a knowledge base from shipwrecks.

It is hard to believe today that in the early days of the Council on Underwater Archaeology (CUA) you could find Peter Throckmorton, Pilar Luna, Robert Marx and George Bass all sharing bottles of wine and swapping stories about shipwrecks. The early pioneers co-authored sections of UNESCO's *Underwater Archaeology: A Nascent Discipline* (Paris, 1972). That bonhomie has long since disappeared, replaced by suspicion and jealousy. Today, the battle lines are so clearly drawn that you would never encounter the different camps in a room together – unless it was a courtroom.

As the field became more politicized, government agencies saw an opportunity to step in and take control of the resource. Unfortunately, dogma based on unsubstantiated theory – not grounded in evidence – was promoted as fact in the development of protocols for management of underwater cultural heritage resources. As a result, many discussions in policy circles and government agencies now seem to focus on myths and convenient half-truths. These include:

- The myth of *in situ* preservation.
- The misperception that for-profit companies are incapable of high-quality scientific work.
- The mistaken belief that academics always adhere to archaeological protocols and publish their work.
- The misconception that treasure hunters are the greatest danger to shipwrecks.
- The false perception that shipwrecks are gravesites.

Truth, it is said, is the first casualty of war and when war broke out over underwater cultural heritage the adage was once again proven correct.

I was lucky enough to enter this field in the 1980s, when all the varied camps were still talking. At my first Society for Historical Archaeology (SHA) conference in 1988, I met treasure hunters like Robert Marx and archaeologists George Bass and John Broadwater, while the CUA film festival that year featured videos from both camps. In 1991, we presented the results of our archaeological work conducted solely using robotics on the deep-sea Tortugas shipwreck to the backdrop of a standing-room only crowd.

In those days, when the archaeologists, treasure hunters and deep-ocean technicians were all communicating, it felt like we were all on the verge of entering an exciting new era of underwater exploration. I was a young entrepreneur who had been passionate about history and shipwrecks since my youth and naturally saw an opportunity to combine all these interests and skills. At the time, I felt welcome at the SHA conference and many of the archaeologists I met there were thrilled that we were bringing advanced technology to the table. The fact that we were a for-profit company seemed less important than the access to a new world of shipwrecks to study.

Today, in contrast, the annual SHA conference engages in the deliberate censorship of academic presentations by any archaeologist who has ever worked with a for-profit shipwreck company. This new insular world ignores any data that does not come from its own fold. As a result, the attendees remain uninformed about some cutting-edge advances in technology that are being refined for deep-sea archaeology and they lose out on a world of new information about shipwrecks that is opening up through the efforts of companies like Odyssey.

When ICOMOS first started formulating an international convention for the protection of underwater cultural heritage in the early 1990s, it was George Bass, founder of the Institute of Nautical Archaeology, who first advised me to pay attention to pending moves to bureaucratize underwater cultural heritage. Dr. Bass also invited me twice to Texas A&M University to give guest lectures to both INA undergraduate and graduate students on our advances in deep-ocean technology for archaeology.

Then something changed. During the mid-1990s, the protection of shipwrecks and underwater cultural heritage began to take on the aura of a religious crusade. As with any crusade, reasonable dialogue between dissenting views ground to a halt. The new initiative to underwater archaeology moved to UNESCO, where it morphed into what is today the UNESCO Convention on the Protection of Underwater Cultural Heritage 2001. I was appointed to the US delegation for the negotiation of the Convention and so had a front row seat during the years of negotiations in Paris. As the process advanced, it was somewhat disconcerting to see what started out as a relatively straightforward Code of Ethics for underwater archaeology evolve into a politicized set of regulations, promoted and drafted for the most part by desk-bound cultural heritage managers and lawyers.

Of approximately 300 people involved in the UNESCO negotiations, I do not think I met more than a dozen people with extensive underwater archaeology experience. The opinions of explorers and archaeologists who had substantial fieldwork experience were marginalized in favor of the creation of a regime that would serve to enlarge bureaucracies and gobble up budgets for the oversight and regulation of shipwrecks, rather than fieldwork and exploration. The consequence of this new direction was clear: it would serve to significantly curtail archaeological fieldwork and demonize private sector shipwreck exploration.

During the second year of negotiations, I asked UNESCO whether I could give a presentation to the entire assembly to share the archaeological work that we were conducting as a for-profit company. To the credit of Lyndel Prott, who chaired the sessions on behalf of UNESCO, and thanks to the late Robert Blumberg who was the leader of the US delegation, I was given the stage for an evening presentation.

I began my presentation by posing a single question on a slide: How Many Shipwrecks Are There In the World?

In order to manage any resource, one first needs to quantify and characterize the resource. Trying to develop a management plan without that data is like trying to develop a plan to manage a forest when you do not know whether it contains 1,000 or 1,000,000 trees. I asked the assembled experts if anyone in the audience had any idea how many shipwrecks existed in the world. No one answered.

In preparation for the presentation I had examined all the literature I could find on the subject and, surprisingly, I failed to locate a single estimate for the number of shipwrecks in the world cited by any author or in any reference book. Based on studies for various areas of the world, where tens of thousands of shipwrecks were reported within relatively narrow time spans and limited geographical zones, I proposed a theory to the assembled group. I asked whether anyone in the hall imagined that less than an average of 1,000 shipwrecks per year had occurred during the past 3,000 years that man had been exploiting the oceans, rivers and lakes of the world for transportation – and no one disagreed. I also commented that I could easily imagine the number being five times that amount, but my goal that night was to develop a baseline that all the assembled experts could agree upon.

I then drew a big circle on the lecture hall board and wrote above it '1,000 shipwrecks x 3,000 years = 3,000,000 shipwrecks'. Once again, I polled the audience and did not find any single person among the hundreds of assembled experts who disagreed with that figure as a baseline. On the next slide, I listed 'Stakeholders'. As with any resource, in order to devise a management plan you must decide on the stakeholders in the resource.

On my list I wrote:

Fishing: including those that utilize the resource unintentionally (collateral damage to sites by trawlers, etc.) and intentionally (shipwrecks create artificial reefs and structures that attract fish, which are caught either by line, nets or spearfishing).

Tourism and Recreation: including sites that are visited by scuba divers, viewed though glass-bottom boats and subs or are used in conjunction with tourist attractions and/or exhibits.

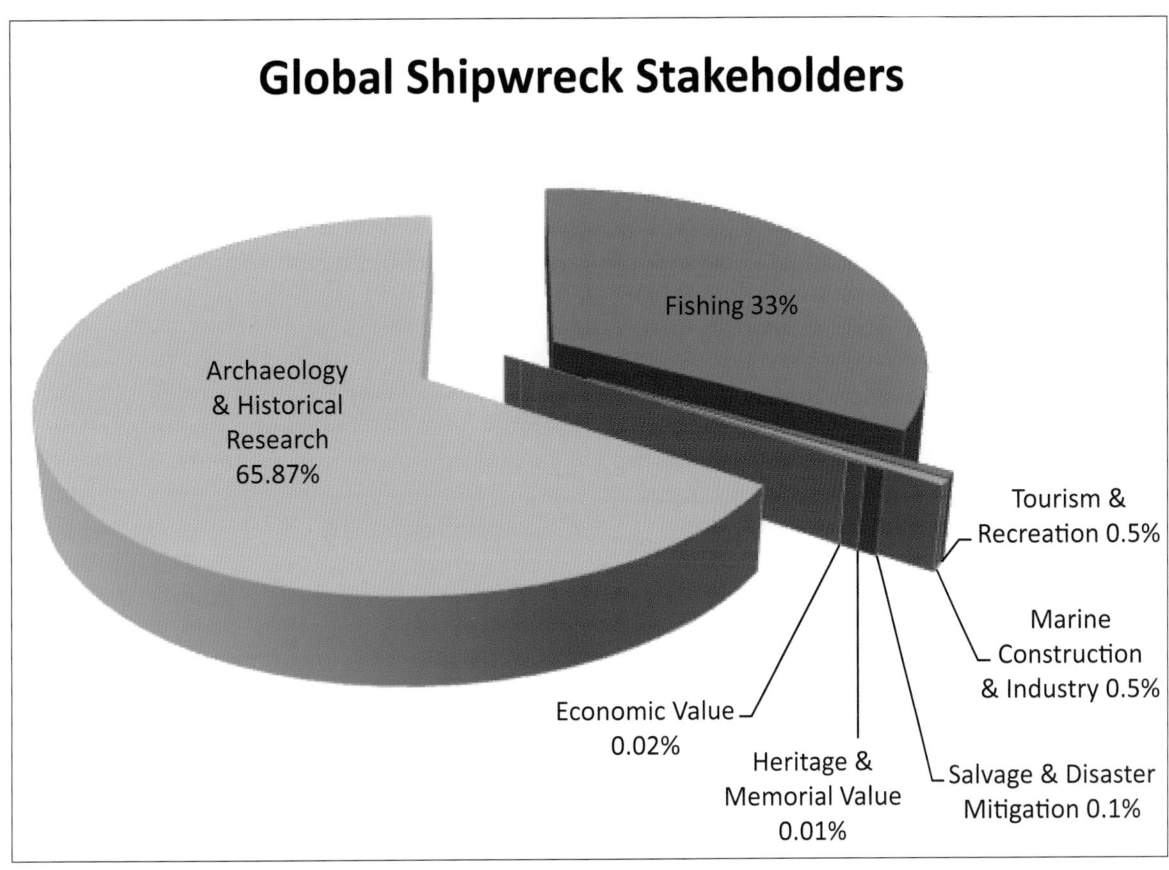

Fig. 1. Global stakeholders among the estimated total 3 million shipwrecks worldwide.

Marine Construction and Industry: dredging, aggregates, fiber-optic cable and pipelines, windfarms, etc. This category includes industrial activities that may require the removal of shipwrecks or inadvertently damage sites in the course of operations.

Salvage and Disaster Mitigation: shipwrecks that are intentionally recovered or destroyed because of the risks they pose as natural obstacles or pollutants.

Heritage and Memorial Value: sites that are set aside to commemorate specific disasters or the loss of a shipwreck of great communal heritage value.

Economic Value: shipwrecks that contain cargos or artifacts that warrant recovery based on economic merit and yield significant monetary value above and beyond the cost of their recovery.

Archaeology and Historical Research: shipwrecks that are excavated or studied for the knowledge that can be gained from their archaeological contexts.

After delineating all of these user groups and stakeholders, I proceeded to draw a large pie chart of the size of these groups to provide a basis for discussion. While this was intended to be a very rough estimate, I did not receive any argument from the audience relating to my assumptions. My percentages and logic for applying these values were as follows (Fig. 1):

1. Fishing: based on the fact that the vast majority of shipwrecks lie within coastal waters and that many of the sites that are not completely buried show signs of disturbance by fishing or are exploited by fishermen, I granted this user group a large percentage of the resource that could be affected: 33% (990,000 wrecks).

2. Tourism and Recreation: many shipwrecks in coastal waters accessible to dive boats are either dived regularly or at least occasionally. Substantial overlap would exist

between this category of user and fisheries' exploitation, so I incrementally added only 0.5% to this category for sites that would be targeted specifically by this group above and beyond those affected by fishermen. While this still accounts for 15,000 shipwrecks, I believe this is a reasonable number considering that over a million divers are active in the US alone: 0.5%

3. Marine Construction and Industry: the impact on shipwrecks is difficult to predict because most sites damaged by dredging and marine construction may go unnoticed and, especially if constructed of wood, may simply be destroyed during the dredging of channels, aggregate mining or marine construction. Due to the amount of construction taking place throughout the world, I suggested that 15,000 shipwrecks will also be affected in this manner: 0.5%

4. Salvage and Disaster Mitigation: an impact source for a statistically insignificant number of shipwrecks to date, but a category that is likely to become a major issue in the future. Many 20th-century wrecks lost during the world wars and in other accidents still contain either dangerous pollutants, chemicals or live munitions. As access to the deep ocean gets easier and many of these steel wrecks deteriorate, these materials will become a serious problem and salvage activities will be demanded to mitigate the potential pollution and dangers they pose. This number could equal 3,000 shipwrecks or more worldwide: 0.1%

5. Heritage and Memorial Value: ships associated with historical events, battles or disasters hold a special place in our culture as memorials. The obvious examples of these types of vessels include the *Titanic*, the USS *Arizona* and the *Edmund Fitzgerald*. These ships are part of a category that through public pressure will be left alone or remain *in situ*, although with recent revelations about the rapid deterioration of the *Titanic* the idea of memorials *in situ* may change. This number could equal 300 ships: 0.01%

6. Economic Value: this class of shipwrecks is the most controversial and widely recognized of all categories but, ironically, represents a tiny minority of the resource. While there are myriad tales of shipwrecks laden with 'treasure', the reality is that many of these are legends or undocumented accounts. The numbers of shipwrecks that can be documented as having sunk with cargos sufficiently valuable to justify their recovery on purely economic criteria are surprisingly small. Most valuable shipwrecks in shallow waters, where access is easy, have already been discovered or were salvaged at the time of their loss. Those that lie in deep water require the investment of millions of dollars of capital and advanced equipment for recovery and archaeological excavation. Odyssey has one of the most extensive libraries of shipwrecks in the world, and there is only a number in the hundreds of shipwrecks that actually meet our criteria to justify the investment and expenditure for recovery and/or archaeological excavation in terms of the gold, silver or other valuables that can be recovered to counterbalance the enormous expense of the science and proper recovery techniques. I estimated that 600 ships worldwide might fit these criteria: 0.02%

7. Archaeology and Historical Research: basically, once all other categories have been taken into account, this user group has access to all remaining shipwrecks or those not destroyed by one of the other stakeholders without proper excavation techniques. In the case of destruction by fisheries or marine construction – or those that are kept off limits for investigation as memorials or dive sites – the stakeholders' interests are often mutually exclusive. Ironically, despite the attacks on stakeholders interested in shipwrecks of economic value, virtually every piece of information that can be gleaned from a site archaeologically can still be obtained in cooperation with an economic user group member: 65.87% (1,976,100 wrecks).

After laying out my case for recognizing these stakeholders and user groups to the assembled crowd, I presented them with a series of slides demonstrating how Odyssey conducts deep-sea archaeology using robotics. I explained that in the course of an excavation we were able to save as much data as the 'Archaeology and Historical Research' group was able to extract from a site during their own archaeological excavations.

At the end of my presentation, I posed the following final question. Taking all this information into consideration, why were so many members assembled at the UNESCO event obsessed with a tiny user group of the resource and the sole partner that possesses the potential to save the most archaeological and historical information from shipwrecks? Based on the eventual outcome of the negotiations and the final draft of the UNESCO Convention on the Protection of Underwater Cultural Heritage 2001, it would seem that few people in the crowd followed my logic that day.

Yet interestingly enough, in a press release distributed by UNESCO at the end of the session, UNESCO 'borrowed' my 3,000,000 figure as the number of estimated shipwrecks worldwide. That number is often referenced and cited today and has become a stock basis for many estimates and debates set forth in the world of cultural heritage management. While it is interesting that my hypothesis has now become 'fact', it is also a reflection of the process that governments follow in developing models used to manage resources and of the wider willingness to jump to conclusions about the role of the 'Economic Value' stakeholders in shipwreck studies.

This second volume of scientific and archaeological papers related to our projects, *Oceans Odyssey 2*, is presented with pleasure as further and ongoing proof that there really is a place for commercial archaeology out there and that profit and sustainable science can go hand in hand in underwater archaeology – as it does in virtually every other field in the world.

Greg Stemm
Co-Founder & CEO
Odyssey Marine Exploration
Tampa, April 2011

Introduction

Oceans Odyssey 2 continues the core objective of Odyssey Marine Exploration to make its work accessible as widely as possible in a comprehensive and timely manner. This philosophy is all the more important in the field of deep-sea shipwreck archaeology, where sites are inaccessible to most of the world's marine scientists, let alone the general public. Today's egalitarian ideal of public outreach in marine archaeology, promoted through the transformation of some sites into underwater parks where divers should "take only photos and leave only bubbles", is currently a utopian dream in deep waters well beyond the reach of SCUBA divers. The Odyssey Marine Exploration Report series is making progress in converting previously unreachable depths into an accessible past.

This volume combines the publication of primary archaeological data with thematic studies. The documentation of sites using Remotely-Operated Vehicles as the eyes and hands of the archaeologist working beyond depths accessible to divers triggers great debate and strong feelings about commercial organizations' use of archaeologists, sophisticated technology, legal frameworks and, of course, the expense of operations and financial sustainability of working in deep-sea environments.

'Underwater Cultural Heritage & UNESCO in New Orleans' (Chapter 1) expands on a series of conference papers and round-table discussions presented on 11 February at Underwater Intervention 2010. Its eight contributions by a variety of interested parties – archaeologists, university professors, lawyers and businessmen involved in commercial archaeology – reflect divided opinions about the ethics of commercial archaeology, but also a common concern about the apparent 'one size fits all' interpretation by some heritage bodies of the UNESCO Convention on the Protection of the Underwater Cultural Heritage (2001).

The practical problem of how to fund the extreme costs of studying shipwrecks and submerged settlements in deep waters worldwide is developed further by Greg Stemm and David Bederman (Chapter 2), who propose the creation of a private curatorship scheme. Their model provides a possible financial solution for dealing with the crippling costs of archiving and storing archaeological collections 'in perpetuity'. Despite the strong reactions that commercial archaeology generates, it is becoming increasingly clear that an 'out of sight, out of mind' mentality is inappropriate, myopic and unsustainable. With ever-increasing access to data has come the inescapable realization that deep-sea wrecks are at risk from natural deterioration, as well as from marine industries and offshore fishing impacts.

Stephen Johnston's analysis of the wooden carpenter's rule from Site 35F (Chapter 3), a wreck of *c.* 1660-90 in the Western Approaches associated with a cargo of elephant tusks and copper *manilla* bracelets, demonstrates the quality of artifacts that have generally been destroyed by fishing impacts in Odyssey's 'Atlas' shipwreck survey area. The site has been heavily damaged by scallop dredges, amongst other forms of bottom gear. The survival of one of this rule's arms (the other has been lost to the ravages of the deep) was an act of extreme good fortune rather than environmental preservative conditions. This form of English timber and board measure, bearing logarithmic lines of numbers on its edges, is seemingly the earliest example discovered on any shipwreck.

While the question of the management of the wreck of the First Rate Royal Navy HMS *Victory* (1744) awaits a political decision, Odyssey is maintaining its commitment to understanding the ship, its life, crew, loss and wreckage, exemplified here through two studies of the warship's guns and the conservation of the 12-pounder and 42-pounder recovered from the site in 2008 (Chapters 4-5). Charles Trollope presents a compelling picture of the cannon's historical and archaeological rarity, dissecting the complex pattern of how this unique collection came to be cast at the Royal Brass Foundry, Woolwich, by Andrew Schalch to the design of Surveyor General Colonel John Armstrong, which included an early example of 'borrowing' French naval artillery blueprints. In this regard, Balchin's *Victory* reveals itself to have been a trail blazer for naval architects' subsequent chasing of Gallic inspiration in the Georgian generation following the loss of England's greatest warship from the age of sail – the only archaeologically recorded First Rate of that period known worldwide.

Oceans Odyssey 2 also presents the final publication of Odyssey's survey and excavation of Site 33c, the wreck of an armed privateer discovered in 2008 at a depth of around 80m in the western English Channel. Identified through its bronze bell as the Bordeaux-based *La Marquise de Tourny*, a corsair that both traded and fought in local waters and as far as French Quebec during the War of the Austrian Succession and beyond (1744 to the late 1740s/early 1750s), the remains of the wreck are a sad sight. Its ceramic, glass and domestic assemblages are no longer preserved and only the most durable of artifacts were identified: almost exclusively concreted iron ballast ingots and iron cannon. This pattern of very poor preservation unfortunately seems to be typical for the English Channel environment and is apparently related to extensive beam trawler traffic in the area. The privateer ship owes what survives to its durable and heavy ordnance and ballast, and so provides a clear image of the even more ignoble fate of other ships lost in this region. Very little of a hull that lacks comparable overlying heavy and durable assemblages is likely to survive to denote the site of a lost vessel in these heavily fished waters.

Nevertheless, Neil Cunningham Dobson and the Odyssey team have reconstructed in detail the archaeology and history of the life and times of *La Marquise de Tourny* (Chapter 6) from badly preserved artifacts (glass fragments and lead hull sheathing) to the bell and a study of the ship's cannon, including one iron swivel gun recovered by Odyssey. The presence of extensive iron ingot ballast defining the site's surface, in conjunction with an absence of other sets of material culture obviously identifiable as cargo, suggests that *La Marquise de Tourny* was possibly transporting an organic cargo (now deteriorated) locally between Bordeaux and the French ports along the eastern Channel when she foundered. This profile is complemented by a detailed study of the rationale underlying the art of privateering during the War of the Austrian Succession (Chapter 7), which demonstrates the archaeological significance and value of Site 33c as only the fourth privateer wreck of this period scientifically excavated and published and the only one located off the UK.

A glazed pot snagged in a shrimp fisherman's trawl net led to Odyssey's discovery in 2003 of a fascinating shipwreck located at a depth of 370m, 70 nautical miles off Jacksonville, Florida, in the Atlantic Ocean. A return visit to Site BA02 in 2005 revealed that extensive impacts from trawling had damaged the wreck and substantially transformed its formation in the interim two years. The resultant rescue project and post-excavation research (Chapters 8-11) identified the 23 x 12m wreckage as associated with a small East Coast schooner lost in the mid-19th century.

Analysis of the 1,025 ceramic wares, clay tobacco pipes and glass products visible on the surface of the site, and the representative sample recovered, revealed that Site BA02 was transporting a primary cargo of British ceramics, largely manufactured in Staffordshire, alongside American spirits, mineral water, condiments, colognes and medicinal products packaged in glass bottles. Various building materials were also discovered, including glass window panes and white lead in wooden kegs, in addition to various kegs apparently holding tobacco pipes, lead musket balls and possibly leather shoes.

Artifacts and historical analysis point to a best-fit scenario for the Jacksonville 'Blue China' schooner as New York based, while recorded storm models indicate that the great hurricane of 7-9 September 1854 (an infamous black year for East Coast maritime insurance agents) was a possible cause of the ship's loss. As the only example of a New York schooner associated with its cargo – a class of vessel that was the 'workhorse' of this great city's rise to economic greatness – Site BA02 symbolizes the problematic ongoing dichotomy in deep-sea shipwreck management between preferences for *in situ* preservation and monitoring on the one hand and the clear need for intrusive excavation and its sponsorship on the other to save human knowledge.

Oceans Odyssey 2 ends with World War II, represented by Axel Niestlé's study and reassessment of the fate of six German U-boats examined in the Western Approaches and western English Channel during Odyssey's 2008 'Atlas' Shipwreck Survey Project (Chapter 12). Between June 1944 and May 1945, the English Channel witnessed intense naval operations during the final phase of the German U-boat campaign against allied shipping. Operating close to the coastline and along the cross-Channel convoy supply lanes, German schnorkel-equipped submarines suffered grievous losses. A high percentage of U-boats went down with all hands under circumstances that remain obscure today: in the heat of battle, historical documentation was often necessarily incomplete, resulting sometimes in major distortions in the true narrative of how historical events unfolded.

The five wreck sites examined displayed different levels of preservation due to wartime damage, natural degradation and the detrimental impact of fishing. Based on authoritative evidence obtained during Odyssey's ROV surveys, the wrecks have now been identified as the former German U-boats U 325, U 400, U 650, U 1021 and U 1208. Odyssey's expedition results have corrected previous errors in the operational history of the German U-boat campaign in the western English Channel during the final phase of the war. The survey project stands out as a fine example of successful teamwork between marine archaeologists and historians rewriting naval history.

Dr Sean A. Kingsley
Director, Wreck Watch Int.
London, April 2011

Underwater Cultural Heritage & UNESCO in New Orleans: An Introduction

Sean Kingsley
Director, Wreck Watch Int., London, UK

1. Introduction

In the course of the marine archaeology session held at the Underwater Intervention conference in New Orleans on 11 February 2010, a panel discussion was convened to explore the perceived merits and potential pitfalls of UNESCO's Convention on the Protection of the Underwater Cultural Heritage 2001 (henceforth the Convention or CPUCH).[1]

Over the last decade the Convention has attracted major interest, debate and intrigue. Irrespective of which countries have and have not ratified this instrument (27 to date, with a further four going through the acceptance phase),[2] it has become a significant fulcrum point for discussing the management of underwater cultural heritage in the early 21st century. There is no reason to expect an abrupt sea change in the next decade.

CPUCH incites extreme opinions and, perhaps unexpectedly amongst scientists, a wide range of emotions. The New Orleans event was no different due to the co-presence of archaeologists, who have witnessed first-hand the wanton pillage of shipwrecks, and commercial archaeologists who argue that the controlled for-profit sale of some 'trade goods' (but not unique 'cultural goods') is a realistic and robust model for shipwreck archaeology. In the Odyssey Marine Exploration structure this applies particularly to deep-sea sites, where access is prohibitively expensive and technologically challenging for most academic and government entities.

Due to the 'closure' of all airports along the northeast coast of America because of a snow blizzard, several panelists were unable to attend the conference. The eight individual contributions in this paper thus unite the opinions of the original panelists, plus a few additional specialists – a diverse and eclectic range of experts, some with overlapping professions, including three archaeologists, three university professors, two lawyers and two businessmen involved in commercial archaeology:

- Prof. Filipe Castro – Center for Maritime Archaeology and Conservation, Texas A & M University, USA.
- Prof. David Bederman – K.H. Gyr Professor of Private International Law, Emory University School of Law, USA.
- John Kimball – International and Maritime Litigation and ADR Practice Group Leader, Blank Rome, LLC; Adjunct Professor, School of Law, New York University, USA; US delegate to CPUCH.
- Greg Stemm – CEO, Odyssey Marine Exploration, USA, and US delegate to CPUCH.
- James Sinclair – Director, SeaRex Inc., USA.
- Daniel De Narvaez – Naval Historian and Investigator, Colombia.
- Dr Sean Kingsley – Director, Wreck Watch Int., United Kingdom

2. CPUCH Versus Treasure Hunters

UNESCO's initiation of the Convention in 2001 has been interpreted as a defensive strategy with three goals: to eliminate the undesirable effects of the law of salvage; the exclusion of a 'first come, first served' approach to heritage found on the continental shelf; and to strengthen regional cooperation (Scovazzi, 2002: 154). Top of this list is the international community's concern over advances in deep-sea technology during the last 20 years, causing the Convention to be geared specifically to "provide a detailed legal regime for controlling the activities of treasure hunters in international waters" (Dromgoole, 2006: xxvii).

This remains a central tenet, although reading between the political lines, CPUCH also seems to be a reaction to past generations' unbridled recovery of artifacts and structural remains. The resource has been perceived as having been exploited without sufficient concern about conservation, storage, curation, display or publication.

The recovery of substantial wooden hull remains may be pinpointed as an additional motivation underlying these newly formalized policies. Behind closed doors there is a general consensus that certainly no European country wants, or can afford, another *Mary Rose*, despite its enormous educational and touristic benefits. Its titanic expense

– some £500,000 every year since 1982 for preserving the timbers, and an extra £35 million for completing the curation of its artifacts and building a dedicated ship museum – still haunts many heritage managerial meetings. The extrapolation that every wreck lifted might turn into another *Mary Rose* money pit is an inaccurate yet extant perception.

Dr Colin White, a former Director of the National Maritime Museum at Greenwich (White, 1994: 180), has argued that ship preservation went wild after 1949, when history was ransacked to provide reasons for preservation as crowd pullers. He proceeded to caution against raising ships with great exuberance: "The fact is that underwater camera and satellite-link technology now exists which renders the tearing of wrecks from their sea-beds as obsolete an operation as the ripping out of infected tonsils."

Collateral motivations aside, it is the stereotype of uncontrolled, large-scale shipwreck plunder or recovery for the commercial sale of artifacts as the primary objective that united many countries under the CPUCH banner. The extent of the negative reaction to 'treasure hunting' has been particularly strongly expressed by Robert Grenier in an ICOMOS publication (Grenier, 2006: x):

> "An inventory of all the wrecks who have been subject to excavation or salvage since the invention of the aqualung (autonomous deep-sea diving suit) half a century ago demonstrates that no historic wreck has ever been saved by commercial contractors or treasure hunters; only archaeologists have succeeded in this task. At the very most, treasure hunters have "saved" objects of commercial value at the cost of the destruction of the archaeological context, which is the real danger. These people exploit historic wrecks as if they were mines of precious metals. The countries that compromise with them, attracted by the promise of receiving 10% and even up to 50% of the spoils, in fact, recuperate only a minimal part of the historic value of the wreck, as 90 to 95% of this value is destroyed in most cases. These wreck salvagers are in fact like proverbial wolves guarding the flock. Why not conserve 100% of what belongs to the nation?"

Dr. Grenier assumes an extremist, though far from unique, position. The issue UNESCO faces, and which dominated discussions at the New Orleans conference in February 2010, is the reality that unbridled treasure hunting is simply not considered a legitimate activity by any of the legitimate stakeholders in underwater cultural heritage management. The new breed of commercial marine archaeologist may rely on capital investment, stocks and private investment, and the lure of profit from the sale of select artifacts, but some commercial companies have proven highly proficient at excavating, recording and interpreting shipwrecks.

Today some commercial companies undeniably possess the combined sophistications of technology, personnel and experience to fuse for-profit ventures with science, whereby wreck contexts are respected and recorded and site plans and pottery statistics compiled. Nanhai Marine Archaeology, for instance, has worked closely with the Malaysian government to record and recover elements of ten wrecks dating between the 11th and 19th centuries (Brown and Sjostrand, 2002; Sjostrand, 2007). Artifacts are transparently available for sale, with government sanction. If the site plan of the cedar and pine Desaru wreck's hull of *c.* 1830, 34 x 8m, typifies this company's archaeological capabilities across the board, then their recording exceeds most contract-led projects and equals university standards. The site's 69,726 ceramic wares have also been comprehensively quantified. Artifacts from the Desaru ship are on display at the Maritime Archaeology Malaysia exhibition at Muzium Negara in Kuala Lumpur.[3]

The discovery of the *Henrietta Marie* by the Armada Research Corporation in 1972 on New Ground Reef, 56km west of Key West in Florida, has literally opened a new chapter in understanding the 17th-century triangular slave trade. More importantly, it has become a sociological focus for the West's modern confrontation of its shameful past. Initially funded through commercial investment for underwater surveys searching for the 1622 Spanish fleet, site research continues to this day. Although the project has been criticized by some scholars because the results have not been principally disseminated through academic papers, but through the Mel Fisher Maritime Heritage Society website (Webster, 2008: 10),[4] extensive scientific data has been obtained, ranging from 90 sets of iron shackles to over 300 English pewter wares, 11,000 trade beads, six elephant tusks and 28 examples of 'voyage-iron' bars. These are now recognized as 'signature assemblages' of the slave trade (Moore and Malcom, 2008).

Finally, the commercial archaeology company Odyssey Marine Exploration is recording deep-sea wrecks (spatially accurate photomosaics, site plans, descriptions of contexts, artifact catalogues) to standards that facilitate detailed historical interpretations of sites. The survey work on the wreck of HMS *Victory*, lost in the English Channel in 1744 (Cunningham Dobson and Kingsley, 2010), and the excavation of site E-82, the possible wreck of HMS *Sussex* in the Straits of Gibraltar, reveal that such organizations match, and in cases exceed, standards set on shallow-water sites. The environmental and marine biological non-intrusive work on site E-82, in particular, coupled with contextual recording, has set new standards for deep-sea shipwreck archaeology (Cunningham Dobson *et al.*, 2010).

This careful and concerned approach to underwater

cultural heritage is a world apart from the hit and run image depicted above by Robert Grenier, although it must be acknowledged that standards are far from uniform across the entire commercial marine archaeology field. In light of the above new brand of commercial marine archaeology, a significant element of the debate in New Orleans centered around defining the ethical fine line between science and commerce. Many panelists and members of the audience felt that UNESCO has failed to recognize and encourage debate of this new world order.

3. Crossing the Lexicon

Anybody with a passion for the sea and its submerged archaeological heritage should support the basic premise of the UNESCO Convention of striving to shore up protection and dissemination of knowledge about our shared past. Profound differences in philosophy surround the Convention, but at its core it has the potential to serve society in the right spirit by promoting the existence and perilous condition of underwater cultural heritage. The protocol unites a collage of ideas and ideals that have been debated and applied for decades. Almost all of the initiatives have a long track record of being tried and tested. Without wishing to be even remotely comprehensive, these include inter-regional cooperation, the creation of marine parks for controlled public access and outreach, sanctions, public outreach, personnel training, the formulation of project plans and the establishment of appropriate centralized authorities.

Publications and discussions, as aired in New Orleans in February 2010, are making it increasingly clear that a rift exists, however, between the objectives of the Convention, as UNESCO intends it to be utilized, and its interpretation within the scientific and cultural heritage community. A problem of language, rationale and meaning exists, particularly in regard to the following ambiguous points (excluding areas of fundamental philosophical differences):

1. Who is CPUCH designed for: government heritage organizations and contract archaeology companies or also university-led projects?
2. The concept of *in situ* preservation (Article 2.5; Annex Rule 1) has assumed the status of a sacred cow in many circles and elicits strong reactions. Again, for whom is this conceived? To mentor countries with fledgling marine archaeology units or also sophisticated organizations with a track record of successfully organizing and publishing major excavations, such as NOAA, English Heritage, DRASSM and the Israel Antiquities Authority? Are major universities that have pursued research-led projects for decades and contribute to the writing of long-term history expected to adhere to *in situ* protocols, such as the Institute of Nautical Archaeology, Texas A&M University; the Leon Recanati Institute for Maritime Studies, University of Haifa; the Centre for Maritime Archaeology, Southampton University; or the Centre for Maritime Archaeology, University of Oxford, to name but a few.
3. How is the encouragement of "the public awareness, appreciation, and protection of the heritage" (Article 2.10; cf. also Annex Rule 7) practically possible beyond territorial waters, where site monitoring – even in marine parks – is physically complex and financially expensive? What models exist for comparison? Can and will awareness of underwater cultural heritage finally make its way into the UK Marine and Coastal Access Act 2009? The absence of any mention, let alone policy, regarding underwater and coastal cultural heritage in UNESCO's own World Heritage Marine Programme (Douvere, 2010), stands as a warning about the very real logistics of getting wrecks, submerged prehistoric camps and Roman ports onto governmental and organizational agendas.
4. Within which legal and financial structures can countries be expected to protect or prohibit access to underwater cultural heritage in the Exclusive Economic Zone and on the Continental shelf (Articles 9.1, 10.2)?
5. The idea that State parties should "notify the Director-General and any other State with a verifiable link, especially a cultural, historical or archaeological link, to the underwater cultural heritage concerned of any seizure of underwater cultural heritage that it has made under this Convention" (Article 18.3) may prize Pandora's Box off its hinges. For instance, would this permit Lebanon to influence fieldwork on Phoenician wrecks being excavated off Spain, or Greece to claim rights over statuary looted by Roman aristocrats and lost during transshipment overseas in the 1st century AD? Would France be permitted to claim the return of the 700kg Neupotz hoard of 1,000 silver and bronze bowls and other vessels wrecked down the Rhine in Germany after being looted by the Alamanni tribe in the late 3rd century AD (Kingsley, 2006)?
6. How will UNESCO objectively manage decisions, data flow and databases, and on what criteria will the Scientific and Technical Advisory Body (STAB) operate (cf. O'Keefe, 2009: 58)? Who will fund this initiative?

No doubt much of the above will come out in the wash, based on real-time practical experiences. For now, a feeling remains in many heritage and scientific circles that sections of the Convention are an unenforceable set of Utopian rules and regulations compiled by legal teams who incorporated minimal fundamental input from archaeologists. If the initiative is compared to terrestrial archaeology, where countries would react with outrage to any supposition that they need to be centrally supervized so intimately from abroad, many marine archaeologists with decades of experience and contribution are highly concerned about why they are suddenly being forcefully re-educated in their core competencies.

The Utopian argument matters because it is likely to lead to inappropriately politically-motivated managerial strategies. The primary example of a misreading of the Convention, which has already led to its use as political propaganda in some circles, is the reading of Article 2.5 on applying *in situ* preservation as the first managerial option. In the UK, for instance, the Joint Nautical Archaeology Policy Committee (JNAPC) has strongly promoted Article 2.5 as the obligatory rationale for preserving *in situ* the wreck of HMS *Victory* (1744) in the English Channel and leaving it untouched. Their language refers to the Article as the 'preferable' route (Williams, 2006), or virtually obligatory (Yorke, 2009: 21), thus using artistic license to extrapolate the Article's true meaning (see Kingsley, 2011: note 1). UNESCO's perceived preoccupation with *in situ* preservation is considered by some people to be the "main principle" of the Convention (Sokal, 2005). This is simply not the case, and is not borne out by the history of negotiations behind the Convention.

Many of the profound differences that currently divide maritime archaeology user groups are not insurmountable, especially if the spirit of cooperation rightly championed by UNESCO is truly respected. On the matter of inclusiveness, Williams (2009: 66) has speculated about the possible mutual benefits of UNESCO nominating observers to the Convention's Scientific and Technical Advisory Body from the Western Maritime States that have not ratified the Convention, especially those with indigenous deep submergence technology:

> "Such participation in the implementation of the Convention could only serve to promote a greater understanding of its value and potential by those States that view it with such misgivings. Considered in this light, the relatively slow adoption of the Convention, especially by the leading maritime States, should not be seen as an immediate failure."

Many participants in the Underwater Intervention 2010 marine session shared this sentiment and hoped that the doors of Paris are not closed to their passion and the scientific contributions of the private sector.

4. Underwater Intervention 2010, New Orleans: Differences of Opinion

The seven papers presented below represent a cross-section of legal, academic and commercial-oriented opinions about the origins, inspiration and workability of the UNESCO Convention on the Protection of the Underwater Cultural Heritage (2001).

Filipe Castro cautions that besides the problem of the often too rapid dispersal of the collections, the business model of commercial archaeology has an internal contradiction that is difficult to address: as objectives, maximizing profit and maximizing the quality of the recording, recovery and conservation of all artifacts are difficult to reconcile. The net result is all too often site destruction and an absence of publications to 'cold store' knowledge for present and future generations. However, Prof. Castro also expresses concern about the repressive emphasis in the UNESCO Convention on some points, notably an insistence on *in situ* preservation, and the establishment of unrealistic goals. Whilst welcoming the Convention as a step in the right direction, Castro warns that prohibitions rarely stimulate the desired end result.

David Bederman emphasizes that contrary to the high profile of the UNESCO Convention in current underwater cultural heritage managerial circles, it actually currently speaks for a small and geographical selective number of countries. Focusing on UNESCO's Draft Operational Guidelines (DOG's), adopted at the Meeting of Convention of the Protection of the Underwater Cultural Heritage States Parties in December 2009, Prof. Bederman argues that putting these recommendations into practice is potentially impossible. Unclarified definitions of State vessels and the expansive demand for protection of all underwater cultural heritage over 100 years old leaves extensive room for real-time managerial concern at the national level. Some of the limits of the Convention's language are contradictory and the Convention fails to legislate for circumstances where intrusive intervention is unavoidable to save heritage from myriad threats other than from 'treasure hunters'.

John Kimball highlights significant flaws in the implications of CPUCH that are likely to limit its effectiveness, in particular the creation of new coastal State rights and regulatory authority over underwater cultural heritage located in Exclusive Economic Zones and on continental shelves. Prof. Kimball argues that the Convention fails to provide adequate protection for military shipwrecks consistent with customary international law. In light of such new coastal State regulatory authority that improperly alters UNCLOS' carefully constructed balance of rights and interests, it is unlikely that many major Western Maritime States, such as the USA, will sign the Convention.

Greg Stemm considers the UNESCO Convention's 'one size fits all' policy for State signatories an unrealistic form of management. As well as questioning the practicalities and ethics of blanket designating every trace of mankind over 100 years old as culturally significant, Stemm proposes getting the public actively involved in curatorship through private ownership as a means of managing sprawling museum and excavation collections that otherwise rarely, if ever, see the light of day. Odyssey's wreck of the SS *Republic* is presented to exemplify the advantages of this model. Stemm cautions that eradicating the age-old system of salvage to reward groups for risking their capital and resources will deincentivize anyone from taking this initiative, except using government resources, potentially leaving major sites and regions unexplored and susceptible to looting or natural destruction.

Based on his decades of fieldwork in marine archaeology, James Sinclair considers UNESCO's zealous preoccupation with treasure hunters to be a highly biased managerial tool. The days of the uncritical extraction of 'booty' from shipwrecks has passed and modern professional salvage and commercial archaeology companies impose sets of scientific objectives on sites, in which the contextual recovery of high-value material is just one. Sinclair considers the neglect of additional impacts on shipwrecks (natural, electrochemical, physical deterioration and trawler damage) that are more extensive in scope to be a serious weakness of the Convention. He again regards the preoccupation with *in situ* preservation to be a failure to understand the realities of underwater preservation and advises that current initiatives to manage museum collections and archives through deaccessioning in the USA are likely to promote the private stewardship of artifacts and commercial models following recording and the creation of permanent digital records.

Sean Kingsley perceives much common sense and wisdom within the UNESCO Convention, which is essential for developing national regimes in need of 'off the shelf' managerial solutions. However, he cautions that single strategy solutions are unlikely to work for all regions due to varying geographical and constitutional circumstances. A positive outcome of the renewed consideration of *in situ* methods has been a growing awareness that the underwater heritage resource has to be qualified before it can be managed. Dr Kingsley proposes that UNESCO needs to go further by reducing ambiguities about what needs protecting by formulating a formal value system to qualify sites' importance. With the old-fashioned era of treasure hunting effectively dead, Kingsley advises that UNESCO would be better served to distinguish between commercial companies that produce accountable reports and pure salvage companies with little interest in history or archaeology.

Daniel De Narvaez presents a deeply considered example of how the UNESCO Convention cannot work as 'all things to all men' through a case study of Colombia. De Narvaez expresses caution that the Convention flies in the face of former well-established laws and protocols. Covering 926,660 square kilometers of sea and touching the borders of nine other countries, some of which are involved in ongoing disputes over marine territories, it is instead localized looting in remote regions and the unrecorded natural exposure and deterioration of sites that is a major challenge for Colombia. The combination of unusually extensive high-value cargoes in its waters, coupled with their shallow location in depths of under 20m, is the major threat. Colombian law already claims ownership of all shipwrecks within its Economic Exclusive Zone, while the Supreme Court does permit some commercialization of maritime artifacts. For Colombia to sign the UNESCO Convention would thus actually run contrary to its own legal constitution, a factor that might affect other countries' participation once they look at CPUCH in light of their own constitutions.

Notes

1. The author extends his sincere gratitude to Greg Stemm, Mark Gordon, Laura Barton and John Oppermann for convening the New Orleans session on the UNESCO Convention on the Underwater Cultural Heritage in New Orleans 2010 and for ensuring its smooth running, and to Odyssey Marine Exploration for sponsoring the event. This set of reports was edited by Sean Kingsley, Wreck Watch Int.
2. See: http://portal.unesco.org/la/conventionasp?KO=1520&language= E&order=alpha.
3. See: http://www.mingwrecks.com/Desaru.html.
4. See: http://www.melfisher.org/henriettamarie.htm.

Bibliography

Brown, R.M. and Sjostrand, S., *Maritime Archaeology and Shipwreck Ceramics in Malaysia* (National Museum, Kuala Lumpur, 2002).

Cunnigham Dobson, N. and Kingsley, S., 'HMS *Victory*, a First-Rate Royal Navy Warship Lost in the English Channel, 1744. Preliminary Survey & Identification'. In G. Stemm and S. Kingsley (eds.), *Oceans Odyssey: Deep-Sea Shipwrecks in the English Channel, the Straits of Gibraltar and the Atlantic Ocean* (Oxford, 2010), 235-80.

Cunningham Dobson, N., Tolson, H., Martin, A., Lavery, B., Bates, R., Tempera, F. and Pearce, J., 'The HMS *Sussex* Shipwreck Project (Site E-82): Preliminary Report'. In G. Stemm and S. Kingsley (eds.), *Oceans Odyssey: Deep-Sea Shipwrecks in the English Channel, the Straits of Gibraltar and the Atlantic Ocean* (Oxford, 2010), 159-90.

Douvere, F., *World Heritage Marine Programme. The Future 2010-2013* (UNESCO, Paris, 2010).

Dromgoole, S., *The Protection of the Underwater Cultural Heritage. National Perspectives in Light of the UNESCO Convention 2001* (Brill NV, Leiden, 2006).

Grenier, R., 'Introduction: Mankind, and at Times Nature, are the True Risks to Underwater Cultural Heritage'. In R. Grenier, D. Nutley and I. Cochran (eds.), *Underwater Cultural Heritage at Risk: Managing Natural and Human Impacts* (ICOMOS, 2006), x-xi.

Kingsley, S., 'Barbarian Loot Beneath the Rhine', *Minerva* 17.5 (2006). 16-18.

Kingsley, S., 'UNESCO, Commerce & Fast-Food Maritime Archaeology'. In G. Stemm and S. Kingsley (eds.), *Oceans Odyssey 2. Underwater Heritage Management & Deep-Sea Shipwrecks in the English Channel & Atlantic Ocean* (Oxford, 2011), 20-23.

Moore, D.D. and Malcom, C., 'Seventeenth-Century Vehicle of the Middle Passage: Archaeological and Historical Investigations on the *Henrietta Marie* Shipwreck Site', *International Journal of Historical Archaeology* 12 (2008), 20-38.

O'Keefe, P., 'The UNESCO Convention on the Protection of the Underwater Cultural Heritage: a Future for our Past? The Implementation of the 2001 Underwater Convention', *Conservation and Management of Archaeological Sites* 11.1 (2009), 58-60.

Scovazzi, T., 'Convention on the Protection of Underwater Cultural Heritage', *Environmental Policy and Law* 32.3-4 (2002), 152-57.

Sokal, M.P., 'International Law for the Protection of the Underwater Cultural Heritage: Can our Past be Salvaged?', *Culture Without Context* 16 (2005): http://www.mcdonald.cam.ac.uk/projects/iarc/culturewithoutcontext/issue16/papa-sokal.htm.

Sjostrand, S., *The Wanli Shipwreck and its Ceramic Cargo* (Department of Museums, Malaysia, 2007).

Webster, J., 'Slave Ships and Maritime Archaeology: An Overview', *International Journal of Historical Archaeology* 12 (2008), 6-19.

White, C., 'Too Many Preserved Ships Threaten the Heritage'. In M. Bound (ed.), *The Archaeology of the Ships of War* (International Maritime Archaeology Series Volume I, Oswestry, 1994), 179-83.

Williams, M.V., 'The UNESCO Convention on the Protection of the Underwater Cultural Heritage: An Analysis of the United Kingdom's Standpoint'. In *The UNESCO Convention for the Protection of the Underwater Cultural Heritage. Proceedings of the Burlington House Seminar, October 2005* (JNAPC, 2006), http://www.jnapc.org.ukBurlington%2House%20Proceedings%20final%20text.pdf.

Williams, M., 'The UNESCO Convention on the Protection of the Underwater Cultural Heritage: a Future for our Past? Towards a Two-speed Implementation?', *Conservation and Management of Archaeological Sites* 11.1 (2009), 60-67.

Yorke, R., 'Odyssey's Victory is Archaeology's Dilemma', *British Archaeology* May/June (2009), 19-21.

Fig. 1. The cover of UNESCO's booklet publicizing its Convention on the Protection of the Underwater Cultural Heritage.

Archaeologists, Treasure Hunters, and the UNESCO Convention on the Protection of the Underwater Cultural Heritage: a Personal Viewpoint

Filipe Castro
Frederick R. Mayer Faculty Professor II of Nautical Archaeology, Nautical Archaeology Program, Texas A&M University, USA

Differences between archaeologists and treasure hunters often stem from a misunderstanding about what archaeologists do. We try to reconstruct past cultures through the study of their material remains. We are interested in archaeological sites and contexts, and the most interesting artifacts we study seldom have market value. In other words, archaeologists are not antiquarians.

I have spent almost 20 years fighting treasure hunters. My involvement in this fight started in Portugal in the early 1990s when treasure hunting was legalized there. My first reaction was trying to understand the treasure hunter's viewpoints and objectives, but that was not easy. Some dismissed us altogether as natives of a poor country. Others promised to raise an entire caravel and put it in an aquarium. Others claimed that they were going to salvage fabulous treasures and give us half of everything they would find. To my astonishment, people believed most of these tall stories.

My experience with treasure hunters was therefore not a positive one. I saw them lying for money, destroying archaeological sites without a thought for what they were doing, fooling their investors and bragging about it, stiffing local populations, and scamming politicians with invented stories and fake promises. I saw them claiming the right to do whatever they wanted, as if they owned the planet. I met the kind that is more prone to make declarations to the media than to actually dive. And I met treasure hunters that worked in silence, salvaged real cargos, sold them discretely, and made real money.

At times archaeologists work with treasure hunters in order to fulfill contractual obligations to governments or lend some expertise to their work. Some come out and complain about the frustrations of working in for-profit ventures: to maximize profit and to do good archaeology are directly opposite objectives. Few publish reports. Everywhere secrecy has been the rule, even when reports are produced and sometimes even published. The quality of most reports is poor: fuzzy data, bad or incomplete site plans, no sections, no complete artifact catalogues, no recording of hull remains, and no conservation of artifacts without market value.

Like me, other archaeologists cringe before this reality. Imagine us patiently working to try to understand vanished cultures and the differences and similarities between them and those of the present, gathering data, studying the expressions of humanity contained in every different society, looking for patterns that may enhance our knowledge of what it means to be human… and being asked to accommodate the reasons of those who want to destroy the fragile, rare and non-renewable archaeological evidence for profit, or for fun, or for both.

It is easy to imagine how treasure hunters' interests may come across as shallow, or ignorant, or naive, or selfish, and this situation fosters the development of a holier-than-thou attitude. Together with a professional tribal feeling, this attitude may blur reality into an Orwellian vision: archaeologists good/treasure hunters bad, and develop an unhealthy self-righteousness among archaeologists. Who can sympathize with those that want to destroy archaeological sites for short-term profit, and leave a planet without history to their own children?

These high moral grounds called for a holy war and in the process we stopped asking a few important questions: what is the difference between a treasure hunter and an archaeologist who does not publish his or her excavations? Why have so many bureaucrats become prohibitionists in their old age? Why do we still allow 19th-century nationalistic feelings to linger among the community? Why is the circulation of primary data so hampered outside the United States?

It was in this context that from the 1970s onwards a growing number of archaeologists gathered around organizations such as ICOMOS and UNESCO, and in 2001 produced a Convention on the Protection of the Underwater Cultural Heritage. In March 2010 it had been ratified by 27 states.

The legitimacy of its authors is not in question: they were appointed by their governments, the majority of which are parliamentary democracies. But perhaps because a significant number of archaeologists involved in its drafting were bureaucrats, the resulting text can be interpreted as a repressive tool that pushes conservation *in situ* with a blind and stubborn optimism. Worse, together with a commendable call for an end to the destruction of the world's submerged cultural heritage, it sets the bar too high for archaeologists: Rule 1 of the Annex states: that "...activities directed at underwater cultural heritage... may be authorized for the purpose of making a significant contribution to protection or knowledge or enhancement of underwater cultural heritage." I am afraid that as all repressive rules, this Convention may invite arbitrary behavior, nepotism, and even corruption.

Despite all criticisms, I am actually glad that there is a Convention, and I find that most of the text of the Annex is well crafted, fair and relevant. But we must not stop here. We need a generation of young archaeologists and excavations to train them. We need to emphasize Rules 30 and 31 of the Annex, which focus on schedules and destinations for reports, and fight for a rapid and clear flow of information worldwide. The culture of secrecy that so often surrounds archaeologists is hurting us. Treasure hunters are decades ahead of archaeologists when it comes to public relations strategies. The world of nautical archaeology is a small world: we need ethical standards that make principles applicable to everybody and not only treasure hunters and those who do not have friends in their country's bureaucracies.

The next years will show us whether the Convention will help protect anything. Prohibitions alone seldom stop activities that are socially accepted, such as looting and treasure hunting.

In the meantime, Odyssey is changing the landscape, publishing reports and submitting them to public scrutiny. This is a development that we should follow closely. In documenting and publishing their salvage operations, they are placing themselves above the archaeologists that do not publish their excavations on the archaeology decency scale. Having spent the best part of the last two decades complaining against treasure hunter's secrecy, I applaud Odyssey's new policy and look forward to starting a constructive dialogue, solidly based on printed and published reports. In a democratic world we may all disagree, but we must acknowledge the opinions of our opponents and take close note when they use private resources that are of public interest and benefit.

Fig. 1. The Pepper Wreck under excavation in 1999: a Portuguese Indiaman lost at the mouth of the River Tagus, Portugal, and probably identifiable as the Nossa Senhora dos Máritires, *lost in 1606. Photo: Guilherme Garcia.*

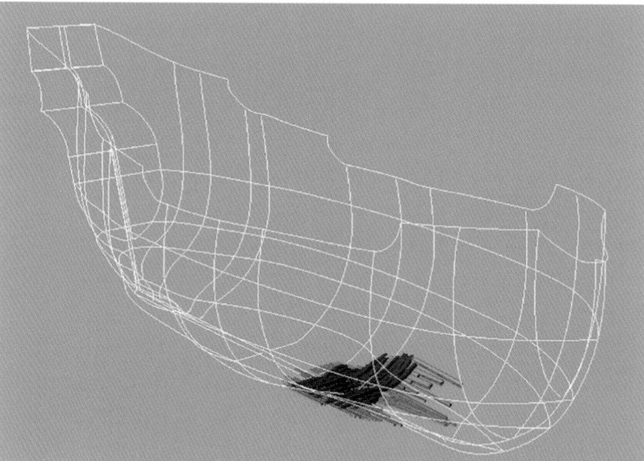

Fig. 2. The hull remains of the early 17th-century Pepper Wreck feature inscribed carpenter marks, which allowed a tentative reconstruction of the ship based on contemporary ship treatises. Traditionally such subtle primary data is lost or neglected during projects conducted by treasure hunters, who ignore elements of social archaeology in favor of trophy hunting. Photo: Kevin Gnadinger.

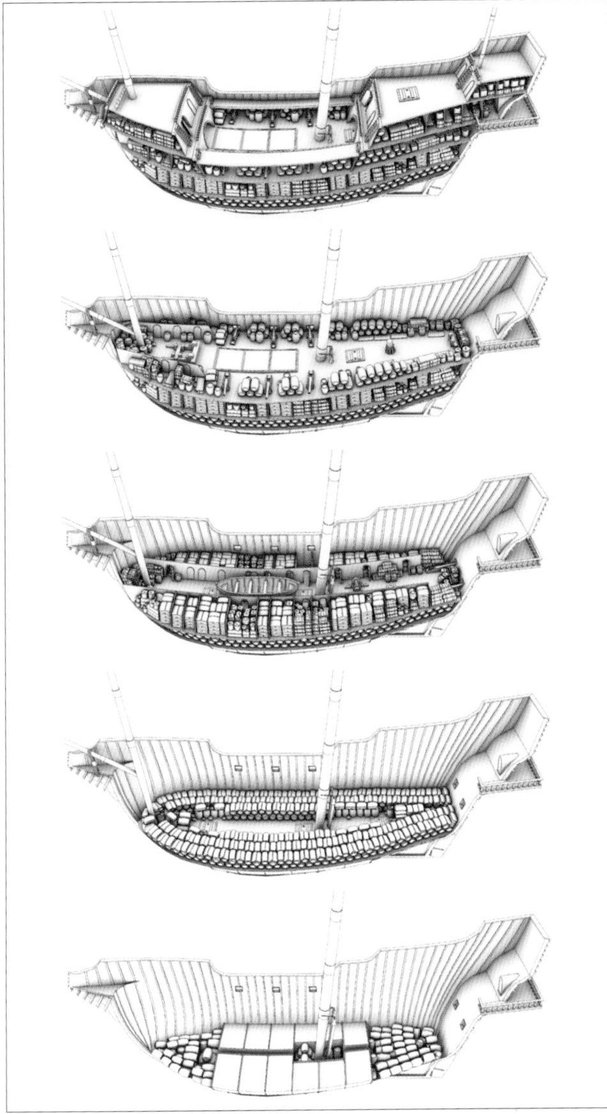

Fig. 3. A 3D reconstruction of the Pepper Wreck. Tentative load configuration studies reveal how small the inhabiting space was for the 450-person crew and passengers who departed from India to Lisbon on the Nossa Senhora dos Máritires *in 1606. Photo: Audrey Wells.*

Fig. 5. A small collection of Wan-li porcelain plates was found still packed, with straw mats between them, on the early 17th-century Pepper Wreck. Photo: Center for Maritime Archaeology and Conservation, Texas A&M University.

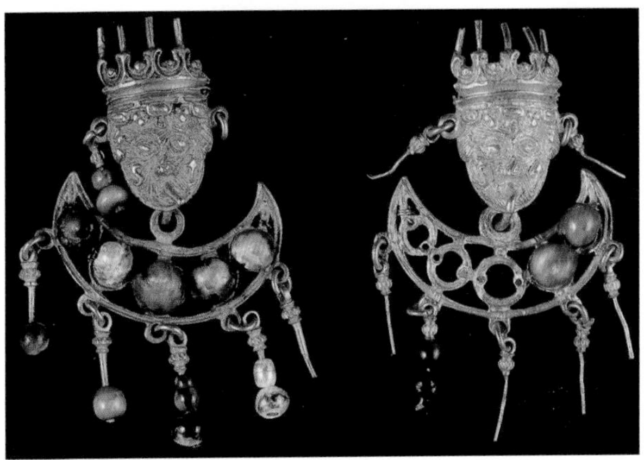

Fig. 6. A pair of earrings found on the early 17th-century Pepper Wreck by avocational archaeologist Carlos Martins, who declared the site to the authorities in 1992. Photo: Center for Maritime Archaeology and Conservation, Texas A&M University.

Fig. 4. Three astrolabes from the early 17th-century Pepper Wreck found on and near the shipwreck site. Such crucial artifacts are typically sold by treasure hunters, rather than retained and studied. Photo: Center for Maritime Archaeology and Conservation, Texas A&M University.

The UNESCO Convention on the Protection of Underwater Cultural Heritage: Operational Guidelines & Implementation Challenges

David J. Bederman
K.H. Gyr Professor of Private International Law, Emory University, Atlanta, *USA*

The UNESCO 2001 Convention on the Protection of Underwater Cultural Heritage (CPUCH) entered force in January 2009, with the deposit of the twentieth ratification, accession or acceptance of the treaty instrument. The number of States Parties remains small, and the group of countries bound rather selectively from the perspective of geography and commitment to maritime heritage. Nevertheless, it is important to examine the prospects for future implementation of CPUCH's provisions. This very short contribution does so from the institutional perspective of UNESCO's Draft Operational Guidelines ('DOGs'), adopted at the Meeting of CPUCH States Parties in December 2009 (UNESCO, 2009). At the same time, I examine here the very real – and what I regard here as potentially insuperable – difficulties in practically fulfilling the Convention's goals of protecting underwater cultural heritage.

One glaring deficiency of the DOGs is that they fail to refine further the definition of 'underwater cultural heritage' as set forth in CPUCH (UNESCO, 2001 art. 1(1)(a)). The expansive treatment of underwater cultural heritage (UCH) as "all traces of human existence having a cultural, historical or archaeological character which have been partially or totally under water, periodically or continuously, for at least 100 years" has been vigorously criticized in the literature (Bederman, 1999: 30; Forrest, 2002: 31). Nor did the DOGs give further guidance as to the definition of "State vessels", either for purposes of immunity from salvage and coastal state protection, or from the requirements of shipwreck reporting and other response measures (UNESCO, 2001 arts. 1(8), 7(3), 10(7), 12(7), 13). This set of provisions was amongst the most controversial in CPUCH, and largely led many maritime powers to decline to sign or ratify the instrument (Bederman, 2000: 31; Blake, 1996: 45; Carducci 2002: 96; O'Keefe, 2002).

But even insofar as the DOGs seem to be limited to sketching out the modalities of the 'State cooperation mechanism' and the 'operational protection of UCH' in CPUCH, they really do not achieve that objective (UNESCO, 2009: 15, 21). A stated goal of CPUCH is to bar the "commercial exploitation" of underwater cultural heritage (UNESCO, 2001 art. 2(7), Rule 2). This is confirmed in the DOGs (UNESCO, 2009: 9). But these do not even attempt to amplify on the language of CPUCH Rule 2 that allows "provision of professional archaeological services or necessary services incidental thereto" in the recovery of underwater cultural heritage, as well as permitting "deposition of underwater cultural heritage… provided such deposition does not prejudice the scientific or cultural interest or integrity of the recovered material or result in its irretrievable dispersal" (UNESCO, 2001 Rule 2). "Deposition" in the sense used by CPUCH Rule 2 means the ultimate disposal of recovered underwater cultural heritage. This was a crucial piece of compromise language in CPUCH, and acknowledged the practical reality that States would need to rely on private enterprise and incentives in order to optimally protect underwater cultural heritage (Bederman, 2004; Dromgoole, 2003: 18).

Even more shockingly, the DOGs appear to ignore willfully the fact that underwater cultural heritage is presently in danger in some regions and situations, yet elsewhere establishes a threshold for action that may be too high, given the circumstances. The DOGs do allow "safeguarding measures" to be taken when heritage is "in immediate danger" (UNESCO, 2009: 21). But "immediate danger" is then defined in this convoluted fashion: where "convincing and controllable conditions exist which can reasonably be expected to cause damage or destruction… within a short delay of time and which can be eliminated by taking safeguarding measures" (UNESCO, 2009: 22). This provision is transparently aimed at the threat of looting, but utterly ignores other ongoing, long-term, and systemic threats, including trawl damage and environmental degradation. This exposes the distinction between "activities directed at" underwater cultural heritage, as opposed to those merely "incidentally affecting" it, as false and meaningless (UNESCO, 2001 art. 1(6) & (7)).

As for CPUCH's State cooperation mechanism, some elements are helpfully elaborated in the DOGs. The goals of the mechanism to encourage reporting, declarations of interest, consultation, and action are noted (UNESCO, 2009: 7-8). But, in truth, the main focus is on reporting and the roll-out of a new database (at www.unesco.org: UNESCO, 2009: 8, 33-48). The concept is that States Parties to CPUCH will record underwater finds through the database and then countries will "declare" their status as an "interested State." Only time will tell if this streamlined reporting mechanism for discoveries, activities, and declarations of interest will function effectively.

Ironically enough, even in proffering these modest reporting modalities, the DOGs expose some crucial theoretical weaknesses in the CPUCH regime. One of these relates to how interested States Parties establish – in the ubiquitous phraseology of CPUCH – a "verifiable link, especially a cultural, historical or archaeological link, to... underwater cultural heritage" that is to be managed (UNESCO, 2001 arts. 6(2), 7(3), 9(5), 11(4), 12(6), 18(3)&(4)). In this regard, the DOGs merely noted that a "link" can be "verified" by "scientific expertises [sic], historic documentation, or other adequate documentation" (UNESCO, 2009: 17) And, rather obviously, the DOGs observe that if a State Party discovering UCH "gives only little information on [a]... site... or artefact in a report, it can only [expect] a small amount of proof concerning the verifiable link from another State Party that declares its interest in being consulted concerning its protection" (UNESCO, 2009: 17). The proposed UNESCO database is singularly unhelpful in eliciting definitive details about the "supposed [cultural] origin" of underwater cultural heritage, lumping it all as being of either African, Asian, European, Arab, American, or Australian origin (UNESCO, 2009: 39).

Lastly, the DOGs leave maddeningly vague the process by which "coordinating States" are appointed under CPUCH, and their decision-making authority (UNESCO, 2001 arts. 10 & 12). This problem is especially acute for underwater cultural heritage situated beyond any nation's exclusive economic zone (EEZ) or continental shelf, but (in such circumstances) the DOGs indicate the appointment of a coordinating State will be "by consensus" and that, after appointment, that State "is responsible for... further consultation... and the coordination and implementation of the protection measures decided" (UNESCO, 2009: 21). The DOGs suggest that the coordinating State acts as a kind of fiduciary for all interested States in underwater cultural heritage, but "does not gain new jurisdiction from its position..." (UNESCO, 2009: 23).

This language – as with many of the other aspects of the CPUCH DOGs discussed above – is virtually guaranteed to cause mischief in the future. The prospects for practical implementation of CPUCH by States Parties thus remain in doubt.

Bibliography

Bederman, D.J., 'The UNESCO Draft Convention on Underwater Cultural Heritage: A Critique and Counter-Proposal', *Journal of Maritime Law and Commerce* 30 (1999), 331-54.

Bederman, D.J., 'Rethinking the Legal Status of Sunken Warships', *Ocean Development and International Law* 31 (2000), 97-125.

Bederman, D.J., 'The UNESCO Convention on Underwater Cultural Heritage: Panacea or Peril for Resource Managers?'. In J.R. Richman and M. Forsyth (eds.), *Legal Perspectives in Cultural Resource Law* (2004), 140-61.

Blake, J., 'Protection of Underwater Cultural Heritage', *International and Comparative Law Quarterly* 45 (1996), 819-43.

Carducci, G., 'New Developments in the Law of the Sea: The UNESCO Convention on the Protection of Underwater Cultural Heritage', *American Journal of International Law* 96 (2002), 419-34.

Dromgoole, S., '2001 UNESCO Convention on the Protection of Underwater Cultural Heritage', *International Journal of Maritime and Coastal Law* 18 (2003), 59-108.

Forrest, C.J.S., 'Defining "Underwater Cultural Heritage",' *International Journal of Nautical Archaeology* 31 (2002), 3-11.

O'Keefe, P.J., *Shipwrecked Heritage: A Commentary on the UNESCO Convention on the Protection of Underwater Cultural Heritage* (London, 2002).

UNESCO, 2001: *United Nations Educational, Scientific and Cultural Organization, Convention on the Protection of Underwater Cultural Heritage (CPUCH)*: available at www.unesco.org and *International Legal Materials* 40 (2002), 41.

UNESCO, 2009: *United Nations Educational, Scientific and Cultural Organization, Meeting of States Parties, 2d Sess., Doc. UCH/09/2.MSP/220/5 rev., Draft Operational Guidelines for UNESCO CPUCH* (20 October 2009).

Living with the Convention on the Protection of the Underwater Cultural Heritage: New Jurisdictions

John Kimball

Partner, Blank Rome LLP; Adjunct Professor, School of Law, New York University, USA[1]

Despite its laudable aims, the Convention on the Protection of Underwater Cultural Heritage (CPUCH) has significant flaws that are likely to prevent it from being effective either in the short term or over the long haul. All of these points were known when the Convention was drafted and its adoption reflects a considered decision by UNESCO to accept the text nonetheless.

The Convention creates expansive new coastal State jurisdiction over underwater cultural heritage-related activities in wide areas outside of the traditional limits of national jurisdiction. It also fails to provide adequate protection for military shipwrecks consistent with customary international law. As a result of these provisions, the United States and other major maritime nations do not support the Convention and likely will not become parties, thereby limiting its effectiveness.

For vessels flagged in States that have ratified the Convention, their activities will be subject to significant new regulations and reporting requirements. The Convention's provisions may also have an effect on the operations of vessels flagged in non-State Parties. CPUCH contains the broad requirement that States Parties take "all practicable measures" to ensure that their nationals and vessels flying their flag not engage in activities which are not in conformity with the Convention's provisions and the Rules of the Annex, and establishes broad authority to impose sanctions for violations of measures a State has taken to implement the Convention, "wherever they occur."

The Convention also broadly requires States Parties to "use the best practicable means" at their disposal to prevent or mitigate activities which may inadvertently or incidentally physically disturb or otherwise damage underwater cultural heritage. Also, included within the Convention's regime for activities occurring within a State's Exclusive Economic Zone, on the Continental Shelf and on areas of the seabed outside of national jurisdiction, is the requirement that the master of any vessel flagged by a State Party who discovers or intends to engage in activities directed at underwater cultural heritage report such discoveries or activities to the State Party in whose waters the activities take place.

It remains to be seen how signatories to the Convention will implement these provisions, especially those concerning inadvertent or incidental activities. For example, vessels which inadvertently drag an anchor or a trawl net through a shipwreck could be at risk of sanctions. At a minimum, shipowners and managers of vessels flagged by States Parties should expect flag State inspections to include reviews of measures involving underwater cultural heritage activity and reports. Until some practice has been developed in this area, shipowners and managers of vessels flagged by, or operating in the jurisdiction of, States Parties should be aware of the potential risks and exercise caution when planning and conducting any underwater activities.

The Convention also contains control-of-entry and non-use provisions that affect all vessels. It requires State Parties to prohibit the entry into their territory or the possession of underwater cultural heritage that was not recovered in compliance with the Convention's provisions. The use of a State Party's territory, including its maritime ports, by vessels which engaged in activity directed at underwater cultural heritage (not conducted in compliance with the Convention) is also prohibited. The Convention further authorizes the seizure of underwater cultural heritage found in a State's territory that has been recovered in a manner not in conformity with the Convention.

Accordingly, shipowners and managers of vessels involved in activities directed at underwater cultural heritage must be aware of which nations are States Parties when planning their vessel's movements, including the designation of potential ports of refuge. Otherwise they run the risk of inadvertently bringing their vessels within the Convention's authority. Vessels that transport artifacts recovered underwater, even possibly container vessels, also should be aware of the possibility of having cargo seized and sanctions imposed if they enter the jurisdiction of State Parties. Shipowners should consider the extent to which these requirements may affect their operations. One solution for avoiding them is to reflag in a country that has not ratified the Convention.

The Convention contains several key provisions that are unacceptable to the United States and the other maritime nations that voted against its adoption or abstained from voting. In particular, these nations object to the Convention's creation of new coastal State rights and regulatory authority over underwater cultural heritage located in Exclusive Economic Zones and on continental shelves, and are concerned that the Convention does not provide adequate protection for sunken warships.

With respect to jurisdiction, the United States and other maritime nations oppose the Convention because, in effect, it establishes a "cultural heritage zone" beyond 24 miles and the outer edge of the continental shelf, in which coastal States have direct authority to regulate access to underwater cultural heritage. The view of the United States and other maritime nations is that such new direct coastal State regulatory authority would improperly alter UNCLOS' carefully constructed balance of rights and interests.

With respect to sunken warships, military aircraft and other national vessels, the view is that the Convention would alter customary international law and practice regarding title to such vessels. It also permits coastal States to recover such vessels located in internal waters or territorial seas without the consent of the flag State or even an obligation to notify them. The United States' position is that the Convention should instead codify customary principles of international law, which provide that title to sovereign vessels and aircraft, wherever located, remains vested in the original flag State unless expressly abandoned and is not lost through the passage of time. The US does not wish to see the salvage or recovery of such vessels or aircraft permitted without the express consent of the flag State.

As the late Robert Blumberg, the head of the United States delegation to the panel of experts who negotiated the Convention's text, put it, "Ultimately, the Convention will not be effective unless it is broadly ratified and implemented throughout the international community, including by countries in which the most advanced undersea technology resides and whose nationals are most active in regard to underwater cultural heritage" (Blumberg, 2006). Because of their objections to expansive jurisdictional provisions or concerns about the lack of warship protection, many leading maritime nations most likely will remain outside the CPUCH regime. As a result, the Convention's Rules and other positive provisions may ultimately have only limited impact on the protection of underwater cultural heritage.

Notes

1. The author is a partner of Blank Rome LLP and an Adjunct Professor at New York University Law School. The author chaired the Study Group established by the Maritime Law Association of the United States to consider UCH and served as a member of the United States delegation to the working sessions of experts at UNESCO where UCH was drafted. The author also served as Rapporteur of the Working Group established by the Comité Maritime International to study UCH.

Bibliography

Blumberg, R.C., 'International Protection of Underwater Cultural Heritage'. In M.H. Nordquist, J.N. Moore and K-C. Fu (eds.), *Recent Developments in the Law of the Sea and China* (Leiden, 2006), 491-514.

Protecting the Past: UNESCO Versus the Private Collector

Greg Stemm
Chief Executive Officer, Odyssey Marine Exploration, Tampa, USA

The UNESCO Convention contains some valid archaeological principles, but loses its way when it tries to dictate a one size fits all policy for State signatories. This flies in the face of the legal rights of countries that might choose to consider the sale of select duplicate artifacts as part of their deaccessioning and collections management policy, and creates problems for States, including Australia, France, Ireland and the UK, that retain a reward system, either monetary or in kind (Firth, 2002: 72; Le Gurun, 1999: 54, 59; Jeffery, 1999: 8).

The Odyssey Marine Exploration commercial model is one that achieves the archaeological goals and principles behind CPUCH, but is nevertheless potentially outlawed, depending on the interpretation of the Annex rules. We distinguish between 'Trade Goods' and 'Cultural Artifacts' internally as a matter of policy. Only artifacts that fit our Trade Good definition are offered for sale. This is a category characterized by large quantities of mass-produced objects, such as coins, bottles, pottery and other mass-produced cargo (Figs. 1-2). Our company policy is to retain a representative sample of Trade Goods. Duplicates are only sold to private collectors after thorough study and recording, which makes all information that can be collected available for study in the future (Figs. 3-6). Everything else is defined as the cultural collection, which is strictly retained in permanent collections and never irretrievably dispersed.

In my opinion, the general concept of CPUCH, which states that every trace of mankind over 100 years old is culturally significant, is unrealistic and cannot be justified intellectually, be policed or afforded by society. On land it would be absurd to consider that all traces of man are so culturally significant that they could never be privately owned or traded. Why does it change because an object has ended up underwater?

I do not believe that most museums or institutions have an interest in retaining giant collections of tens or hundreds of thousands of bottles, coins, bricks or plates in perpetuity. The real cost of storage must take into account the prices of real estate in areas where the archives are stored. For instance, in the British Museum's neighborhood of Bloomsbury, rental space costs an average of £50 per square foot per year. Our cultural collection from the SS *Republic* shipwreck (1865), comprising 14,414 artifacts, including 8,429 bottles (Gerth, 2006), as well as plates, cutlery, tools and unique personal possessions like tea sets, grooming items and keys (Cunningham Dobson *et al.*, 2010; Cunningham Dobson and Gerth, 2010; Vesilind, 2005), is all stored and conserved to the highest museum standards. The majority of the collection takes up about 1,000 square feet of space in our conservation lab.

The UNESCO Convention would require (Article 2.6, Annex Rules 32-34) that sufficient funds for storing the *Republic* artifacts in perpetuity would need to be funded in advance of excavation. At £50,000 per year, just setting aside funds for the next 50 years (much less in perpetuity) would demand £2.5 million in funding just for space for the *Republic* collection if it were stored in the British Museum. Of course, there are less expensive places, but in many cases where artifacts are stored in public buildings in high-rent city districts, the real cost of storage is hidden.

What happens when hundreds or thousands of similar shipwreck collections need homes? I believe that the only rational solution to this dilemma is to allow the public to get actively involved in curatorship. UNESCO's bizarre prohibition against "commercial exploitation… for trade

Fig. 1. A sample of 2,775 ironstone wares was excavated from the Republic *shipwreck site and has been retained within Odyssey's permanent collection. Photo: © Odyssey Marine Exploration.*

Fig. 2. Brown and green glass beer or ale bottles in situ *on the wreck of the* Republic*. Odyssey defines the thousands of glass bottles excavated from the shipwreck as trade goods, but keeps representative samples in the permanent collection. Photo: © Odyssey Marine Exploration.*

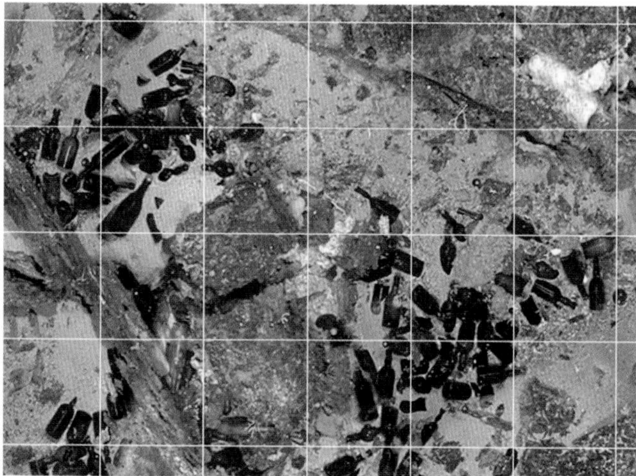

Fig. 3. During excavations on Odyssey projects a virtual grid is generated over live video coverage of shipwrecks, such as here on the Republic *site, so the exact locations and contexts of all of artifacts – whether trade goods or cultural artifacts – can be mapped. Photo: © Odyssey Marine Exploration.*

or speculation" (Annex Rule 2) seems to be related more to a misguided collectivist policy than any practical real-world model, and is virtually impossible to define legally.

Much of the archaeology conducted in the world today is accomplished by for-profit companies, typically through rescue excavations conducted to 'remove' sites standing in the way of commercial development. The very nature of being in business is an act of trade and speculation – and archaeology is big business. In 2003-04 private developers sponsored the vast majority of UK archaeology, spending £144 million, compared to £19 million spent by the central government and the European Union, and around £25 million by local government. In each case, these activities were the result of "commercial exploitation", albeit of the real estate where the site was located, but certainly driven by "commercial exploitation" nonetheless.

The greatest weakness in the principles behind CPUCH is the blatant prejudice against private ownership and collectors as a viable cultural heritage management tool. On land, in most countries a thriving and vital regime for managing historically and culturally significant property and buildings exists by allowing people to own culturally significant structures – and care for them as their own private property.

It is a simple fact of human nature that people cherish and take care of the objects they own. A wide choice of models exists to examine the positive results of private ownership and curatorship in other fields. Fossils, coins, stamps, art, bank notes, antiques – virtually every trace of nature and mankind that is collected by humans – demonstrate the success of an active and vital community of collectors who conserve, document and, most importantly, publish as much information as possible on their collections.

I believe that the coins we recovered from the SS *Republic* have achieved maximum protection. We documented the X, Y and Z position of every artifact on the site (Fig. 3). We have conserved, recorded, quantified and documented the coins with high-resolution photos that will allow any coin aficionado of the future to inspect every die variation and scratch without paying a fortune for storage and insurance (Figs. 4-6). Then we placed them in the hands of collectors who are passionate about studying and sharing knowledge from them.

The *Republic* excavation led to the recovery of over 8,000 liberty-seated half-dollar silver coins that were minted in New Orleans in 1861 (Bowers, 2010: 90-1). This allowed experts to look at every single coin and identify the tiniest traces of die variations, a painstaking exercise that was accomplished by private collectors and funded by Odyssey (cf. Wiley, 2005 for the die form's complexity). These results were published in the *Gobrecht Journal*, dedicated to the study of coins that feature the sculptural art of Christian Gobrecht, a die engraver at the US Mint (Wiley, 2006: 36-7). This journal is published by private collectors and is one of thousands published by the dedicated private collecting community. I do not think you can justify that these coins would be better off unseen in a museum vault than in the hands of these passionate collectors, with a virtual record retained in perpetuity on a dedicated website, easily available for future study.

Fig. 4. The numismatic team documenting and conserving some of the 51,404 gold and silver coins recovered from the wreck of the SS Republic. *Photo: © Odyssey Marine Exploration.*

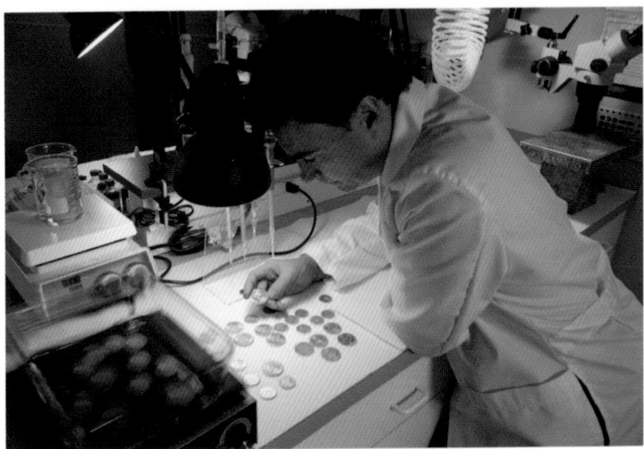

Fig. 5. Gold coins under conservation by a numismatic expert in the laboratory of Numismatic Conservation Services. Photo: © Odyssey Marine Exploration.

Private ownership encourages study and publication. If you visit the website Amazon.com and search for books on 'coins', you will find over 15,000 entries. Change the query to 'shipwrecks' and only 5,000 entries come up. Interestingly, the majority of these 5,000 books relate to shipwreck projects that were commercial in nature and funded by the private sector. 'Underwater Archaeology' generates about 750 entries. While this is not a conclusive scientific study, it demonstrates the existence of a vibrant market for the exchange of knowledge in the coin collecting world that has apparently not suffered from private ownership. Where is the justification for claims that private collectors are not diligent and responsible curators?

Odyssey has discovered hundreds of shipwrecks ranging from Punic to Roman sites and privateers to Colonial trading ships. Our policy is to record the site, and then either pick up a small selection of diagnostic artifacts for study and permanent retention or, in the majority of cases, leave the site undisturbed *in situ*. A typical example of our operations in action is the Atlas Shipwreck Survey Project (2005-2008). Other than highly endangered material on site 35F, a mid-17th century armed merchant vessel lost in the Western Approaches with a rare cargo of elephant tusks and copper *manilla* bracelets, and heavily damaged by scallop dredges (Kingsley, 2010: 220, 223, 228-30), from which 58 artifacts have been recovered, a total of 60 other artifacts from 267 shipwrecks (bricks, bottles, hull spikes, bells) have been recovered during this survey project in the English Channel covering thousands of square miles, all recorded properly and reported to the UK Receiver of Wreck as required by law.

The purpose of salvage law has always been to reward individuals and groups for risking their capital, resources and even lives to return items lost in the sea to the benefit of society. Doing away with any reward system or private ownership will serve to deincentivize anyone from taking this initiative, except using rare government resources. Based on my own observations this is not a use of public funds that is endorsed by the public, especially in today's economy. We can only hope that one day, faced with the reality of the benefits of private curation, UNESCO and CPUCH signatories will adjust their policies to redefine "cultural, historical or archaeological character" and "commercial exploitation" to develop a more rational policy for managing shipwrecks and collections – and give the public and the private sector their due for being responsible and able curators of our underwater cultural heritage.

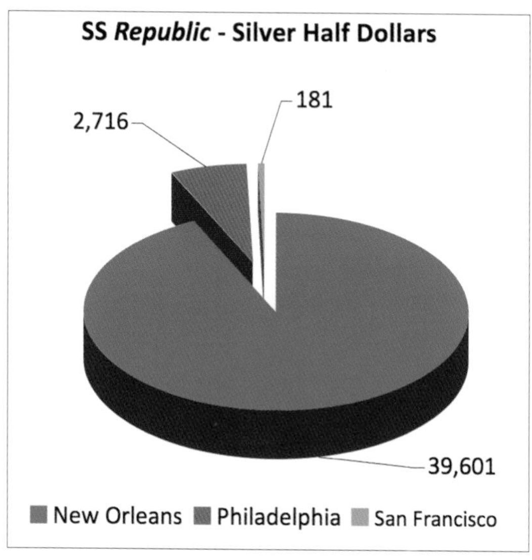

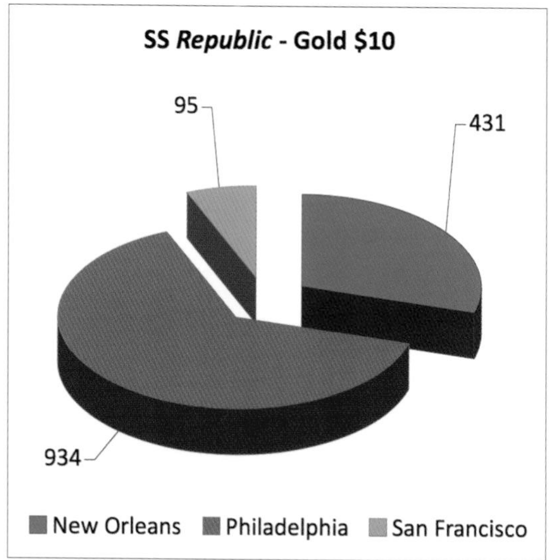

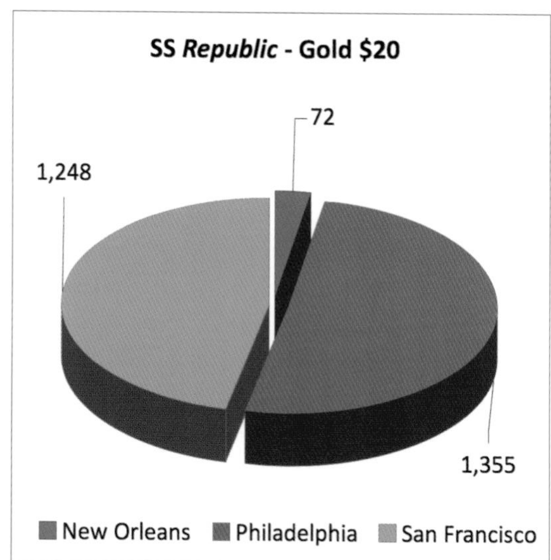

Fig. 6. Photography, cataloguing and quantification of the Republic coin collection enabled the relative types of all coins from the wreck to be quantified by mint and die varieties. Photo: © Odyssey Marine Exploration.

Bibliography

Bowers, Q.D., 'The SS *Republic* Shipwreck Excavation Project: the Coin Collection'. In G. Stemm and S. Kingsley (eds.), *Oceans Odyssey. Deep-Sea Shipwrecks in the English Channel, Straits of Gibraltar & Atlantic Ocean* (Oxbow Books, Oxford, 2010), 69-100.

Cunningham Dobson, N., Gerth, E. and Winckler. J.L., 'The Shipwreck of the SS *Republic* (1865). Experimental Deep-Sea Archaeology. Part 1: Fieldwork & Site History'. In G. Stemm and S. Kingsley (eds.), *Oceans Odyssey. Deep-Sea Shipwrecks in the English Channel,*

Straits of Gibraltar & Atlantic Ocean (Oxbow Books, Oxford, 2010), 1-24.

Cunningham Dobson, N. and Gerth, E. 'The Shipwreck of the SS *Republic* (1865). Experimental Deep-Sea Archaeology. Part 2: Cargo'. In G. Stemm and S. Kingsley (eds.), *Oceans Odyssey. Deep-Sea Shipwrecks in the English Channel, Straits of Gibraltar & Atlantic Ocean* (Oxbow Books, Oxford, 2010), 25-68.

Firth, A., *Managing Archaeology Underwater. A Theoretical, Historical and Comparative Perspective on Society and its Submerged Past* (BAR Int. Series 1055, Oxford, 2002).

Gerth, E., *Patent Medicines, Bitters, & Other Bottles from the Wreck of the Steamship Republic* (Shipwreck Heritage Press, 2006).

Jeffery, B., 'Australia'. In S. Dromgoole (ed.), *Legal Protection of the Underwater Cultural Heritage: National and International Perspectives* (London, 1999), 1-18.

Kingsley, S.A., 'Deep-Sea Fishing Impacts on the Shipwrecks of the English Channel & Western Approaches'. In G. Stemm and S. Kingsley (eds.), *Oceans Odyssey. Deep-Sea Shipwrecks in the English Channel, Straits of Gibraltar & Atlantic Ocean* (Oxbow Books, Oxford, 2010), 191-234.

Le Gurun, G., 'France'. In S. Dromgoole (ed.), *Legal Protection of the Underwater Cultural Heritage: National and International Perspectives* (London, 1999), 43-63.

Vesilind, P.J., *Lost Gold of the Republic* (Shipwreck Heritage Press, 2005).

Wiley, R.E., 'Die Marriages of 1861-O Half-Dollars', *The Gobrecht Journal* 32.94 (2005), 3-29.

Wiley, R.E., 'Coining Authority and Rarity for Die Marriages of 1861-O Half-Dollars', *The Gobrecht Journal* 33.97 (2006), 34-49.

Threats to Underwater Cultural Heritage – Real & Imagined

James Sinclair, MA
SeaRex Inc., Florida, USA

1. The UNESCO Convention: Antiquated Ideas

The UNESCO Convention on the Protection of Underwater Cultural Heritage is based on ideas that are already antiquated. The thought that the greatest threat to the resource is the professional salvage industry is absurd – the professional historic shipwreck salvage industry is extremely selective in its efforts and targets very specific shipwrecks. Realistically, the overwhelming majority of shipwrecks in the world are of little interest to most professional salvors.

While regulations are necessary for activities aimed at a resource with perceived financial, historical and emotional value, the CPUCH rules are burdensome, punitive in nature and without the ability or will to enforce them. Rules such as these tend to have the exact opposite effect. Divers who find artifacts of real intrinsic value are now much less likely to report them for fear of the legal ramifications. Experience demonstrates that a system that rewards finders of such material/sites is much more likely to produce the effect that the current Convention is seeking to promulgate.

2. Threats to Underwater Cultural Heritage - Real & Imagined

The image projected by the authors of the UNESCO Convention is that of a 'cultural resource' under threat. However, the focus of this 'treaty' is not on those threats that are the true scourge of these resources and properties. Instead, serious consideration should be given to natural environmental threats, as well as those anthropogenically inflicted.

Shipwrecks and lost cargos are predominantly manmade objects that, with few exceptions, undergo rapid chemical and natural deterioration once lost in the sea. After an undetermined amount of time this process slows, but does not – as far as can be determined – cease completely. The oceans are enormous planetary engines of weather, biology and geology – the greatest recycling engine in the world. The action of the seas on cultural objects is an entire complex field within corrosion sciences.

One of the most outrageous statements that the UNESCO Convention advocates is that *in situ* preservation should be considered as a first option. This runs counter to what the overwhelming reality of shipwreck situations demand. If the working committees involved in the drafting and promulgation of this treaty had included any corrosion scientists in their fact-finding research, this idea would have been immediately discarded as a realistic first option for management.

The hard data behind corrosion studies in material science confirms the reality regarding chances of preserving cultural objects lost to marine environments through purely electrochemical and physical site qualifications. Increasingly, we are also observing vast amounts of damage already caused by commercial fishing/trawling activities. If we truly want to 'protect and save' underwater cultural heritage, we need to find creative ways of managing these sites, which must include the recovery and preservation of objects associated with them. All options should remain on the table.

Fig. 1. The copper-sheathed bows of the wreck of a 23m-long English merchantman of c. 1810, with MIR II in the foreground, investigated in 2001 by SeaRex Inc's James Sinclair at a depth of 4,800m in the North Atlantic Ocean. This is the deepest pre-modern shipwreck found to date and reflects the contribution that commercial companies make to exploring and understanding cultural heritage in deep seas. Photo: courtesy & © Woods Hole Oceanographic and Deep Ocean Expeditions 2001.

3. 'Treasure Hunting' as an Evolving Endeavor

The UNESCO Convention is attempting to eradicate "treasure hunting and indiscriminate salvage". I heartily agree that 'treasure hunting', as historically defined by the archaeological community, needs to be ended, even though blanket prevention is an impossibility. But the Convention fails to discriminate between the reality of different forms of commercial activities. The traditional image of treasure hunting groups is no longer valid. In their wake professional shipwreck recovery groups have evolved in a milieu of ever-stricter regulations and oversight. Those entities that now seek to do this work are nothing like their 20th-century ancestors.

Fig. 2. The bows of the wreck of the deep-sea English merchantman of c. 1810 contained a cargo of coconuts and glass bottles. Photo: courtesy & © Woods Hole Oceanographic and Deep Ocean Expeditions 2001.

Despite the fact that the shipwreck salving of the previous century has greatly changed (technologies, methodologies, motivations of companies involved in the commercial recovery and management of underwater cultural property and resources), the same rhetoric denigrating private sector efforts remains. The situation is highly reminiscent of the struggle for legitimacy by commercial contract archaeology groups within the wider field of academic and institutional archaeology 20 years ago. Those who held positions of power within the broader field demeaned contract archaeology as inferior to their standards. Yet now the same companies that struggled so mightily perform the majority of archaeological work in nearly every industrialized country.

The challenge for commercial shipwreck exploration and recovery groups today is to show the various agencies tasked with oversight that no single strategy is correct for the entire UCH/Submerged Historic Properties resource. Indeed, managers must consider a pallet of options for management before final decisions are reached.

Fig. 3. Detail of domestic assemblage wares in the stern of the deep-sea English merchantman of c. 1810, including ceramic plates, a stoneware bottle and an hourglass. Photo: courtesy & © Woods Hole Oceanographic and Deep Ocean Expeditions 2001.

4. Collections Management Issues

One of the greatest false premises that the Convention codifies is the rule against the "barter, trade or sale" of underwater cultural heritage. In this the realities of modern collections management challenges are discounted. In the USA many archaeologists have been very carefully taught the credo that the archaeological record is not for sale at any price. Any irretrievable dispersal of parts of a collection has been envisioned to degrade somehow the meaning and thus archaeological value of the whole assemblage. As a result some often seemingly absurd collections have been preserved; from bags of soil for 'future analysis' to thousands of fragments of a type of mayonnaise jar from the 1960s, for such was US Federal Law.

We are now at the end of the first decade of a new century and the global economic situation is less secure. Budgets have been slashed across all spectrums of the heritage industry, and some of the hardest hit programs are those tasked with storing excavated artifacts. Each artifact in a museum or archive takes up space and therefore represents an expense. Financial managers are looking very hard at how these archives are used and by whom. There is a growing realization that it is no longer tenable to retain everything for perpetuity.

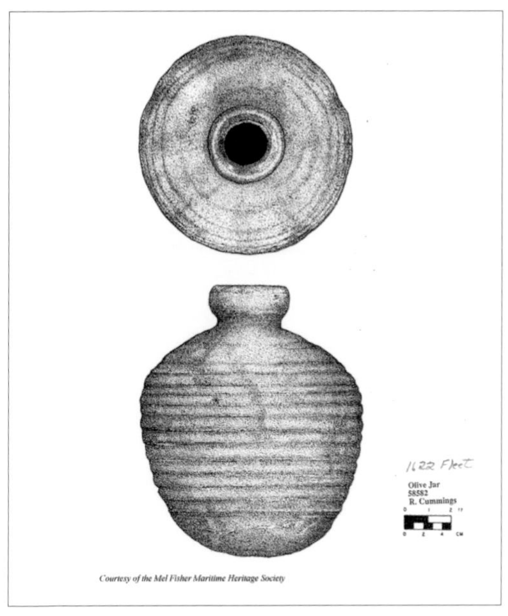

Fig. 5. The wreck of the Atocha *has produced an important collection of olive jars that contribute to understanding of the development of the container's typology. Photo: © Mel Fisher Maritime Heritage Society, Inv. No. 58582a.*

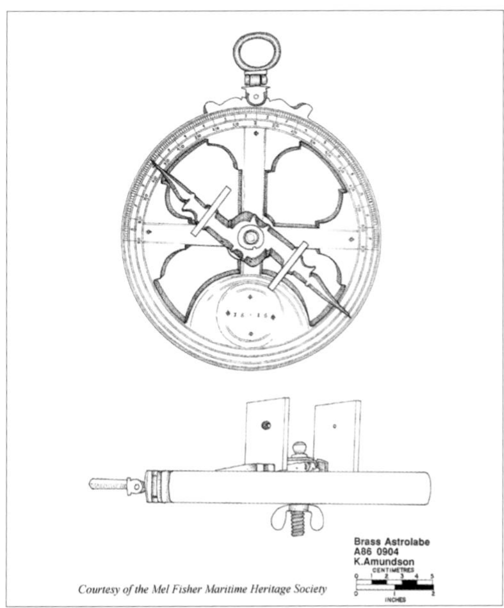

Fig. 4. The wrecks of the Nuestra Señora de Atocha *and* Santa Margarita *from the* Tierra firme *fleet lost off the Florida Keys in 1622 have yielded the largest collection of Colonial Spanish artifacts recovered and studied from the sea. A significant part of the collection, such as this well-preserved astrolabe, has been professionally drawn. Photo: © Mel Fisher Maritime Heritage Society, Inv. No. 86a-0904a.*

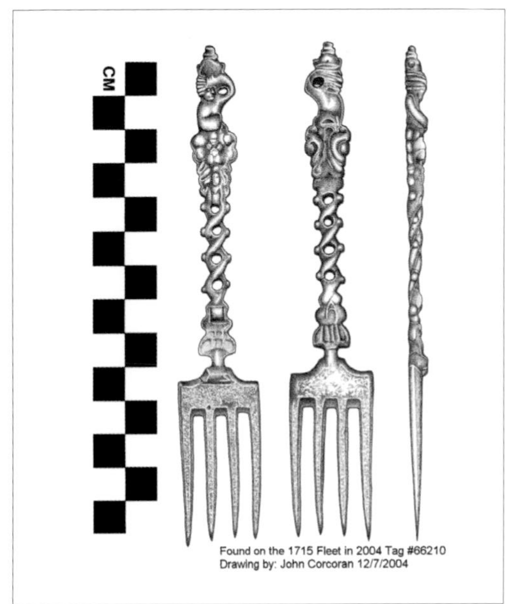

Fig. 6. A decorated silver fork from a wreck associated with the 1722 Spanish fleet off the Florida Keys. Photo: © Mel Fisher Maritime Heritage Society, Inv. No. 04-1715-66210.

In fact in the USA national collecting policies are presently being rewritten (cf. Warner, 2009; Warner and Sonderman, 2010). Many objects once defined as part of a permanent collection will now be deaccessioned. The culling of 'redundant' collections will force archaeologists and curators alike to make value judgments about the relative worth of objects, something that for a very long time they have been loath to do.

Fortunately, technological advances will greatly mitigate the specter of loss. Systems for the capture and storage of data are today at a level that could only be dreamed of a decade ago and will continue to develop. We can now create a virtual collection or assemblage archive of sufficient detail to more than satisfy most researchers. So one of the greatest arguments against the private sector utilization of these cultural properties through sale or dispersal will soon become a standard part of nearly all archaeology in the USA.

The future may lie in innovative ideas, such as private curatorship, with large numbers of private citizens serving as owners and caretakers of parts of the collective heritage of mankind, all interconnected through modern technology and financial self-interest to the museums that hold the master virtual archive. Instead of being a static collection on shelves, these artifacts will become more of a living, breathing heritage co-managed by varied private owners and collectors.

Bibliography

Warner, Mark., *Sandpoint Archaeology Project Collection Management Protocol* (University of Idaho, 2009).

Warner, M. and Sonderman, R., 'Drowning In Artifacts: a Discussion on Deaccessioning and the Implications for Historical Archaeology' (*SHA 2010 Conference on Historical and Underwater Archaeology, Amelia Island Plantation, Jacksonville, Florida, January 6-9, 2010*).

UNESCO, Commerce & Fast-Food Maritime Archaeology

Sean Kingsley
Director, Wreck Watch Int., London, UK

1. 'Fast Food' Archaeology

No marine archaeologist working today could contest the merits of taking a 'time out' to assess where the discipline is heading in the 21st century. As an incentive for soul searching and fresh ideas, the UNESCO Convention on the Protection of the Underwater Cultural Heritage is a force for good. Myriad countries with non-existent or unstructured underwater heritage programs desperately need an 'off the shelf' guide as the Convention provides.

A problem arises when UNESCO is seen to speak with the authoritarian voice of a global watchdog. Different countries inhabit localized geographic realities, varying degrees of looting, funding streams and established managerial traditions that make any idea that all underwater cultural heritage can be managed using unitary policies unrealistic.

This is where the Convention demands clarity. Single solutions create 'fast-food' archaeology. For instance, the territorial waters of Israel are notoriously shallow. Almost all of the 200 wreck sites along the 230km-long coastline lie in depths of under 10m and, in the case of over 15 Canaanite to Early Islamic wrecks in the port of Dor, in less than 4m (Figs. 2-4). Such sites are easily accessible by all. Some 60% of wrecks have already been looted across Israel and by 2012 little maritime heritage will survive *in situ* in these shallows (Kingsley, 2004: 27-33).

For this reason the marine branch of the Israel Antiquities Authority favors artifact recovery (Fig. 1). Coupled with academic research, which necessitates the removal of assemblages, *in situ* would be both a destructive and scientifically unenlightening tool. It is no coincidence that the optimum data available anywhere in the Mediterranean about the transition from shell-first ships built with mortise and tenon technology towards a frame-first philosophy around the 6th century AD comes from Israel courtesy of intrusive exploration (Kingsley, 2002: 86-94; Mor and Kahanov, 2006).

2. Quantifying the Past

One positive side effect arising from CPUCH's promotion of *in situ* preservation as a primary managerial option is a move towards quantifying regional underwater heritage.[1] Countries including Australia, Ireland, France, Israel, Italy, the UK and USA hold extensive databases that have quantified the resource by location, date and form. Such knowledge is just a beginning.

UNESCO could make conceivably its most important contribution to underwater cultural heritage by establishing a worldwide standardized value system for qualifying 'importance', along the lines developed by English Heritage in the UK. Period, rarity, documentation, group value, survival/condition, fragility/vulnerability, diversity and potential are all integrated non-statutory criteria adopted by the Advisory Committee for Historic Wreck Sites and the Department for Culture, Media and Sport to assess the importance of wrecks.[2] A further layer of high level values is also considered (Dunkley, 2008: 24-5):

- Evidential: a wreck's potential to yield primary evidence about past human activity.
- Historical: how the present can be connected through a wreck to past people, events and aspects of life.
- Aesthetic: how people derive sensory and intellectual stimulation from a wreck site.
- Communal: the meanings of wrecks for the people who relate to them and whose collective experience or memory it holds (eg. commemorative and symbolic values).

The first phase needed worldwide today for underwater cultural heritage management by national organizations and contract companies alike is without doubt this regional quantification of the resource and the formal qualification of its value. This would create a relatively objective means of assessing what may be left *in situ*, to a degree abandoned to time and tide, and what simply must be protected or recovered for present and future science, education and indeed recreation and entertainment.

Fig. 1. A vast hoard of Mamluk and Hellenistic metal wares and coins was recovered from shallow water wrecks off Megadim along the Carmel coast, Israel, to prevent them being looted. Intrusive excavation is an essential managerial tool in the marine archaeology of Israel.

Fig. 2. Recovery of an early 7th-century AD Byzantine bronze steelyard from Dor, Israel, bearing Greek inscriptions, enabled the Christian owner to be identified as 'Psates of Rhion'. Photo: Sean Kingsley.

3. Hunting 'Treasure Hunters'

One of the most hostile initiatives of the UNESCO Convention is its undisguised broadside on 'treasure hunters'. This is an area of veritable over-emphasis. The bad old days of unrestricted large-scale plunder and the quarrying of high-value cargoes is a thing of the past. It began to fade in the 1980s with the *Atocha* and *Margarita* shipwreck project, which were the first 'treasure hunting' operations to employ academically-trained archaeologists as part of their team.

Curiously, however, far more information has been published about Spanish wrecks in the 'Americas' initially discovered or managed through commercial models, including final reports and studies of pottery and gold bars (cf. Barto Arnold and Weddle, 1978; Craig and Richards, 2003; Earle, 1979; Lyon, 1979; Marken, 1994;

Mathewson, 1986; Pearson and Hoffman, 1995), than for any Colonial-era wreck of 16th-19th century date in Spanish waters. One is hard pressed to identify any preliminary report from Spain, let alone a final publication.

There is no doubt that commercial companies including Arqueonautas (Mirabel, 2006), Maritime Explorations (Blake and Flecker, 1994; Flecker, 1992), and Nanhai Marine Archaeology (Brown and Sjostrand, 2002; Sjostrand, 2007) are making major contributions to the field today, while Odyssey Marine Exploration has set new standards for pioneering custom-tooled technology and recording using Remotely-Operated Vehicles in the deep (Stemm and Kingsley, 2010). All of these companies rely on select artifact sales to cover costs of operations and indeed to generate profits. By the letter of the UNESCO Convention law, these activities are taboo and should be outlawed.

A major issue of false perception prevails. All of the above companies conduct contextual archaeology and do not rip high-value cargoes out of wrecks. Their reports reveal that the recovery of mass-produced 'trade goods' for sale is just one – albeit highly significant – set of interlocking scientific objectives. Further, the governments of Indonesia, Malaysia, Philippines, Singapore, Thailand and Vietnam consciously embrace commercial models based on the split share of cargoes as a core model to save shipwreck heritage long-term (Flecker, 2002). In parts of Southeast Asia, where finances are particularly limited, this is the most robust way to combat looting, trawling and site dynamiting. The West has to be cautious not to preach to governments who have specifically and legally chosen this path.

Commerce is not as perilous as some interpreters of the UNESCO Convention promote. Witness the five unique oared galleys of the late 3rd-4th centuries AD excavated in Mainz, Germany, during the construction of an extension to the Hilton Hotel and now on display in the custom-designed Museum of Ancient Ships (Pferdehirt, 1995).

Meanwhile, the foundations for a new control center for the Rome-Genoa national railway in Pisa exposed 30 wrecks dating between the 1st century BC and the 7th century AD in December 1998 at a cost of £9.3 million (Sedge, 2002: 158-70). Gino Nunes, the President of the Provincia di Pisa, has realistically observed (Bruni, 2000: 9) that:

> "The archaeological, historical and artistic heritage contained and partly concealed in Pisan territory could constitute an inexhaustible resource with potential benefits which are not solely cultural. For this reason we believe that private companies should also be actively involved in operations for the preservation and appreciation of the area's historical and artistic heritage. Safeguarding a cultural heritage is an operation that entails investment, but can also create wealth."

Fig. 3. Recording hull remains beneath ballast on the late 6th century AD Dor D shipwreck, Israel. Over 15 wrecks lie within this harbor and many are exposed naturally after winter storms, when they become vulnerable to looting. Recording and select recovery is the preferred regional managerial option. Photo: Sean Kingsley.

Fig. 4. Tenons on the hull of the late 6th century Dor D shipwreck were left loose in mortises and were unpegged. The same harbor has yielded 6th-century wrecks that are of entirely frame-first construction. The commercialization of the Holy Land wine trade was a major stimulus behind the shift away from shell-first shipbuilding. Photo: Sean Kingsley.

Fig. 5. The 'Jesus Boat', a 1st-century Roman fishing boat excavated and recovered from the western shore of the Sea of Galilee has provided key information about inshore seafaring at the time of Jesus and also stimulated the local economy. Photo: Sean Kingsley.

Fig. 6. The port of Byzantine Constantinople under excavation at Yenikapi, Istanbul, during a $2.6 billion project to build a metro link between the European and Asian shores of the Bosphorus. Some 32 shipwrecks of the 5th-11th centuries AD have been identified during the $24 million rescue excavation. Several hulls will be lifted for study and eventual display. Profit and archaeology are inevitable and natural bedfellows.

Even UNESCO acknowledges that "The attraction of the historic significance, beauty and authenticity of underwater sites can have a considerable economic importance for many regions", naming the Roskilde, *Mary Rose*, Bodrum, Vasa and Hedeby museums as key attractions.[3]

The core of the commercial debate, in truth, is the same that enshrouds the Elgin Marbles: open the gates to change and a tidal wave might consume us in an unbridled free-for-all. It is a serious anxiety, but a situation that is best debated and managed, not outlawed. The history of collecting proves that an intellectual demand has always existed for ownership of part of the past. But it is not an insatiable hunger and can be controlled. Uncontrolled, it runs the risk of disappearing underground unmonitored.

If commercial archaeology companies working underwater create project plans, fully publish results after comprehensive recording and cataloguing, retain all rare cultural goods permanently, deposit statistically valid samples of assemblages in museum collections, offer complete and intact collections as the first option to museums, and promote outreach through educational programs, popular magazines and television documentaries, it would be hypocritical to suggest that they are making any less of a contribution than most national heritage organizations or contract firms that promote little and publish less than 80% of sites. As Marie Curie once wrote, "Nothing in life is to be feared, it is only to be understood. Now is the time to understand more, so that we may fear less."

Notes

1. At a session on 'In Situ Preservation' convened at the Institute for Archaeologists' annual conference on 14 April 2010, Ulrike Guérin, Secretary of the UNESCO Convention on the Protection of the Underwater Cultural Heritage, emphasized that contrary to some misinterpretation UNESCO has never proposed that *in situ* preservation should be the 'preferred' managerial option. It is an option that should be considered as a primary possibility. She also expressly stated that intrusive excavation is not disallowed.
2. See: http://www.english-heritage.org.uk/server/show/nav.20794.
3. See: http://www.unesco.org/en/underwater-cultural-heritage/the-heritage/museums-tourism.

Bibliography

Barto Arnold, J. and Weddle, R., *The Nautical Archaeology of Padre Island. The Spanish Shipwrecks of 1554* (New York, 1978).

Blake, W. and Flecker, M., 'A Preliminary Survey of a South-East Asian Wreck, Phu Quock Island, Vietnam', *International Journal of Nautical Archaeology* 23.2 (1994), 73-91.

Brown, R.M. and Sjostrand, S., *Maritime Archaeology and Shipwreck Ceramics in Malaysia* (National Museum, Kuala Lumpur, 2002).

Bruni, S. (ed.), *Le navi antiche di Pisa* (Florence, 2000).
Craig, A.K. and Richards, E.J., *Spanish Treasure Bars From New World Shipwrecks, Volume One* (En Rada Publications, Palm Beach, 2003).
Dunkley, M., 'The Value of Historic Shipwrecks'. In I. Radic Rossi, A. Gaspari and A. Pydyn (eds.), *Proceedings of the 13th Annual Meeting of the European Association of Archaeologists (Zadar, Croatia, 18-23 September 2007)* (Zagreb, 2008), 18-28.
Earle, P., *The Wreck of the Almiranta. Sir William Phips and the Search for the Hispaniola Treasure* (London, 1979).
Flecker, M., 'Excavation of an Oriental Vessel of c. 1690 off Con Dau, Vietnam', *International Journal of Nautical Archaeology* 21.3 (1992), 221-44.
Flecker, M., 'The Ethics, Politics, and Realities of Maritime Archaeology in Southeast Asia', *International Journal of Nautical Archaeology* 31.1 (2002), 12-24.
Kingsley, S., *A Sixth-Century A.D. Shipwreck off the Carmel Coast, Israel. Dor D and Holy Land Wine Trade* (BAR Int. Series 1065, Oxford, 2002).
Kingsley, S., *Shipwreck Archaeology of the Holy Land. Processes and Parameters* (London, 2004).
Lyon, E., *The Search for the Atocha* (New York, 1979).
Marken, M.W., *Pottery from Spanish Shipwrecks, 1500-1800* (University Press of Florida, Gainesville, 1994).
Mathewson, R.D., *Treasure of the Atocha* (London, 1986).
Mirabal, A., *Intermediate Report on Underwater Archaeological Excavations off the Island of Mozambique and Mogincual, from April to November 2005* (Arqueonautas, 2006).
Mor, H. and Kahanov, Y., 'The Dor 2001/1 Shipwreck, Israel – a Summary of the Excavation', *International Journal of Nautical Archaeology* 35.2 (2006), 274-89.
Pearson, C.E. and Hoffman, P.E., *The Last Voyage of the El Nuevo Constante. The Wreck and Recovery of an Eighteenth-Century Spanish Ship off the Louisiana Coast* (Louisiana State University Press, 1995).
Pferdehirt, B., *Das Museum für Antike Schiffahrt* (Mainz, 1995).
Sedge, M.H., *The Lost Ships of Pisa* (New York, 2002).
Sjostrand, S., *The Wanli Shipwreck and its Ceramic Cargo* (Department of Museums, Malaysia, 2007).
Stemm, G. and Kingsley, S. (eds.), *Oceans Odyssey Deep Sea Shipwrecks in the English Channel, Straits of Gibraltar & Atlantic Ocean* (Oxbow Books, Oxford, 2010).

The UNESCO Convention for Protecting Underwater Cultural Heritage: a Colombian Perspective

Daniel De Narvaez
Naval Historian & Investigator, Bogota, Colombia

Colombia was one of the six nations initially selected to draft the UNESCO Convention on the Protection of Underwater Cultural Heritage, an avid promoter and wholehearted supporter as the regional leader of the GRULAC, the Latin-American and Caribbean group. Colombia's representative at UNESCO, former Minister of Culture Juan Luis Mejia, asserted his relentless effort and interest in the following way:[1]

> "In three aspects we can summarize the obstacles that needed to be overcome to reach an agreement: the fear of many States that this Convention would undermine the 1982 Law of the Sea Convention; the Colonial concept of other States had that considered the rights of the "flag state" to be unlimited in time; and the third, and most difficult of all, the pressure of marine treasure hunting companies that tried to eliminate all legal barriers that limit its devastating action and whose ultimate goal is profit."

In retrospect, it is sad to say that the Convention has produced catastrophic results that have trampled venerable maritime concepts such as the Law of Finds, the Law of Salvage and property rights, necessary concepts that have remained prevalent among maritime nations since Phoenician times, rewarding the recovery of property lost at sea. As a result, the Convention has created a system that makes the recovery of artifacts from historic wrecks virtually impossible for developing nations and, instead, exposes historic wrecks to destruction if left unprotected. The Convention is based on several assumptions, all of which have been seriously challenged, primarily in nations that have so far adhered, such as the case of Panama. Several other assumptions are clearly wrong.

1. Threats to Colombian Underwater Cultural Heritage

Colombia possesses an immense marine area covering 926,660 square kilometers, with borders touching Ecuador, Panama, Costa Rica, Nicaragua, Honduras, Jamaica, Haiti, the Dominican Republic and Venezuela. Major unresolved boundary disputes are still pending with a few of these nations, presently disputed in international tribunals. The threat to underwater cultural heritage in Colombian waters is very real: dredging, erosion, looting and the destruction of marine archeological material has resulted in the permanent loss and destruction of valuable cultural material.

Colombia's marine areas have immense potential for extracting oil and mineral deposits and also contain hundreds of historical wrecks submerged on its ocean floor. An estimated 1,200 Colonial-era documented shipwrecks lie within its territorial waters, EEZ and on its Continental shelf.[2] A significant proportion of these contain great amounts of gold, silver and uncut emeralds. Most of the Colonial silver from the Viceroyalty of Peru aboard the South Sea fleet, and all the gold from the very rich Chocó and Cauca districts, sailed across what are now Colombian waters, and a significant part of these sank.

The privileged confluence of the Spanish Pacific trade routes and the *Tierra Firme* fleet routes that crossed through Colombian waters has accumulated immense wealth on the seabed. The galleons concerned were menaced by innumerable shoals and reefs, producing hundreds of wrecks that have been protected until recently by the isolated location of these uninhabited landmasses. Quitasueño shoal, for example, is a totally submerged 64km-long coral reef, which became a marine cemetery harboring hundreds of historic wrecks during the eras of Discovery and Colonialism.

Most of the objects that lie on the ocean floor are fragile and rapidly decaying and to assert that these objects need to be left on the ocean floor as common cultural heritage only shows arrogance and contempt. What percentage of the Colombian population can presently dive to maximum depths to view these wrecks, compared to the thousands who could visit them inside a museum? According to the naval historian Claudio Bonifacio, 110,000 tons of gold lie on the world's ocean floors.[3] While this figure seems surprisingly high, there is no question that in general the seas contain an immense collection of valuable and historically significant artifacts.

One of the main criticisms of the UNESCO Convention is the core principle of considering '*in situ* preservation' to be the first option before allowing any activity on submerged heritage. Wrecks lying, for example, in the Mediterranean Sea are better protected from looters due to the greater depth of its waters. Researchers believe that 80% of Caribbean wrecks rest in depths of less than 20m, whereas the greater majority of Mediterranean sites are likely to be located in depths of more than 30m, where they are better protected naturally from divers and looters. This principle of *in situ* preservation is obviously more applicable to European and Mediterranean nations rather than to the Caribbean.

2. Beyond Territorial Waters

Most of the countries present at the UNESCO Convention negotiations were ready to extend the jurisdiction of the coastal State to include underwater cultural heritage found on the continental shelf and EEZ.[4] For Colombia, this extension of the jurisdiction of coastal states (in regard to Nicaragua, for example) beyond the limits of territorial waters could undoubtedly alter the delicate balance embodied in UNCLOS between the rights and obligations of the coastal state and its neighbor. Of particular negative consequence to Colombia, due to its immense treasure-rich EEZ, is Article 9, Paragraph 5 of this Convention, which states that:

> "Any State Party may declare to the State Party in whose exclusive economic zone or on whose continental shelf the underwater cultural heritage is located its interest in being consulted on how to ensure the effective protection of that underwater cultural heritage. Such declaration shall be based on a verifiable link, especially a cultural, historical, or archaeological link, to the underwater cultural heritage concerned."

Both Venezuela's and Nicaragua's continental shelves are immersed inside Colombia's EEZ, and the possibility that Colombia would be obligated to "consult" with these countries, that are currently disputing title to extensive marine areas where valuable shipwrecks are known to lie, would be a nightmare for any foreign relations ministry and would certainly create a great deal of internal political turmoil. Furthermore, a recent ruling by the Colombian Supreme Court regarding the controversial Sea Search Armada case (for the rights over the famous *San Jose* galleon)[5] has produced new jurisprudence that contradicts the UNESCO Convention's position by stipulating Colombian title over all shipwrecks in its EEZ.

Another transcendental consequence of this 2007 ruling is the clear differentiation the Supreme Court has made between what it has determined to be "cultural patrimony" artifacts that cannot be commercialized and those that can be commercialized, again in clear contradiction to the proposed absolute ban established in UNESCO's CPUCH.

3. Sovereign Immunity

Odyssey Marine Exploration's recent legal proceedings in Tampa, Florida, have demonstrated the vulnerability that former Spanish colonies are now exposed to by Spain's arbitrary claims as a consequence of the fine line between a military mission and a commercial mission by State ships. Spain is using this perceived ambiguity as a valuable weapon camouflaged under the concept of Sovereign Immunity, which might allow it to try to acquire new rights to the immense wealth that lies on Colombia's ocean floor. The concept of Sovereign Immunity, as applied to Spanish historic wrecks lost in Colombian waters, has gained a new dimension in the UNESCO Convention that can only be used to the detriment of the title of Colombia's underwater cultural patrimony, in clear opposition to its Constitution.

4. Commerce & Shipwrecks

Lastly, the prohibition against commercialization in Article 2.9 of CPUCH, tied to the all-inclusive controversial definition of underwater cultural heritage as "all traces of human existence", makes the recovery of exposed or threatened shipwrecks an almost impossible prospect for countries where Ministries of Culture have very limited funding and where financing would have to be at the expense of more urgent social needs.

Several Colombian historic wrecks contain huge amounts of gold and silver bars or rough uncut emeralds that possess little intrinsic cultural or museological value following recording and study, which, if they were allowed to be commercialized, would facilitate the prompt recovery of major cultural patrimony and irreplaceable historic artifacts that could fill museums and cultural centers. The commercialization of trade goods and uncut emeralds of no cultural or archeological significance is surely a small price to pay to finance the recovery and preservation of hundreds of historic wrecks now possibly being plundered and vulnerable to disappearing forever.

5. Conclusion

Between 29 November and 1 December 2004 the Ministry of Culture of Colombia organized and hosted a Latin-American and Caribbean meeting in Bogota, with the participation of very high-level UNESCO personalities, such as Mr. Guido Carducci,. Its recommendations were "To invite the governments of Latin America and the Caribbean that have not done so, to begin the internal process towards the ratification of the UNESCO Convention..."[6] More recently, on 24 November 2008, another meeting was held in Cartagena with the participation of renowned marine archaeologists, such as Marc-André Bernier from Parks Canada and Chris Underwood from the Nautical Archaeology Society.

Despite these initiatives it would seem that concerns and contradictions remain in respect to Colombia's position on its underwater cultural heritage. If validation of the UNESCO Convention is adhered to, it would bring about countless constitutional problems with our oceanic neighbors, breaking the current balance and relative geopolitical stability.

Notes

1. See: http://www.pensamientoiberoamericano.org/articulos/4/97/3/apuntes-sobre-las-politicas-culturales-en-america-latina-1987-2009.html.
2. See: http://mesaculturalantioquia.files.wordpress.com/2009/03/politicas-culturales-en-colombia_marta-elena-bravo.pdf.
3. See: http://www.buceo21.com/REPORTAJES entrevistas/102bonifacio.htm.
4. Scovazzi, T., 'Convention on the Protection of Unde water Cultural Heritage', *Environmental Policy and Law* 32.3-4 (2002), 152-57.
5. Corte Suprema De Justicia Sala De Casación Civil Magistrado Ponente Carlos Ignacio Jaramillo Jaramillo Bogotá, D.C., cinco (5) de julio de dos mil siete (2007). Ref: Expediente 08001-3103-010-1989-09134-01.
6. Memorias Seminario-Taller Regional De America Latina Y El Caribe Sobre La Convencion De La UNESCO Para La Protection Del Patrimonio Cultural Subacuatico, 57. See: http://www.sinic.gov.co/SINIC/Publicaciones/Archivos/Patrimoniosubacuatico.pdf.

Virtual Collections & Private Curators: A Model for the Museum of the Future

Greg Stemm
Chief Executive Officer, Odyssey Marine Exploration, Tampa, USA

David J. Bederman
K.H. Gyr Professor of Private International Law, Emory University School of Law, Atlanta, USA

Many museum collections are today experiencing an unprecedented crisis in storing and curating enormous collections, a significant percentage of which often lie outside the remit of contemporary collecting strategies. Public funds for the acquisition, conservation, preservation, display and storage of such museum objects are becoming increasingly restricted.

On the basis of Odyssey Marine Exploration's extensive research into deep-sea shipwrecks, for which a robust commercial model is obligatory to enter and research this extremely expensive scientific arena, this paper proposes a new managerial tool: a Private Curatorship program ('PC'). The policy and legal implications of museums deaccessioning certain types of collections for private stewardship are discussed as well as the substantial qualifications and legal restrictions that would accompany private curatorship.

1. Introduction

Many museum collections today are in a state of crisis unprecedented in the history of curatorship. Public funds for the acquisition, conservation, preservation, display and storage of museum objects (particularly archaeological or historical objects) are scarce and the costs for proper care and treatment of collections have been skyrocketing. Many museums today are placed in the unenviable position of choosing between various initiatives – such as infrastructure building, program development, visiting installations, new acquisitions or preservation of existing collections – recognizing that it is impossible to accomplish all of these objectives with the funds available from public agencies, member support or philanthropic institutions.

The time is ripe to propose a new paradigm for collections management, one that takes advantage of technological innovation, public/private partnerships, notions of individual stewardship for historical objects, and the ultimate objective of any museum: the preservation of knowledge for future generations. This paper discusses the policy and legal implications of deaccessioning certain types of collections by museums or governments for private stewardship, or conditioning acquisitions of new collections, based on the concept that a certain selection of objects in such collections can be owned, curated and stewarded by private individuals under a pre-determined set of legal restrictions.

The basic concept is that there are collections that consist (to a certain degree) of largely duplicative or fungible objects. In these situations, it is not always a preferable option for a museum to retain ownership, and thus assume the expensive and resource-intensive responsibility of conservation and curatorship over the entire collection. Instead, a museum might consider keeping a representative sampling of such a collection (perhaps around 10% of all objects comprising the collection or, at a minimum, the finest exemplars of objects) and designating the remainder for a Private Curatorship program ('PC'). The museum would then transfer title to the remaining objects (either individually or in sub-collection units) to private collectors.

Ownership would come with substantial qualifications under this PC concept. First, the private owners would agree to curate and conserve the artifacts under specified conditions and modalities as a condition of their acquisition. Second, the private owners would agree to pay for the expense of the artifacts being digitally imaged and catalogued in a database maintained by the museum for future researchers – creating a virtual collection and archive. Third, the private owner would agree to make their objects available for actual physical inspection, study and (non-intrusive and non-destructive) testing by researchers, qualified and approved by the museum, on reasonable terms of visitation. Fourth, these conditions would run with the objects in perpetuity, meaning that if a private owner sold the artifacts to another collector, the transaction would be reported to the museum and the same restrictions would apply to all subsequent owners. In exchange for agreeing to these PC restrictions, the private owner otherwise receives fee simple title to the object(s), along with a guarantee of provenance and marketable title.

This paper will briefly explore this new collections management concept and will primarily focus on the policy and legal implications of collections derived from underwater cultural heritage (UCH) sources, in light of new international cultural heritage trade and collection management developments.

2. Museum Collections & Artifacts in Danger

It is beyond doubt that many collections of artifacts held by museums and libraries in the United States and throughout the world are disintegrating and degrading because of poor conservation, improper storage, and a lack of funds for curatorship. In the United States this is confirmed by a Heritage Preservation/Institute of Museum and Library Services/New York Public Library report issued on 6 December 2005 (Heritage Preservation, 2005). According to this survey of 3,370 museums, libraries and archives, many did not have the most basic environmental or climate controls to protect artifacts, only one in five had paid staff devoted to conservation, and only one in three had an up-to-date assessment of the overall conditions of their collections. Shockingly, nearly 65% already reported extant damage to their collections. The report estimated that 270 million books and journals, 189 million scientific specimens, 153 million photographs, 4.7 million works of art and 13.5 million historical objects were at risk and in need of immediate care.

Put quite simply, the old museum model of a physical location where history and knowledge are stored and displayed forever, where collections are never deaccessioned, and where there are ostensibly endless resources (space, technology, money and time) for conservation and curatorship, is unsustainable. Intelligent and wise choices need to be made now as to the proper allocation of resources to collections management, and we need to consider the possibility that private stewards may be in a superior position to curate certain kinds of collections, under specified legal and technical conditions. This is not simply a matter of 'out-sourcing' what had previously been viewed as essential museum functions and services. Rather, it is imperative that we rethink the relationship between a museum and its public.

Figs. 1-2. Black glass beer bottles (H. 24.5cm & 20.3cm) and champagne-style bottles (H. 25.4cm and 30.8cm) from the SS Republic, *wrecked in 1865 at a depth of 500m off southeast America. A sample of 8,529 glass and stoneware bottles of repetitive types was recovered, all of previously recognized forms. They are defined as trade goods due to a combination of their high-volume on the wreck and commonness within archaeology and antiques circles.*

Figs. 3-4. The wreck of the Republic *contained an extensive cargo of white ironstone china produced in Staffordshire, England, including mugs (H. 9.5cm) and slop jars (H. 31.5cm). Some 2,775 examples were recorded and recovered. Status: trade goods.*

3. Policy Concerns with Deaccessioning Collections or Privatizing Collections Management

In America the deaccessioning of collections is no longer regarded as a breach of public trust by a museum, gallery or similar institution. Instead, it is considered an essential part of collections management. Among the criteria for deaccessioning objects and, indeed, of acquisitions policy, are considerations of the following factors: whether the object is no longer relevant to the museum's mission; the object has deteriorated beyond usefulness; the object is hazardous to other collections or staff; or the object is wrongly attributed or even potentially a fake. Perhaps the most significant factor is whether there are multiple examples of the same (or substantially similar items) in the collection (cf. Malaro, 1998; Weil, 1998).

The US policies of relevant standard-setting and best-practices bodies for museums, libraries and archives have all recognized changes in deaccession policies which permit disposition of objects or artifacts into other museums or into private collections under appropriate circumstances. Moreover, it has been recognized that under certain conditions it may be entirely appropriate to privatize or transfer ownership to private individuals or private museum collections under certain aspects of collections curation and conservation. As long as acquisition/deaccession decisions are made consistently in light of relevant policies and guidelines, it would be permissible to assign to private ownership parts of museum collections that are redundant or duplicative, for which the cost of conservation and storage is prohibitive and in instances when the gains from curating and exhibiting the entire collection are limited.

The situation in the United Kingdom, by contrast, remains more stringent and rooted on a "strong presumption against disposal" (Besterman, 1992: 30), a term preferred in the UK to deaccession. Thus, the *Report of the Committee of Enquiry into the Sale of Works of Art by Public Bodies* (1964), chaired by Viscount Cottesloe (paragraph 30) stated that (Loynd, 1987: 122):

> "When a work of art is given to a museum or gallery for general exhibition, the public thereby acquires rights in the object concerned and these rights cannot be set aside. The authorities of the museum or gallery are not the owners of such an object in the ordinary sense of the word; they are merely responsible, under the authority of the courts... If they attempt a sale in breach of trust it is the function of the Attorney-General to enforce the trust and protect the

rights of the public in the object by taking proceedings in the Chancery Division."

This 'law' of trust is today incorporated into the annually published Museum's Association Code of Practice for Museum Authorities and in the Museums and Galleries *Guidelines for a Registration Scheme for Museums in the United Kingdom* (1988). The Museum Authority's Code of Practice outlines strict procedures to be followed where disposal is proposed (Ewles, 1991: 37).

In reality, the above opinion has never been tested in court. Although many museum professionals view these protocols as definitive statements of the legal basis on which they hold collections, they are not legally binding because only acts of parliament and statutory instruments have the absolute force of law. It should also be emphasized that the *Report of the Committee of Enquiry into the Sale of Works of Art by Public Bodies* is confined to gifts "for public exhibition" and thus does not cover material in museum storage.

The British Museum Act (1963) governing the British Museum and Natural History Museum permits exchange, gift or other disposal of duplicates, printed material after 1850 for which there is a photographic record and of material useless due to damage, physical deterioration or infestation. More general permission exists for Trustees to dispose of items that in their opinion are "unfit to be retained and when disposal would not be to the detriment of students." Similar rules are in place under the National Heritage Act (1983) for the Victoria & Albert Museum, the Science Museum and via the Merseyside Museums & Galleries Order (1986). The Museum of London Acts (1965 and 1986) permit exchange, sale or other disposals of duplicates, or objects no longer required for museums purposes, but requires a two-thirds majority of the Museum's Board (Babbidge, 1991a: 256). None of these Acts include controls over disposal that are as rigorous as those advised by the Museums & Galleries Commissions *Guidelines for a Registration Scheme for Museums in the United Kingdom*. Legally, only the National Gallery and Tate Gallery are expressly forbidden from disposal of items in collections within the UK (Babbidge, 1991a: 255).

Charitable trusts can protect collections by law, however (Babbidge, 1991b), and trustees in England and Wales wishing to dispose of assets need the consent of the Charity Commission or the courts (Ewles, 1991: 37). If permission is not sought, action can be taken by the Attorney-General. Overall, the UK situation has been termed a blunt and ineffectual instrument (Loynd, 1987: 122).

Fig. 5. A lead spigot (L. 11.7cm) from the wreck of the Republic *(1865). Status: trade good.*

Fig. 6. The 51,414 coins onboard the Republic *(1865) are the archetypal trade good category. Every coin was fully recorded and the entire collection quantified by type, date and mint origin.*

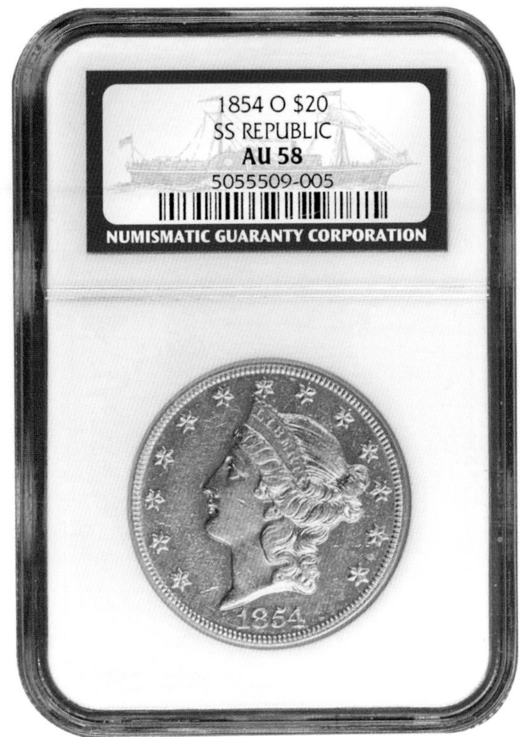

Figs. 7-8. A gold $20 and silver 50-cent coin from the wreck of the SS Republic *(1865). After conservation, every coin from this site was 'slabbed' to protect it long-term from atmospheric pollution, wear and tear.*

4. Case Study for Underwater Cultural Heritage

Objects derived from underwater cultural heritage (UCH) sources present special problems and opportunities for the policy of private curatorship presented in this paper. Collections derived from shipwreck resources may often be generally divided into two categories.

'Trade Goods' are those artifacts which are duplicative and fungible items carried on board vessels as freight before they were sunk, whether in the form of specie, bullion, ceramic wares, amphoras or shipping crates. These are typically characterized by large quantities of machine or handmade items that are nearly identical, and often reflect types of artifacts that are already widely collected by the private sector and are well published (Figs. 1-11).

'Cultural Artifacts' are artifacts that were part of the ship or its contents that reflect naval architecture and ship design, ship handling and seamanship, maritime life and the personal effects of crew and passengers (Figs. 12-21). This category may reflect more unique artifacts that are not necessarily duplicative or fungible. Obviously, some of these objects may be truly unique and would not be subject to a policy of subsequent deaccession or private curatorship considered here.

Relevant standards and best practices have evolved as to UCH collections management. The 1996 International Council of Monuments and Sites (ICOMOS) Charter for the Protection and Management of Underwater Cultural Heritage, takes a relatively uncompromising view of the subject. Article 13 of the ICOMOS Charter, on the curation of UCH collections, provides that:

> "The project archive, which includes underwater cultural heritage removed during investigation and a copy of all supporting documentation, must be deposited in an institution that can provide for public access and permanent curation of the archive. Arrangements for deposition of the archive should be agreed before investigation commences, and should be set out in the project design. The archive should be prepared in accordance with current professional standards. The scientific integrity of the project archive must be assured; deposition in a number of institutions must not preclude reassembly to allow further research. Underwater cultural heritage is not to be traded as items of commercial value."

While the prohibition of trade in UCH could be interpreted as absolute, it should be understood in the context of ensuring the integrity of collections and providing for a collection to be effectively studied by subsequent researchers in the future.

The 2001 UNESCO Convention on the Protection of Underwater Cultural Heritage (CPUCH) takes a far more nuanced approach to this subject. While article 2(7) states that "Underwater cultural heritage shall not be commercially exploited," the term "exploit" has a wide range of meanings and so it needs to be placed in the context of other provisions. Article 18(4) notes that disposition of UCH artifacts should "be for the public benefit, taking into account the need for conservation and research; the need for reassembly of a dispersed collection; the need for public access, exhibition and education." The Annex to CPUCH, which articulates rules concerning activities directed at underwater cultural heritage, has a number of provisions relevant to the policy discussed here. Rule 2 provides:

> "The commercial exploitation of underwater cultural heritage for trade or speculation or its irretrievable dispersal is fundamentally incompatible with the protection and proper management of underwater cultural heritage. Underwater cultural heritage shall not be traded, sold, bought or bartered as commercial goods.
>
> This Rule cannot be interpreted as preventing:
>
> ...(b) the deposition of underwater cultural heritage, recovered in the course of a research project in conformity with this Convention, provided such deposition does not prejudice the scientific or cultural interest or integrity of the recovered material or result in its irretrievable dispersal; is in accordance with the provisions of Rules 33 and 34; and is subject to the authorization of the competent authorities."

Rules 33 and 34 provide together that:

> "project archives, including any underwater cultural heritage removed and a copy of all supporting documentation shall, as far as possible, be kept together and intact as a collection in a manner that is available for professional and public access as well as for the curation of the archives... The project archives shall be managed according to international professional standards, and subject to the authorization of the competent authorities."

Neither the ICOMOS Charter, nor UNESCO's CPUCH, are binding authority for a museum in the United States or for any country that is not a signatory to the Convention. Indeed, the United States Government has declared that it has no intention of ever signing the UNESCO Convention. Despite the Burlington House Declaration issued by various heritage managers in London in 2006 as a call for the government to sign CPUCH, and which resulted in an informal consideration of the Convention's Annex as best practice, the government of the United Kingdom still shows no inclination to ratify the Convention.

Fig. 9. A spirits bottle (H. 26cm) from the mid-19th century 'Jacksonville Blue China' wreck recorded at a depth of 370m off southeast America. Status: trade good.

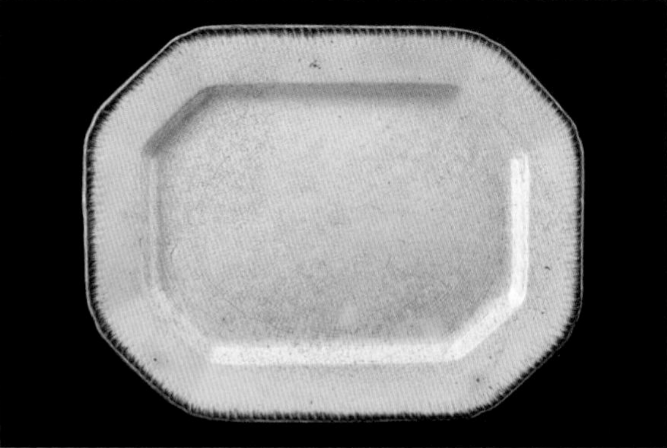

Figs. 10-11. A blue shell-edged English soup plate and platter (W. 24.2cm and 34.7cm) from the 'Jacksonville Blue China' shipwreck, whose cargo included soup plates, plates and platters. Status: trade goods.

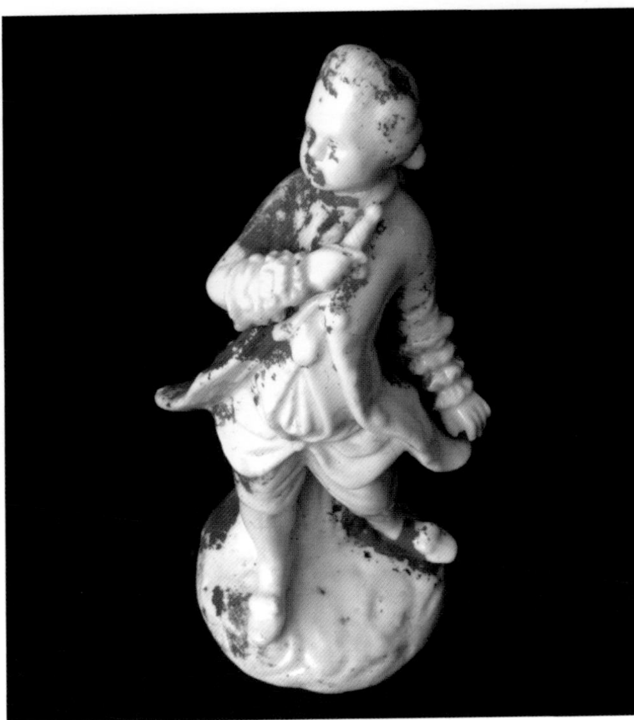

Fig. 12. A porcelain male figurine from the SS Republic *(1865), probably of French origin and the counterpart to a male/female matching pair, both without pigment or paint in the 18th-century Rococo style (H. 13.4cm). Although both were low value products in 1865 and remain inexpensive on today's antiques market, these objects are defined as cultural artifacts due to their low frequency on the wreck.*

Fig. 13. One crate of 96 religious artifacts on the Republic *(1865) included porcelain kneeling angels with the remains of its red paint still visible (H. 6.5cm). All seven examples of angels were retained for Odyssey's permanent collection. Status: cultural artifacts.*

In any event, neither the ICOMOS Charter nor the UNESCO CPUCH would seem to preclude an underwater cultural heritage collections management policy of the type described here. As long as:

A. Acquisition/deaccession policies are made with a view to the duplicative/fungible nature of certain classifications of UCH artifacts.
B. A virtual repository is made for the entire collection.
C. There is a means provided for researchers to examine all objects in a collection.
D. The collection is not "irretrievabl[y] dispers[ed]."

Under these circumstances a system of Private Ownership Curation and Stewardship (PC) should be permissible, even under these very restrictive articulations of collections management policies and best practices.

Before a UCH collection is even considered for the PC model, a systematic decision will need to be made about the fungible/redundant nature of the objects comprising the collection. The collection as a whole will need to be catalogued and studied. Variations among different individual artifacts/objects in the collection or sub-collections will need to be analyzed. A statistical sampling of artifacts will need to be conducted in order to ascertain what number of retained artifacts would constitute a 'representative sampling' of the collection as a whole. Examples of the finest objects from the collection would have to be designated. Sub-collections reflecting representative groups of artifacts would need to be identified.

5. Modalities of Restrictive Covenants for Objects Subject to a PC Policy

Essential to any collections management scheme which relies on private curators is a set of restrictions governing the object. Such restrictions will fall into a few different categories. One general and undelegable obligation for the PC owner is to apprise the museum of any change in the ownership status of the object, contact information for the owner, location of the display or storage of the object, or condition of the object. Each object would be assigned a unique ID number and label (perhaps coupled with a RIF, radio frequency tag) to facilitate the management process.

1. First, the private owners would agree to curate and conserve the artifacts under specified conditions and modalities as a condition of their possession. It is intended that the conditions of curatorship would vary with different classifications of objects. For collections derived from

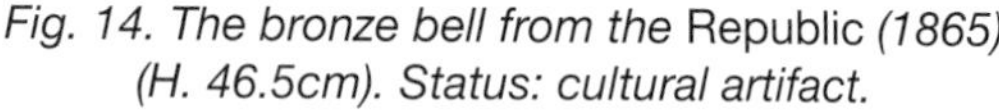

Fig. 14. The bronze bell from the Republic *(1865) (H. 46.5cm). Status: cultural artifact.*

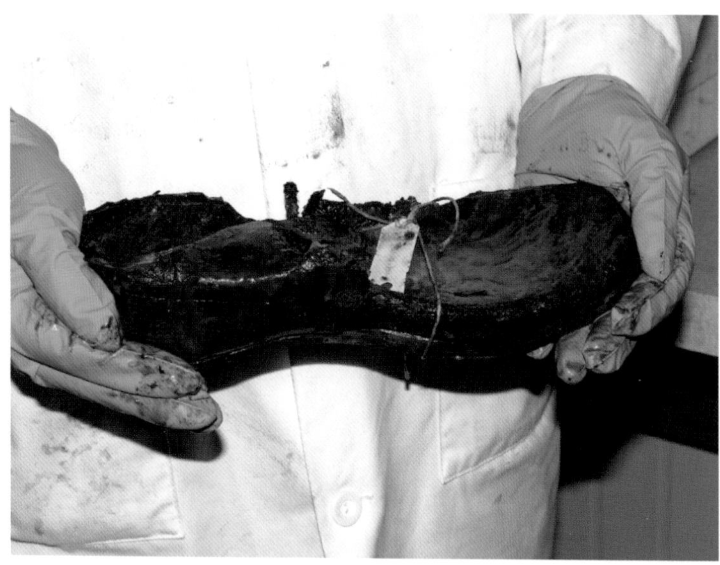

Fig. 15. A leather shoe from the Republic *(1965) (L. 26.1cm). Status: cultural artifact.*

UCH, it would be safe to assume that before deaccession or allocation to a private owner under a PC plan, the object would have been successfully stabilized after its recovery from an aquatic environment (whether freshwater or saltwater), properly conserved, recorded and documented. Additionally, as has been discussed above and considered further below, the object would, as part of the documentation process, have also been preliminarily studied, catalogued, and imaged. Presumably the object will be in a condition (or nearly so) of being capable of display. Finally, the museum curators would need to have a sufficient understanding of proper curation techniques for the object concerned, so that it would be possible to effectively instruct a private curator about its proper handling and treatment. The PC deed of trust would specify the proper way in which the object must be displayed, stored and conserved.

Under the PC policy, a private curator would be under an obligation to take all necessary and reasonable steps to curate the object and conserve it properly to reasonable standards. Under the deed of trust, dependent on the significance of the artifact a PC owner may be required to file an annual report about the condition of the object in a format specified by the museum, with a photographic record (such might be accomplished by a web-based reporting system).

An additional requirement might be that every ten years (or within another specified time frame) the PC owner would be obligated to take affirmative steps to have the condition of the object surveyed by a museum staff member (or a designated conservator or organization to undertake such a task), in what will be referred to here subsequently as 'sabbatical inspections'. Obviously, this will entail costs for the owner (such as arranging transport of the object to the museum or to reimburse the expenses of a party undertaking the inspection). Also, at regular intervals, the museum will have to update the owner about changes in knowledge or technology regarding the proper curation of the object.

2. *Second, as part of the purchase price of the piece, the private owners would pay for the expense of the artifact being digitally imaged and catalogued in a database maintained by the museum for future researchers, in what might be termed a virtual collection.* Part of the fee paid for the private owner to acquire a PC object (which will also reflect the market value for such objects, if ascertainable, as adjusted by the PC restrictions) would be to recapture the costs for the museum to establish a virtual database for the collection. The database will be publicly accessible through a user- and researcher-friendly interface through the web.

At a minimum, the database entries would include the ID information for the artifact, all standard cataloguing information (dimensions, a narrative characterization of the object, provenance data, etc.), as well as digital visual

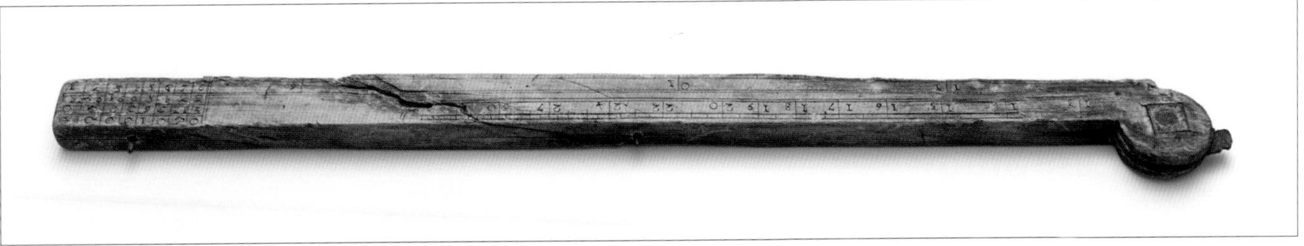

Fig. 16. A unique c. *mid-17th century wooden folding rule from Site 35F in the Western Approaches to the English Channel (L. 30.7cm). Status: cultural artifact.*

images of the artifact taken from all angles, at the highest possible resolution specifications and performances, and any other imaging data. The database will also include references to the stabilization, conservation, and curation history of the artifact, including the annual and regular inspection reports for the object. Any researcher notes for the object will be included. Data concerning the current ownership and location of the object will generally not be publicly available through the database (for privacy and security concerns), but, as will be discussed in point 3 below, will be known to the museum. As 3D technology evolves, three dimensional recording might also be utilized as a mechanism for storing data.

3. *Third, the private owner would agree to make his/her objects available for actual inspection, study and (non-intrusive and non-destructive) testing by researchers, qualified and approved by the museum, on reasonable terms of visitation.* Most researcher inquiries about a collection will be answered either through study of the representative sampling of exemplary objects maintained on premises by the museum, or through consultation of the virtual collection through the database. On occasion, though, an accredited researcher may approach the museum with a study query that involves the actual viewing of objects in the possession of PC owners. In such circumstances, it may be incumbent on the museum to vet the research plan, subjecting it to peer review and evaluation. Only in the event of an approved plan by an accredited researcher would the museum make contact with the affected PC owners to arrange a visitation.

When such a visitation has been sought on reasonable terms of access, it would be incumbent for the PC owner to allow it. The researcher (or sponsoring institution) would bear the costs of the visitation. The researcher will be allowed to inspect, examine, study and handle the object. The researcher may not conduct any form of intrusive or destructive test on the object, unless firstly the museum has expressly approved such in the research plan and has expressly queried through the peer review process whether such testing is absolutely necessary for the accomplishment of the research plan, and secondly the PC owner has consented to such in writing, after being fully informed of the risks and benefits of such testing through a process of consent.

The museum, and the affected PC owner(s), would receive the results of the research and copies of any published studies about the collection objects. Such notes and studies would be included as part of the collection database.

4. *Fourth, these conditions would run with the objects in perpetuity, meaning that if a private owner sold the artifacts to another collector, the transaction would be reported to the museum and the same restrictions would apply to all subsequent owners.* These restrictions and conditions would be reduced to terms in the bill of sale from the museum to the PC owner. Although technically a bill of sale, because it does convey title over the object to the PC owner, it will also be referred to here as a deed of trust. The restrictions in the bill of sale/deed of trust will run with the object in perpetuity. A current PC owner is free to sell, gift or bequeath the object to another owner (whether an individual or legal person: corporation, trust, foundation, or partnership), but the restrictions will follow the object along the chain. It will be required that any subsequent transaction involving the object include all of the PC restrictions.

The bill of sale might also contain a reversionary clause by which title will revert back to the museum under one of three extraordinary conditions. First, should a current owner (if an individual) die intestate and the object would otherwise escheat to the state, or (if a legal person) cease to exist, liquidate or wind-up without a legal successor, the object would be returned to the museum's ownership. Second, if a current owner is found to have legally abandoned the object, it would be returned to the museum's ownership. Third, should a court of competent jurisdiction find that any or all of the PC restrictions are unenforceable or unconstitutional in a *cy pres* action (used to challenge unlawful provisions of trusts and estates), then the artifact would be returned to the museum's ownership and the money paid presumably returned.

6. Legal Enforceability of Restrictive Covenants for PC Artifacts: the United States Law as a Case Study

The PC restrictions are, legally speaking, a restrictive covenant or equitable servitude that will run with ownership of the personal property. Such restrictions are usually disfavored in law because they obviously enough interfere with the free purchase and sale of goods. Nevertheless, in the case of the USA they have been upheld when narrowly tailored and where consistent with public policy: see *P. Lorillard Co. v. Weingarden,* 280 F. 238, 238-40 (W.D.N.Y. 1922). Public policy grounds have been broadly construed by courts: see *Nadell & Co. v. Grasso,* 175 Cal. App.2d 420, 346 P.2d 505 (1959). It is highly doubtful that any court would disagree that the public policy objectives of the PC restrictions – maintaining cultural heritage not only for the interests of a private owner, but also for the benefit of society at large – are anything but laudable.

The essential element of all these rulings is that a subsequent purchaser had adequate notice of the restrictions at the time of purchase or transfer. See *In re Waterson, Berlin & Snyder Co.,* 48 F.2d 704, 708 (2d Cir. 1931) ("one who takes property with notice that it is to be used in a particular way receives it subject to something resembling an equitable servitude. Courts in the United States have enforced rights resembling an equitable servitude binding on a third party who has acquired personal property from one who is under a contract to use it for a particular purpose or in a particular way"). The PC restrictions outlined above would certainly be well known with the purchase and ownership of any historical artifact or museum-grade object.

Privity of contract is not necessarily required as an element in these equitable servitude for personalty (moveable private property) cases. See *Nadell,* 175 Cal. App.2d at 431; *Clairol, Inc. v. Sarann Co., Inc.,* 146 U.S.P.Q. 726, 734 (Pa. Common Pleas 1965); *Waring v. WDAS Station, Inc.,* 327 Pa. 433, 448- 56, 194 A. 631 (1937). That means that the PC restrictions would notionally be enforceable, even if not expressly included in the bill of sale between a subsequent seller and subsequent purchaser. (Obviously, the PC restrictions would be embodied in the bill of sale from the museum to the first private owner. It should be a condition of the original sale that all subsequent transactions include all of the PC restrictions.)

These sorts of equitable servitudes in personalty have been upheld, or at least recognized, under Florida law. See *Tri-Continental Financial Corp. v. Tropical Marine Enterprises, Inc.,* 265 F.2d 619, 626 (5th Cir. 1959) ("Where

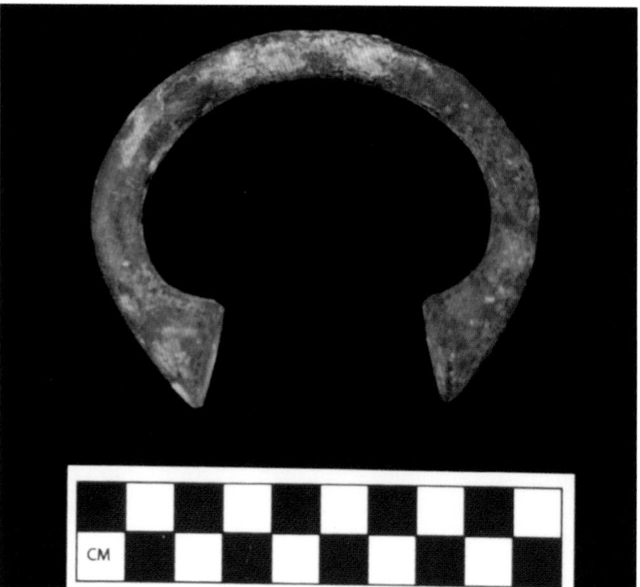

Fig. 17. One of nine copper manilla currency bracelets (L. 8.9cm) from the c. mid-17th century Site 35F in the Western Approaches to the English Channel. All have been retained in Odyssey's permanent collection. Status: cultural artifact.

Fig. 18. Ginger jars from Canton of c. 1840-60 from the mid-19th century 'Jacksonville Blue China' wreck (H. 15.3cm). These low frequency objects on the site have been retained as cultural artifacts in Odyssey's permanent collection.

Fig. 19. English slip-decorated earthenware mugs (H. of large mug 11.4cm) from the 'Jacksonville Blue China' wreck. Status: cultural artifacts.

Fig. 20. A 1st-2nd century AD amphora from a Roman wreck in the Western Mediterranean. Odyssey will sometimes recover a small sample of artifacts from ancient sites to aid in dating and identification. All are retained for study or donated to museums. Status: cultural artifacts.

restrictive covenant with respect to the use of property, real or personal, is valid, it may be enforced by injunction but only as against one under obligation not to violate the covenant. Since a purchaser with notice gets title subject to the restriction he may be enjoined from using the property in violation of the restriction") (citing *Weissman v. Lincoln Corp.*, 76 So.2d 478, 481 (Fla. 1954)). Florida courts have certainly recognized covenants not to compete in regards to some sorts of personal property. *Rinker Materials Corp. v. Holloway Material Corp.*, 167 So.2d 875 (Fla. App.1964), cert. denied, 173 So.2d 145 (Fla.1965); *Kofoed Public Relations Associates, Inc. v. Mullins*, 257 So.2d 603 (Fla. App.1972), cert. denied, 263 So.2d 230 (Fla.1972).

A properly drafted restrictive covenant or equitable servitude, embodying the PC restrictions, should thus be enforceable under Florida law or in any state of the Union. In America the PC bill of sale/deed of trust would designate Florida law as the law of the contract, and designate a Florida court as the forum for resolution of any disputes. A judgment procured in any state of the Union would be enforceable elsewhere under principles of comity and full faith and credit. In anticipation that the artifact might be sold abroad, a clause could be added to the original bill of sale/deed of trust that, in the event a subsequent owner of the artifact is located outside of the United States, the PC restrictions would be enforced via international arbitration, designating an arbitral forum (such as the International Chamber of Commerce in Paris), as well as the applicable law of the contract.

The most reasonable means of legally enforcing the PC restrictions, in the event that a subsequent private owner fails to abide by them, is to secure an equitable injunction compelling compliance. This might be useful in the event that a subsequent owner is grossly uncooperative in any attempts to arrange visitation of the object by an accredited researcher. It may be a less useful legal mechanism in the event that a subsequent purchaser fails to record the transaction, file annual updates on the object, arrange for sabbatical (seven-year or 10-year) inspections or properly conserve or curate the artifact. Nonetheless, in extraordinary circumstances the museum – as the original owner of an artifact – might seek an injunction against a subsequent owner to seek compliance with one or more of the PC restrictions, and to prevent transfer of title in the artifact without being in compliance with the restrictions.

7. Inducements for Compliance with Restrictive Covenants: Provenance & Marketability

A far more credible and efficient means of enforcing the PC restrictions will be to rely on market mechanisms and enlightened self-interest, rather than the threat of injunctive proceedings. It is probably safe to assume that those parties that seek to become owners-curators-stewards of objects from a collection will be well meaning and public-spirited. Although they will be paying a market price for ownership, they will also be allowed to possess, display and conserve an object that usually would only be found in a museum or similar collection.

The primary reason why artifact owners will comply with the PC restrictions is that it will be in their own self-interest to do so. The reporting and sabbatical inspection provisions would actually enhance the value of an object by ensuring that it is kept in a fit condition, and that the latest knowledge of curatorship and conservation is available to the PC owner. Allowing a research visitation for the artifact likewise may increase the object's value, if it is found to possess some unique characteristic that was not previously known or appreciated.

Moreover, having the artifact as part of a comprehensive collection database serves two vital functions for the PC owner. First, it establishes the provenance of the object. In today's antiquities markets having a clear chain of title/custody and an established provenance for an object (that proves that it was lawfully excavated, recovered and acquired) is vital and potentially significantly increases the value of the piece. International restrictions on the trade of illegally excavated artifacts are increasing. Just as importantly, US authorities are now starting to aggressively enforce these rules, including the application of foreign excavation restrictions on artifacts in the hands of US collectors. While such rules are not necessarily applicable to UCH-sourced collections now (at least those recovered from sites more than 24 nautical miles from shore or in international waters), there is always the risk that a UCH-derived object will be confused for one recovered on land or for material recovered illegally from another country's territorial waters. Entry of an object into a collection database would obviate such provenance concerns.

Similarly, a PC owner benefits from the marketability of title conferred by having an object of reputable pedigree in relation to the collection database. Although most PC owners will likely tend to keep their artifacts, there will undoubtedly be sales transactions. In such circumstances, an established provenance and clear chain of title will inure to the benefit of current and subsequent PC owners.

In short, it may be an effective mechanism for the enforcement of the PC restrictions for the museum to threaten the 'de-listing' of the object(s), rendering them not in good standing with the collection registry. Such should only be done in the most egregious of circumstances, such as willful refusals for an object to be subject to sabbatical inspections or research visitations, or with the knowledge that an artifact has been allowed to seriously degrade in condition owing to the neglect of the PC owner. Obviously, it is to be hoped that such events would be rare and that, instead, the vast majority of PC owners would care for, display, preserve and (dare we say) love the object as much as any museum curator.

8. Conclusion

This paper is intended to help chart a course for a new approach to collections management for museums, one that recognizes today's realities of museum operations and the possibilities of new public-private partnerships for the curation of certain types of objects. The concept of Private Curatorship (PC) of historic artifacts has the potential to revolutionize the relationship between museums and the public. Through such a program, the public becomes an extension of the museum curation staff and allows them to invest resources and time in the long-term maintenance of a museum's collection – which in turn provides a solution to one of the most vexing problems confronting museums and cultural heritage managers in the world today.

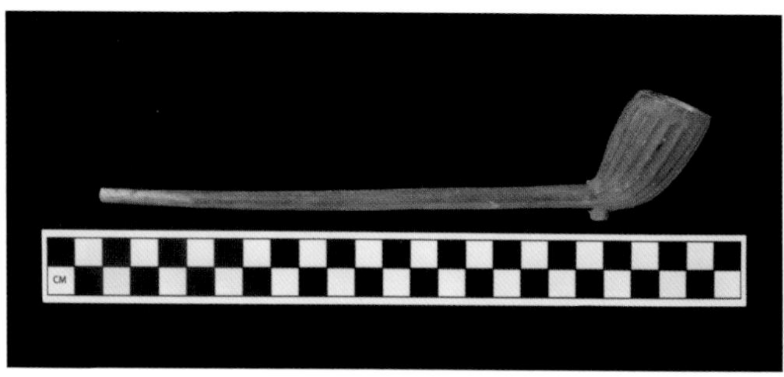

Fig. 21. A clay tobacco pipe from the mid-19th century 'Jacksonville Blue China' wreck. Status: cultural artifact.

Bibliography

Babbidge, A., 'Disposals from Museum Collections. A Note on Legal Considerations in England and Wales', *Museum Management and Curatorship* 10 (1991a), 255-61.

Babbidge, A., 'Legal, Decent and Honest?', *Museums Journal* (September 1991b), 32-34.

Besterman, T., 'Disposals from Museum Collections. Ethics and Practicalities', *Museum Management and Curatorship* 11.1 (1992), 29-44.

Heritage Preservation 2005: *A Public Trust at Risk: The Heritage Health Index Report on the State of America's Collections* (Heritage Preservation, Institute of Museum and Library Services & New York Public Library, 2005): http://www.heritagepreservation.org/hhi/HHI summary.pdf.

Ewles, R., 'Disposal and Registration', *Museums Journal* (September 1991), 37.

Loynd, M., 'The Law', *Museums Journal* 87.3 (1987), 122-3.

Malaro, M., *A Legal Primer on Managing Museum Collections* (Smithsonian Institution Press, Washington, 1998).

Weil, S. (ed)., *A Deaccession Reader* (Smithsonian Institution Press, Washington, 1998.)

A Note on the Wooden Carpenter's Rule from Odyssey Shipwreck Site 35F

Stephen Johnston
Museum of the History of Science, University of Oxford

In 2006 Odyssey Marine Exploration recovered one half of a wooden folding rule from site T7a35f-5, a shipwreck heavily impacted by the offshore fishing industry and located at a depth of 110m in the Western Approaches to the English Channel. The 1ft-long object is one half of a distinctive type of carpenter's joint rule with a design that is characteristically English. The artifact is extremely rare and the earliest example found on a shipwreck. The very limited comparative examples on land suggest a possible date of manufacture for the instrument between the 1660s and 1690s.

1. Scale Identification

The 1ft-long wooden artifact recovered by Odyssey Marine Exploration in 2006 from site 35F in the Western Approaches to the English Channel is a single arm from an originally 2ft-long folding rule (Figs. 1-3). It features a series of lines, numbers and letter abbreviations incised into three sides. These scales (Kingsley, 2008) are the key to identifying and dating the instrument.

1. Side A has three scales (Figs. 1, 3, 5-10):

   a. An inch scale [0]-12, divided to unit, half, quarter, eighth and numbered by 1. This would have continued to 24 on the missing leg.

   b. A pair of scales labelled C and D (Fig. 10), standing for 'Circumference' and 'Diameter'. The two scales share the same format: each begins with a subdivided segment and then a scale of equal parts from [0] to the limit imposed by the length of the rule.

2. Side B has three elements (Figs. 2, 3, 11-15):

   a. The end of a line of board measure running from 12 (at the hinge) to 36, each unit subdivided to half. The scale ends 4in from the end of the leg (4 x 36 = 144 = 1ft square).

   b. The beginning of a line of timber measure from 9 to 12 (at the hinge), each unit subdivided to quarter.

   c. A table of timber undermeasure. This is continuous with the timber line and supplies values for 1 to 8in, which the rule cannot accommodate on the scale line.

3. The edge carries a logarithmic line of numbers 1-10 (Fig. 4). The missing leg would have carried the same scale to make a double radius line 1-100.

2. Mathematical Formulas

Side B for timber and board measure was designed to be used for measuring areas and volumes. This particular format was established during the 17th century as an adaptation of a design first published by Leonard Digges in 1556 (Knight, 1988; see Johnston, 1994 for the 16th-century development, and Johnston, 2006 for a detailed study of an unusual straight carpenter's rule of 1635). The complete instrument would have had a board line running from 7 to 36, with a table of undermeasure from 1 to 6in at the end of the missing leg. The timber line would have run on to 36 on the other leg, terminating 1 1/3in from the end.

The logarithmic line of numbers on the edge was first published by Edmund Gunter in the 1620s. In the form found here, which appeared on a range of instruments in the 17th century, it would have been used with a pair of dividers or compasses as a general-purpose calculator – in effect, a slide rule.

The most distinctive scales are those marked C and D (Fig. 10). They would have been used with compasses or dividers and are interrelated. If the circumference of a log had been measured with string, the scales provided the diameter without calculation. These scales would have been matched by another pair on the missing leg, most likely labelled SE for 'Square Equal' and SW for 'Square

Fig. 1. Site 35F wooden folding rule side A with an incised inch scale numbered [0]-12 inches and divided into half, quarter and eighth units.

Fig. 2. Site 35F wooden folding rule side B incorporates three elements. Inner scale: the end of a line of board measure running from 12 to 36, each unit subdivided to half. Outer scale: beginning of a line of timber measure from 9 to 12, each unit subdivided to quarter. Far left: table of timber undermeasure.

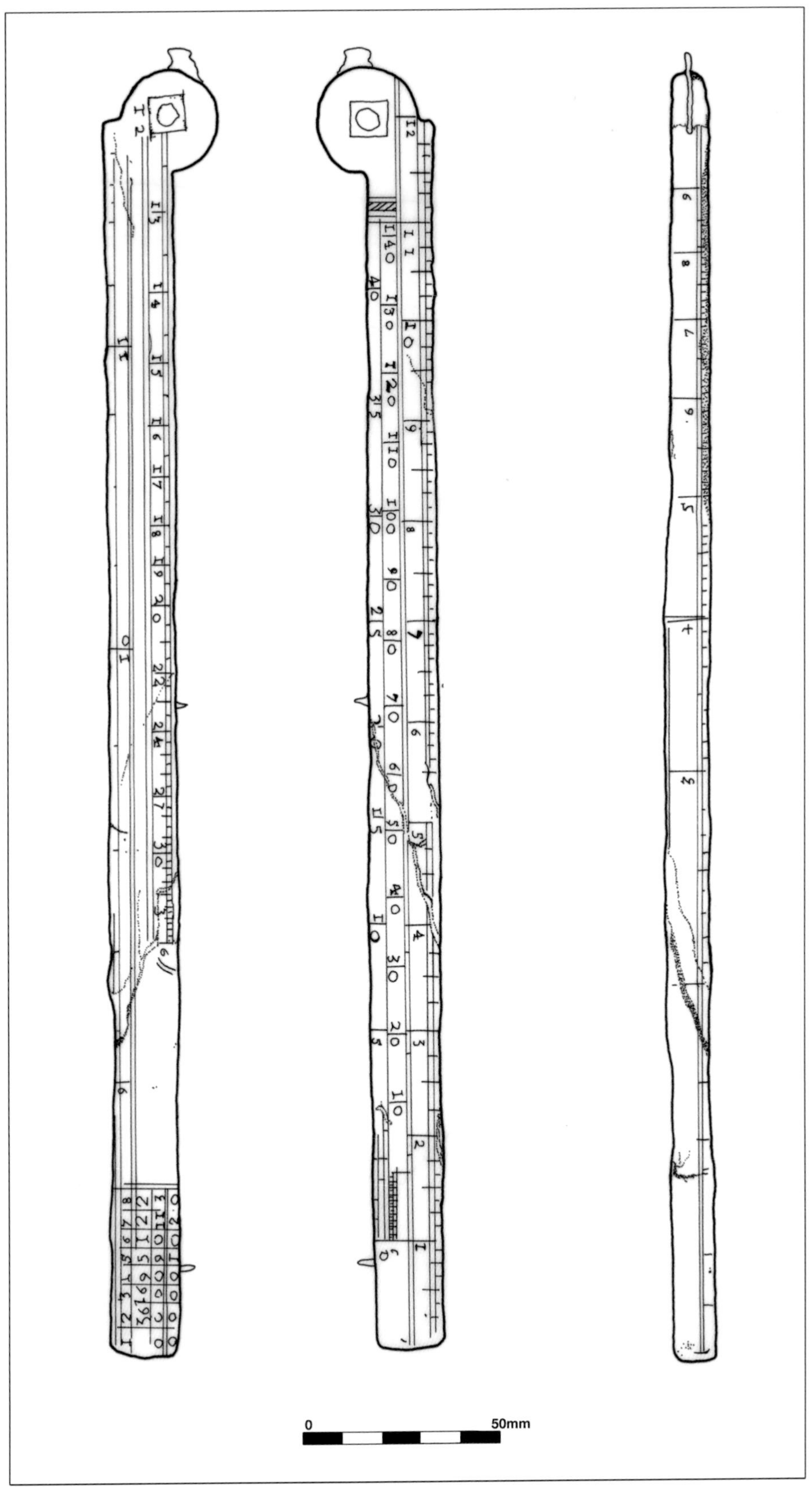

Fig. 3. Drawing of the one arm of the wooden folding rule from site 35F (inv. no. 0010). Left: Side B. Centre: Side A.

Within'. Given any one of these four dimensions, the others can be determined without arithmetic.

For example, to find the diameter of a log with a circumference of 108in, first one foot of a pair of dividers would have been placed on the 100 mark of C, while the other foot would have been extended to the 8 division on the subdivided segment. Keeping the dividers separated, this length would have been transferred to the D scale so that one foot was on a numbered division and the other was in the subdivided segment: the rule would show about 34½in as the diameter. The C scale is simply the D scale multiplied by ϖ (pi), since C = ϖD. The approximation used here is not the standard one of 2 2/7, but a less accurate one of about 3 1/8. (The disparity is easily seen from the scales. When 2 2/7 is used, the divisions for 100 and 30 coincide since, taking account of the subdivided segments, they actually represent 110 and 35.)

The SE and SW scales would have been constructed in a similar way. The square equal provided the side of a square whose area equalled the circle defined by the circumference; squaring this value (easily done with the logarithmic line) provided the cross-sectional area of the circular log. The square within (also known as the inscribed square) gives the side of a square that fits within the circle and hence provided an indication of the usable timber that could be extracted from the log.

3. Historical Context & Chronology

The presence of the C and D scales provides the best clue for dating the instrument. They were first referred to in print in 1661 by the mathematical instrument maker John Brown, who provided an explanatory diagram. Brown's discussion was introduced without fanfare as simply 'The use of four scales, called Circumfence [sic], Diameter, Square equal, Square inscribed'. This brief account appeared in his *The Description and Use of a Joynt-Rule* (London, 1661: 87, 107-8) at the end of a chapter entitled 'The use of certain lines for the mensuration of superficial and solid bodies, usually inserted on Joynt-Rules for the use of Work-men, of several sorts and kindes', which suggests that the scales were already known by this date.

There is some evidence, however, from surviving instruments that these scales were a relatively recent innovation. The Science Museum collection in London retains an instrument (inv. 1954-292) to the same design as the 35F example, which is dated to 1659 (Fig. 16). The four scales are fully labelled as circumference, diameter, square equal and square within. This suggests a degree of unfamiliarity regarding terminology, which had evidently been overcome by the time the 35F example was manufactured and could use the abbreviations C and D.

The Science Museum example remains the earliest currently known that features all four scales. A unique instrument, however, in the National Museums Scotland, Edinburgh (inv. 1978-92), incorporates three of the scales found on the site 35F example. This is a 3ft, three-fold brass carpenter's rule, evidently made in London but inscribed '1655 Robert Trollap of yorke free mason' (Fig. 17). Like the 35F example, it was designed for board and timber measure, and also has an inch scale and a double radius logarithmic line of numbers. It includes three unlabelled scales for circumference, diameter and square equal. There is space where a fourth scale for square within could have been inserted. Its absence suggests that the four-scale pattern, as exemplified on the site 35F wooden rule, was created in the later 1650s.

Prior to their introduction as scales on rules, the problem of the interrelation of these four dimensions had been treated as a topic for the logarithmic line of numbers. When first announcing the logarithmic line in 1623, Edmund Gunter's *De sectore & radio. The Description and Vse of the Sector in Three Bookes. The Description and Vse of the Cross-Staffe in other Three Bookes* (London, 1623: 35-6) provided problems interrelating the circumference, diameter and square equal. Presumably Gunter was the inspiration for the scales on the 1655 instrument now in Edinburgh.

In 1645 Edmund Wingate expanded Gunter's logarithmic problems in *The Use of the Rule of Proportion in Arithmetique and Geometrie* (London, 1645: 65-6) to include the inscribed square. He was followed in 1656 by John Brown's *The Description and Use of the Carpenters-Rule together with the Use of the Line of Numbers (inscribed thereon) in Arithmatick and Geometry* (London, 1656: 53-5), which described the function of the straight 2ft carpenter's rule. Brown, therefore, may have been responsible for the instrument pattern that the 35F example follows.

How long-lived was this particular pattern of carpenter's rule? The characteristic set of four scales was mentioned as an optional extra for joint rules by John Brown in 1677 and they were still current in 1688 when he added their use to a new impression of his *The Description and Use of the Carpenters-Rule*. The latest example of an instrument carrying the 'circle-square' scales currently known is dated to 1685 and is held today at Colonial Williamsburg (inv. 1997-100). In addition to a set of four unlabeled circle-square scales, this carries the familiar complement of board, timber and logarithmic scales, but in a different physical format: it is a three-fold rule, with two 9in wooden legs and a (now broken) folding brass extension piece to complete the full 2ft length (Figs. 18-19).

Fig. 4. Detail of the side edge of the folding rule incised with a logarithmic line of numbers 1-10. (The missing leg would have carried the same scale to make a double radius line 1-100.)

Fig. 5. Detail of the hinge end of side A.

Fig. 6. Detail of the hinge mechanism at the folding end of side A.

Figs. 7-8. Detail of side A.

Fig. 9. The end section of side A.

Fig. 10. Detail of the end section of side A with a pair of scales incised 'C' and 'D', standing for 'Circumference' and 'Diameter'.

Figs. 11-13. Detail of side B.

Fig. 14. End section of side B with table of undermeasure at right.

Fig. 15. Detail of table of undermeasure on side B.

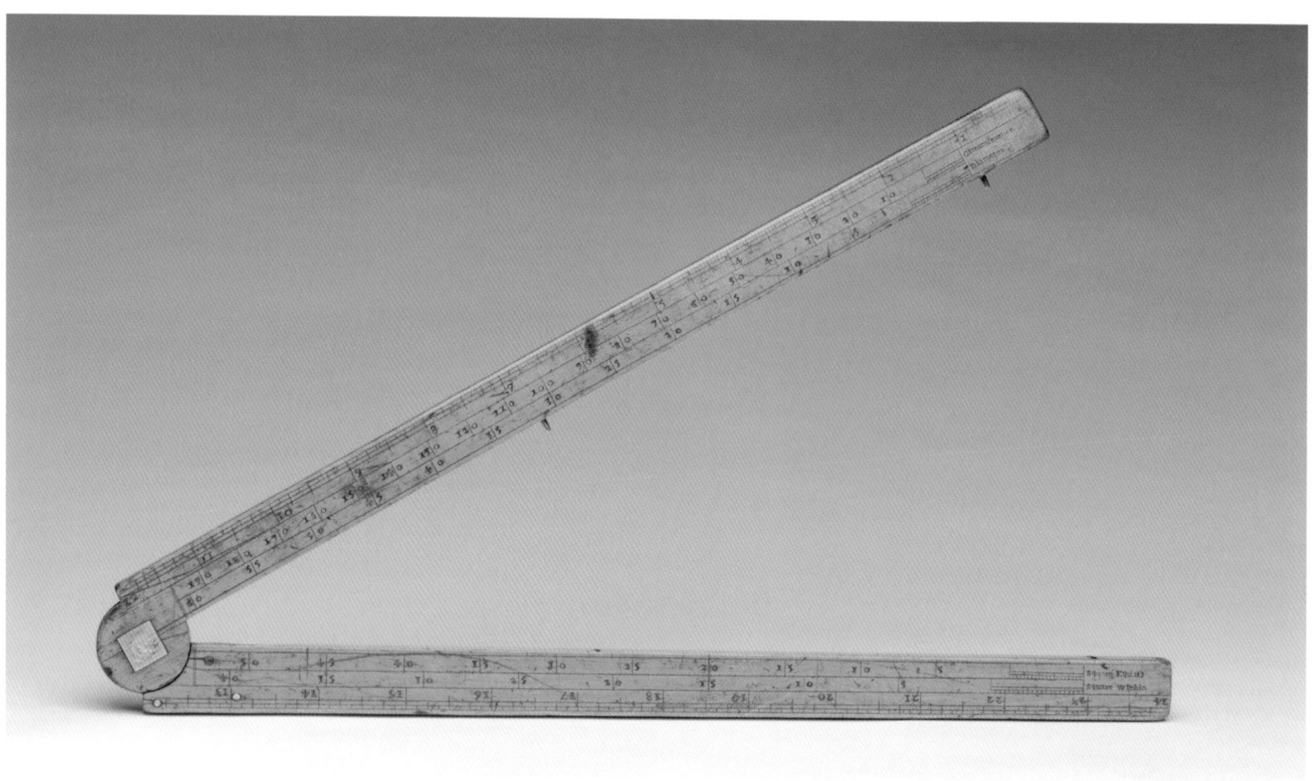

Fig. 16. An intact wooden folding rule in the collections of the Science Museum, London, was crafted to the same design as the site 35F instrument, and is dated by an inscription to 1659. Its four central scales are fully labelled as circumference, diameter, square equal and square within. Photo: © Science Museum, London (inv. 1954-292).

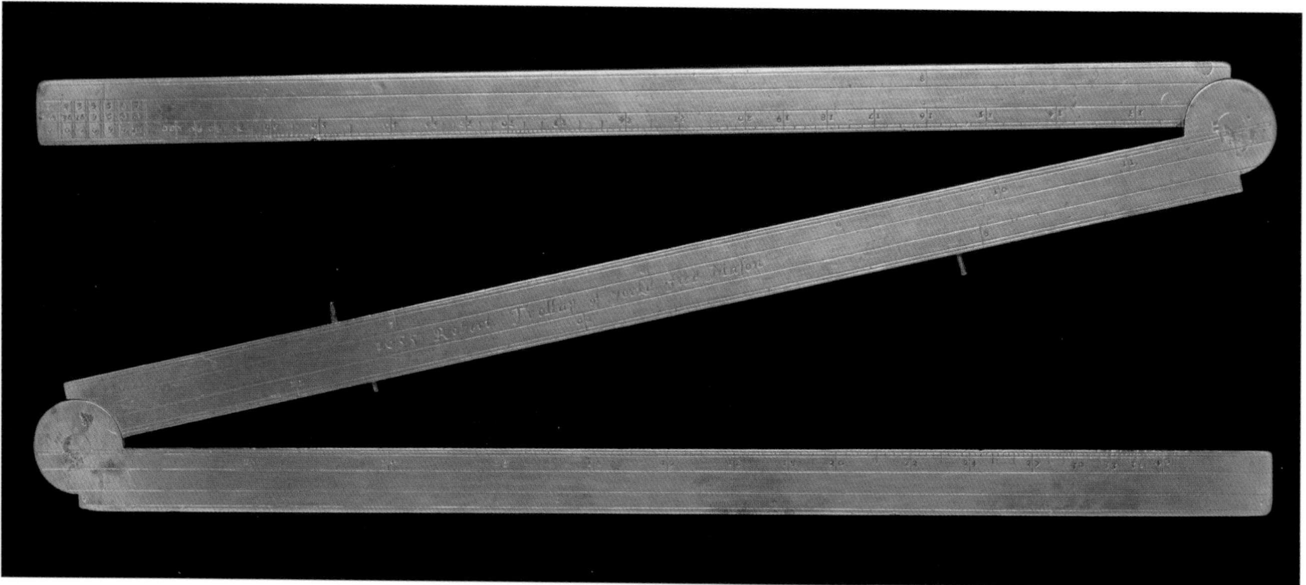

Fig. 17. A unique 3ft, three-fold brass carpenter's rule in the National Museums Scotland, Edinburgh. It shares scales with the site 35F example and appears to be a prototype for the overall design. Though crafted in London, it is inscribed '1655 Robert Trollap of yorke free mason'. Photo: © National Museums Scotland (inv. 1978-92).

Fig. 18. A three-fold rule at Colonial Williamsburg (inv. 1997-100) with inch scale to 18in and the remains of a 6in brass extension piece. The central 'circle-square' scales are unlabelled. Photograph: permission of the Colonial Williamsburg Foundation.

Fig. 19. Detail of the three-fold rule at Colonial Williamsburg signed 'Robart Blake 1685', with an alternating stamped fleur-de-lys. Blake may have been the owner, rather than maker. Photograph: permission of the Colonial Williamsburg Foundation.

Fig. 20. A two-fold, 2ft rule engraved 'N P 1678' in the collection of Colonial Williamsburg (inv. 1995-18). This carries the same arrangement of scales as the site 35F rule, here showing the face with timber and board lines and tables. Photograph: permission of the Colonial Williamsburg Foundation.

It seems reasonable to place Odyssey's site 35F rule in the period between the 1660s and the 1690s. Although no more than an educated hunch, the 1670s or 1680s might be considered most likely. The closest known surviving example is found at the Science Museum, London, dated to 1674 (inv. 1936-33). Another similar example at Colonial Williamsburg is dated to 1678 (inv. 1995-18) (Fig. 20). Both Williamsburg examples have differently applied brass protective end-pieces, perhaps suggesting a different workshop style. The expansion of manufacture could be further investigated by a closer comparative study of the punched numeral forms, as well as additional variations in constructional detail. There are presumably further surviving examples currently lying unidentified in other public and private collections. These may in time shed additional light on the origins of the site 35F rule.

Acknowledgements

Figs. 1-2 and 4-15 are by Lisa Payne. The drawing of the wooden folding rule (Fig. 3) is by Sean Kingsley.

Bibliography

Brown, J., *The Description and Use of the Carpenters-Rule together with the Use of the Line of Numbers (inscribed thereon) in Arithmatick and Geometry* (London, 1656).

Brown, J., *The Description and Use of a Joynt-Rule* (London, 1661).

Brown, J., 'A Supplement, Containing the Description and some Uses, of a convenient Two-foot Joynt-Rule: Upon which are inscribed divers Lines and Scales, sutable to all sort of Artificers occasions'. In William Leybourn, *The Line of Proportion, commonly called Gunter's Line, made easie. A Second Part* (London, 1677).

Brown, J., *The Description and Use of the Carpenters-Rule: together with The Use of the Line of Numbers commonly called Gunter-Line* (London, 1688).

Gunter, E., *De sectore & radio. The Description and Vse of the Sector in Three Bookes. The Description and Vse of the Cross-Staffe in other Three Bookes* (London, 1623).

Johnston, S., 'The Carpenter's Rule: Instruments, Practitioners and Artisans in 16th-century England'. In G. Dragoni, A. McConnell and G.L'E. Turner (eds.), *Proceedings of the Eleventh International Scientific Instrument Symposium* (Bologna, 1994), 39-45.

Johnston, S., 'Reading Rules: Artefactual Evidence for Mathematics and Craft in Early-modern England'. In Liba Taub and Frances Willmoth (eds.), *The Whipple Museum of the History of Science: Instruments and Interpretations* (Cambridge, 2006), 233-53.

Kingsley, S., *A Folding Rule from Odyssey Marine Exploration's Shipwreck Site 35F: a Preliminary Note* (Odyssey Marine Exploration, unpublished, 2008).

Knight, R., 'The Carpenter's Rule', *Newsletter of the Tools and Trades Society* 20 (Winter, 1988), 12-19.

Wingate, E., *The Use of the Rule of Proportion in Arithmetique and Geometrie* (London, 1645).

Brass Guns & Balchin's *Victory* (1744): the Background to their Casting

Charles Trollope, FSA
Colchester, United Kingdom

The 41 bronze cannon discovered and recorded by Odyssey Marine Exploration on the surface of the wreck of Balchin's *Victory* in the western English Channel are unique examples preserved from a First Rate Royal Navy warship active in the early Georgian period. The quantity of the guns and their unity from a single dedicated batch manufactured by Andrew Schalch at the Royal Brass Foundry in Woolwich are unparalleled in surviving collections. Furthermore, they are extremely rare examples of hybrid guns designed by Colonel John Armstrong based on the former Borgard system and a template obtained from the French.

Balchin's *Victory* was built and equipped at a seminal moment in the history of gun founding. The ship was the last fitted with a full complement of purpose-made brass cannon. Those onboard the First Rate *Royal George* and *Britannia*, by contrast, were a cosmopolitan collection of antique English cannon and prizes seized from enemy ships over the course of decades.

1. The Background

At the end of the Second Dutch War (1665-67) it was clear to the Royal Navy that the iron guns in service were not adequate for the demands of the new style of naval warfare, which expected opposing fleets to fight in line at a distance as opposed to in a general melee. In 1670 the Board of Ordnance introduced a new series of guns more suited to this style of naval warfare, which would prove to be an outstanding design and would continue in service for the next 100 years. This series of 1670 was cast in all sizes up to and including the largest calibre (Trollope, 2005), the 'cannon of seven', which was used to arm some of the new First Rate warships (the earlier name for a 42-pounder that referred to the 7in of the bore's diameter).

The drill required gun teams of up to 14 men for a 42-pounder to work in coordination to maintain the gun in action at the best rate possible. The performance of the guns at the range where a hit was likely allowed the 42- and 24-pounders – when fired at a flat trajectory with a point-blank range of some 250 yards (Kinard, 2007: 113) – to smash through the timbers of the opposition and cause havoc, with the solid shot knocking over men, guns and causing a shower of deadly splinters to spread across the danger area. Shots from 42-pounders or 24-pounders would make a hole that could cause a disastrous leak if located at the waterline or below. The 12-pounders and 6-pounders were designed to cause damage to the upper deck levels.

While the iron guns had needed an upgrade to the new enhanced design, the same was not true for the brass equivalents. The greater tensile strength of brass when compared to brittle iron, and coupled with the fact that many of the brass guns cast after 1587 had been cast with excess metal to control the violence of the recoil, made it unnecessary to manufacture new brass guns after 1670. Such brass guns that were already in circulation continued in use.

Brass cannon, however, had inherent deficiencies as described in Captain Franc Stoney and Captain Charles Jones's *A Text-Book of the Construction and Manufacture of the Rifled Ordnance in the British Service* (London, 1872: 29-31):

> "*Bronze*, or rather that particular kind called "*gun-metal*", consists of an alloy of about 90 parts of copper and 10 of tin… it is deficient in hardness, being readily indented and abraded by the projectile, and expanded by the force of the explosion, this softness being increased as the material becomes heated from continuous firing…
>
> The want of uniformity in large bronze castings is due to the fact that copper and tin do not form one definite alloy in the proportion of ten to one (the theoretical proportion in gun-metal), but will form numbers of alloys varying in the richness of either metal. The specific gravity and temperature of fusion of the two metal being also very different, it follows that they separate more or less from one another while cooling, and thus are formed those tin spots and porous patches which have hitherto led to the failure of this material..."

From 1670 solely for prestige purposes, and to make use of perfectly good brass guns still in circulation, four out of the seven contemporary First Rate Royal Navy warships retained their brass armament. This consisted of English guns dating back to as early as 1587, plus French, Dutch and the occasional Spanish cannon captured in the various wars of the 17th century.

Historically, when First Rates with brass ordnance were rebuilt the brass guns were retained for the new ship, while those with iron ordnance received a new cast set. As the predecessor to Sir John Balchin's *Victory* had been a Second Rate equipped with iron guns, a new set of brass or iron was required for the new *Victory*, which was to be both a First Rate and the flagship of the fleet. The large stock of worn out and captured brass guns held by the Board of Ordnance (PRO Supp 5-1), unsuitable for a warship of such high status, made the casting of a new brass set the right and necessary choice on prestige and economical grounds.

Old and unusable brass guns were viewed as scrap and not as historic pieces. To buy the raw copper and tin needed for a single gun cost £60, as compared to an iron gun cast from iron ore, whose production and delivery cost £20. From 1660 into the first half of the 18th century the price of cast iron guns ranged from £14 to £20 depending on urgency in peace and war. Brass guns varied from £30 to £40 when cast from old guns in hand, of which £4/10s to £8 was required for the quality hand finishing of the embellishments. Prize guns were bought in at £70 to £80 per ton from naval captains. Those taken in battle on land obviously cost nothing (cf. PRO WO51). To cast a brass cannon from a captured and re-used enemy gun cost about the same as iron. Since the Board of Ordnance already possessed the necessary brass metal, the expense of casting was the only point needing factoring in to the new manufacture. Britannia ruled the waves, and with her 100 brass guns *Victory*'s role was to remind the world of this feat.

2. Changing the Guard

By 1715 the Stuart Dynasty had been replaced by the Hanoverians and personnel in or close to the Board of Ordnance who understood the reasons for the gun design of 1670 were either dead or out of office. The Duke of Marlborough was back in the position of Master-General of the Ordnance. The senior engineer from his campaigns, Brigadier General Michael Richards, became Surveyor-General, and Colonel Albert Borgard (cf. Caruana, 1982), a Dane by birth, was employed to produce a complete system of artillery, guns, gun carriages, carts and ammunition.

Borgard belonged to the European school of artillerists who thought that gunpowder exploded instantaneously and therefore the area of maximum chamber pressure was confined to the space occupied by the gunpowder charge only and thus did not extend any further down the bore. Therefore, in his view, the first reinforce only needed to be positioned at 2/7th of the gun's length. He chose to ignore the design of the 1670s that had extended the first reinforce lengths.

Figs. 1-2. A 42-pounder brass cannon C33 (bottom) and 12-pounder C28 (top) recovered from the wreck of Balchin's Victory.

Fig. 3. Royal arms of King George I on 42-pounder cannon C33.

Fig. 4. Royal arms of King George II on 12-pounder cannon C28.

Borgard's designs in both brass and iron extended from the half-pounder swivel gun up to and including the 42-pounder. While brass guns produced to his designs proved safe due to the tensile strength of brass, no iron guns were ever taken into service above the 24-pounder calibre because the first reinforce was too short to accommodate the area of maximum chamber pressure without the length of the guns being extended by an extra 1-2ft to a length that a ship could not reasonably accommodate. Extending the gun also extended the first reinforce but did not simultaneously increase the size of the gunpowder charge.

Brigadier General Michael Richards died in 1721 and was replaced by Colonel – later Major General – John Armstrong as Surveyor-General. Armstrong dispensed with the services of Colonel Borgard and took the design of ordnance into his own hands. Brass guns continued to be cast to the Borgard pattern for some years to come. Armstrong reduced the metal on the iron guns of Borgard's design to save weight, with predictable results – the new guns started to burst.

3. Borgard Pattern Brass Guns

The casting of brass guns to Borgard's pattern (cf. BM Kings 261) in 1716 did not get off to an auspicious start. The cannon included two 24-pounders and were to be cast by Mathew Bagley at his foundry in Moorfields, where a crowd of eminent persons gathered to view proceedings. Regrettably the molds used were still damp and a disastrous eruption occurred. Mathew Bagley and many others were killed and even more injured, including Borgard (cf. PRO WO51-98 for payments for Borgard's injuries). As The *Mercurius Politicus* of 18 May 1716 announced (Hogg, 1963: 246-7):

> "Several gentlemen were invited to see the Metal run, which being a very great and curious Piece of Art, a great many Persons of Quality came to see it, and some General Officers of the Army among the rest... About 11 at night the Metal being ready, was let go... the burning Metal no sooner sunk down to the Bottom of the Mould, but with a Noise and Force equal to that of gunpowder, it came pouring up again, blowing like the Mouth of a *Volcano*, or little *Vesuvius*. There was in the place about 20 Men, as well as Workmen as Spectators, 17 of whom were so burnt that nothing more horrible can be thought of, neither can Words describe their Misery. About 9 of the 17 are already dead, the other 8 are yet living, but in such a condition that the Surgeons say they have very small hopes of above 2 of them."

Fig. 5. Latin inscription 'SCHALCH FECIT' along the base ring of 12-pounder cannon C28.

Fig. 6. The date of '1726' on the base ring of 42-pounder cannon C33.

Fig. 7. The date of '1734' on the base ring of 12-pounder cannon C28.

Fig. 8. Dolphin handle on 42-pounder cannon C33.

Fig. 9. Gun deck position '28' incised onto the trunnion of cannon C28. Balchin's Victory *had 28 x 12-pounder guns on the upper deck and this gun would have been the last in the circuit of the deck. Numbering usually started at the entry port and worked clockwise round the ship.*

As a direct result of this disaster the Board of Ordnance took the decision to take the casting of brass guns into their own hands, and the Royal Brass Foundry was commenced in 1716. Accordingly, the Ordnance Journal Book of 19 June 1716 reports how (PRO WO 47/29):

> "It having for many years been the Opinion of the most experienced Officers that the Government should have a Brass Foundery of their own, and whereas Mr. Bagley's Foundry is the only own for Casting Brass Ordnance and liable to dangerous Accidents, w[ch] can't be prevented.
>
> It is therefore order'd that a Proposal and Estimate be made for Building a Royal Brass Foundery at His Majesty's Tower Place at Woolwich; and the Charge thereof Defrayed out of the £5,000 given this Year by Parliament for recasting Brass Ordn[ce] and y[t] no time be lost herein, inasmuch as there are but 2 12 Pounders, and not 1 18 or 24 Pounder for Land Service."

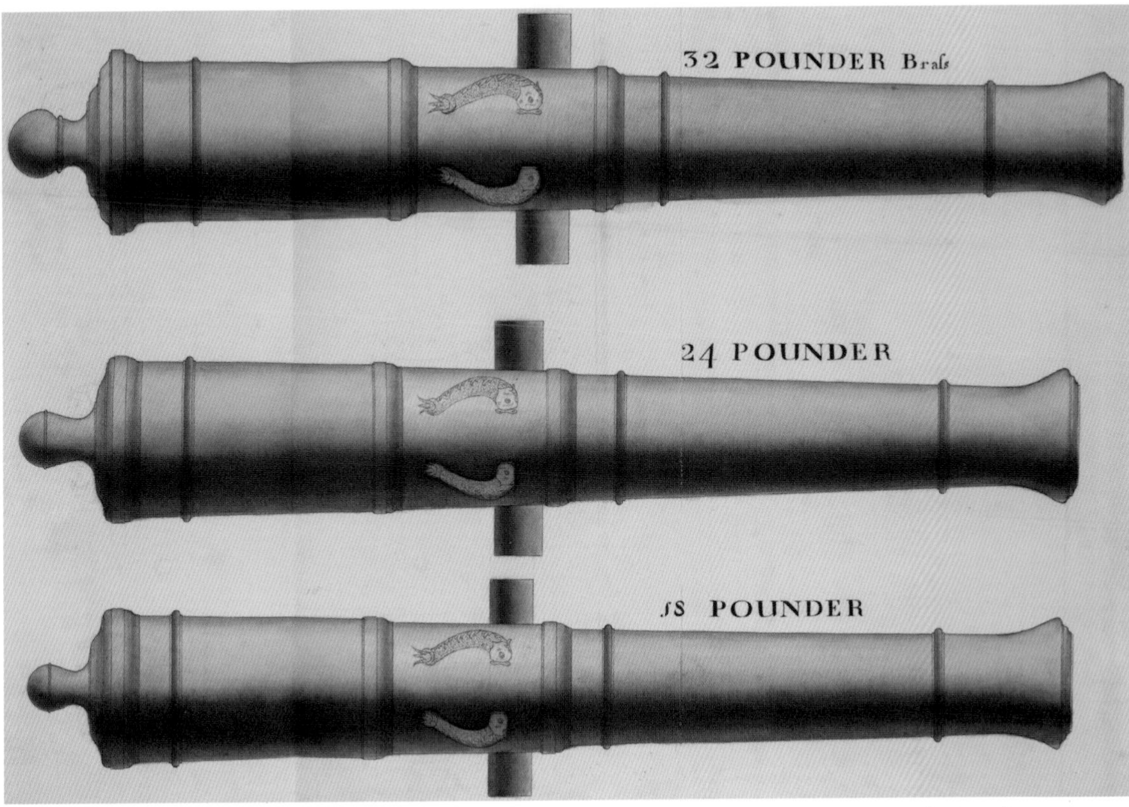

Fig. 10. Templates for 32-, 24- and 18-pounder cannon to be used in gun manufacture by the Royal Brass Foundry, Woolwich. Photo: © The British Library, London (BM Kings 261).

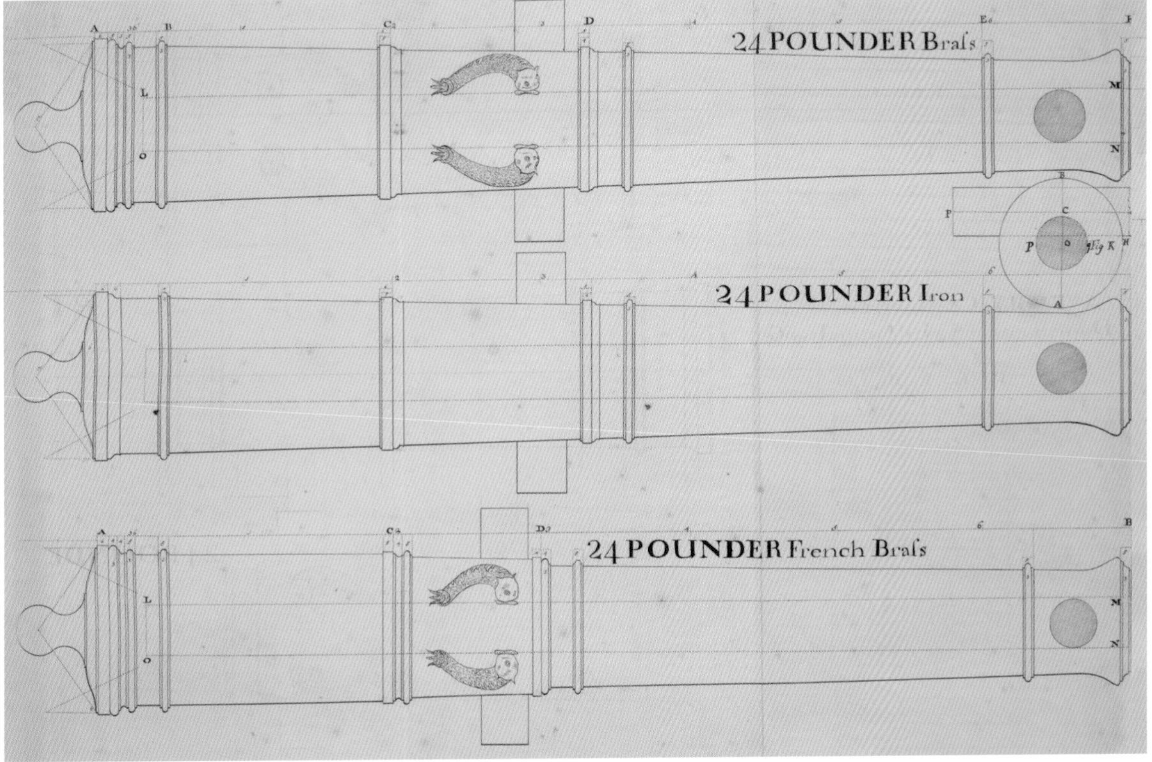

Fig. 11. Templates for 24-pounder cannon to be used in gun manufacture by the Royal Brass Foundry, Woolwich, based on a blueprint obtained by Colonel John Armstrong in Paris in 1727. Note the French gun lines at bottom. Photo: © The British Library, London (BM Kings 261).

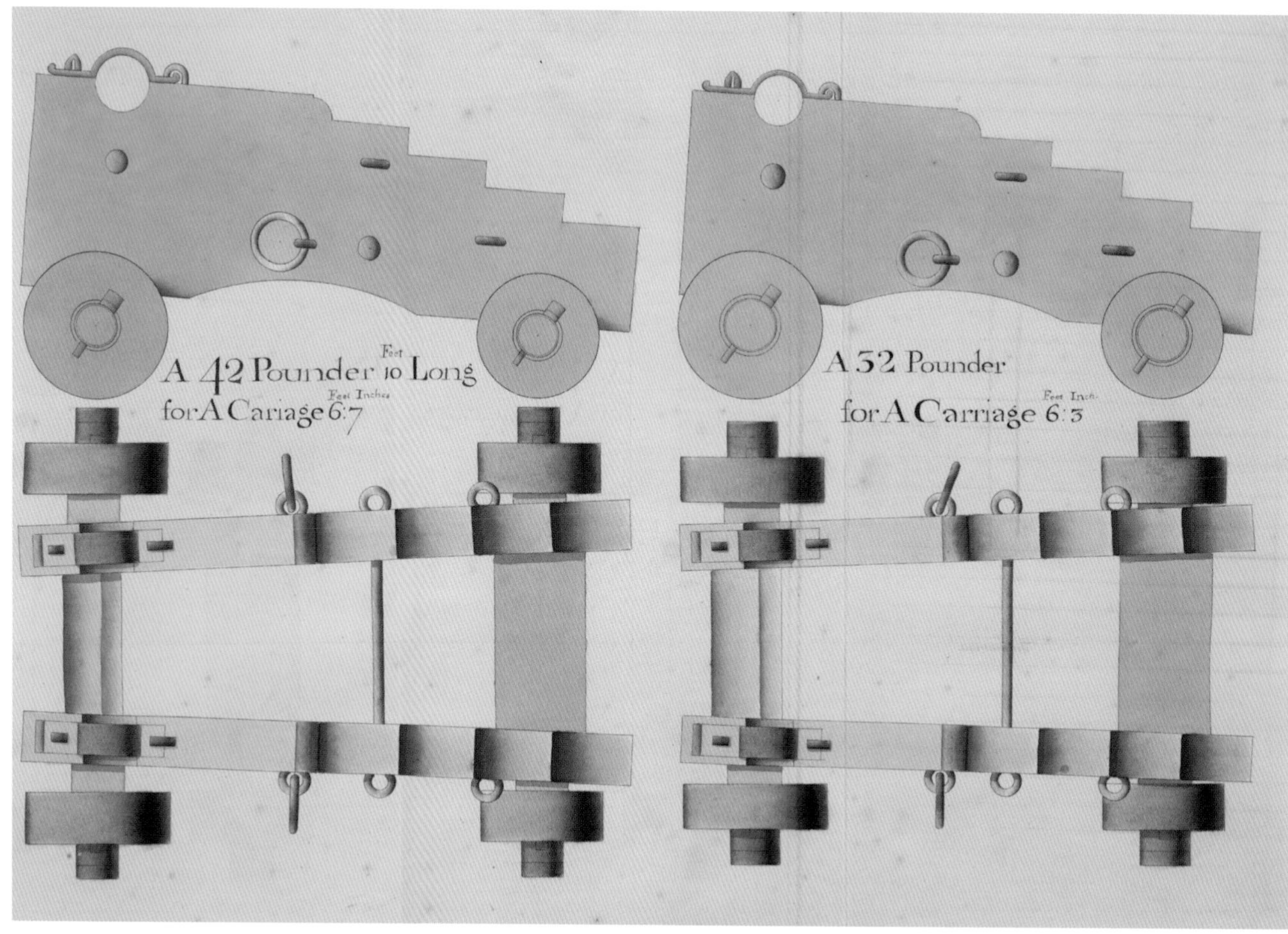

Fig. 12. Templates for 42- and 32-pounder gun carriages to be used on Royal Navy warships. Photo: © The British Library, London (BM Kings 261).

The Royal Brass Foundry opened in 1717, with Andrew Schalch recruited as Master Founder and receiving a salary of 5*s*. a day, which was upgraded to £219 per annum after 1 April 1718, once the Board of Ordnance was satisfied by his skill and competence (Hogg, 1963: 251, 259; Kennard, 1986). Casting started with a variety of small items and small mortars on 16 October 1717, and large guns began to be cast a year later.

It was in 1722 that Schalch started to cast a complete set of 100 brass guns for a First Rate warship, a task that would take him a total of some 12 years (when combined with the requirement to cast an additional 400 guns, mortars and howitzers). Those cast up to and including 1727 were manufactured to the Borgard pattern. The batch of guns post-dating 1727 were manufactured to the new design introduced by Armstrong. Some 15 of the 42-pounders, all the 24-pounders, all of the 12-pounders (although one on Balchin's *Victory* is a later addition: Cunningham Dobson and Kingsley, 2010: 248, 261), and all 6-pounders mounted on Balchin's *Victory* should have been produced to the Borgard design.

4. Colonel John Armstrong's Gun Design

Colonel Armstrong's career had been largely spent as an engineer specializing in the building, attacking and knocking down of fortresses. The closest that he had ever got to studying guns first-hand was to site and build batteries and then direct the battery's fire. Such guns would have been designed to the earlier 1670 series.

On assuming the position of Surveyor General, Armstrong had clearly recognized that the Borgard gun design had a greater weight than the 1670 series and, quite reasonably, attempted to reduce their weight. The English practice since 1670 had been to make the first reinforce of a cannon to cover a length that covered the area of maximum chamber pressure, which was more than 2/7th of the gun's total length (see Section 2 above). However, by reducing the weight produced to the Borgard system, Armstrong introduced a major structural flaw into the cannon design, which was his undoing. As noted above, because of his design iron guns started to burst onboard ship. Armstrong had a serious problem.

As a consequence, all casting of iron guns was stopped and none were accepted for proof between 31 December 1724 and 25 April 1729. The brass guns then being cast for the *Victory* to the Borgard pattern were all 6-12in longer than had been accepted during the previous 50 years and so were safe.

Armstrong's problem was solved when he received instructions from George I to go on a diplomatic trip to Paris on the king's behalf. He set out for Paris on 3 April 1727 and returned after 49 days on the 21 May (for the record of Armstrong's journey to Paris, see PRO WO 51/122). In his baggage on his return he had drawings of the latest French gun designs (for a drawing of his 24-pounders imitating those of Paris, see BM Kings 261, Fig. 11).

Armstrong anglicized these drawings, changed the gun button design and had a set of scale models cast, which he received on 30 June 1729 (WO 51/121). The Colonel set the gun casters and the Brass Foundry to work to produce the brass and iron guns needed, and the first delivery of iron guns passed proof on 25 April 1729. Armstrong's designs, with minor modifications, continued in production into the 1790s, when they were replaced in turn by General Blomefield's designs.

Fig. 13. Cannon C22 perched on top of a second bronze gun on the wreck of Balchin's Victory.

Fig. 14. Bronze cannon C15 and C19 on the wreck of Balchin's Victory. *The conger eel inhabiting the gun's bore is common to all of the other site cannon.*

5. The Guns on Balchin's *Victory*

The decision to build the First Rate *Victory* was clearly taken before 1722 because on 29 June 1722 Armstrong wrote to the Admiralty (PRO ADM 1/4006) to confirm that this warship's brass guns were to conform to the current regulations laid down in 1715 (as extracted from a notebook by Lieutenant James *c.* 1722: RAI G3n 1a and ADM 1/4005) and that both the 42-pounders and the 24-pounders were to be 10ft long. By this date the first of *Victory*'s three 42-pounders had already been cast to the Borgard design at Woolwich. The comment added by the Admiralty, on Armstrong's letter after receipt, confirms the above.

Armstrong's next letter to the Admiralty, dated to 9 July 1722 (PRO ADM 1/4006), pointed out that of the brass guns on the three other operative First Rates of the era, the *Royal George*, *Royal Sovereign* and *Britannia*, only 53 conformed to the current establishment. He thus proposed casting additional guns to correct this anomaly. The fourth First Rate, the *London*, was rebuilt in 1706 and again in 1721, but never received her brass guns. These cannon remained stockpiled ashore.

The state of the armament of the three First Rates cited above accounts for the additional guns cast at the same time as those for *Victory* and explains why the 12-pounder recovered by Odyssey Marine Exploration in 2008 dates to 1734 (Cunningham Dobson and Kingsley, 2010: 248, 261). Those guns cast from 1727 onwards are of the John Armstrong design, but of necessity had to conform to the lengths of the guns already cast. Otherwise, the differences between Borgard and Armstrong's designs were mostly minor and lie in the style of decoration, the royal cipher and muzzle swell.

Balchin's *Victory* may have been carrying additional 3-pounders of 4ft 6in length above the quarterdeck, as was the practice on previous and subsequent First Rates. The 6-pounder of 9ft length is not an ideal signal gun. A set of 3-pounders was cast in 1729 alongside some of the *Victory*'s guns and may potentially have been exploited instead of (or as well as) the 6-pounders. Only time and future fieldwork on the wreck site will tell.

The supply of guns of greater length and weight, as compared with 17th-century standards, added an additional 18+ tons weight to a warship above the waterline. While this may not seem to be a great addition, when combined with the reduction below the waterline of provisions eaten and water and beer drunk, plus broadsides fired (each broadside requiring approximately 1 ton's weight of powder and shot), this disproportionate, unbalanced upper weight may have been a contributing factor to *Victory*'s loss after just five months at sea. This mathematical conundrum remains a matter for a naval architect to calculate.

It is interesting to note, and may be nothing more than a coincidence, that immediately after the launch of Balchin's *Victory*, in the year before he died Armstrong conducted experiments to determine the correct length and weight of guns necessary to achieve optimum performance (records of Armstrong's expenses in these exercises are listed in PRO WO 51/139). As a direct result of these experiments his successor reduced the length of Royal Navy cannon once again. As a consequence, the 42-pounders and 24-pounders cast in the 1760s for the *Royal George* measured 9ft 6in in length and her total ordnance was lighter in weight: her 12-pounder and 6-pounders on the upper deck now weighed 19 tons less than *Victory*. Lessons had been learned and applied for the naval protection of the realm.

6. Conclusion

In the era that covers the history of naval ordnance applicable to use on the First Rate warship Balchin's *Victory*, four cannon series may be considered relevant in general:

- Borgard, 1715-22
- Borgard modified by Armstrong, 1722-27
- Armstrong, 1728-33
- Armstrong modified by himself, 1733-44

Due to changes in personnel, naval tactics and the pivotal transition in the medium of gun casting from brass to iron, Balchin's *Victory* was built and equipped at a seminal moment in the history of gun founding. The ship was the last fitted with a full complement of purpose-made brass cannon. The guns onboard the First Rate *Royal George* and *Britannia* were a cosmopolitan collection of English cannon and prizes seized from enemy ships over the course of decades. Thus, their armament technically was comprised of brass antiques of which hardly any two were alike, and included English 12-pounders and 6-pounders of Henry Pitt (1591), Dutch 12-pounders of Johannas Burgherhuys and Arent Vander Put (1616), and Spanish 6-pounders of Ferdinando de Valdesteero (1623).

As a result of the normal practice of melting brass guns down for re-use, very few cannon from this pivotal era survive for study today. The *Britannia*'s guns were all melted down. Although the *Royal George* of 1756 possessed a full set of newly cast brass guns when launched, her ordnance had been reorganized and was mixed by the time she sank. The 49 brass cannon salvaged from the *Royal George*'s iron and brass guns off Spithead between 1782 and 1843 (27 x 24-pounders and 22 x 12-pounders) were similarly almost all melted down, with one brass 24-pounder and six brass 12-pounders left unsalvaged on the seabed (Codrington, 1840: 167). The few retained or sold by its salvors, rather than returned to the Admiralty for melting, comprise the limited examples preserved in museums and storerooms today.

Balchin's *Victory* is thus a highly unique site in the history of naval ordnance (Figs. 1-9, 13-18):

Fig. 15. Bronze cannon C13 on the wreck of Balchin's Victory, *contextualized with wooden remains.*

Fig. 16. Bronze cannon C7, C8 and C12 on the site of Balchin's Victory.

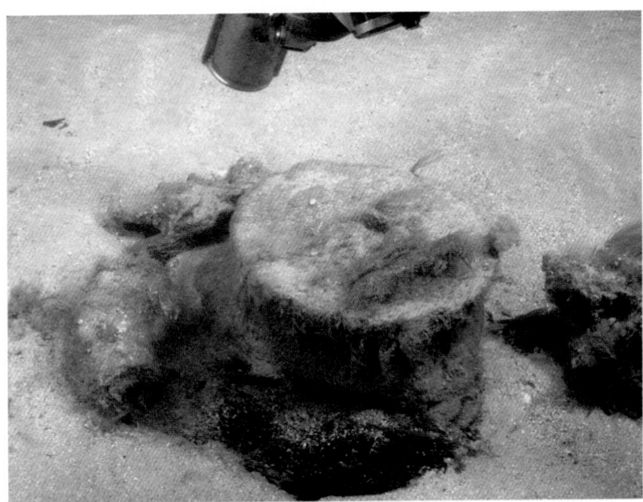

Fig. 17. A wooden carriage truck in situ *on the wreck of Balchin's* Victory.

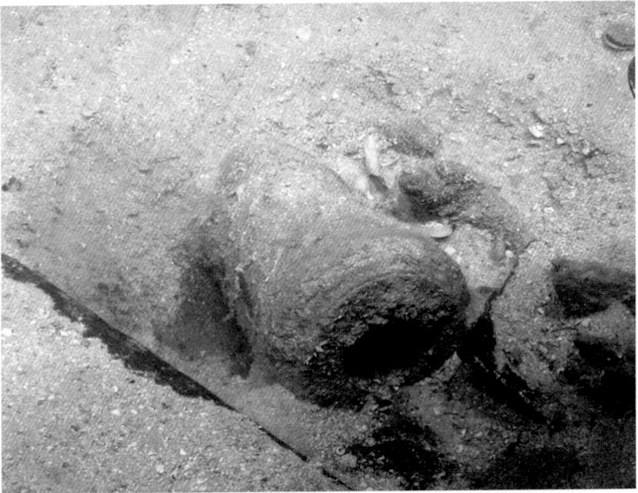

Fig. 18. Bronze cannon C37 on the wreck of Balchin's Victory*, contextualized with wood remains.*

1. The last Royal Navy First Rate warship in British history to be armed with a single batch of brass cannon when lost (rather than a geographically and chronologically diverse collection of English and foreign antiques).

2. By far the most complete collection of English cannon cast by any founder at Moorgate, Woolwich or anywhere else in existence.

3. The largest surviving collection of cannon produced by the Master Founder Andrew Schalch at the Royal Brass Foundry, Woolwich.

4. The only wreck site of a First Rate Royal Navy warship with an intact collection of cannon known in the world.

The rarity of the Balchin's *Victory* cannon is compounded by the survival of very few comparable examples on museum display or in storerooms worldwide. All of this warship's 28 lower-deck 42-pounders were cast between 1722 and 1728 specifically for the *Victory* and thus no other comparative examples exist in museums. Of the thousands cast in England in the 17th and 18th centuries, the only one in existence on land today is the single example recovered so far from the wreck of Balchin's *Victory*. No brass 42-pounders were installed on the First Rate warship *Royal George* when she foundered off Spithead in 1782, having been replaced in spring 1782 or the year before with iron 32-pounders (Codrington, 1840: 23-24).

All of the 28 middle-deck 24-pounder sea service guns commissioned for the *Victory* were cast between 1719 and 1724. No comparable cannon for this period survive in museums, although several 24-pounders are known from the *Royal George*. The earliest is dated to 1743 and differs in detail from those cast for the *Victory*: it bears in relief the arms of John, Duke of Montagu, Master General of the Ordnance (from 1740-2 and 1742-49), with its base ring inscribed with name of the founder and the date ('A. SCHALCH FECIT 1743'); the cascabel is incised with the weight of '51-1-0'. The royal arms of King George II are present on the first reinforce and a brass plate near the muzzle states that this gun was recovered from the *Royal George* by Anthony Dean in 1834. The cannon is now at Southsea Castle (Blackmore, 1976: 72).

Some 34 12-pounders were cast between 1719 and 1729, plus a few more in the 1730s. Only one survives in the Rotunda collection at Woolwich, dated to 1739. No 6-pounder or 3-pounder sea service guns exist from this period.

Apart from the two guns raised by Odyssey Marine Exploration from the *Victory*, only three other English-manufactured naval cannon dating to the reign of King George I survive on land. One 32-pounder of 1719, bored to 7in, exists in Tangier; an English 13in mortar cast in 1726 by Andrew Schalch, bearing the arms of George I on the reinforce is still extant (Blackmore, 1976: pl. 65); and an 8-inch howitzer captured at Yorktown in October 1781 and, dating to 1727, with the royal arms of George I on the chase and the coat of arms of John, Duke of Argyll, Master General of Ordnance from 3 June 1725 to 10 May 1740, on the breech, is preserved in the Colonial National Historical Park, Virginia (Borresen, 1938: 237, 239).

Other than that, a remarkable collection of 31 small brass 3-pounders survives at Fort Belvedere, of which 27 were cast by Andrew Schalch between 1729 and 1747. A further few 3-pounders are preserved in Lisbon. Notably, however, all of these 3-pounders were designed for and used in land service. In this regard, they had a wholly different function to *Victory*'s naval guns.

Bibliography

Blackmore, H.L., *The Armouries of the Tower of London. I. The Ordnance* (London, 1976).

Borresen, T., 'The Markings of English Cannon Captured at Yorktown', *Journal of the American Military History Foundation* 2.4 (1938), 235-39.

Caruana, A.B. 'Albert Borgard and British Artillery of 1675-1725', *Arms Collecting* 20.3 (1982), 77-94.

Codrington, E., *A Narrative of the Loss of the Royal George at Spithead, August 1782; Including Tracey's Attempt to Raise her in 1783, Her Demolition and Removal by Major-General Pasley's Operations in 1839-40-41-42 & 43, Including a Statement on her Sinking Written by her then Flag-Lieutenant, Admiral Sir C.P.H. Durham* (S. Horsey, Sen., London, 1840, 7th ed.).

Cunnigham Dobson, N. and Kingsley, S., 'HMS *Victory*, a First-Rate Royal Navy Warship Lost in the English Channel, 1744. Preliminary Survey & Identification'. In G. Stemm and S. Kingsley (eds.), *Oceans Odyssey: Deep-Sea Shipwrecks in the English Channel, the Straits of Gibraltar and the Atlantic Ocean* (Oxford, 2010), 235-80.

Hogg, O.F.G., *The Royal Arsenal. Its Background, Origin and Subsequent History Volume 1* (Oxford University Press, 1963).

Kennard, A.N., *Gunfounding and Gunfounders* (Arms and Armour Press, 1986).

Kinard, J., *Weapons and Warfare* (Santa Barbara, 2007).

Trollope, C., 'Design and Evolution of English Cast-iron Guns 1660 to 1725', *Journal of the Ordnance Society* 17 (2005), 49-58.

Balchin's *Victory*: Bronze Cannon Conservation Report

Frederick Van de Walle
Director of Conservation, Odyssey Marine Exploration, Tampa, USA

In 2008 Odyssey Marine Exploration recovered two bronze cannon from the shipwreck of Admiral Sir John Balchin's *Victory* in the Western English Channel in cooperation with the UK Ministry of Defence. A conservation program was subsequently initiated within Portsmouth Naval Base before both guns were formally handed over to the MOD in March 2010 after concluding a transaction with Odyssey, which gave the MOD possession of the artifacts. Conservation is currently continuing at the Mary Rose Trust under MOD management.

This report outlines the conservation strategy developed by Odyssey Marine Exploration and also details the theory that was recommended to be put into practice to complete the conservation. This theory is also relevant to any future recovery of cannon from the wreck of Balchin's *Victory*.

1. Introduction

In April 2008 Odyssey Marine Exploration examined an interesting target in the western English Channel using side-scan sonar and a magnetometer as part of its ongoing Atlas Shipwreck Survey Project. Subsequent visual investigation using the Remotely-Operated Vehicle (ROV) Zeus, complemented in September and October by an ROV pre-disturbance survey, identified a substantial concentration of wreckage covering an area of 61 x 22m comprised of disarticulated wooden planking, iron ballast, two anchors, a copper kettle, rigging, two probable gunner's wheels and, most diagnostically, 41 bronze cannon (Figs. 17-18).

Two of these guns were recovered in October 2008 (Cunningham Dobson and Kingsley, 2010: 248, 261, 262). An examination of the site and its material culture in relation to a desk-based assessment led to the conclusion that Odyssey had discovered the long-lost wreck of Admiral Sir John Balchin's First Rate Royal Navy warship, HMS *Victory*, lost in the Channel on 5 October 1744. Elaborate royal arms of King George I and George II, as well as the founder's dates of 1726 on the recovered 42-pounder cannon and 1734 on the 12-pounder, place the wreck precisely within the timeframe of HMS *Victory*'s construction and operation.

The dimensions of the recovered cannon are:

- Cannon C33 (42-pounder): L. 3.4m and muzzle and trunnion diam. 17.8cm (7in). Decorated with the royal arms of King George I and inscribed with the founder's name SCHALCH and the date of 1726. Elaborate dolphins (Figs. 4-5, 10-12, 14-16).
- Cannon C28 (12-pounder): L. 3.12m and muzzle and trunnion diam. 11.5cm (4.5in). Decorated with the royal arms of King George II and inscribed with the founder's name SCHALCH and the date of 1734. Elaborate dolphins (Figs. 6-9, 13).

2. Pre-Treatment Conditions

Following recovery from the seabed the cannon were kept submerged in fresh water on the research ship the *Odyssey Explorer* and during relocation to a conservation facility in Portsmouth Naval Base, where they were immersed in stainless steel tanks supported on wooden blocks to prevent scratching and movement (Fig. 1). The bores were flushed with a water hose to remove loose sand and debris.

The two cannon are both in a similar state of preservation (Figs. 4-16). They have not undergone severe degradation in terms of corrosion processes and physical damage. Both are intact, with only small pieces of bronze fractured away from the surface. Upon recovery, little marine growth was observed on the cannons' surfaces. Cuprous chloride (CuCl) and cuprous sulphide (Cu_2S) are usually the prevalent corrosion products identifiable on bronze immersed in a marine environment. Smaller amounts of cupric

Fig. 1. The 12-pounder bronze cannon C28 undergoing conservation in its tank at Portsmouth Naval Base in 2009.

chloride, $CuCl_2$, cuprous oxide, Cu_2O, malachite, $Cu_2(OH)_2CO_3$, and azurite, $Cu_3(OH)_2(CO_3)_2$, are likely to be found (Gettens, 1964: 550-57).

The first stage in the electrochemical corrosion of copper alloys is the production of cuprous ions. These, in turn, combine with chloride in the seawater to form cuprous chloride as a major component of the corrosion layer on the surfaces. Cuprous chlorides are highly unstable mineral compounds that will continue to corrode chemically when exposed to air. In the presence of moisture and oxygen, cuprous chlorides are hydrolyzed to form hydrochloric acid and basic cupric chloride (Oddy and Hughes, 1970: 188). The hydrochloric acid, in turn, will attack the metal to form more cuprous chloride. This process is commonly referred to as 'bronze disease'.

3. Conservation Treatment Theory

Desalination is the process whereby soluble salts are removed from a find, typically through repeated immersion in distilled or deionized water. Certain salts, such as some chlorides, nitrates, and sulphates, are easily soluble in water and can be absorbed into porous materials. Desalination is necessary when finds derive from environments known to have a high level of soluble salts, such as marine contexts, privies, areas of brackish water and certain terrestrial sites.

Even when soluble salt contamination is obvious, complementary treatment may be required if the soluble salt crusts hold a fractured object together, support vulnerable pigment or otherwise create unstable conditions. In such cases other forms of conservation treatments may be necessary before desalination can be carried out. For metals that require desalination, it may be necessary to use chemical baths other than water, since water itself can stimulate rapid corrosion.

If desalination is carried out poorly or incompletely the treatment can cause damage; the surface can crack and the patina can change color. Additionally, in cases where the salt content is very high, osmotic pressure caused by the differences in salt content between the find and the desalination bath can damage the find unless steps are taken to reduce these differences.

There are three different chemical treatments available that were appropriate for considering stabilizing the two cannon recovered from the *Victory*, while leaving the corrosion layers intact:

- Treatment with sodium sesquicarbonate
- Treatment with sodium carbonate
- Treatment with benzotriazole

Sodium sesquicarbonate treatment was chosen to treat the two guns from *Victory* because it has the desirable result of not removing the green patina on the surface of the cannon and is most suitable for treatment of marine copper alloys. Treatment with benzotrialzole is appropriate as a stage to follow the sodium sesquicarbonate treatment. The cuprous chloride components of copper and its alloys are insoluble and cannot be removed by washing in water alone. When bronzes or other copper alloys are placed in a 5% solution of sodium sesquicarbonate, the hydroxyl ions of the alkaline solution react chemically with the insoluble cuprous chlorides to form cuprous oxide and neutralize any hydrochloric acid by-product formed by hydrolysis to produce soluble sodium chlorides (Organ, 1963: 100; Oddy and Hughes, 1970; Plenderleith and Werner, 1971: 252-53).

These chlorides are removed each time the chemical solution is changed. Successive rinsing continues until all the chlorides are removed. The object is then rinsed in several baths of de-ionized water until the pH of the last immersion is neutral. For the initial immersion, the sodium sesquicarbonate is mixed with tap water. De-ionized water is used for subsequent immersions. If the chloride contamination is extensive, baths prepared with tap water can be used until the chloride level in the solution approximates the chloride level of standard tap water. De-ionized water is then substituted. This procedure is very economical when processing

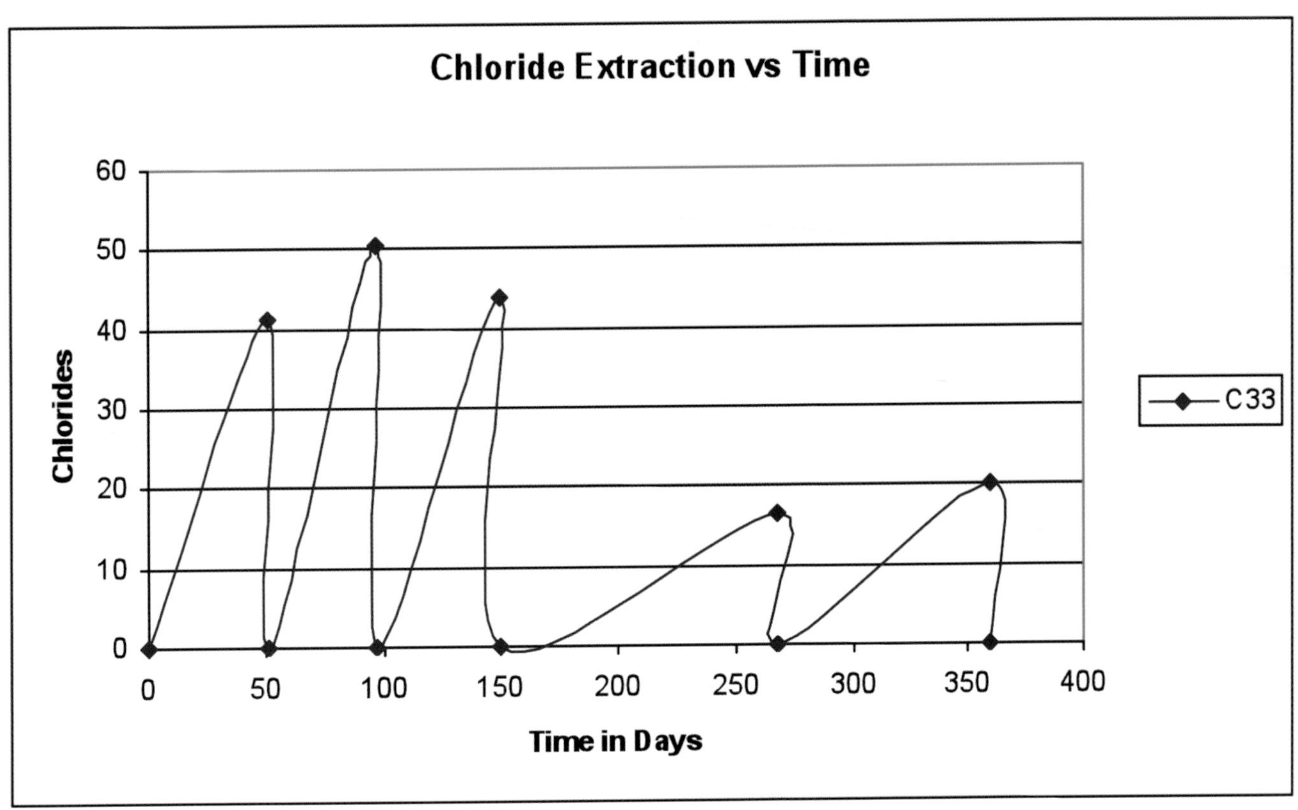

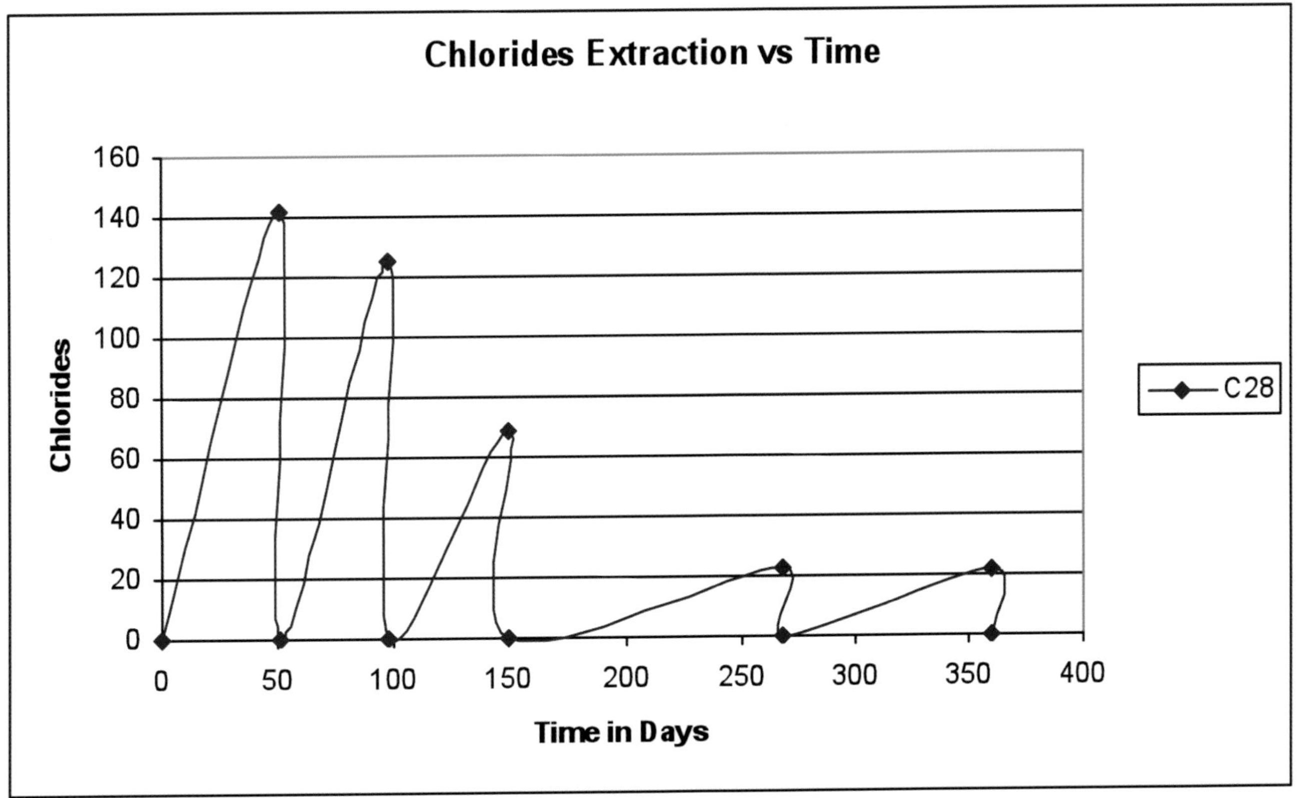

Tables 1-2. The speed of chloride extraction versus time in days recorded for Victory's *two recovered cannon.*

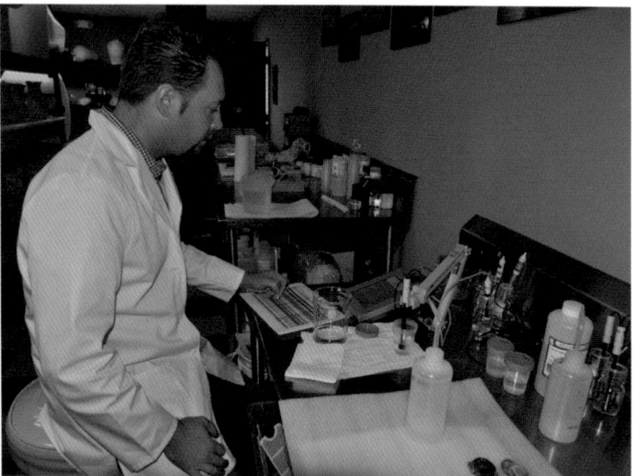

Fig. 2. Odyssey's chief conservator Fred van de Walle recording levels of chloride ion extraction within sodium sesquicarbonate solution using a Fisher Scientific Accumet XL50 meter.

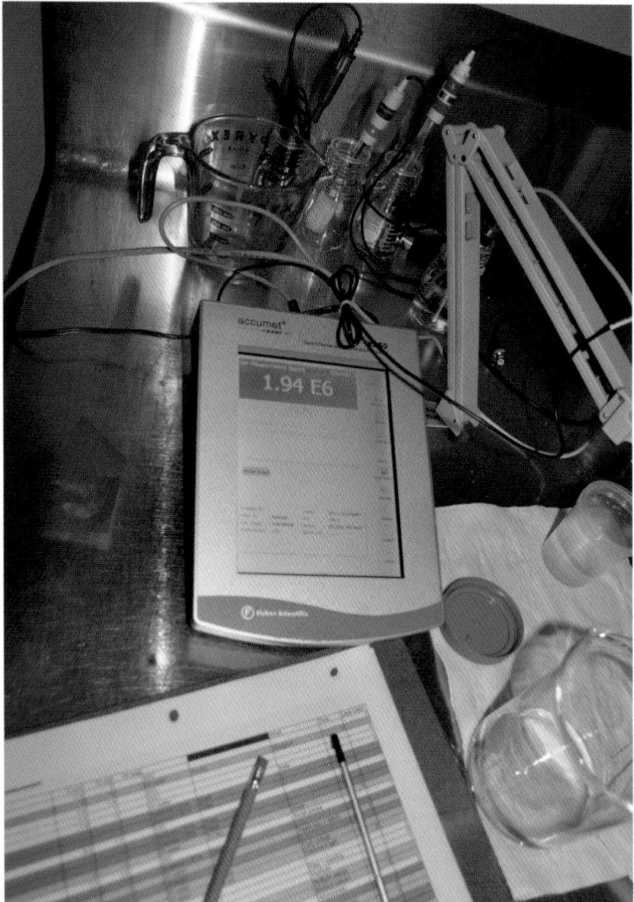

Fig. 3. Detail of the Fisher Scientific Accumet XL50 meter used to record levels of chloride ion extraction within the sodium sesquicarbonate solution covering the cannon from Balchin's Victory *undergoing conservation.*

objects that require months (or perhaps years) of treatment, such as the two cannon recovered from HMS *Victory*.

Immediately upon recovery from the wreck, both of the *Victory*'s cannon were stored in stainless steel tanks holding tap water (Fig. 1). After arrival at the secure storage facility in the Royal Naval Base in Portsmouth, the cannon were submerged in a 5% solution of sodium sesquicarbonate in tap water. The amount of chlorides extracted from the solution has been measured approximately every 10 weeks by analyzing solution samples (Figs. 2-3, Tables 1-2).

4. Analysis

Salt levels in desalination baths need to be measured to assess the progression of the desalination process and to determine the end point. The removal of the chloride ions from the *Victory*'s cannon can be said to be the principle goal of the stabilization treatment. Chloride ion extraction from the sodium sesquicarbonate solution was monitored using a Fisher Scientific Accumet XL50 meter with an ion specific electrode, which is able to measure amounts of chloride in a sample by electrolytical means, and its accuracy is trusted to be ±5ppm within the range of 10-400ppm (Figs. 2-3).

Tables 1-2 show the speed of chloride (Cl^-) extraction versus time (in days) recorded so far for the *Victory*'s recovered cannon. These measurements demonstrate that chlorides are being extracted as rapidly as would be expected using this treatment. After one year of treatment in sodium sesquicarbonate, the chloride levels had dropped from the initial measurements of 41.2 ppm to 20.2 ppm and 142 ppm to 21.6 ppm. When no more chlorides are being extracted by the chemical treatment, the desalination process will be complete. At the current rate from when Odyssey Marine Exploration began the conservation of *Victory*'s cannon, the likely completion date for the desalinization process would be within a total period of 24 months from the very start of the treatment.

5. Odyssey's Conservation Strategy

Under Odyssey's management the two cannon were documented, measured and desalinated in sodium sesquicarbonate in tap water. The following steps were also recommended for the cannon's continued conservation and preservation after they were turned over to the MOD and placed in their care. These phases are also applicable to any future recovery and conservation of *Victory*'s extensive cannon collection.

Fig. 4. Detail of the relatively non-encrusted royal arms Of King George I on 42-pounder cannon C33.

Fig. 5. Detail of the crown on the royal arms of King George I on 42-pounder cannon C33.

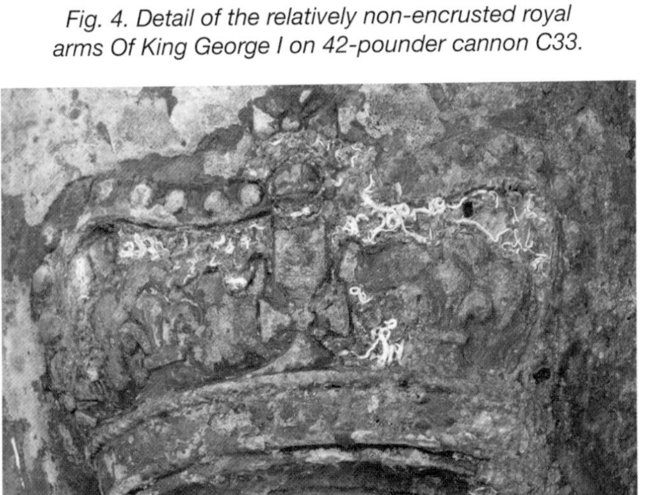

Fig. 6. Detail of the concreted crown on the royal arms of King George II on 12-pounder cannon C28.

Figs. 7-8. Detail of the fleur de lis, lions and harp within the quadrants on the royal arms of King George II on 12-pounder cannon C28. Note the extensive concretion.

Encrustations, corrosion products and debris should be removed mechanically from the cannon to reveal the preserved surface of the metal and the inside of the bore. A cleavage line between the original metallic surface and the encrustation was formed on the seabed, which makes identification of the Georgian surfaces and the removal of post-depositional concretion fairly easy.

In modern conservation practice, superficial encrustation is often deliberately left adhering to the surface of the artifact due to its fragility or to avoid damaging its surface. Careful mechanical cleaning and rinsing in water may be all that is required to remove this remaining superficial encrustation. Encrustation can also be removed by soaking the object in 5-10% citric acid with 1-4% thiourea added

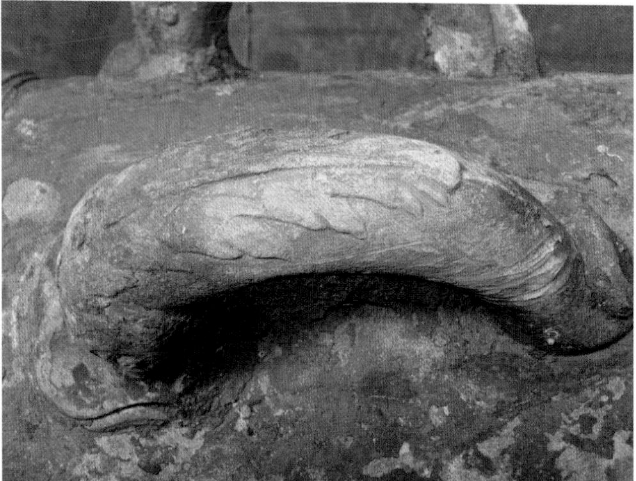

Figs. 9-10. Dolphin handles from 12-pounder cannon C28 (top) and 42-pounder C33 (bottom). Note the far greater concretion on the former gun.

as an inhibitor to prevent metal etching (North, 1987: 233; Pearson, 1974: 301; Plenderleith and Torraca, 1968: 246). If applied, citric acid should be used cautiously because it can dissolve cupric and cuprous compounds within the artifact. In this process cannon are completely submerged in the solution of citric acid until the encrustation is removed. If this acid treatment is considered to be too severe, the cannon can be soaked in a 5-15% solution of sodium hexametaphosphate (Plenderleith and Werner, 1971: 255) to convert the insoluble calcium and magnesium salts in the encrustation to soluble salts, which subsequently can be washed away.

Tap water should be used until the chloride level in the solution approximates the chloride level of standard tap water. De-ionized water should then substituted. The same procedure with a solution of 5% sodium sesquicarbonate is repeated until the chloride levels are sufficiently low.

When desalination is complete, the cannon should be put through a series of hot rinses in de-ionized water until the pH of the last rinse bath is neutral. Because copper tarnishes in water (Pearson, 1974: 302), Odyssey planned to wash the cannon in several baths of denatured ethanol. If a water rinse is used, any tarnish could be removed with 5% formic acid or by polishing the area with a wet paste of sodium bicarbonate.

A benzotriazole (BTA) treatment should follow the chemical treatment to create a barrier between the remaining cuprous chloride and moisture in the atmosphere. The benzotriazole forms an insoluble, complex compound with cupric ions (Madsen, 1967; Plenderleith and Werner, 1971: 254). The precipitation of this insoluble complex over the cuprous chloride forms a barrier against any moisture that could activate the cuprous chloride and cause bronze disease. A solution of 1-3% BTA dissolved in ethanol or water is recommended. After the cannon are

Fig. 11. Detail of the tail of one of the dolphin handles from 42-pounder C33.

Fig. 12. Detail of the button of 42-pounder C33.

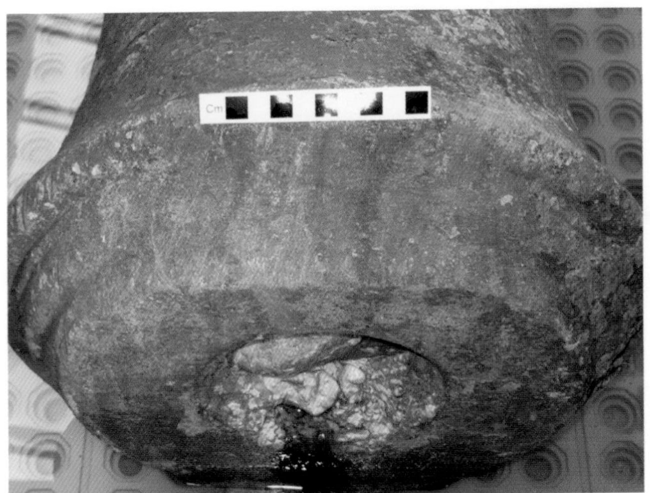

Figs. 13-14. Detail of the muzzles of 12-pounder cannon C28 (left) and 42-pounder C33 (right). Note the eroded upper surface of C28 and the dense concretion on the interior of its lower mouth.

Fig. 15. Early Georgian-era damage to the mouth of 42-pounder C33.

Fig. 16. Delaminated bronze on the surface of 42-pounder C33.

removed from the solution, they should be wiped off with a rag saturated in ethanol to remove excess BTA. If any fresh corrosion appears, the process would need to be repeated until no adverse reaction occurs (Green, 1975; Hamilton, 1976; Merk, 1981; Sease, 1978; Walker, 1979). Following BTA treatment, the cannon can be polished to any degree desired and then should be dehydrated in acetone or a water-miscible alcohol and coated with clear acrylic lacquer or microcrystalline wax.

Assuming that the two cannon from HMS *Victory* are destined for exhibition, an optimum storage area would need to include controls for temperature, relative humidity, pollutants, pests and other degradative factors. In particular, rapid and extreme changes in humidity and temperature will cause cycles of shrinkage and expansion of the cannon and remaining salts. These can cause significant damage and encourage degradation. It is therefore important that the storage system be able to maintain stable temperature and relative humidity levels, and that when fluctuations do occur they are slow and gradual.

Silica gel is the most commonly used desiccant in storage and display cases because it is efficient and relatively inexpensive. This is an amorphous silica crystal capable of absorbing and holding large quantities of atmospheric moisture when properly prepared and used. It can maintain a very low relative humidity (ie. less than 20% RH), as long as the gel is used in the correct proportions, monitored and regenerated periodically. There are two forms of silica gel: non-indicating gel, which is clear, and indicating gel, which is colored and experiences a color change as it becomes saturated. The indicating silica gel can be used to quickly and easily monitor the relative humidity in the storage environment, as the color change is clearly visible. Indicating gel is usually significantly more expensive than non-indicating gel, so a cost-effective approach is to mix one part indicating gel with three parts non-indicating gel.

6. Conclusion

The extremely long time required for washing finds in sodium carbonate and sodium sesquicarbonate treatments often discourages their use, but the process provides very satisfactory results and does not prevent other treatments, like electrolysis, from being carried out in the future. The sodium sesquicarbonate treatment is also used because, unlike other cleaning treatments, it does not remove the green patina on the surface of cupreous objects. This means that the end result should be cannon retaining their original surface color, as opposed to over-polished surfaces, which are common in many ordnance collections. Regardless of preliminary treatments, an application of BTA should be an inherent step in the conservation of all cupreous metal artifacts.

Following 12 months of conservation, the *Victory*'s cannon were formally handed over to the UK Ministry of Defence and were relocated to the Mary Rose Trust for ongoing treatment. This article details Odyssey Marine Exploration's conservation strategy – completed and planned, and in no way anticipates the preferences adopted by the Mary Rose Trust. The above practice and theory is intended to be applicable to any future recovery of bronze cannon from the wreck of Balchin's *Victory*.

Figs. 17-18. Some of the cannon on the wreck of Balchin's Victory *are almost completely devoid of concretion (top), whilst others are densely concreted.*

Bibliography

Cunnigham Dobson, N. and Kingsley, S., 'HMS *Victory*, a First-Rate Royal Navy Warship Lost in the English Channel, 1744. Preliminary Survey & Identification'. In G. Stemm and S. Kingsley (eds.), *Oceans Odyssey: Deep-Sea Shipwrecks in the English Channel, the Straits of Gibraltar and the Atlantic Ocean* (Oxford, 2010), 235-80.

Gettens, R.J., 'Mineral Alteration Products on Ancient Metal Objects'. In G. Thomson (ed.), *Recent Advances in Conservation* (London, 1963), 89-92.

Gettens, R.J., *The Corrosion Products of Metal Antiquities* (Smithsonian Institution, Washington, 1964).

Green, V., 'The Use of Benzotriazole in *Conservation*'. *In Conservation in Archaeology and the Applied Arts* (London, 1975), 1-15.

Hamilton, D. L., *Conservation of Metal Objects from Underwater Sites: A Study in Methods* (Texas Antiquities Committee Publication No. 1, Austin, 1976).

Madsen, H.B., 'A Preliminary Note on the Use of Benzotriazole for Stabilizing Bronze Objects', *Studies in Conservation* 12 (1967), 163-67.

Merk, L.E., 'The Effectiveness of Benzotriazole in the Inhibition of the Corrosive Behavior of Stripping Reagents on Bronzes', *Studies in Conservation* 26 (1981), 73-76.

North, N.A., 'Conservation of Metals'. In C. Pearson (ed.), *Conservation of Marine Archaeological Objects* (London, 1987), 207-52.

Oddy, W.A. and Hughes, M.J., 'The Stabilization of Active Bronze and Iron Antiquities by the Use of Sodium Sesquicarbonate', *Studies in Conservation* 15 (1970), 183-89.

Organ, R.M., 'The Consolidation of Fragile Metallic Objects'. In G. Thomson (ed.), *Recent Advances in Conservation* (London, 1963), 128-34.

Pearson, C., 'The Western Australian Museum Conservation Laboratory for Marine Archaeological Material', *International Journal of Nautical Archaeology* 3.2 (1974), 295-305.

Plenderleith, H.J. and Torraca, G., 'The Conservation of Metals in the Tropics', *The Conservation of Cultural Property. Museum and Monuments* 11 (1968), 237-49.

Plenderleith, H.J. and Werner, A.E.A., *The Conservation of Antiquities and Works of Art* (Oxford University Press, 1971).

Sease, C., 'Benzotriazole: A Review for Conservators', *Studies in Conservation* 23 (1978), 76-85.

Walker, R., 'The Role of Benzotriazole in the Preservation of Antiquities'. In *The Proceedings of the Symposium for the Conservation and Restoration of Metals, Edinburgh, Scotland, March 1979* (Scottish Society for Conservation and Restoration, Edinburgh, 1979), 40-44.

La Marquise de Tourny (Site 33c): A Mid-18th Century Armed Privateer of Bordeaux

Neil Cunningham Dobson
Odyssey Marine Exploration, Tampa, USA

In 2008, Odyssey Marine Exploration discovered an unknown wreck at a depth of around 80m in the western English Channel (Site 33c). A pre-disturbance survey was conducted, including the recording of surface features and the production of a photomosaic. The presence of a blue glass *flaçon* bottle and *fleur de lis* decoration along an iron swivel gun recovered from the site suggested a possible French nationality for the vessel. The discovery of the ship's bronze bell, inscribed with the name *La Marquise de Tourny* and the date of 1744, confirmed that Site 33c represented a ship that had once been a Bordeaux-based privateer.

La Marquise de Tourny may have been sailing short-haul between Bordeaux and the French Channel ports when she was lost during a storm in the late 1740s or early 1750s. No cargo is evident on the site and the abundance of iron ballast may reflect the original presence of an organic consignment such as coffee or sugar, which no longer survives. Other than the dense concretions surrounding iron ballast and cannon, the wreck is poorly preserved in shallow sediments, compounded by damage caused by trawlers. Evidence suggests that Site 33c comprises the rare remains of the wreck of a French corsair. Beyond two outstandingly preserved wrecks undergoing excavation off St. Malo, France, and the comprehensive excavation of the French *Machault* by Parks Canada, Site 33c is the only other privateer of this period that has been examined archaeologically.

1. Introduction

During the 2008 season of Odyssey Marine Exploration's Atlas Shipwreck Survey Project in the western English Channel, the *Odyssey Explorer* located a significant and previously unknown shipwreck (Fig. 1). Initial investigation of site MUN-T1M33c-1 (henceforth Site 33c) using the Remotely-Operated Vehicle Zeus revealed a spread of over 20 cannon and several masses of amorphous, linear iron concretions. During the initial survey the ship's bell was located lying on its side just west of the wreck nucleus. The artifact was recovered and sent for conservation to the York Archaeological Trust. Initial conservation exposed various French symbols, a date of 1744, and most of the letters of the ship's name *La Marquise de Tourny.*

Although lying within the outer limits of diving range, environmental conditions such as strong currents and poor visibility made the use of an ROV a highly suitable archaeological tool for investigating this site. A photomosaic was produced and a cannon and concretion measurement survey conducted, from which a master site plan was generated. A small iron swivel gun was recovered to assist identification of this vessel. In 2009 a FADE survey (Odyssey's sub-sediment metallic detection system) was initiated to locate and plot buried features.

2. Site Characterization

Site 33c was discovered on 26 April 2008 during a program of high-resolution side-scan and cesium magnetometer survey and was investigated using an ROV. A total of 16 ROV dives were conducted during several visits in 2008. Over 2,000 still photographs were taken and 67 DVD's and 27 High-Definition tapes recorded during a total dive time of 66 hours and 36 minutes.

Conditions on the first dive (Dive 402) were extremely challenging.[1] Bottom currents and very low visibility complicated the initial non-disturbance survey. However, a spread of iron cannon was recorded exposed on the sea bottom in association with extensive spreads of large concretions (Figs. 19-21). Conditions on the site remained poor throughout the next five survey dives, when two artifacts were recovered to help date and identify the nationality of the shipwreck. The first artifact recovered was a section of lead sheet, probably a hull repair patch, located near the left hand muzzle of cannon C-21 (inv. no. MUN-A-08-0001-SF; Fig. 67). The second artifact recovered was a small shard of glass from a common form of bottle recorded close to the right-hand side of cannon C-22 (inv. no. MUN-A-08-0002-GL).

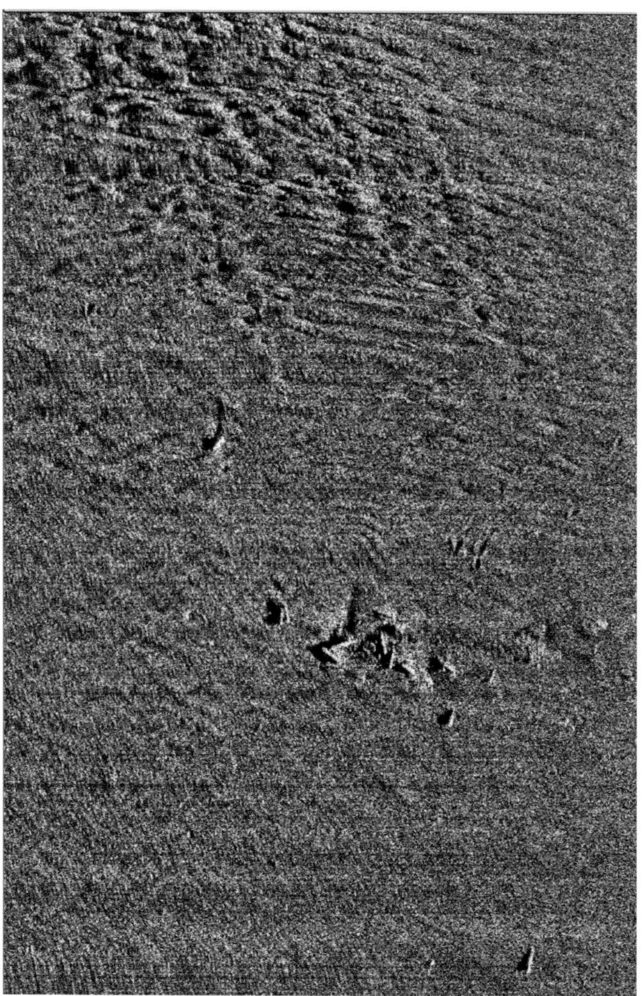

Fig. 1. A side-scan sonar image of Site 33c, which manifests as a series of linear features and anomalies at center. Sand ripples are present in the background.

Fig. 2. The Odyssey Explorer *on assignment in the western English Channel.*

Site 33c lies approximately 100km southeast of Plymouth, England, in the western English Channel at a depth of around 80m (Fig. 3). It lies beyond the territorial seas or contiguous zone of any country and is within an area of high commercial fishing activity. The visible extent of the site densely covers an area of 35 x 25m, oriented along a northwest to southeast axis. During spring tides a current of 0.1-1.2 knots flows across the site. The surface features consist of 25 iron cannon ranging in length from 1.05-3.17m and 13 large multi-concreted areas, each measuring up to 3.5 x 3.0m (Tables 1-2; Fig. 6). Two of the cannon, C-01 to the northeast and C-22 to the southwest, lie over 35m away from the nucleus of the site and have most probably been displaced by trawlers. Very few areas of limited ship timbers survive. Fishing net fragments and modern garbage are snagged on concretions and cannon and partially buried within the shipwreck's matrix (Figs. 12-14, 29, 32, 43, 45).

The seabed is composed of a heavily abraded, shell-rich sedimentological matrix consisting of areas of gravel, flint and small stones intermixed with coarse sands (Fig. 11). The sediments are shallow: an average depth of 15cm, and apparent 40cm maximum, covers the compact seabed. Small clusters of surface rocks and boulders are also present. The wreck site is extremely dynamic and subjected to ongoing periods of exposure, re-cover and scouring.

3. The Bell Recovery

One month after the initial discovery, the *Odyssey Explorer* returned to continue the site survey. During Dive 423, with underwater visibility at only about 2m, Zeus discovered the ship's bell lying on its side and partly buried in sand sediment (Fig. 54). Its position was approximately 8-9m from cannon C-25 on a bearing of 270° (Fig. 6). The bell seemed to be in good state of preservation, with letters present on its surfaces but unreadable due to the low underwater visibility. The decision was thus made to recover the object for purposes of site identification. The bell was recorded *in situ* and the surrounding sediments cleared to free it for recovery in a custom-fabricated box. Visibility was once again very poor during Dive 424, the result of seasonal and tidal/current conditions. The bell was lifted by the ROV manipulator arms and secured in the recovery container. Once on deck, the artifact was relocated to the *Explorer*'s dedicated on-board laboratory for recording, first-aid conservation and storage.

This copper alloy bell measures 46.70cm in height, 41.07cm in width and weighs 52kg (Fig. 55). Close study confirmed its good state of preservation, with only

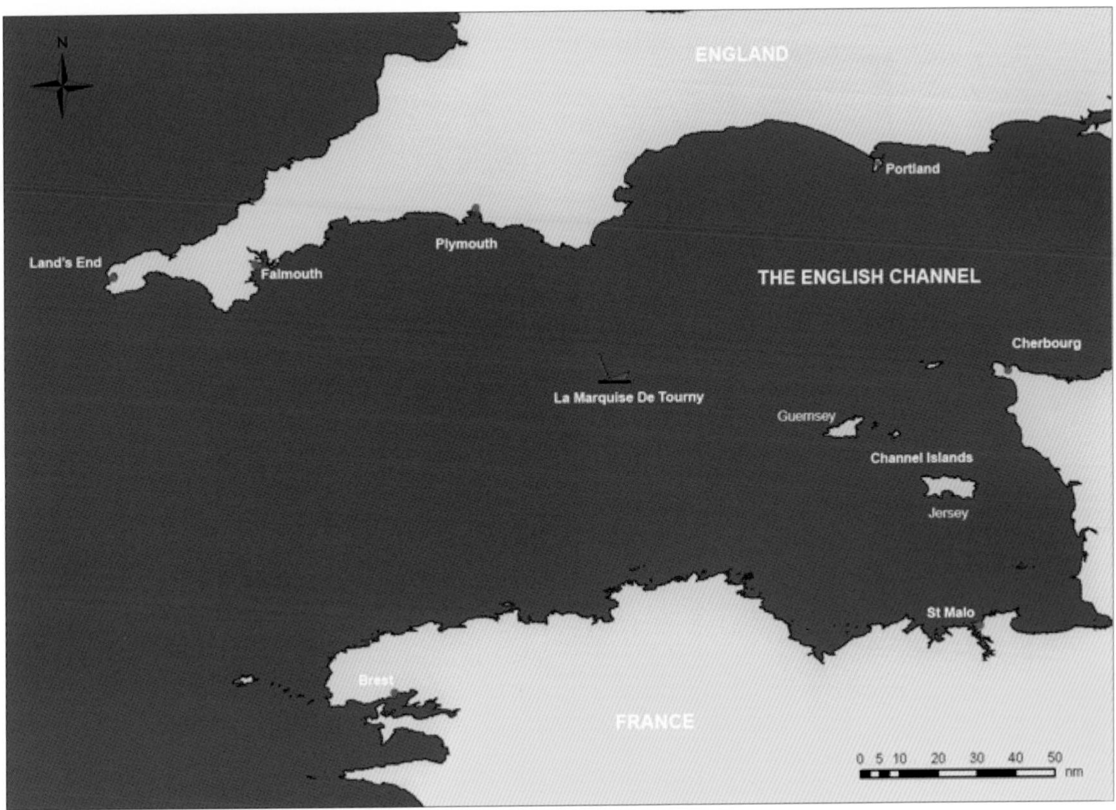

Fig. 3. The location of Site 33c in the western English Channel.

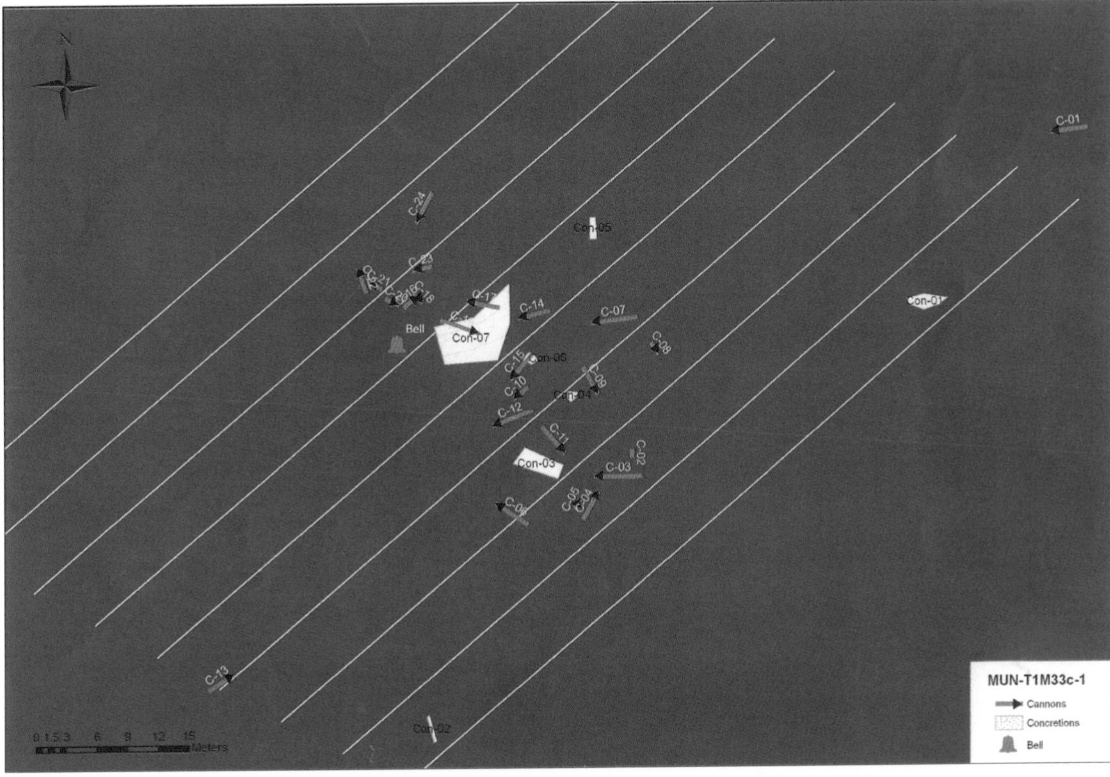

Fig. 4. An electronic grid with 5m spacing intervals, running northeast to southwest, was established for the ROV Zeus to survey Site 33c systematically.

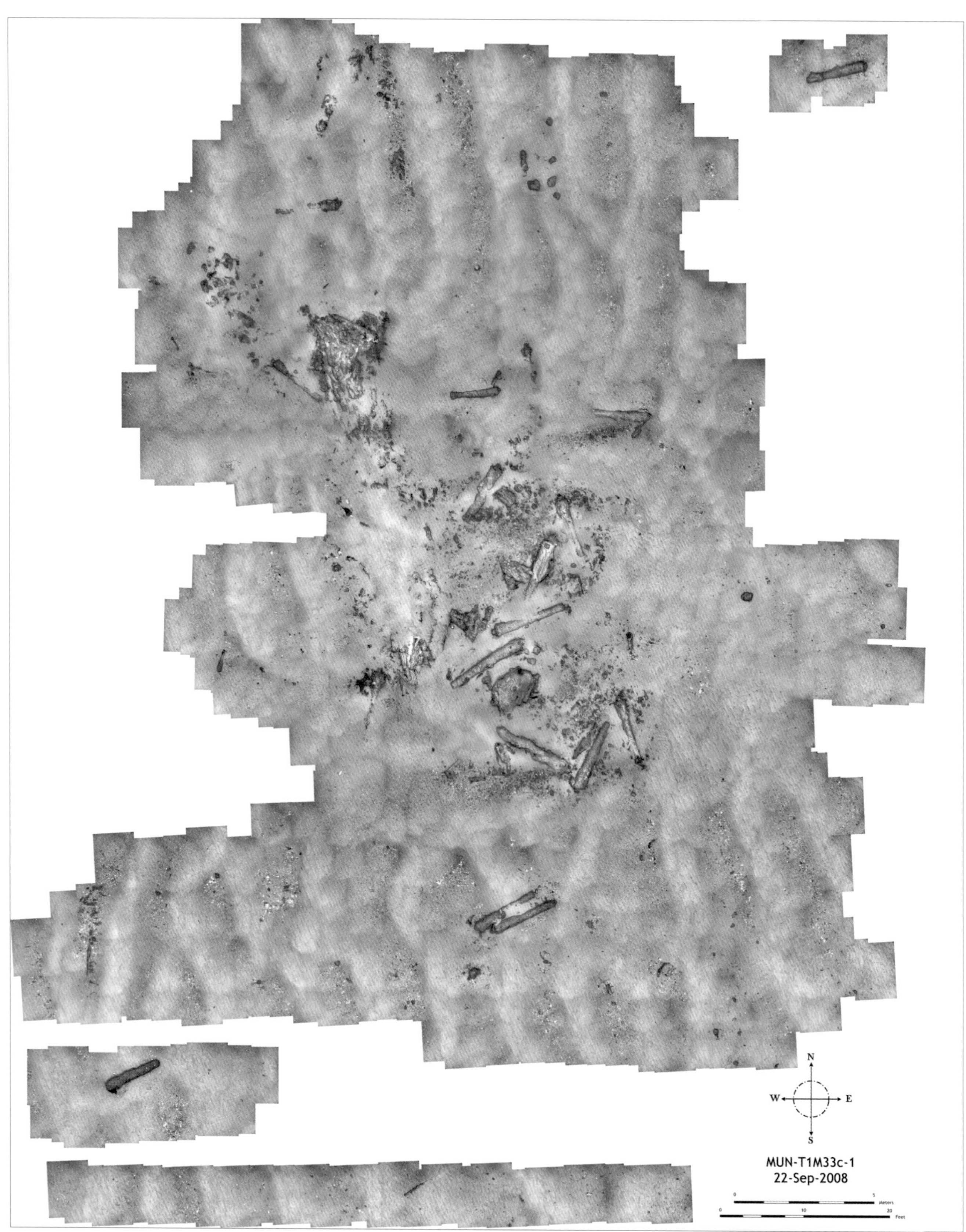

Fig. 5. Photomosaic of Site 33c, composed of 1,417 digital photographs covering an area of 1,220 square meters.

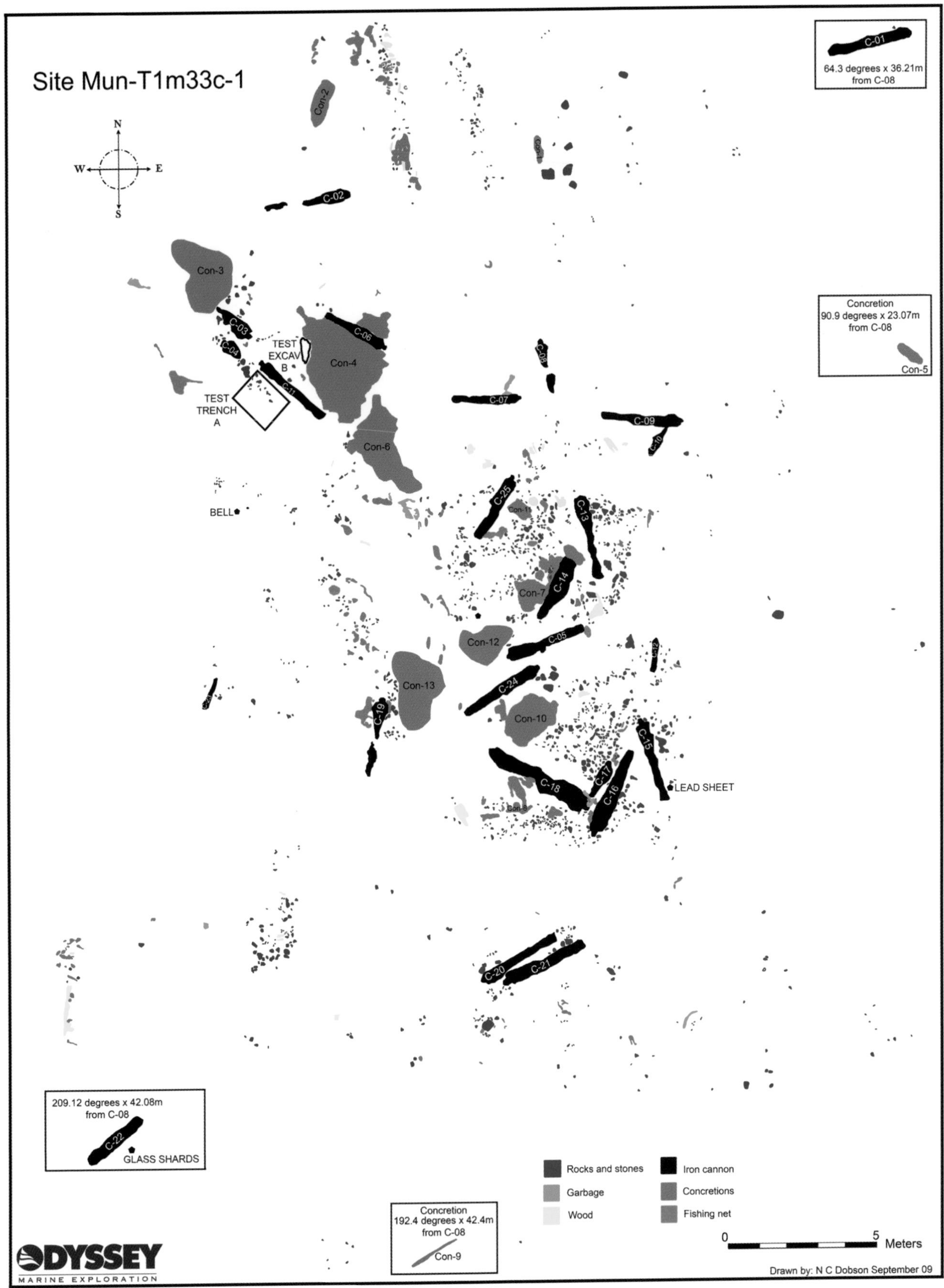

Fig. 6. Plan of shipwreck Site 33c.

Figs. 7-8. The ROV Zeus custom-tooled with the FADE system for detecting sub-bottom metallic anomalies, its wings folded (top) and expanded (below) ready for use.

a thin cover of marine growth in areas and minor damage to the lower edge. A crown-shaped suspension ring consisting of two single and two double canon rings surmounts the top of the bell (Fig. 59). The inside was in a similar condition to the exterior. Below the shoulder, between two horizontal lines, a partially identifiable inscription (2.3cm high) runs around the entire circumference of the bell. Although difficult to read due to corrosion and marine encrustation, it initially appeared to contain Latin letters, possibly the name of the ship. Light surface washing revealed the following letters:

-A M- - -ISE DE - - - -A- - - - FECIT 1744

Positioned 1.4cm below this lettering are two horizontal lines set 1.2cm apart. A further 12.0cm below these two lines are six horizontal lines occupying a band width of 3.4cm. At a height of 2.8cm above the base of the bell is another horizontal line. Of particular interest is the area between the top and lower bands along the waist of the bell, where four molded symbols project beyond the surface metal. Spaced evenly around the sides were a curved fish/dolphin, a roundel, a Calvary cross, and three *fleur de lis* (Figs. 60-63).

The fish/dolphin motif is representative of the Christian faith. If a fish, it represented Christ and if a dolphin symbolized resurrection and salvation. The roundel symbol reflects the rotating force of Christian divine power. The Calvary cross symbolizes the Rock of Golgotha where Christ was crucified, while the three *fleur de lis* are representative of the Virgin Mary. Although all of these symbols are common within Christianity (Ferguson, 1961: 15, 18, 183), since 1147 it has been generally accepted that *fleur de lis* set in this configuration are indicative of the French monarchy. This tentatively suggested that the nationality of the bell was French.

Once recording and documentation of the bell were completed, the artifact was secured in a plastic container holding a solution of sodium sesquicarbonate (a corrosion inhibitor) until the *Odyssey Explorer* reached the next port of call, where it was shipped to the York Archaeological Trust conservation laboratory in north England after being declared to the UK Receiver of Wreck.

4. Phase 1 Site Survey

When the *Odyssey Explorer* returned to the site five weeks later, sea bottom conditions and visibility had improved, although a dense particulate algae layer was suspended in the water column. Project plans were designed to survey the site visually to determine its extent, main features and to conduct a photomosaic survey. A virtual grid composed of survey lines spaced at 5m intervals, and running northeast to southwest, was established and followed by the ROV Zeus (Fig. 4). Cannon and large concretions were waypointed using Winfrog (navigation survey software). Measurements of cannon were recorded and features photographed (Table 1).

The survey revealed that the site consists of a large spread of 25 iron cannon, 1.05-3.17m long, intermixed with 13 large concreted masses (0.85 x 0.25m to 3.5 x 3.0m), some of which cover areas of 2-10 square meters and appeared to consist of approximately 1m-long cylindrical iron concretions (Tables 1-2; Figs. 19-42). A minimum of 167 examples of these linear concretions are visible on the site's surface, although the merging of concretions and unseen stratigraphy severely complicates identification. The total volume of ballast ingots may be closer to

Survey Feature	Muzzle Heading	Length (meters)
Cannon C-01	255	2.90
Cannon C-02	275	2.81
Cannon C-03	310	1.54 partly buried
Cannon C-04	132	0.84 partly buried
Cannon C-05	72	2.70
Cannon C-06	300	2.33
Cannon C-07	270	2.35
Cannon C-08	171	1.94 partly buried
Cannon C-09	268	2.81
Cannon C-10	48	1.33 swivel gun
Cannon C-11	312	2.88
Cannon C-12	186	1.28 partly buried
Cannon C-13	344	2.75
Cannon C-14	210	2.22
Cannon C-15	164	2.79
Cannon C-16	22	3.17
Cannon C-17	212	1.33
Cannon C-18	306	3.00
Cannon C-19	12	2.52
Cannon C-20	61	2.93
Cannon C-21	64	3.00
Cannon C-22	50	2.25
Cannon C-23	24	1.05
Cannon C-24	239	2.83
Cannon C-25	216	2.45

Table 1. Measurements and orientations of cannon recorded on Site 33c.

500-600 individual pieces. No evidence of any other cargo was discovered and no anchors were present. Some red galley brick fragments were seen, but no potsherds recorded. No visible wooden ship structure survives, other than minor small sections of timbers (Figs. 11, 46-47). The site offers no visible indication as to which part of the wreck signifies the bow or stern. The shipwreck measures approximately 35 x 25m and, taking into account the number of cannon, the wreck may be interpreted as the remains of a moderately armed 25-gun sailing vessel.

Survey Feature	Length (meters)	Character
Con-01 Concretion	0.85 x 0.25	1 unknown
Con-02 Concretion	1.60 x 0.50	2 ingots/cannon?
Con-03 Concretion	2.20 x 1.50	1 unknown
Con-04 Concretion	3.50 x 3.00	88 ingots & 2 cannon
Con-05 Concretion	1.00 x 0.25	6 ingots
Con-06 Concretion	2.50 x 1.80	----
Con-07 Concretion	1.20 x 0.60	20 ballast ingots
Con-08 Concretion	2.60 x 1.50	4 unknown
Con-09 Concretion	1.80 x 0.15	1 unknown
Con-10 Concretion	2.00 x 1.60	25 ingots
Con-11 Concretion	1.00 x 0.8	5 ingots
Con-12 Concretion	1.50 x 1.30	4 unknown
Con-13 Concretion	2.00 x 1.40	21 ingots
T-01 Timber Area	2.50 x 1.00	Planking

Table 2. Measurements of concretions and planking area recorded on Site 33c.

Some limited test trenching was conducted in an attempt to locate hull remains or artifacts that could support a date or nationality (Figs. 6, Figs. 42-47). Additional partly buried cannon and concretions were discovered, as well as modern rubbish in the form of parts of plastic sheet, sacking and tin cans trapped in the shipwreck's matrix.

Along one edge of concreted area Con-4, a small test excavation revealed 10cm below the surface a layer of stones and flint nodules overlying a dark organic layer at a total depth of 15-20cm (Fig. 44). Close by at cannon C-11 a second test trench (1.45 x 1.17m and 0.30m deep) exposed the same stratigraphy and sediment composition (Fig. 42). Excavation to a depth of 30cm revealed some small disarticulated and unidentifiable abraded ship's timbers. Both areas excavated were devoid of artifacts.

As part of Odyssey's standard site investigation procedure, a photomosaic survey was conducted (Dives 492, 493 and 498). A total of 1,417 digital photographs were taken by the ROV Zeus across an area of 1,220 square meters during a period of 10 hours. Images were taken with a 50% overlap, with the ROV flying at an altitude of 2.7-3.2m above the seabed, with a line spacing of 0.8m, and were stitched together digitally to produce the final photomosaic (Fig. 5).

Using the site photomosaic as a reference source, a measurement survey of all visible cannon and large concreted areas was conducted (Dive 494). The ROV manipulator arms (the tips of which are geo-spatially coordinated with the ROV transponder) were placed at the end of each cannon and at selected points, enabling the maximum length and widths of the concretion features to be measured (Tables 1-2). A software program calculated the distance between the arms via the ROV's navigational system. The compass heading of each gun's muzzle was also recorded. For the concretions the ROV took positions that were later plotted in ARC GIS software.

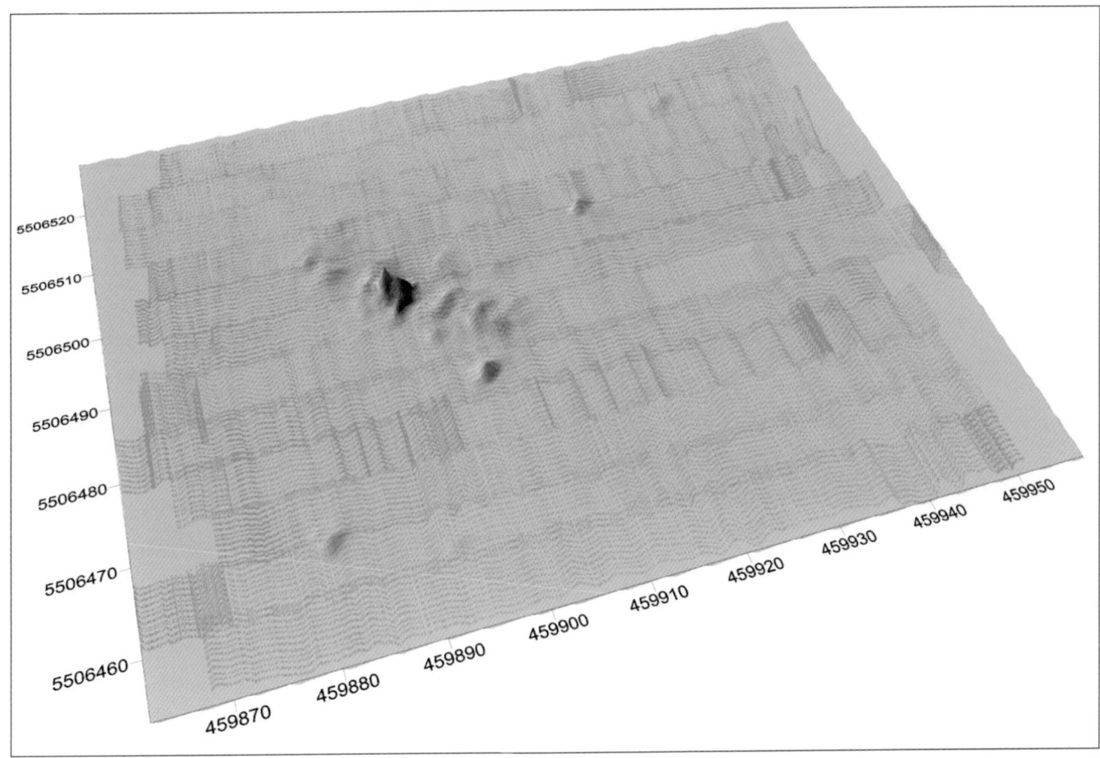

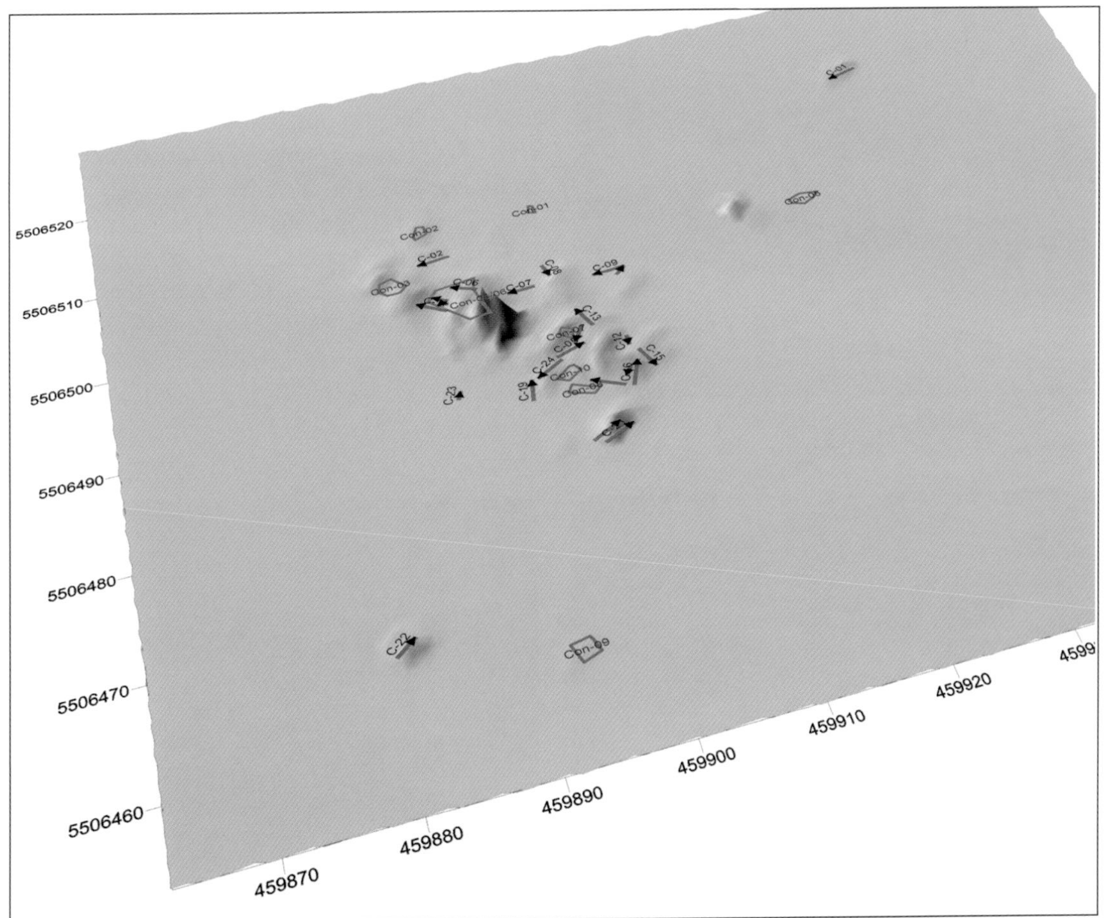

Figs. 9-10. The positions of targets plotted by the FADE system on Site 33c (top), with visible surface metallic archaeological remains superimposed over them (bottom), demonstrating precise matches.

Fig. 11. The sea bottom matrix on Site 33c consists of very coarse sands intermixed with flint nodules and pebbles. Between 5-40cm of sediment maximum covers the archaeological remains. Disarticulated plank fragments are present at top center.

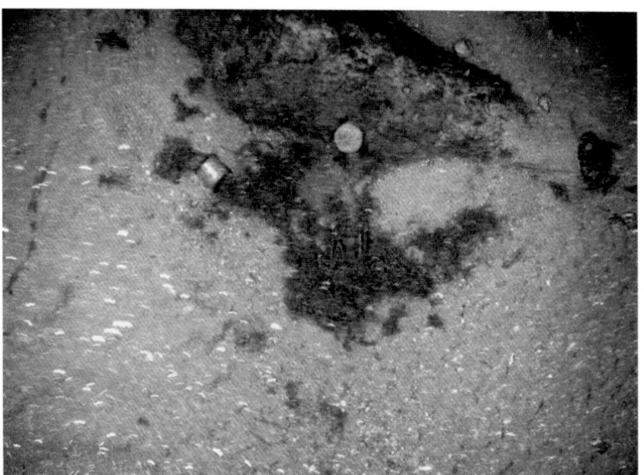

Fig. 12. A pile of fishing net and a tin can snagged on cannon C-19.

5. Cannon C-10 Recovery

While the bell was undergoing conservation and its inscription remained tantalizingly undeciphered, the decision was taken to recover a cannon to examine if it bore any date, a maker's mark or decoration that might facilitate dating and identification of the ship. C-10 located to the northeast of the wreck, and believed most likely to be a swivel gun, was selected for this purpose. The gun concretion was lying on the seabed with the muzzle oriented at 48° (Figs. 48-49). It lay at an angle off the southern side of the cascabel of cannon C-09 and was completely exposed and seemingly unattached to any other structures or artifact. Using its SeRF excavation tool, the ROV carefully removed the sediment from around the base of the gun. Less than 10cm below the surface a layer of small stones and flint nodules was recorded, confirming that the object was not associated with any artifacts or structure, but lay on the compact seabed and would thus permit a straightforward recovery that would not disturb any underlying archaeological contexts.

A recovery box was placed on site, which was rubber mat-lined to protect the gun during the lifting process. The ROV was positioned at the muzzle end, while its dredge system excavated around and below the muzzle, creating space to rig up a rope-lifting strop (Fig. 50). (Rope or canvas slings/strops are the preferred lifting gear for this type of operation because wire can easily cut into the concretion and damage a cannon's surface.) Zeus then moved to the cascabel end, where a similar process was carried out (Fig. 51). The rope strops were connected to the ROV and the gun flown to the recovery basket (Figs. 52-53). With the artifact secured within the recovery basket, Zeus and the gun were winched to the surface. Placement in the recovery basket ensured that the cannon was successfully supported and protected during its lift through the water/air interface and onto the deck of the *Odyssey Explorer*.

Fig. 13. A section of fishing net snagged on C-25.

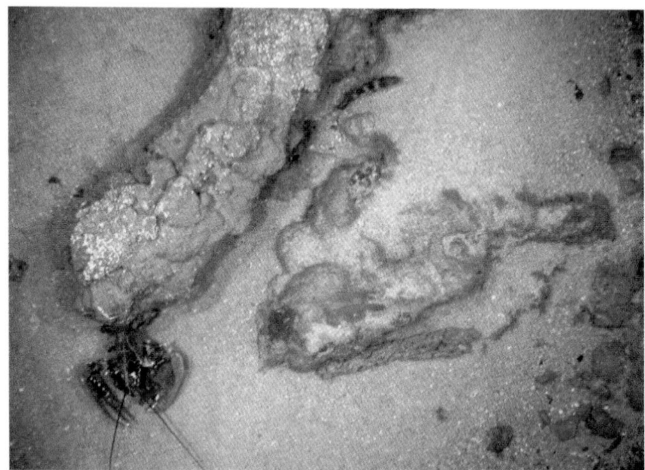

Fig. 14. A length of fishing net cable snagged on Con-8.

On reaching the research ship's deck, the gun was removed from the recovery basket, photographed, measured and documented (Fig. 68). Prior to the removal of its concretion, the object was weighed at 82kg and measured at 1.07m in length. The concretion was carefully removed using a small chisel and hammer (Fig. 69). The cascabel button proved to be broken and part of one trunnion was missing. The exposed gun measures 1.03m and weighs 54kg. Visible on the breech is a round nipple, 1.3cm in diameter, and a 6cm long gunner's 'V' mark. On the first reinforce is an 8 x 6cm incised *fleur de lis* motif, and a similar type and size of symbol is repeated on the second reinforce (Figs. 70-71). The muzzle end is damaged, so a section of concretion was left attached for removal and conservation under laboratory conditions. No other markings were discovered and the cannon was placed in a tub of fresh water with a pH of seven pending transfer to the conservation laboratory at the York Archaeological Trust.

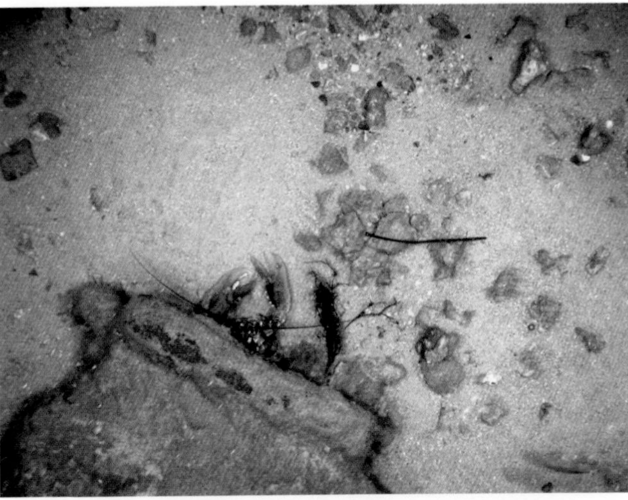

Fig. 16. Lobsters are common across Site 33c, both on the open seabed and inhabiting cavities between and below concretions.

6. Phase 2 Site Survey

Especially interesting amongst the wreckage, as visible on the site's master photomosaic, were cannon C-01 (36.21m from C-08 muzzle at an angle of 64.3°), C-22 (42.08m from C-08 at an orientation of 209.12°) and concretion Con-5 (23.07m from C-08 at an angle of 90.9°). The off-site positions of cannon C-01 and C-22 may indicate that both have been dragged by fishing trawling activities. This scenario is in line with the degraded nature of the site and corresponds with its location within extensive European commercial fishing grounds, where displaced cannon have been observed associated with other wrecks investigated by Odyssey.

During the survey of cannon C-22, the neck of a glass bottle was observed protruding above the sediment,

Fig. 17. A monkfish (Lophius piscatorius Linnaeus) *on Site 33c. Note the concreted cannon in the background lying on top of parallel-set iron ballast blocks.*

Fig. 15. Cavities between and below concretions are extensively inhabited by conger eels on Site 33c.

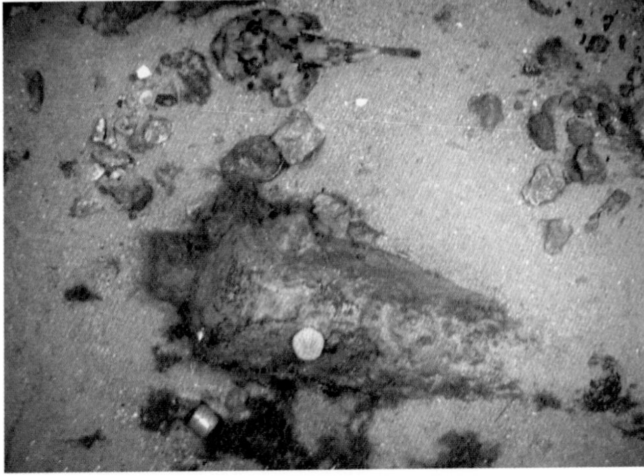

Fig. 18. A monkfish next to cannon C-19.

Fig. 19. A typical view of Site 33c (Con-4), characterized by dense concentrations of rectangular iron ballast blocks.

Fig. 20. Concreted rectangular iron ballast blocks associated with two encrusted iron cannon (center right and bottom left) within Con-4.

Fig. 21. Concreted rectangular iron ballast blocks within Con-4, with a possible cannonball in the center foreground. The site's concretions are extensively inhabited by brown crabs.

about 0.5m from the southeast edge of the gun (Fig. 65). Using the ROV limpet suction tool to gently dust away the surrounding sediment, it was freed from the seabed and proved to be a neck and shoulder fragment from a blue-colored square bottle. It was recovered to the surface for documentation and photography (Fig. 66) and returned to the site on the next dive.

Close study of concretion Con-5 identified what appeared to be a series of five iron cylinders (Figs. 22-23). The feature was not connected to any ship's structure or artifacts and was lying in a shallow scour pit, seemingly also dragged to this location, most likely by trawling activity.

Zeus next investigated the outer edges of concretion Con-4 between cannon C-06 and C-11 (Test Trench A: Dives 496 and 497; Figs. 25, 42) in order to establish whether any ship's hull underlay it, thus contributing to the question of whether the concreted area was cargo or ballast. Excavation demonstrated that the stratigraphy was identical to that recorded elsewhere across the site. A strand of polypropylene fishing-net rope was again uncovered, snagged on the concretion and seabed matrix. Further abraded black disarticulated ship's timbers were uncovered at a depth of 15cm.

Some 15m west of cannon C-20 and C-21, and 12m southwest of C-19, a 3 x 1m area of hull timbers was exposed (Figs. 46-47). Zeus dusted off the light top sediment layer to expose the wood in an attempt to determine its character. Approximately 5-15cm of vertical loose mobile sediment was removed. The wood was black in color and the surfaces highly abraded. This section of timbers appeared to consist of two frames and two hull planks, otherwise disarticulated. Following photography, the area of planking was backfilled. Although small patches of disarticulated ship's timbers were discernable beneath light sediment covering other sections of the wreck site, only in this area were limited interconnected planks encountered. The hull remains are evidently badly preserved, partly due to the thin level of sediment covering the seabed.

Figs. 22-23. Con-5 consists of around five linear iron concretions and lies next to an undefined circular object.

7. The 2009 Survey Season

In the 2009 Atlas Shipwreck Survey Project season, Site 33c was revisited. During Odyssey shipwreck search operations, side-scan targets and magnetometer hits are investigated using an ROV. In many cases no visual targets are located on the seabed, and only a magnetometer hit betrays the presence of wreckage. To examine these types of targets, it is necessary for an ROV to be fitted with metal detecting equipment.

Odyssey has custom-tooled the ROV Zeus with a 'FADE' system. This tool is capable of locating, tracking and measuring the relative positions of sub-bottom ferro-magnetic objects by means of their intrinsic magnetism and consequent distortion of the Earth's magnetic field. The FADE system consists of three major elements: a sensor array of magnetic gradiometers and fluxgate sensors, a subsea electronics package and a surface computer workstation and display.

The FADE apparatus consists of 12 sensors fitted at 63cm intervals along a frame composed of two 2.43m side wings and a 2.3m frame in front of the ROV (Fig. 7). When conducting a survey the wings are extended to create a scanning surface slightly more than 7m in length (Fig. 8). The FADE survey of and around Site 33c was undertaken following the lines of a digitally produced electronic grid survey box measuring 80 x 12m long with 6m spacing lines. The ROV was flown along these lines and the position of ferrous targets plotted (Fig. 9). After the dive a map of the FADE hits was compared with the physical positions of the cannon and concretions and was found to match directly (Fig. 10). Some of the buried FADE hits were investigated and found to consist of unidentifiable iron concretions buried at depths of 5-15cm.

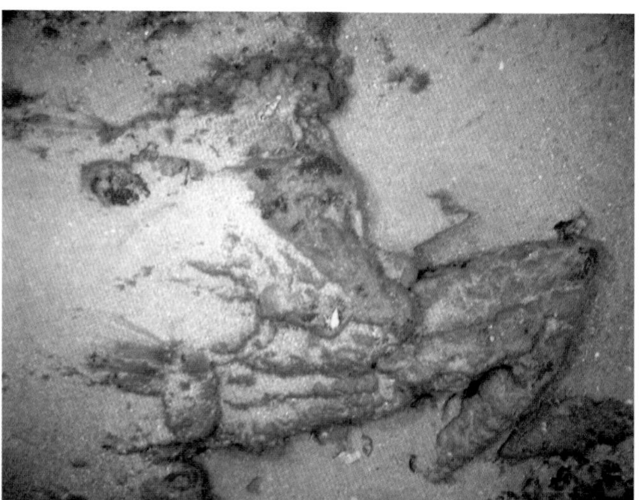

Fig. 24. A pile of concreted rectangular iron ballast blocks within Con-13.

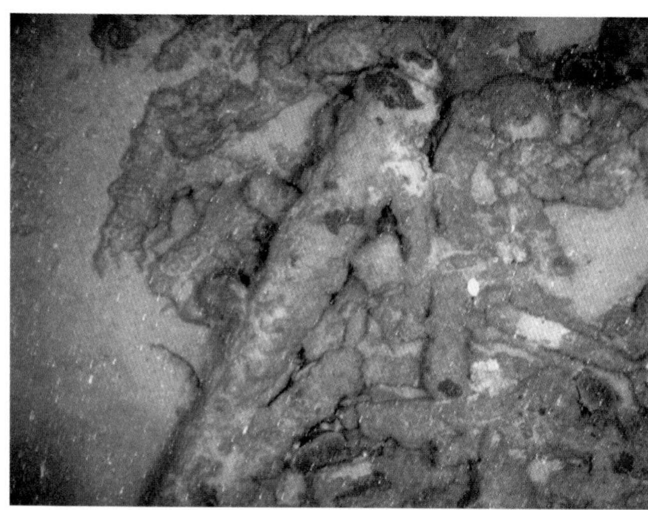

Fig. 25. Cannon C-06 lying on top of concreted rectangular iron ballast blocks within Con-4.

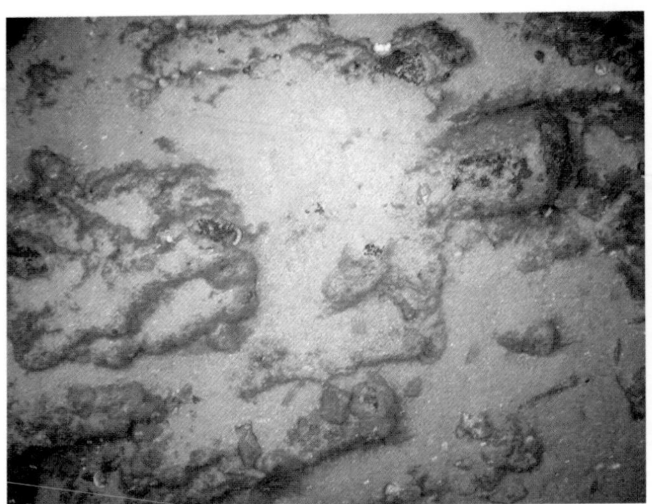

Fig. 26. Possible broken cannon amongst concreted rectangular iron ballast blocks within Con-6.

Fig. 27. Concreted iron cannon C-15.

Fig. 28. A concreted iron cannon on Site 33c.

Fig. 29. Concreted iron cannon C-21 and C-20 with a modern tin can behind.

Fig. 30. Concreted iron cannon C-01.

Fig. 31. Concreted iron cannon C-22.

Fig. 32. Concreted iron cannon C-19, with snagged plastic and fishing net.

Fig. 33. Concreted swivel gun C-17 in situ.

Fig. 34. Detail of concreted swivel gun C-17, with its yoke still attached.

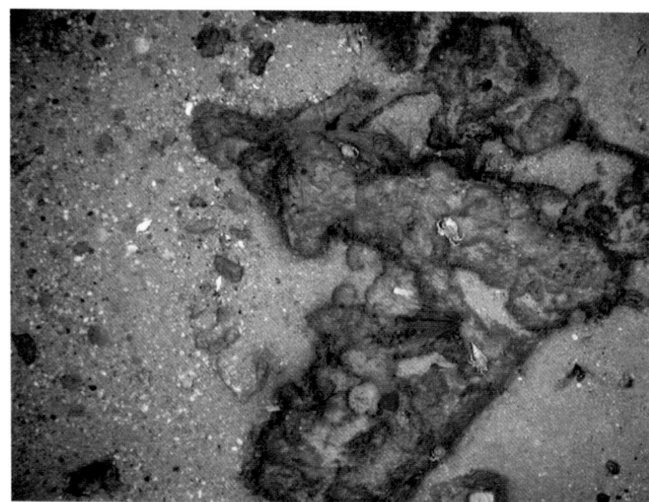

Fig. 35. A possible concreted swivel gun.

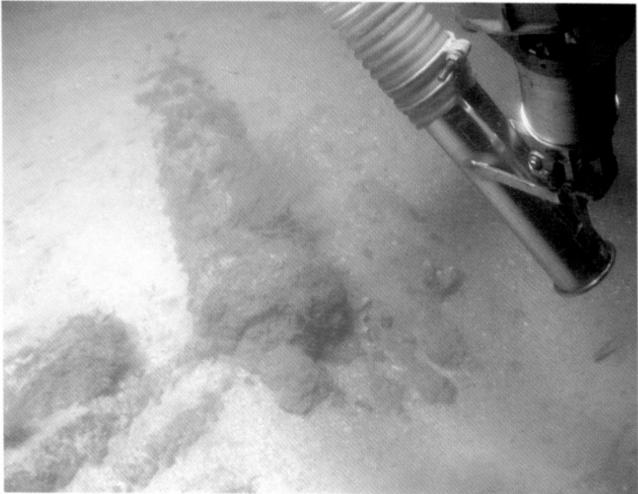

Fig. 36. Detail of the cascabel end of concreted cannon C-16.

Fig. 37. Detail of the cascabel end of concreted cannon C-04.

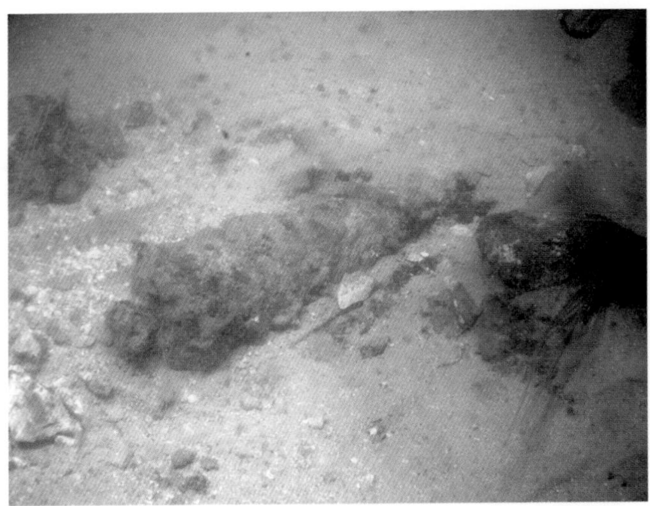
Fig. 38. Concreted iron cannon C-20.

Fig. 39. Detail of the cascabel end of iron cannon C-01 within very shallow sand sediments and lying directly on top of the seabed composed of flint nodules and pebbles.

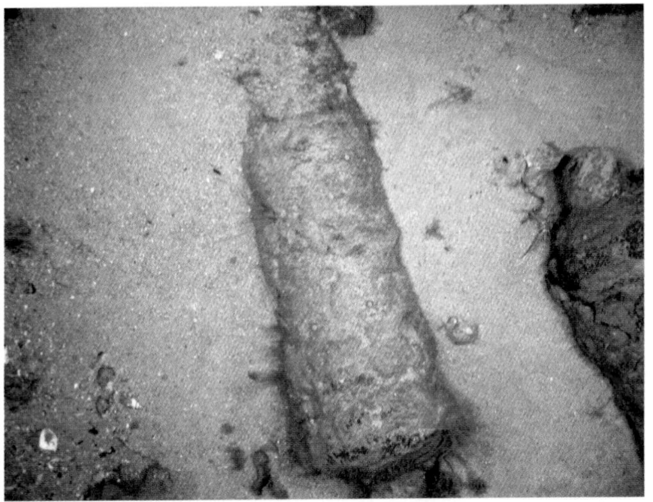
Fig. 40. Detail of the cascabel end of concreted cannon C-05.

Fig. 41. Detail of the cascabel end of concreted cannon C-14.

Fig. 42. Trial Trench A exposed at a depth of 0-20cm a section of synthetic fishing net snagged on cannon C-11 alongside part of a possible wooden barrel stave.

Fig. 43. Modern rubbish/snagged fishing net exposed in Trial Trench B.

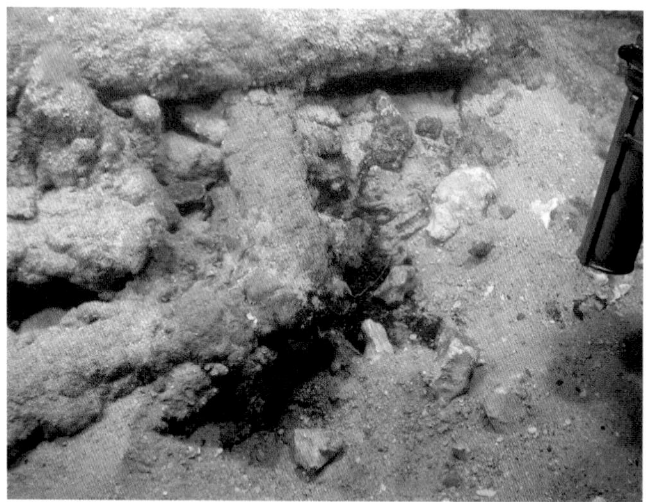

Fig. 44. Trial Trench B encountered a layer of natural flint and pebbles within 5cm of the surface.

Fig. 45. A modern workman's glove encountered next to Trial Trench B.

Figs. 46-47. An area of limited hull planking at the southwestern limit of Site 33c before and after trail trenching.

Figs. 48-49. Swivel gun C10 in situ *prior to recovery, lying partially buried in a 10cm deep matrix of sand alongside cannon C9.*

Figs. 50-51. Following excavation around and below cannon C10, ROV Zeus threaded and tied rope strops around both ends of the gun to facilitate lifting.

Figs. 52-53. ROV Zeus flies cannon C10 to the nearby recovery basket, which was lined with rubber matting to cushion the gun during its recovery.

8. Post-Survey Research

A. The Ship's Bell

One of the most crucial diagnostic artifacts recorded on Site 33c was the ship's bell, which clearly bears a date of 1744 and a partly legible name or Latin phrase (Figs. 55-57). Its dimensions are:

- H. 46.70cm
- Max W. 41.07cm
- Weight 52kg
- Inscription H. 2.3cm
- Fish symbol 4.9 x 4.8cm (Fig. 60)
- Roundel symbol 4.4 x 4.4cm (Fig. 61)
- Cross symbol 11.8 x 7.8cm (Fig. 62)
- Three *fleur de lis* symbols, each H. and W. 3.1 x 2.7cm (Fig. 63)

Sent to the York Archaeological Trust in England for conservation, the bell's copper alloy was reported to be in good condition with a thin encrustation of marine growth in some areas and a thin layer of corrosion on the surface. Minor areas of physical damage to the lower edge of the bell were also observed. Symbols and an inscription were visible but, due to the concretion and corrosion, were not readily identifiable.

The artifact was subjected to mechanical cleaning to remove the light concretion and corrosion. The bell was then desalinated by intensive washing in tap water and distilled water. Once all the salt was removed from the metal, the artifact was scheduled to be dried and coated in a protective coat of microcrystalline wax.

Mechanical cleaning of the inscription revealed the following inscription (with its translation below) (Figs. 56-58):

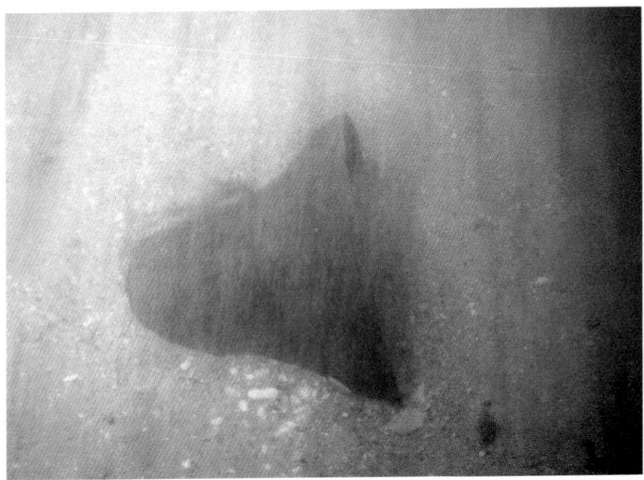

Fig. 54. The ship's bell in situ *on Site 33c.*

Fig. 55. The bell (H. 46.70cm) of La Marquise de Tourny *during conservation.*

LA MARQISE DE TORN- A-DE- R- FECIT 1744

(THE MARQISE OF TORN ???? MADE 1744)

Initial research into this name and date revealed the existence of a French corsair called *La Marquise de Tourny* (see Section 10 below). Illustrations of a French 74-gun warship's main bell and watch-bell depict objects of similar shape and design with comparable symbols. French naval bells were typically manufactured at a brass foundry in Rochefort, but in addition were supplied to the navy by private contractors (Boudriot, 1986: 115, 126). If cast at the Royal Foundry at Rochefort, records may survive. Considering the name in context with the *fleur de lis*, the working hypothesis was that Odyssey had discovered a French vessel.

The bronze bell recovered from Site 33c falls within the timeframe of the golden age of bell-founding between the third decade of the 17th century and the mid-18th century. Ship's bells were traditionally crafted of copper and tin (13 parts copper to four of tin or approximately 80/20%). Applications of higher percentages of tin improved the tone, but rendered the metal brittle. Similarly, too much copper softened the alloy (Nichols, 1928: v, 63).

Ships' bells are relatively common finds on wrecks as far afield as England, France, America, Poland, Portugal, Norway and Polynesia, and typically display a conservative design that makes the formulation of an evolutionary typology ineffective. The earliest historical reference to a ship's bell is a record of Henry VIII's *Henri Grace à Dieu* in 1485.

Figs. 56-57. The name 'DE TORNY' and 'FECIT 1744' molded onto the top of the ship's bell.

Ten years later, an inventory of the warship *Regent* revealed that this ship carried two "wache bells" (Wede, 1972: 2).

At times of crisis, the sounding of the bell warned of danger, fire, fog or an enemy ship. In his *Marine Dictionary* (Hamburg, 1793), J.H. Roeding described the use of bells on ships as primarily serving to identify the passage of time during the day (Wede, 1972: 4):

> "Since on ships the day is divided into 48 half-hours, each half hour is struck on the bell... At each change of watch, namely after four hours have elapsed and the sand in the half-hour glass has run out eight times, the bell is rung to awaken the watch below to come up. At six o'clock at night, the bell is rung for prayer, and as soon as it is over, it is sounded again for dinner. If sudden danger threatens the ship, the alarm is given by ringing the bell to call all hands on deck."

Comparisons of Site 33c's two single and two double canon rings can be drawn with the bells of the *Forsigtigheten* of 1784 and the Copenhagen ship the *Constantia Maria* of 1801 (Wede, 1972: 1, 21). The closest parallel to the Site 33c suspension ring is the bell of the *Henrietta Marie*, an English merchant slave ship wrecked in the summer of 1700 some 55km off Key West, Florida. In this instance, the ship's name runs along the bell's waist. Anatomically, however, the shape of the Site 33c bell is nearest to that recovered from the wreck of the 100-gun English warship the *Royal George*, which sank with great loss of life while being heeled over for repairs at Spithead, Portsmouth, in 1782 (Kingsley, 2008).

This robust crown form, however, was a stylistic preference and by no means serves as a chronological indicator or a reliable dateable criterion for the 18th century. Thus, the 1ft-tall bronze bell from the *Concorde*, wrecked off Beaufort Inlet, North Carolina, in 1718, and believed to be of either Spanish or Portuguese origin (but crafted in the New World), displays a tall single-frame suspension ring, as does the ship's bell of 1745 found at a depth of 170m on a probable Dutch shipwreck along the Ormen Lange pipeline route off northwest Norway (Bryn *et al.*, 2007: 112, 114). Bells of 1792 from the *San Josef*, captured by Nelson at the Battle of Cape St. Vincent in 1797, the *Nostra Senora del Rosario* lost off Paignton, Devon, in 1794 (Larn and Davis, 1977), and the small watch bell from the French ship *L'Astrolabe*, which sailed *c.* 1778-1828, similarly incorporate single, usually plain rectangular suspension rings.

Fig. 58. A rolled-out and interpreted view of the Latin inscription on the bell of the wreck of La Marquise de Tourny.

Fig. 59. Detail of the two single and two double canon rings on the top of the ship's bell.

Fig. 60. A dolphin or fish molded onto the side of the bell.

The combination of the cross, fish and roundel are unlikely to be meaningful in combination as reflectors of a founder or patron. All three are typical symbols of Christian art. The Calvary cross symbolizes Jesus' crucifixion. The fish represents Christ himself – the five Greek letters forming the word 'fish' (ICHTHYS) being the initial letters of the Greek term 'Jesus Christ God's Son Saviour'. If this motif is actually a dolphin, this marine creature appears in Christian art more frequently than any other sea creature as the symbol of resurrection and salvation. The wheel-like roundel represents the rotating force of divine power (Ferguson, 1961: 15, 18, 183).

Given the deeply superstitious tendencies of mariners, it is most logical that these three symbols are apotropaic. Bells had a reputation in sailing folklore of safeguarding ships' crews from the dangers of the deep. A Dutch engraving by Philip Galle, published *c.* 1560, depicts a sea crawling with sea creatures and bells at the stern of a ship next to a Latin inscription reading, "On the ship of Erythreus that sails the sea in the prow and in the poop the greatest of bells hangs. I ring to warn of cetaceans, balenas and sea monsters which threaten the ship." In a similar vein, in his *Traites des Cloches* of 1721 Jean Baptiste Thiers wrote that "Bells are rung… to drive away the demons of the air… to dissolve thunders, storms, and tempests which is not done by their nature, but by the divine virtue given them when they are blessed" (Wede, 1972: 2).

This interpretation of the protective power of the bell's symbols leaves the *fleur de lis* motif as the only motif reflecting the owner's origins. The *fleur de lis* is common in England, France and Spain, but its form in triplicate, with two symbols above a centered one below, is recognizable in the French coat of arms. This variant is also recorded on the small watch bell of the French ship *L'Astrolabe*, which sailed *c.* 1778-1828 with *fleur de lis* decoration.

Fig. 61. A roundel molded onto the side of the bell.

Fig. 62. A Calvary cross molded onto the side of the bell.

Fig. 63. Three fleur de lis *molded onto the side of the bell.*

The botanical lily is a symbol of purity and, associated with the Trinity through its tripartite representation, originally symbolized the Virgin Mary. Following a decree of Louis VII in 1147, the *fleur de lis* became connected with the monarchy and started to appear on royal seals. However, the motif is far from exclusively connected with the French throne: 20 armorials of the 13th-15th centuries depict no fewer than 6,000 examples, with the majority concentrated in northern France, and especially Brabant (Kingsley, 2008).

B. A French Glass Flaçon

Study of the blue glass sherd and glass bottle neck fragments located adjacent to cannon C-22 has revealed another French connection for Site 33c (Figs. 64-66). The dimensions of the neck of bottle MUN-A-08-0002-GL are:

- Fragment L. 5.0cm
- Fragment W. 4.0cm
- Mouth Diam. 2.7cm
- Lip Th. 0.7cm
- Body Th. 0.3cm

Both derive from a type of glass known as '*verre bleu*' or '*verre fougère*' manufactured mainly in southern France. As the name infers, *verre fougère* glass wares were produced from a mixture of sand and potash derived from the ashes of ferns (McNally, 1979: 2). The southwestern forest regions of Gresigne in Languedoc, in particular, were important glassmaking areas between the 15th and 18th centuries (Van den Bossche, 2001: 227, 397), where wood and fern resources were abundant. Burnt fern contains high quantities of potash, which is a basic alkali ingredient in glass making that produces a typical blue-green color, hence the term '*verre bleu*' or '*verre fougère*' for these wares (cf. Chopinet, 2004).

However, in reality a scientific analysis of a blue-green bottle fragment has identified glass composition relying on soda-lime. Soda was more readily available in the coastal regions of France, where it could be produced from the ash of various seaweeds. By contrast, potash was more accessible in the form of bracken and wood ash in the interior, and was more economical for the *petites verreries* (Harris, 1979: 89).

Blue-green bubbled glass *verre fougère* case bottle *flaçons*, mouth-blown into dip-molds and similar to the Site 33c fragment, reached peak popularity in the mid-18th century (Hume, 1969: 70). The base from a bottle of this form has been recovered from the wreck of La Natière 2, a French privateer lost off St. Malo in 1749 (L'Hour and Veyrat, 2002: 96), and the form traveled widely into the French provinces. Examples are common across America from Nova Scotia to Michigan and Charlotte.

This form of glass, for instance, has been excavated in a latrine pit abandoned in 1719 at the fort and chateau site of St. Louis in Canada[2] and, more extensively, has been documented across the Fortress of Louisbourg in two French occupation periods (1713-45 and 1749-50). The Site 33c example is identical to Louisbourg's Type 5 *flaçon* with its short tubular neck and a very gently outward-sloping neck wall. Lip diameters vary from 3.0-3.2cm (with bore diameters of 1.7-2.2cm), neck heights are 3.0-3.2cm and shoulder diameters range from 7.0-9.0cm (Harris, 1979: 100, 134). French *flaçons* also traveled inland in the Americas up the Illinois River valley.

Flaçon bottles were present amongst the galley remains excavated on the *Machault*, lost in 1760 on the Restigouche River, Canada, which interestingly was another Bordeaux privateer. An identical neck of a *flaçon* with a cork still inserted in its mouth is associated with the wreck of the *Queen Anne's Revenge*, lost in Beaufort Inlet, North Carolina, in June 1718 (Carnes-McNaughton and Wilde-Ramsing, 2008: fig. 2), amongst 402 fragments of comparable square case bottles. With a lip diameter of 2.8cm, its mouth is just 1mm smaller than the Site 33c example. Records from Louisbourg suggest that these bottles contained olive oil, while scientific studies of contents and preserved labels indicate broader contents of apothecary and household products, toilet water, perfumes and spirits.

Verre fougère tablewares were produced in small wood-burning glasshouses in France, which typically possessed just one furnace and four to six pots utilized to melt glass. These small ventures commonly employed no more than 20 people. Some *petites verreries* specialized solely in glass bottles, while others manufactured a broader set of tablewares and window glass, where bottles were a sideline. The more ambitious *petites verreries* produced large and small bottles, bowls, condiment containers, decanters, tumblers, goblets, inkwells, lamps and lamp chimneys, pitchers, plates, urinals, and vases in both clear and blue-green glass. In the first half of the 18th century they may also have supplied the perfumeries of southern France and the growing export trade in toilet waters. Records refer to a variety of items shipped in glass to the colonies, ranging from olives to anchovies, capers, marinated tuna, olive oil, vinegar, liquors, *eau de vie* and toilet water (Harris, 1979: 87-88).

The Site 33c type of bottle was also produced in the larger *grosses verreries* of Normandy and northwestern France, but in a heavier coarser green glass (*gros verre*) favored in the mineral water, liquor and wine trades. These ventures were owned and operated by *gentilshommes verriers*, minor nobility who employed common workers. A typical Normandy *grosses verreries* of 1740 would produce 70 tons of common green glass for every 150-200 tons of window panes.

Excavations conducted at Louisbourg since 1960 have uncovered 1,200 vessels of blue-green bubbled glass, of which imported French *flaçons* comprise 70% of the glass sample and occur in at least nine different types and several sizes. A combination of the archaeological evidence and local historical sources indicate that these wares were coveted by the upper and middle classes – king's officers, merchants, *habitant-pecheurs* and inn keepers – but were not accessible to the lower level inhabitants (Harris, 1979: 93, 100).

A curious secondary use for French *flaçons* was recorded by Lieutenant Maynard during the pirate Blackbeard's final battle in the late 1710s (Carnes-McNaughton and Wilde-Ramsing, 2008: 16):

> "When the lieutenant's sloop boarded the other, Captain Teach's men threw in several new-fashioned sort of grenadoes, viz., case bottles filled with powder and small shot, slugs, and pieces of lead or iron, with a quick match at the end of it, which, being lighted outside, presently runs into the bottle to the powder. As it is instantly thrown on board, it generally does great execution, besides putting all the crew into a confusion..."

The meager glass small finds from the wreck of *La Marquise de Tourny* complement the emerging image of French domestic wares closely reflecting the national origins of this French privateer.

Fig. 64. A fragment of blue verre fougère *glass found adjacent to cannon C22.*

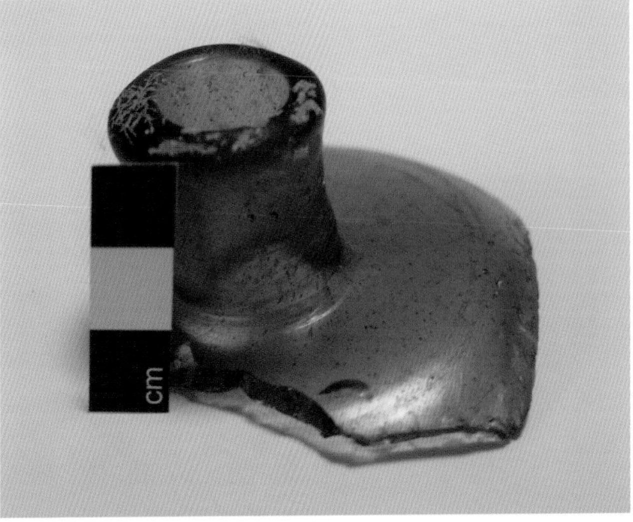

Figs. 65-66. The neck of a blue verre fougère *glass case* flaçon *(MUN-A-08-0002-GL) found adjacent to cannon C22,* in situ *and after recovery.*

C. Lead Hull Patches

One lead patch fragment was recorded on Site 33c on the edge of concretion Con-4, and a second example with two nail holes visible on the outer edge was recovered from the site (inv. no. MUN-A-08-0001-SF; Fig. 67): L. 20cm, W. 18cm and Th. 0.5cm.

Lead has long been used to protect and patch ships' hulls. The Romans, Portuguese, Spanish, and later the English all relied on this system. Lead was used to line parts of the sternpost and the rear face of the rudder and to protect parts of the anchor (Lavery, 1987: 61, 62), but more extensively to create a sealing layer between Teredo shipworms and the wooden hull below the waterline.

Both lead patches from Site 33c feature nail holes and most probably functioned as hull repair or protection patches for parts of the hull. No evidence that the hull was fully, or indeed significantly, sheathed in lead or copper has been detected. The absence of large-scale coppering on Site 33c reflects a likely pre-1779 date for the ship. Following the Royal Navy's successful experimental sheathing placed over the lower hull of the 32-gun frigate the *Alarm* in 1758, coppering became standard on British warships and across Europe in 1779. By 1782 Admiral Rodney was able to attribute much of his success over the French navy at the Battle of the Saints to the greater speed and maneuverability achieved by the Royal Navy's coppered ships (Bingeman *et al.*, 2000).

By the time *La Marquise de Tourny* was launched in 1744, the use of lead to patch leaking or vulnerable hulls was well over 1,500 years old. First used on the later 4th century BC Kyrenia shipwreck lost off northeast Cyprus, whose entire outer hull was sheathed with lead affixed by regular rows of copper tacks (Katzev, 1970: 9), lead sheathing in various scales became common practice for all nations. Historical and archaeological data indicate that lead sheathing was commonly, if not universally, applied to Portuguese and Spanish ships voyaging to the East and West Indies during the 16th century.

Fig. 67. Lead patch MUN-A-08-0001-SF (L. 20cm).

The 'Angra B' Iberian 16th or 17th century wreck documented off Porto Novo in the Azores was lead lined (Crisman, 1999). Thousands of fragments of lead sheet (0.5-0.9mm thick with a weight of 6.57kg per square meter) are associated with the scattered remains of the *Santa Margarita,* a *naos* of the *Tierra Firme* fleet lost off Florida Keys in 1622. An estimated vast 2,134kg of lead, or 325 square meters, would have been required to sheathe this ship (Malcom, 2000-2001).

Due to its weight, lead became less popular in the 18th century as a means of entirely sheathing lower hulls, although patching endured, as recorded on the 1718 wreck of the *Queen Anne's Revenge* in Beaufort Inlet, North Carolina (Welsh, 2008: 2). Of comparable age and nationality to Site 33c, rolled strips of lead have been recovered from the outstandingly preserved early 18th-century corsair wrecks of La Natière off St. Malo, France, alongside 1ft-square lead sheets pre-coated with oakum in preparation for repairing hulls (L'Hour and Veyrat, 2003: 316).

D. Iron Swivel Gun

Following the recovery of the swivel gun from Site 33c, the artifact was weighed and documented, providing the following measurements (Fig. 69):

- Total L. 85.5cm
- First Reinforce L. 26.0cm
- Second Reinforce L. 18.0cm
- Chase L. 36.0cm
- Muzzle L. 5.5cm
- Bore Diam. 4.0cm
- Trunnion L. 4.0cm, Depth 3.5cm
- Breech L. 3.8cm
- Base ring L. 17.5cm, W. 1.0cm

The surface of the gun was kept wet while the concretion layer was removed mechanically on board the *Odyssey Explorer* research ship, revealing iron surfaces bearing incised symbols on the first and second reinforces. The iron surface was soft and brittle, suggesting that the cast iron had undergone graphitization. The conservation plan for the gun, which was dispatched to the York Archaeological Trust, included the removal of the remaining concretion

Fig. 68. Swivel gun C-10 after safe recovery onto the deck of the Odyssey Explorer.

Fig. 69. Swivel gun C-10 after preliminary cleaning.

followed by desalination using a combination of electrolytic reduction and intensive washing using caustic soda as a corrosion inhibitor. Once chloride levels had been reduced below 50ppm, the gun was to be dried and coated with a corrosion inhibitor, such as tannic acid. The fractured cascabel was to be treated in a similar manner and adhered back in place.

The muzzle was found damaged, so the concretion covering that section of the gun was left untouched to be removed under conservation laboratory conditions. To determine the caliber, the trunnions were measured at 4.0cm wide, which converts to an imperial measurement of 1.57in and equates to a half-pounder cannon, most likely a swivel gun. No evidence of any swivel mountings or tillers was observed or discovered during the excavation of this gun, but may be associated with C17 (Fig. 34).

Swivel guns are small pieces of artillery that were mounted on a swiveling stand or fork and rotated to be aimed in some cases using a tiller fitted to the cascabel end. Average lengths of such guns were 34-36in with bores of 1.5-1.75in. They were in effect a short-range anti-personnel weapon that typically fired shot weighing 0.50-0.75lbs and grapeshot (Tucker, 1989: 98).

Used as portable wall artillery in land fortifications, and as an early form of ordnance at sea, swivel guns can be traced back to the late 14th century. By the end of the 17th century thousands of naval vessels, privateers and merchant vessels were armed with this type of ordnance. On many small warships they comprised a major component of the primary armament. Privateers and pirate ships carried swivel guns as their only ordnance because their objective was to capture ships intact and to avoid sinking them (Gilkerson, 1993: 50, 58, 76).

They made versatile weapons and were mainly situated on stanchions or on the rails at the high ends of a vessel and along the main deck. On warships they were mounted on platforms between the lower mast and topmast. In these positions they could be used effectively to rain fire down on the main deck of a vessel. Steel's 1794 treatise *The Elements and Practice of Rigging and Seamanship* illustrates the only known plan of a top platform with accommodations for a swivel battery of a Royal Navy 38-gun frigate (Gilkerson, 1993: 75, 80, 82). Two swivel guns to each top platform was standard issue in the French Navy by the end of the 18th century. These locations were very effective, as exemplified by the famous rail-to-rail engagement of John

Fig. 70. Detail of a gunner's 'V' near the muzzle and a fleur de lis *crudely incised onto the first reinforce of swivel gun C-10.*

Fig. 71. Detail of a second fleur de lis *crudely incised onto the second reinforce of swivel gun C-10.*

Paul Jones's French vessel the *Bonhomme Richard* against HMS *Serapis* in 1797 off the northeast coast of England (Gilkerson, 1993: 83).

This gun type was not only a weapon of war. Swivels were used on the quarterdeck of a ship for signaling duties, for the recall of boats and shore parties, and as a signal to warn of danger, such as fog, icebergs and reefs. By 1812 their design had generally changed towards shortened, thickened and simplified forms (Gilkerson, 1993: 62).

Other than the *fleur de lis*, no further markings, names or dates were present on the Site 33c swivel gun. Full conservation may reveal more information. The most common marks recorded on these guns denoted their deadweight. In France and the Netherlands the weight of a gun was marked in pounds. The fact that a French pound weighed more than an English pound, but not as much as a Dutch pound (Gilkerson, 1993: 63), sometimes enables gun nationalities to be determined. Makers' marks, dates and weights were often incised onto the face of a trunnion, but both these and other numbers and marks can appear elsewhere. One of the trunnions on the Site 33c swivel gun was unfortunately broken prior to the wreck's discovery, and so any associated information is lost.

The *fleur de lis* motif encountered beneath the gun's concretion displays the hallmarks of mid-18th century manufacture. The symbol was a common sign used by royal foundries before 1789, incised or cast onto the cannon or cast on one trunnion alongside two letters representing the name of the foundry (Chartrand, 2003: 39-40). By 1748 the French cannon foundries were in a bad state for a number of reasons (Pritchard, 1987b: 145). The exclusive right to supply cast-iron guns to the navy disappeared with the demise of the Landouilette de Logiviere family, whose monopoly led to the loss of skilled labor at the forges and coincided with a decline in the size and arming of the naval fleet after 1715. The War of Spanish Succession ended in 1713, and France was preoccupied with economic and naval recovery rather than manufacturing guns.

The nationality of the Site 33c gun remains an unanswered question. Rudolf Roth (pers. comm. March 2010) has suggested that it resembles a Swedish half or three-quarter pounder swivel gun of the mid-18th century. These were manufactured in large quantities for export to the Dutch and British. If the Site 33c swivel gun is a Swedish product, then its presence on *La Marquise de Tourny* would suggest that it was reused following capture from a prize of war, possibly a Dutch or British ship. The *fleur de lis* symbols on the cannon are very crudely incised and not centered. Roth suggests that their shape could have served to disguise a former VOC mark.

Alternatively, the Site 33c cannon could be a French

iron swivel gun, a larger version of which is preserved at the entrance to the harbor of Bequai Island, south of St. Vincent in the West Indies (Charles Trollope, pers. comm. March 2010). Throughout the 18th century the French lost large numbers of their guns to the British, who considered them low grade and dangerous. After the War of the Austrian succession these captured French guns were sold back to the enemy, but after the Seven Years War were melted down for cannonballs and used in action against the French in later wars.

Considering that *La Marquise de Tourny* was built and based in Bordeaux (see Section 10 below), it would be reasonable to conclude that Site 33c gun may have been manufactured in one of France's royal foundries, such as Rancogne, Planchemenier or Perigord in southwestern France.

The cannon assemblage on Site 33c is of high archaeological and historical significance because few examples of French iron cannon from this period survive. Further study of the swivel gun, and the possible future recovery and identification of a larger cannon from the wreck, may add to the compelling history of French cannon manufacture and use on a mid-18th century privateer.

Fig. 72. A portrait of Louis Urbain Aubert de Tourny, royal 'intendant' to Bordeaux between 1743 and 1757. From: L'Héritier, 1920.

9. Site 33c: The Ship's Origins

The core question of the historical identity of *La Marquise de Tourny* and the background of the ship that bore her name can be traced to Bordeaux in France. In the 18th century Bordeaux was the largest and most important city in the southwest of the country. The end of the War of Spanish Succession in 1713 was a significant event that facilitated its growth, liberating its merchants who vigorously participated in the expanding trade with the French West Indies.

Bordeaux's riverine port and merchant quarters were transformed into a vast international center of trade and trans-shipment. Commodities from all over France and northern Europe streamed into town, where they were stored and eventually exported to the West Indies, including wine, olive oil, silk, wheat, machine parts and cannon made in the foundries of nearby Perigord. Bordeaux supplied the French West Indies with the majority of its vital necessities during the 18th century.

Sugar and coffee were brought back to France by the Bordeaux merchants and, along with other Colonial goods, were re-exported to England, Ireland, northern Europe and throughout France. Many other European trade goods were also imported into Bordeaux on returning vessels. No other French port city came close to matching Bordeaux's trade supremacy, and many of the merchants became wealthy from maritime commerce (Auerbach, 2000: 144, 151-57).

Under French law royal agents who served the king in each of his provinces were classified as 'intendants' and were relied on to achieve administrative unification and centralization under the French monarchy. Their authority extended over every sphere of provincial administration. Bordeaux's intendants were collectively known as '*de grands administrateurs*' and it was under their guidance and tutelage that the city was transformed into a modern

Fig. 73. View of the promenades of Bordeaux from the sea. The Marquis de Tourny developed the town into one of the finest in France. From: Binaud, 1999.

commercial hub. Directed by the province's three most famous intendants, namely Boucher (1720-1743), Tourny (1743-1757) and Dupré (1776-1785), the port city developed from a cramped medieval town into a spacious modern city (Auerbach, 2000: 140).

The second of Bordeaux's three famous intendants, Tourny (1743-1757), was the dignitary in whose honor *La Marquise de Tourny* privateer was named (Auerbach, 2000: 140). Louis Urbain Aubert de Tourny was born in Andelys in 1695 and died in Paris in 1760 (Fig. 72). Initially Master of the Requests, in 1730 he became governor of Limoges and in 1743 rose to the position of Governor of Guyenne to Bordeaux. Tourny was named as Councilor to the State in 1757. The Marquis De Tourny can largely be credited with transforming Bordeaux into the most beautiful city in France (Fig. 73), expanding the quays on the Garonne, creating wide avenues, open spaces, public gardens and building a prominent theater (Auerbach, 2000: 140).

It was customary, if not especially common, for the powerful merchants of Bordeaux to lend the name of their wives to privateers (L'Héritier, 1920: 200), such as *La Marquise Damon* mentioned in texts of 1748-50, *La Marquise de Cassigny* (1781) and *La Marquise de Lafayette* (1782) (Binaud, 1999). From the name on the bell of Odyssey's Site 33c, and from the date of 1744 molded onto it, it is reasonable to conclude that a local privateer was named after his wife, *La Marquise de Tourny*. Historical documentation to a vessel bearing this name endured into the late 18th century, when sources referred to a frigate being built in imitation of the construction plans of *La Marquise de Tourny*, which was upheld as a fine example of a corsair built for speed that later ships needed to replicate (Ducère, 1895: 301-302). This reference, although a little ambiguous, also discusses the placement of guns on the first or second deck of vessels.

10. The Life & Times of *La Marquise de Tourny*

Current information available about the frigate *La Marquise de Tourny* is vague. A published record of the ship's life (Binaud, 1999: 279-81) contains omissions for 1744, when the ship was likely built and launched, for 1748, and for the crucial date of her loss. According to the Bordeaux archives, *La Marquise de Tourny* was built by Geslain from the port of Rochefort, was owned by Dubergier and Audat (Beaurepaire, 2002: 304) and was classified as a 460-ton frigate (Archives départementales de la Gironde, 6B 98 157v). Launched during the War of the Austrian Succession, *La Marquise de Tourny* inevitably functioned as a privateer with an official letter of marque from the war commission (as in Fig. 74), but was simultaneously on merchant service (Table 3).

Very little is known about the movements of this ship and the record is complicated further by the existence of two other contemporary privateers bearing an almost identical name. Alongside *La Marquise de Tourny* existed *Le Marquis de Tourny*, named after Louis Urbain himself and listed in 1746 as under the command of Captain Joseph Mallac and owned by Alauze & Co. Finally, *Le Grand Marquis de Tourny* is referred to in Bordeaux in 1756, owned by Pierre Baour and sailed under Captain Louis Boyries (Binaud, 1999: 280, 281). The name of this latter ship was no doubt an homage to the 'greatness' that the Marquis had brought to a now fully rebuilt Bordeaux.

To reconstruct the life and times of *La Marquise de Tourny* – the least known of the three ships bearing this general name – it is essential to examine the other two, for which far more extensive historical evidence survives. Research in the French-Canadian archives has revealed the complex history of the movements of *Le Marquis de Tourny* in 1748, which serves as a key touchstone for the life of its sister ship.

Entries for 26 January 1748 confirm that the brother ship was scheduled to sail to Quebec in Canada with a crew of 47 (Archives départementales de la Gironde 6B 309 119v). An entry dated 4 September 1748 cites a letter sent by a M. d'Ailleboust to a government minister, which detailed the loss of provisions and trouble imposed on d'Ailleboust (Archives nationales d'outre-mer, COL C11A 92/fol.331-332v). Records dating to 12 October and 27 October 1748 refer to losses incurred when the vessel was taken as a prize. Further correspondence of 29 October describes merchandise lost aboard the vessel (Archives nationales d'outre-mer, COL C11A 92/fol.137). The ship seems to have made such heavy losses that at an undated point in time between 1745 and 1749 a petition was produced in Bordeaux for the return of merchandise seized from *Le Marquis de Tourny* (Binaud, 1999: 58).

La Marquise de Tourny, by contrast, proved relatively successful as a privateer, capturing the following merchant vessels from the English and Dutch enemy:

- The *Fitney*, 1746 (Bordeaux Archives, 6B 1991)
- The *Bonne Esperance* of Amsterdam, 1746 (Bordeaux Archives, 6B 1990)
- The *Charleston* of Liverpool, 1746 (Bordeaux Archives, 6B 1989)
- The *Mortimer*, 1747 (Bordeaux Archives, 6B 1992)

N°236 LOUIS JEAN-MARIE DE BOURBON, DUC DE PENTHIEVRE, Gouverneur et Lieutenant-General pour le Roy en sa Province de Bretagne, Amiral de France, A Tous ceux qui ces présentes Lettres verront, Salut. Sçavoir faisons, Que Nous avons donné Congé à S[r]. Laurens Domé Maistre & Capitaine du Navire nommé Le Marquis de Tourny de Bordeaux du port de quatre cent soixante tonneaux ou environ, monté de vingt pieces de Canons & de Pierriers, estant de présent au Port de Bordeaux, de faire équipper en Guerre & Marchandise led. Navire l'armer & munitionner de toutes choses necessaires, le charger de telles marchandises que bon lui semblera, pourvû qu'elles ne soient ni prohibées ni défendues, pour aller trafiquer a Quebeck et autres colonies françoises & en ce faisant, faire la Guerre aux Ennemis de l'Estat, à tous Corsaires, Pirates, Forbans, gens sans aveu, & autres qui voudront empescher la liberté du Commerce aux Sujets du Roy; pourra aussi courir sur les Vaisseaux, Barques & autres Bâtimens de Mer, tant François qu'Etrangers, faisant le Commerce Etranger & prohibé aux Isles Françoises de l'Amerique, les réduire par la force des armes, les prendre & amener dans l'Isle la plus prochaine du lieu où la prise aura été faite, après avoir toutefois donné caution de même que s'il armoit en guerre, sans quoi la presente Commission ne lui pourra être délivrée; à la charge par ledit Sieur Domé de garder & faire garder par ceux de son Equipage les Ordonnances de la Marine, porter & faire porter pendant son voyage le Pavillon des Armes du Roy & les nostres, faire enregistrer le present Congé au Greffe de l'Amirauté le plus proche du lieu où il fera son armement, y mettre un Rôlle signé & certifié de luy, contenant les noms & surnoms, naissances & demeures des hommes de son Equipage, faire son retour audit lieu ou autres Ports des Isles de l'Amerique ou de France, y faire son rapport pardevant les Officiers de l'Amirauté, & non autres, de ce qui se sera passé durant son voyage, nous en donner avis, le tout conformément au Reglement rendu par Sa Majesté le vingt-troisième jour de Juillet 1720. Prions et requerons tous Rois, Princes, Potentats, Etats, Republiques, Amis, Alliés & Confederez de cette Couronne, leurs Amiraux, Gouverneurs de leurs Provinces, Villes, Ports, Havres, & Passages, Capitaines, Chefs & Conducteurs de leurs Vaisseaux & Equipages & autres leurs Officiers & Sujets qu'il appartiendra, de donner audit S[r]. Domé toute assistance, passages & retraite en leurs Ports avec sondit Vaisseau, & ce qu'il aura pû conquerir, offrant de faire le semblable lorsque Nous en serons par eux requis. Mandons et ordonnons aux Vice-Amiraux, Lieutenans-Generaux des Armées Navales, Chefs d'Escadres, Capitaines de Vaisseaux, & à tous autres Officiers de Marine qu'il appartiendra, de laisser seurement & librement passer ledit Sieur Domé avec sondit Vaisseau & Equipage, & tout ce qu'il aura pû conquérir pendant son voyage en vertu du present Congé, sans lui donner ni souffrir luy estre fait ou donné aucun trouble ni empêchement, mais au contraire tout le secours, ayde, faveur & assistance dont il aura besoin: & ne servira le present Congé que pour un seul voyage. En temoin dequoy Nous avons signé ces Presentes, & à icelles fait apposer le Sceau de nos Armes & contre-signer par le Secretaire generale de la Marine. A Bordeaux le vingt sixieme jour du mois de janvier mil sept cent quarante huit.

Je soussigné Receveur de S.A.S. Monseigneur l'amiral au Departement de Bordeaux Certiffie avoir delivré la presente Commission a Bordeaux le vingt six janvier mil sept cent quarante huit.

Reçu soixante livres

L.J.M. de Bourbon.

PAR SON ALTESSE SERENISSIME,

Fig. 74. The letter of marque dated 26 January 1748 for the privateer Le Marquis de Tourny, *the brother ship of the vessel wrecked at Site 33c, (PRO HCA 32/129).*

In turn, French ships were ready prey for the enemy in the War of the Austrian Succession (cf. Kingsley, 2011) and although the avoidance rate of *La Marquise* remains unknown, certainly *Le Marquis de Tourny* ran into serious trouble. An entry of April 1748 in the *Gentleman's Magazine* (1748: 174) records that:

> "The Marquis de Tournay, 500 tons, 20 guns, 180 sailors besides soldiers, from Bordeaux to Canada, with naval stores, and sale goods, taken by London privat. and brought to Portsmouth."

The detailed itinerary of this privateer in the first quarter of 1748 is clarified by French manifests and bills of lading seized along with *Le Marquis de Tourny* and enclosed in a mail sack labeled "Messieurs Fatin & Compaignie, Notaire Royale Place STE Colombe à Bordeaux. Double Alliance." After being taken by the *London* privateer, all of these communications were translated into English and this rich archive survives in the Public Records Office at Kew (PRO HCA 32/129). The complex web of manifests provides a fascinating possible comparative window into the otherwise unqualified movements of the ship wrecked at Site 33c.

Headed for Quebec under the command of Laurens Domé, *Le Marquis* evidently never made it out of home waters. According to a bill of lading signed at Bordeaux on 29 January 1748, *Le Marquis de Tourny* had taken onboard a consignment of men's shoes, boots, shirts, handkerchiefs, stockings, Sogovia caps and linen from Brittany, Ucholet and Laval. To this were added fishing lines, linen and metal wares on 2 February. By 2 April a further bill of lading signed at Rochelle reveals that the corsair was lying off L'Isle d'Aix on the west coast of France and had just loaded a further 34 barrels of shot.

The same documentation includes an invoice for Bordeaux wine, salt pork, salt and flour laden on *Le Tourny* intended to re-stock foodstuffs consumed on the king's frigate *La Frippone* by 30 passengers during the pending 80-day voyage from France to Quebec. Captain Domé was charged with delivering the provisions upon the order of Monsieur de Tilly. The receipt for these outward goods, in a convoy in which *Le Marquis de Tourny* and the frigate *La Friponne* were presumably sailing together, was signed by Captain Domé at Rochefort on 18 March 1748.

A further bill of lading for yet more wine, brandy, salt pork, olive oil and vinegar was signed by Captain Domé at Rochefort on 22 March 1748 and seems to refer to provisions intended for the *Laurent*, which was being fitted out at Quebec and for which *Le Marquis de Tourny* was charged

Captain	Ship	Commission	Date	Ship-owner	Prizes Taken
Jean Blondel	*La Marquise de Tourny*	War	Jan 1745	Dubergier & Audat	
Louis Terie de Clermont (Prevost)	*La Marquise de Tourny*	War	1746		3
Julien Gusliez & Guillaume Masselous (Prevost)	*La Marquise de Tourny*	War	1747		1
Barthes	*La Marquise de Tourny*	War	1749		1

Table 3. History of La Marquise de Tourny *as cited in official documentation of Bordeaux (tabulated from Binaud, 1999: 279-81).*

with delivering provisions into the king's warehouse. A final consignment of linen was added on 6 April 1748 as the ship was anchored off L'Isle d'Aix.

The frigate was clearly on a war footing in this voyage, delivering staple military foodstuffs to French Quebec, as well as carrying luxury clothing. Legal oaths made by the Customs Officers Robert Knipper and Joseph Seal Tidesmen in the port of Portsmouth confirm that *Le Marquis de Tourny* was boarded there on 23 April. This outward-bound Bordeaux privateer was thus lost between the second and third week of that month.

If these largely organic commodities provide a comparative understanding of the outward-bound goods, itinerary and geography of *La Marquise de Tourny* during the War of the Austrian Succession, what consignments did the Bordeaux corsairs return home with from the French colonies? The seizure of *Le Grand Marquis de Tourny* as a prize by the *Liverpool* privateer on 18 June 1757 reveals that this ship was inward bound to Bordeaux from St. Domingo with a cargo of sugar, coffee, indigo and logwood valued at £20,000 (*Gentleman's Magazine*, July 1757: 337; Williams, 2004: 127-8). This was a typical cargo composition for incoming French merchant vessels and corsairs.

However, the final resting place of *La Marquise de Tourny* lies around 50km off the English coast and approximately 60km west-northwest of Guernsey (Fig. 3). She was evidently not outward bound to the French Colonies of the Americas, nor to the West Indies, and was too far east to have been heading directly home for Bordeaux (unless she encountered extreme storm trouble). The implication is that *La Marquise* may have been involved in a short-haul mercantile venture when disaster struck.

One conceivable explanation of what this French privateer was doing in the western English Channel when she foundered may lie in the town of St. Malo on the north-western coast of France, south of the Channel Isles. St. Malo was a renowned center for merchants, sailors and privateers and, for centuries, was involved in private wars with the Channel Isles (Timewell, 1970: 205). The French privateers of St. Malo ran highly successful operations and were seen as a great threat to English and Dutch shipping. It is possible that *La Marquise de Tourny* was carrying a shipment of supplies for St. Malo or was transporting goods to the French Channel ports of Cherbourg, Dunkirk or Calais further east up the English Channel when trouble struck.

In association with the 25 cannon recorded on the wreck, Site 33c contains 13 large concreted features (Fig. 6), which appear to comprise iron ballast ingots (167 single pieces visible with a total on-site volume estimated at 500-600). These features display the following dimensions:

- Concretion-4: average ingot length 60-80cm
- Concretion-7: average ingot length 60-70cm
- Concretion-10: average ingot length 80-90cm
- Concretion-13: average ingot length 70-80cm
- Average widths of all these objects: 10-20cm

The ballasting of mid-18th century merchant vessels, frigates and warships is not a well documented subject. Certainly the Royal Navy's lack of iron ballast surprised the French master shipwright Blaise Ollivier during his trip to Britain's dockyards in 1737 (Roberts, 1992: 167-9):

> "They do not use iron kentledge to ballast their ships save for long commissions, and in those ships which have insufficient space in the hold to accommodate earth ballast. I confess

that when I saw at Deptford Dockyard that great quantity of kentledge of which I spoke… I believed that the English knew how to make good use of it…. I have asked the reason of several officers; they replied that iron ballast stiffens all the movements of the ship, especially the rolling. Upon receiving this reply I enquired as to how the ballast is stowed, and was shown it on either wise of the keelson to larboard and to starboard of this timber. We used to find the same inconvenience in our own ships when we stowed the ballast as the English do, but now that we lay it along the rungheads our ships have an easier motion. The English admit that if iron kentledge did not make the movement of their ships so harsh it would be more advantageous to ballast their ships with kentledge than with gravel or earth, since the weight of the iron is farther removed from the centre of motion, and because the weight of the stores stowed atop the ballast is carried lower down."

In contrast to Ollivier's dismissal of Britain's unsophisticated ballasting system, other scholars consider Britain to have exceeded France's knowledge. Franck Goddio has thus argued (1999: 95) that "the English technological advance in iron and steel compared to France, where in the middle of the 18th century, ballast comprised scrap cast iron cannons and old obsolete cannonballs, to which 50-100 lb. pigs of iron were only added around 1760".

In reality, archaeology has demonstrated a near concurrent evolution. Iron ballast pigs comparable to those highly conspicuous on Site 33c have been recorded on the 1744 and 1748 wrecks of the Royal Navy warships *Victory* and *Fowey* (Cunningham Dobson and Kingsley, 2010: 245-7; Skowronek *et al.*, 1987: fig. 3). On the wrecks of multinational long-distance merchant vessels dated very closely to *La Marquise de Tourny*, iron ballast has been recorded on the 600-ton French East Indiaman the *Prince de Conty*, lost off Brittany in 1746 (L'Hour and Richez, 1990: 75), and also on the *Sussex*, an English East Indiaman wrecked at Bassas da India in the Indian Ocean in 1738 (Bousquet *et al.*, 1990: 83).

Revealing data relating to ballasting merchant vessels with such kentledge has been recorded on the wreck of the *Griffin*, a 499-ton English East Indiaman built in the Blackwall dockyard in 1761 and sunk in the Sulu Sea, the Philippines. The ship was loaded with 30 tons of iron ballast of widely varying dimensions (set on a bed of stone ballast), with lengths of 38-101cm and weights of 23-122kg following the removal of concretion. All of the pigs bear mold marks of 'Elk Ridge', named after a foundry established by Caleb and Edward Dorsey in the county of Howard in Maryland, USA. In 1761 this colony had eight main furnaces producing 2,500 tonnes of cast iron and ten foundries casting 66 tonnes of iron bars (Goddio, 1999: 95-7).

The iron bars recorded across the surface of Site 33c are very similar to the *Griffin* site and, in conjunction with the absence of any visible cargo, are compatible with the shipment of an organic consignment such as *Le Marquis de Tourny* was transporting in 1757 and which typified those imported from the Americas and West Indies back to France. Whether or not this kentledge was of saleable or permanent form cannot be proven except perhaps with the recovery and study of select examples (cf. Kingsley, 2011 for further comparative analysis).

In conclusion, the evidence suggests that *La Marquise de Tourny* was built in 1744 and remained active until at least 1749, after the War of the Austrian Succession ended in April 1748 with the Treaty of Aix-La-Chapelle. She outlived the war, after which the letters of marque dried up. The privateers had retracted their guns. By reverting to a typical long-distance merchant vessel, uninvolved in matters of State, the unspectacular movements of *La Marquise de Tourny* are unlikely to have been chronicled beyond the ship captain's logs and customs books.

Since the economy of the privateer involved seizing enemy ships intact and forcing them into a home port, the logical explanation is that *La Marquise de Tourny* ended her life wrecked by a storm at the end of the 1740s or in the early 1750s. If she was still plying the seas in 1756, when the Seven Years War started, it seems reasonable to assume that her adventures may have appeared in contemporary literature.

11. French Frigates & Corsairs

Corsairs such as *La Marquise de Tourny* were light and nimble three-masted frigates with the majority of their armament set on a single gun deck, but with additional guns on the poop and forecastle. The number of guns carried varied between 20 and 56, but 30 to 40 was most common. The term 'frigate-built' implies the disposition of the decks of such merchant ships featuring a descent of four or five steps from the quarterdeck and forecastle into the waist of the vessel, as distinct from those whose decks were built on a continuous, uninterrupted line along the entire length of the ship, which are termed 'galley-built' (Falconer, 2006: 160).

Frigates could not compete militarily with ships of the line in naval engagements, but their design enabled them to sail at greater speed, which made them perfect scouts or escort vessels for protecting merchant convoys from other privateers. They also cruised the oceans as merchant raiders in their own right and were the choice of vessel for privateers because of their speed and maneuverability.

It was the opinion of many 18th-century naval officers

that French warships were the finest in the world (Pritchard, 1987a: 1). In general, French frigates had a reputation for being faster than British frigates in optimum sea conditions, but were usually less suited to heavy weather or long-distance cruises. British ship captains were attracted to the capture of French frigates because they brought in greater prize money than those of other nations (Saxby, 1993: 334-35). In 18th-century Britain it became common practice to convert captured prizes into naval vessels and, in some cases, these vessels were exploited as templates for the construction of English ships (Pritchard, 1987a: 1).

The following ships are examples of captured French frigates dating to the era of *La Marquise de Tourny* that became Royal Navy vessels. The *Médée* is a significant example of a prize sold on as a privateer (Boudroit and Berti, 1992). It was also the first modern single-decked frigate to mount 26 8-pounder cannon (Pritchard, 1987a: 12).

- *Médée:* a 26-gun design by Blaise Ollivier, with 26 x 8-pounder guns, launched February 1741 at Brest; captured by the Royal Navy on 4 April 1744 and sold on as the privateer *Boscawen* rather than added to the Royal Navy.
- *Panthère*: a one-off 20-gun design of 1743 by Jacques-Luc Coulomb, with 20 x 6-pounder guns, launched February 1744 at Brest; captured by the Royal Navy in 1745 and converted into HMS *Amazon*.
- *Volage*: a 24-gun design by Pierre Morineau, with 24 x 8-pounder guns, launched 1 April 1741 at Rochefort; captured by the Royal Navy on 4 April 1746, but retaken by the French the following day and deleted from record books on 1753.
- *Renomée*: launched 19 December 1744 at Brest; captured by the Royal Navy on 27 September 1747 and converted into HMS *Renown*.
- *Emeraude:* a 28-gun design by Chaillé with 24 x 8-pounder and 4 x 4-pounder guns. Launched on 10 June 1744 at Le Havre, captured by the Royal Navy on 21 September 1757 and converted into HMS *Emerald*.

The above corsairs, as well as *La Marquise de Tourny*, were operative during the War of the Austrian Succession, which began in October 1739 but was just the latest in the endemic hostility between Britain and France between 1689 and 1815. At the start of this conflict the Royal Navy was far superior in strength to the French Navy, having a force of 110 ships of the line compared to France's 35 men-of-war. The French navy was so stretched providing escorts for its convoys that its corsairs emerged as an independent tool of combat to cripple trade, just as they had done during the War of Spanish Succession of 1701-14 (Russell, 1970: 33).

Privateering can be traced back to the medieval period. Essentially it emerged as a system whereby a person from one country who had been victimized by an individual of another nationality could seek compensation for his losses. With a government license known as a 'letter of marque and reprisal' (cf. Fig. 74), ships could be armed and search out merchant ships of the offending country for seizure as 'prizes'. This entitled the 'prize takers' (privateers) to sell the captured ship and cargo at auction and pocket the proceeds, which would then be divided between captain and the crew. Initially privateering was designed for effecting private compensation on the high seas, regardless of whether or not a state of war existed between nations. However it soon evolved into an instrument of war in its own right (Sechrest, 2001: 6).

A vessel with a letter of marque could act in two ways. Firstly as a privateer whose sole purpose was to seek out and capture vessels of enemy nations or, secondly, as a merchant vessel primarily transporting cargo but which was sufficiently armed should the opportunity arise to take a prize (Sechrest, 2001: 7-8). Either way, privateering followed a strict code of rules based on naval standards (cf. Kingsley, 2011). Those who failed to adhere to these regulations, or were not in possession of a letter of marque, were branded as pirates, which was punishable by death. French privateering was so respectable and profitable that the Catholic bishops of St. Malo and Nantes retained financial interests in such enterprises (Russell, 1970: 23).

Historical records indicate that the majority of French privateers were privately owned. However, vessels and officers of the French navy were sometimes seconded to private individuals and consortiums that ran privateers. In these cases the cost of such operations was met by the State, but the wages and victualing were the responsibility of the privateer (Timewell, 1970: 200).

12. Guernsey Privateers

For many centuries the Channel Isles were a major center of smuggling. During wartime the islanders indulged in privateering and in peacetime smuggling (Saunders, 1930). Both England and France smuggled goods through the Channel Isles and through this entrepôt traded with each other, even during war.

Guernsey, the second largest of the Channel Isles, located 48km west of Normandy, lies close to the wreck site of *La Marquise de Tourny*. During the 150 years of almost unabated hostilities between the reign of King Louis XIV and the end of the Napoleonic era, the sailors of Guernsey were actively engaged in privateering and were a scourge to French trade (Timewell, 1970: 199). Their most notable success was the seizure of *La Vierge du Bon Port*, an East Indiaman lost off St. Malo in 1666.

The Guernsey corsair came into prominence during the War of Spanish Succession (1701-14), when their main role was preventing French privateers from disrupting England and Holland's maritime trade. During this war the Guernsey privateers took 608 French prizes and their neighbor, the island of Jersey, seized a further 152 (Russell, 1970: 30). In most cases the firing of cannon warning shots was sufficient to induce the surrender of a potential prize.

What made the Guernsey privateers so successful was their geography: located close to the French coast, they had an intimate knowledge of local waters. With small and fast vessels at times acting in threes, they were expert at forcing the chase aground and then hauling her off with the tide (Timewell, 1970: 205). For the Guernsey privateers, ships carrying naval stores destined for Calais, Dunkirk, St. Malo and other French ports were common prizes, but the most sought after and lucrative prey were inward bound European craft making for Bordeaux, Nantes and Rochelle – precisely the route sailed by *Le Marquis de Tourny* and likely its sister ship wrecked at Site 33c. The captain of *La Marquise de Tourny* would have been wary of the threat of the Channel Isles as a natural and, at times, human hazard as he navigated these waters during what would turn out to be the ship's final voyage.

13. Privateering Engagements

Privateers operated under a code of rules. Their main aim was capture and not destruction. Such an approach transferred ownership, but left the property intact. Privateers used various methods to range alongside their targets (sailing close to another vessel on her beam whilst both were underway). An unsuspecting French vessel would be hailed by a French-speaking Guernsey privateer crew, for instance, only to find out too late that an enemy lurked in its shadow (Timewell, 1970: 199).

Deception was a valuable weapon and privateers usually carried various national flags and false sets of papers. When sighting a target they would fly the flag of the same nation or an ally to enable them to approach by stealth. Warning shots would then be fired and the privateer crew would board and take the ship. It was advantageous for corsairs to have large crews, 20-30 to man the sails and cannon and a large number to comprise the boarding party. It was not uncommon for privateers to sail with crews of 120 or more (Sechrest, 2001: 15).

Such underhand masquerading using foreign flags was exactly how the Bordeaux-based *Le Grand Marquis de Tourny* was captured by the British *Liverpool* privateer on 10 June 1757 (Williams, 2004: 127-8):

Fig. 75. An18th-century three-masted, 30-gun French frigate, which would have resembled the corsair La Marquise de Tourny.

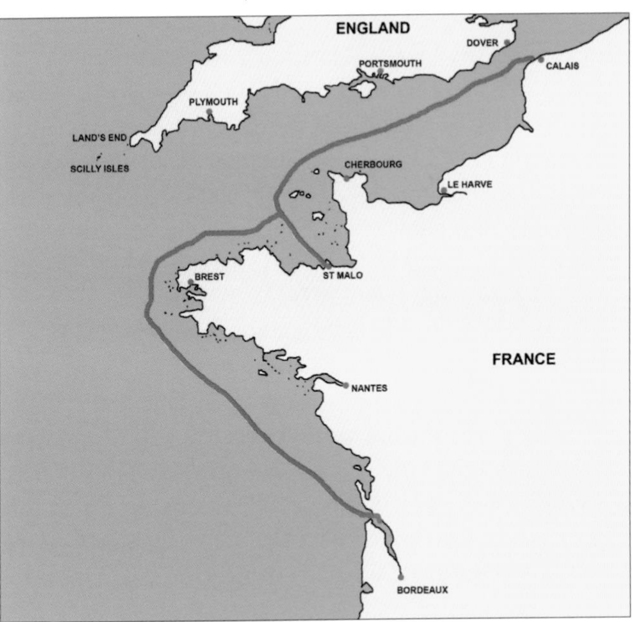

Fig. 76. The possible route of the final voyage of La Marquise de Tourny *from Bordeaux up the Channel towards the ports of northern France.*

"in lat. 48°O 18 mins. long., from London, made a sail from the masthead bearing S. from us, called all hands to quarters, and gave chase with all sails set. At 8, the ship hauled up her courses, and my appearance seemed to prepare for action. At 10, they threw out a French ensign and fired a gun. We answered them only with French colours, but they, not trusting us, began to fire their stern chase pretty briskly, upon which we gave them two of our bow chase. The ship yawed and gave

> us her larboard broadside. Several of their shot went through our sails, and one of the crossbar shots (a six-pounder) struck the fore topmast and fell upon our deck. We immediately gave her both our broadsides, upon which she struck. Sent our boats on board the prize for the prisoners. On examination she appears to be the *Grand Marquis de Tourney*, Francis Dellmar, commander, from St. Domingo for Bordeaux; is pierced for 24 guns (20 upon the upper deck and 4 upon the lower deck), but has only 12 six-pounder mounted. She came out of St. Domingo with 31 sail, under convoy of six men-of-war, one of 80 guns, four of 74 guns, and a frigate of 36 guns, who saw them through the windward passage and then left them. Found on board the prize, Captain John Mackay, and his crew, of the *Sarah*, brig, bound from Bristol for Boston, whom they had taken on the 3rd ult…"

What could a merchant vessel do when attacked by a privateer? The answer is very little. It was not part of a merchant vessel or crew's duty to defend itself. The best they could hope for was to escape without engaging in a skirmish. Avoidance tactics included sail quartering (the wind more or less on the quarter) with the sails drawn (inflated by the wind to advance the vessel on her course). This offered the best and swiftest course for a merchant vessel to flee. Another method when under fire was to lead the braces (ropes attached to the end of a yard to haul it aft, rotating the sail) and other necessary ropes below deck and through the gratings. This would keep all the crew below deck and allow them to have some control of the sails until the ship was safely out of cannon and musket range (Leyland, 1911: 272, 274).

If a merchant vessel could not escape and boarding was imminent, then the best tactic was to force the privateer to board the vessel over the quarter (Leyland, 1911: 275). This allowed the incoming privateers less area of a ship to attack and gave the merchant vessel time to work the sails, defend the main deck and hopefully escape. In reality, the majority of attacks ended with the merchant vessel giving itself up without sustaining any damage or loss of men.

14. Conclusion

Site 33c was discovered by Odyssey Marine Exploration in 2008 in the Western English Channel and is a previously unreported shipwreck. A pre-disturbance survey program and very limited trial trenching identified the site as the final resting place of the Bordeaux-based *La Marquise de Tourny*, a merchant vessel and privateer. The 25 iron cannon recorded on the wreck's surface confirms that it was armed very similarly to *Le Grand Marquis de Tourny*, which records confirm carried 24 guns. Like *Le Marquis de Tourny*, it probably also had an approximate 460-ton burden.

The presence of extensive iron ingot ballast defining the site's surface, in conjunction with an absence of other obviously identifiable cargo, suggests that *La Marquise de Tourny* was likely transporting an organic cargo when she foundered, which has now deteriorated. The *Liverpool* privateer's seizure in 1757 of another Bordeaux privateer, *Le Grand Marquis de Tourny*, reflects the common import of sugar, coffee, indigo and logwood, of which the first two products would certainly not remain preserved within the environment where Site 33c lies. Potential storm activity aside, the location of Site 33c well within the English Channel is incompatible with an outward-bound vessel sailing to the Americas or West Indies. Similarly, this route is eastward of a return trip directly into the port of Bordeaux.

The absence of official Admiralty documentation or reports in British newspaper related to this ship suggests that she may well have managed to escape being taken as a prize during her lifetime. Amongst the prize papers for the Austrian War of Succession, there are no entries for *La Marquise de Tourny (High Court of Admiralty Index to Prize Papers 1739-1748,* London, 1973). The geography of the ship's final resting place suggests she was heading up or out of the Narrow Seas on the French side of the Channel when she was lost. The presence of a French glass *flaçon* and the *fleur de lis* decoration on the recovered swivel gun supports a French pattern of ownership. The most likely hypothesis based on current evidence is that *La Marquise de Tourny* was undertaking a short-haul voyage with re-exported organic produce to the French coastal towns of St. Malo, Cherbourg, Dunkirk or Calais, further east up the English Channel, when she was lost.

Historical sources from Bordeaux reveal that *La Marquise de Tourny* was still in operation in 1749, when she took a prize of war (Binaud, 1999: 279-81). The naval circumstances of this seizure are obscure, especially since this year post-dates the end of the War of the Austrian Succession. Currently, it seems reasonable to propose that *La Marquise de Tourny* was lost in the late 1740s or in the early 1750s. She is not listed in known historical documentation for the Seven Years War, which started in 1756 and thus may provide a *terminus ante quem* for her loss. Technically, it seems more probable that she was conducting a merchant venture when she sank rather than privateering – although this cannot be ruled out categorically.

Archaeologically, Site 33c is extremely sparse. The most common features on the wreck's surface are the iron concretions. No pottery is present, nor was any identified during select trial trenching. Hull remains are almost non-existent. The site formation is consistent with a poorly preserved wreck that has been extensively dragged out by trawlers, which are common in the area. Many of the artifacts from the site may be in the collections of fishermen who dragged them up from the deep.

The wreck of *La Marquise de Tourny* is an echo of a long-forgotten time and place, the glory years of Bordeaux, which was extensively rebuilt in the style of Paris under the ambitious eye and direction of Louis Urbain Aubert de Tourny, the town's royal 'intendant' between 1743 and 1757. Within one year of taking office, one of Bordeaux's new corsairs was christened in his wife's honor. In a cruel twist of fate the new ship would outlive the intendant's wife. Within two years of the privateer's launch, the Marquise herself died suddenly aged 50 on 17 March 1746 and her body was interred in the Church of Notre-Dame de Puypaulin (L'Héritier, 1920: 319). The name of that lady, whose formal title alone was found molded onto a bronze bell at the bottom of the western English Channel, was Jeanne-Claude Cherouvrier des Grassieres.

Acknowledgements

The contents of this paper would not have been possible without the assistance and professionalism of many of my workmates and colleagues. Dr. Sean Kingsley for his editorial wisdom and additions to the research. *Odyssey Explorer* captains Keith Herron and Michael Wainman and their officers and crew, who always make my stay on the ship a safe and pleasurable one. Senior Project Manager Tom Dettweiler and Project Managers Andrew Craig and Mark Martin for their continuing support and for making it all happen out on site. ROV supervisors Ewan Bason, Eric Peterson and Gary Peterson, and ROV Technicians David Dettweiler, Jeff Thomas, Olaf Dieckhoff, Roberto Blach, Jesus Vasques Perez, Jose Rodrigeuz, and Paul Money, whose skill and professionalism never fail to amaze me.

For collecting and managing the data and images a big thanks goes to Data Manager Gerhard Seiffert and his team of Data Loggers: Dave Kamm, Tom Money, Frederick Fretzdorff, James McIsaac and James Hagen. Where would we be without our surveyors Kris Allen, Jim Gibeaut, Chris Heke, Ryan Wells and Mike Matthews, who constantly maintained accurate positioning of the ship and the ROV. Special thanks to Project Manager Ernie Tapanes and his side-scan technicians, Brett Hood and Zach Antonissen, for their great diligence in locating targets and producing amazing side-scan images.

I wish to extend my sincere gratitude to the vision and support of Greg Stemm, co-founder and Chief Executive Officer of Odyssey Marine Exploration. To Mark Gordon, Laura Barton and John Oppermann for their ongoing support and energetic encouragement. I would like to acknowledge the archival research conducted by Mark Musset, Simon Davidson and Patrick Lize. Much appreciation to Alice Copeland for her proofreading prowess. A big thank you to Melissa Dolce for the layout of this paper. A special thank goes to Ian Panter and Mags Felter at York Archaeological Trust for their conservation of the bell and swivel gun and their hospitality when I visited their lab. Thanks are also extended to Jason Williams, President of JWM Productions, and the Discovery Channel.

Notes

1. Odyssey's ROV dive log system is consecutively numbered and on this site Dive 402 is in effect Dive 1.
2. See: Verre Fougere in Canada, http://www.pc.gc.ca/eng/lhn-nhs/qc/saintlouisforts/natcul/ arch1a/arch1e.aspx.

Bibliography

Auerbach, S., *"Encourager le Commerce et Répandre les Lumières": the Press, the Provinces and the Origins of the Revolution in France: 1750-1789* (Doctor of Philosophy Dissertation, Louisiana State University, 2000).

Beaurepaire, P.-Y., 'L'Europe des lumières maçonniques: construction, réseaux et représentations'. In C. Villain-Gandossi (ed.), *L'Europe à la recherche de son identité. Actes du 125e Congrès national des sociétés historiques et scientifiques, Lille, 10-15 avril 2000* (Paris, éditions du CTHS, 2002), 305-16.

Binaud, D., *Les corsaires de Bordeaux et de l'estuaire: 120 ans de guerres sur mer* (Atlantica, Biarritz, 1999).

Bingeman, J.M., Bethell, J.P., Goodwin, P. and Mack, A.T., 'Copper and Other Sheathing in the Royal Navy', *International Journal of Nautical Archaeology* 29.2 (2000), 218-29.

Boudroit, J., *The Seventy-Four Gun Ship. Vol. 2* (Collection Archéologie Navale Francaise, Paris, 1986).

Boudroit, J. and Berti, H., *Frégate de 18. La Venus, 1782* (Collection Archéologie Navale Française, Paris, 1979).

Bousquet, G., L'Hour, M. and Richez, F., 'The Discovery of an English East Indiaman at Bassas da India, a French Atoll in the Indian Ocean: the *Sussex* (1738)', *International Journal of Nautical Archaeology* 19.1 (1990), 81-85.

Bryn, P., Jasinski, M.E. and Soreide, F., *Ormen lange. Pipelines and Shipwrecks* (Oslo, 2007).

Carnes-McNaughton, L. and Wilde-Ramsing, M.U., *Queen Anne's Revenge Shipwreck Project. Preliminary Glassware and Bottle Analysis from Shipwreck 31CR314, Queen Anne's Revenge Site* (Underwater Archaeology Branch Office of State Archaeology Department of

Cultural Resources, State of North Carolina, 2008).

Chartrand, R., *Napoleon's Guns, 1792-1815: Heavy and Siege Artillery* (London, 2003).

Chopinet, M.H., 'Evolution des alcalins dans les mélanges vitrifiables depuis le 18e siècle', *Verre* 9.6 (2004), 38-45.

Crisman, K., '*Angra B*: the Lead-sheathed Wreck at Porto Novo (Angra do Heroismo, Terceira Island, Azores-Portugal)', *Revista Portuguesa de Arqueoloqia* 2.1 (1999), 255-62.

Cunningham Dobson, N. and Kingsley, S., 'HMS *Victory*, a First-Rate Royal Navy warship Lost in the English Channel, 1744. Preliminary Survey & Identification'. In G. Stemm and S. Kingsley (eds.), *Oceans Odyssey. Deep-Sea Shipwrecks in the English Channel, Straits of Gibraltar & Atlantic Ocean* (Oxbow Books, Oxford, 2010), 235-81.

Ducère, E., *Les corsaires sous L'ancien regime* (Bayonne, 1895).

Falconer's New Universal Dictionary of the Marine, 1815 Edition (London, 2006).

Ferguson, G., *Signs & Symbols in Christian Art* (Oxford University Press, 1961).

Gilkerson, W., *Boarders Away II: Firearms of the Age of Fighting Sail* (Lincoln, RI, 1993).

Goddio, F., 'The Wreck, from Reality to the Documents'. In F. Goddio and E.J. Guyot de Saint Michel, *Griffin. On the Route of an Indiaman* (London, 1999), 57-115.

Harris, J.E., *Eighteenth-Century French Blue-Green Bottles from the Fortress of Louisbourg, Nova Scotia* (National Historic Parks and Sites Branch, Parks Canada, 1979).

Hume, I.N., *Glass in Colonial Williamsburg's Archaeological Collections* (Colonial Williamsburg Archaeological Series, 1969).

Katzev, M.L., 'Kyrenia 1969: A Greek Ship is Raised', *Expedition* 12.4 (1970), 6-14.

Kingsley, S.A., *The Ship's Bell from Odyssey Marine Exploration's Site 33C: Preliminary Considerations* (Unpublished Odyssey Marine Exploration Report, 2008).

Kingsley, S.A., 'The Art & Archaeology of Privateering: British Fortunes & Failures in 1744'. In G. Stemm and S. Kingsley (eds.), *Oceans Odyssey 2. Underwater Heritage Management & Deep-Sea Shipwrecks in the English Channel & Atlantic Ocean* (Oxford, 2011), 109-42.

Krisman, K., 'Angra B: the Lead-sheathed Wreck at Porto Novo (Angra do Heroismo, Terceira Island, Azores-Portugal)', *Revista Portuguesa de Arqueologia* 2.1 (1999), 255-62.

Larn, R. and Davis, R., 'Ships Bell found at Paignton, Devon', *International Journal of Nautical Archaeology* 6.1 (1977), 71-2.

Lavery, B., The *Arming and Fitting of English Ships of War 1600-1815* (London, 1987).

Leyland, J., 'Fighting Instructions for 'Merchantmen', 1706. "An Old Fighting Merchant Seaman",' *Mariner's Mirror* 1.4 (1911), 271-75.

L'Héritier, M., *L'Intendant Tourny (1695-1760), Vols. 1 et 2* (Bordeaux, 1920).

L'Hour, M. and Richez, F., 'An 18th century French East Indiaman: the Prince de Conty (1746)', *International Journal of Nautical Archaeology* 19.1 (1990), 75-9.

L'Hour, M. and Veyrat, E., *Un corsaire sous la mer. Les épaves de la Natière, archéologie sous-marine à Saint-Malo. Volume 3. Campagne de fouille 2001, l'épave Natière 2* (Edition Adramar, 2002).

L'Hour and Veyrat, E., 'Ships and Private Shipyards through the Archaeological Evidence of the Wreck off La Natière (Saint-Malo, Brittany, France)'. In C. Beltrame (ed.), *Boats, Ships and Shipyards. Proceedings of the Ninth International Symposium on Boat and Ship Archaeology Venice 2000* (Oxford, 2003), 314-19.

Malcom, C., 'Lead Hull-Sheathing of the *Santa Margarita*', *The Navigator: Newsletter of the Mel Fisher Maritime Heritage Society* 16.1 (December, 2000/ January, 2001).

McNally, P., *French Table Glass from the Fortress of Louisbourg, Nova Scotia* (National Historic Parks and Sites Branch, Parks Canada, 1979).

Nichols, J.R., *Bells Thro' the Ages; the Founders' Craft and Ringers' Art* (London, 1928).

Pritchard, J., 'From Shipwright to Naval Constructor: The Professionalization of 18th-Century French Naval Shipbuilders', *Technology and Culture* 28 (1987a), 1-25.

Pritchard, J.S., *The Ordnance Problem From Louis XV's Navy, 1748 -1762: A Study of Organization and Administration* (McGill-Queens University Press, 1987b).

Roberts, D.H. (ed.), *18th Century Shipbuilding. Remarks on the Navies of the English & the Dutch from Observations Made at their Dockyards in 1737 by Blaise Ollivier, Master Shipwright to the King of France* (Jean Boudriot Publications, Rotherfield, 1992).

Russell of Liverpool, Lord, *The French Corsairs* (London, 1970).

Saunders, A.C., *Jersey in the 18th and 19th Centuries* (Jersey, 1930).

Saxby, R., 'British & French Watercraft – Comparison of the British 'Frigate' and the French 'Frégate' of the 18th Century', *Mariner's Mirror* 79.3 (1993), 334-35.

Sechrest, L.J., 'Privateering and National Defense: Naval Warfare for Private Profit', *Independent Institute Working Paper* 41 (2001), 1-39.

Skowronek, R.K., Johnson, R.E., Vernon, R.H. and

Fischer, G.R., 'The Legare Anchorage Shipwreck Site – Grave of HMS *Fowey*, Biscayne National Park, Florida', *International Journal of Nautical Archaeology* 16 (1987), 313-24.

Spencer, S., *Arming the Fleet, US Navy Ordinance in the Muzzle Loading Era* (Annapolis, 1989).

Timewell, H.C., 'British watercraft – Guernsey, Channel Islands, 'Privateers', 1665-1815', *The Mariner's Mirror* 56.2 (1970), 199-218.

Tucker, S., *Arming the Fleet, US Navy Ordinance in the Muzzle Loading Era* (Annapolis, Maryland, US Naval Institute Press, 1989).

Van den Bossche, W., *Antique Glass Bottles, Their History and Evolution (1500-1850)* (Woodbridge, 2001).

Wede, K., *The Ship's Bell. Its History and Romance* (New York, 1972).

Welsh, W.M., *Queen Anne's Revenge Shipwreck Project. Lead Studs from Shipwreck 31CR314: Queen Anne's Revenge Site* (Underwater Archaeology Branch Office of State Archaeology, State of North Carolina, 2008).

Williams, G., *History of the Liverpool Privateers and Letters of Marque with an Account of the Liverpool Slave Trade, 1744-1812* (McGill-Queen's University Press, 2004).

The Art & Archaeology of Privateering: British Fortunes & Failures in 1744

Sean A. Kingsley
Wreck Watch Int., London

Two shipwrecks discovered by Odyssey Marine Exploration in the English Channel in 2008 are embedded in the history of the War of the Austrian Succession (1739-48) and specifically the year 1744. The First Rate Royal Navy warship HMS *Victory* was lost in the western English Channel on 5 October that year, while returning from escorting to sea one outgoing commercial convoy and liberating another blockaded down the River Tagus in Lisbon.

The date of 1744 inscribed on the bell recovered from Site 33c in the same part of the Channel, alongside the name *La Marquise de Tourny*, revealed that Odyssey had also discovered the wreck of a Bordeaux corsair launched in the year when France joined the war. Both ships actively participated in the protection of trade and the art of privateering. This article contextualizes both wrecks by examining the objectives, character, structure and scales of privateering and securing prizes during the War of the Austrian Succession before discussing the few comparable wrecks to assess whether it is realistic to refer to an archaeology of privateering.

1. Introduction

The year 1744 occupies an emotive year in both Britain's maritime history and in the recent fieldwork of Odyssey Marine Exploration. In May 2008 the company discovered the wreck of Admiral Sir John Balchin's *Victory*, the finest early Georgian flagship and First Rate of kings George I and George II that was lost during a storm in the western English Channel on 5 October 1744 (Cunningham Dobson and Kingsley, 2011). In the same waters Odyssey also located Site 33c, whose bell identified the wreck as the remains of *La Marquise de Tourny.* Although this Bordeaux-based corsair also probably succumbed to the elements in the late 1740s or early 1750s (Cunningham Dobson, 2011), by a twist of fate the bell's inscription reveals that this ship was launched in 1744.

As one ship started its life, another vanished under the most tragic of circumstances. Nevertheless, the histories of both are intertwined in the War of the Austrian Succession and by privateering in a year of extreme highs and lows. On 29 March 1744 King George II had issued a declaration of war against the French king. The long-brewing war and signing of letters of marque had brought great expectations to the captains and crews of privateers, a romantic profession that gripped the imagination of the public. As the *Gentleman's Magazine* announced from Bristol in September 1744:

> "Nothing is to be seen here but Rejoycings for the Number of *French Prizes*, brought into this Port. Our Sailers are in high Spirits and full of Money; and while on Shore spend their whole time in carousing, visiting their Mistresses, going to Plays, Serenading, *&c.* dressed out with laced Hats, Tossels, Swords with Sword-Knots, and every other jovial way of spending their Money."

In early autumn 1744 Britain was still riding the crest of a wave of patriotic pride. The rejoicing had started on 15 June 1744, when the 60-gun warship the *Centurion* glided undetected through both the fog and looming French fleet in the English Channel to slip into Spithead. Commanded by Commodore George Anson, the *Centurion* had just completed the most famous circumnavigation of the globe since the heady days of Sir Francis Drake. Despite an appalling loss of life and the entirety of the rest of his squadron, Anson returned home after three years and nine months with one of the greatest treasures seized at sea following an act of breathtaking privateering – as defined in its broadest sense. At Cape Esperitu Santo in Philippine waters the *Centurion* had taken the Spanish treasure ship *Nuestra Senora de Cobadonga*, loaded with 2.6 million pieces of eight. It was the most valuable prize seized during the War of the Austrian Succession (Figs. 1-6). Anson became a national hero (Heaps, 1973; Pack, 1960).

The *Cobadonga* was just one of many hundreds of enemy French and Spanish merchant vessels and corsairs boarded on the high seas in the name of king and country. *La Marquise de Tourny* is one of several examples of precisely the kinds of corsairs that chased the British and, in turn, were pursued. The war on trade was in fact not just private:

Fig. 1. The War of the Austrian Succession started successfully with Admiral Edward Vernon's capture of Porto Bello in November 1739, commemorated in a copper alloy medal. Photo: © National Maritime Museum, Greenwich, London (Inv. E3195-1 and E3195-2).

men of war were equally embedded in capturing prizes and Admiral Balchin onboard the *Victory* and his fleet attacked and seized merchant vessels during the cruise to Lisbon and Gibraltar between July and September 1744.

Fig. 2. Lord George Anson (1697-1762), who circumnavigated the world between 1740 and 1744 to capture the Nuestra Senora de Cobadonga, *the richest prize taken in the War of the Austrian Succession. Painting attributed to Thomas Hudson, pre-1748. Photo: © National Maritime Museum, Greenwich, London (Inv. BHC2517).*

To date few wrecks of privateers of any nation have been surveyed or excavated. For the period under discussion, scientifically recorded and published sites are restricted to just four wrecks, all of which are French: two sites off La Natière in the infamous corsair haven of St. Malo (early and mid-18th century), Odyssey's Site 33c (late 1740s/early 1750s) and the *Machault* in the Gulf of St. Lawrence, Canada (1760). This article examines the structure, objectives and background to privateering in England around 1744, before comparing the above wrecks in an attempt to examine whether it is realistic to define an archaeology of privateering.

2. Historical Background

The War of the Austrian Succession (1739-48) was triggered by the pressures of 18th-century colonial trade between Britain and Spain, whereby distant lands were exploited primarily for the goal of commerce, rather than for forging civilization or building empires. A doctrine of monopoly was designed to maximize profits. Figures demonstrate that by 1750 England was importing 22% of its manufactured goods, 41% of its drink and tobacco and 36% of semi-manufactured goods (Clarkson, 1974: 128).

Produce was typically shipped raw, so the profits of processing materials into finished forms accrued to the home manufacturer. Exports in finished form from the colonies were discouraged by heavy import duties, which were prohibitively high for the natives of the West Indies: for instance, 15 shillings per counterweight for raw sugar

Fig. 3. The Capture of Nuestra Senora de Cabadonga. *Painting by Samuel Scott. Photo: © National Maritime Museum, Greenwich, London (Inv. BHC0360).*

(muscovado), as opposed to £4.18s 8d for refined sugar. A similar disincentive prevailed through the Molasses Act of 1733 (Richmond, 1920: 1).

The colonial superpowers often operated beyond the line of the law. On the one hand England happily ignored the commercial restrictions formalized by the Treaty of Utrecht, notably in the case of the South Sea Company that exceeded its treaty rights and encouraged an extensive smuggling trade through the ports of North America (Richmond, 1920: 2). On the other, the Spanish coastguard patrolling the Caribbean needed little incentive to flout legal niceties and intercept English vessels.

The tales of the Spanish *guarda-costas*'s crimes and misdemeanors saturated the British and American newspapers throughout the 1730s, infuriating Britain. Matters came to a head in October 1731, when Captain Robert Jenkins of the *Rebecca* was seized off Havana during a return trip from Jamaica to London with a shipment of sugar. As the *Pennsylvania Gazette* of 7 October 1731 reported (Swanson, 1991: 11):

"They broken all her Hatches, Lockers and Chests, in which finding nothing to their Purpose, their Lieutenant ordered Capt *Jenkin*'s Hands to be tied, as also his Mate's, and seized them to the Foremast, and then cut and violently beat a Mulatto Boy (his Servant) to extort a Confession of there being Money in the Ship; but he confessing nothing, they began with Capt. *Jenkins*, putting a Rope about his Neck, and another about the Boy's, which they fastened to him, and hoisted them up to the Fore-Yard... and after keeping him hanging for a short space, they let him fall down again on the Deck, and asked him if he would not then confess where his Money was. But he still told them he had none; on which he was hoisted up a second time, and swiftly let down again, and being then asked the same Question, he replied as before, adding that they might torture him to Death, but he could not make any other Answer: They threatened to burn the Ship, and him and his People in it, for that they were obstinate Hereticks...

When he recovered, their Lieutenant came to him with Pistols and a Cutlass in his Hands, went to him, crying, Confess, Confess, or die... The Lieutenant then took hold of his left Ear, and with his Cutlass slit it down; and then another of the *Spaniards* took hold of it, but gave him the Piece of his Ear again, bidding him carry it to his Majesty King *George*. Others were then given for scalping of him, but finding his Head close shaved, they forbore executing that part of his Sentence."

The attacks on British shipping were particularly acutely felt amongst the merchants and tradesmen of the City of London, who lobbied the government to issue letters of marque and reprisal (Anderson, 1995: 39). Seven years after his trauma at sea, Captain Jenkins was called to the House of Commons in March 1738 to display his severed ear in a carefully staged political show trial. Britain wanted satisfaction and once Spain failed to pay the £95,000 compensation for British losses in the Caribbean in the winter of 1738-9 under the Convention of El Pardo, matters reached boiling point and the memory of 1731 was rekindled to start the War of Jenkins' Ear (Swanson, 1991: 10). Although Britain formally declared war on 19 October 1739, letters of marque against Spanish trade started to be issued from July (Starkey, 1990: 120). The war with Spain seamlessly transitioned into the War of the Austrian Succession, and with France's entry into the fray in March 1744 England would be locked for nine years in the nation's purest ever trade war.

Due to the relative small sizes of naval fleets by modern standards, and the rarity of fleet engagements, privateers played a crucial role during wartime in disrupting enemy commerce. Juxtaposed against the reality that the Battle of Toulon of February 1744 was the only major action of the war at sea was the endless scheming and swarming world of the individual entrepreneur. Outlawed since 1713, the privateers were back in business. Between 1739 and 1748 a total of 1,582 letters of marque would be issued authorizing British private vessels to engage enemy shipping (Starkey, 1990: 120).

3. The Structure of Privateering

As piratical as it sounds, privateering was a legal form of private enterprise in which individuals deployed their own resources to attack and seize vessels and the goods of foreign subjects, over which they acquired the rights to the property appropriated. The practice was not random, but was officially sanctioned under the law of the sea (Petrie, 1999). Privateering was a business opportunity, a tool of war and a factor of diplomacy between nations and has been subdivided into three categories, the Channel privateer, the deep-water private ship of war and the expeditionary force (cf. Starkey, 1990: 36, 38).

Fig. 4. Crowds cheer the 32 wagons of Spanish treasure captured by Commander George Anson from the Nuestra Senora de Cobadonga *as they are transported to the Tower of London in 1744. Photo: Rischgitz/Getty Images.*

Fig. 5. A King George II Lima half-crown minted in London as part of the currency struck from the Spanish silver captured by Admiral Lord George Anson from the Nuestra Senora de Cobadonga *prize on 20 June 1743. Photo: National Maritime Museum, Greenwich, London (Inv. E3818-1 and E3818-2).*

Controls over the profession included the necessity for privateer commanders to provide bail to guarantee the good conduct of their crews. This surety had been fixed in 1674 at £3,000 per vessel with 150 or more men and at £1,500 for a lesser complement. To ensure that a ship's capture was lawful, judges of the Admiralty Court demanded that between three and four members of a prize's crew, including the master and mate, were taken to the homeport to be sworn in, examined and interrogated. Local officials authorized by an Admiralty Court warrant required the captives to respond to a set of up to 34 'standard interrogatories', which had to be recorded within five days of a warrant's issue (Starkey, 1990: 24-5). Figures from the Vice-Admiralty Court for Massachusetts, Rhode Island, New York, Pennsylvania and South Carolina for the period 1739-48, when 148 of 192 privateer cases were won, demonstrate that while prize status was not guaranteed, in 77% of cases heard in this colony enemy ships were successfully condemned (Swanson, 1991: 42).

To deliberate on judgments Courts required supportive documentary data, including passes, sea briefs, charters and bills of lading from captured prizes. From the issue of a letter of marque to a prize's final condemnation, a privateer's business was completely sanctioned and controlled by the High Court of Admiralty (Starkey, 1990: 24-25). These legal formalities explain why so much information survives for the brother ship of *La Marquise de Tourny, Le Marquis de Tourny*, seized by the *London* privateer in 1748, and, conversely, why it would seem that the former Bordeaux corsair was probably never captured by the British.

Behavior at sea was expected to be highly disciplined, equaling Royal Navy standards. As the new Prize Act of 1744 demanded, "All offenses committed by any officer or seaman on board any privateer or merchant ship taking letter of marque, during the present war with Spain and France, shall be punished in such manner as the like offences are punishable on board his Majesty's ships of war". Regulations demanded that "swearing, Drunkenness and Prophaness be avoided" on privateers (Swanson, 1991: 67).

Despite these requisite strict measures, countries took every measure to encourage the art of privateering. Although the 1708 Prize Act remained the basis of law, whereby the Crown relinquished its right to shares in the profits of privateering and offered bounties to entrepreneurs engaged in the capture of enemy men of war (Starkey, 1997: 127), by a new clause of 1740 the navy paid crews of any British predator £5 sterling for every seaman on board an enemy warship (Swanson, 1991: 37).

Whereas the Crown and Admiralty had taken traditionally 3% of a prize, in the War of the Austrian Succession privateers were granted the entire property. The French followed suit in 1743, a development that had immediate results pending their declaration of war in 1744. As the *Pennsylvania Gazette* (27 October 1743) reported, this carrot was so advantageous that "Bretagne alone engages to fit out 500 Ships in Case of War with England." By 1748 the Dutch government incentivized its privateers by exempting its crews from naval impressment and by offering bounty money against French predators (Swanson, 1991: 15-16, 37, 221).

Fig. 6. A gold medal made by Thomas Pingo commemorating the Battle of Cape Finisterre in 1747 and Admiral George Anson's 1740-44 circumnavigation of the globe. Obverse: bust of Anson crowned by Victory on the prow of a galley. Reverse: Victory standing on a sea monster over a small globe and the legend 'CIRCVMNAVIGATION'. Photo: National Maritime Museum, Greenwich, London (Inv. E3354-1 and E3354-2).

The distribution of bounty secured from enemy prizes was rooted on the Convoys and Cruizers Act of 1708, which established the sliding scale of prize money for the next 100 years. The net sum was divided by eight. The captain received three-eighths, but if a prize capture was directed by a flag officer, one of those eighths diverted to him. Since this was generally the case, in reality a captain could expect a one-quarter split. Another eighth was divided equally amongst lieutenants, the captain of the marines and master. A further eighth went to the warrant officer, boatswain, gunner, carpenter, purser, chaplain, surgeon, master's mate, junior officers and quartermaster. An additional eighth was divided between the petty officers: the boatswain's mate, gunner's mate and tradesmen (caulkers, ropemakers, sailmakers). The rest was split among the remaining quarter (Hill, 1998: 201).

Compared to regular commercial trade, privateering was lucrative. The capture of a single prize of average value yielded an annual profit of more than 130% on the capital invested in a privateering venture (Swanson, 1991: 15-16, 37, 221). In an age when an able seaman received a salary of about £20 a year, £5,000 could set a man up for life (Hill, 1998: 178). Given that ordinary Spanish ships listed in the *Supplement to the Gentleman's Quarterly* of 1741 (Vol. XI: 698) were valued at 3,500*l.* per vessel, a captain of a privateer and his investors in theory could become rich overnight. (This article retains the original use of *l.*, the mid-18th century symbol of the British pound, as it appears in its original usage.) By 14 August 1744, the *Daily Post* calculated that the prizes taken in the war since its start were valued at £3 million. The 308 French, 226 Spanish and 195 enemy ships of unrecorded nationality captured by American privateers alone in the North American colonies between 1739 and 1748 equated to a value of £968,972 (Swanson, 1991: 181).

A common source of quick revenue was accepting ransoms on captured ships, such as in the case of the *Mary* heading from Carolina to the Orkneys taken on 3 July 1744, which was ransomed for £1,000 sterling (*Gentleman's Magazine*, July 1744: 367). Sales, however, were by far the most common outcome. In the war years, both the sale of captured ships and cargo were advertized extensively in the English press, which published details about the name of the prize, composition of its consignments and location of auction 'by the candle' – most notably for prizes seized by Royal Navy warships (Figs. 11-14, 16). An entry in the *Daily Advertiser* of 25 July 1744 is typical of the entries:

> "*For Sale by the* CANDLE, At Garraway's Coffee-House in Exchange-Alley, on Wednesday the 1st of August, at Four O'Clock in the Afternoon,
> 219 Casks of French Sugars
> About 15 Tons of Coffee,
> 7360 Pricks of Tobacco, more or less,
> 1 Cask of Indigo,
> 12 Rolls of Varinex Tobacco,
> 2 Cases of Citron Water,

Fig. 7. The total volume of prizes of all nations taken during the War of the Austrian Succession, 1739-1748.

1 Case of Brass and Iron Locks, and Iron Ware.
Being the Cargo of the Ship Chevalier Bart, from Martinico, taken by his Majesty's Ship Monmouth, Henry Harrison, Esq, Commander.

The above Goods to be view'd at Galley-Key from Monday the 30st instant to the Time of Sale, which will be begin at Twelve o'Clock.

Abraham Lestourgeon, *Broker, in Lawrence-Poultney-Lane.*"

The privateering war was global in scope. New World privateers sailed the Atlantic from Newfoundland to Florida and from the east coast of Mexico to French Cayenne. American cruisers chased prizes in the privateer-infested waters of Britain and Europe. Statistics published for 1745 reflect the scope of the seizures (*Supplement to the Gentleman's Quarterly*, 1745: 696). Of 565 Spanish and French ships carried by the English into 54 cited ports, 36 were brought into Dover, 35 into Lisbon, 24 into Leghorn, 20 into Rhode Island, 19 into Portmahon, 18 into Plymouth, 17 into Antigua, 16 into Barbados, 15 into Bristol, 14 into Jamaica and 11 into New York (with the names of 202 harbors not cited). Of 507 English ships seized by French and Spanish privateers and carried into 34 reported harbours, 71 were taken into St. Malo, 44 into Brest, 24 to Martinico, 23 into Porto Rico, 22 to Bayonne, 20 into Morlaix, 19 to Dunkirk, 11 to Hispaniola, 11 to Dieppe and 10 to Vigo (plus 180 harbor names not specified). Seemingly every patch of open water was fair game.

4. Scales of Privateering & Prizes

During the war of 1739-48 some 2,828 British privateers went to sea (Swanson, 1991: 26-7, 54) and just over 6,800 English, French and Spanish craft were seized by all sides. An abundance of newspapers of the age provide a compelling image of the scales and dynamics of privateering through both first-hand letters and journalistic news.

The *Gentleman's Quarterly* highlighted the rising threat in August 1740, when "The *Spanish* Privateers are all round our Coast, they have taken a Boat and two Sloops on the *Norman Coast*, treated the Passengers in a barbarous Manner, and left them quite naked, a Woman in particular they used most cruelly. These Rovers have no more than 40 Men in a Boat, but they row with sixteen Oars, and are upon you as soon as they are seen."

British unease was unabated in 1742 when an extract from a letter written in Bordeaux and published in the *London Evening Post* on 24 April reported that:

"By our last Letters from St. Sebastian's we are inform'd, there are no less than eight English Prizes lately carried in there;

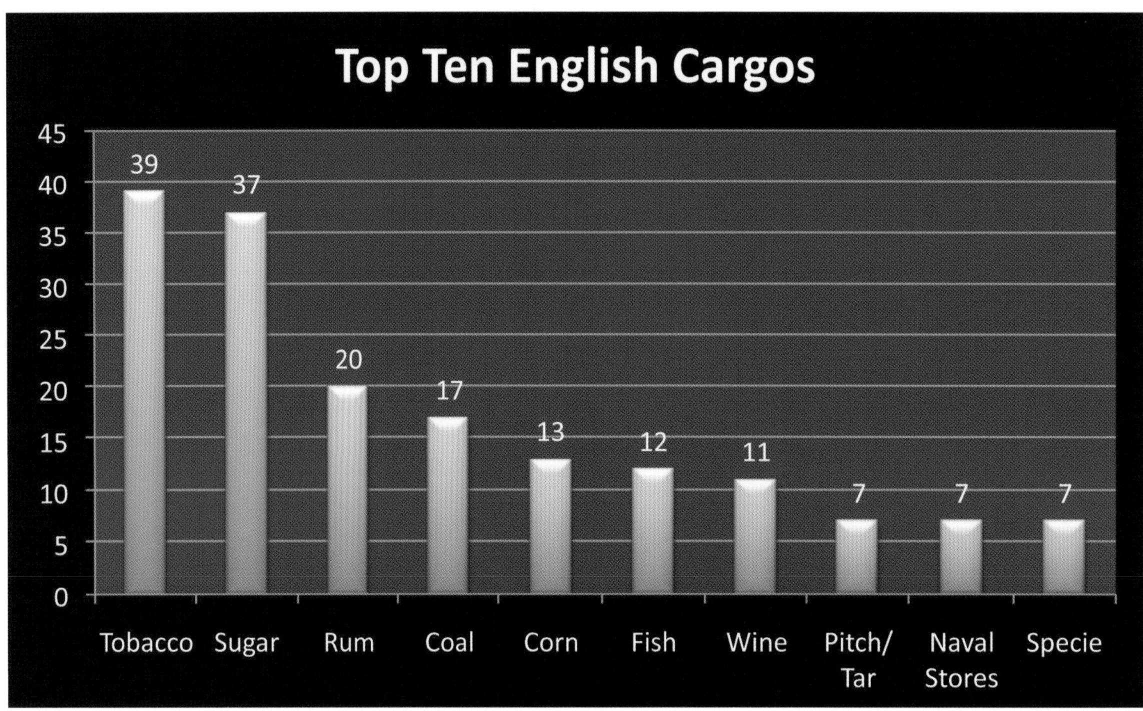

Fig. 8. The top ten most numerous English cargos taken by the French and Spanish during the War of the Austrian Succession, 1739-1748.

> one with Rice from Carolina; one outward bound for Newfoundland; one from Ireland for Madeira; two with Sugar from the American Plantations... The Capture of so many Ships lately by the Spaniards, scarce a Post arriving without a melancholy Account of more or less being taken, justly gives the Merchants great Uneasiness, and justifies the Reasonableness of their Complaints against the Misconduct of carrying on the War, the ill Effects of which daily appear, and will require some Time to rectify".

Prize lists published consistently throughout the war over a total of 127 pages of the *Gentleman's Quarterly* provide a solid picture of the relative scale of seizures and losses, even if the quality of the data varies across time. In some issues nationalities, cargos and the name of the capturing ship are meticulously reported, while in others such data is lacking. In some cases listings are published in condensed type across double columns on single pages, compared to the typical single column pages, with information seemingly sacrificed in favor of superior stories. A clear bias towards the careful reporting of enemy prizes taken is also obvious, whereas lists of English losses rarely furnish comparable details about cargo composition and wealth, presumably for purposes of propaganda and morale at the exclusion of the depressing truth about diminishing losses. Overall, however, the newspaper devoted remarkable space to the war of privateering. This major primary set of data within the *Gentleman's Quarterly* comprises the source material for the quantification of the economics of privateering in the War of the Austrian Succession discussed in this article.[1]

The balance of annual statistics demonstrates that no one nation won the privateering war. Up to 1741 Spain seized 337 ships, valued at 35,000*l.* each, amounting to a total prize value £1.179 million, while the English took 250 ships valued at £1.749 million for the same period (*Gentleman's Quarterly*, 1741). Overall, a total of 6,917 ships were seized on all sides between 1739 and 1748, or 6,809 if retaken English ships are factored into the equation (which crews presumably did not profit from, but were returned to the original owner).

Spanish and French forces captured a total of 3,493 English ships accounting for 51.3% of all prizes, whereas the English in turn took 3,316 Spanish, French and other enemy craft representing 48.7% of all losses. These consisted of 1,953 French ships (58.9% of all enemy prizes), 687 Spanish ships (20.7%) and 676 others (20.4%: 184 of non-French and non-Spanish nationality and 492 of unknown origin; Fig. 7). Rich cargos were naturally the ultimate prey and only 1.0% of all ships captured during the war were sailing solely in ballast.

A. English Prizes

The character of a total of just 268 cargos of the 3,493 English ships captured is reported in the *Gentleman's Quarterly*, comprising 51 different types of commodity, which can be sub-divided into the following general categories:

- Alcoholic Drinks: 36 (13.4%)
- Ballast: 2 (0.7%)
- Foodstuffs: 100 (37.3%)
- Metals: 7 (2.6%)
- Non-Edible Dry Goods: 99 (36.9%)
- Very Rich Cargos: 14 (5.2%)
- War Shipments: 10 (3.7%)

The top three most extensive cargos taken were tobacco (39), sugar (37) and rum (20), which were often enormous shipments. The consignments are generally of international character and do not reflect uniquely English manufactured goods (Fig. 8). Exceptions include one cargo of cider and 17 of coal. The English prizes are not registered as having been particularly rich: of 14 high-value examples, just seven contained specie. Unsurprisingly, French and Spanish privateers logically sought as a preference incoming merchant vessels carrying exotic wares over long distances. Of the 268 English cargos registered, 111 originated in the West Indies and Americas (41.4% of the total English cargos).

The variety and scale of the losses were nevertheless impressive. In April 1746, for instance, 1,100 hogsheads of sugar and 10 tons of sugar being transported by the English *Dreadnought* and *Lyon* from Barbados to London were lost. While sailing between Africa and Jamaica with 354 slaves in May 1746, the *Fortune* of Liverpool was taken by a Martinico privateer and carried to Porto Cavallo. In the same month a shipment of stone quarried in Portland for the new Westminster Bridge was captured by a French privateer and ransomed for 200*l.*, and the 881 hogsheads of sugar captured on the *New Ranger*, Montserrat to London, and taken into Brest, was judged to be the most valuable sugar ship ever bound to England. Its quality was presumably superior to the above 1,100 hogsheads of sugar or the *Gentleman's Quarterly* reporters had short memories.

Irrespective of the fact that merchant vessels sailed in convoys to maximize safety, facilitate protection and to try to avoid being picked off individually by enemy predators, prizes captured in groups were not uncommon. In July 1746, 14 English sails were taken between Orkney and Shetland by just one French privateer of 20 guns, and further afield 40 sails from North America for the Leeward Isles were seized by Martinico privateers. A report of January 1747 describing the previous month referred to the prizes streaming into Bayonne, France, where "Within a month past 30 English ships have been brought into this port, following one another like sheep. You may judge of the value of their fleeces by the following particulars, *viz.* 3500 hogsheads of sugar, 1200 hogsheads of tobacco, 5000 quintals of fish, several puncheons of rum, and a great quantity of beef..."

An example of a rich and politically sensitive seizure that held the potential to impact seriously the course of the war were the 24,000 zechins (gold Venetian coins) and diplomatic dispatches for the king of Sardinia captured by the French in August 1747. Onboard the same vessel, which was driven ashore at St. Remo, was an English admiral and General Schulemberg. A cargo of "horses and equipage of a nobleman" taken in November 1747 was an unusual prize, while the loss of the *Dominco d'Amico* of 24 guns in February 1748, en route from London to Naples and taken by the Algerines, was considered a particularly heavy blow. The loss to the merchants of Naples was computed at 100,000 ducats and to the merchants of Leghorn, London, and Civita Vecchia another 300,000 ducats. In January 1748 a cargo of 400 barrels of gunpowder and ordnance stores dispatched from the Tower of London for Plymouth was captured.

Privateering was not restricted to far off places; English craft were often pursued outrageously close to the shores of Britain. In November 1746 a French corsair took the brigantine *Duke of Cornwall* belonging to the Falmouth custom's house in Gerran's road near the port. December 1747 witnessed a French privateer of just four guns and 45 men seizing a boat laden with coal near Ardroth in Scotland, which it ransomed for "4 sheep, a leg of beef, and 72 bottles of ale..."

B. Spanish Prizes

The quantity of cargos captured by the English as reported amongst the 687 Spanish prizes in the *Gentleman's Quarterly* is about equal to those on English prizes. Although slightly larger at 280 cargos, the 41 different categories of consignments are more limited, being ten less numerous:

- Alcoholic Drinks: 9 (3.2%)
- Ballast: 1 (0.4%)
- Foodstuffs: 21 (7.5%)
- Metals: 13 (4.6%)
- Non-Alcoholic Drinks: 16 (5.7%)
- Non-Edible Dry Goods: 87 (31.1%)
- Very Rich Cargos: 100 (35.7%)
- War Shipments: 33 (11.8%)

The three most extensive cargos seized were war stores, such as ammunition, gunpowder and pistols (33), cocoa

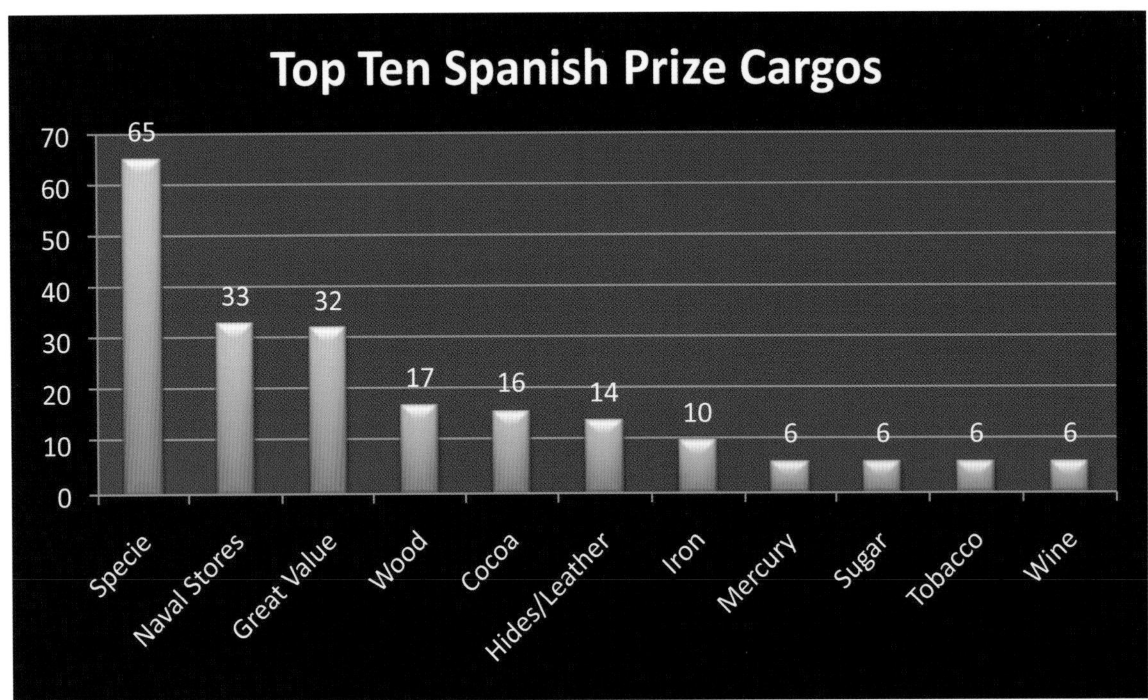

Fig. 9. The top ten most numerous Spanish cargos taken by the English during the War of the Austrian Succession, 1739-1748.

(16) and hides/leather (14). This excludes monetary shipments, which naturally comprised a high ratio of Spanish prizes compared to English and French losses (Fig. 9). Some 32 cargos and ships are simply described as very valuable or of great value, while 65 contained specie. Some 33% of Spanish prizes thus contained 'treasure', compared to 5.2% of English and 8.3% of French prizes. The chance of striking it rich by taking a Spanish ship was not literary hyperbole. Some 66 Spanish cargos were Colonial (23.6% of total Spanish cargos, excluding specie), and included both exotic and staple commodities such as cochineal, indigo, mercury, snuff, tortoiseshell, ostrich feathers and wood.

Cargos taken by the English between September 1739 and December 1741 reflect the scales and character of the Spanish losses. In this period Admiral Haddock took one ship with 700 barrels of gunpowder and 10,000 arms and brass cannon valued at 11,000*l*., as well as 100,000 pieces of eight in a register ship. In early 1745 the 350-ton, 16-gun *Maria Fortuna*, bound from Cadiz to Buenos Aires, was captured with a cargo value of 100,000*l*. and insured for 550,000 dollars. As a bonus its passengers included the Governor of Paraguay. The capture of dignitaries was a useful source of securing enemy intelligence, and in early 1745 the English struck lucky again when the 20-gun *Elephant* and its 140 men were taken en route from Mississippi to Rochfort. As well as a primary cargo of indigo, hides, logwood and tobacco, 20,000 pieces of eight were secured plus the Superintendant of Mississippi and his wife and family.

An equally impressive prize was the *St. Joseph N.S. Granado*, sailing from Cartagena to Havana in May 1745, which was captured after three days by the *Kouli Kan* privateer and carried into Lisbon. The ship was found to contain eight chests of silver holding 24,551 dollars, one chest of gold, 50,436 further dollars, all registered, plus 17,250 dollars and three bars of golden contraband, all alongside a very large cargo of sugar, cocoa, snuff, hides and tobacco. The *St. Joseph* was described as the richest prize taken by a privateer since the war had started.

The *Postilion* of Alicante, a Spanish register ship from Vera Cruz to Cadiz, was seized in July 1745 with a large quantity of cochineal valued at 200,000 pieces of eight. A further rich Spanish ship was captured by a privateer of Rhode Island, "laden with many tons of copper plate, and a great quantity of valuable China, besides 30,000 dollars, and a case of wrought plate, of some 1000 ounces..." The reference to china is intriguing. Although Oriental ceramics were finding a receptive market in the West during the

1740s, only one French and one Spanish cargo of china were listed amongst all of the 6,917 ships within the current database of prizes, which is unlikely to be an accurate reflection of commercial reality. Why was this category of product so under-represented? The conspicuous presence of Chinese porcelain documented on the wrecked cargos of the Compagnie Française des Indes's *Prince de Conty* (1746), the 50-gun *Maidstone* English warship (1747) and the *Amsterdam* (1749) more accurately reflects the physical reality of the trade in Chinese porcelain in this period (de Maisonneuve, 1992: 22-24; L'Hour, 2005a; Marsden, 1972: 93).

The Spanish ship the *St. Zirioco* "suppos'd for Scotland, with 2500 muskets, and bayonets, 100 barrels of powder, 150 quintals of musket balls, some boxes of horseshoes and flints, and 7 chests of Spanish money, about 24,000 dollars in gold and silver, among the gold many pistoles folded singly in papers" taken by the *Tryal* privateer of Bristol in October 1745, is another revealing anomaly. Two months later another Spanish ship, the *St. Pedro* from St. Andero for Scotland, was intercepted by the *Ambuscade* privateer of Captain Cool containing 2,500 muskets, 100 chests of gunpowder, 70 chests of ball, and 1,219 pistols, which were carried into Crookhaven, Ireland. By aiming for Scotland Spain was replicating a strategy of the Spanish Armada of 1588, whereby the country's Catholic, anti-English sympathies were exploited. These seizures successfully helped doom the Second Jacobite Rebellion of 1745 aimed at putting Bonnie Prince Charlie on the throne of Britain (pers. comm. Lange Winkler, October 2010).

By far the richest prize taken during the entire war (other than Anson's capture of the *Cobadonga*, see Section 6 below) was commandeered in May 1746 by a Royal Navy warship, which joyfully found a million sterling in bullion in its hold. In July of the same year, cochineal, indigo, hides, snuff, gold, silver and the Governor of Guatemala in New Spain were captured by the *Dublin* privateer westward of the Azores on the 400-ton, 18-gun Spanish register ship the *N.S. de Begona* from Havana to Cadiz, which was brought into Dublin. The latest attested Spanish prize captured by the English in August 1748, notably several months after the signing of the Treaty of Aix-La-Chapelle on 18 April 1748 (Browning, 1994: 344), was the *Jesus Maria Joseph* from Vera Cruz for Havana and on to Europe with 161 chests of silver and two chests of gold taken by the *Bethell* frigate and carried into Fyall in the Western Islands.

C. French Prizes

French ships comprise the most abundant category of enemy prizes taken by the English during the War of the Austrian Succession and by far the most numerous volume of recorded cargos. A total of 852 French consignments are cited in the *Gentleman's Quarterly*, over three times more numerous than for Spanish or English prizes, and consist of 69 different categories:

- Alcoholic Drinks: 104 (12.2%)
- Ballast: 5 (0.6%)
- Foodstuffs: 260 (30.5%)
- Metals: 5 (0.6%)
- Non-Alcoholic Drinks: 105 (12.3%)
- Non-Edible Dry Goods: 250 (29.3%)
- Very Rich Cargos: 71 (8.3%)
- War Shipments: 52 (6.1%)

At double the volume of any other commodity, the 163 cargos of sugar comprised 19.1% of all registered French shipments (Fig. 10). By relative value, for Britain sugar was the most important colonial import from the West Indies. Domestic English consumption was on the rise. Whereas 364 Bristol firms had imported 60,214 counterweight of sugar in 1681, 338 firms were importing 129,306 counterweight of sugar in 1742 (Price, 1996: 491). Across England consumption rates increased from about 4lbs per head in 1700-09 to reach 11lbs by 1770-79, compared to just over 2lbs per head used in France in the latter period (Price, 1998: 81-2).

The war interrupted the start of a rapid rise in sugar imports, which doubled in the London markets between 1740 and 1769. Different qualities of sugar existed, with a preference for the fine produce of St. Kitts and Barbados over the below aveage sugars of Jamaica and especially Antigua. As the House of Lascelles and Maxwell summarized in September 1756:

> "The Jamaica Sugars, are in general very low and weak in quality, and not esteemed here nor abroad, which is chiefly owing to a want of care, and slovenliness in the making of them. The Planters in the Leward Islands are careful and industrious, and their Sugars are in request, and we can sell them as fast as they are landed. Indeed the Sugar Bakers seldom work Jamaica Sugars without mixing them in the pans with those of the Leward Islands."

The war naturally stalled the import of supplies and caused the price of sugar in England to rise in July 1744 from 34s. to 41s for Jamaican muscovados (Pares, 1996: 227, 232, 237). Captured French cargos were happily welcomed by Britain's sweet tooth.

Other highly represented French consignments included coffee (78), indigo (67), wine (58), war stores and soldier recruits (52, of which soldiers 15), cotton (37),

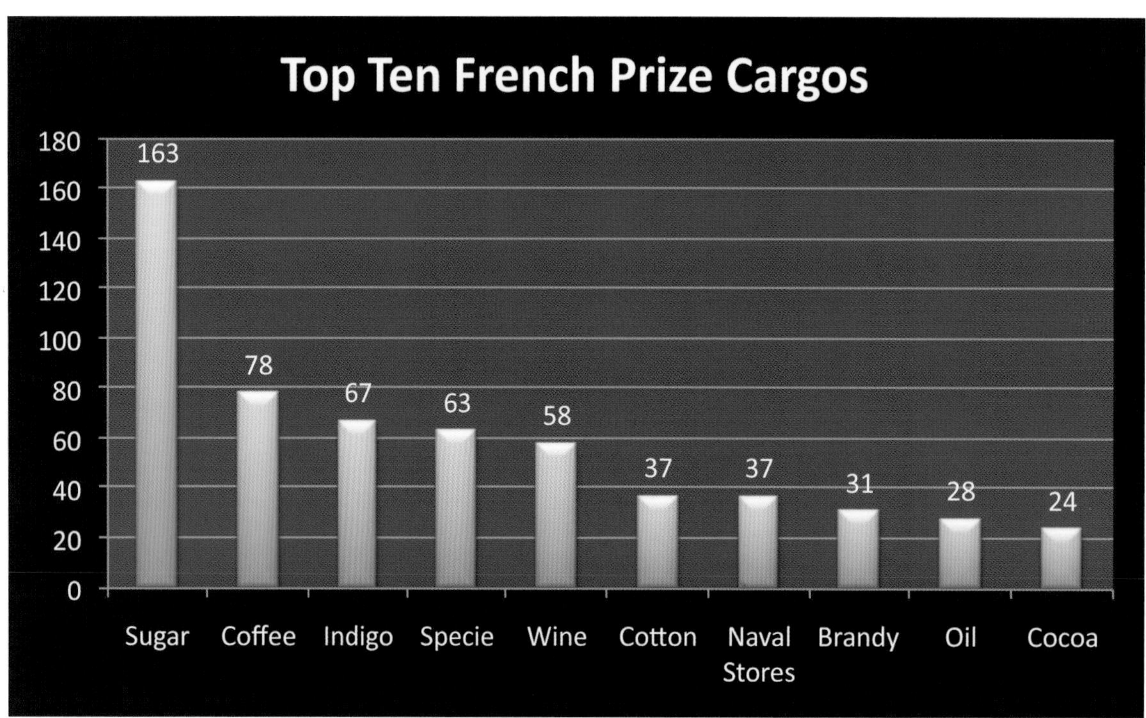

Fig. 10. The top ten most numerous French cargos taken by the English during the War of the Austrian Succession, 1739-1748.

brandy (31), oil (28), hides/furs (25) and bale goods (19). Eight ships were generally described as very rich and 63 carried some form of specie (7.4%), higher than the 5.2% figure for English prizes but far lower than the 33% for Spanish ships. Not surprisingly given its extensive Colonial territories, some 420 of the French prize cargos originated in the West Indies and Americas (49.3% of the total).

The French also seemingly dominated the trade with Africa. The prizes include 13 cargos of slaves and seven of elephant tusks, compared to none for Spanish vessels and five slaves and one elephant tusk shipment amongst the English prizes. Nantes was the dominant French port in the triangular slave trade, and between *c.* 1700-92 92 ships operating in and out of this port were wrecked (Ducoin, 2005). Nevertheless, the war caused French imports from Africa to decline sharply from £3,775,000 in 1743 to just £31,000 in 1745 (Villiers, 1996: 260).

The high presence of indigo cargos warrants comment. Again, this was a much-needed bonanza for Britain, where the production of woolen goods outstripped all other industrial activities, just as linen did in Scotland and Ireland. The need for a constant flow of dyestuffs was essential to the domestic economy. In the period covered by the War of the Austrian Succession, Britain experienced a crisis in supply after the West Indies abandoned the cultivation of dye products in favor of the far more lucrative sugar. Imports from the Americas declined accordingly from 48% in 1722-24 to 25% in 1752-54 with the result that British dye-salters had to secure supplies from France, whose West Indian colonies had continued production (Price 1998: 82).

The following newspaper entries provide a balanced reflection of the typical character and scale of the French prizes, and of France's particular specialty of concealing specie. On 18 April 1744 a French ship of 200 tons sailing from Havana to Old Spain with a valuable cargo of 25,000 pieces of eight, found concealed in bags of snuff, was taken by a Charlestown privateer. *La Victoire* of 36 guns and 145 men was captured in March 1746 with 100 chests of silver en route from Cape François to Port Louis. The cosmopolitan, multiple inward and outward bound consignments dispatched in single ships between France and its American colonies is represented by the *Jean Baptist,* Marseilles to Cape François, which was taken into Philadelphia by the Marlborough privateer in June 1746 and was found to contain 250 hogsheads of wine, 400 casks of oil, 250 boxes of soap and 200 boxes of candles, alongside cordials, gold lace and clothing. By May 1747 the *Gentleman's Quarterly* announced that officials had computed that the English held 11,000 French sailors as prisoners.

D. Other Prizes

English ships also captured a further 255 cargos comprising 42 different categories of commodity from six other nations. Several consignments are registered as deriving from smuggler ships, and the provenance of a large quantity is simply listed as unknown: Danish 4 (1.6%), Dutch 45 (17.6%), German 7 (2.7%), Italian 11 (4.3%), Prussian 2 (0.8%), smugglers 16 (6.3%), Swedish 15 (5.9%) and unknown 155 (60.8%). These can be subdivided into the following general categories:

- Alcoholic Drinks: 40 (15.7%)
- Ballast: 3 (1.2%)
- Foodstuffs: 45 (17.6%)
- Metals: 12 (4.7%)
- Non-Alcoholic Drinks: 23 (9.0%)
- Non-Edible Dry Goods: 51 (20.0%)
- Very Rich Cargos: 52 (20.4%)
- War Shipments: 29 (11.4%)

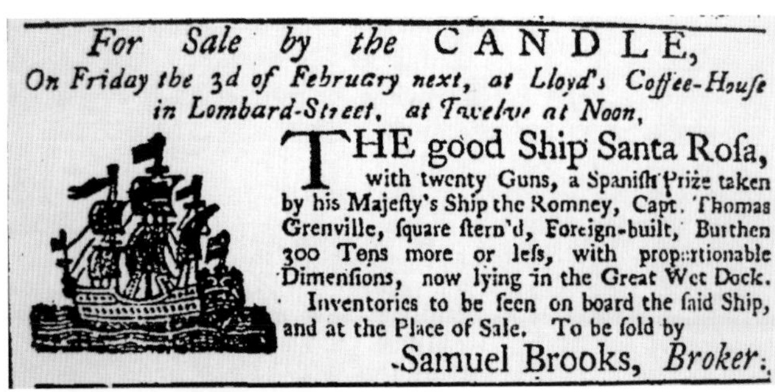

For Sale by the CANDLE,
On Friday the 3d of February next, at Lloyd's Coffee-Houſe in Lombard-Street, at Twelve at Noon,

THE good Ship Santa Roſa, with twenty Guns, a Spaniſh Prize taken by his Majeſty's Ship the Romney, Capt. Thomas Grenville, ſquare ſtern'd, Foreign-built, Burthen 300 Tons more or leſs, with proportionable Dimenſions, now lying in the Great Wet Dock.

Inventories to be ſeen on board the ſaid Ship, and at the Place of Sale. To be ſold by

Samuel Brooks, *Broker.*

Fig. 11. An advert for the sale on 3 February 1744 at the Lloyd's Coffee-House, London, of the 300-ton Santa Rosa *Spanish prize taken by the* Romney *English warship* (Daily Advertiser, *25 January 1744).*

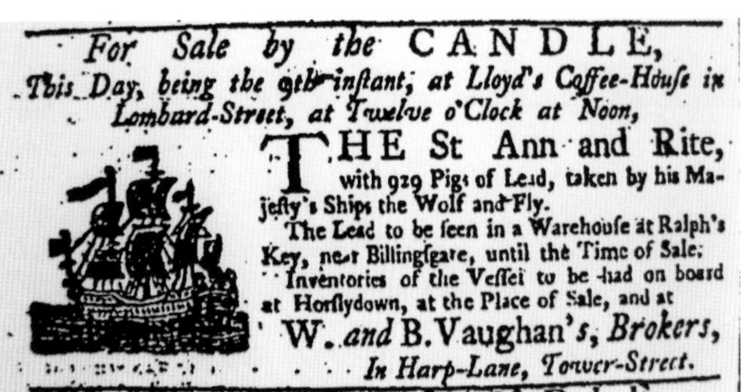

For Sale by the CANDLE,
This Day, being the 9th instant, at Lloyd's Coffee-Houſe in Lombard-Street, at Twelve o'Clock at Noon,

THE St Ann and Rite, with 929 Pigs of Lead, taken by his Majeſty's Ships the Wolf and Fly.

The Lead to be ſeen in a Warehouſe at Ralph's Key, near Billingſgate, until the Time of Sale; Inventories of the Veſſel to be had on board at Horſlydown, at the Place of Sale, and at

W. *and* B. Vaughan's, *Brokers,*
In Harp-Lane, Tower-Street.

Fig. 12. An advert for the sale on 9 May 1744 at the Lloyd's Coffee-House, London, of 929 lead ingots taken with the St. Ann and Rite *prize by the* Wolf *and* Fly *English warships (*Daily Advertiser, *9 May 1744).*

Of these prize cargos, 59 originated in the West Indies and Americas (23.1% of the total other consignments). Sugar is especially well represented (19), as well as cocoa (13) and indigo (11). Examples of non-French and non-Spanish foreign cargos captured by the English include 27 chests of silver, each containing 4,000 pieces of eight, taken out of a Genoese ship valued at 20,000*l.* in 1741 and 200,000 pieces of eight belonging to the Spanish captured off the Western Isles from the Swedish ship the *Samuel Lynn* in October 1743.

The English simultaneously kept a close eye on local craft breaking the embargo on the import of the goods of enemy states. So in June 1745 a smuggling cutter of Hastings was taken into Dover by the *Eagle* privateer after being caught en route to Bologne with money to buy a French cargo. Another smuggling cutter of 40 tons and armed with 14 swivel guns was seized by a custom-house sloop on the coast of Sussex in August 1745 laden with three tons of tea, 400 half anchors of brandy and some mountain wine and claret. In September 1745 a vessel was listed as "A smuggling boat, with a cargo of tea and brandy, and the cargo of another boat, making together 800 lb. of tea, and 300 half anchors of brandy."

For Sale by the CANDLE,
On Friday next, the 11th instant, at Lloyd's Coffee-Houſe in Lombard-Street, at Twelve at Noon,

A Spaniſh Privateer, now lying at Portſmouth, call'd Nueſtra Senora d'Eſclavitud, Burthen about 100 Tons leſs or more, taken by his Majeſty's Ship the Fox, Capt. Robert Erſkine, Commander. The Veſſel was formerly known at Liſbon by the Name of the Black Prince's Schooner, and was built for Sailing, in which ſhe has been ſeldom outdone, tho' often tried. She attack'd the Fox firſt, taking her for a Merchant Ship. She is mounted with four Braſs Guns and two Iron Guns, carrying four-pound Shot; ſix Braſs Pedereroes, carrying three-pound Shot, with three Braſs Chambers to each Pedereroe, and twelve Iron Pedereroes. She has a Parapet or Breaſt-Work forward, which ſerves for a Cover to her Men, and whereon ſhe can mount the ſix Braſs Pedereroes, which with the two Chace-Guns, make eight directly in Front, and by her great Length, her whole Artillery may be fought on one Side. She rows with twenty-eight Oars, and is exceedingly well found; and will be ſold with or without about thirty Tons of Lead Ballaſt, fix'd in the Hold.

Inventories will be left at Lloyd's and Sam's, in London; and with Mr. William Serjeant, at Portſmouth. To be ſold by

W. *and* B. Vaughan, *Brokers.*

Fig. 13. An advert for the sale on 11 May 1744 at the Lloyd's Coffee-House, London, of the Spanish 27-gun galley prize the Nuestra Senora d'Esclavitud, *"built for Sailing, in which she has been seldom outdone", and taken by the* Fox *man-of-war* (Daily Advertiser, *9 May 1744).*

5. Royal Navy 'Privateering'

The role of Royal Navy officers and warships in the war of privateering is often overlooked despite the reality that in the War of the Austrian Succession ships of the line aggressively sought out prizes, largely to protect the English trade but equally to line the pockets of a commander and crew.

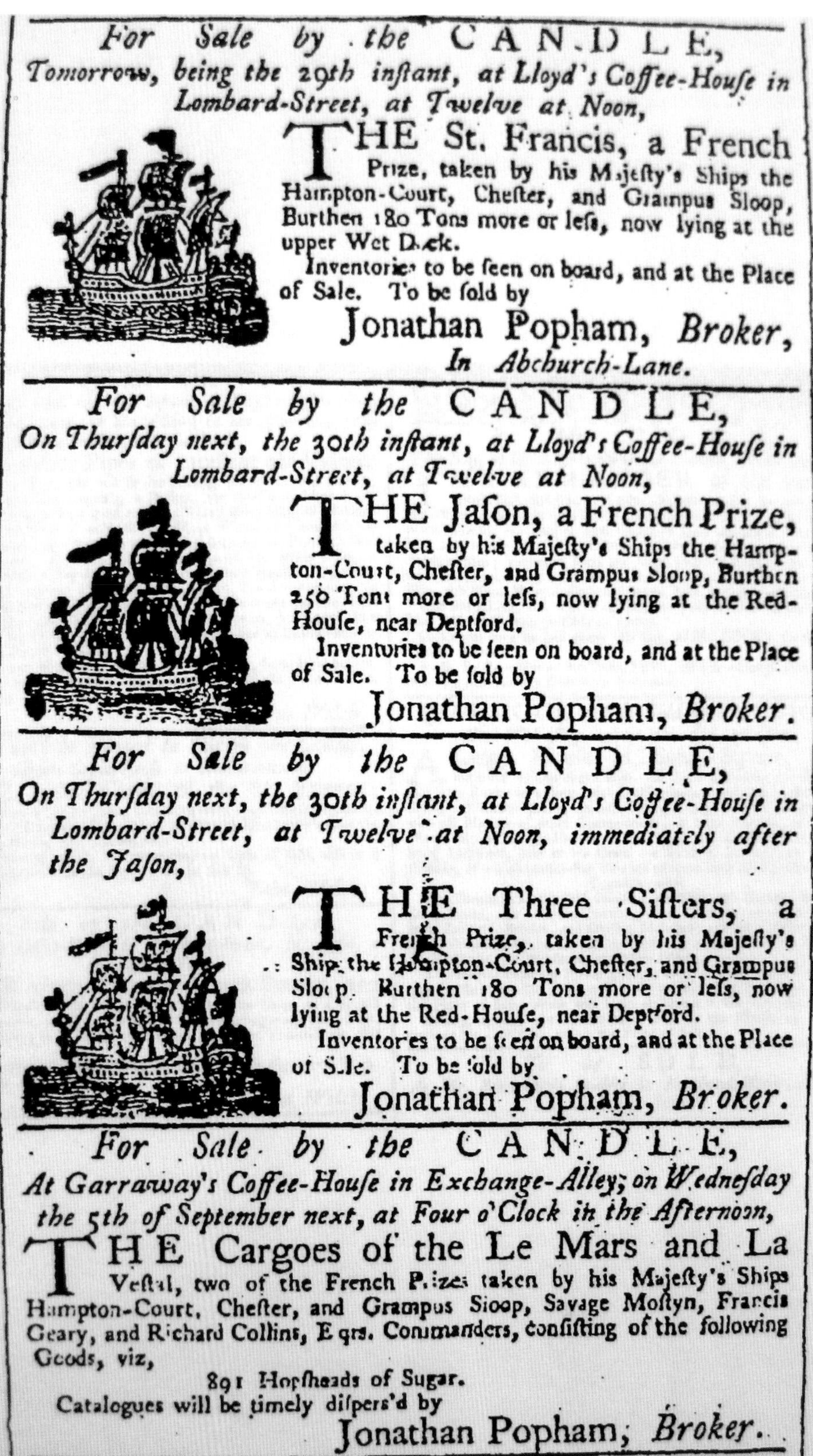

For Sale by the CANDLE,
Tomorrow, being the 29th instant, at Lloyd's Coffee-House in Lombard-Street, at Twelve at Noon,

THE St. Francis, a French Prize, taken by his Majesty's Ships the Hampton-Court, Chester, and Grampus Sloop, Burthen 180 Tons more or less, now lying at the upper Wet Dock.

Inventories to be seen on board, and at the Place of Sale. To be sold by

Jonathan Popham, *Broker,*
In Abchurch-Lane.

For Sale by the CANDLE,
On Thursday next, the 30th instant, at Lloyd's Coffee-House in Lombard-Street, at Twelve at Noon,

THE Jason, a French Prize, taken by his Majesty's Ships the Hampton-Court, Chester, and Grampus Sloop, Burthen 250 Tons more or less, now lying at the Red-House, near Deptford.

Inventories to be seen on board, and at the Place of Sale. To be sold by

Jonathan Popham, *Broker.*

For Sale by the CANDLE,
On Thursday next, the 30th instant, at Lloyd's Coffee-House in Lombard-Street, at Twelve at Noon, immediately after the Jason,

THE Three Sisters, a French Prize, taken by his Majesty's Ships the Hampton-Court, Chester, and Grampus Sloop. Burthen 180 Tons more or less, now lying at the Red-House, near Deptford.

Inventories to be seen on board, and at the Place of Sale. To be sold by

Jonathan Popham, *Broker.*

For Sale by the CANDLE,
At Garraway's Coffee-House in Exchange-Alley; on Wednesday the 5th of September next, at Four o'Clock in the Afternoon,

THE Cargoes of the Le Mars and La Vestal, two of the French Prizes taken by his Majesty's Ships Hampton-Court, Chester, and Grampus Sloop, Savage Mostyn, Francis Geary, and Richard Collins, Esqrs. Commanders, consisting of the following Goods, viz,

891 Hogsheads of Sugar.

Catalogues will be timely dispers'd by

Jonathan Popham, *Broker.*

Fig. 14. A row of adverts for the sale at Lloyd's and Garraway's Coffee-Houses of the prize ships St. Francis, Jason, Three Sisters, Le Mars *and* La Vestal, *plus some related cargo, in late August and early October 1744. These ships were taken by the* Hampton Court *and* Chester *men-of-war and the* Grampus *sloop, which had been part of Admiral Balchin's fleet (*Daily Advertiser, *28 August 1744).*

In fact, between 1739 and 1748 statistics obtained from the *Gentleman's Quarterly* prize lists reveals that no less than 1,337 Spanish and French ships were taken by Royal Navy ships, which equates to an impressive 40.3% of all prizes captured by the English. The navy's role in the strategy of *guerre de course* was substantial.

With their irrefutable firepower, numerous key prizes were seized (Figs. 11-14, 16). Between 1739 and 1741, for instance, Captain Warren of the *Squirrel* got his hands on a French ship with 1,387 pistols, 290*l.* in silver, 200 ounces of plate and 700 barrels of flour, cocoa, gold and silver lace for Cartagena. In the same period Captain Thompson of the *Success* captured a cargo of cochineal, hides, 170,000 dollars and 60 bars of gold and silver. Rummaging through paperwork also aided intelligence. On 8 May 1744 communications on a Spanish tender taken by HMS *Montague* revealed that Admiral Torres was making his way to Europe with his squadron and 16 million pieces of eight.

Following the daring capture of the *Nuestra Senora de Cobadonga* by Commander Anson, it was yet another Royal Navy warship that took what was alleged to be the second richest cargo of the war in early 1745:

> "The *Conception*, a French ship of 400 tons, 20 guns, and 326 men, from Carthagena for the Havana, having on board 800 serons of Cocoa, in each of which was deposited a bar of gold, 68 chests of silver coin, containing 310,000 pieces of eight, wrought plate of equivalent value, a compleat set of church plate, a large quantity of gold buckles and snuff-boxes, a curious two-wheel'd chase of silver… a large quantity of pearls, diamonds, and other precious stone, above 600 l. weight of gold, &c. which made it the richest ships taken since the war, except the Acapulco ship taken by admiral Anson. This valuable prize was taken by the Rose man of war of 20 guns, capt. Frankland, after a very smart engagement of 11 glasses, in which the Conception had 110 men killed, and the Rose five, and carried into Charles Town, South Carolina."

The 22-gun *Notre Dame de Deliverance* from the South Seas was captured by HMS *Sutherland* and *Chester* in September 1745 and carried into Louisbourg with "in gold and silver above 300,000*l.* and a cargo of Peruvian wool, cocoa, and jesuits bark". His Majesty's fleet of the *Kent, Advice, Lion, Oxford, Eagle, Hector, Dolphin* and *Hampton Court* enjoyed vast success in July 1747, when 48 French ships were taken homeward-bound from St. Domingo carrying 48 consignments of sugar, 30 of indigo, four of cotton, seven of hides, 24 of coffee, one cochineal and one leather.

The capture of rich prizes often involved serious loss of life, not least the taking of the 70-gun Spanish man of war *Glorisio* in November 1747, which had just arrived at Ferrol from Havana. An initial chase with the *Dartmouth*

For Sale by the CANDLE,
At the New Inn in Dartmouth, on Wedneſday the 7th of November next, at Ten o'Clock in the Morning,

THE good Ship the Deux Amis, a French Prize, not two Years old, taken by the Boſcawen Privateer, Burthen 360 Tons more or leſs, a prime Sailor, with twenty-one Carriage-Guns, proportionable Dimenſions, and well found, now lying at Dartmouth.

At the ſame Time will be ſold the following Prize Goods.

208 Hides in the Hair, in four Lots, landed out of the Deux Amis Prize, from the Havanna;
880 Buſhels of French Salt;
16 Pieces, containing 1530 Gallons of French Brandy, landed out of the Fortune from Nantz, taken by the Young Ceres Privateer.

The Brandy to be put up one Caſk in a Lot.

The ſaid Goods to be ſeen at Dartmouth till the Time of Sale.
Inventories of the Ship to be had at the Place of Sale, at Lloyd's Coffee-Houſe in Lombard-Street, and of

Charles Rogers, *Broker.*

Fig. 15. An advert for the sale at the New Inn, Dartmouth, of the French armed merchant vesssel Deux Amis *and several prize cargos on 7 November 1744* (Daily Advertiser, *31 October 1744).*

For SALE by the CANDLE,
At the FOUNTAIN TAVERN in Portſmouth,
On Monday the 29th of Auguſt, at Nine o'Clock in the Morning;

THE following Goods taken by a Squadron of his Majeſty's Ships, commanded by Lord *Anſon* and Sir *Peter Warren, viz.*

295 Hogſheads, 3 Butts, 11 Cheſts French Red Wine
17 Hogſheads, 1 Butt Ditto White ditto
90 Butts Spaniſh White ditto
200 Quarter Quarter Caſks, 8 Butts Brandy
199 Cheſts, 10 Caſks Olive Oil
41 Hogſh. White Wine Vinegar
180 Barrels Flour
414 Barrels, 62 Tierces Pork
334 Barrels, 59 Tierces Beef
8 Pieces White Silk
1 Piece Black Velvet
17 Pieces Scarlet Camblet
1908 Pair Linnen Spatterdaſhes
426 Linnen Frocks
366 Canvas Trowſers
630 Reams Paper
152 Pier and Chamber Looking Glaſs
586 Laced Hats

3000 Cartouch Boxes
1000 Buff Slings
480 Buff Belts
568 Muſkets
144 Piſtols
500 Powder Horns
289 Serviceable Iron Cannon from 6 to 42 Pounders, 2 Unſerviceable
A large Quantity of Iron Shot ſuitable to the Cannon
102 Barrels and Caggs of Bullets, and ſmall Shot
34 Copper Pans for Sugar Boilers
50 Iron Plates for Hatters
797 Iron Pots of all Sizes
65 Caſks of Nails
19 Hogſheads, 45 Barr. Bozin
12 Hogſheads, 23 Barr. Pitch
46 Barrels, 11 Hogſh. Tar

With Carpenters, Joyners, and Smiths Tools, Stock Locks, Padlocks, Tin-plates, Hungary and Compound Waters, Drugs and Medicines, Beans, Peas, Calavancies, Rice, Gunners Stores of all Sorts and ſundry other Goods.

Catalogues will be Timely delivered at the Place of Sale; and by

WILLIAM and BENJAMIN VAUGHAN, *And* JONATHAN POPHAM, *Brokers.*

Fig. 16. An advert for the sale of several cargos at the Fountain Tavern, Portsmouth, on 29 August 1748, taken by English warships commanded by Lord Anson and Sir Peter Warren (General Advertiser, *3 August 1748).*

ended up with the Royal Navy warship blowing up and all its crew but one being lost. The *Russel* man of war subsequently prevailed and got its hands on the reward of £1.3 million in specie being transported by the Spanish warship. Towards the end of the war in March 1748 one of the last enemy prizes to be captured was the *Union*, a Spanish register ship of 30 guns sailing from Havana to Cadiz with 360,000 dollars, cocoa, cochineal, snuff and hides that was taken by HMS *Bristol.*

6. The Voyage of the *Centurion*

Inspired by Admiral Vernon's early naval success in the war of taking the Spanish-held town of Porto Bello, Panama, in November 1739 (Rodger, 2004: 236), the Admiralty continued to consider grand acts of shock and awe (Fig. 1). Nowhere was the strategic central role of the Royal Navy in the privateering war more brazen than in the round the world voyage of the *Centurion* between 1740 and 1744, which was an almost suicidal example of a highly ambitious attempt to drive a stake straight through the heart of Spain's commercial empire. Overtly dangerous and of dubious impact beyond raising national morale, the venture would be the last act of naval privateering sanctioned by any English government.

The scheme was formalized on 18 October 1739, and in the words of Sir John Norris (Heaps, 1973: 23):

> "This morning I and Mr Kemp were at Sir Charles Wager's with his secretary Mr Gashry and Mr Naish, who opened up to us his sentiments of meeting the Spanish ships from Acapulco at the port of Manila, where they always come to, and likewise are built there and make their outset from thence. And that if a proper strength could be fitted to sail from hence by Christmas we might reach the place before they would arrive with their usual money which is two million sterling or thereabouts. That the Spaniards in the fort and port of Manila were about 150 soldiers; that about 300 soldiers above the ship's complement that should be sent might take the said place, and by removing the Spanish government and garrison, and a good useage to the natives, the place would be easily kept. That by its situation the most beneficial trade can be carried on to China, and if His Majesty should after possession give it to the East India Company an allowable consideration might arise from it."

Commodore George Anson was well experienced for the job of commander of the mission, having served in the Royal Navy since the age of 15 (Fig. 2). He had served under Sir John Norris in the Baltic and North Sea and in 1724 was put in command of a frigate protecting commerce off North America (Anson, 1905). The commodore was appointed to the 60-gun warship *Centurion* in 1737. The ship had been built in 1732 for a crew of 400 men, was short and beamy, with cannon on two decks.

The squadron of five men-of-war, one sloop and two store ships set out on 18 September 1740. En route several prizes were seized following an extremely painful voyage where the crews had to deal with unsuitably old sailors, scurvy, bad weather and pursuit by the Spanish fleet of Pizarro. On 8 September 1741 the *Centurion* captured the *Nuestra Senora de Monte Carmelo*, a rich merchant vessel of 450 tons carrying a large cargo of sugar, cloth and £1,800 in dollars and plate. A month after spotting mainland Chile on 30 September 1741, the *Centurion* captured a second prize, the *Santa Teresa de Jesus*, bound from Guayaquil to Callao with a valuable cargo and £170 of silver. The *Tryal* went on to take the 260-ton *Nuestra Senora del Carmine* on 11 November and its cargo of steel, iron, wax, pepper, cedar and bale goods bound for Callao from Paita and worth 400,000 dollars (Pack, 1960: 49-58).

Anson produced a complete account of his ultimate success whilst still on board the *Centurion* after returning safely to St. Helen's on 14 June 1744, which summarized the taking of General Don Jeronimo de Mentero's *Nuestra Senora de Cobadonga* of 550 men, 36 mounted guns and 28 four-pounders (*Daily Advertiser*, No. 4187; Fig. 3):

> "The South-West Monsoon being set in on the Coast of China before I had refitted his majesty's Ship, made it impossible for me to proceed to Europe till the Month of October. I therefore determined, although I had not half my Complement of Men, to Cruize for the King of Spain's Galleon, which was expected from Acapulco with Treasure to Manila. After having finished the necessary Repairs of my Ship, on the 18th of April, I made the best of my Way for Cape Spiritu Santo, being the Land to the Southward of the Streights of Manila... having cruized thirty-one Days, on the 20th of June I got Sight of her, and gave Chace, she bearing down upon me before the Wind, when she came within two Miles she brought to, to fight me, and after an Engagement of an Hour and half, within less than Pistol-Shot, the Admiral struck his Flag at the Main-Topmast-Head: She was called the Nuestra Senora del Caba Donga, Don Geronimo Montero, Admiral, had 42 Guns; 17 of which were Brass, and 28 Brass Pedereroes, 550 Men, 58 of which were slain, and 83 wounded; her Masts and Rigging were shot to pieces, and 150 Shot passed through her Hull, many of which were between Wind and Water, which occasioned her to be very leaky."

Anson's return to London caused a sensation. The enormous treasure captured was paraded in a Roman triumphal style parade of 32 wagons through St. James's, the Strand and Cheapside before being deposited in the Tower of London (Fig. 4). When finally counted, the plunder consisted of "2,600,000 Pieces of Eight, 150,000 Ounces of Plate, 10 Bars of Gold, and a large Quantity of Gold and Silver Dust; in the whole to the Amount of 1,250,000*l.* Sterling" (*Gentleman's Magazine*, June 1744). This monetary windfall compared extremely favorably against the entire budget of the navy, which amounted to £2,813,586 in 1745 (Heaps, 1973: 254). No greater prize has ever been captured before or since (Fig. 5).

7. Balchin's *Victory* & Royal Navy Prizes in 1744

The seek and capture mission of the *Centurion* was an extreme example of long-distance Royal Navy privateering. Far less predatory and typical of the times were warships undergoing cruises with multiple objectives. Disrupting foreign trade was typically combined with the captain and crews' own personal financial ambitions. The year 1744 was no different to the rest of the war and in fact witnessed the zenith of enemy prizes taken: 550 French and Spanish ships compared to 539 in 1747, the next highest year. By contrast 431 English ships were seized, the third highest annual figure for the duration of the war.

The newspapers especially relished the tales of Royal Navy warships bloodying the enemy's nose. In 1744, for instance, the *Daily Post* of 22 May reported that "The *Roebuck* took Spanish ship, the *St. Jago*, of 400 tons laden with Ammunition, Stores &c. besides 30,000 Pieces of Eight, and carry'd her into Lisbon." Meanwhile, Captain Mitchell of the *Worcester* man of war took four French Ships of great value bound from the Canaries to St. Omers, and carried them into Gibraltar. Soon after, the *Newcastle* seized a French ship sailing from Alexandria to Marseilles "being richly laden, she having on board upwards of 90,000 Dollars in Specie" alongside a cargo worth 20,000*l.* (*Daily Advertiser*, 11 June 1744).

The following month "According to private Letters from Cadiz, they had Intelligence there, that a Register-Ship which sailed from thence in April last for America, has been taken by an English Man of War. It is said, that 200,000 Pieces of Eight have been insured on this Ship at Genoa" (*Daily Advertiser*, 13 July 1744). August was equally busy, when the Court of Admiralty announced that two Spanish prizes had been captured by the *Princessa* and *Deptford* in the Bay of Biscay (*Daily Post*, 9 August 1744). A week later the *Deptford* and *Humphries* cruising off Barcelona captured a further three Spanish prizes worth £50,000 (*Daily Post*, 13 August 1744). At the same time a French ship transporting 7,000 barrels of white sugar and 1,600 bags of coffee was seized by an English man-of-war and carried into Leghorn (*Daily Advertiser*, 16 August 1744).

The cruise of Admiral Sir John Balchin's First Rate warship *Victory* towards Lisbon and on to Gibraltar yielded equal success. As part of its core role as the flagship of the Channel fleet, the *Victory* had been charged with protecting British trade from early on in the war. Thus, on 25 June 1741 Admiral Norris was in command of this flagship and a large fleet, and set out from *Spithead* because, as the *Gentleman's Quarterly* confirmed, "'twas hoped to root out the Privateers of St. Sebastians, and deliver our Ships, of which they took too many this Month..."

Captain Thomas Trevor's log of the *Duke* (ADM 51/282), under the command of Admiral Stewart, Vice Admiral of the Red, described the beginning of a privateering attack within Balchin's fleet on Friday 12 August 1744 at the start of the *Victory's* final voyage, after Admiral Sir John Balchin had assumed command that summer:

> "At 7pm saw 25 sails. At 5am on Sunday 12... the *Hampton Court, Augusta* and *Fly* sloop [in *Victory's* fleet] gave chase. At 2pm still carrying on the chase under hard squalls and rain showers. On Monday 13 August the chase proved to be two English privateers and six French merchant ships. The *Captain* took possession of the *Intrepid*, the *Augusta* of the *Flower*, and the *Hampton Court* of the *Bon Enfant* and St Lawrence. The Dutch took the *Moderate* and *Le Searne*."

Captain Roger Martin's log of the *St. George* (ADM 51/854) confirmed that "the other two were Engs privateers, who had been chasing the 6 sail of French, which had occasioned them to bear down to us...", the interesting inference being that the privateers and Royal Navy fleet were perhaps preying on the same ships. This is again indicated by the *Gentleman's Magazine* of August 1744, which described the skirmish as consisting of "Two Martinico Ships out of Six for France, 4 of which engaged with the Prince Charles Privateer, Capt. Gwynn, for above 4 Hours, to whom, after his losing 6 Men and 18 wounded, they struck; but next Day all of them were taken by Sir John Balchen's Fleet in Lat. 46.40."

The master's log of the *Duke* (ADM 52/576) provides further detail of the chase and the nature of the vessels seized (Fig. 17):

> "S^r: John Balchen hoisted his flagg... at ½ past 5 d^o: came up w^th: the Chase which prov'd to be 2 English Privateers and 6 s^e: of French Marcht: ships – from Cape Franceis Laden w^th: Sugar, Coffee, and Indigo, where taken by ye fleet Viz –
> Le Intrepide ¬.. by ye Captain
> Le Flore ...... Augusta
> La Laurence .. Hampton Court
> Le Bons Enfant . Ditto

> Le Monarch ..... Dutch
> Le Siren .... Dutch"

The captain's log of the *Augusta* (ADM 52/537) confirmed that the master of the "Flora" was Reymard Challiblier, whose 250-ton, 24-gun ship was bound from Cape François to Nantes with a crew of 40 men and a cargo of sugar and indigo. The master's log of the *Duke* related that the four prizes were accompanied to shore by the *Hampton Court,* which departed from the fleet on Saturday 18 August. The skirmish took place around 40 leagues west of Land's End, but seems to have continued after this initial capture. The *Daily Advertiser* of 23 August 1744 (No. 4316) thus informed its eager readers that:

> "Letters from on board the Sunderland, Man of, belonging to Sir John Balchen's Squadron, dated the 18th instant, in the Latitude 45.56, mention, that they had taken six Ships from Martinico, and were in Pursuit of four more, which they were in Hopes of coming up with; and that Ship which the Sunderland boarded had a great Quantity of Money on board...'

While the *Hampton Court* sailed home, both Balchin's fleet and other British squadrons continued to round on the enemy trade. The *Baltimore* carried into Lisbon a rich ship from Bordeaux with 14 guns and 90 men, and "There was found in one of the Hogheads of Sugar taken out of the Martinico Ship taken by the Dartmouth-Galley, about 7000 Dollars, which had been conceal'd" (*Daily Advertiser,* 25 August 1744). Meanwhile, from Balchin's original fleet "The Princess Amelia, Capt. Jandine, took a French Felucca of Malta, bound for the Streights from the Levant, who took out 1,000 l. in Specie; and the Ship, ransomed for 70,000 Livres, is since taken by the Oxford Man of War" (*London Evening-Post,* 28-30 August 1744). The additional prizes that the *Hampton Court* claimed, as listed on 28 August (ADM 106/993/115), were the *Jason, Duc Penthuise, Le Mars, Le Solide, St. Francois, Le Vestal, Trois Soirs* and *Jenette* (Fig. 14). The circumstances under which this English man-of-war took these vessels – on the way back to England after leaving Balchin's fleet or in a second rapid cruise thereafter – remains unclarified.

Back home, the question of prize possession was heating up. The *Hampton Court* had reached port, seemingly with the additional prizes it captured after departing Balchin's fleet, and the Dutch Commodore Baccherst had quickly traveled to town "from the Dutch Squadron now with Sir John Balchen's Fleet, in Order to settle some Disputes

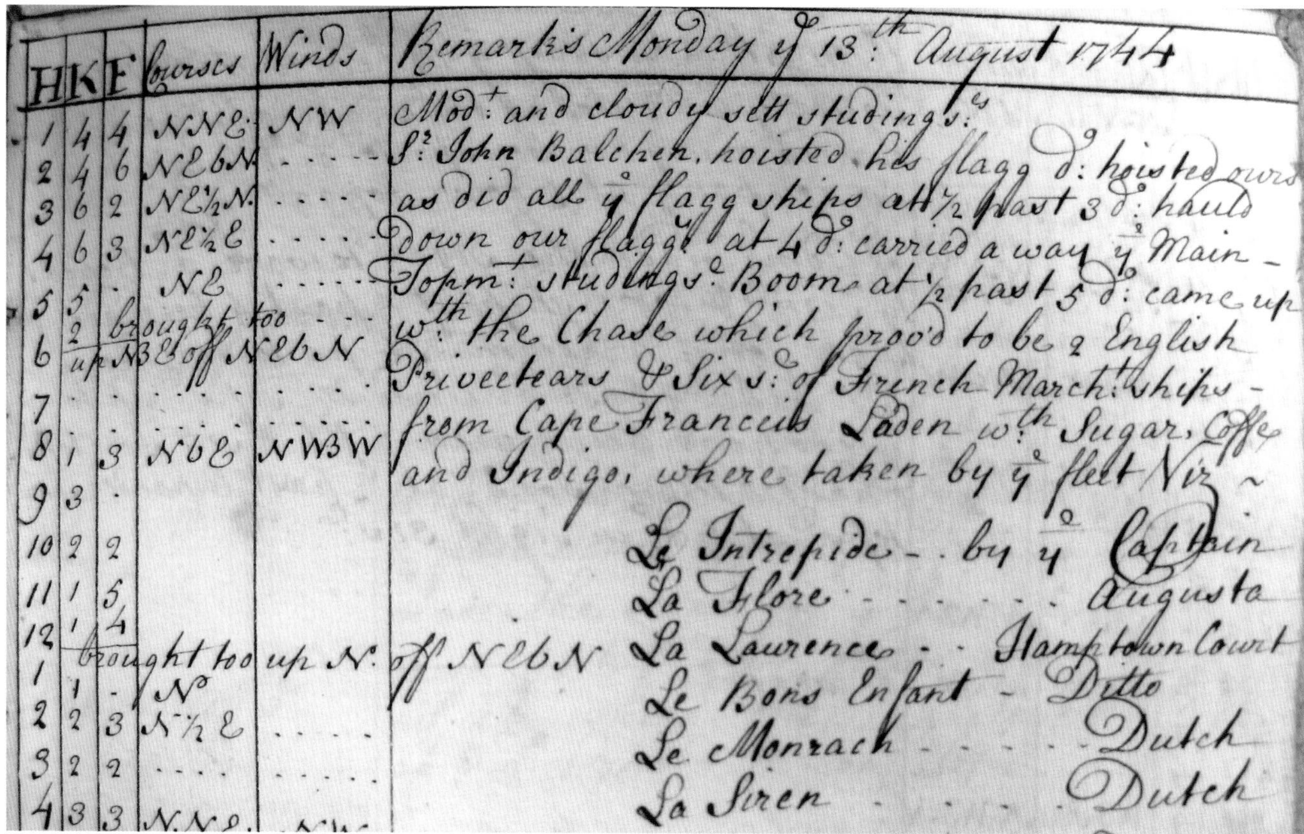

H	K	F	Courses	Winds	Remarks Monday ye 13th August 1744
1	4	4	NNE	NW	Mod: and cloudy sett studings:
2	4	6	NEbN	....	Sr John Balchen hoisted his flagg d: hoisted ours
3	6	2	NE½N	....	as did all ye flagg ships at ½ past 3 d: hauld
4	6	3	NE½E	....	down our flagg at 4 d: carried a way ye Main -
5	5	.	NE	....	Topmt studdgs Boom at ½ past 5 d: came up
	2	brought too			wth the Chase which prood to be 2 English
6	up N3E off			NEbN	Priveetears & Six s: of French Marchtships -
7	.	.		....	from Cape Francois Laden wth Sugar, Coffe
8	1	3	NbE	NWbW	and Indigo, where taken by ye fleet Viz ~
9	3	.			Le Intrepide - by ye Captain
10	2	2			La Flore .... Augusta
11	1	5			La Laurence .. Hampton Court
12	1	4			
	brought too	up N:	off NEbN		Le Bons Enfant - Ditto
1	1	-	N°		
2	2	3	N½E	....	Le Monrach ..... Dutch
3	2	2	....	....	
4	3	3	NNE.		La Siren ..... Dutch

Fig. 17. Entry in the master's log of the Duke *(ADM 52/576) for the chase of the French prizes caught by Admiral Balchin's fleet on 10 August 1744.*

between some of our Men of War, two Dutch Ships, and one of our Privateers, about the taking the two Martinico Ships, which struck to all the aforesaid Ships one after another" (*Daily Advertiser*, 31 August 1744). The implication is that the allies were concerned about being short-changed of potential prize money.

Following admiralty law, the hatches of these prizes would have been sealed until British customs officers could formally assess their contents. The wait was well worthwhile because "In rummaging the Tessier, a Martinico Ship, taken by the Hampton Court and the Chester Men of War, there have been found conceal'd in the Ballast 28,000 Dollars and two Casks of Gold, reckon'd 25,000 l." (*Penny London Post*, 31 August - 3 September 1744). More joy followed: "We hear there were found on board one of the St. Domingo Ships, that struck to the Dutch Men of War along with Admiral Balchen, above 60,000 Pieces of Eight" (*London Evening-Post*, 4-6 September 1744). Towards the end of September "On examining the Le Lux del Francis, a French Prize, taken by his Majesty's Ships the Dreadnought and Hampton Court [both of Balchin's fleet], there was found conceal'd in the Ballast five Bags off Dollars, valued at 12000l." (*Penny London Post*, 17-19 September 1744).

Back at sea the blitz on trade continued unabated. From Balchin's fleet the *Jersey* man-of-war took into Gibraltar two Spanish ships bound from Bordeaux to Toulon (*Daily Post*, 3 September 1744). Coincidentally, a merchant vessel also called the *Victory* "of 450 Tons, from Martinico for Marseilles, laden with white Sugar, Coffee, Cacao, &c. was taken the 17th of July, by his Majesty's Ship the Guernsey, and sent into Leghorn. This Prize is thought to be worth 40000 l. Sterling" (*Daily Advertiser*, 13 September 1744).

Although these few weeks give the impression of British successes, these were tempered by proportionate ship seizures by the Spanish and French. Around 31 August 1744 reports from Cartagena filtered home of nine Dutch ships "laden with Ammunition for the English Fleet" taken in the Straits of Gibraltar, including a "large Sum of Money [that] was found on board these Ships hid in the Powder Barrels, which 'tis said, was design'd for the Court of *Turin*" (*Daily Advertiser*, 15 September 1744). On the very day that the *Victory* was lost in a storm on 5 October, dispatches from Paris confirmed that the Brest squadron had taken two English warships and 14 transports laden with provisions and ammunition for the Mediterranean fleet (*Daily Advertiser*, 8 October 1744).

Admiral Balchin's fleet would have clearly benefited financially from the prizes captured early in his cruise to Lisbon. The extent to which Sir John was personally concerned with monetary windfalls remains a matter of debate. If the *Penny London Post* of 12 November 1744 was faithful to reality, then the battle-hardened admiral had his eye on just one goal at Gibraltar after safely escorting the liberated victualing convoy into the Mediterranean towards Admiral Matthews – defeating the enemy:

> "The late brave and worthy Sir John Balchen, a little before he left the Mediterranean, was told by an Officer as a Piece of good News, that M. Torres was expected on that Coast; to which the gallant old Man answer'd, very briskly, *Believe me To-, I had rather fight* Six French *Men of War than carry Six of the richest* Galleons *to* Britain."

These were brave words: Torres' squadron was convoying 16 million pieces of eight. Nevertheless, these are the last recorded words of Sir John Balchin, Admiral of HMS *Victory*, before his flagship sank in the western English Channel on 5 October 1744.

8. The Life of *La Marquise de Tourny*

The absence of any documentation for *La Marquise de Tourny*, whose wreck Odyssey Marine Exploration discovered at Site 33c (Cunningham Dobson, 2011), within records at the Public Records Office or in any captured prize lists in the UK, including the detailed entries in the *Gentleman's Quarterly*, strongly suggests that the ship escaped British privateers and warships during the course of its life. By contrast, both its sister and brother corsairs, *Le Marquis de Tourny* and *Le Grand Marquis de Tourny*, were captured: the former in 1744 and 1748 and the latter in 1757.[2] The documentation for these ships provides the most opportune means of reconstructing the routine of *La Marquise de Tourny* in her capacity as an armed private merchant vessel.

Like *Le Marquis de Tourny* it is highly probable that the sister ship ventured to the Americas to supply the French colonies of Quebec and further afield to the West Indies (Fig. 20). *Le Marquis de Tourny* was captured by the *London* privateer and taken into Portsmouth on 23 April 1748, where it was boarded by customs officers. The processing of the cargo evidently took some considerable time because the cargo was only advertized by 'sale by the candle' in the *General Advertiser* on 3 August 1748 and was listed in the following order as consisting of (Fig. 18):

- Brandies, bales of linen, cottons, rattines, blankets, canvas and vitry
- Men and women's shoes

For *SALE* by the *CANDLE*,
At the Royal Exchange Coffee-house in Threadneedle-Street,
Sometime the latter End of August,

THE Cargoe of the *Marquis de Tourny*, taken by the *London* Privateer, *J[illegible] [illegible]* Commander, as it now lies at Guernsey, and there to be delivered, consisting of various Goods, suited for the Guinea, West-India, and New-England Trade, as

Brandies, Bales of Linnen, Cottons, Rattines, Blankets, Canvas, Vitry.

Men and Wemens Shoes
Silk and mill'd Hose
Silk Handkerchiefs and Pieces of Cambrick, Gold and Silver Lace
Ribbons, Shirts, Hats
Playing Cards, Nails
Earthen and Glass Ware
180 Barrels Gunpowder
Cases of Glass

Candles, Salt
Pitch, Tar, Rozin, and Oyl
About 600 Brass and Copper-Kettles and Stewpans
264 Forrest or Fowling-Pieces
With a Set of new Sails, Cables and Cordage, intended for a 40 Gun Man of War building at Canada
And sundry other Goods.

Particulars of which will be published, and Catalogues delivered in due Time, at Mr. Peter Dobree's, Merchant in Guernsey (under whose Care the Cargoe is) at the Place of Sale, and by

D H. S. AUGIER, *Broker*.

Whalebone-Court, where Samples may be seen.

Fig. 18. An extensive advert for the sale of the cargo of the Marquis de Tourny *at the Royal Exchange Coffee-House in Threadneedle-street, London, at the end of August 1748* (General Advertiser, *3 August 1748*).

For SALE by the CANDLE,

At the Bath Coffee-house in Liverpool, on Tuesday the 20th Instant, at Eleven o'Clock in the Forenoon, the following Goods, being the entire Cargo of the Grand Marquis de Tournay, a French Prize from St. Domingo, taken by the Liverpool Privateer, Capt. William Hutchinson Commander, viz.

FOUR Hundred and ninety-four Hogsheads, 13 Tierces, 4 Barrels, Sugar; 19 Butts, 35 Hhds. 30 Tierces, 83 Barrels, Coffee; 2 Butts, 7 Hhds. 24 Tierces, 31 Barrels, 4 Anchors, Indigo; 22 whole Hides tann'd; 1117 half ditto; 8 1 half Tons Logwood.

Samples of the aforesaid Goods to be seen to the Time of Sale, at the following Places, viz.

In Liverpool at Mr. Hardware's, Merchant; in London, at No. 2, Dyers-Hall, Thames-street; and at the Place of Sale, the three preceding Days; where Catalogues may be had, and of

MARK HUDSON, Sworn Broker,
Laurence Pountney Lane, Cannon-street.

Fig. 19. An advert for the sale of the cargo of the Grand Marquis de Tournay *at the Bath Coffee-House, Liverpool, on Tuesday 20 September 1757 (*Public Advertiser, *9 September 1757).*

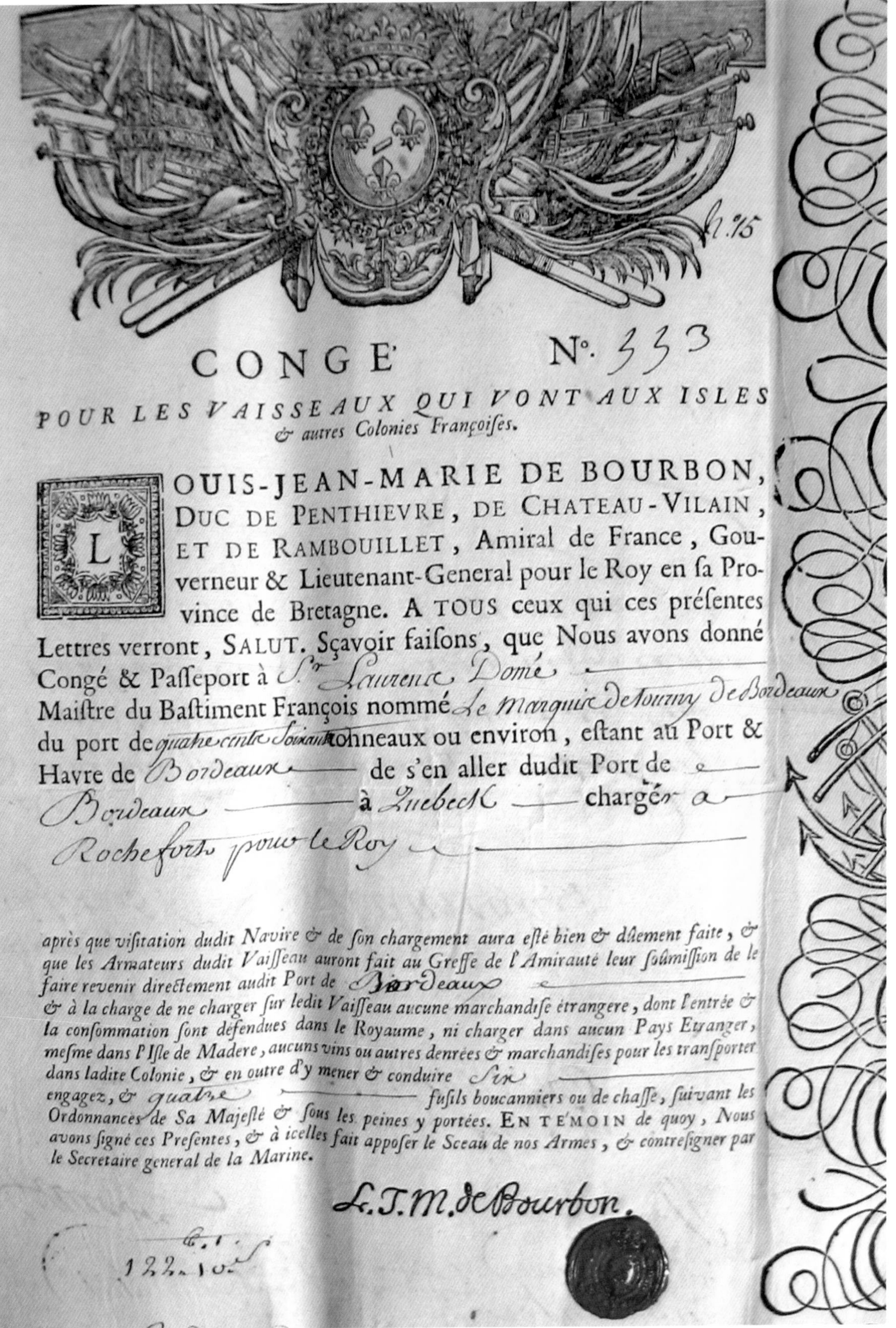

CONGE' N°. 333

POUR LES VAISSEAUX QUI VONT AUX ISLES
& autres Colonies Françoises.

LOUIS-JEAN-MARIE DE BOURBON, DUC DE PENTHIEVRE, DE CHATEAU-VILAIN, ET DE RAMBOUILLET, Amiral de France, Gouverneur & Lieutenant-General pour le Roy en sa Province de Bretagne. A TOUS ceux qui ces présentes Lettres verront, SALUT. Sçavoir faisons, que Nous avons donné Congé & Passeport à Sr Laurence Domé Maistre du Bastiment François nommé Le Marquis de Tourny de Bordeaux du port de quatre cents soixante tonneaux ou environ, estant au Port & Havre de Bordeaux de s'en aller dudit Port de Bordeaux à Quebeck chargér a Rochefort pour le Roy

après que visitation dudit Navire & de son chargement aura esté bien & dûement faite, & que les Armateurs dudit Vaisseau auront fait au Greffe de l'Amirauté leur soûmission de le faire revenir directement audit Port de Bordeaux *& à la charge de ne charger sur ledit Vaisseau aucune marchandise étrangere, dont l'entrée & la consommation sont défendues dans le Royaume, ni charger dans aucun Pays Etranger, mesme dans l'Isle de Madere, aucuns vins ou autres denrées & marchandises pour les transporter dans ladite Colonie, & en outre d'y mener & conduire* six *engagez, &* quatre *fusils boucanniers ou de chasse, suivant les Ordonnances de Sa Majesté & sous les peines y portées.* EN TEMOIN *de quoy, Nous avons signé ces Presentes, & à icelles fait apposer le Sceau de nos Armes, & contresigner par le Secretaire general de la Marine.*

L.J.M. de Bourbon.

122..10

Fig. 20. An export permit for the safe passage of the Marquis de Tourny to sail from Bordeaux to Quebec, dated 26 January 1748 (PRO HCA 32/129).

- Silk and mill'd hose
- Silk handkerchiefs and pieces of cambrick, gold and silver lace
- Ribbons, shorts and hats
- Playing cards and nails
- Earthen and glass ware
- 180 barrels gunpowder
- Cases of glass
- Candles and salt
- Pitch, tar, rozin and copper kettles and stewpans
- 264 forrest or fowling pieces
- A set of new sails, cables and cordage intended for a 40-gun man-of-war being built in Canada
- Sundry other goods

For unspecified reasons, *Le Marquis de Tourny* had been escorted to Guernsey. By coincidence, the cargo was put under the care of Mr. Peter Dobree, a local merchant and most likely a relative of Nicholas Dobree, who had informed the Admiralty of the discovery of wreckage from Balchin's *Victory* on the Channel Isles in October 1744 and who was the man who accused the Alderney lighthouse keeper of luring the ship to its fate by failing to keeps the lights burning. The auction advertisement states that cargo was to be shipped back to London for sale at the end of August at the Royal Exchange Coffee-house in Threadneedle Street.

The translated letter of marque seized with *Le Marquis de Tourny* leaves no doubt that despite its extensive commercial and State consignments, it was simultaneously a functioning privateer. The document's translation as part of condemning the ship as a prize in 1748 records that:

> "Louis-Jean-Marie de Bourbon, Duke of Penthievre, Governor and Lieutenant-General for the King in his Province of Brittany, Admiral of France, to all to whome these presents shall come, Greeting. We make known, that we have given leave to M. Lawrence Domé master and Cap[n] of the ship named *Le Marquis de Tourny* of Bordeaux of the burthen of four hundred sixty tons or there abouts, mounting twenty guns and no swivels, was lying in the harbour of Bordeaux to cause the said ship to be fitted out for war and trade to arm and provide her with all things necessary to load her with such goods as he shall think proper provided they are not prohibited of forbidden, to go and trade at Quebeck and other French colonies, and in so doing to make war upon the enemies of the State, upon all Rovers, Pirates, Robbers, lawless people and others who would hinder the Liberty of the Commerce of the King's subjects; he may also cruize upon the vessels, barks, and other shipping, as well French as foreign carrying on a foreign and prohibited trade to the French islands in America, to conquer them by force of arms, to take and carry them to the island, the nearest to the place where he shall have taken then prize, having first given the same bond as if he was fitted out for warr... we have signed these presents and have there unto caused the seal of our arms to be countersigned by the Secretary General of the Marine at Bordeaux cause the 26th of January 1748.
>
> Delivered at Bordeaux the 26th of January 1748 – Registered in the Registry of the Admiralty of Bordeaux the 26th of January 1748.
>
> L.J.M. de Bourbon
> By his most serene Highness Romieu [?]"

If the fate of *Le Marquis de Tourny* furnishes a partial mirror image of the kind of cargos *La Marquise de Tourny* would have transported during its lifetime out of Bordeaux, the capture of *Le Grand Marquis de Tourny* in 1757 inbound from St. Domingo offers insights into the kinds of commodities possibly shipped homeward. The cargo of the 1757 ship, captured by the *Liverpool* privateer, was advertized for sale in the *Public Advertiser* of 9 September 1757 at the Bath Coffee-house in Liverpool and consisted of (Fig. 19):

- 494 hogheads, 13 tierces, 4 barrels of sugar
- 19 butts, 35 hogsheads, 30 tierces and 83 barrels of coffee
- 3 butts, 7 hogsheads, 24 tierces, 31 barrels and 4 anshers of indigo
- 22 whole tanned hides
- 1,117 half-tanned hides
- 8.5 tons of logwood

This cargo typified homeward bound French merchant vessels. Sugar, coffee, indigo and logwood were common products of the colonies. Curiously, after the sale the auctioneers seem to have experienced troubles disposing of the purchased commodities. The *Public Advertiser* of 25 October 1757 recorded how:

> "The Managers of the Defiance private Ships of War, John Dyer, Commander, do hereby give Notice to the Purchasers of Goods by the Marquis de Tourney, the Jupiter, the Jeune Pierre, and the Nymph, who have not yet taken their Lots away, that if they do not do so in fourteen Days from this Day, the said Lots will be put up to Sale again, and the former Purchasers will be called upon, for any Expense or Loss that may arrive on that Occasion, agreeable to the Terms of Sale, and those who have taken away their Lots, and have not paid in their Money, will lose the Benefit of the Dscompt."

The comparative historical data for the Bordeaux-based

Le Marquis de Tourny and *Le Grand Marquis de Tourny* are crucial for reconstructing the possible cargo shipped by *La Marquise de Tourny* and its privateering history before she sank in the western English Channel. Within the constraints of the wreck's marine environment, consisting of shallow coarse sediments, almost all of the above organic produce – from cloth to foodstuffs – which comprised the majority of the shipments, would not be expected to be preserved in the archaeological record of Site 33c.

9. The Archaeology of the Privateer

Despite the vast numbers of privateers that blitzed the oceans of several continents during the War of the Austrian Succession, precious few of their wrecks have been discovered or recorded. In fact, privateer wrecks are restricted to the *Machault* off Canada, two corsairs lost off St. Malo and now *La Marquise de Tourny*. The other three sites display superior preservation that enables aspects of *La Marquise de Tourny*'s potential organic cargos and original character as a corsair to be more widely envisioned.

Little data are available about other wrecks of privateers, such as *La Charmante*, wrecked in the Bay of St. Malo, France, during a privateering expedition in November 1702. Limited fieldwork on the site, which includes deposits of wood, pottery, lead hull sheathing and 140 mainly copper coins, has been conducted by DRASSM (Douillez, 2005).

The wreck of the privateer *L'Alcide*, lost in Morlaix Bay, France, in 1747, is important due to its close date to *La Marquise de Tourny*. The 180-ton, 25m long and 9m wide corsair was built in St. Malo in 1746 and was armed with 20 cannon. Excavated over three campaigns from 1985-87, human remains were found and recorded on site alongside cannon, ceramic and pewter assemblages of kitchen and table wares, apothecary objects, grey and faience unguent bottles, parts of swords, a sounding lead, navigation tools and grey glass bottles from Normandy (Appriou and Bozellec, 1997; Bozellec and Jegou, 2005). The finds have not been scientifically published.

Significantly post-dating the War of the Austrian Succession, and thus excluded from this analysis, are several additional wrecks of privateers. These include the 170-ton *Defence* mounting 16 6-pounders, which participated in the Penobscot Expedition and was lost possibly on its maiden voyage on 14 August 1779 in the largest military and naval effort mounted by the Americans during the War of Independence (the fleet of 1,000 militia and 43 vessels also included 12 privateers). While retreating from besieging the British garrison of Majabagaduce, the *Defence* was lost in Stockton Harbor. As much as 40% of the vessel's structure is preserved in mud, including the stump of the foremast and the brick cooking stove with its copper cauldron still *in situ* (Switzer, 1998: 183). The possibility is currently being examined that the deep-sea 'Mardi Gras' wreck in the Gulf of Mexico was the American privateer *Rapid* lost in 1813 (Ford *et al.*, 2010: 95). Finally, the 67m-long, three-masted Confederate privateer the CSS *Alabama* lies in 58-60m off Cherbourg, where it was lost in 1864 (L'Hour, 2005b).

The following section focuses on the *Machault* in Canada's Gulf of St. Lawrence, the two La Natière wrecks off St. Malo and *La Marquise de Tourny* to examine whether it is feasible to refer to an archaeology of privateering through the composition of artifact assemblages, ship's structures and ordnance.

A. The Corsair Wrecks of St. Malo

Since 1999 DRASSM has been excavating two wrecks of French corsairs lost in depths of 9-19m and situated 20m apart at La Natière, 1 nautical mile from the fortification wall of St. Malo in northern Brittany (Fig. 21). Both sites are extremely well preserved, spread over an area of approximately 1,000 square meters (L'Hour and Veyrat, 2003a: 314), and have yielded an extraordinary volume and diversity of finds from part of the skeleton of a six month old monkey from Gibraltar to a three-pointed tricorn hat that once adorned a wooden figurehead and intact sections of both hulls. By the end of the 2003 excavation season a total of 1,666 artifacts had been recovered from both wrecks: 1,294 from La Natière 1 and 372 from La Natière 2 (L'Hour and Veyrat, 2003a: 315; 2004: 34). The smaller volume of finds on the second site is a result of 18th-century salvage. Two more as yet unidentified wreck sites off St. Malo, La Natière 3 and La Natière 4 (L'Hour and Veyrat, 2005a), promise the continuation of fresh knowledge in future generations.

The wreck of La Natière 1 consists of the starboard side of a ship preserved from the keel up to the gun deck. Dendrochronological dating reveals a construction date after the winter of 1702-03 (L'Hour and Veyrat, 2005a: 246). Although as yet unconfirmed in the academic literature, DRASSM has announced that the site is identifiable as the wreck of the 300-ton royal frigate *La Dauphine*, which was built in Le Havre in 1703 before King Louis IV entrusted the ship to private merchants to fit out as a privateer. *La Dauphine* was returning from an Atlantic campaign when it was lost at the entrance to the port of St. Malo on 11 December 1704.

The starboard side of the ship wrecked at La Natière 2 survives from the keel up to the second deck and has

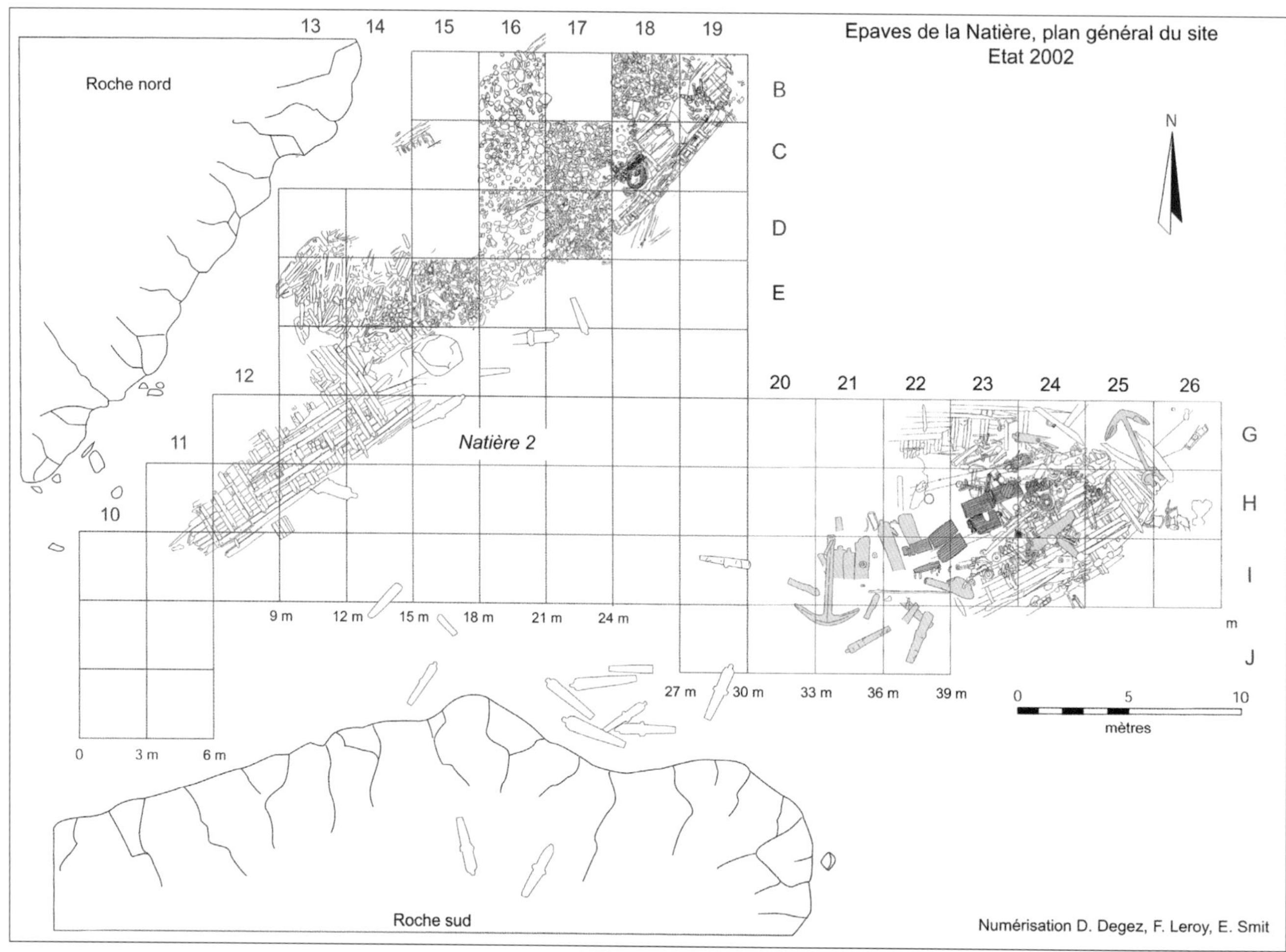

Fig. 21. Site plan of the wrecks of La Natière 1 and 2 off St. Malo, France. Both served as corsairs and have been identified respectively as the La Dauphine *(1704) and* L'Aimable Grenot *(1749). From: L'Hour and Veyrat, 2003b: 107.*

been identified as the frigate *L'Aimable Grenot* lost on 6 May 1749 at the entrance to St. Malo. Built in Granville, Nomandy, in 1747, this large frigate of 400 tons was fitted out as a privateer until the end of the War of the Austrian Succession in 1748, after which she traded with Spain and was en route for Cadiz when she sank.

Although La Natière 1 (*La Dauphine*, 1704) precedes *La Marquise de Tourny* by a generation, it is nevertheless a key comparative site because it is unusually well preserved and was still operating as a privateer when it was lost. Wrecked in 1749, La Natière 2 (*L'Aimable Grenot*) is precisely contemporary with the wreck of *La Marquise de Tourny* and would have similarly retained an element of its original domestic assemblage, as well as its principal ordnance, alongside its commercial cargo, at the time of loss.

The wreck of *La Dauphine* is one of the most extraordinarily well-preserved Colonial wrecks ever recorded. Organic remains range from the hull itself to a coconut, bundles of rope, an excessive 24 brooms, large areas of basketry, numerous carpenters tools, wooden buttons still attached to woolen cloth, oak barrels composed of nine staves, leather shoes, an English gunner's rule inscribed with a date of 1648 and bearing the initials 'IC' (thought to relate to John Chatfield, a manufacturer of scientific equipment active in London from 1630-50: L'Hour and Veyrat, 2005b), double and single wooden sheave blocks, a cannon axle and truck, wooden dice and a remarkable smoking pipe protected within a pistol-shaped wooden case.

Alongside the sailors' wooden bowls and spoons, the captain and higher ranking crew used pewter wares, including 19 plates found in the 2000 and 2002 seasons, plus an additional 20 further examples discovered in 2003. Some are inscribed with the maker's mark of Joseph Hoodges of London and dates of 1691 and '170?' (presumably for 1700). The ship carried a bronze mortar and pestle, notably identical to that from the *Machault*, and associated with an apothecary kit, and bowls, a sieve and cauldron, all made of copper. Faunal analysis reveals that the crew consumed beef, pork, lamb, chicken, birds and rabbit. Wine was also apparently readily available, and 25 glass onion bottles were found in the 2003 season. The pottery assemblage includes a Dutch 'Bellarmine' jug and the ship was carrying a set of 70 merchants' weights when she sank.

A 4m-long iron anchor with v-shaped arms is associated with the wreck of *La Dauphine*, and its iron cannon set side by side along the keel resemble possible saleable ballast. The hull had been protected in places with lead sheathing, and seven sheets examined measure between 29.5 x 26cm and 33 x 28cm and 0.35-0.5cm thick. A grappling hook may once have been used for boarding enemy craft (L'Hour and Veyrat, 2001: 55, 91, 93, 94, 96, 100, 101; 2003b: 42-3, 57, pl. 4-25).

Despite a lower volume of finds, the wreck of *L'Aimable Grenot* (1749) is equally fascinating as an example of a well-preserved ship launched as a privateer. In many ways, and despite the 45-year gap between the two sites, the material culture of La Natière 2 is not dissimilar to the earlier corsair. Again the sailors dined off wooden bowls, while higher status pewter wares are represented by spoons, eight plates and two candlesticks. The ship was again carrying an apothecary's kit and a diverse collection of white faience unguent pots from Rouen, onion, case and elongated glass bottles, including green glass *flaçons* with corks in place comparable to the example from *La Marquise de Tourny.*

Bottles and stoneware jars originated in Normandy and small tripod pots and pitchers from Saintonge in southwest France. The ship's galley hearth bricks measured 22.5-23 cm long, 10.5-11cm wide and were 5cm thick. The wood remains included a 15 x 5.5m section of exposed hull, a Christian cross, combs, buttons, pump wheels, carpenters tools and sheave blocks. *L'Aimable Grenot* was stocked with a complement of bronze merchants' weights at the time of her loss. Parts of pistols have been recorded and the site is associated with an iron anchor with bow-shaped arms and its wooden stock still in place (L'Hour and Veyrat, 2002: 23, 35, 40, 44, 47, 57, 95, 96, 98-103).

By far the most graphic point of comparison between the wrecks of *La Marquise de Tourny* and *L'Aimable Grenot* is a 1m-high mound of iron ingots restricted to the western end of La Natière 2, covering an area of 6.5 x 5.5m and associated with granite, flint, calcerous and black quartzite ballast stones. The site contains between 600 and 1,000 ingots with an estimated total mass of 30-50 tons. Almost 100 ingots have been extracted from their dense concretions and a wide diversity of dimensions identified from 42-92cm long, 9-19cm wide, mainly 7-9cm tall and weighing 25-110kg (Figs. 22-23). The ingots bear molded inscriptions on their top surfaces, which read 'Step.^{n}. Onion', 'Step.^{n}. Onion 1746', 'POTUXENT 1746' and 'POTUXENT 1747' (L'Hour and Veyrat, 2002: 27-31).

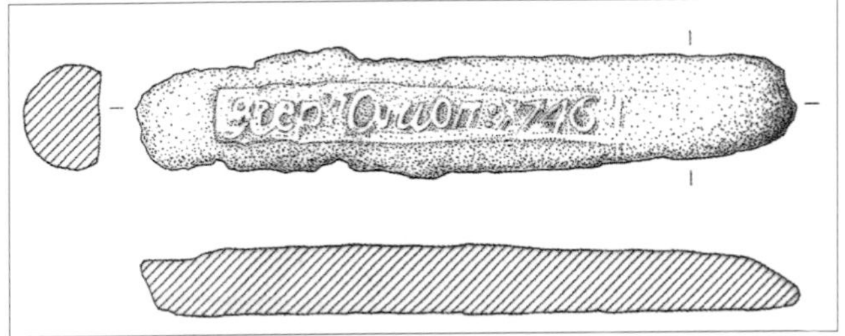

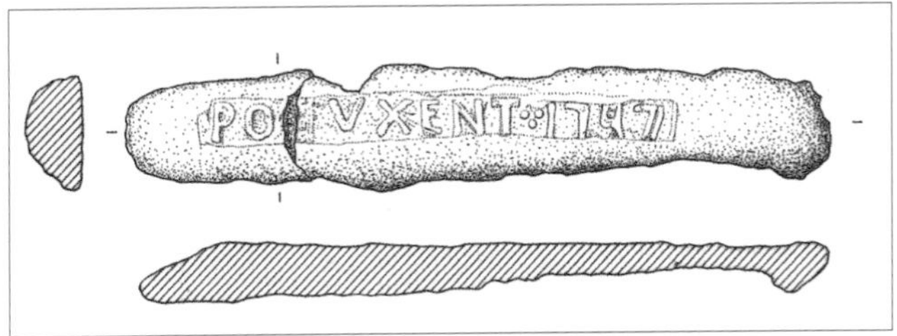

Figs. 22-23. Examples of up to 50 tons of iron ingots transported as saleable ballast on the wreck of L'Aimable Grenot *(1749) off St. Malo, France. Some bear the maker's marks 'Step.n. Onion 1746' and 'POTUXENT 1747', revealing the source of manufacture in Maryland. From: L'Hour and Veyrat, 2002: 88-89, nos. 977 & 980.*

This ballast on *L'Aimable Grenot* originated in the same American state as the 30 tons of inscribed iron ballast carried by the 499-ton English East Indiaman the *Griffin,* wrecked in the Sulu Sea, the Philippines, in 1761, which derived from the 'Elk Ridge' foundry in Maryland (Goddio, 1999: 95-7). The iron was originally processed in the Patuxent Iron Works along the Patuxent river in southern Baltimore and in the foundry of Stephen Onion, established in 1745 along the Gunpowder river in north Baltimore.

Impurities in English pig iron restricted its use to non-commercial ships' ballast, but Colonial expansion led to the emergence of an English-backed iron industry in Maryland in 1715. Five years later a group of English investors, including Stephen Onion, founded the Principio Company and Principio Iron Works. By 1726 eight furnaces and nine forges were operating across Maryland, which in 1736 were exporting 2,458 tons of iron. Notably, seven iron ingots recovered from the French corsair the *Machault* were also stamped 'Step.n. Onion 1746' and are typologically identical to those on La Natière 2. Three others are marked 'PATUXENT 1755', while another two stamped '1755 YORK' were probably manufactured in York County along the Susquehannah river near the Gunpowder and Patuxent rivers in northern Maryland. An estimated 90% of the iron ingots processed in the foundries of Maryland were used for ballasting English ships returning to Europe with cargos of American tobacco (L'Hour and Veyrat, 2002: 27-34).

L'Aimable Grenot was the third in a successive line of corsairs to be fitted out for privateering during the War of the Austrian Succession by Léonor Couraye Duparc. The *Charles Grenot* was wrecked in 1745, after which *Le Grand Grenot* was equipped with funds raised from merchants in Rouen, Granville, St. Malo, St. Brieuc and Morlaix and set out from St. Malo for its first privateering campaign with 40 pieces of artillery on 3 March 1746. Due to its great success in seizing prizes, a third ship, *L'Aimable Grenot,* was launched on 29 January 1747 and undertook two privateering campaigns before the end of the war a year later. The third 390-ton corsair was manned by a crew of 374 and armed with 40 cannon of 4-8 pounders, 250 muskets and 150 sabres. Between the ship's two privateering campaigns of 18 August and 18 November 1748 at least 12 cannon were removed, and the end of the war resulted in a further decrease in the size of its ordnance (L'Hour and Veyrat, 2002: 69-72). *L'Aimable Grenot* was seemingly lost en route to Cadiz on a commercial venture.

B. The Machault

The *Machault* was originally another example of a Bordeaux corsair that sank in the Restigouche river off Chaleur Bay in the Gulf of St. Lawrence, Canada, in July 1760 and was extensively excavated by the Underwater Research Unit of Parks Canada Archaeological Research Division between 1969 and 1972 (Fig. 24). Submerged within soft, silt sediments, an extraordinary variety of organic artifacts, tools, munitions and hull survived.

The 500-ton *Machault* had sailed for Canada in April 1760 with king's supplies, similar to the dual role of the *Marquis de Tourny* in 1747 and undoubtedly its sister ship too, as part of an attempt to retake Quebec – lost in 1759 – from the English. The French fleet was attacked by the English 74- to 20-gun warships the *Fame, Dorsetshire, Achilles, Repulse* and *Scarborough*. The *Machault* exploded and burned on 8 July 1760. Its demise marked the last naval engagement on the high seas between France and England during the Seven Years' War, as well as the last major naval encounter between these two European powers on the North American continent (Zacharchuk, 1972; Zacharchuk and Waddell, 1986: 15-19).

The *Machault* was launched in Bayonne in 1758 as a privateer and was later refitted as a convoy vessel. It measured 39-41m in length and was 11m wide and 5.5m high between the bilges and the deck. Frames, floor timbers and inner and outer planking were built of red oak, while at 9cm outer strakes were especially thick to protect the hull from enemy fire (Sullivan, 1986: 11).

An extremely diverse collection of artifacts and hull remains were recovered from the *Machault,* which (although not strictly operating as a corsair in 1760 but as a heavily armed frigate transporting commodities and naval stores on behalf of the king) offers a rare insight into the archaeology of French privateers operating in Canada at the end of the French Colonial era. Food, ammunition, pitch and nails were stored in 29cm-high oak kegs bound with two sets of seven willow hoops fixed to each end of barrels with iron nails. Other goods were shipped in rectangular oak chests measuring 130.6 x 53.5cm. Non-bulk commodities were discovered still wrapped in bales. Soft packages were bound with cord or metal hoops to which 2.5cm-diameter lead seals were fixed. The hand-knit woolens, a wool tuque, wool stockings, silk ribbon bows, a 17m length of rolled silk ribbon, a roll of twill-woven wool and cotton are key physical parallels to the cargo forms shipped to Canada a decade earlier.

The wreck of the *Machault* also yielded numerous shoe and knee buckles, a French silver garter buckle, cuff links, brass or pewter buttons and almost 500 new men's shoes. The contents of the carpenter's chest and a caulking mallet with spare heads and associated caulking irons were retrieved, alongside brass candle holders and snuffers, bone and horn hair combs, wrought-iron curling tongs, a pewter syringe, a bronze metal and pestle, metallic Dutch tobacco boxes engraved with biblical scenes, smoking pipes attributed to R. Tippet of Bristol, other spurred TD examples, and a third category made by Gottfried Aust of North Carolina, whose bowls were molded into the form of human effigies.

The wreck contained several dozen intact cooking pots, green-glazed French ceramic pitchers, French and English glass bottles, pewter beakers, almost 500 French ceramic bowls and plates stacked in the hold, plus a cargo of English white salt-glazed stoneware bowls, Chinese porcelain bowls, London tea wares and Chinese eggshell porcelain tea bowls and saucers. Bricks from the galley structure were found still mortared together.

Extensive standing rigging survives, such as an iron futtock plate attached to a three-hole deadeye, wooden sheaves and a mast truck. A one frame wide cross-section of the hull was cut away and lifted for exhibition, as well as a length of keel/keelson with some 10ft of framing and ceiling planking attached desired to display the system of cargo stowage inside, plus "any pieces, such as the rudder and stern assembly, which were considered of interest". A total of 40 tons of structural material was lifted from the wreck of the *Machault* (Zacharchuk and Waddell, 1986: 53). A myrtle broom may once have been used to sweep the decks clean.

Privateers were equipped with extensive sets of ordnance, and the original list of 1757 for the fitting of the *Machault* referred to a complement of 24 12-livre deck cannon, two six-livre guns for the forecastle, six swivel

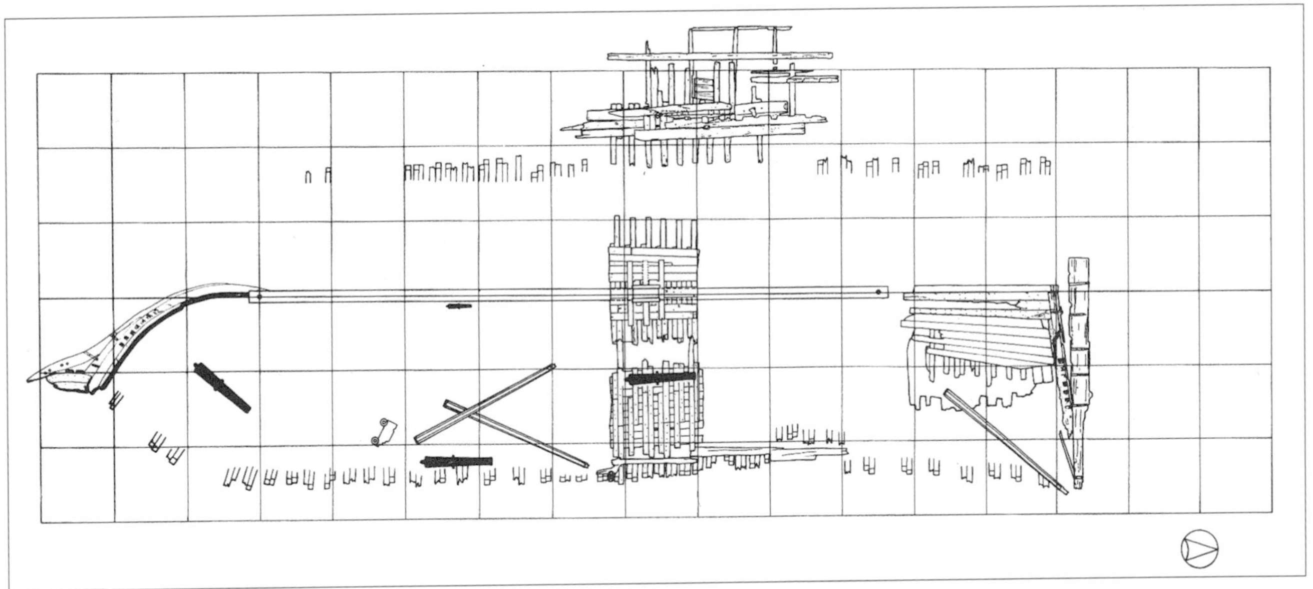

Fig. 24. Schematic site plan of the wreck of the French corsair-built Machault, *blown up by English forces in the Gulf of St. Lawrence, Canada, in 1760. From: Zacharchuk and Waddell, 1986: 38.*

guns, 800 12-livre cannonballs, 120 hand grenades, plus muskets, sabres and boarding axes. Extensive ordnance covered the wreck. The small arms included a minimum of 11 French *fusils grenadiers* and 10 Model 1733-34 cavalry pistols, a minimum of 10 sabres and seven *à la mousquetaire* swords for hand-to-hand combat, at least two British Long Land Pattern muskets, plus scabbards. Especially evocative of boarding parties are the site's blunderbuss, an iron hand grenade with a wooden fuse and an intact wrought-iron boarding axe.

The *Machault* fielded 26 guns when it was built, but may have been carrying 32 cannon when it sank in 1760. The three 12-livre cast-iron cannon lifted each weigh 1,364kg. Two are identical and measure 2.77m in length with bores of 12cm diameter and, precisely like the swivel cannon from *La Marquise de Tourny*, were incised with *fleur de lis* on the first reinforce, the second reinforce and muzzle parts of the tube (Fig. 25). Two identical iron swivel guns were recovered, each 92cm long, with bores of 3.54cm and 3.89cm. One was found *in situ* along the starboard side of the ship towards the bows with its yoke still attached to the trunnions. One cannon carriage, two trucks and a swivel gun yoke completed the cannon-related fittings recovered (Bryce, 1984: 42, 47).

Some 553 iron cannonballs were lifted from the wreck, 56 multiple-shot iron and lead balls, thousands of lead pellets, six hand grenades, 58 mortar bombs, 53 bar shots, 15 star shot, three linked shot and eight canvas ammunition bags. Of the cannonballs, 538 are French and 15 possibly British, of which 304 are 12-livre cannonballs (11.3-11.7cm diam, 5.5kg each). A further 48 of the cannonballs (8.8-9.3cm diam, each 3kg weight), and 186 four-livre balls (7.8-8.0cm, each 1.9kg), would have been used for the swivels, of which 94 were cast with *fleur de lis* symbols. The iron bar, link and star shot was designed to bring down the rigging and sails of enemy ships. The

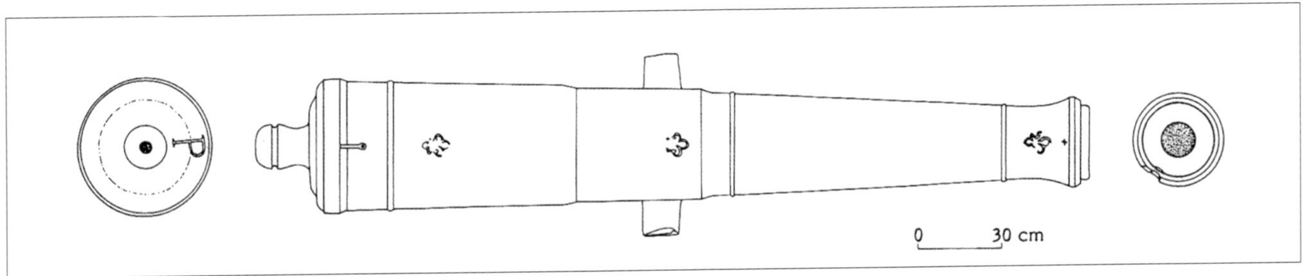

Fig. 25. A French iron 12-livre cannon from the wreck of the Machault *(1760). Note the* fleur de lis *decoration. From: Bryce, 1984: 42, no. 56.*

Machault also carried hollow cast-iron mortar bombs filled with gunpowder for firing from mortars. These presumably served as part of the cargo of naval stores (Bryce, 1984: 51).

C. La Marquise de Tourny

La Marquise de Tourny operated under comparable geopolitical circumstances to the *Machault* and *L'Aimable Grenot*. All three corsairs were built in France and sought out enemy prizes and carried commercial cargos either during the War of the Austrian Succession or within 15 years of its cessation. While *La Marquise de Tourny* had a burden of 460 tons, *L'Aimable Grenot* was smaller at 390 tons and the 500-ton *Machault* slightly larger.

The two *fleur de lis* symbols coarsely incised onto the reinforces of the recovered swivel gun from Site 33c are stylistically comparable to the decoration on a 12-pounder iron cannon and cannonballs from the *Machault* (Bryce, 1984: 42, 51) and on the bronze merchants' weights from *L'Aimable Grenot* (L'Hour and Veyrat, 2002: 99) and may be considered a calling card of French naval privateers and presumably warships too. The swivel gun recovered by Odyssey from Site 33c is stylistically comparable to those from the *Machault* and very similar in size: 85.5cm long with a bore width of 4.0cm compared to 92cm long and with bores of 3.54cm and 3.89cm for the 1760 wreck off Canada. Blue *flaçon* glass bottles are represented on all three shipwrecks and patches of lead hull sheathing are registered on both Site 33c and on the wreck of *La Dauphine*. Such hull protection typifies all classes of craft of the era and is in no way specific to privateers.

The most notable and unexpected point of archaeological similarity on all three of the contemporary French corsairs is the most mundane: the presence of American iron ballast ingots. The possibility that the iron ballast on *La Marquise de Tourny* originated in Maryland, as confirmed on the wrecks of the *L'Aimable Grenot* and the *Machault*, is strong but requires archaeological confirmation through the recovery and study of examples from Site 33c. This pattern, however, would favor the presence of a final voyage commencing in the Americas for *La Marquise de Tourny*, a commercial sphere that her brother ship, *Le Marquis de Tourny*, had operated within in 1748. Considering the location of the shipwreck, it is also not inconceivable that *La Marquise de Tourny* was heading for St. Malo itself when disaster struck.

In all other respects, the wreck of *La Marquise de Tourny* is a very poor relative to the other sites discussed due to its extremely low level of archaeological preservation: Site 33c displays almost no hull survival, the cargo and domestic assemblage are no longer present, and the absence of extensive clusters of cannonballs, shot and lead is equally puzzling. Not only are no organic objects present, but no ceramic vessels or even sherds were encountered, other than a few fragments of durable thick galley brick. The single neck of a blue glass *flaçon* and a couple of patches of lead hull sheathing recorded on the surface of the site and in several soundings are an extremely low volume of finds.

Several interlocking reasons for the specific formation of Site 33c may be proposed. First, the absence of the wide variety of cannonball sizes and small arms registered on the two wrecks off La Natière and on the *Machault* favor the view that *La Marquise de Tourny* was not operating as a corsair at the time of her loss, which implies a date beyond the end of the War of the Austrian Succession in 1748 and before the Seven Years War in 1754. Unlike the *Machault*, *La Marquise de Tourny* is unlikely to have been carrying naval supplies for a French war initiative, but was still equipped with her ordnance. The abundance of iron ingots points to an incoming journey from the Americas with an organic cargo, which has completely deteriorated today.

Second, the shallow sediments, localized at an average of 15cm and maximum of 40cm, do not favor high levels of preservation on Site 33c. However, the absence of multiple pottery and glass sherds, which would be anticipated to be at least detected typically wedged in crevices between ordnance and ballast, is anomalous. Despite the significant depth of Site 33c in around 80m, the site formation typifies the most highly dynamic of shallow-water sites located on rocky seabeds, where currents heavily scramble wreckage. Obviously this is invalid in the current case, which leads to the conclusion that the site has been disturbed by some other phenomenon.

Site 33c's formation is most rationally explicable through extensive post-depositional disturbance caused by the offshore fishing industry. Fishing net fragments are snagged on concretions and cannon, and were identified buried within the shipwreck's matrix. Two of the cannon, C-01 and C-22, lie over 35m away from the site and may have been dragged by trawlers. Vessel Monitoring Systems data recorded by satellite observed 109 fishing vessels operating within 1,000m of Site 33c and 27 within 500m of the wreck just for the period between 2000 and 2008: 72.5% beam trawlers, 10.1% lobster/crab potters and 4.6% scallop dredges. The wreck of *La Marquise de Tourny* thus serves as another unfortunate example of the serious impacts inflicted on internationally important shipwrecks in the western English Channel. Reconstructions of the anatomy and history of this badly preserved wreck rely heavily on comparative archaeology and historical sources.

10. Conclusion

The archaeology and image of the world of the corsair and the privateer are often misunderstood. C.B. Norman succinctly summarized the exaggerated perception in *The Corsairs of France* (London, 1887: 3):

> "He is generally depicted as a rollicking dare-devil whose waistbelt was a perfect armoury and whose pockets were full of doubloons. Eschewing nearer seas he sailed the Spanish main, seized all craft that came within his reach, treated his prisoners with the utmost generosity, sometimes with the most refined cruelty, and generally ended his career by being compelled to 'walk the plank' after falling a victim to a ship of war, which disguised as a 'Quaker' enticed the unsuspecting Corsair alongside her well-manned decks. Nothing can be more erroneous. The Corsair was a recognized and important factor in the wars of the past centuries, when naval estimates assumed more modest proportions than they do in this the later quarter of the Nineteenth Century. The rules which governed his conduct were clear and well defined."

Throughout the War of the Austrian Succession privateers on all sides disrupted shipping and enriched their crews and the sentiments of the *Observator* of 10 June 1702 remained valid four decades later: privateering was still one of the "props of this island, being both so useful & necessary to trade and navigation, and to the poor of these kingdoms" (Starkey, 1990: 253). In the final analysis following nine years of prize hunting, however, the concept of privateering proved to be a short-term, false economy. Neither side enhanced its colonial trade and each party received very heavy losses.

Anson's expeditionary force that circumnavigated the world to attack Spanish ports and vessels and ultimately to seek the world's richest contemporary treasure ship resulted in unacceptable fatalities and would be the last time the Royal Navy dispatched warships to try and cripple trade by hunting down individual ships. Of the six men-of-war that began the epic voyage, bearing 236 guns and manned by a crew of 1,510 people (Hervey, 1750: 184), increased to a total of 1,939 with the hands on two victualling ships, only the *Centurion* made it home to England. Some 1,051 of the crew died of disease and exposure, including all 500 Chelsea pensioners that the Admiralty had unwisely imposed on Anson (Pack, 1960: 20).

The voyage of the *Centurion* had little political, strategic or economic influence on the outcome of the war. The capture of the *Cobadonga* may have cheered the hearts of England, but hardly turned the political tide. While the public lapped up the story of the venture, the sailors were even forced to go to Court for a share of the prize. The supernumeraries who had been commanded by superior officers to abandon their own warships and join the *Centurion* were by law not entitled to the money from the Spanish galleon because they did not comprise the official complement of the *Centurion*. For all their hard work, they came away with nothing despite appealing to the House of Lords. As one of the supernumeraries wrote, "we had more terrible engagements in the courts of law than we ever had on the high seas" (Heaps, 1973: 253).

Product	1722-1724	1752-1754
Coffee	£123,000	£53,000
Cotton	£45,000	£56,000
Dyestuffs	£155,000	£98,000
Oil	£26,000	£43,000
Silk	£50,000	£94,000
Skins & Hides	£34,000	£46,000
Sugar	£928,000	£1,302,000
Tea	£116,000	£334,000
Tobacco	£263,000	£560,000

Table 1. Comparative values of English commodity imports from Asia, Africa and America (annual averages) (compiled from Price, 1998: 100).

Long-term, however, the effects of the experience were wide-ranging. Of the expeditions officers, six went on to become admirals and George Anson made First Lord of the Admiralty to become the 'father of the Royal Navy', introducing a suite of improvements in ships, equipment and conditions. In 1747 he reformed naval war tactics and a year later rolled out the first uniforms for officers. Anson went on to introduce the Line of Bearing, founded the Articles of War, which lasted till 1865, and established the Royal Marines. The coppering of ships' hulls was also his initiative (Anson, 1912: 182, 185; Pack, 1960: 1, 5-6).

Unexpectedly, arguably the most enduring by-product of the round-the-world voyage of the *Centurion* was the impact of the suffering and death of the crews from scurvy. When Anson left England in 1739 the cause of the disease was unknown and the only medicine available was a useless and violent purgative called Dr. Ward's Drop and Pill. The loss of life from the disease recorded on Anson's expedition was so acute that Dr. James Lind of Haslar Naval Hospital was inspired to study the disease and publish his *Treatise on the Scurvy* in 1753, which he dedicated to Anson and which proved convincingly that the simple remedy was a lemon or an orange, but not a lime. It would nevertheless take the conservative Admiralty a further 40 years to issue lemon juice to crews who had been on salt provisions for six weeks (Heaps, 1973: 13).

On the domestic front the War of the Austrian Succession has been defined as a sterile conflict, which ended few of the European rivalries. The struggle between Prussia and the Habsburgs in Germany remained as bitter as ever. As the Austrian statesman Count Wenzel Anton von Kaunitz wrote, "We are entering a house made of cardboard. We shall have to see whether we think of making from it something more solid" (Anderson, 1995: 210). The dream of expanding British trade proved equally illusory.

Even if the British capture of Louisbourg reduced France's transatlantic trade to a trickle by the end of the war (Johnston, 1983), this was a small return for the ultimate cost of the war and was counterbalanced by the loss of Madras and the failure to exert any further commercial control over the French West Indian islands (Anderson, 1995: 218). Some 100,000 soldiers and perhaps as many as 400,000 civilians died during the war and by 1747 stock prices in Britain had dropped ominously to levels not witnessed since 1724 (Browning, 1994: 328, 376). On balance, privateers' capture of enemy ships did not enhance England's position in colonial trade. Even if England did take an impressive 3,316 Spanish, French and other ships, the enemy in turn captured 3,493 English vessels. The net product was a stalemate.

Moreover, King George II's war badly disrupted long-distance trade. Commerce between France and the West Indies did drop by nearly 50% between 1743 and 1745 and Cuban tobacco to Spain fell by 17% in 1745-49. The total value of Havana's non-peninsular commerce declined by 54% in the years 1735-40. Britain though was equally hit hard. Exports from the British West Indies to Britain fell by 18% in 1744 and from North America by 25%. Caribbean purchases of British goods dropped by 37% and North American consumption by 23% in 1744 (Swanson, 1991: 184, 186).

As the dangers of preying privateers escalated, so freight costs and insurance rates rocketed. In 1740 freight charges on Chesapeake tobacco cargos rose by 35% over peacetime levels. By spring 1748 Charlestown merchant Henry Laurens reported that it cost 86% more to ship a ton of rice to London than in 1739 when the war had started. Within the sphere of West Indian sugar trade, the busiest concern in the colonies, the cost of shipping a hundredweight of sugar from Barbados to London increased by 29% when war with Spain was announced; at the height of the war it peaked at double the peacetime freight costs. The mood of autumn 1744 was well captured by the American merchant John Reynell, who complained that "Trading is Exceeding dead here; hardly anything goes forward but Privateering" (Swanson, 1991: 188, 190).

The heavy commercial losses inflicted on all sides are comprehensively reflected by the obsessive lists of privateer captures published throughout the war in the *Gentleman's Quarterly*. They are not, however, entirely accurate statistics for the volumes and characters of cargos in circulation. The very low frequency of references to shipments of Chinese ceramics vastly underestimates the flow of what must have been a considerable bulk commodity carried as space fillers amongst larger cargos.

The under-representation of shipments of tea is a more inexplicable anomaly. Only three cargos of tea are registered amongst the French prizes of 1739-48 and none amongst the Spanish or English consignments. Two more shipments are listed under unknown prizes and six as smugglers taken by English ships. This pattern exposes the problems inherent amongst the newspaper sources. Whereas coffee was not the drink of choice in England, where still as late as 1756-75 almost 94% of this imported commodity was re-exported to the Low Countries, Germany and northern Europe (Price, 1998: 86), tea was highly popular (Table 1).

Tea imports monopolized by the East India Company would increase one hundredfold in value from some £80,000 in 1699-1701 to £848,000 in the period 1772-4 (Price, 1998: 83). The 1740s was a pivotal decade in the establishment of tea in the sitting rooms of middle England. In 1713 the East India Company had established trade links with Canton and tea consumption doubled in the 1730s and 1740s. This trend is mirrored in the import of tea service equipment, such as tea kettles, teapots, and teaspoons, which were only found in 10% of the households of Kent after 1720 but by the 1740s were registered in 74% of Kentish homes (Overton *et al.*, 2004: 106).

Britain's favorite hot beverage continued to reach kitchens throughout the war despite some sharp fluctuations: in 1740 the East India Company sold 1.653 million pounds weight of tea in Britain, 691,000 lbs in 1742, 911,000 lbs in 1743, 2,463,000 lbs in 1745 and 282,000 lbs in 1747 (Mui and Mui, 1986: 184). The very low presence of cargos of tea in lists of captured English prizes is again possibly explained by an apparent unwillingness to publicize British losses as gushingly as in the case of enemy losses. Or was tea transported on better armed or convoy-protected East Indiamen? The sources discussed in this paper thus need to be used with a degree of caution.

Finally, is it realistic to refer to an archaeology of privateering? The very few wrecks of ships launched or lost as privateers currently recorded or published seriously hinder this discipline. The subject is also complicated by the reinvention of privateers as merchant vessels outside times of wars. Hence, neither seemingly *La Marquise de Tourny*, the *Machault* or *L'Aimable Grenot* were technically cruising for prey when they were lost at sea. The *Alcide* is an exception but no scientific report of the wreck has as yet materialized. This leaves *La Dauphine* as the only known and well published corsair recorded for the 18th century, yet pre-dating 1739 by 35 years is only of general comparative interest to the War of the Austrian Succession.

Despite these reservations, the cannon and guns and cannonballs inscribed with *fleur de lis* on the *Machault*, as well as the ship's preserved cloth and lace, serves as an important physical source for reconstructing the kinds of cargo once carried by *La Marquise de Tourny*. The Dutch 'Bellarmine' jug and English gunner's rule, glass bottles and pewter wares on the French *Dauphine* caution against blindly accepting material culture found on any privateer – such as Site 33c's blue glass *flaçon* neck – as indicative in isolation of a wrecked vessel's nationality.

Unexpectedly, and fortuitously considering the very poor level of Site 33's preservation, it is the iron ballast that serves as an intriguing touchstone for future research. Its form is conspicuously comparable to the iron ballast ingots manufactured in Maryland found on *L'Aimable Grenot* and *La Machault* and reflects the dual role of corsairs in war and trade operating between Europe and the Americas.

For now, Odyssey has completed its preliminary investigation of the wreck of *La Marquise de Tourny*. Future missions could concentrate on additional analysis of the iron cannon and the matter of whether moulded inscriptions survive on the upper surfaces of the iron ballast. Beyond that, with its organic cargo, small finds, wooden rigging blocks and even pottery destroyed or deteriorated by time and tide, and further destroyed by endemic beam trawling and other forms of fishing, Site 33c is an example of a wreck within the western English Channel that has been mechanically ground down to the stage where little tangible evidence survives. Merely the most robust objects endure on the site of the world's deepest privateer, an inglorious end to its daring life during the War of the Austrian Succession.

Acknowledgements

As ever, great appreciation to all the offshore management, archaeological and technical team that produced the primary data that made the research into Site 33c possible (as listed at the end of *OME Papers* 17), and hence this accompanying study. Great credit is due to Greg Stemm and Mark Gordon at Odyssey for choosing to initiate and support the survey of this rare wreck form. In addition to both of them, I offer further sincere thanks to Laura Barton and John Oppermann at Odyssey Tampa for their support and enthusiasm of this project. It remains on ongoing pleasure to work with Odyssey's Director of Field Archaeology, Neil Cunningham Dobson.

I am indebted to Richard Keen for discussing the St. Malo corsairs from La Natière site with me and to generously making several reports available. Kathy Evans patiently and efficiently processed and made sense of the documentation captured from the *Le Marquis de Tourny* in 1748, which was sourced by Patrick Lize and Simon Davidson; Lange Winckler generously commented on this text and clarified certain points, and John Griffith generated the VMS fishing data related to the Site 33c region. Many thanks to Alice Copeland for proofreading this text. The research into *La Marquise de Tourny* was initially enthusiastically kick-started by Jason Williams and his team at JWM Productions, with whom, along with the Discovery Channel, it has been a pleasure to work. As ever, Melissa Dolce has toiled relentlessly and with great charm on the design of this report. All errors within this Paper are my own.

Notes

1. The specific sections of the *Gentleman's Quarterly* examined for obtaining statistics about captured privateers of all nations between 1739 and 1748 are: *Supplement to the Gentleman's Magazine for the Year 1741*, Vol. XI, 689-98; *Gentleman's Magazine*, January 1743, Vol. XIII, 23-24; August 1743. Vol. XIII, 419-20; August 1743, Vol. XIII, 473-75; *Supplement to the Gentleman's Magazine for Year 1743*, 699-700; *Gentleman's Magazine*, May 1744, Vol. XIV, 260-66; June 1744, Vol. XIV, 310-12; July 1744, Vol. XIV, 365-67; August 1744, Vol. XIV, 422-24; January 1745, Vol. XV, p.49: list of privateers; February 1745, Vol. XV, 79-80; March 1745, Vol. XV, 153-54; April 1745, Vol. XV, 211-12; May 1745, Vol. XV, 262-63; June 1745, Vol. XV, 302-303 and 330; July 1745, Vol. XV, 351-52; August 1745, Vol. XV, 436-37; *Supplement to the Gentleman's Magazine for Year 1745*, Vol. XV, 691-96; *Gentleman's Magazine*, February 1746, Vol. XVI, 63-64; April 1746, Vol. XVI, 180-82; May 1746, Vol. XVI, 238-39; June 1746, Vol. XVI, 285-86; July 1746, Vol. XVI, 347-48; September 1746, Vol. XVI, 458-60; November 1746, Vol. XVI, 582-84; December 1746, Vol. XVI, 695-98; February 1747, Vol. XVII, 91-2; April 1747, Vol. XVII, 195-96; May 1747, Vol. XVII, 235-36; June 1747, Vol. XVII, 287-88; July 1747, Vol. XVII, 333-35; September 1747, Vol. XVII, 429-32; October 1747, Vol. XVII, 482-83; November 1747, Vol. XVII, 532-33; *Supplement to the Gentleman's Magazine* for the Year 1747, Vol. XVII, 606-609; *Gentleman's Magazine*,

January 1748, Vol. XVIII, 35; February 1748, Vol. XVIII, 83; March 1748, Vol. XVIII, 126-28; April 1748, Vol. XVIII, 173-74; May 1748, Vol. XVIII, 226-27; June 1748, Vol. XVIII, 267-69; July 1748, Vol. XVIII, 322-23; August 1748, Vol. XVIII, 367-68; September 1748, Vol. XVIII, 418-19; *Supplement to the Gentleman's Magazine for the Year 1748*, Vol. XVIII, 593-94.

2. The *Gentleman's Magazine* for 1744 (Vol. XIV, 592) reported that the *Marquis de Tourny*, Captain Gorer, from St. Domingo for France, was captured and carried into Jamaica. In turn, in December 1746 the "Marquis de Tournay" took the *Charlton* from Cork to Antigua and the *Fanny* from Liverpool to Africa (*Gentleman's Magazine*, December 1746, Vol. XVI, 696-97).

Bibliography

Anderson, M.S., *The War of the Austrian Succession 1740-1748* (Harlow, 1995).

Anson, G., *The Taking of the Galleon. From Lord Anson's Voyage* (London, 1905).

Anson, W.V., *The Life of Admiral Lord Anson. The Father of the British Navy 1697-1762* (London, 1912).

Appriou, D. and Bozellec, E., *L'Alcide corsaire de Saint Malo. La guerre de course et l'histoire d'une corvette de 1745 à nos jours* (Coop Breizh, 1997).

Bozellec, E. and Jegou, J-C., 'Le naufrage d'un corsaire Malouin en baie de Morlaix: L'*Alcide* (1747)'. In L'Hour, M. and Veyrat, E. (eds.), *La mer pour mémoire. Archéologie sous-marine des épaves Atlantiques* (Paris, 2005), 252-3.

Browning, R., *The War of the Austrian Succession* (Stroud, 1994).

Bryce, D., *Weaponry from the* Machault. *An 18th-Century French Frigate* (Parks Canada, Ottawa, 1984).

Clarkson, L.A., *The Pre-Industrial Economy in England 1500-1750* (London, 1974).

Cunningham Dobson, N., '*La Marquise de Tourny* (Site 33c): A Mid-18th Century Armed Privateer of Bordeaux'. In G. Stemm and S. Kingsley (eds.), *Oceans Odyssey 2. Underwater Heritage Management & Deep-Sea Shipwrecks in the English Channel & Atlantic Ocean* (Oxford, 2011), 69-108.

Cunningham Dobson, N. and Kingsley, S., 'HMS *Victory*, a First-Rate Royal Navy warship Lost in the English Channel, 1744. Preliminary Survey & Identification'. In G. Stemm and S. Kingsley (eds.), *Oceans Odyssey. Deep-Sea Shipwrecks in the English Channel, Straits of Gibraltar & Atlantic Ocean* (Oxbow Books, Oxford, 2010), 235-81.

de Maisonneuve, B., 'Excavation of the Maidstone, a British Man-of-War Lost off Noirmoutier in 1747', *International Journal of Nautical Archaeology* 21.1 (1992), 15-26.

Douillez, D., 'L'épave de la Pierre des Portes ou le naufrage de la *Charmante* (1702)'. In L'Hour, M. and Veyrat, E. (eds.), *La mer pour mémoire. Archéologie sous-marine des épaves Atlantiques* (Paris, 2005), 24-5.

Ducoin, J., 'Le commerce négrier et les risques maritimes de la traite: l'example Nantais'. In L'Hour, M. and Veyrat, E. (eds.), *La mer pour mémoire. Archéologie sous-marine des épaves Atlantiques* (Paris, 2005), 174-77.

Ford, B., Borgens, A. and Hitchcock, B., 'The 'Mardi Gras' Shipwreck: Results of a Deep-Water Excavation, Gulf of Mexico, USA', *International Journal of Nautical Archaeology* 39.1 (2010), 76-98.

Goddio, F., 'The Wreck, from Reality to the Documents' In F. Goddio and E.J. Guyot de Saint Michel, *Griffin. On the Route of an Indiaman* (London, 1999), 57-115.

Hervey, F., *The Naval History of Great Britain; Including the Lives of the Admirals* (London, 1750).

Heaps, B., *Log of the Centurion* (London, 1973).

Hill, R., *The Prizes of War. The Naval Prize System in the Napoleonic Wars, 1793-1815* (Stroud, 1998).

Johnston, A.J.B., *The Summer of 1744. A Portrait of Life in 18th Century Louisbourg* (Parks Canada, Ottawa, 1983).

L'Hour, M., 'Périr à Locmaria: le naufrage du *Prince de Conty* (1746)'. In L'Hour, M. and Veyrat, E. (eds.), *La mer pour mémoire. Archéologie sous-marine des épaves Atlantiques* (Paris, 2005a), 166-7.

L'Hour, M., 'Naufrage d'un corsaire Confédéré devant Cherbourg: L'*Alabama* (1864)'. In L'Hour, M. and Veyrat, E. (eds.), *La mer pour mémoire. Archéologie sous-marine des épaves Atlantiques* (Paris, 2005b), 256-7.

L'Hour, M. and Veyrat, E., *Un corsaire sous la mer. Les épaves de la Natière, archéologie sous-marine à Saint-Malo. Volume 2. Campagne de fouille 2000* (Edition Adramar, 2001).

L'Hour, M. and Veyrat, E., *Un corsaire sous la mer. Les épaves de la Natière, archéologie sous-marine à Saint-Malo. Volume 3. Campagne de fouille 2001, l'épave Natière 2* (Edition Adramar, 2002).

L'Hour and Veyrat, E., 'Ships and Private Shipyards through the Archaeological Evidence of the Wreck off La Natière (Saint-Malo, Brittany, France)'. In C. Beltrame (ed.), *Boats, Ships and Shipyards. Proceedings of the Ninth International Symposium on Boat and Ship Archaeology Venice 2000* (Oxford, 2003a), 314-19.

L'Hour, M. and Veyrat, E., *Un corsaire sous la mer. Les épaves de la Natière, archéologie sous-marine à Saint Malo. Volume 4. Campagne de fouille 2002, l'épave Natière 1* (Edition Adramar, 2003b).

L'Hour, M. and Veyrat, E., *Un corsaire sous la mer. Les épaves de la Natière, archéologie sous-marine à Saint Malo. Volume 5. Campagne de fouille 2003, l'épave Natière 1* (Edition Adramar, 2004).

L'Hour, M. and Veyrat, E., 'L'histoire d'un *piège à bateaux*: les épaves de la Natière (XVIIIe s.)'. In L'Hour, M. and Veyrat, E. (eds.), *La mer pour mémoire. Archéologie sous-marine des épaves Atlantiques* (Paris, 2005a), 246-49.

L'Hour, M. and Veyrat, E., 'L'artillerie de mer et l'échelle de cannonier de l'épave de la Natière 1'. In L'Hour, M. and Veyrat, E. (eds.), *La mer pour mémoire. Archéologie sous-marine des épaves Atlantiques* (Paris, 2005b), 250-1.

L'Hour, M. and Veyrat, E., 'La construction dans les chantiers privés: l'example de l'épave Natière 1'. In L'Hour, M. and Veyrat, E. (eds.), *La mer pour mémoire. Archéologie sous-marine des épaves Atlantiques* (Paris, 2005c), 284-7.

Marsden, P., 'The Wreck of the Dutch East Indiaman *Amsterdam* near Hastings, 1749. An Interim Report', *International Journal of Nautical Archaeology* 1 (1972), 73-96.

Mui, H.-C. and Mui, L.H., 'Smuggling and the British Tea Trade Before 1784'. In S.L. Engerman (ed.), *Trade and the Industrial Revolution, 1700-1850. Volume II* (Cheltenham, 1996), 161-90.

Norman, C.B., *The Corsairs of France* (London, 1887).

Overton, M., Whittle, J., Dean, D. and Hann, A., *Production and Consumption in English Households, 1600-1750* (London, 2004).

Pack, S.W.C., *Admiral Lord Anson. The Story of Anson's Voyage and Naval Events of his Day* (London, 1960).

Pares, R., 'The London Sugar Market, 1740-1769'. In S.L. Engerman (ed.), *Trade and the Industrial Revolution, 1700-1850. Volume I* (Cheltenham, 1996), 227-43.

Petrie, D.A., *The Prize Game. Lawful Looting on the High Seas in the Days of Fighting Sail* (Naval Institute Press, Annapolis, 1999).

Price, J.B., 'The Imperial Economy, 1700-1776'. In P.J. Marshall (ed.), *The Oxford History of the British Empire. Volume II. The Eighteenth Century* (Oxford University Press, 1998), 78-104.

Price, J.M. and Clemens, P.G.E., 'A Revolution of Scale in Overseas Trade: British Firms in the Chesapeake Trade, 1675-1775'. In S.L. Engerman (ed.), *Trade and the Industrial Revolution, 1700-1850. Volume II* (Cheltenham, 1996), 457-99.

Richmond, H.W., *The Navy in the War of 1739-48. Volume I* (Cambridge University Press, 1920).

Rodger, N.A.M., *The Command of the Ocean. A Naval History of Britain, 1649-1815* (London, 2004).

Starkey, D., *British Privateering Enterprise in the Eighteenth Century* (University of Exeter Press, 1990).

Starkey, D.J., 'A Restless Spirit: British Privateering Enterprise, 1739-1815'. In D.J. Starkey, E.S. van Eyck van Heslinga and J.A. de Moor (eds.), *Privates and Privateering. New Perspectives on the War on Trade in the Eighteenth and Nineteenth Centuries* (University of Exeter Press, 1997), 126-40.

Sullivan, C., *Legacy of the* Machault. *A Collection of 18th-Century Artifacts* (Parks Canada, Ottawa, 1986).

Swanson, C.E., *Predators and Prizes. American Privateering and Imperial Warfare, 1739-1748* (University of South Carolina Press, Columbia, 1991).

Switzer, D.C., 'The *Defence*'. In M. Bound (ed.), *Excavating Ships of War* (Oswestry, 1998), 182-93.

Villiers, P., 'The Slave and Colonial Trade in France Just Before the Revolution'. In S.L. Engerman (ed.), *Trade and the Industrial Revolution, 1700-1850. Volume I* (Cheltenham, 1996), 259-85.

Zacharchuk, W., 'The Restigouche Excavation. An *Interim Report', International Journal of Nautical Archaeology* 1 (1972), 157-63.

Zacharchuk, W. and Waddell, J.A., *The Excavation of the* Machault. *An 18th-Century French Frigate* (Parks Canada, Ottawa, 1986).

The Jacksonville 'Blue China' Shipwreck (Site BA02): A Mid-19th Century American Coastal Schooner off Florida

Ellen Gerth, Neil Cunningham Dobson
Odyssey Marine Exploration, Tampa, USA

Sean A. Kingsley
Wreck Watch Int., London, UK

During the survey for the wreck of the sidewheel steamer the SS *Republic*, Odyssey Marine Exploration discovered the remains of a merchant vessel, Site BA02, located at a depth close to 370m, 70 nautical miles off Jacksonville, Florida. The wreck was brought to Odyssey's attention by fishermen, whose nets had snagged ceramic wares over the last 40 years. A small selection of artifacts was recovered in 2003 and the wreck arrested in court. The site was revisited by Odyssey in 2005 and due to observed additional impacts caused by fresh dragging of trawl nets in the interim years further diagnostic material culture was recorded in relation to its contexts prior to select recovery to identify and date the site before the wreck became even more extensively disturbed and data lost.

Site BA02 is interpreted as containing the remains of a small American coastal schooner that was transporting a consignment of British ceramics manufactured in Staffordshire in the decade 1850-60 alongside American glass wares and building materials. The most plausible theory is that the ship was lost in a hurricane, with the storms of September 1854 the most likely scenario. The vessel appears to have been a two-masted schooner typical of the East Coast's thriving regional maritime trade based in New York. The Jacksonville 'Blue China' shipwreck reflects the lure of high status, yet relatively cheap, Staffordshire and US products that prevailed across middle class America and permeated down into the lower classes.

1. Introduction

During Odyssey Marine Exploration's research into the deep-sea waters of the Atlantic Ocean off Florida, a glazed earthenware jar snagged in a trawlerman's net at a depth of more than 350m was brought to the company's attention. Odyssey designated Site BA02 a target meriting further investigation. The wreck was subsequently discovered 70 nautical miles east-southeast of Jacksonville, Florida, at a depth of 367m on the periphery of the Atlantic Ocean's Gulf Stream current (Figs. 1-3) and was surveyed by Odyssey as part of the search operations that ultimately led to the discovery of the sidewheel steamship the SS *Republic* (Cunningham Dobson *et al.*, 2010; Cunningham Dobson and Gerth, 2010).

The wreck first appeared as an acoustic image on 11 July 2002 obtained using an EdgeTech DF1000 towed side-scan sonar unit (Fig. 1). The target was subsequently examined visually with a Deep Ocean Engineering Phantom Ultimate Remotely-Operated Vehicle (ROV) on 29 January 2003 and proved to consist of a relatively coherent shipwreck composed of a low-lying mound of hull and conspicuous deposits of blue and white decorated ceramics, various ceramic bowls and pots, and glass bottles. Three artifacts were recovered for purposes of an admiralty 'arrest' of the site and provisionally to date and characterize the ship (a bowl and jug, which proved to contain a glass tumbler).

On 28 April 2003 an eight-hour dive was conducted using the Phantom ROV with the primary objective of producing a video survey. Three additional diagnostic artifacts were selected for recovery from the northern end of the wreck: a large stoneware jug and two ceramic Canton ginger jars decorated with blue ornamental designs. These were recovered on 29 April after the completion of the site ROV video survey.

Site BA02 consisted of a large, low-lying mound, initially estimated at measuring approximately 30 x 10m, with a relief of some 1.5m above the seabed. A large quantity of articulated hull structure was observed in various stages of deterioration and further sections underlay the sand substrata. A large concentration of ceramics and glass bottles was clustered near the southern end of the site,

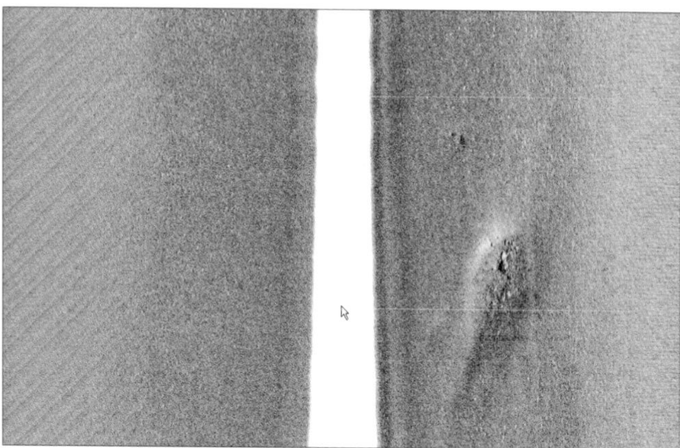

Fig. 1. Side-scan image of Site BA02 (2003).

identified as the bows through the presence of two concreted iron anchors. Numerous encrusted iron concretions were scattered across the site. The displacement evident amongst the artifacts reflected severe impacts caused by modern fishing trawls. The initial survey suggested the presence of a merchant ship at Site BA02, possibly a coastal trader. An admiralty arrest was filed to protect the site from external disturbance and to provide Odyssey with the legal basis to re-visit the wreck at a later stage.

During a break from operations on the wreck of the *Republic* in 2005, the *Odyssey Explorer* – now equipped with far more technologically advanced archaeological tools and a highly sophisticated ROV – was dispatched to re-examine and re-assess the condition of additional wrecks located in the vicinity, including the Jacksonville 'Blue China' wreck. During this inspection the project team was alarmed by obvious signs of fresh impacts caused by trawlers dragging nets directly through the site in the intervening two years. Little of the formerly observed contexts remained undisturbed, and the substantial cargo of ceramics had been heavily smashed and scattered across the sea bottom (Fig. 119).

The 2005 visit had planned only to check the status of the site during an interval of relative quiet in the midst of the season's multiple hurricanes. However, it was clear that Site BA02 now appeared to be in imminent danger of large-scale data loss based on the alarming damage perceived. As a result, the decision was reached to use a small window of fair weather to conduct a rescue archaeology operation. Odyssey's deep-sea archaeological resources were deployed with a dual objective. Firstly, to obtain as much data as possible from the wreck in the limited weather window, including the recovery of diagnostic artifacts and intact examples of all the ceramic types represented in an attempt to characterize the vessel. Secondly, to test Odyssey's latest versions of data logging software, photomosaic production capabilities and other archaeological methods.

This report presents the results of the 2003 and 2005 seasons, analyses of the artifact distributions and a summary of the ceramic and glass wares in order to define the type of craft lost at Site BA02, the site impacts, cargo character, date, wreck event and origins. More detailed specialist reports on the ceramics, glass wares and tobacco pipes are published in Chapters 9-11.

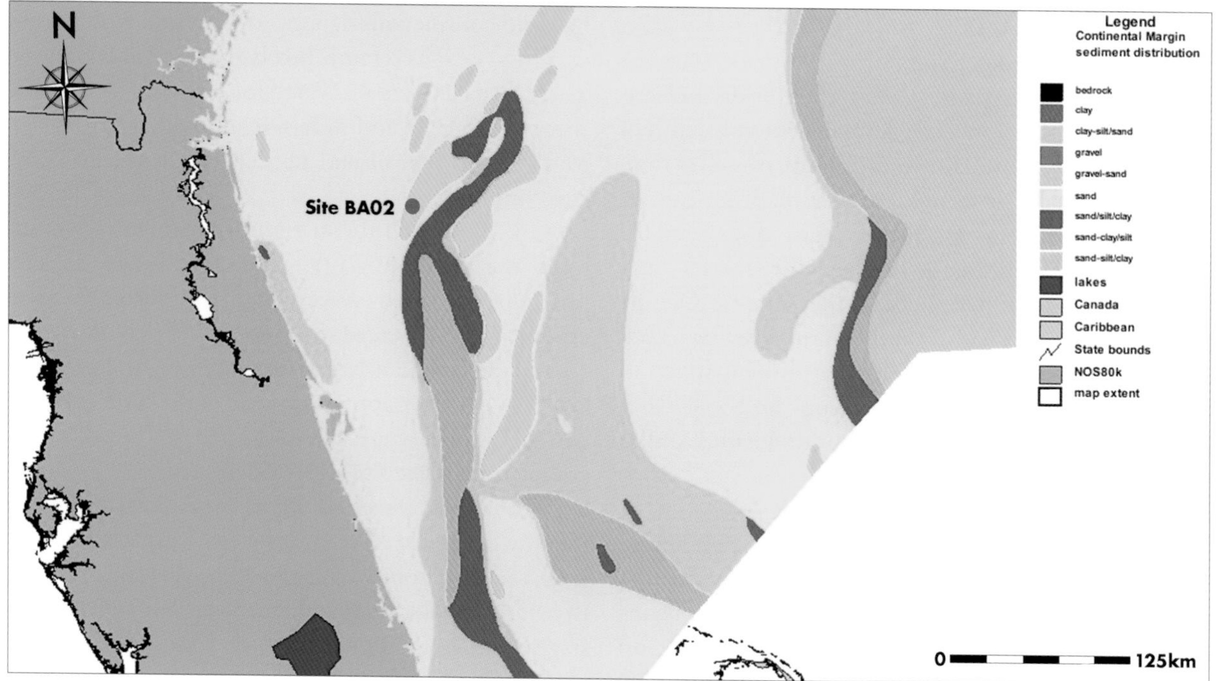

Fig. 2. Site BA02 in relation to its sedimentological context.

2. Technology & Archaeological Tooling, 2005

The 2005 Site BA02 survey was conducted from the 76m-long, 1,431 gross-ton research vessel the *Odyssey Explorer* and relied on the newly acquired and custom-tooled Remotely Operated-Vehicle Zeus. A primary influence on the selection of this ROV system was the complexity of operating among the strong currents of the Gulf Stream. A system capable of efficiently working in this environment required mass, powerful maneuvering thrusters and strongly constructed manipulator arms. Simultaneously, an ROV needed to be well balanced to work amongst delicate artifacts and shipwreck structure.

The Soil Machine Dynamics Ltd (SMD) ROV acquired by Odyssey and renamed Zeus fitted this purpose perfectly (8 tons, 3.7 x 3.1 x 2.38m, depth range 2,000m). Zeus' propulsion system consists of eight reversible hydraulic thrusters: four 43cm-diameter units aligned on the horizontal plane and four 30cm-diameter units operating on the vertical plane. The speed of each thruster is controlled via electro-hydraulic valves, making Zeus highly maneuverable. The vehicle frame is constructed from aluminum and buoyancy is provided by molded syntactic foam.

For survey operations Zeus was fitted with a Kongsberg Simrad Mesotech 6,000m Digital Sonar and additionally with transducer/receivers fitted for navigation and survey. For manipulation, two Schilling Conan seven-function master/slave manipulator arms were installed on the front of the ROV, one to each side (reach 1.79m, working arc of 120°, lifting capacity 170kg). The ROV was equipped with a dredge pump for excavation, a limpet suction device for artifact recovery and a Sediment Removal and Filtration System (SeRF). Tools such as scales were deployed from stowage positions built into the center of the vehicle's underside.

For the Site BA02 project Zeus was configured with seven cameras, four used by the ROV pilot to monitor the vehicle's navigation and three for dedicated archaeological recording. These consisted of an Atlas High Resolution Color Camera, an Insite Pacific Inc. Scorpion Digital Camera and a Deep Sea Systems HDTV Camera. These high-resolution cameras, combined with Halide Mercury Incandescent (HMI) lighting, supplied the archaeologist and ROV operator with high quality images. The main cameras incorporated pan and tilt controls. Various color monitors and a large format plasma screen in the Offline Room enabled the archaeologist to observe close-up images of artifacts on the wreck site only a few millimeters in size. This equipment was employed to produce a high-resolution photomosaic of the site consisting of 395 individual digital photographs before the intrusive phase commenced.

The project incorporated a unique data logging system, DataLog®, developed by Odyssey to record all events and activities, such as artifact manipulations and dive observations, by entering logs through drop-down menus accompanied by a typed comment. The program automatically logs key dive events, including time, date, dive number and X, Y, Z spatial coordinates of Zeus' movements at any one time. Every second of each dive was also recorded in triplicate on high-capacity digital video disk. Archaeological features, contexts and artifacts of particular interest were recorded in addition on DVD and High Definition tape, complemented by still photography.

Artifacts undergoing recovery were individually placed using the limpet suction device into an off-site Fourplex, a large metal lifting basket sub-divided into separate context-specific units designed to hold plastic containers. Each unit, and each division within it, was numbered, so all could be reliably tracked from context to Fourplex and onto the *Odyssey Explorer* using DataLog. Once recovered to the surface, the artifacts were recorded, logged on a spreadsheet and photographed. By formulating this sub-sea and surface recording systems, working in tandem with a separate inventory and management database maintained by the project conservator, Odyssey's archaeologists can track the history of any single artifact from its initial observation on the sea floor to its final destination and disposition.

Fig. 3. Cross-section of Site BA02 in relation to its depth and gradient.

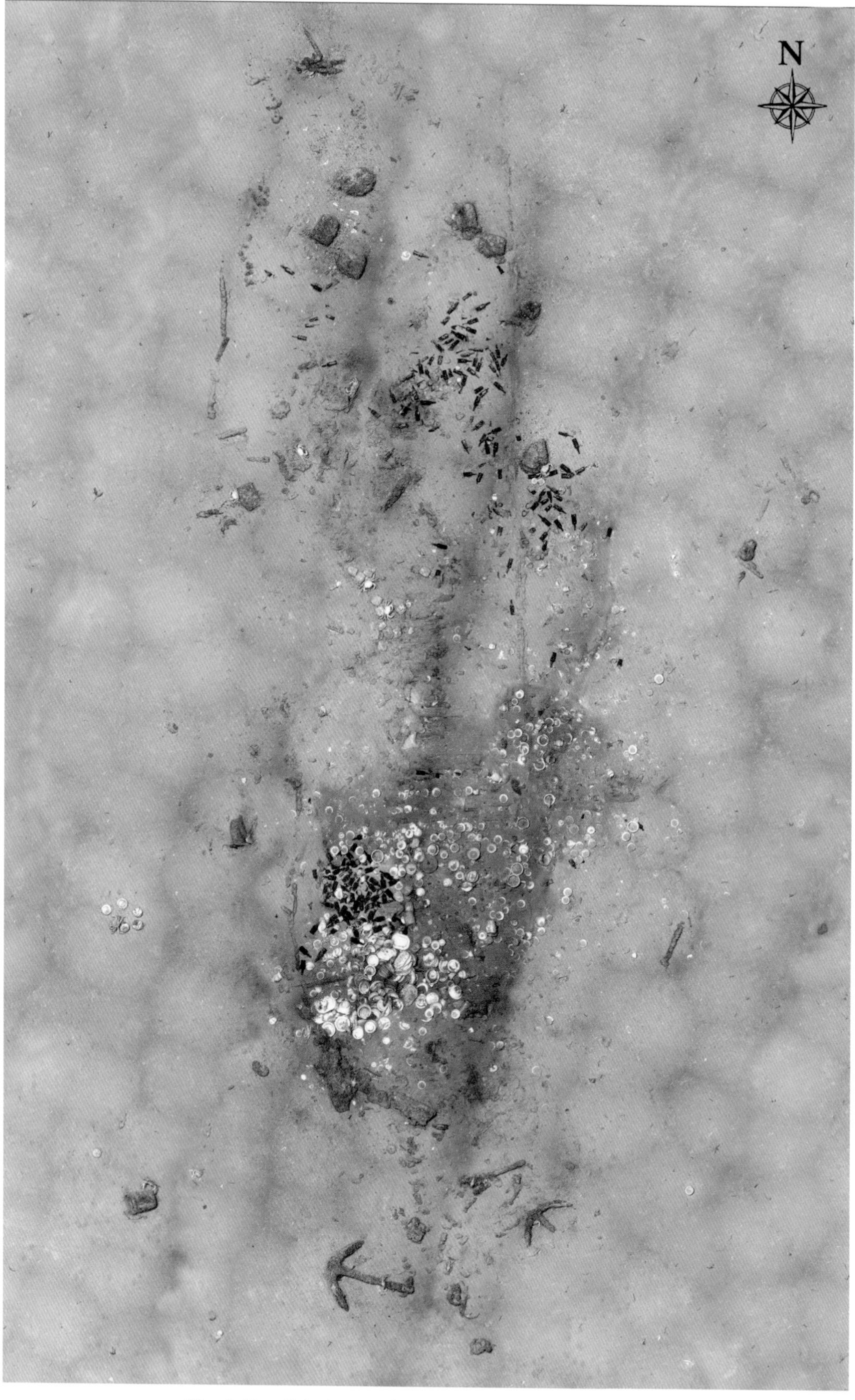

Fig. 4. Pre-disturbance photomosaic of Site BA02 (2005).

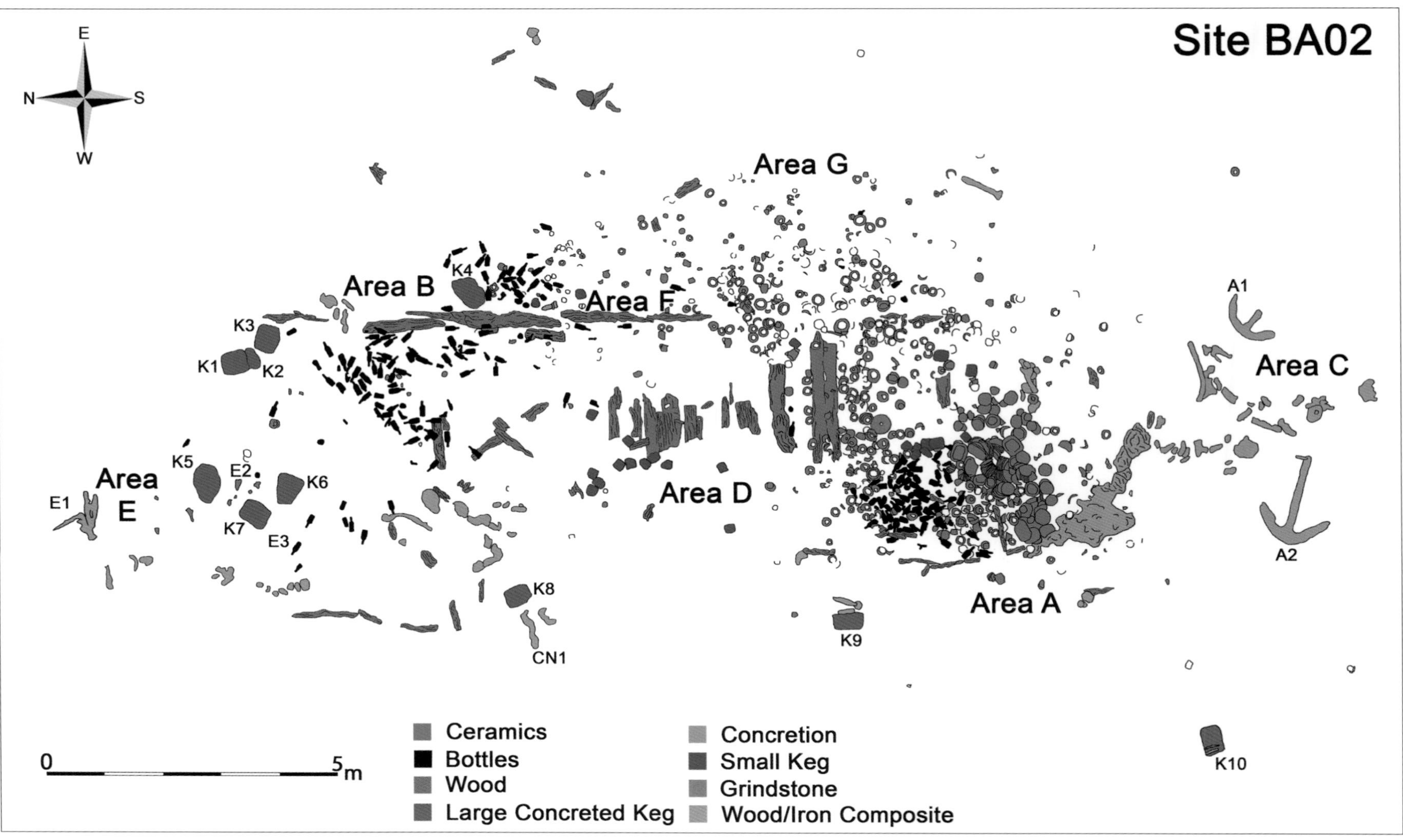

Fig. 5. Plan of Site BA02.

3. The Marine Environment

The ship wrecked at Site BA02 came to rest at a depth of 367m, some 70 nautical miles east-southeast of Jacksonville, Florida, in the Atlantic Ocean's Gulf Stream current and topographically within the 'Atlantic'-type continental margin (Kennett, 1982: 27-30; Figs. 2-3). The continental margin in this macro region sub-divides into three distinct morphological zones: a northern region extending from the Grand Banks to north of Long Island, a middle strip from north of Long Island to Cape Hatteras, and a southern one stretching from Cape Hatteras down to the Florida Panhandle. Between Maine and Florida the continental margin consists predominantly of basins and platforms, the latter covered by thin layers of sediment and numerous horsts and grabens of probable Triassic age. South of Cape Hatteras, the dominant topographic features of the continental margin are carbonate platforms between the Cape and the Puerto Rico Trench.

The northernmost carbonate platform is the Blake Plateau, a surface attached to the broader Florida Platform that projects down to a depth of 850m from the Florida-Hatteras slope (Kennett, 1982: 345-46). The Jacksonville 'Blue China' wreck lies on the Florida Platform, right at the edge of the Blake Plateau. Depth and slope data supported by an overlay of bathymetry on the US Geological Survey website and loaded into ARC GIS indicate that the wreck lies on its continental rise.

The Florida Platform is located on the south-central section of the North American Plate, extending to the southeast from the North American continent separating the Gulf of Mexico from the Atlantic Ocean. It is defined by the surrounding 91m isobath, spans more than 565km at its greatest width and extends southwards for more than 725km at its maximum length. A thick sequence of mid-Jurassic to Holocence siliciclastic-bearing carbonates and siliciclastic sediments, unlithified to well lithified, overlie the weathered surface of much of the platform.[1]

With a breadth of nearly 300km, the Blake Plateau Basin is one of the widest along the whole margin and covers an area of 127,700km^2. Sedimentary rocks characterize its geology and Jurassic to Cretaceous carbonates subsist over the plateau. Lower and Upper Cretaceous limestones and dolomites are present along the Blake Escarpment (Miall, 2008: 486-87; Pratt and Heezen, 1964: 721; Sheridan, 1987: 257).

The Blake Plateau first started to form in the early Tertiary, when the strong Florida Current began to flow through the Straits of Florida across what was then a deepwater continental shelf, cutting off the supply of continent-derived sediment to the outer shelf. Although some sediments were deposited on the outer Blake Plateau in the later Tertiary, the combined flow of the Florida Current and the Antilles Current, which merge over the southern Blake Plateau to form the Gulf Stream, has prevented most deposition over the plateau and has deeply scoured its base.[2]

The sediments covering the continental shelf can be classified into two groups based on age and their relation to the depositional environment: near-shore deposits of modern origin and in equilibrium and relict sediments (70% of the sediment cover) in disequilibrium. Modern sands are deposited in the nearshore part of the shelf, within approximately 6km of shore, and are subsequently dispersed by currents. Seaward of this area on the central and outer portions of the shelf are relict sediments. Unlike the modern sands these exhibit a coarse character, iron staining, and dissolution pitting from subaerial weathering (Kennett, 1982: 308-309).

The geological province in which the Jacksonville 'Blue China' wreck lies is beyond the southernmost Ice Age glacial advance and is thus devoid of the glacial till and gravelly outwash that predominate further north. It also does not display the fluvial sediment and reworked coastal deposits present off the central Atlantic states. Rather, South of Cape Hatteras skeletal and clean quartzitic sands typify the shelf sediments, with carbonates increasing southwards. The Blake Plateau is a northern continuation of the Bahama Bank carbonate province, whose carbonate distribution varies according to the local abundance of shells in an otherwise quartzose shelf environment (Pratt and Heezen, 1964: 724-25). Fine, silty sands form a near-shore belt and carbonates increase offshore. Sediments are richer in quartz and poorer in feldspar, a result of the erosion of coastal plain areas by rivers (Kennett, 1982: 311-12).

Localized maps of the continental margin sediments off the East Coast of North America demonstrate that Site BA02 is situated in an area of iron silicate sands, where the calcium carbonate content varies from 50-95% (Kennett, 1982: 311). United States Geological Survey coastal mapping reveals that this area of the seabed consists of surface deposits of sand, sand/silt/clay and that the wreck site is most closely aligned with an area of gravel sand. DVD footage captured during the 2005 site survey shows that the sediments are highly coarse and mixed with abundant large and fragmented shell and ripples characteristic of sand substrata. The wreck is rich in rock crab (*Cancer irroratus*), vermillion snapper (*Rhomboplites aurorubens*), with some limited conger eel documented below hull structure on the southern flank (Figs. 30, 37, 44, 113-117).

4. Site Description, 2005

The Jacksonville 'Blue China' shipwreck lies in waters affected by the flow of the Gulf Stream current, where bottom currents range from 0.5-1.0 knots. The deep seabed environment is sparsely populated by flora and fauna. Folklore amongst local fishermen abounds in tales of surface currents trapping disabled ships, creating a regional graveyard of wrecks. Site BA02 is the only disruption to a relatively featureless bottom plain beneath the rolling Atlantic waves. The wreck mound is oval in shape, 23.05 x 11.65m, and has an elevation of around 1.5m above the sea floor, with the centerline oriented north to south and the bows positioned to the south (Figs. 4-5).

Minimal modern rubbish overlying the wreck includes plastic rubbish bags, a beer can, and sections of cloth/canvas, some of which may be parts of sails. The bottom matrix consists of shallow deposits of sediment overlying hardpan, although the sediments – including dense fragmented shell and what appear to be pulverized pottery fragments – deepen northwards along the wreck to around 50cm thick. No stone or iron ballast was identified after large sections of the hull, including the keel, were uncovered. The ship was evidently fully loaded on its final voyage.

Site BA02 exhibits direct and indirect evidence of trawl impacts. The former includes physical trawl furrows on the eastern side of the keel, especially the southeastern quadrant, drag marks cut into the sea bottom matrix, and smashed artifacts and ship's structure. Indirect evidence comprises an absence of benthic organisms, which are slow to develop and spread, and the 'desert-like' surroundings of the wreck (pers. comm. Tom Dettweiler, 15 February 2005). Since no photomosaic was produced in 2003 when the site was initially discovered, comparative analysis of the change in its level of preservation is not easily quantifiable. The level of site impact is discussed in further detail in Section 12.

The most extensive concentration of cargo is situated towards the bow end of the site in Area A in a dense cluster of pottery and glass wares covering an area of 4.1 x 1.9m (Figs. 5-6, 13-14). The repertoire of the stowed ceramic wares is clearly limited. In the southern half of Area A within a concise zone measuring 1.9 x 1.9m were at least 231 ceramic vessels, restricted in form to 109 shell-edged Type 1A and Type 1B whiteware plates and soup plates (40 within a single stack), 16 Type 1C octagonal shell-edged whiteware platters and 105 Type 2A dipped whiteware bowls (Figs. 15, 17-22, 47-48). A single Type 2B dipped jug lies outside the hull to the west. This is the only section of the wreck where shell-edged wares occur (Fig. 47). Seven Type 4C white granite/white ironstone china wash basins, five still stacked in two sets of three and two, are also present to the south of Area A (Fig. 50). All of these ceramics are of British origin (see Section 7 below).

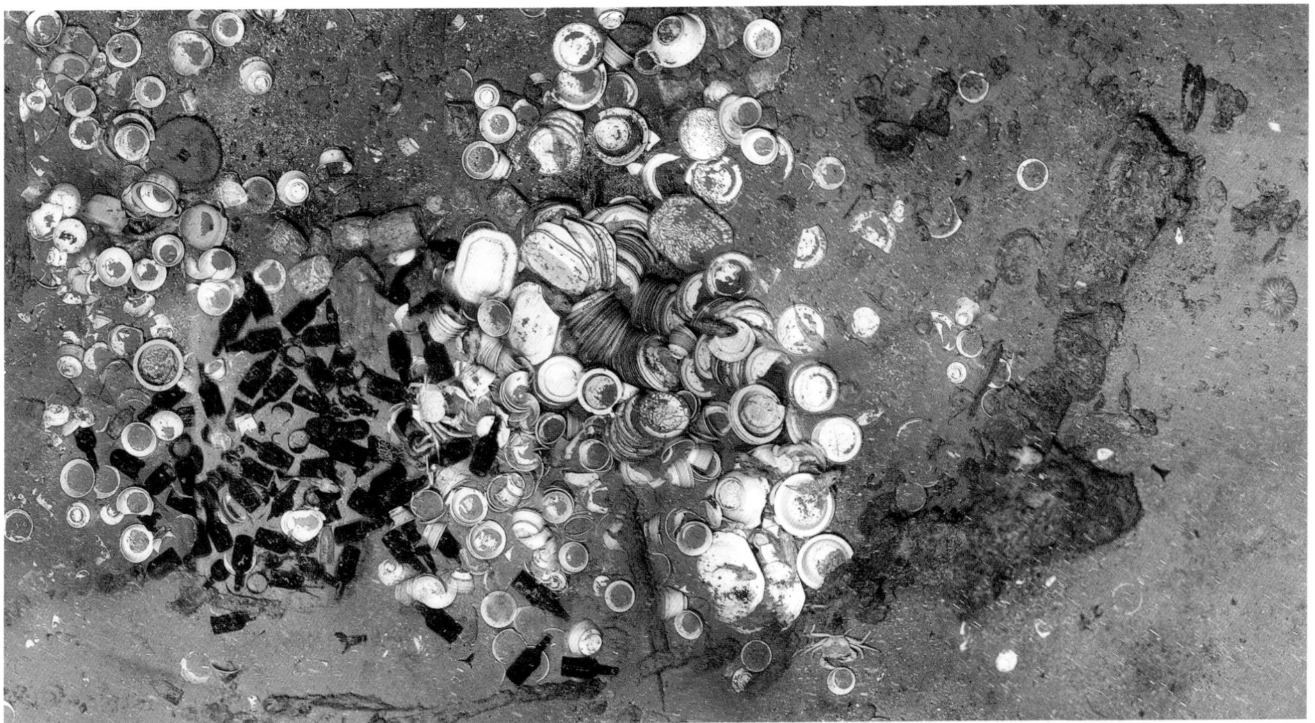

Fig. 6. Photomosaic detail of Area A: shell-edged earthenware plates, soup plates and platters to the south, mixed with dipped whiteware bowls, and a cluster of dark glass bottles to the north. Note the structural remains at east (foreground) and far south (far right, possible stem assembly with hatch rollers to its left), and wooden kegs to the east, which helped preserve this part of the wreck from trawler damage.

The wreck's four Type 6 Canton ginger jars were discovered some 0.5-0.8m north and northwest of the northern end of Area A along a 1.8m-long line (Figs. 22, 51), giving the impression of having rolled to these points of deposition from height, perhaps having originally been stacked on the very top of the Area A ceramic cargo hold, a pattern that would have befitted the comparatively high value of these more expensive porcelain wares. Contextualized with the ceramics in the northern half of Area A, covering 2.0 x 1.9m, are 65 Type 1 black glass liquor bottles, three transparent glass tumblers and two Type 3 transparent long-necked sauce/utilitarian bottles. One Type 6 green glass cologne bottle is present on the southern flank of the main ceramics cluster (Figs. 6, 13-14, 23, 53, 54).

The concentration of cargo in Area A, including material still stacked (albeit having fallen on its side), and the far more dispersed nature of ceramics and glass wares across the rest of the site, is an unbalanced and thus artificial pattern that cannot reflect the ship's original stowage. This relationship is the result of the wreck's unique site formation. Most of the site has been heavily impacted by bottom trawling gear (see Section 12 below).

However, the Area A deposit has been cushioned by an extensive 2.38m-long section of durable concreted iron (seemingly sheathed around a wooden core) to the south, possibly related to the largely decomposed stem (Figs. 6, 29). To the west is a comparable iron/wood part of hull structure, 2.9m-long and seemingly delineating the outer edge of the starboard hull, but today heavily ground down (Fig. 17). This is bisected at 90° by an iron/wood structure resembling a bulkhead divider. The eastern flank of Area A has similarly been protected by a deposit of small wooden kegs, 10 intact examples of which survive, each measuring between 16.8 x 16.8cm and 21 x 17.8cm, intact to the north but now highly fragmented to the south (Figs. 6, 14, 16). This eastern section beyond Area A is densely covered with a white organic deposit, all that remains of additional kegs struck by trawls. Area A owes its current preservation to a combination of fortunate localized geographical conditions.

A second less extensive concentration of cargo occurs to the north of the stern section of the wreck in Area B, where 115 Type 1 black glass liquor bottles cover an area of 5.7 x 3.9m and straddle both the eastern and western side of the keel (Figs. 5, 7, 24, 25). Although these have been scattered by trawlers and are far more loosely clustered, this deposit gives the impression of having been stowed midship in the stern. Area B is bounded on the north and east by four

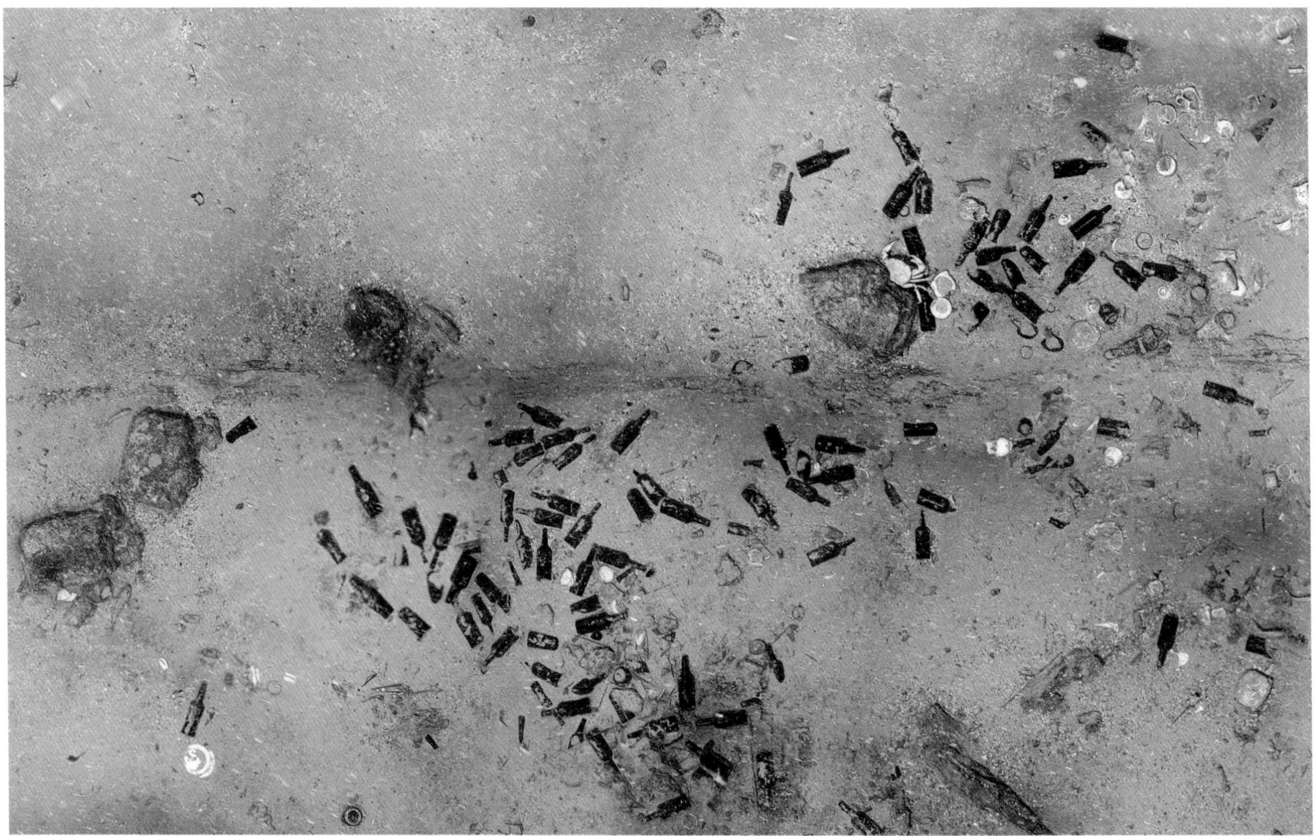

Fig. 7. Photomosaic detail of Area B: a cluster of dark glass bottles, tobacco pipes and large kegs K1-K4 with the buried keel visibly running north/south.

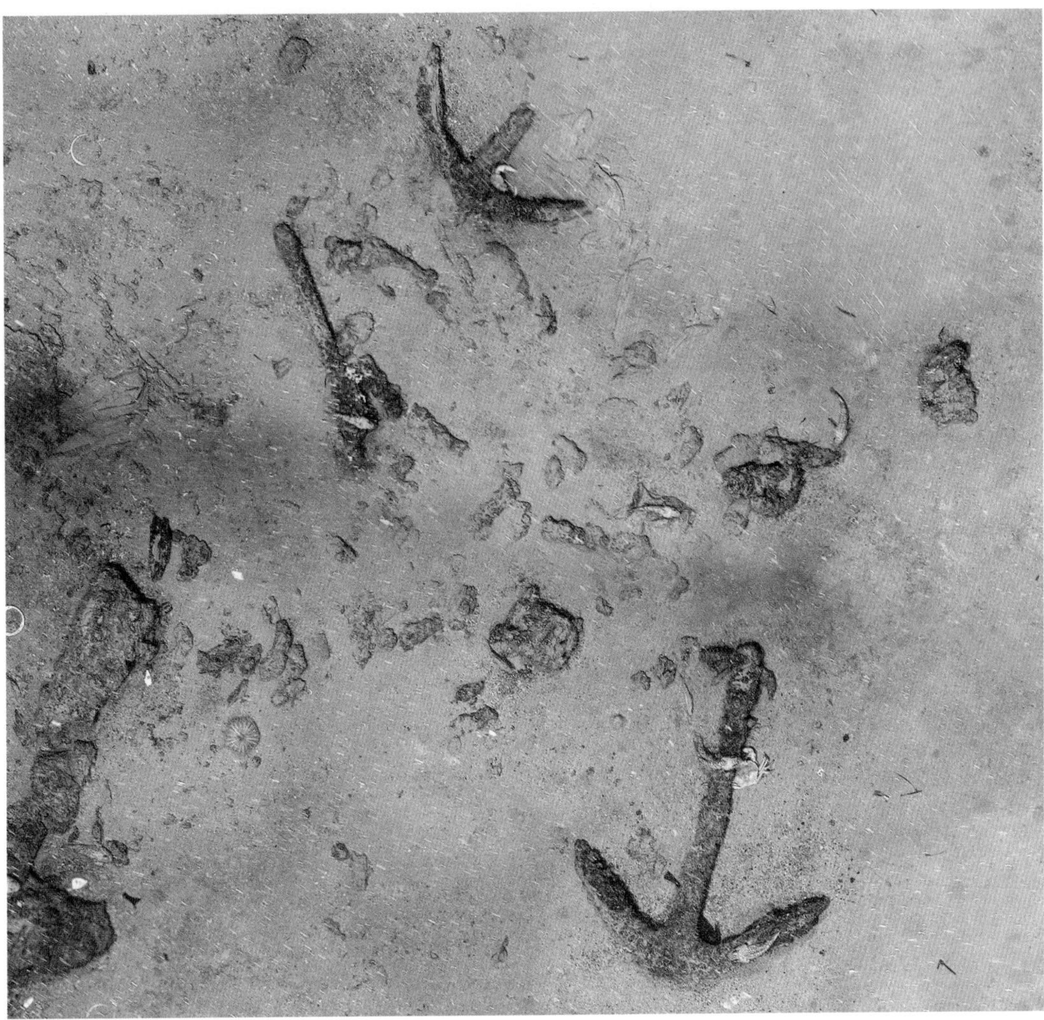

Fig. 8. Photomosaic detail of Area C: two iron anchors at the bows with the possible stem assembly towards the north (far left).

large wooden kegs (K1-K4), concreted through their iron hoop binding, holding unknown contents and each measuring approximately 48 x 38cm (Figs. 7, 26). (Additional examples on the site may point towards a content of musket shot and/or tobacco pipes.)

The two easternmost kegs, K3 and K4, have been seemingly struck and flattened by a trawler. Mixed amongst the bottles in Area B are 39 clay tobacco pipes, 33 within the confined limits of Area B1, 3.0 x 2.2m, and all of the ribbed Type 1 variant (see Section 8 below; Fig. 24). This is the epicenter of the scatter of 63 pipes on Site BA02 and suggests storage within one or two crates possibly stowed in this location (Fig. 52). In addition, seven of the eight ceramic salve jars and covers visible on the surface of the wreck are confined to Area B1 (Fig. 50). Two Type 4 Sand's Sarsaparilla medicine bottles lie on the western edge of keg K1 and two glass oil lamps with bases were identified 1.5m to its northwest (Fig. 55). No Types 2 or 3 dipped or underglaze painted wares whatsoever are present in the stern section of the site in either Area B or E.

Two iron anchors are visible at the southernmost section of the site in Area C, one intact (A2) and the second (A1) with just its arms and lower shank preserved (see Section 5). No wood underlies the anchors. This zone is covered with around 33 small concretions of differing sizes and appears to have been heavily impacted by trawls (Figs. 5, 8, 27, 28).

Area D immediately north of Area A contains 14 small square wooden kegs of similar dimensions to those bordering the eastern flank of Area A (16.8 x 16.8cm and 21 x 17.8cm), identified as containing white lead. All but three are clustered in the northern half of Area D within an area covering 1.53 x 1.50m (Figs. 5, 9, 30). The southern half, Area D2, is characterized by remains of an additional cargo of stacked rectangular glass window panes, each measuring some 29.8 x 25.1cm and visible across a limited area of 1.78 x 1.27m. In the two main piles preserved on the surface of the wreck the panes are stacked five to six high (Figs. 31, 53, 74). Underlying both the kegs and glass is a 3.4m-long section of articulated hull consisting of at least 14 wooden frames aligned east/west. The hull section is 0.93m wide before it is concealed by the overlying cargo (Figs. 30, 31). A lead ingot, a section of canvas and a blue-paneled cologne bottle are associated with Area D (Fig. 75).

Area E is especially interesting because of the presence of an eclectic deposit of domestic assemblage clearly belonging to the captain and crew and once stored in the ship's cabin (Figs. 5, 10, 55). A 88cm-long tripod-shaped iron concretion, perhaps resembling part of surveying/astronomy equipment, marks the extreme north end of the site in Area E1 and from between its legs were recovered a portable brass telescope with a wooden outer tube sheath and two brass pocket compasses (Figs. 33, 76-83).

Some 2.9m due south and immediately north of the large keg K6 in Area E2 a rich deposit was examined, consisting of a glass salt cellar, a glass inkstand, part of a brass and glass sextant and a brass hinge (Figs. 34-35, 55, 84-86). To the southwest of keg K7 a cluster of six Type 1 ribbed tobacco pipes was recorded in Area E3, while another six were scattered around the north and east of keg K5 (Figs. 36, 52). A seventh example concreted to K6 may reflect the original form of their stowage within kegs. Two light aqua Type 3 sauce/utilitarian glass bottles lie on the northwestern side of keg K7 (Fig. 53). Two cupreous sail thimbles were located between Areas B and E (Figs. 43, 55, 95-99). The presence of the navigational and domestic wares, which would typically have been stored in a galley cabin, confirms the identification of the north end of the site as the position of the ship's stern.

Area F on the eastern, port side of the wreck is characterized by a spread of glass window panes covering a 1.8 x 1.2m section of wreckage and located parallel to the cluster present at the northern end of Area D (Figs. 11, 38, 53). This class of cargo was evidently originally stacked on both sides of the keel in the center of the ship. Area F coincides with the densest presence of glass tumblers that merges with the northwestern side of Area G (44 in total on Site BA02: two examples in Area A, one in Area B, four in Area D, four in Area E, seven in Area F, 25 in Area G, one next to concretion CN1; Fig. 54).

From the northeastern edge of Area A an uninterrupted deposit of largely scattered ceramic wares continues in Area G for a main range of 6.7 x 3.0m from the southwest to northeast, but with outlying deposits covering a total length of 8.5m (Figs. 12, 39-40). Cargo ceramics in Area G are far less nucleated, and bottom trawlers have seemingly heavily impacted this part of the site, which has manifested in the survival of lines of intact and broken pots lying along trawl lines (Fig. 119). Notably, no Type 1 shell-edged whitewares or glass bottles are present in this

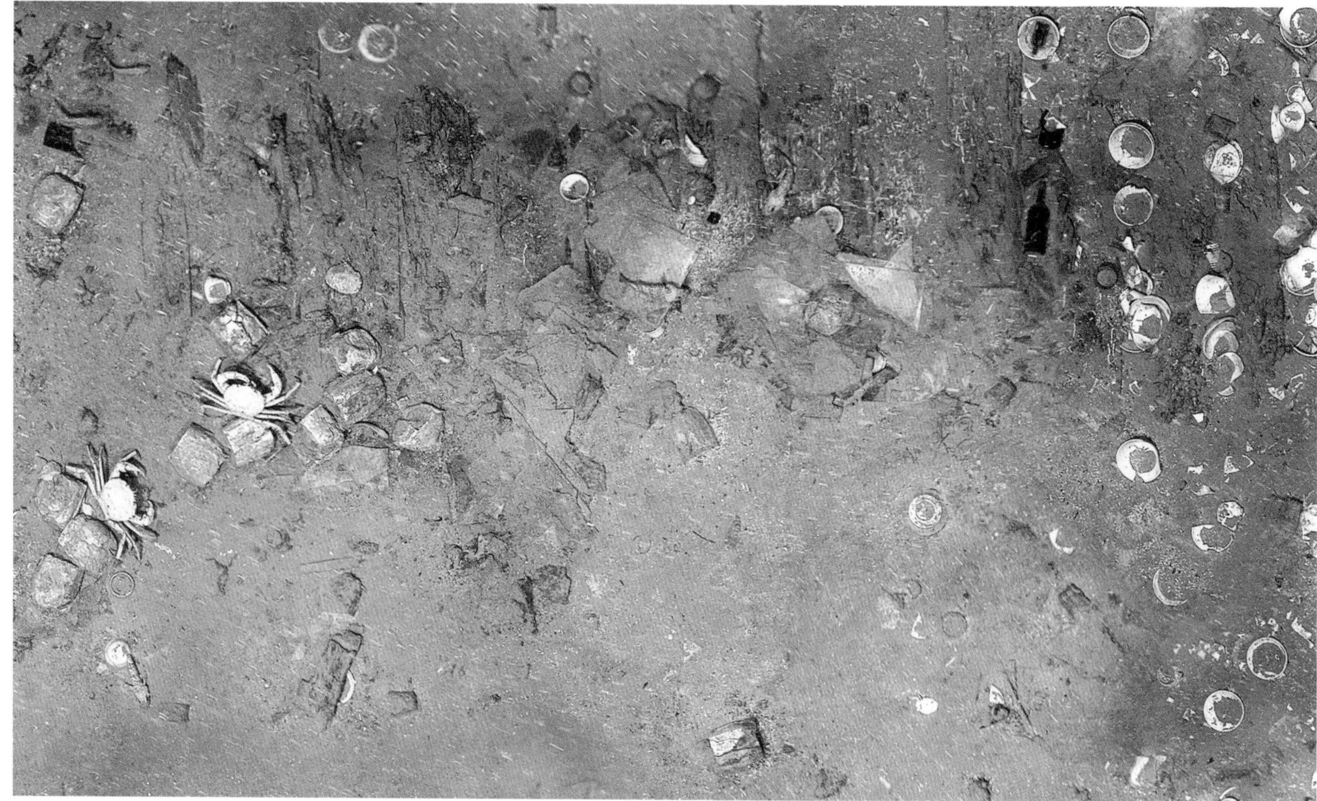

Fig. 9. Photomosaic detail of Area D: glass window panes overlying wooden frames at right and center, with wooden kegs to the north (at left).

zone, which is characterized by three types of ceramics: 10 Type 5B yellow ware chamber pots are restricted to the southwestern half of Area G in a 3.1m-long east/west linear band (Fig. 51); the most numerous cargo form are Type 2A dipped ware bowls confined to the central and southwestern sections of Area G, but with nine Type 2B dipped ware jugs and one Type 2C dipped ware mug more widely diffused to the northeast (Fig. 48); Type 3 underglaze painted whitewares used for tea service are heavily concentrated to the northeast within a 8.6 x 2.5m north/south band (that includes its extension across Area F and into Area B; Fig. 49); spreads of Type 4 white ironstone chamber pots, bowls and basins are present throughout this zone (Fig. 50). A 7.2m-long and 0.7m-wide narrow band of 25 scattered glass tumblers extends down the northwestern side of this zone, terminating at the northern end of Area A (Fig. 54). A cluster of eight ribbed tobacco pipes along the keel line at the center of Area G may reflect the presence of another decomposed crate of these wares (Fig. 52).

The ship form present at Site BA02 was a sailing vessel that did not rely on powered machinery. No wire rigging has been identified, an absence that is indicative of a pre-Civil War timeframe (Murphy, 1993: 204), thus prior to *c.* 1861. The absence of cannon signifies that the vessel was neither a privateer nor an armed merchantman. It is most suitably characterized as a coastal or, less likely, a trans-oceanic trading craft.

The single intact anchor's length points towards a vessel of 100 tons or less. The length of the visible keel remains measures 17.6m, which probably reliably equates to the original keel length. The visible hull remains measure 2.5m in width between the keel and the starboard frame edges in Area D. Despite its small magnitude, the ship was relatively heavily framed (Fig. 32): the wooden frames exposed near the middle of the wreckage between Areas D and F display sided dimensions ranging from 12-14cm (4.7-5.5in), with spacing of 11cm (4.3in). For a vessel of 100 tons the Rule VIII hull construction requirements cited in the *American Lloyd's Register of American and Foreign Shipping* (1865: xv) indicated that floors needed to measure a minimum of 9in and frames 4.5in at the plank shear and 8in at the throat. Again, this information is suggestive of a small vessel, probably under 100 tons.

5. The Anchors (Area C)

Two concreted iron anchors are associated with Site BA02 and define the southernmost flank of the wreck (Area C). Both were evidently still lashed to the bows when the ship sank (Figs. 4, 5, 8). Anchor A1 is located 2.2m northeast of the end of the visible articulated wreckage (defined by the eastern tip of a large sub-rectangular iron concretion that may be part of the stem assembly). A1 is broken and only a section of the crown, arms and the lower shank are preserved (surviving L. 57.7cm, shank W. 11.6cm; Fig. 28). The arms are gently rounded, 58.7cm long, and measure 1.1m between the fluke tips. A second section of concreted iron lying just 78cm to its southwest, surmounted by a ring, seems to be the missing section of the shank (L. 1.12m, Th. 9.4cm). This suggests a total length for anchor A1 of 1.69m, which is consistent with the dimensions of anchor A2.

Anchor A2, 1.65m long, is intact and lies 2.31m due south of the tip of the possible stem structure and 2m

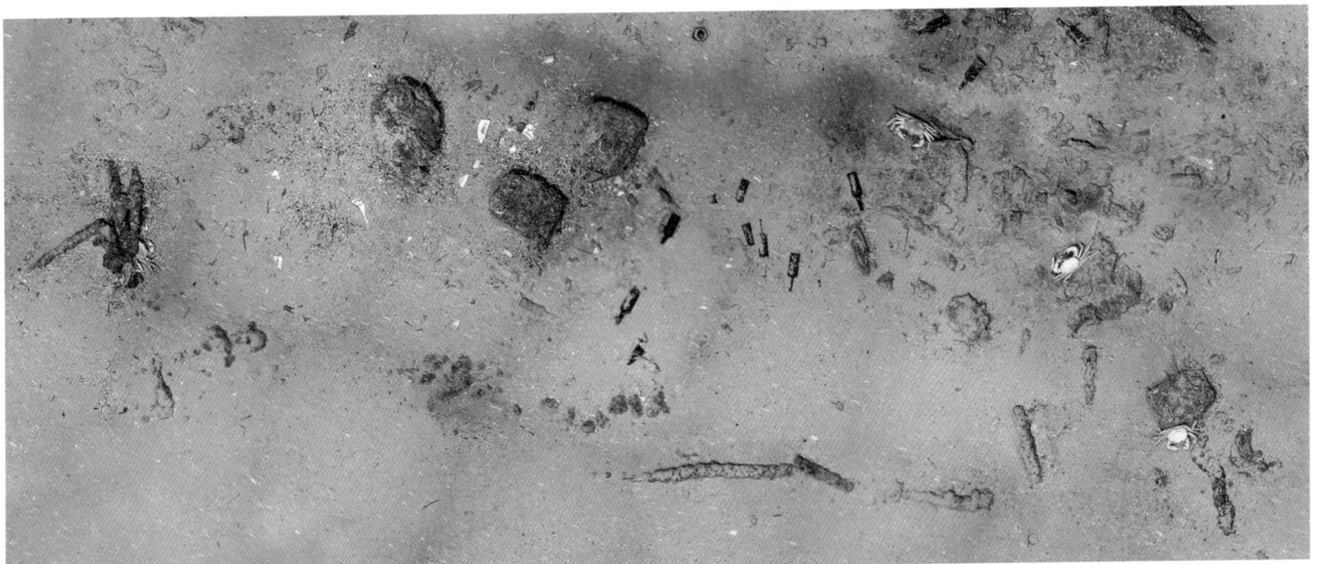

Fig. 10. Photomosaic detail of Area E in the stern: a concreted tripod (E1, far left), large kegs K5-K7, and at far right keg K9 and CN1, a concreted feature, possibly a rudder gudgeon.

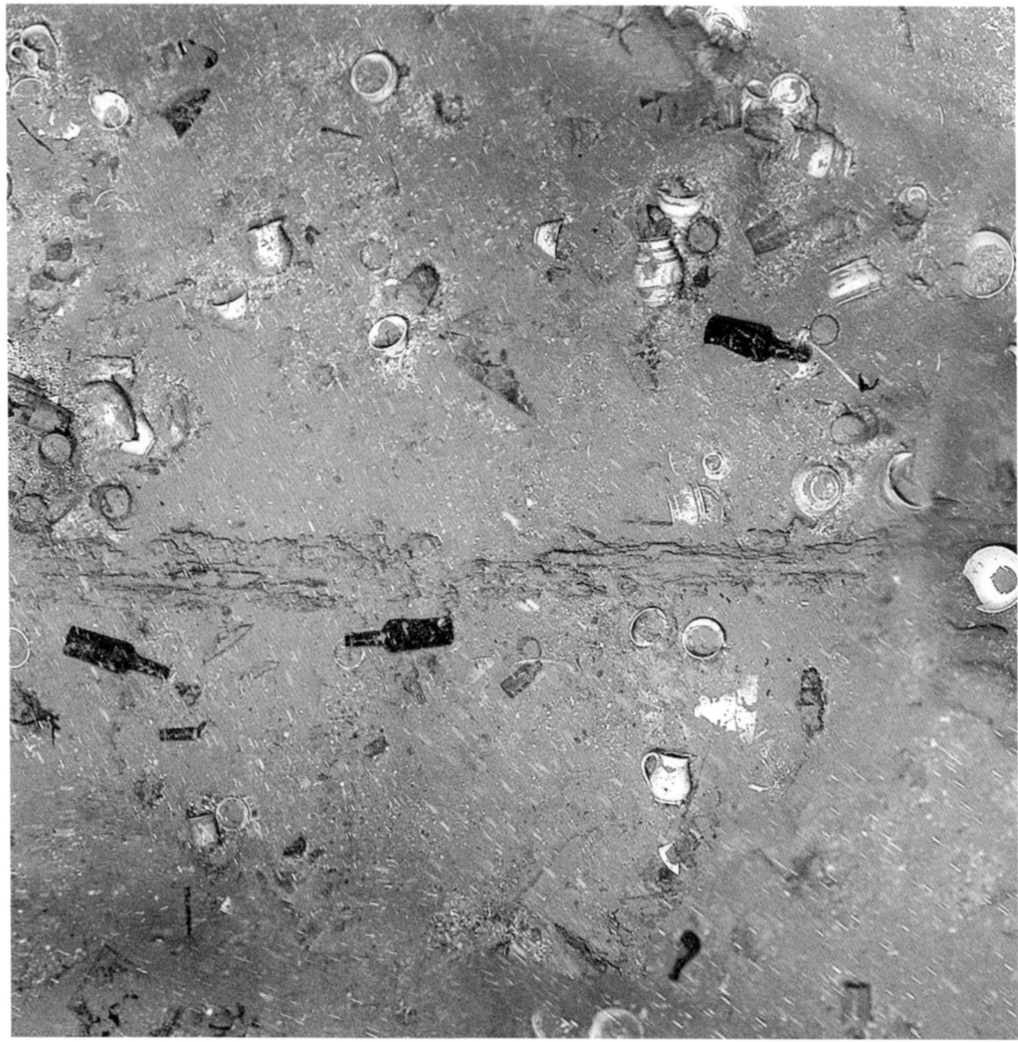

Fig. 11. Photomosaic detail of Area F: the north/south running keel at center surrounded by underglaze painted whiteware cream jugs, sugar bowls and tea bowls (tea service cargo) and glass window panes in the foreground.

west of A1 (Fig. 27). A small hawser ring (Diam. 23.1cm) survives at the top of the shank (Th. 12.6cm). Its arms, 64.9cm long, assume a more v-shaped profile than A1 and the flukes incorporate widened palms. The width between each of the two 12.6cm-wide arms is 1.3m.

Neither A1 nor A2 is associated with an iron stock, which suggests a reliance on a form of technology exploiting two pieces of oak sandwiched around the iron shank and bolted together, with the joint reinforced by iron hoops. A2 appears to feature a protrusion known as a 'nut' (Dover, 1998: 67), a design concept intended to help prevent the stock from sliding down the shank while in operation.

The use of anchors as diagnostic artifacts reflecting origins and chronology is infamously problematic. Anchor shape is not specific to places of origin and anatomy changed little over time (Marx, 1975: 97; Potter, 1972: 62). Potter (1972: 62) has proposed that the presence of an iron stock signifies a general post-1820 date. Marx (1975: 97), by contrast, argues that iron replaced wooden stocks as early as the mid-1800s. Within the British Navy, wooden anchor stocks were superseded by iron for anchors weighing less than 1,500lb in the early 1800s (Murphy, 1993: 229-30, 288). The apparent absence of iron stocks on Site BA02 demonstrates that this guide is far from uniformly applicable. No iron stocks were recorded on the wreck of the sidewheel steamer the SS *Republic*, wrecked off Georgia in 1865 (Cunningham Dobson *et al.*, 2010: 9, 17, fig. 12).

In terms of anchor forms in circulation around the time of the loss of the Jacksonville 'Blue China' wreck, the 1819 *Young Sea Officer's Sheet Anchor* (Dover, 1998: 67) lists an inventory of "one Sheet Anchor, one Spare Anchor, two Bower Anchors, one Stream Anchor, and one Kedge" for "Men of War, East Indiamen, and large Ships in the Southern Trade". The same source unhelpfully stated that "In the Merchant Service, the Anchors and Cables sometimes differ in Size and Number." Coasters, for example, which is directly applicable to Site BA02, "and particularly in the Coal Trade from the North to London," carried "two BOWER anchors, and in Vessels of two hundred Tons and upwards, a spare or waist Anchor." Murphy (1993: 288) has observed that regulations around 1850 mandated that ships "carry at least two bower anchors, a stream anchor and a smaller kedge anchor", while Tomlinson (1854: 46) reported in the decade when the Jacksonville 'Blue China' ship foundered that "Smaller vessels, such as brigs, cutters, and schooners, have only three or four anchors."

The 'sacred' sheet anchor was the largest and strongest and was only employed in extreme emergencies, such as the wildest gales. The bower anchors were nearly the same size as the sheet anchor and were referred to as the best bower, the small bower and spare anchor. The stream anchor weighed one-fourth to one-fifth the weight of the others and was relied on for holding the vessel in station in rivers or in moderate strength streams. Finally, the kedge anchor was half the size of the stream and was used for kedging, the process by which a vessel moved itself in the face of contrary currents or winds. This involved hauling this anchor out ahead of the vessel in a small boat, dropping it and drawing the ship ahead by pulling on the cable (Tomlinson, 1854: 46).

Identification of the type of anchors present on Site BA02 requires a determination of weight, the major factor in classification. A formula from *c.* 1854 provided a means of estimating anchor weight from the length, as follows: anchor weight in cwt (one counterweight equates to 110lb]) = anchor length in feet^3 x 0.0114 (Tomlinson, 1854: 47). This formula was suggested along with the caution that "for large anchors the result is too small, because the thickness is greater in proportion." Applying this formula to the intact Jacksonville 'Blue China' anchor A2, which measures just over 1.6m in length, yields an estimated weight of 190lb.

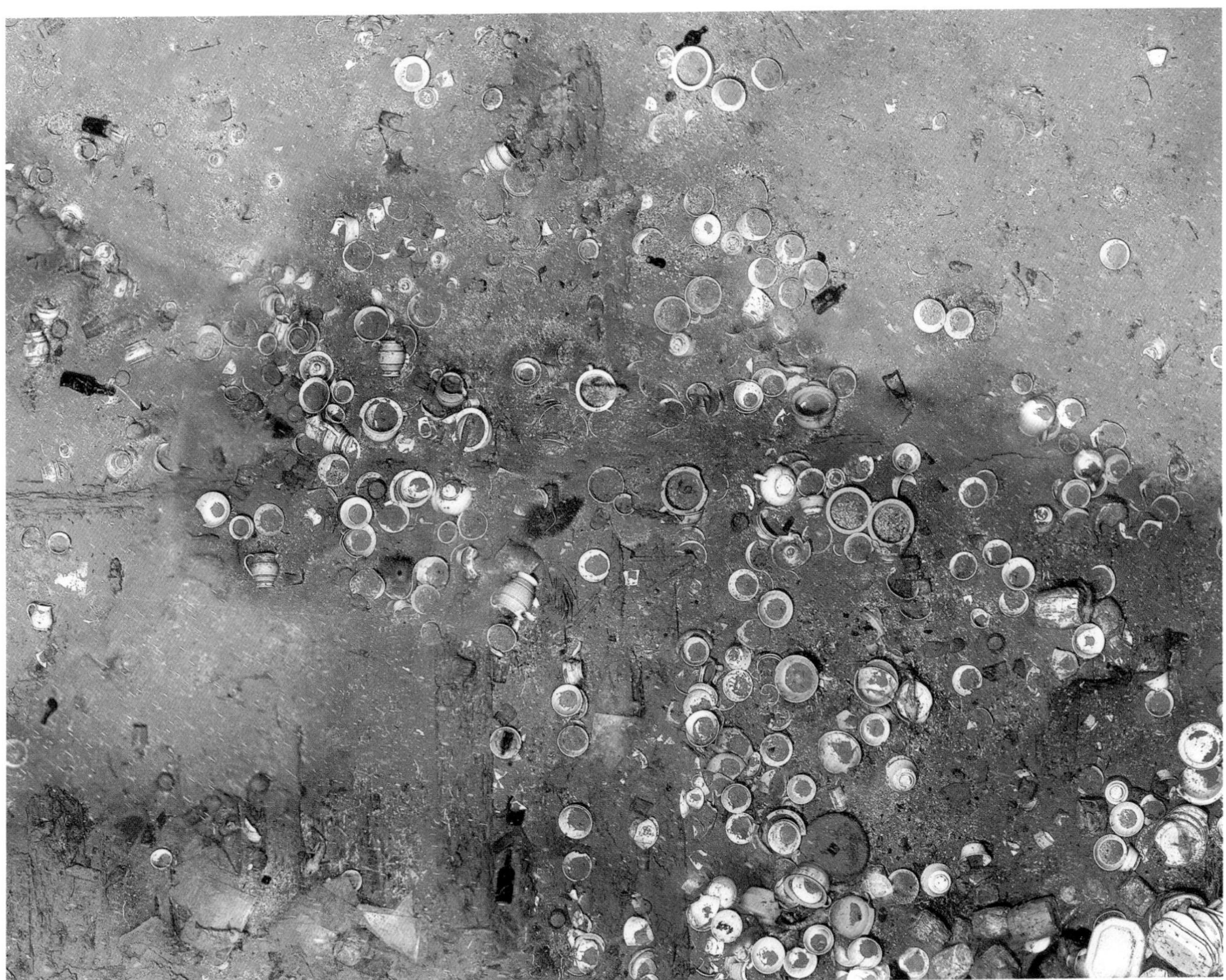

Fig. 12. Photomosaic detail of Area G: scattered white ironstone china, dipped yellow chamber pots, whitewares, and glass tumblers at left. Area A is visible at bottom right and Area D at bottom left.

Figs. 13-14. Overview of Area A: shell-edged earthenware plates, soup plates and platters to the south, mixed with dipped whiteware bowls, white ironstone china and a cluster of dark glass bottles to the north. Wooden kegs and dipped yellow ware chamber pots flank this zone.

Fig. 15. Detail of Area A from the south.

Fig. 16. Detail of Area A from the northeast, with the grindstone in the foreground flanking this zone.

Fig. 17. Concreted structural remains to the west of Area A (far right).

Fig. 18. Detail of shell-edged earthenware plates, soup plates and platters, dipped whiteware bowls, and white ironstone china chamber pots and basins in Area A.

Figs. 19-20. Detail of stacks of shell-edged earthenware plates, soup plates and platters in Area A.

Fig. 21. Detail of stacks of dipped whiteware bowls in Area A.

Fig. 22. Two of the four Canton ginger jars in situ *on the western flank of Area A.*

Fig. 23. Detail of dark glass bottles to the north of Area A.

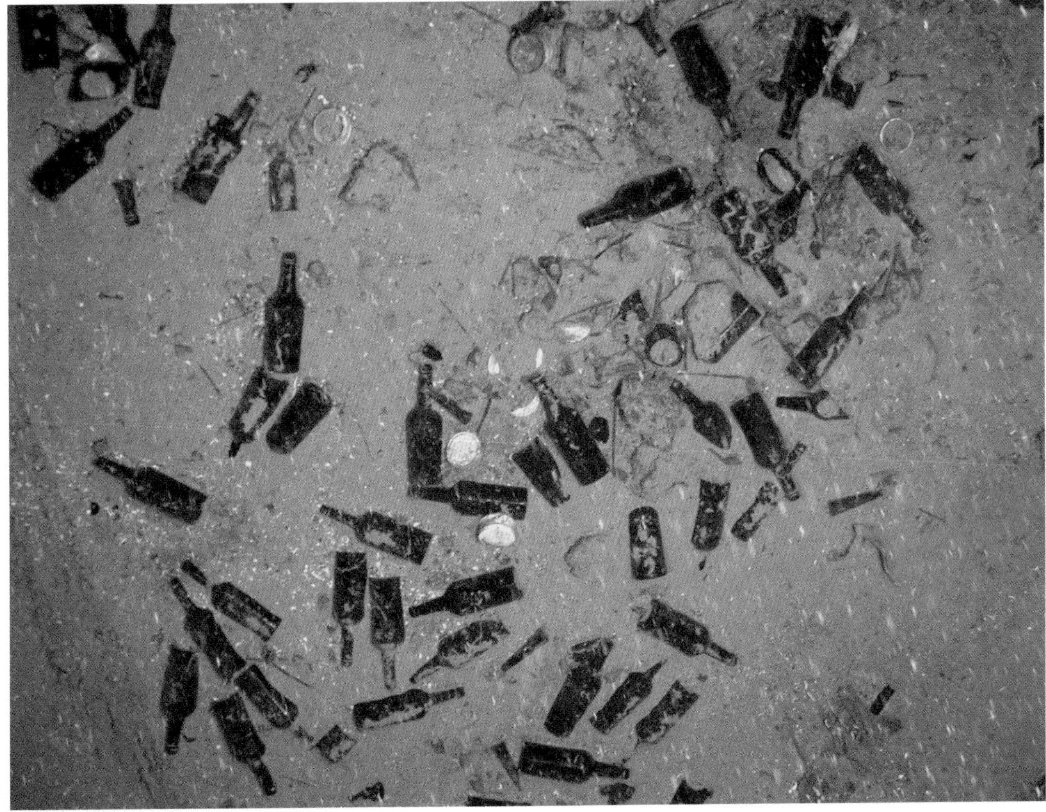

Fig. 24. Detail of scattered dark glass bottles in Area B, mixed with fluted tobacco pipes. The keel runs north/south at far left.

Fig. 25. Detail of dark glass bottles and underglaze painted whitewares (tea service) to the south of Area B.

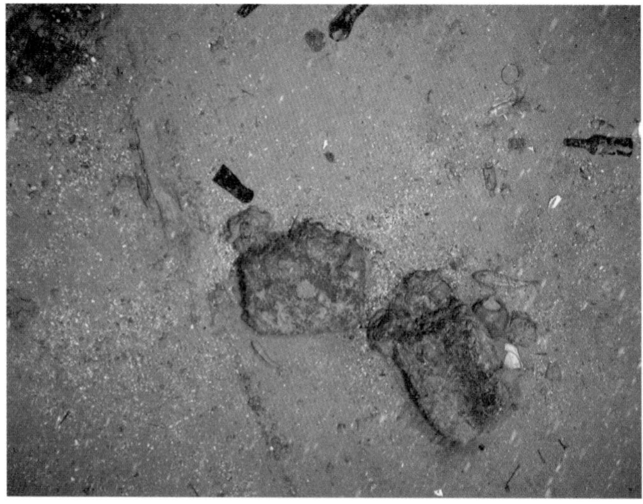

Fig. 26. Large wooden kegs K1-K3 with concreted iron hoops to the north of Area B, with the buried keel to their east.

Fig. 27. Anchor A2 in the bows at the southernmost end of Site BA02.

Fig. 28. Anchor A1 in the bows at the southernmost end of Site BA02, with its probable broken shank behind.

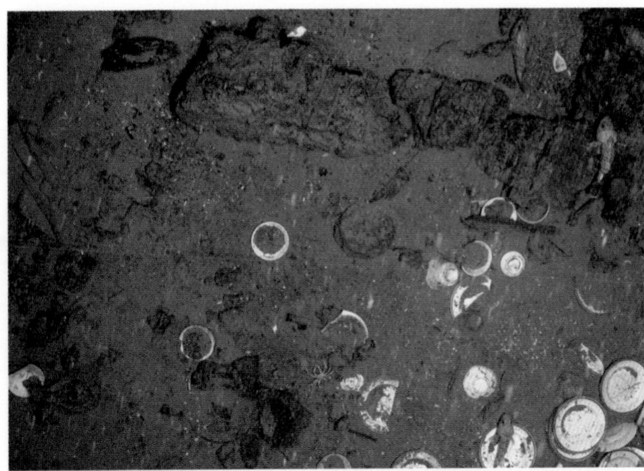

Fig. 29. Areas A and C are divided by a long section of concreted timber, possibly part of the stem assembly structure.

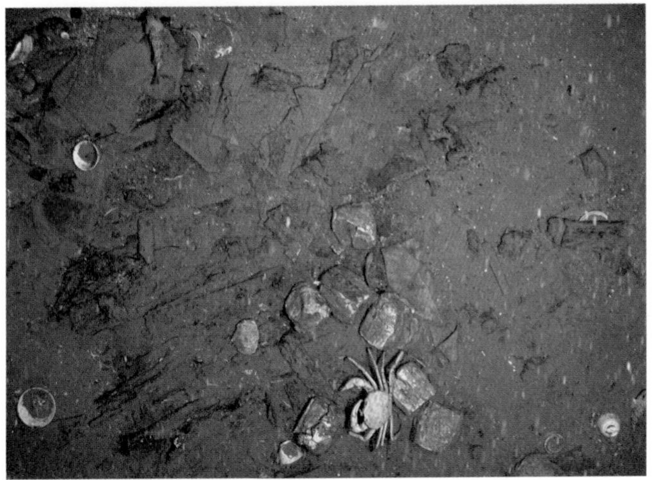

Fig. 30. Area D from the north with glass window panes overlying wooden frames (top) and wooden kegs in the foreground.

Fig. 31. Vertical view of glass window panes in Area D2.

Fig. 32. Hull remains in Areas D and F: the keel runs north/south (at left) flanked by a series of at least 11 starboard frames attached to underlying strakes (at right). Keel and frames are no longer interconnected.

Fig. 33. Detail of feature E1 to the north of Area E in the stern, a concreted tripod possibly used for navigation/surveying purposes and originally stowed in the ship's main cabin.

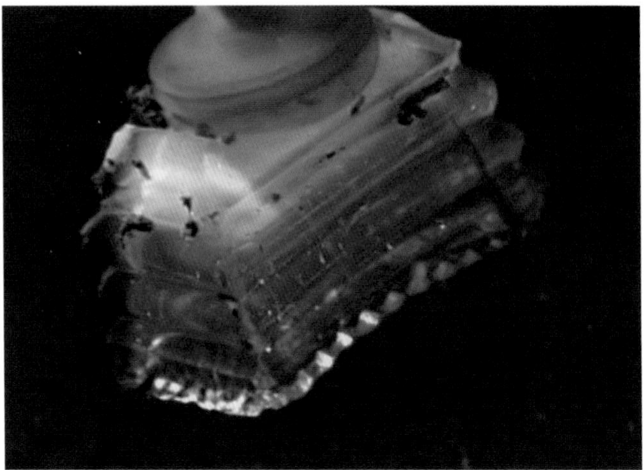

Fig. 34. A glass salt cellar being recovered from Area E2 by the ROV Zeus' limpet suction device.

Fig. 35. A glass inkstand under examination by the ROV Zeus in Area E2.

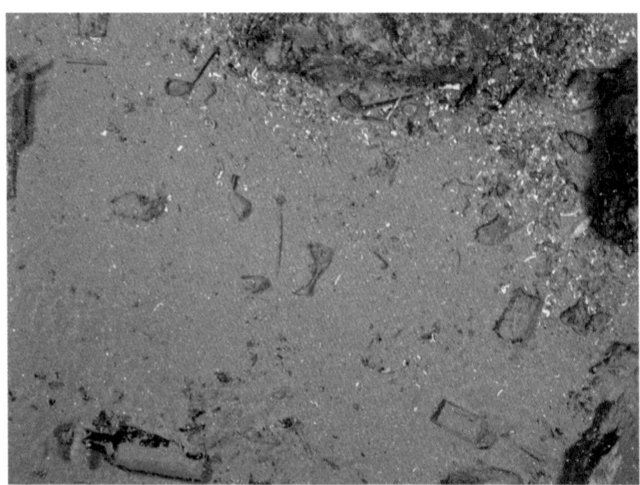

Fig. 36 (middle left). Detail of feature E3 in Area E in the stern: glass bottles and tobacco pipes clustered around large keg K7.

Fig. 37 (middle right). Detail of concretion CN1 to the south of Area E to the west of the wreck, possibly identifiable as remains of a rudder gudgeon.

Fig. 38 (bottom left). Various glass bottles and two sides or bases of wooden crates in Area F.

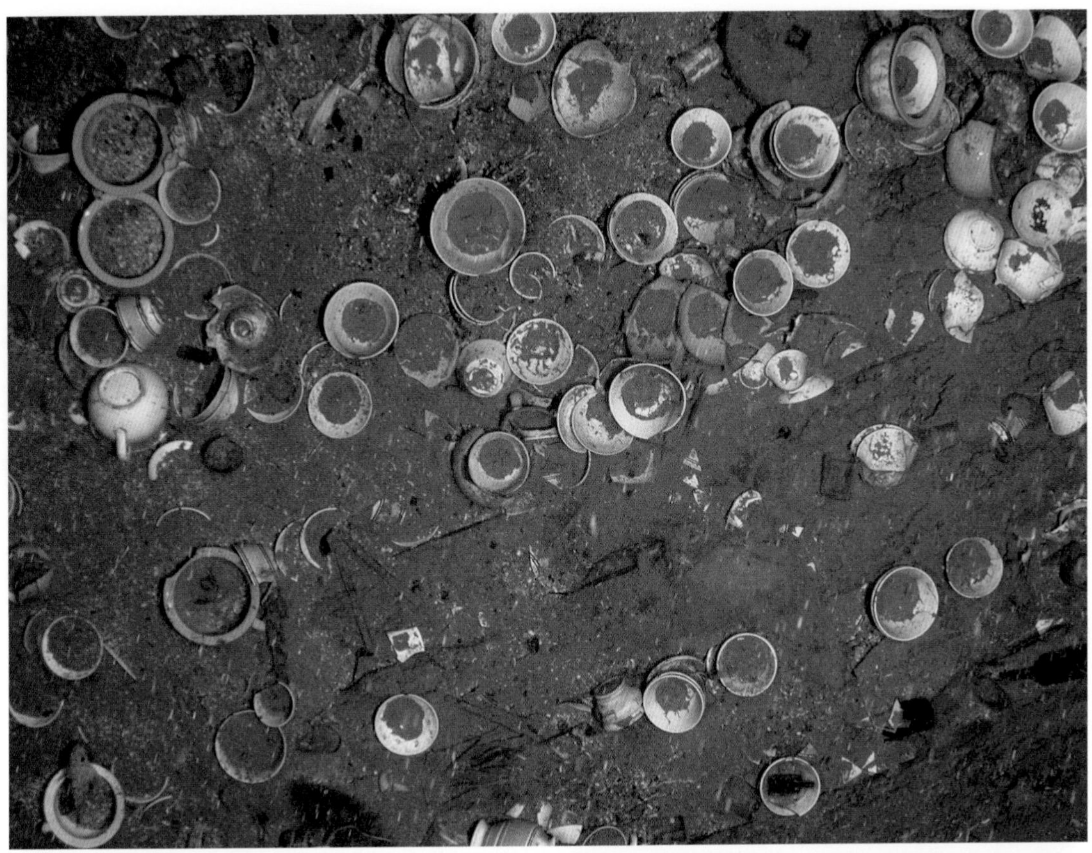

Figs. 39-40. Scattered underglaze painted floral tea saucers and tea bowls, dipped yellow ware chamber pots and dipped whiteware bowls across Area G, directly overlying flattened wooden strakes.

Fig. 41. Detail of the grindstone in Area G surrounded by dipped yellow ware chamber pots and dipped whiteware bowls.

Fig. 42. Detail of a cluster of lead ingots on the northwest flank of Area G in association with a wooden keg, dipped ware jug and underglaze painted whiteware cups and saucers.

Fig. 43. Detail of a cupreous sail thimble in situ *between Areas D and E.*

Fig. 44. A wooden hatch roller in situ *in the bows to the south of the wreck.*

When the two bowers were 'weighed' (raised off the sea floor) on a working vessel, they would have been secured on either side of the bow with the arms square to the hull. When stowed, the inner arms of the bowers overlay the gunwale (Dover 1998: 67; Tomlinson, 1854: 46). Harland (as cited in Dover, 1998: 126) noted that in Darcy Lever's day, *c*. 1819, bower anchors were generally the same size, but "one of the Bowers was designated 'Best Bower'. This, the 'working' anchor, was carried on the larboard (port) side, and had two cables bent to it." By contrast, Murphy (1993: 288) stated that "bowers were normally carried on deck for ready deployment in coastal waters. The stream and kedge anchors would likely be below decks."

As a consequence of the displacement and destruction of cultural material by the dragging of trawl nets across Site BA02, surface material cannot be assumed to remain in its original disposition. The absence of any snagged or otherwise lost nets suggests that no part of the site has been sufficiently rigid to withstand dragging, but it seems reasonable to work under the assumption that larger and heavier objects would have been displaced to a lesser degree than smaller and lighter ones.

The wreck's centerline, as demonstrated by the preserved keel, extends north/south. The presence of one intact and one broken anchor at the southern end of the site is taken to denote the reliable position of the bows. The lack of wood underlying them is consistent with their having fallen off the bows following the hull's collapse, rather than classification as spares stowed below deck. This identification is also reflected by their close proximity to each other at what is believed to be the forward end of the wreck. Intact anchor A2 seems to have been attached to the starboard bow, while A1 lies along

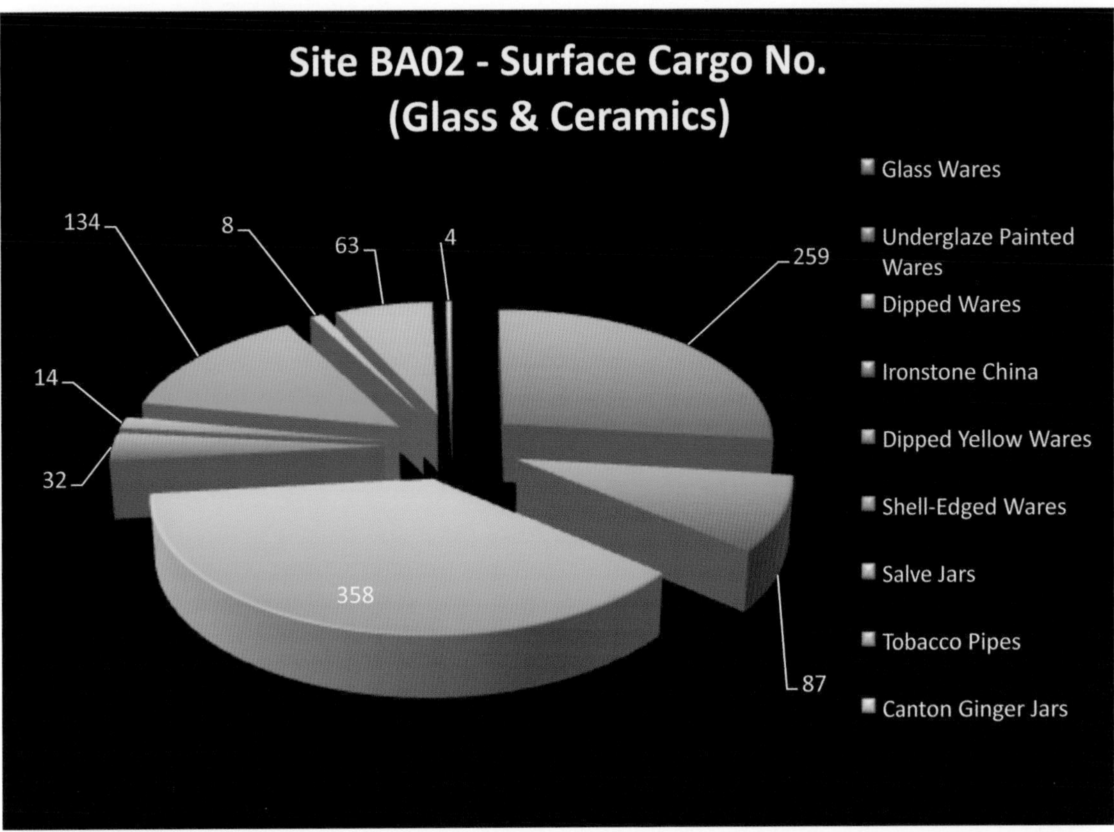

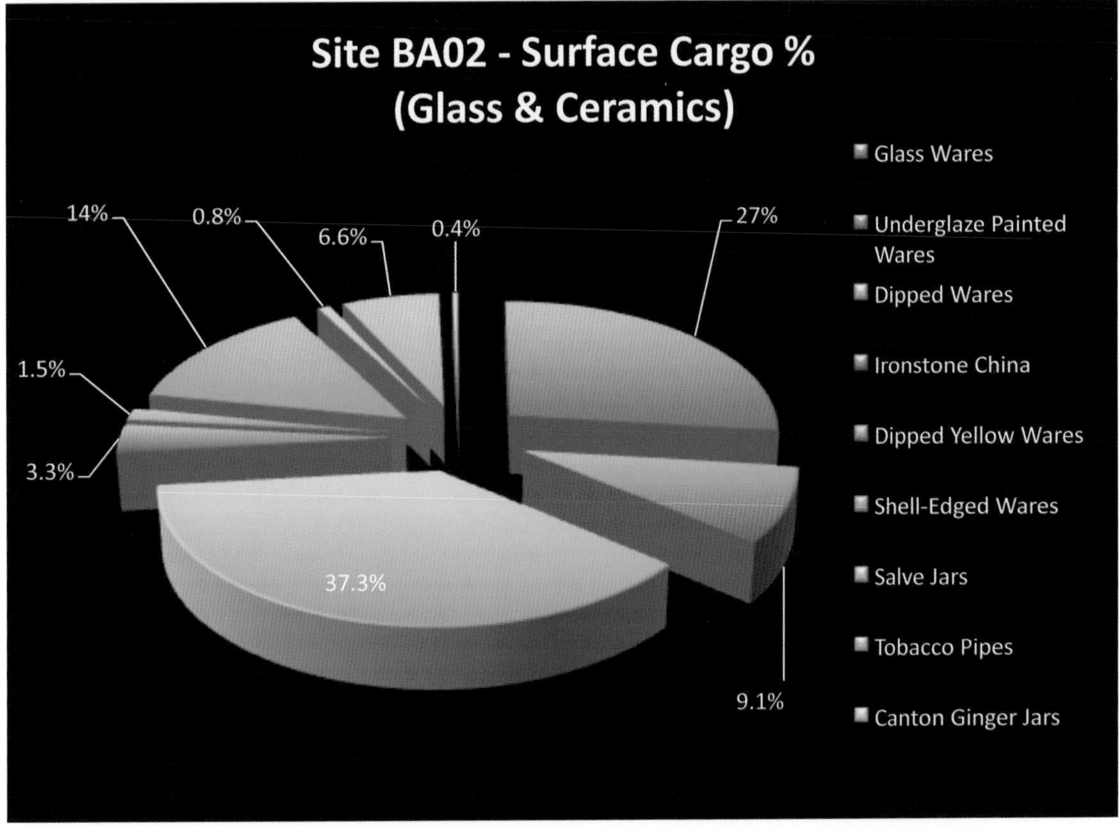

Figs. 45-46. The Jacksonville 'Blue China' shipwreck: surface cargo ceramics and glass cargo volumes as visible on the site photomosaic (by number and per cent).

the direct axis of the keel suggesting possible trawl dragging from portside in a northeast to southwest direction. This theory is in line with the sterile nature of the southeast quadrant of the wreck site, which has been heavily stripped of material culture.

Paasch's Illustrated Marine Dictionary of 1885 described merchant vessels as carrying bower, stream and kedge anchors of differing number and weight dependent on the size of a ship. In addition, he specified that "for a Sailing-Vessel of 100 tons" the usual complement of anchors would consist of two bowers from 5-6cwt each, one stream of about 2cwt and one kedge of around 70lb weight. With 1cwt equating to 110lb, the 190lb intact Site BA02 anchor currently seems to represent a stream anchor from a 100-ton sailing vessel or a bower from an even smaller sailing vessel.

6. Ceramic Cargo: Introduction

The diversity in type and quality of ceramic and glass cargo recorded on Site BA02 typifies a modest coastal trader, almost certainly of American origin, transporting goods on an established route to customers along the Atlantic and Gulf coasts or conceivably further into the Caribbean. The ceramic wares are largely British-made products, most likely from the Staffordshire potteries that would have been imported initially through the major American ports, such as New York, Philadelphia, Boston and Baltimore. From there they were repackaged and shipped down the Southern coast for resale to other merchants or smaller distributors (pers. comm. William Sargent, 6 March 2003; pers. comm. Jonathan Rickard, 12 July and 28 August 2006). Inland and Southern dealers also frequently traveled to the East Coast ports to choose their purchases.

While many Staffordshire manufacturers established pottery outlets in several US cities, American importers and agents also played an essential role in the transatlantic ceramics trade. By the 1850s the bulk of Staffordshire exports was handled by New York ceramic importers and dealers, who controlled the distribution network for the internal American market. For example, the Staffordshire-based ceramic merchant John Hackett Goddard of Longton purchased ceramics from British manufacturers, while his US partners John Burgess and Robert Dale operated the American wholesale ceramic outlets from Baltimore and New York. Goddard typically toured the Staffordshire potteries to determine what wares would best suit his American customers and regularly sent out samples to his American-based partners (Ewins, 1997: 88-91, 105-107, 109).

The wares of Kentucky and Ohio that did start to compete with the products of Staffordshire were virtually

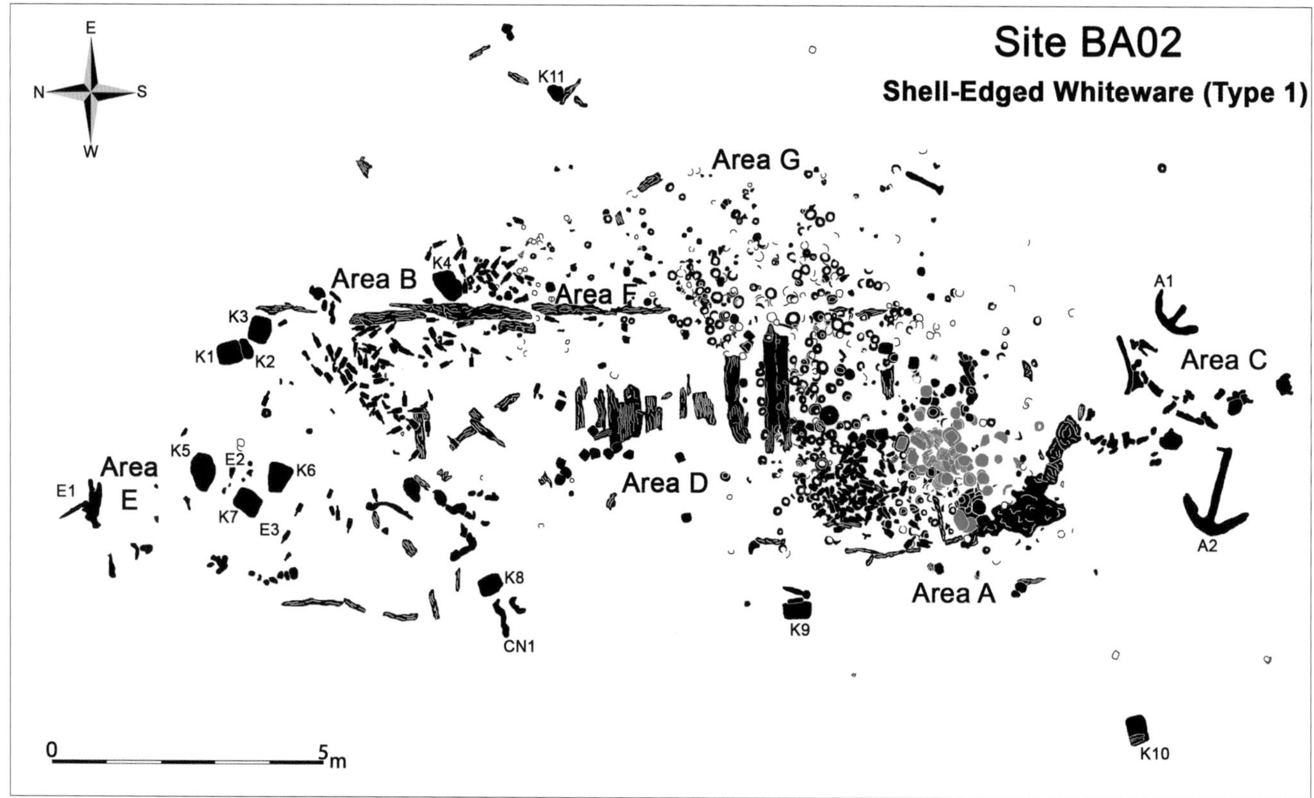

Fig. 47. The distribution of British shell-edged whitewares (Type 1) on Site BA02.

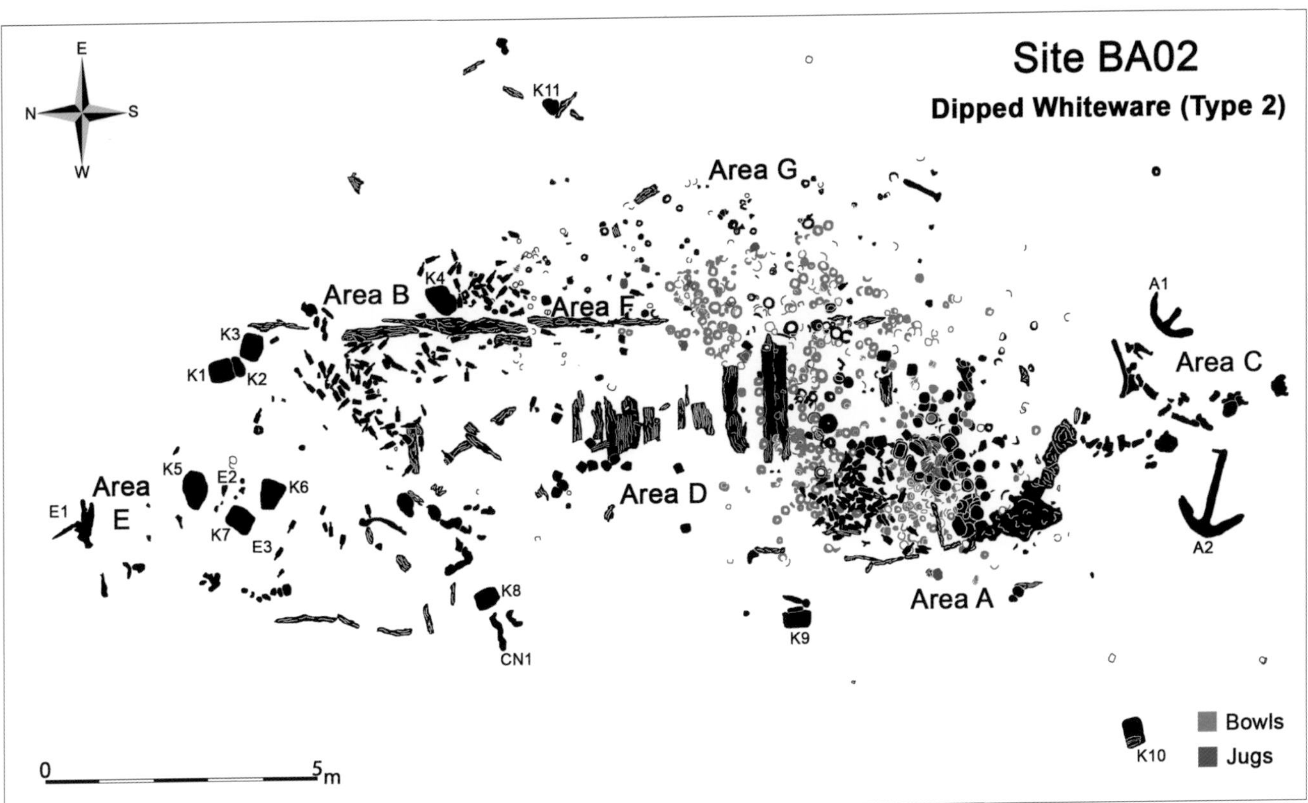

Fig. 48. The distribution of British dipped whitewares (Type 2) on Site BA02.

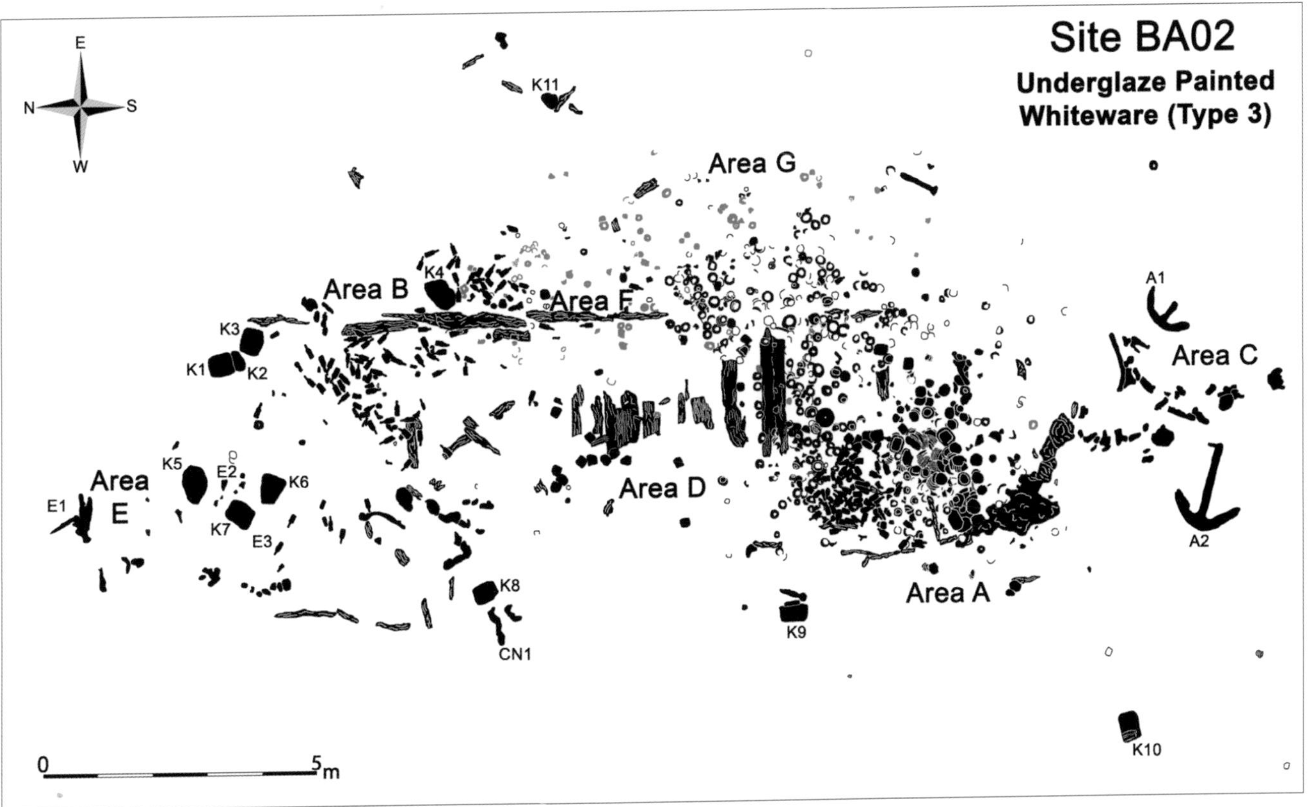

Fig. 49. The distribution of British underglaze painted whitewares (Type 3) on Site BA02.

all yellow wares, unlike the predominant British whitewares recovered from Site BA02. The latter on the wreck were produced from white firing clay, sources of which were not commercially exploited in the United States until later in the 19th century (pers. comm. Jonathan Rickard, 12 July 2006). Current data regarding the ownership and home port of the vessel wrecked at Site BA02 point towards a coastal trader originating in a port located on the Northern Atlantic Seaboard (pers. comm. Jonathan Rickard, 28 August, 2006). New York remains the most likely point of departure.

The artifacts recovered from Site BA02 have been conserved in Odyssey's laboratory in Tampa. Some have been incorporated into the company's interpretive traveling exhibits and the best examples of each duplicated class, plus unique objects such as all four Canton ginger jars, remain in Odyssey's permanent collection within the secure, climate-controlled storage of the curatorial facility in Tampa, where they are available for study.

7. Ceramic Typology Summary

The most conspicuous artifacts on the Jacksonville 'Blue China' shipwreck site are concentrations of ceramics clustered at the southern bow end in Area A and extensive scatters to its northeast in Area G: everything from circular plates and soup plates to octagonal platters, colorful banded bowls, tea service cups, saucers, creamers and sugar bowls, chamber pots and wash basins (Figs. 47-51). Except for a few examples, the assemblage encompasses the full range of British tea, table and toilet earthenwares most common on North American archaeological sites between the 1850s and 1860s.

The pre-dusting site photomosaic displays a minimum of 703 ceramic wares on the surface of the wreck (Figs. 4, 45-46). The surviving consignment, as visible on the pre-disturbance site photomosaic, consisted of:

- 134 shell-edged whitewares, Staffordshire, England (Type 1; Fig. 47).
- 358 dipped whitewares, Staffordshire, England (Type 2; Fig. 48).
- 87 underglaze painted whitewares (tea service), Staffordshire, England (Type 3; Fig. 49).
- 40 white granite/white ironstone, Staffordshire, England (Type 4; Fig. 50).
- 14 dipped yellow wares, Staffordshire, England (Type 5; Fig. 51).
- Four porcelain Canton ginger jars, China, (Type 6; Fig. 51).

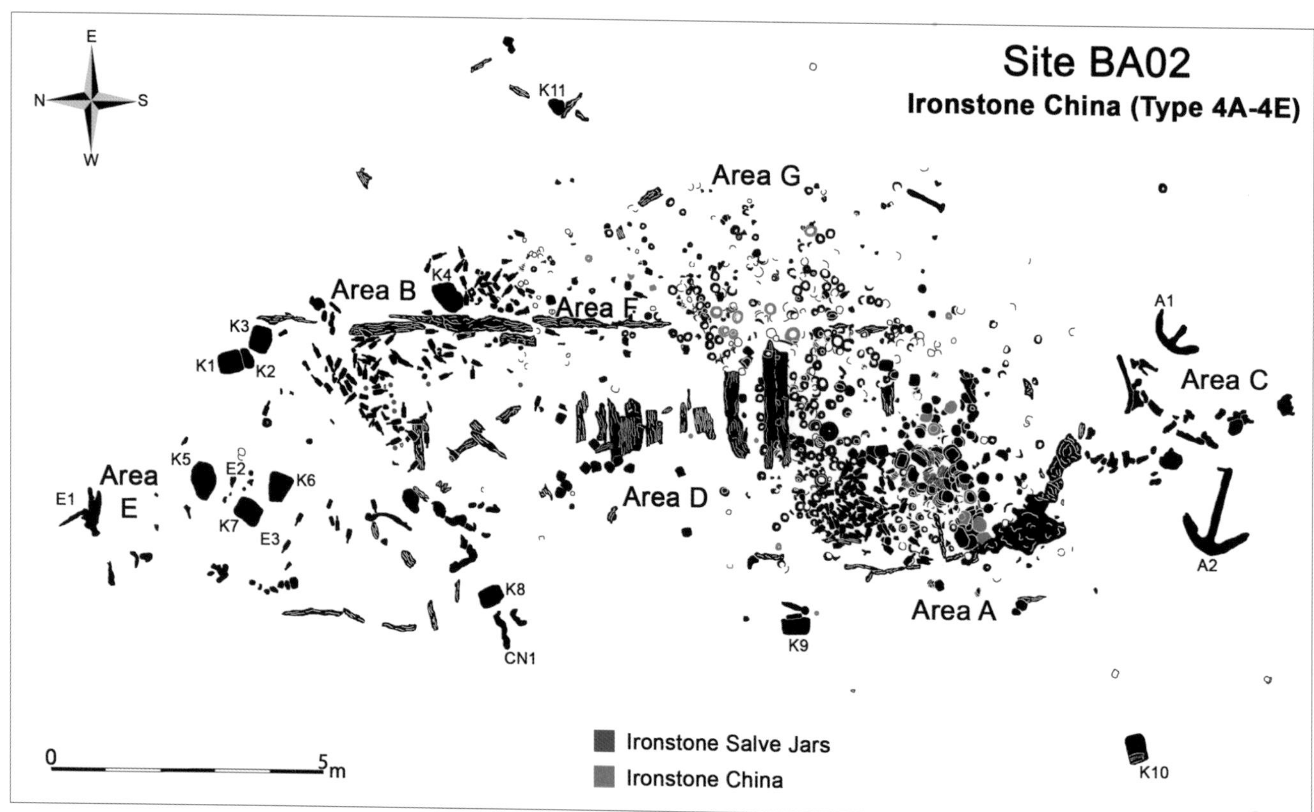

Fig. 50. The distribution of British white granite/ironstone china (Type 4) on Site BA02.

- Three stoneware vessels (two salt-glazed and one Bristol-glazed example), American/European (Types 8-10; Fig. 62).
- 63 clay tobacco pipes (Fig. 52).

A sample of 318 examples of these ceramic wares was recovered for study, enabling a further class, transfer-printed whiteware, to be added as Type 7. The ten different types of ceramic ware are classified largely by their decorative scheme, which accords to the names they were given by mid-19th century potters, merchants and consumers. The assemblage comprises largely earthenware, including shell-edged ware, dipped wares, painted wares, undecorated white granite/white ironstone china, yellow ware, and transfer-printed wares (as defined in Miller, 1988: 172), plus limited porcelain Canton ginger jars and stoneware. With the exception of a few individual examples, such as two European stoneware vessels and one American stoneware jug indicative of domestic assemblage used by the small crew, the ceramics were largely being shipped as cargo, having first arrived in one of the major American ports such as New York or Boston (Tolson *et al.*, 2008: 166). The below summarizes Ellen Gerth's detailed site pottery report published separately in Chapter 9.

The Jacksonville 'Blue China' Type 1 ceramic form consists of a sample of 153 recovered British blue shell-edged earthenware plates, soup plates and octagonal platters/serving dishes (Figs. 56-57, 62). This comprised the second largest concentration of earthenware among the cargo after Type 2. Initially marketed for upper middle class families and sold as complete dinner services, British shell-edged ware very quickly became available to the masses. The earlier shell-edged pearlware, in particular, resembles Chinese porcelain, yet was far less expensive and thus accessible across the class divide. The simple decorative pattern comprised a molded rim, frequently with blue or green underglaze paint, which excelled at framing the food on the otherwise all-white plate.

British shell-edged earthenware was produced and exported in vast volumes between 1780 and 1860 to such an extent that it permeated almost every American household. In terms of quantity it was one of the most successful developments in ceramic production throughout the Industrial Age of the 18th and 19th centuries (Hunter and Miller, 1994: 443; Miller, 2000: 91). The historical records of Staffordshire potters complement the widespread archaeological distributive evidence from land sites. Surviving invoices of American merchants reveal that shell-edge products accounted for more than 40% of dinnerware sold in America between 1800 and the eve of the Civil War in

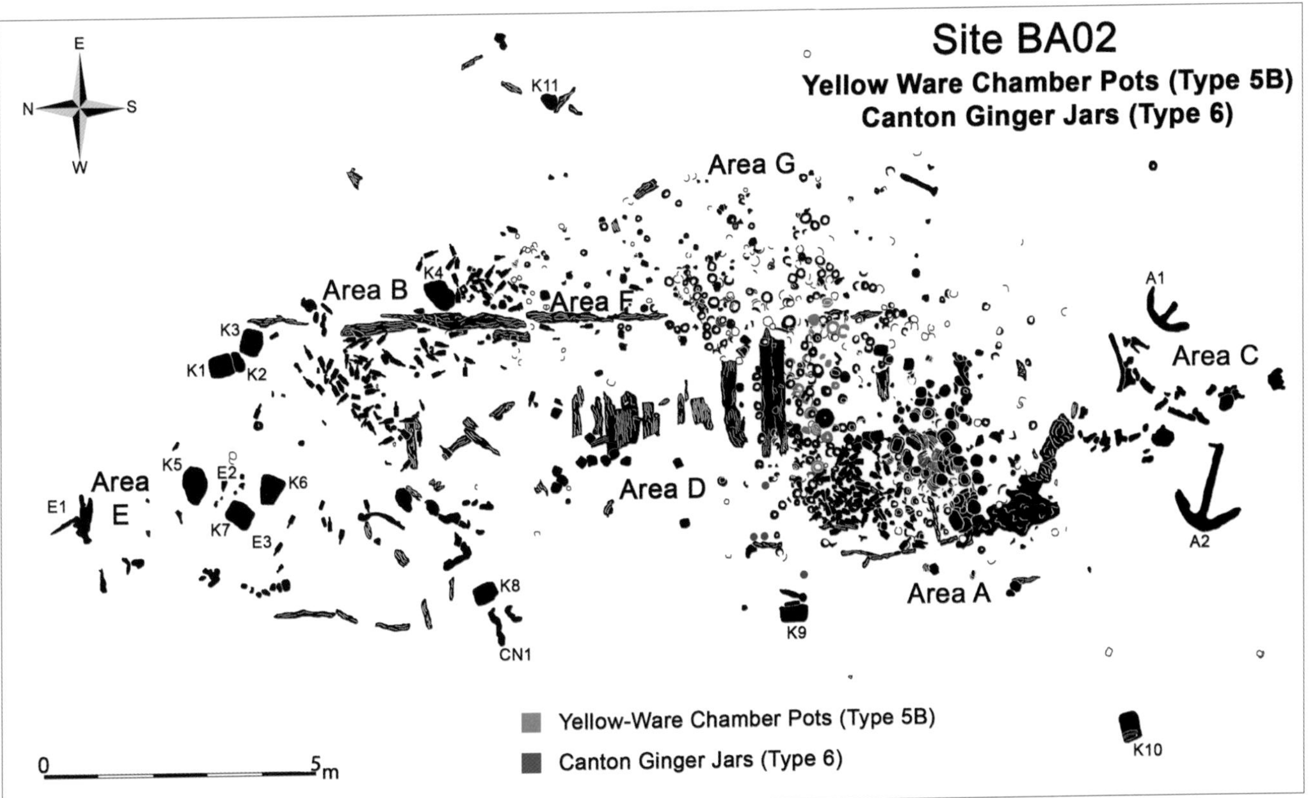

Fig. 51. The distribution of British dipped yellow wares (Type 5) and Canton ginger jars (Type 6) on Site BA02.

1861 (Hunter, 2008: 9; Hunter and Miller, 1994: 441; Tolson *et al.*, 2008: 167). They were the main staple of mid-19th century tablewares used by the average American consumer household.

The shell-edged examples recovered from the Jacksonville 'Blue China' shipwreck are heavy whitewares that feature unscalloped, straight rims impressed with simple repetitive lines colored blue, indicative of shell-edge production in the 1840s to 1850s. Over 50 British manufacturers representing all the major Staffordshire potters have been identified as producing shell-edged ware, which was also one of the standard products of potteries in Leeds, Castleford, Northumberland, Bristol and Devonshire (Hunter and Miller, 1994: 434).

The Type 2 ceramics sample recovered consists of 48 British slip-decorated utilitarian earthenware bowls, mugs and jugs referred to as dipped ware in contemporary sources (Figs. 56, 58, 59). The style was first produced by Staffordshire potters in the late 18th century on creamware and pearlware bodies, yet by the mid-19th century was featured on generic whitewares (pers. comm. Jonathan Rickard, 6 December 2010). Along with shell-edged wares, dipped wares enjoyed a long period of popularity as the least expensive imported decorated earthenware available to American consumers between the 1780s and well into the 1850s (Miller, 1988: 178; Rickard and Carpentier, 2001: 115, 133; Tolson *et al.*, 2008: 171). The British manufacture and export of these bold and colorful products was so extensive that sherds of this type occur on nearly every American domestic archaeological site of the period (Rickard and Carpentier, 2001: 115).

The 56 underglaze painted Type 3 British whitewares of *c.* 1845-55 being shipped as cargo on Site BA02 incorporate four different variations of a hand-painted floral motif (Figs. 60, 63). They have been identified as elements of tea sets that include tea bowls (cups in the 'London' shape), saucers, creamers and sugar bowls. No teapots were recovered or observed, although these vessels certainly originally would have been included amongst such shipments (Tolson *et al.*, 2008: 175, 183). These floral-decorated wares have many stylistic characteristics in common with teacups and saucers discovered on other sites and amongst collections bearing the impressed maker's mark 'ADAMS'. Since 1650 the Adams family managed potteries in Staffordshire with production centers located in Tunstall, Burslem and Cobridge, Stoke-on-Trent (Jervis, 1911: 98; Rickard, 2006: 4).

Five different variants totaling 43 examples of Type 4 British undecorated whiteware, otherwise known as white granite/white ironstone, were recovered from the

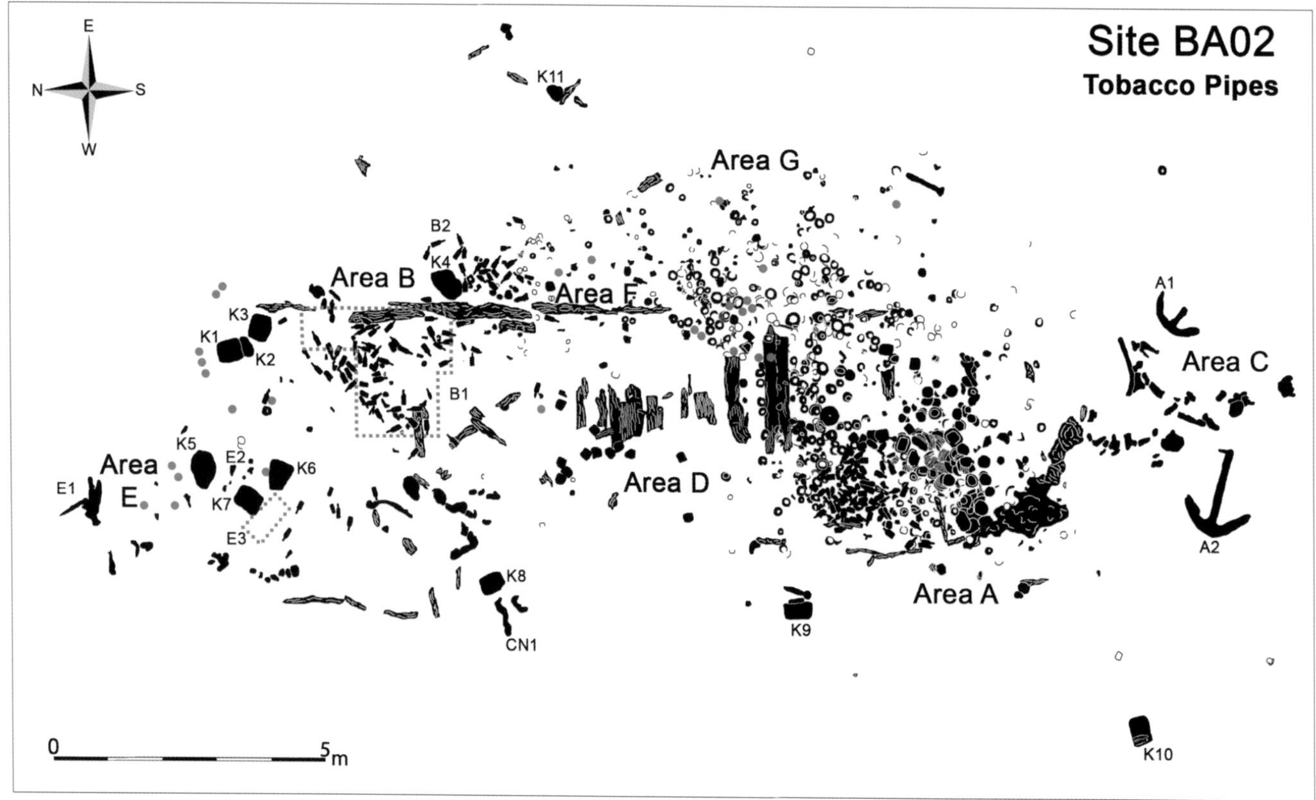

Fig. 52. The distribution of clay tobacco pipes on Site BA02.

Jacksonville 'Blue China' wreck (plates, bowls, chamber pots, wash basins and salve jars with covers; Fig. 60). This heavy, thick-bodied undecorated ceramic ware was mass-produced by England's Staffordshire potters (Blacker, 1911: 177; Godden, 1999: 160-62) and by the mid-19th century had become quite popular among both commercial and domestic American consumers (Miller, 1988: 175).

The preceding stone china and white ironstone wares first introduced in the early 19th century were heavily decorated, often in a Chinese style, and were produced to imitate the popular Chinese export market porcelains in both design and shape (Godden, 1999: 60-62; Miller, 2000: 95). However, the later ironstone forms introduced after 1830, such as those found on Site BA02, were more thickly potted, relief-molded and undecorated utilitarian vessels manufactured largely for the American market (Blacker, 1911: 177; Godden, 1999: 160-62). The ironstone china trade appears to have reached the Western frontier of America by 1839, supplied by a network of wholesalers, some of whom were working in St. Louis, and had strong ties with large-scale wholesalers and importers in Philadelphia and New York. Steady shipments of exports to America began in the early 1840s.

This modest, plain and durable product was highly desired in the 'colonies', where it could be found in various social environments from steamboats to taverns and hotels (Blacker, 1911: 194; Ewins, 1997: 47). The ironstone china discovered on Site BA02 was found stowed as cargo alongside the bulk of the ceramics both at the bow end of the wreck in Area A, where some examples remained stacked *in situ*, and scattered more widely across Area G. It is an important collection that is contemporary with more than 100 examples excavated from the steamboat *Arabia* lost on the Missouri River in 1856 (Hawley, 1998: 203-204) and pre-dates the nearly 3,000 examples recovered from the deep-sea sidewheel steamer the SS *Republic* that sank off southeast North America in 1865 (Cunningham Dobson and Gerth, 2010: 25).

Two forms of Type 5 ceramic artifacts, slip-decorated yellow earthenware chamber pots and a single mug were recovered from a limited east/west band to the south of Site BA02, solely west of the keel to starboard (Fig. 61). Their yellow bodies resemble 'American' yellow ware produced by British immigrant potters who established several workshops in the United States in the 1830s, including potteries at Bennington, Vermont, Trenton, New Jersey, Cincinnati and East Liverpool, Ohio, and Louisville, Kentucky. The North American dipped wares of the period are not easily distinguishable from the yellow-bodied wares produced in potting centers in Great Britain. However, the Site BA02

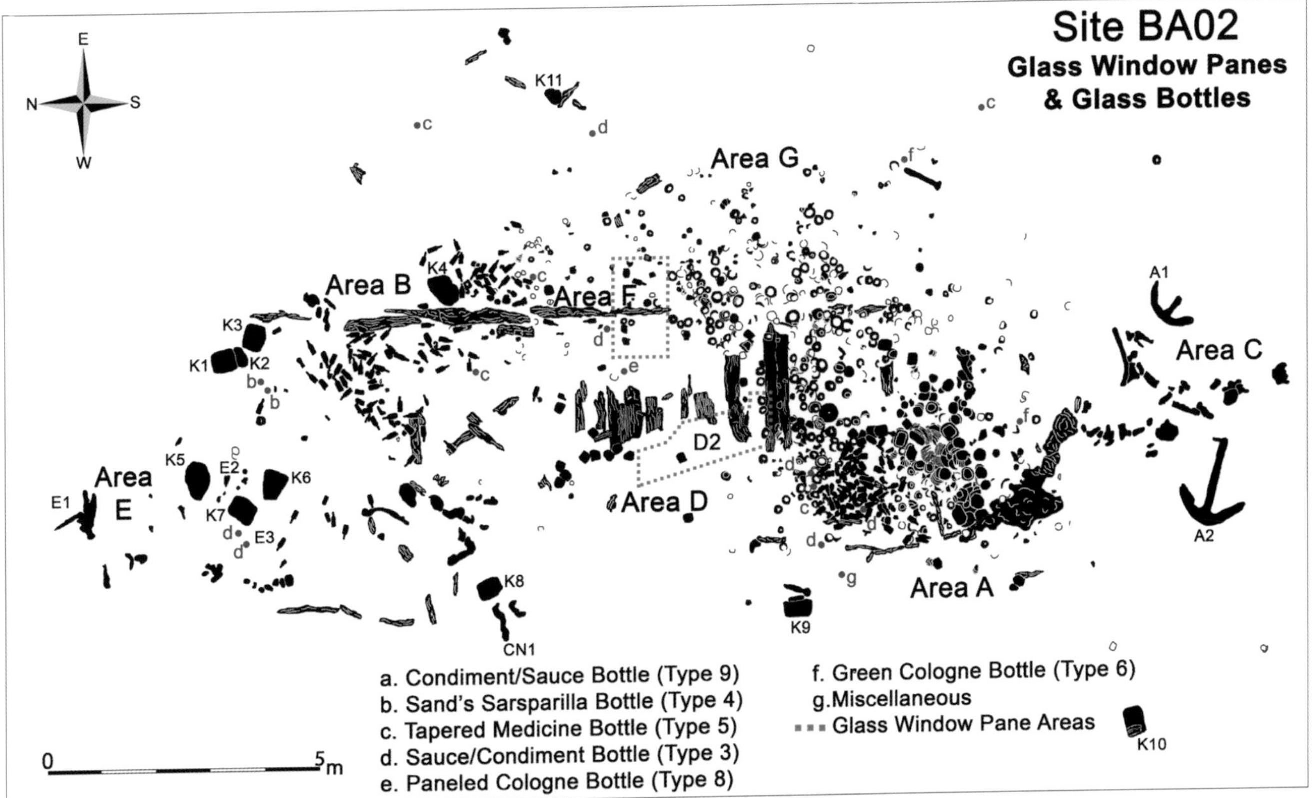

Fig. 53. The distribution of American glass bottles and window panes on Site BA02.

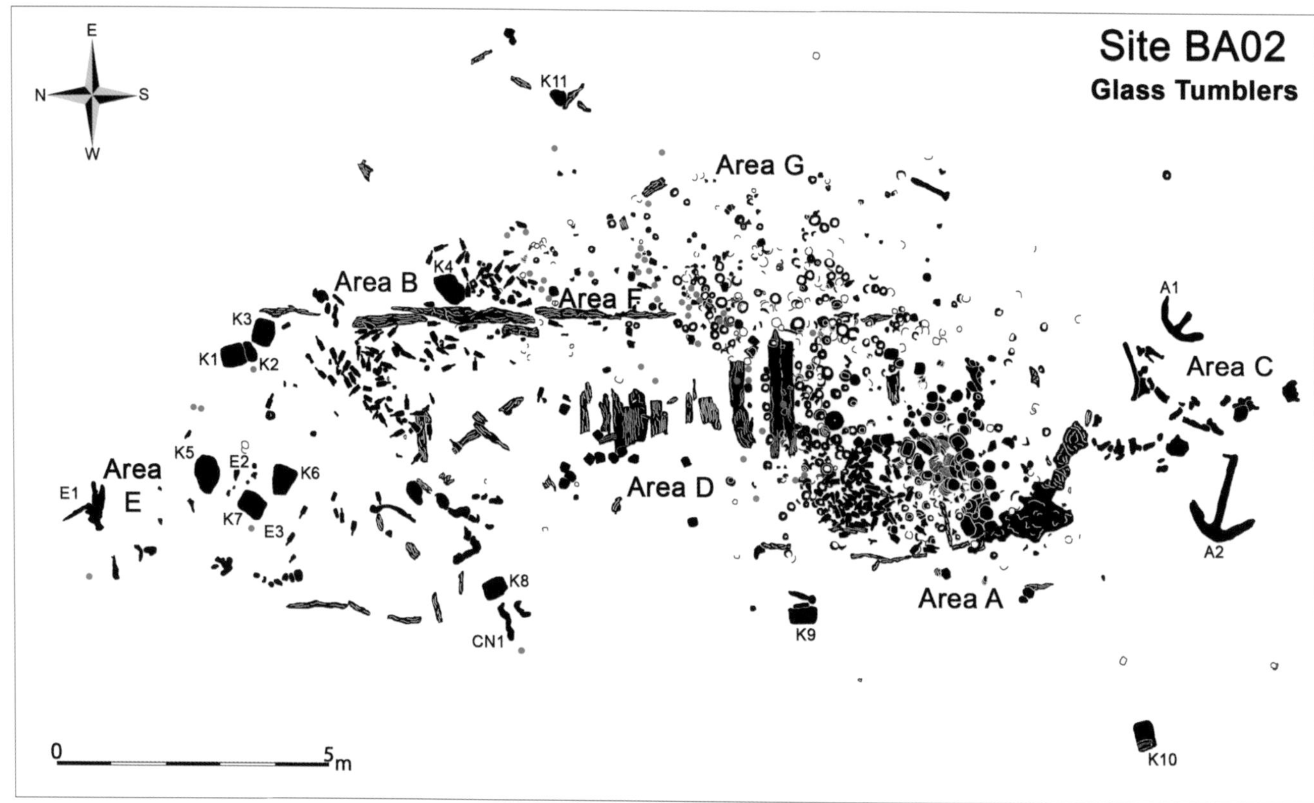

Fig. 54. The distribution of American glass tumblers on Site BA02.

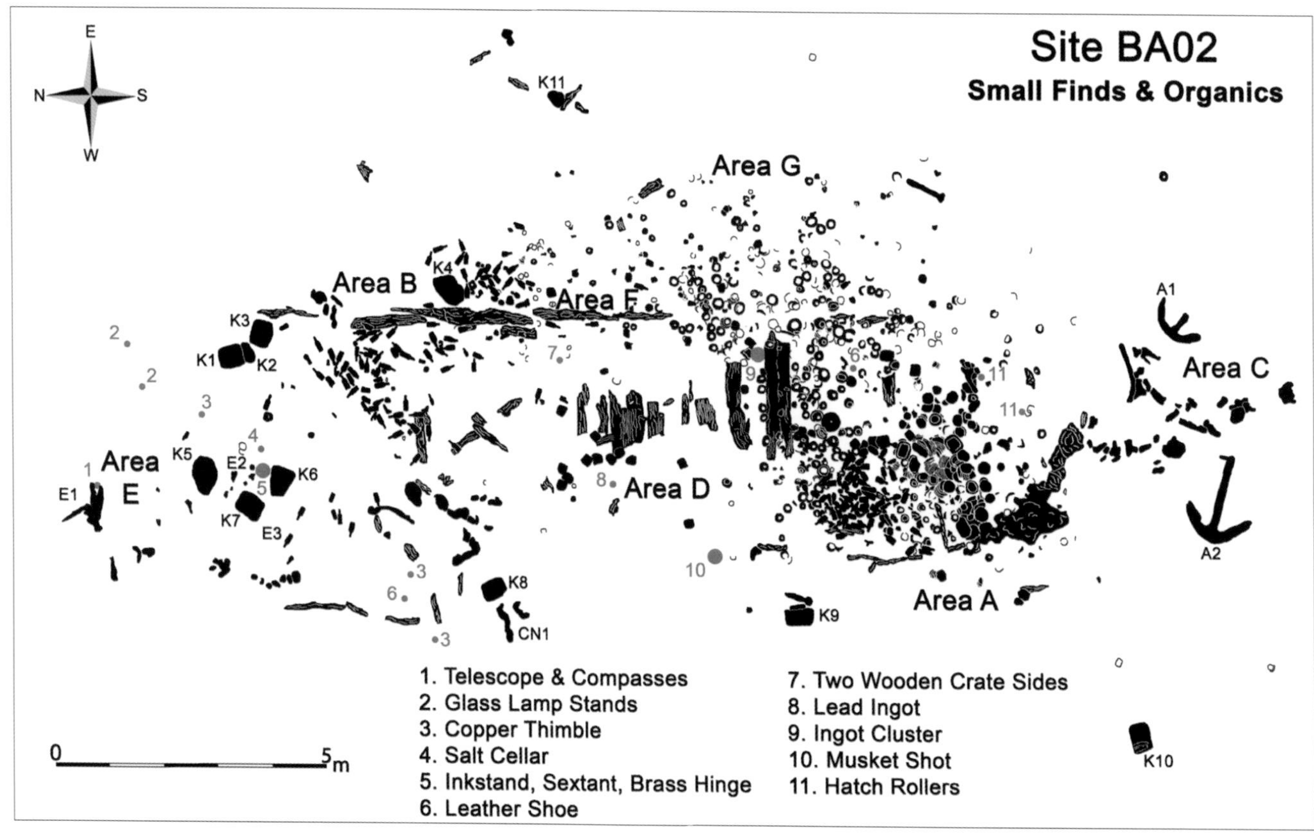

Fig. 55. The distribution of small finds and organic artifacts on Site BA02.

Fig. 56. British shell-edged whiteware platters, soup plates and regular plates (Type 1) with British dipped whiteware jugs on each side (Type 2B) and three Canton ginger jars in front (Type 6).

Fig. 57. British shell-edged whiteware platters, soup plates and regular plates (Type 1).

Fig. 58. British dipped whiteware bowls and mugs (Types 2A and 2C).

Fig. 59. British dipped whiteware jugs (Type 2B).

Fig. 60. British underglaze painted whiteware tea bowls at center (Type 3B) surrounded by white granite/ironstone china chamber pots, wash basins and bowls (Types 4B-4D, 4F).

Fig. 61. British dipped yellow ware chamber pots at center (Type 5B) flanked by British transfer-printed whitewares (Type 7A: 'Asiatic Pheasant' style at left with Primavesi stamp and 'Willow' pattern with Beech, Hancock & Co. stamp at right).

Fig. 62. An American salt-glazed stoneware jug at right (Type 8), alongside a Rhenish mineral water bottle at left (Type 9), flanked by British shell-edged whiteware plates (Type 1).

Fig. 63. British underglaze painted whiteware tea bowls, saucers and a sugar bowl (Types 3A, 3B and 3D).

Fig. 64. Three of Site BA02's four Canton ginger jars (Type 6).

examples are of English manufacture, most likely from the south Derbyshire region renowned for its yellow-bodied wares (Rickard, 2006: 2; Tolson *et al.* 2008: 179). Four of the Type 5 chamber pots feature a distinctive tree-like surface decoration first developed in the late 18th century and known as mocha ware. The widespread popularity of mocha wares amongst American consumers is well documented in early 19th-century records, with contemporary advertisements citing the shipment of mocha to a number of eastern port cities, including Boston and New York, where Staffordshire pottery agents were based. These slip-decorated wares were most fashionable during the period 1795-1835, as documented on American sites.

Porcelain ginger jars originating in Canton, of which four Type 6 examples were found on the southwestern flank of the Jacksonville 'Blue China' wreck at the northwestern edge of Area A (Figs. 56, 64), were popular exports to both America and Britain throughout the mid-19th century. All four are missing their covers and no maker's marks are present. These vessels were frequently used for the export from China of large quantities of crystallized ginger alongside other pickled food items. The hand painted blue underglaze decoration of these wares features a house by the water, a man fishing and a sailing boat. The outline is drawn in light and heavy blue lines and the color washed to lighter shades to contrast with the white porcelain (Tolson *et al.*, 2008: 181). Canton ginger jars of this style are dated to the period 1840-60.

Three examples of Type 7 transfer-printed whiteware plates and a gravy boat were recovered from the wreck – although none were visible on the site photomosaic – and reflect one of the great English innovations in decorated ceramics (Fig. 61). Transfer printing enabled hundreds of sets of dinnerware to be produced at a fraction of the time hand painting took and for a fraction of the cost, thus making these tablewares more readily accessible to middle class families. One of the wreck's plates is a soup plate decorated in the standard 'Blue Willow' pattern, perhaps the most renowned design on early 19th-century pottery and the cheapest transfer-printed pattern available (Miller, 1988: 174). This plate bears the maker's mark 'STONE WARE / B H & Co', which can be attributed to Beech, Hancock & C°., a Staffordshire pottery that began production at the Swan Banks Works in Burslem. The 'B H & C' mark was used from 1851 to 1855 and thus confirms the earliest possible ceramic-based date for the Jacksonville 'Blue China' shipwreck.

A second transfer-printed plate adorned with a bird-and-flower motif known as 'Asiatic Pheasants' was one of the most popular dinnerware patterns of the Victorian era and is most closely paralleled with wares manufactured in Tunstall, Staffordshire, from *c.* 1838-1939. The pattern was also copied along the Clyde in Scotland, the Tyne and Tees in Northumberland, in Yorkshire, London, Devon and south Wales (Tolson *et al.*, 2008: 176). The reverse of this plate is stamped 'F. PRIMAVESI/& SONS/ CARDIFF' and reflects the name of a firm that was active in Wales from 1850 as a pottery agent or dealer.

Three stoneware vessels were recovered from Site BA02 (Fig. 62), including a Type 8 ovoid-shaped American salt-glazed stoneware jug dating to 1850-60 – the sole identifiable American ceramic object from the wreck. This jug form typically stored bulk liquids such as water, wine, rum, vinegar and oil and was a product of the northeastern United States, in particular New York and Pennsylvania. A Type 9 stoneware vessel is a tall cylindrical pouring jug of a type used to hold various fluids better suited to dark, cool environments, including seltzer or mineral water, sarsaparilla, wine, beer, vinegar cider, oil, molasses and even ink. While the origin of this jug is Rhenish, its style is similar to stoneware jugs that bear foreign pottery or company marks most frequently manufactured in Denmark, England, Germany and Sweden.

The third stoneware vessel recovered from Site BA02 is a Type 10 English jar with a so-called Bristol glaze that was the original artifact snagged in a fisherman's net that led to the discovery of the shipwreck. It bears the incised stamp of 'Pearson & Co., Whittington Moor Potteries, near Chesterfield', which was established around 1810. The jar's form of glaze was first developed in Bristol, England, in 1835. Bristol-glazed wares are commonly reported in bottle form from American archaeological sites, although the glaze also occurs on stoneware crocks, jars and other utilitarian items.

Fig. 65. Detail of some of the clay tobacco pipes recovered from Site BA02.

Fig. 66. A Type 1 ribbed clay tobacco pipe.

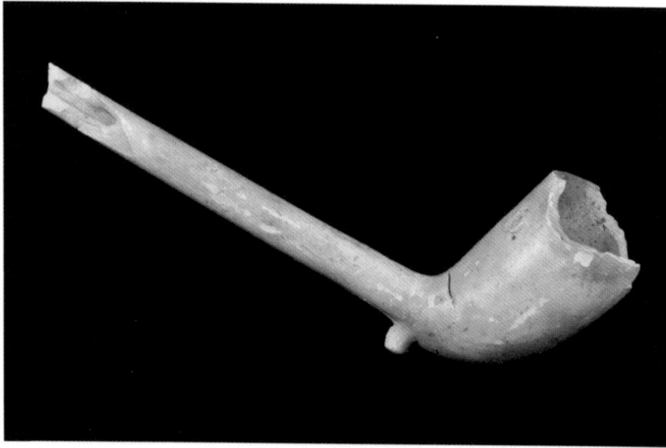

Fig. 67. A Type 2 'TD'-embossed clay tobacco pipe.

8. Clay Tobacco Pipes

The surface of the Jacksonville 'Blue China' shipwreck contained a widely scattered cargo of 63 clay tobacco pipes from which a sample of 16 examples was recovered in two different styles: 13 examples of Type 1 ribbed (also referred to as fluted or cockled) featuring raised vertical lines extending along the bowl and three Type 2 embossed with the letters 'TD' on the back of the pipe bowl (facing the smoker) and otherwise entirely undecorated (Figs. 52, 65-67). The pipes were produced in different two-part molds (pers. comm. Byron Sudbury, 6 November 2009) and all are made from white clay.

The individual examples within the ribbed Type 1 pipe are subtly distinct from each other (Fig. 66). Even though they are essentially typologically comparable, several appear to have been produced in different molds, although probably in the same workshop. Use of multiple molds in a single factory was not uncommon for larger pipe manufacturers (pers. comm. Byron Sudbury, 6 November 2009). The origins of all the pipes remain uncertain due to the pervasive imitation in production that occurred across Europe and America. Comparative excavated examples and historical evidence suggest that they are most likely exports from Britain or Germany, whose pipes made a strong appearance in the United States after 1845, although the Netherlands, Scotland and even America cannot be ruled out.

One of the 'TD'-embossed pipes stands out from the other examples and with the flat trimmed rim of the pipe bowl appears to be of British manufacture (Fig. 67). If indeed British, the pipe is likely to have been made from white ball clay (pers. comm. Byron Sudbury, 6 November 2009 and 4 December 2009), deposits of which are indigenous to Dorset and Devonshire in southwest England. Ball clay was largely used in England, which was a major exporter in the mid-19th century. Although kaolin clay was also available in Britain, with notable sources near Glasgow in Scotland, it was typically reserved for better quality pipes, while ball clay was more common in pipe manufacture (Byron Sudbury, 2006: 27). Given this identification, it is logical to assume that all of the remaining 'TD' pipes come from the same British source.

The emergence of white clay pipes with the initials 'TD' dates back over 200 years and has been correlated possibly with the London pipe maker Thomas Dormer who, along with his sons, produced pipes from the mid-1750s until about 1780. Decades later, 'TD'-marked pipes came to stand for a generic style and not for the actual pipe maker. The initials themselves became a trademark used to denote a certain 'brand' (Cotter *et al.*, 1993: 422; Walker, 1996: 86). Today they represent a major diagnostic

Fig. 68. A variety of glass bottles from Site BA02.

decorative attribute, having been excavated throughout America in contexts dating from the mid-18th century into the early 20th century.

The pipe assemblage from Site BA02 is clearly cargo. The material is highly scattered across the wreck in a zone extending from the northernmost flank in Area E, through Areas B, F and G. Two main clusters occur to the north, with Area B containing 39 pipes (33 in Area B1) and 11 pipes in Area E (six in Area E3). A single Type 1 ribbed pipe bowl observed embedded within the concreted top surface of a large keg in Area E (K6) may reflect their source of stowage. Chapter 10 examines the site's clay smoking pipes in greater detail.

9. Glass Wares

Two large concentrations of glass products define the Jacksonville 'Blue China' wreck and account for a total of 259 cargo wares visible on the surface of the pre-disturbance site photomosaic (excluding the glass window panes: see Section 10 below). An extensive concentration is clustered in the vicinity of its presumed original stowage point in the bows, perceptibly solely within the northern half of Area A (Figs. 5, 6, 53). A more numerous cluster is more widely scattered across the eastern and western flanks of the stern in Area B (Fig. 7). A total of 193 dark glass spirits bottles (including 65 in Area A and 115 in Area B), 18 clear and aquamarine glass bottles and 44 glass tumblers are visible on the surface of the site. The glass cargo includes table and bar wares and individual lamp parts, all of which are American products.

Without incorporating company makers' marks, attributing the Site BA02 glassware to any particular factory is largely impossible, with the exception of a few distinctive patterned examples. All of the glass assemblage is indicative of the two decades between the 1840s and 1860 at the latest, based on shape, form and color. Many of the bottles appear to be pontiled, an attribute that supports this timeframe: pontil scars became uncommon as the 1860s progressed and largely disappeared by the late 1860s or early 1870s as various 'snap case' tools dominated the task of grasping hot bottles for finishing lips. The below descriptions summarize

Fig. 69. A glass salt cellar and variety of glass bottles from Site BA02: Type 9 eight-sided spice or condiment bottles (small variety) (row 1); Type 5 tapered vial-like medicine bottles (row 2); Type 4 rectangular embossed Sand's Sarsaparilla bottles (row 3); Type 9 eight-sided spice or condiment bottles (large variety) (row 4); Type 6 green glass cologne bottles and Type 3 sauce or utilitarian aquamarine bottles (back row). The singular Type 8 cobalt blue 12-paneled cologne bottle is featured in the center of the back row.

the more detailed treatment of the glasswares available in Chapter 11.

The representative sample of glassware recovered from Site BA02 consists of spirits/liquor bottles, a single mineral water bottle, sauce/utilitarian bottles, patent medicine bottles (two different forms), cologne bottles (three types) and condiment/spice bottles (two varieties). None of the bottles' paper or foil labels have survived and just one bottle type incorporates an embossment indicative of the manufacturer. Apart from the sides of two possible wooden packing crates south of Area B, no crates preserve the stenciled names of any companies, the bottled products within or the name of the merchant consignee to whom the goods were being shipped.

A. Glass Bottles

The six Type 1 long-necked spirits bottles recovered represent the largest glass cargo consignment in Areas A and B on the wreck (193 examples visible on the site photomosaic), are dark olive green in color, and often referred to as 'black glass' (Figs. 14, 23). All were found empty without their cork stoppers in place. They are representative of a common liquor/spirits bottle type with bodies that are round in cross-section and whose cylindrical shape evolved generally from wider and squatter to narrower and taller as time progressed (McKearin and Wilson, 1978: 205, 207). This bottle form is generally associated with a variety of liquors ranging from rum to whiskey and brandy and was even commonly used for wine. The bottles' round bodies, an inherently strong shape, are composed of thick glass suited to both maritime trade and typical reuse. The Site BA02 collection displays strong parallels with wares believed to have held brandy excavated from the Hoff Store, which collapsed into San Francisco Bay during the 'Fifth Great Fire' that ravaged the city on 3-4 May 1851 (McDougall, 1990: 58, 60).

A single Type 2 dark olive green mineral water bottle recovered from the wreck, with a relatively heavy and squat body, is typical of mineral water containers designed to survive the rigors of high-pressure bottling, as well as extensive post-bottling handling, again partly due to the tradition of bottle reuse. Such 'black glass' was also especially functional for reducing exposure to heat and light. Often referred to as a 'Saratoga' bottle, this distinctive style was used by hundreds of different 19th-century companies that bottled mineral water, including a large number operating out of Saratoga Springs, New York. The form continued in

Fig. 70. A Type 6 green glass cologne bottle; Type 9 eight-sided spice or condiment bottle (small variety); Type 4 rectangular embossed Sand's Sarsaparilla medicine bottle; Type 3 aquamarine sauce or utilitarian bottle; Type 7 flint glass cologne bottle with a central plume motif; Type 9 eight-sided spice or condiment bottle (large variety); and a Type 5 tapered vial-like medicine bottle (left to right).

use from the earliest bottles made in the 1820s and 1830s until the end of the 19th century (McKearin, 1978: 238).

Two Type 3 sauce/utilitarian bottles, free-blown and light aquamarine in color (Figs. 69-71), were recovered in two slightly different sizes (H. 20.7cm and 21.6cm). This bottle form was also frequently used for any number of products, particularly patent medicines and especially Florida Water cologne. Without any identifying features, including an embossment or paper label, confirming the bottles' contents is not possible. However, long-necked, narrow-mouthed bottles such as these two examples are commonly associated with liquid food products, such as oils and sauces and other non-solid condiments produced by a host of different companies operating in the mid-19th century (pers. comm. Bill Lindsey, 28 January 2010).

Four Type 4 rectangular aquamarine-colored patent medicine bottles are embossed with the company and product name 'SAND'S SARSAPARILLA // NEW YORK' and seem to represent the earliest variant in this production line, which first appeared in the 1840s (Figs. 69, 70). Illustrations depicted in advertisements of 1848 and later feature a slightly modified version with embossed lettering that reads 'SAND'S SARSAPARILLA // GENUINE // NEWYORK' (Fike, 198: 220; *The Gazette of the Union*, 1849: 83). It is possible that both embossed variants were manufactured simultaneously, appearing on the market with some overlap for a period of time.

Abraham and David Sands established their business in New York City in 1836 (Holcombe, 1979: 450) and Sand's Sarsaparilla started to be produced around 1839, as documented in the Sands *Family Recipe & Medical Almanac* published in 1853. Advertisements of 1842 listed their retail and wholesale druggist business as based at several locations under a number of different family names: A.B. & D. Sands Druggists, David Sands & Co., and A.B. Sands & Co. The first two companies apparently served as retail outlets; the latter for the company's wholesale/retail and export business. By 1863 the separate companies were merged as A.B. Sands & Co. Various family members managed the business until it was sold to W.H. Schieffelin & Co. in March 1875 (Fike, 1987: 179).

The wreck's glassware assemblage includes an additional

Fig. 71. A Type 3 aquamarine sauce or utilitarian bottle; Type 9 eight-sided spice or condiment bottle (large variety); Type 6 green glass cologne bottle and a Type 8 cobalt blue 12-paneled cologne bottle (left to right).

Fig. 72. Two glass oil lamp globes and a lamp font and base from the north of Site BA02.

Fig. 73. The two varieties of glass tumblers from Site BA02.

seven Type 5 cylindrical, tapered vial-like medicine bottles, aquamarine in color (Figs. 69, 70). The distinctive bottle shape with a narrow neck and mouth was ideal for the pouring of liquids and was probably an American knock-off imitation of the enormously popular Godfrey's Cordial and Dalby's Carminative. Both of English origins, these soothing syrups were among the many remedies touted for various ailments afflicting infants and young children.

Two Type 6 non-embossed transparent green glass Cologne bottles (with their neck tops broken off) appear to be free-blown wares, possibly with some dip molding utilized to rough out the basic body shape (Figs. 69-71). These bottles are identical to examples discovered in a foundation trench in New Orleans' French Quarter dated to between 1830 and 1850 (pers. comm. Bill Lindsey, 26 January, 2010). Another similar, yet molded variety, dated to the 1880s or 1890s, bears the embossed name 'Lundborg', a prominent 19th-century American perfumer with an establishment in New York City. This bottle type was also used for a number of other products, such as balsam, oil, medicines and liquors like Rosolio (Van den Bossche, 2001: 220).

Included among the cologne bottles recovered from Site BA02 was an additional Type 7 mold-blown, clear glass example possibly made from a higher quality flint (lead) glass produced in the United States between the 1820s and 1860s (McKearin and Wilson, 1987: 11; Fig. 70). The characteristics of a central plume motif date this particular variety from the 1830s to 1865 (McKearin and Wilson, 1978: 396-7). The Jacksonville 'Blue China' cargo also included a stunning Type 8 cobalt blue 12-paneled glass bottle of a style typically associated with cologne or toilet water. The example with its pontiled base dates from approximately the 1830s to the late 1850s and is commonly attributed to the Boston & Sandwich Glass Company, although the type was also produced by a number of glass companies of the era (pers. comm. Bill Lindsey, 2 December 2010; McKearin and Wilson, 1978: 386, 406).

Finally, nine Type 9 spice or condiment bottles were recovered from the wreck site in two different sizes (four larger examples and five smaller) and with slightly different body forms (Figs. 69-71). This bottle type represents the dominant style used for various spices as well as other condiments during the mid to latter half of the 19th century. The unusual eight-sided bottle shape originated in the 1850s or possibly in the late 1840s. The original shape and design, which was subsequently imitated, is believed to have been produced by the J.W. Hunnewell Co. of Boston, Massachusetts (Zumwalt, 1980: 253). The excavation of similar condiment bottles from San Francisco's Hoff Store site is useful in interpreting the Site BA02 examples. The Hoff Store culinary bottles, also recovered in two different sizes, have been identified as containing ground black pepper, suggesting the type of condiment once stored in the bottles recovered from the Jacksonville 'Blue China' shipwreck.

B. Glass Tumblers

Ten short, clear-paneled or fluted bar tumblers (H. 8.7cm and Diam. 8.3cm) recovered from Site BA02 are representative of the more common glassware items produced in great quantities in the 19th century (Figs. 54, 73). The fluted/paneled pattern was apparently manufactured in a number of different styles, as noted by the different factory designations: French flute, reverse flute, gill flute, pillar flute, column, edge flute and so on (Chipman, 1932: 155). The wreck's glass tumblers considerably post-date 1827, when Deming Jarves, using an iron mold, is credited with having produced the first pressed glass water tumbler at the Boston & Sandwich Glass Company in Massachusetts, which he founded in 1826 (Williams, 1922: 9).

The wreck's particular style of glass tumbler form broadly dates from 1845-75 and could have been manufactured in any number of American glass factories producing bar and table wares. An especially likely candidate, however, is one of the New England glass factories, quite possibly the Boston & Sandwich Glass Company itself or its competitor, the New England Glass Company (Spillman, 2006: 16). The Site BA02 examples are believed to be cargo items: the 44 examples visible on the photomosaic are far too numerous for a small crew of around five or less, and five tumblers were also found nested inside ceramic jugs, where they appear to have been packed for maximum spatial efficiency during shipping (Tolson *et al.*, 2008: 172).

Five smooth-sided, pale green bar tumblers (H. 8.7cm, Diam. 6.6cm) were among the recovered glasswares and are again common varieties that were manufactured in quantity in the mid-19th century, notably from 1845-75. Unlike the clear tumblers, these mold-pressed forms appear to feature pontil marks on their bases.

C. Oil Lamps

Site BA02 contained two lamp globes and two fonts at the northern limits of the wreck, some 1-2m north of keg K1 in Area B (Fig. 72). One example is a heavy clear glass lamp pressed in the 'Circle and Ellipse' pattern, with a pressed hexagonal base, which dates from 1840-60 (font H. 16.5cm, Diam. 16.0cm, base H. 21.5cm, Diam. 11.4cm). Similar lamps were produced by the Boston & Sandwich Glass Company and the Pittsburgh firm of McKee and Brothers. The latter featured the lamp in its 1859-60 catalog, noting that a dozen could be purchased with a whale oil burner for $4.00 and with a fluid burner at $4.66 per dozen (Barlow and Kaiser, 1989: 90). This object was plausibly shipped as cargo because a shipboard lamp would have been gimbaled and rigidly mounted.

In addition to the above fonts, the possibility that the ship lost at Site BA02 was carrying a small consignment of lamp parts is supported by the discovery of two additional spherical-shaped lamp globes, also typical of mid-19th century production. Both globes were probably mold-blown and sufficiently generic to have been manufactured by any number of glasshouses processing lighting accessories, including the Boston & Sandwich Glass Company, which began kerosene lamp manufacture in the 1850s. By 1867, most glass factories in the United States were involved in the manufacture of glass lighting devices. The business had become so immense that many glass houses were completely devoted to lamp globes, others to lamp shades and yet more produced just the chimneys (Barlow and Kaiser, 1989: 153, 156; pers. comm. Dorothy Hogan-Schofield, 8 February 2010).

The Second lamp globe is ruby red. No burners or chimneys were found on the site, while lamp stems and brass joint connectors were also conspicuously absent. This raises the possibility that the ship was transporting separate lamp components as cargo, a pattern that was quite common at a time when glass factories specialized in the production of separate glass parts – globes, fonts and bases – for the lamp industry, providing employment for hundreds of workers (Barlow and Kaiser, 1989: 155; pers comm. Jane Spillman, 2006).

D. Beehive Salt Cellar

A single pale opalescent blue pressed glass salt cellar (H. 5.0cm, base 7.7 x 5.0cm; Figs. 34, 69) dating from approximately 1835-60 is attributable to the Boston & Sandwich Glass Company, where fragments have been excavated on the site of the former company factory, indicating that large quantities were manufactured there. This is one of the earliest salt dish forms pressed by the company. The artifact was recovered from shallow surface sediments 20cm northeast of large keg K6.

10. Building Materials: Window Glass & White Lead

In addition to the primary cargo of ceramics and glass bottles, the vessel wrecked at Site BA02 was also transporting building materials. A series of 28 small wooden kegs (16.8 x 16.8cm and 21 x 17.8cm) is located exclusively west of the keel in Areas A and D, which corresponds with the

Fig. 74. Detail of stacked glass window panes in Area D, with crushed wooden kegs in the background.

Fig. 75. Glass window panes in Area D, with a blue cologne bottle and a lead ingot in the foreground and wooden kegs in the background.

ship's starboard side (Figs. 6, 9, 14, 30). Both Area D2 and F contain discrete concentrations of stacked rectangular window glass pane (each 29.8 x 25.1cm; Figs. 9, 11, 30, 31, 53, 74-75).

Although it is not feasible to identify the specific manufacturer of the wreck's window glass because all companies essentially produced virtually the same product, generically the panes were probably cylinder glass, which had been widely adopted in the United States by the 19th century (pers. comm. Jane Spillman, 30 November 2010). At this time America had begun to play a significant role in glass production. Various improvements were underway in the manufacture of flat glass, notably due to its increased use in architecture and commercial and housing construction.

A number of glass houses existed in upstate New York, where over 40 of these businesses were established between the beginning of the 19th century and the 1870s, with at least half of the factories engaged commercially in the manufacture of window glass or bottles, and some producing both. While some of the ventures remained in existence for just a short period of time, a number of the glass establishments operated with varying degrees of success for decades, often under different ownership and management (McKearin and McKearin, 1941: 171).

One such New York establishment producing window glass was the Durhamville Glass Works established in Oneida County in 1845. This factory changed hands several times and in 1895 was acquired by the American Window Glass Company of Pittsburgh, which then closed down the firm (McKearin, 1941: 605). Another contemporary New York establishment producing window glass was the Union Glass Company of Cleveland, which began operations in 1852. Various firms owned the factory until 1899 (McKearin and McKearin, 1941: 608). An earlier New York glass house producing window panes was the Woodstock Glass Manufactory established in 1811, which may have been taken over by the New York Crown and Cylinder Glass Co. before 1836. The latter is also believed to have also purchased a second Woodstock glass house, the Ulster Glass Factory. In 1836 the New York Crown and Cylinder Glass Co. is credited as having employed 50 hands and was making 1,500 boxes of window glass per month. This firm is probably the one remaining factory reported from Woodstock in the 1855 NY State Census (McKearin and McKearin, 1941: 590).

Pittsburgh was also home to many factories manufacturing window glass: 13 glass works in 1837 of which six produced flint glass and the remainder manufactured green and window glass to the value of $700,000 (Thurston, 1876: 129). Included among the early 19th-century Pittsburgh glass ventures dealing in window glass was the Sligo Glass Works established in 1819 by Frederick Lorenz, Sr., but by 1841 operated by William McCully & Co. The factory is believed to have closed down sometime after 1886 (McKearin and McKearin, 1941: 594).

Also listed among the Pittsburgh glass ventures was the window glass house established by Charles Ihmsen in 1814 and by 1836 operated by C. Ihmsen & Co., which erected a vial and bottle factory as well. At this time the factory is reported as possessing eight blowers at the window glass factory, each with an assistant, producing 5,500 boxes of window glass yearly (McKearin and McKearin, 1941: 593). Twenty years later in 1857, Pittsburgh would boast 33 glass factories of which 24 produced window glass (Thurston, 1876: 129).

The breadth of window glass production in both Pennsylvania and New York is highlighted by the quantity of rail shipments in 1863 and 1864. Over 9,000 boxes of window glass were shipped from Pennsylvania, followed by New York with just over 2,000 boxes. While statistics for shipments by boat are not readily available, they are considered to have equaled shipments by rail (Thurston, 1876: 130).

New Jersey also housed many glass factories that produced window glass, including John H. Scott's glass house founded in Estelville, Atlantic County, in 1825. Under changing ownership the factory remained active until about 1877 (McKearin and McKearin, 1941: 597). Contemporary with the Estelville establishment was the Jackson Glass Works of Waterford Township, Camden County, set up in 1827 by Thomas H. Richards. The factory manufactured principally window glass until the 1850s, when it added other glass wares to its production line. The Jackson Glass Works was destroyed by fire in 1877 (McKearin and McKearin, 1941: 598). Camden County was also home to a glass works erected by Coffin & Hay on Cooper's Creek in 1850 that again produced largely window glass and was known as the Sasockson Glass Works (Van Hoeson, 1973: 137).

Among the New Jersey glass houses manufacturing window glass was the establishment launched by William Coffin Sr. and Jonathan Haines in 1817 in Hammonton, Atlantic County. Operated over the years by a number of Coffin family members, the factory shut down in 1857 due to the depression of the late 1850s. In addition to his other ventures, William Coffin Sr. also established with his partner son the Winslow Glass Works, again located in Camden County. The factory operated under a number of different names from 1831 until 1859, when business ceased (McKearin and McKearin, 1941: 594, 600).

Camden County was home to yet another glass house, the Waterford Glass Works launched in 1824 and specializing in window glass. Established by Coffin's former partner Jonathan Haines, the company underwent a series of different ownerships after Haines's death in 1828, and was later reorganized into separate factories in 1870. A decade later the factories were closed (McKearin and McKearin, 1941: 597).

The window panes found at Site BA02 were likely cylinder glass. The cylinder method of glass production was prevalent in the US and permitted the manufacture of up to 6-7ft long cylinders of glass – larger than previous methods (Dodsworth, 2003: 20). Cylinder glass served as the technological bridge between the small wavy panes of crown glass and the wider and optically clear plate glass form (Bock, 1988: 37). As a consequence, the large cylinder-glass window pane replaced the former multi-paned shop windows with their imposing wooden grids. This larger unobstructed Victorian window enabled greater light to penetrate stores and served as an extra enticement to shoppers – a marketing bonus for the hordes of new retailers opening up shops in commercial spaces (Bock, 1988: 36). Courtesy of expanding lines of factory-produced goods, the small city store was quickly becoming a large retail outlet in the early 19th century and general stores were replacing the older frontier trading posts. Coincident with these developments, between 1830 and 1860 the size of the panes used in glass windows increased significantly.

Window glass panes were among the many articles sold by 19th-century wholesale pharmaceutical houses, several of which were based in Buffalo, Chicago and St. Louis. Yet the principal wholesale druggist houses were centered in New York, Boston and Philadelphia, whose overall sales allegedly amounted to $2 million dollars annually in the mid-1800s (Bell, 1856-57: 413). In addition to the traditional diversity of drugs, perfumery, brushes, toilet articles and patent medicines sold in drugstores, these wholesale businesses maintained large stocks of building materials, including immense piles of window glass and thousands of kegs of white lead, and putty alongside a variety of paints and oils.

The technique for packing window panes is summarized in an excerpt from the *Pharmaceutical Journal and Transactions* of 1856-57 (Bell, 1856-57: 413), which helps reconstruct the structure in which the Jacksonville 'Blue China' ship's glass window panes may have been shipped originally:

> "Every imaginable size of glass is put up in wooden boxes by the glasshouses in Pittsburg and New York, from 6 X 7 to 52 X 40, fifty panes in a box – the window glass not coming in huge crates, as in England, but is cut to the desired sizes at the glass works."

The *Pharmaceutical Journal and Transactions* further acknowledged that window glass was an article of very large consumption. In addition to glass panes, white lead in oil stored in 25lb kegs was also essential to the building construction "from the fact that most of the houses in America are built of wood, and in a new country like this, are built in immense numbers" (Bell, 1856-57: 413).

Based on this source it is quite plausible that the intended objective of the white lead discovered at wreck Site BA02 was for use in construction. In liquid form mixed with linseed oil, lead was coated on buildings "to liven them up and save them from decay" (cf. *The Farm Journal*, 1910: 100). White lead was also a vital component in the manufacture of different cement-like putties, which were again indispensable to the 19th-century housing industry and commercial construction (Hopkins, 1913: 325).

The juxtaposition of both products on a single wreck is not unexpected. Records of shipments to New Orleans

Fig. 76. Cupreous and glass compass BC-05-00020-ML (Diam. 4.0cm). Bar codes are used by the Odyssey conservation lab in accordance with company protocol to track all data relating to an artifact from site name and context to conservation history.

Fig. 77. Cupreous and glass compass BC-05-00208-UN (Diam. 4.0cm).

Fig. 78. Compass BC-05-00208-UN in situ *between the legs of a concreted tripod in Area E1.*

from the 'Interior' between 1 September 1849 and 31 August 1850 reveal that 4,887 boxes of window panes reached the Crescent City, as well as 5,979 kegs of white lead, 631 kegs of lead bars and 415,400 lead pigs (De Bow, 1851: 448). In the year ending 31 August 1851, New Orleans consignments from the 'Interior' comprised 16,428 boxes of window glass valued at $82,140, and 325,505 lead pigs, 629 kegs and boxes of lead, plus 1,930 kegs of white lead worth respectively $1,041,616, $12,580 and $13,510 (De Bow, 1852: 147).

11. Miscellaneous Ship's Fittings, Navigational Material & Domestic Assemblage

A relatively low volume of metallic and miscellaneous artifacts of different types and compositions was observed and recovered on Site BA02, including ship's fittings, navigation equipment, raw materials and musket shot. The metallic navigational equipment, limited to the northern surface of the site at the stern, included two disc-shaped lidded bronze containers found in Area E1 within the legs of a concreted tripod, presumably used for surveying or astronomy (Fig. 78). One remains sealed, while the opening of the second example during conservation verified that both artifacts are hand-held compasses (Figs. 76-77). BC-05-00020-ML is a circular cupreous housing composed of a flat lid with a screw thread that connects the object to its base, which features a convex underside. Within is a compass with a central glass mount and a north crosshair at center (lid H. 0.55cm, Diam. 4.0cm, Th. 0.12cm; base H. 1.1cm, Diam. 3.6cm, glass compass Diam. 3.05cm, north crosshair Diam. 0.6cm; weight 34gr). BC-05-00208-UN is a sealed compass (total H. 1.5cm, lid Diam. 4.0cm, base Diam. 3.7cm); the base is slightly convex with two concentric circles incised onto it and a central aperture (0.2mm Diam., weight 36gr).

Within the center of the legs of the same tripod in Area E1 a cupreous single-draw refracting telescope was recovered (BC-05-00031-NL: preserved L. 24.2cm, external draw Diam. 4.0cm, weight 431gr). Located at the northern, stern end of the ship's remains in the vicinity of the former main cabin, this object would have most likely belonged to the captain (Fig. 79). The recovered object includes the eye end and about half of the interior portion of the telescope including the erecting lens (Figs. 81-83). The half of the tube below the erecting lens and the end containing the objective lens are missing. The eyepiece housing (L. 6.4cm, max Diam. 3.5cm, Diam. 3.15cm at the glass eyepiece, max Th. 3.8cm) is pierced with a central glass eyepiece with a 1.55cm-wide central aperture. From here the eyepiece housing broadens through a series of three bands to a 5.8cm wide flange. Inserted into the eyepiece housing is an extremely thinly sheathed cupreous draw, 0.47mm thick, overlying the core draw. The telescope is believed to date from 1820-40. While this 20-year timeframe predates most of the other artifacts discovered at Site BA02, it is a form of instrument that commonly continued in use over a long period of time, with some 19th-century telescopes still in use during World War II (pers. comm. Jeanne Willoz-Egnor, 17 December 2010).

X-rays of the Site BA02 telescope have not revealed any maker's name or mark, but has demonstrated that the two glass elements occupy about one-quarter of the object at each end (Fig. 83). They also revealed a small sliding cover to protect the eye lens and a small knob that would have been used to slide the cover on and off the eyepiece (pers. comm. Jeanne Willoz-Egnor, 17 December 2010). When recovered, the telescope was covered with its original protective wooden tube (Figs. 80-81). A two-draw telescope from the early 19th-century 'Mardi Gras' shipwreck in the Gulf of Mexico, probably manufactured by 'T Harris & Son of London', retains its wooden tube and is very similar typologically (Ford *et al.*, 2010: 91).

One fragment of a sextant sun shield was recovered (BC-05-00009-NL), composed of three cupreous square frame holders attached to a hinge. Inserted into each frame is one green-colored glass, blue (?) and red lens that enabled them to operate as filters individually or in combination (Figs. 84-86). The sextant navigational instrument was invented by John Hadley in 1731, originally as an octant with an arc of 1/8th of a circle, which was enlarged by Captain Campbell in 1757 to 1/6th (Potter, 1972: 63). The objects dimensions are: total artifact L. 6.8cm, rectangular frames 3.36 x 3.34cm, Th. 0.30cm, with a central circular aperture Diam. 2.9cm, hinge L. 2.4cm,

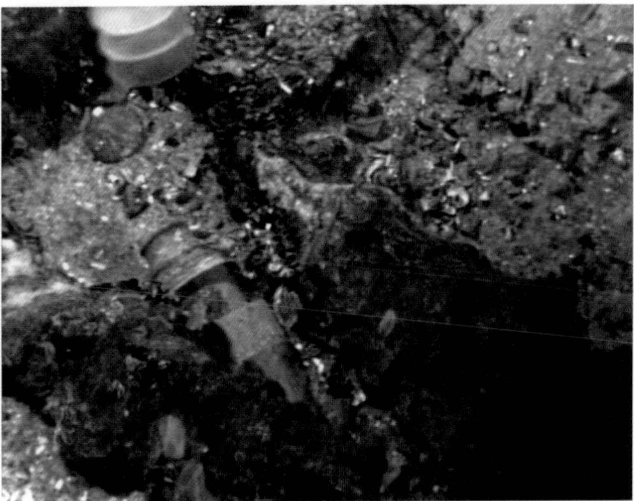

Fig. 79. Telescope BC-05-00031-NL in situ *between the legs of a concreted tripod in Area E1.*

Fig. 80. Telescope BC-05-00031-NL being recovered by the ROV Zeus' limpet suction device. Note the preserved wooden tube.

hinge Th. 0.5 leading to a round rivet 0.67cm Diam. with a central pin 0.34cm wide, circular glass lenses Diam. 2.8cm, Th. 0.18cm. Like the telescope above, the sun shield was found in the stern section of the wreck on the northeast edge of the large keg K6.

A brass plaque from a hanging spring-loaded scale used for weighing (BC-05-00210-ML) consists of the section of a curved front section and upper sides with two rivet holes preserved along the better preserved outer edge (Fig. 87). An inscription runs widthwise along the head of the plaque in capital letters and reads in two lines 'WARRANTIED AND MADE BY' with 'MORTON &' (for Morton & Bremner of New York) stamped in a semicircular curve on the left side before the plaque breaks away (plaque fragment L. 15.0cm, W. 4.1cm, Th. 0.11mm, rivet Diams. 0.45cm; Fig. 88).

The spring scale apparatus with which this artifact

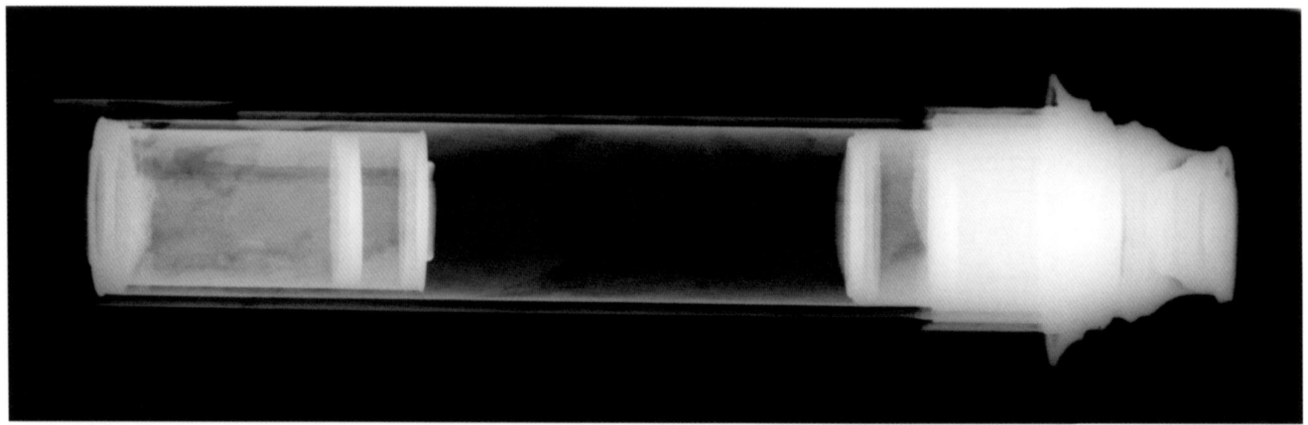

Figs. 81-83. One-draw cupreous telescope BC-05-00031-NL before and after conservation and in x-ray (L. 24.2cm).

was once associated is perhaps the simplest form of weighing instrument known. It simply consisted of a spring fixed at one end with a hook used to suspend the object being weighed at the other and functioned on the tendency of stretched or compressed metal to return to its original position when the load is removed. This concept is derived from Hooke's Law of 1660, which states that the distortion of a metal is proportionate to the load applied. The practical application of Hooke's Law was first put into practice in 1696, when Jacques Ozman produced a 'balance' using the change in length of a coiled spring under load to indicate weight (Graham, 2003: 30).

Later innovations produced a spring balance consisting of a metal tube with a load hook attached to the bottom containing a spring-loaded, graduated bar. As the load was increased, compressing the spring, a greater length of the bar was exposed and the weight could be read from it. Several variations of this design followed, which was a popular and convenient form of weighing used for trade and in households alike. The basic design continued in production until 1960 (Graham, 2003: 30).

Colonel Andrew Augustus Bremner and Major Thomas Morton, both formerly of the Seventh Regiment National Guard, State of New York, were engaged in the manufacture of spring balances and fancy steel goods from 1841 to 1854 (Clark, 1890: 336; Swinton, 2009: 8). According to the *New York Mercantile Union Business Directory 1850-51*, Morton and Bremner were located at 61 Elizabeth Street in New York City. However, by May 1852 the address for their Spring Balance and Steel Manufactory was 389, 391, 393 First Avenue, where it was subsequently destroyed by fire (6 May 1852; *New York Daily Times*).

Following Bremner's retirement in 1854 (Clark, 1980: 226-7; Swinton, 2009: 8), the business continued under Thomas Morton, as clarified in an advertisement in *Scientific American* of 24 September 1859, which offered "Improved Spring balances capable of sustaining from 8 ounces to 1,000 pounds each, suitable for post-office scales, butchers, icemen, grocers, fruit and flower dealers; also much used by leather inspectors....made to order and offered for sale by the manufacturer, Thos. Morton (late Morton & Bremner), 212 Pearl Street, New York".

The discovery on Site BA02 of the remains of the front plaque from a Morton & Bremner spring scale suggests usage aboard the vessel for weighing grocery or other cargo upon receipt or delivery. Its New York place of manufacture further supports the ceramic evidence pointing to this city as the ship's home port. Additionally, the dates in which Morton & Bremner worked together, and subsequently parted ways, significantly narrows down the wreck's date to between the years *c.* 1851 and 1854/5.

Notably also originating in New York are ten identical thin lead bar ingots with rounded edges recovered from a single cluster on the northwest central flank of Area G on Site BA02 (Figs. 42, 55, 89-91). This point of deposition coincides with the easternmost spread of glass window panes and small wooden kegs containing white lead, suggesting original storage in Area D on the starboard side of the ship alongside the building materials. All of the ingots are bent and some display curved horizontal sides. As well as being uniform in shape, the dimensions are relatively consistent. On average, the ingots measure 27.0-28.1cm long and are 1.9-2.1cm wide maximum. The inscription bands are similarly regularized at 23.5-25.8cm long and 1.05-1.2cm wide. The bar thickness, however, does vary overall from 0.49-0.98cm, resulting in weight differentials ranging from 253-358gr. Three exceed 300gr, while seven cluster tightly between 253-286gr (Table 1).

Inv. No.	Length (cm)	Max Width (cm)	Thickness (cm)	Inscription Band Length (cm)	Inscription Band Max Width (cm)	Weight (gr)
BC-05-00029-LD	27.9	1.9	0.63-0.74	23.7	1.05	286
BC-05-00030-LD	27.0	1.97	0.55-0.8	24.2	1.1	260
BC-05-00212-LD	28.0	2.0	0.63-0.94	23.5	1.15	338
BC-05-00213-LD	28.0	1.95	0.64-0.86	23.8	1.1	307
BC-05-00214-LD	28.1	1.98	0.49-0.78	24.0	1.1	253
BC-05-00215-LD	27.8	2.1	0.51-0.71	25.8	1.1	265
BC-05-00216-LD	27.8	2.0	0.49-0.81	23.7	1.15	277
BC-05-00217-LD	27.7	1.95	0.58-0.79	25.7	1.1	270
BC-05-00218-LD	28.1	2.0	0.67-0.98	23.7	1.1	358
BC-05-00219-LD	28.0	2.1	0.51-0.64	23.6	1.2	280

Table 1. Relative dimensions of lead ingots recovered from Site BA02.

Fig. 84. Fragments of a cupreous and glass sextant sun shield from Area E2 (BC-05-00009-NL; total L. 6.8cm).

Figs. 85-86. Sextant sun shield BC-05-00009-NL being recovered from Area E2 by the ROV Zeus' limpet suction device.

Each ingot bears on its upper horizontal surface the mold-impressed name of 'James McCullough. N-Y' (Figs. 90-91). James McCullough was the President of McCullough's Shot and Lead Company, which in 1856 was located at 159 Front Street in New York City. An advertisement in the *New York Times* of 25 October 1856 confirms that McCullough was selling miscellaneous lead products, including bar lead (Wilson, 1857: 518). The company was well known as a major supplier to the Ordnance Department of the Union Army during the American Civil War. Multiple orders of buckshot, elongated balls and round balls of lead were requested from the company by Major Thornton and Captain Crispin of the Ordnance Department between 1861 and 1864. Demand declined after the Civil War and in 1875 McCullough's Lead Company went bankrupt. A second advertisement published in the *New York Times* on 17 March 1875 announced an auction sale for all of the company's goods and machinery (pers. comm. James Blackmon, 11 October 2005).

In light of the absence of any additional clusters, the ingots recovered in a single deposit from the Jacksonville 'Blue China' wreck are best interpreted as domestic assemblage, not due to the minimal differences in dimensions, but because BC-05-00030-LD is sliced off at its left end and possibly burnt at the right end, suggesting shipboard use. A cluster of lead shot was identified at the western edge of Area D in association with remains of a large crushed keg, from which a sample of 38 examples was recovered (Diam. 0.88cm, weight 2.7gr), all representing 30-caliber projectiles (Figs. 92-93). This class of artifact could also have been procured from McCullough's Shot and Lead Company. Extensive spreads of several hundreds of additional pieces of lead shot were observed on the eastern edge of Area D and western Area F overlying hardpan where the hull remains had completely decomposed. Musket shot seemingly shipped in some of the site's large wooden kegs reinforced with iron hoops appears to have been an additional component of the Jacksonville 'Blue China' shipwreck's composite cargo.

The varied ship's fittings include a single robust bronze strap hinge (BC-05-00364-CO; Fig. 94) recorded on the northeast edge of keg K6 in Area E, probably a miscellaneous element of the ship's structure rather than part of a wooden chest reinforce. It is composed of two unequal lengths of bronze, chamfered on all of the outer edges, rotating on a central hinge. The hinge was attached to an object or structure at an angle of about 120°. The longer section is punctuated by four centrally set holes and the shorter length by three holes, one staggered (hinge total L. 32.7cm,

Fig. 87. Brass plaque BC-05-00210-ML from the front of a spring-loaded hanging 'Morton & Bremner' scale (L. 15.0cm).

W. at end 3.5cm, Th. 0.75cm max, hinge W. 3.7cm and Th. 1.38cm with central pin 0.8cm Th., weight 494gr, nail hole heads Diam. 1.2cm and their shaft Th. 0.65cm).

Three cupreous thimble rings with diameters of 7.6-9.0cm that probably served to reinforce the ship's rigging, mooring lines or the corners of sails (Tryckare, 1963: 104) were recovered from the wreck, including one example associated with a well preserved section of rope and canvas (Figs. 43, 95-99). Their measurements are: BC-05-00354-CO, external Diam. 9.0cm, internal Diam. 6.3cm, W. 2.9cm, Th. 0.41cm, weight 294gr; BC-05-00008-CO, external Diam. 8.2cm, internal Diam. 5.8cm, W. 2.7cm, Th. 0.33cm, weight 222gr; BC-05-00209-CO, with fibrous strands of rope/canvas still attached to the outer edge, total artifact Diam. 10.3 x 9.2cm, external thimble Diam. 7.6cm, internal Diam. 5.4cm, rope/canvas Th. 1.7cm, W. 3.0cm, Th. 0.47cm, weight 236gr.

A three-spoked iron wheel fragment of unknown function originates from a wheel or handle once equipped with six spokes (Fig. 100). Other structural finds include a bronze/brass bearing (BC-05-00211-BS; L. 10.8 x 9.9cm, weight 480gr; Fig. 101) composed of wood and cupreous metal that appears to have once been inserted within a wooden plank. A 4.2cm-wide and 0.9cm Th. central cupreous ring with six cylindrical bearings at its center, each 1.2cm wide, is pierced latitudinally with three circular holes, 0.24cm wide. To the outer ring edge into which the bearings are recessed is attached a second ring, Diam. 5.8cm, Th. 0.6cm. Along the artifact's outer edge is a section of wood, Th. 2.1cm, which displays scour marks from friction on both sides. The wood's outer edge is

Fig. 88. Detail of brass plaque BC-05-00210-ML from a weighing scale inscribed "WARRANTIED AND MADE BY MORTON &..." for Morton & Bremner of New York (L. 15.0cm).

Fig. 89. A cluster of ten lead bar ingots from Site BA02 (L. 27.0-28.1cm).

Fig. 90. Detail of a 'James McCullough. N-Y' inscription on a lead ingot.

Fig. 91. Lead bar ingot BC-05-00030-LD bearing the mold-impressed name of 'James McCullough. N-Y' (L. 27.0cm).

riddled with worm holes, 0.2cm wide, and sections of calcareous marine borer shells, 0.19cm wide.

Two heavily degraded mushroom-shaped composite wood/iron hatch rollers were recovered from the southern end of the wreck, 1.5m southeast of the concentration of shell-edged earthenware in Area A (Figs. 6, 44). The original cap survives in place on just one example. Each is pierced with a square hole extending along the central axis from the base to the bottom of the cap. BC-05-00403-SF is 22.7cm long and 17.7cm wide at its single preserved end, with a diameter midway down its length of 7.7cm (Fig. 103). Its central square shaft is 3.2cm wide and lined with a 0.25cm-thick veneer of iron. Four circular nail holes on the base of the preserved end measure 0.5cm in diameter and are set 3.4cm inward of the outer edge. Circular friction marks caused by repetitive rotation are visible at this end.

Just one end of roller BC-05-00402-SF remains intact and both its central barrel and opposite end are heavily degraded (Fig. 102). It measures 23.4cm long and has a diameter of 17.6cm at the intact end. The central square shaft running vertically down the middle of the roller is 3.4cm wide with a 0.33cm iron interior lining. The four nails staggered 3.7cm inwards of the base edge each measure 0.8cm in diameter. Concentric friction marks caused by repetitive rotation are again present on the base.

Both hatch rollers originally may have had an iron core or may have been lined with iron sheet. These objects resemble capstan barrels, but incorporate no obvious holes for capstan bars and have subsequently been identified as hatch rollers (pers. comm. John Broadwater, 1 December 2006). The *Oxford Companion to Ships and the Sea* (1976: 378) defines such objects used on cargo ships as "pivoted in sections which allow the covers to be rolled back, folding together in cantilever fashion at either end of the hatch opening".

The rollers are associated with a heavily degraded composite wood and graphitized iron hatch roller base (BC-05-00169-ML), 19.2 x 18.9cm and Th. 1.8cm and a central aperture 2.9 x 2.9cm, which consists of a wooden core with an iron outer sheathing and is characterized by 16 angled sprockets set 2.4-2.6cm apart (center to center distances). Four symmetrically set circular nail holes are positioned 4.5cm inward of the roller edge, each 0.8cm wide and with a central shaft 0.55cm thick (Fig. 104).

A wood/iron composite hawse pipe (BC-05-00404-SF) consists of a 26.8cm-long section of corroded iron pipe with an asymmetrical lip at one end (presumably the outboard one) mounted through wood (inner pipe Diam. 10.2cm). The preserved circular end is 24.0cm wide, its rim 1.8cm high and 2.0cm thick and the hawse pipe 1.1cm thick (Figs. 105-106). A single circular hole on its edge measures 2.2cm in diameter. Corrosion products from the iron have leached into the wood and preserved the sections closest to the iron. The inner diameter of the pipe, inside which survives a section of iron wire cable, provides an approximation of the maximum size anchor cable used for the vessel.

Apart from the hull remains and two hatch rollers, the organic material observed on the surface of the wreck is restricted to two leather shoe soles with heels, one located 1.2m northwest of keg K8 on the western extreme of the site and the second (BC-05-00006-LR) recorded and recovered 0.9m southeast of the grindstone at the southern, starboard end of the wreck. The heel on the recovered example lacks evidence of any wear, suggesting it had never been worn and conceivably may be a part of a deteriorated larger cargo (Figs. 107-111). While the sole and heel of the shoe are relatively well-preserved, little remains of the uppers, making it difficult to determine the precise style of footwear; yet it appears to have been a man's shoe. The heel of the shoe is made of stacked leather and the top piece is held in place with cut nails and wooden pegs across the breast (pers. comm. Valentine Povinelli, 22 December 2010).

The rounded heel tapers inwards before broadening to a maximum width at its three-quarter length and terminating at a squared off toe. In profile from the side the shoe is gently rounded (L. 26.3cm, squared toe W. 4.5cm, max W. 8.8cm, W. at heel 7.1cm, max H. 5.3cm, Th. of sole 1.15cm, H. of heel 1.9cm). Sets of dual fastening holes, elliptical in shape, 0.18 x 0.13cm, are drilled around the sole's edge.

This single square-toed shoe features a pegged sole, a fabrication method by which the sole was attached using wooden pegs instead of by stitching. The technique of pegging new soles in this manner made its appearance in the United States by 1815 (Bryant, 1897). By 1830 hand pegging was the dominant construction for cheap US shoes (pers. comm. Valentine Povinelli, 13 December 2010). Two decades later this design was no longer accomplished by hand following the invention of the pegging machine by A.C. Gallahue in 1851 (and subsequently improved by Townsend and Sturtevant of Boston). The evenness of the pegging apparent on the recovered shoe suggests the sole was pegged by machine.

The steam-powered pegging machine was used extensively throughout the country and greatly increased

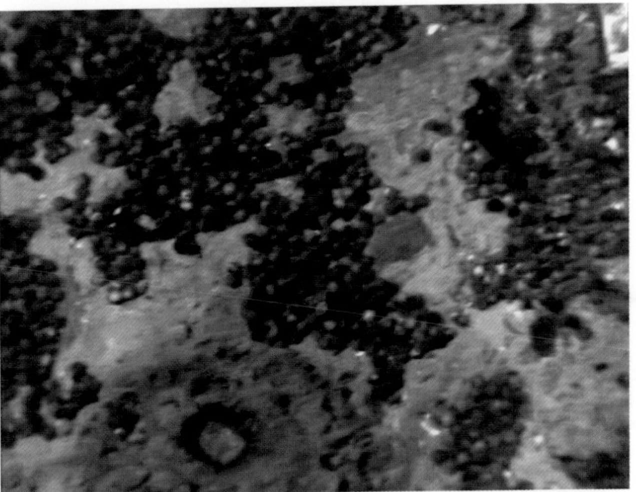

Fig. 92. The sea bottom covered with lead musket shot west of Area D on Site BA02, alongside a cupreous hatch roller base.

Fig. 93. Lead musket shot after recovery from Site BA02.

Fig. 94. Bronze strap hinge BC-05-00364-CO from the northeast edge of keg K6 in Area E (L. 32.7cm).

Fig. 95. A thimble ring in situ on Site BA02.

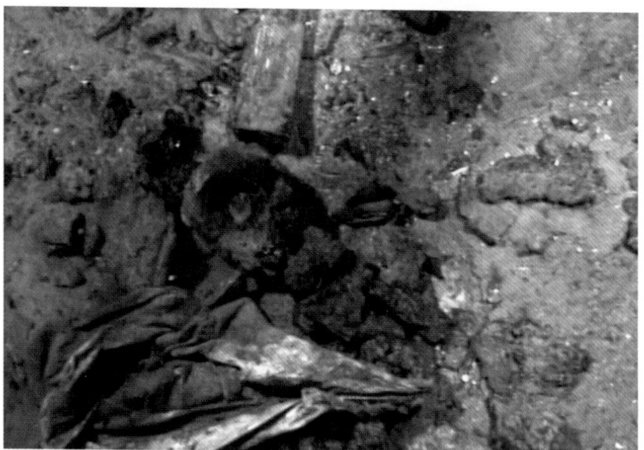

Fig. 96. Thimble ring BC-05-00209-CO in situ alongside wood, concreted iron and canvas, possibly identifiable as a fragment of the ship's sail.

Fig. 97 (top right). Cupreous thimble ring BC-05-00209-CO, with fibrous strands of rope/canvas attached (Diam. 10.3 x 9.2cm).

Fig. 98 (middle right). Cupreous thimble ring BC-05-00354-CO (Diam. 9.0cm).

Fig. 99 (bottom right). Cupreous thimble ring BC-05-00008-CO (Diam. 8.2cm).

Fig. 100. A spoked iron wheel fragment from a wheel or handle once equipped with six spokes.

Fig. 101. Wood and cupreous bearing BC-05-00211-BS (L. 10.8 x 9.9cm).

Fig. 102. Composite wood/iron hatch roller BC-05-00402-SF from the bow area of the wreck (L. 23.4cm).

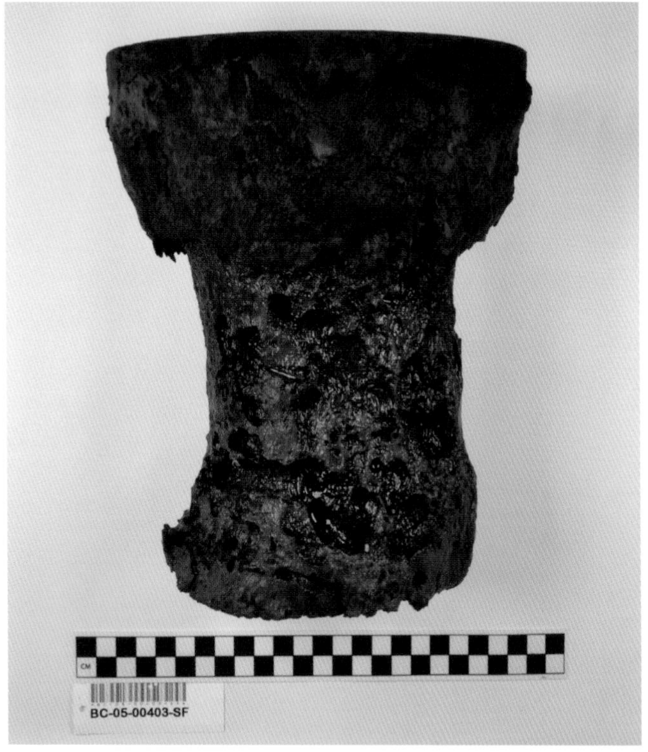

Fig. 104. Wood and graphitized iron hatch roller base BC-05-00169-ML (Diam. 19.2 x 18.9cm).

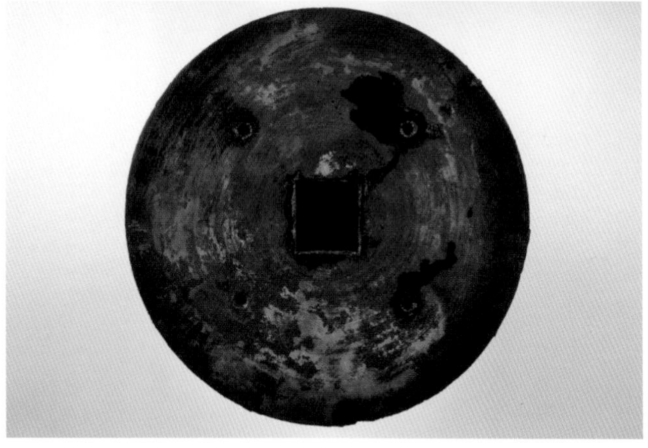

Fig. 103. Composite wood/iron hatch roller BC-05-00403-SF (L. 22.7cm).

Figs. 105-106. Wood/iron composite hawse pipe BC-05-00404-SF (L. 26.8cm).

Figs. 107-111. Leather shoe BC-05-00006-LR from the starboard bow of the wreck (L. 26.3cm).

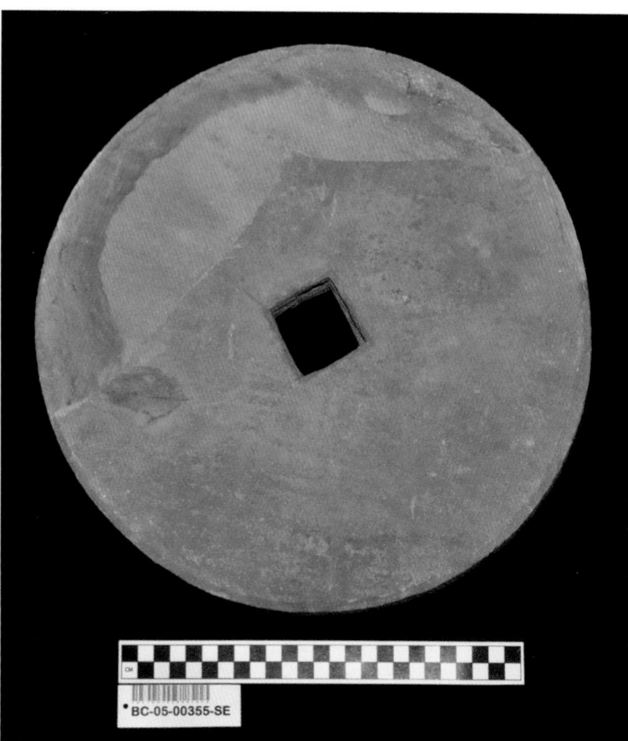

Fig. 112. Grindstone BC-05-00355-SE from the starboard bow of the wreck (Diam. 33.5cm).

the quality and production of pegged shoes. According to Brocket (1882: 220), "It would punch the holes, cut off and shape the peg, and drive them at the rate of 14 per second, and would peg two pair of women's shoes a minute, putting in two rows of pegs if required". By 1872 about 1,700 of these machines were in use across America, largely employed by manufacturers whose predominant convict labor made vast quantities of cheap, but neat looking products. Even for the finest examples, pegged shoes were not the choice of those who were 'delicately reared' (Brocket, 1882: 220).

The sole of the shoe bears an unidentifiable stamp. Some civilian shoes of the era featured hash marks on the sole to indicate size, and during the Civil War contractors and depots stamped their identification mark inside the quarters of the shoe (pers. comm. Valentine Povinelli, 22 December 2010). The purpose of this particular stamp from this time is not apparent.

The square toe of the Jacksonville 'Blue China' wreck's shoe was a recurring style enjoyed over many centuries (pers. comm. Valentine Povinelli, 22 December 2010) as referenced by John F. Watson (1779-1860), a Philadelphia antiquarian and amateur historian best known as the author of *Annals of Philadelphia*. In the 1857 edition, Watson stated that "I came into the world as the first generation of square toed boots were going out of it; and my feet are, at this moment, after an interval of -- years, no matter how many, incased in a pair of square toes No. 2" (Watson, 1884: 199).

Finally, a grindstone (BC-05-00355-SE: Diam. 33.5cm, Th. 6.4cm) with chamfered edges and a square aperture cut through the center for mounting on a rotating axis, 4.7 x 4.5cm, and probably used by the ship's carpenter or boson for sharpening tools, was recovered from the aft section of the shipwreck, just northeast of Area A (Figs. 5, 6, 16, 41, 112). The medium is very coarse and one-quarter of the front side is delaminated and has broken away. Chisel marks are visible across the entire outer edge, with blade widths of 0.3cm. The stone composition has been identified by Prof. Jeffrey Ryan from the Geology Department at the University of South Florida (pers. comm. 9 November 2009) as highly quartzitic sandstone. All of the grains are similar in size, which makes the surface highly homogeneous. The rock most probably originates on the west flank of the Appalachian Mountains between New York and Alabama.

12. Site Impacts

While the principal objective of this report has been to supply documentation related to the archaeological materials recovered from the Jacksonville 'Blue China' shipwreck, it also presents strong evidence for the impacts that trawling can cause wrecks. In this case it is impossible to understand the site formation fully without assessing the scale and character of the fishing impacts. This statement of factual documentation is in no way a comment about the ethics and economics, or a criticism, of the fishing industry, which serves a vital role within society. Without the interest, skilled observations and offshore dedication of fisherman Woody Moore, Site BA02 and the knowledge it contains would never have been accessed. A cooperative reporting scheme rewarding fishermen for reporting and avoiding wreck sites would be a significant move toward protecting deep-ocean shipwrecks and underwater cultural heritage.

The 2005 rescue archaeology conducted on Site BA02 identified a significant amount of impacts inflicted by trawl nets dragged across the wreckage, most obviously visible in the form of at least four parallel furrows cut across the eastern length of the site from north to south (Fig. 119). These have cleared sterile paths through the cargo, leaving behind single straight lines of cleared ceramic wares, all that survive of cargo swept aside by trawl doors and net chains. Little of the original contexts observed in 2003 remained untouched in 2005. Substantial cargo had been smashed and scattered and the ship's structure flattened (Figs. 4, 40,

Figs. 113-114. Rock crab on the surface of Site BA02.

47-52, 118). Only a few relatively deep crevices amongst the hull preserved some stratigraphy below the surface of the sea floor. Limited test excavations revealed that, for the most part, only a single layer of artifacts survives on the site above the hull structure.

Discussions with fisherman Woody Moore (pers. comm., 29 March and 29 September 2010), whose initial inadvertent recovery in his nets of a 'Bristol-glazed' stoneware jar brought the wreck to Odyssey's attention, have revealed the scale of regional fishing. Working out of the port of Savannah, Georgia, he estimates that pottery has been trawled off the wreck for the last 35-40 years and that around four boats of 22.5-30m length regularly fish these waters year round. These fishermen specialize exclusively in red shrimp, which are most abundantly found around the 160-fathom (293m) line depth contour. Over the years Mr. Moore has routinely encountered the rims of abundant ceramic sherds and intact vessels, mostly dishes with blue designs (see British shell-edged earthenware Type 1 in Section 7 above), snagged in his nets at the end of a net drag through the area.

Woody Moore operates out of a twin shrimp trawler, deploying four nets of 16.7m-length each and 113kg: two on the starboard side and two on the port side. Each seam net is equipped with a tickler chain weighing 11.3kg (one tickler per net). The two trawl doors at the head of each net are 2.4m long, 1m wide and weigh 181kg. 'Hangs' or snags caused by his gear becoming caught are not uncommon. As the loss of a net is no small financial matter to commercial fishermen, the careful plotting of such locations is a professional necessity. Over his years of fishing the area around Site BA02, Mr. Moore has established the nature of such hangs (including piles of pipes, sunken aircraft and modern rubbish) by inspecting material recovered in nets. His skill and experience have enabled him to distinguish between airplanes and ships and even between old wooden and modern metallic ship remains.

The nature of layback towing complicates the determination of the exact location of such subsea obstacles. Anything hit by the trawl gear may not be noted until the nets are recovered at the end of a multi-mile long line and found to contain debris. In the event of a 'hard hang', where it is impossible to free the net loose from a seabed obstacle, the required strategy is to stop the ship and recover the trawl. In such a case it is possible to establish the exact location of the hang. Usually, however, only the general area containing a hang is known.

Over the years that the Jacksonville 'Blue China' wreck area has been fished, shrimp trawling gear has undergone major changes that included alterations in rigging. The twin trawl uses four small trawls (two from each outrigger) instead of one larger trawl on each outrigger. This rigging configuration is more efficient and produces greater catches than the double-rigged configuration, but requires extra rigging of an additional bridle and a dummy door, sled or bullet between the paired trawls. The additional rigging can create tangling and handling problems (Watson *et al.*, 1984: 3). Twin-rigged trawls have the advantage that a vessel using four small trawls, rather than two large ones, can tow more total trawl headrope length with the same horsepower. Data on the energy efficiency of shrimp trawl designs indicate that twin trawls sweep a larger total area per gallon of fuel than double rigged trawls (Watson *et al.*, 1984: 8).

The shrimp industry emerged off Florida in 1906, when Solicito Salvador first rigged his boats based in Fernandina, Florida, with otter trawl nets, which enabled his daily shrimp catch to increase tenfold. By 1921 the Salvador Fish Company was shipping shrimp as far away as Los Angeles, Canada and Denmark. By about 1950 most of the potential fishing grounds in the waters adjacent to

Shrimp Type	Year	Weight (lb)	Value ($)
White	2008	3,947,691	9,361,853
Rock	2008	1,875,093	3,950,897
Brown	2008	641,538	1,265,756
Pink	2008	496,376	622,195
Dendrobranchiata	2008	316,706	1,343,279
Royal Red	2008	321,648	627,720
White	1998	2,891,407	8,370,921
Rock	1998	2,199,487	3,001,833
Brown	1998	551,209	1,475,059
Pink	1998	724,125	1,340,149
Dendrobranchiata	1998	439,402	1,311,932
Royal Red	1998	82,291	250,331
White	1988	2,590,546	7,480,369
Rock	1988	2,679,801	1,630,564
Brown	1988	546,000	1,327,858
Pink	1988	134,870	408,379
Dendrobranchiata	1988	0	0
Royal Red	1988	0	0

Table 2. Relative volumes and values of royal red shrimp in relation to other varieties landed in Florida's East Coast in 2008, 1998 and 1988 (as tabulated from the Fisheries Statistics Division of the National Marine Fisheries Service website).

the southeastern United States had been discovered, after which the US shrimp fleet expanded its operations to the east coast of Mexico and into the western Caribbean Sea (Gillett, 2008: 9-10).

Fishermen have been working in the offshore zone in which wreck Site BA02 is located since the early 1960s, although Mr. Moore only starting visiting these grounds in 1977. Since then no drop in yields has been observed: apparently this is not an overfished location (Table 2). In fact, in recent years Mr. Moore has been taking greater catches, which may be explained by improvements in equipment rather than by species population growth. There are currently no quotas in place for this offshore zone and none scheduled for the near future.

The deep-sea fisheries of the southeast United States are rich in rock shrimp and royal red shrimp found in soft bottom environments, primarily fine to medium grain sand made of shell, although both constitute a very small catch compared to other sectors of the overall shrimp fishery (Table 2). The rock shrimp (*Sicyonia brevirostris*) is named after its characteristically tough, rock-like exoskeleton and can be fished year round, but its biological range is restricted to depths in the continental shelf of 25-65m (Harrould-Kolieb, 2007: 1-4). Site BA02 lies beyond these parameters.

The royal red shrimp (*Hymenopeneaus robustus* or *Pleoticus robustus*) is a deep-sea shrimp known for its sweet, juicy flesh and striking red color, popular today as 'sweet shrimp' used in sushi and Asian cuisine. The fishery for royal red shrimp serves a niche market, representing a very small proportion of the overall shrimp industry in southeast America (Table 2). The typical habitat for this shrimp includes sediments transported offshore by the Mississippi and other rivers emptying into the sea and forming blue/black compositions of sand, silt, mud and a more gritty white calcareous mud. Royal red shrimp larvae are carried north by the Gulf stream to settle into adulthood along the Atlantic Coast within a biological range extending along the continental shelf from 180-730m, with peak concentrations found between 250-475m, precisely within the depth of Site BA02. In the southeastern USA the core habitat areas are located off Florida and the northeastern Gulf of Mexico.

Royal red shrimp are harvested by trawl boats dragging four nets that typically leave port for three weeks at a time. Fishermen perceive the royal red shrimp fishery as a more difficult working environment requiring greater investment and specialization that presents higher risks (Harrould-Kolieb, 2007: 6-9). Figures for the period 1978-2004 reveal that 200,000lb of royal red shrimp from the Gulf of Mexico were landed in 1978 and peaked in 1994 at 600,000lb. Catches from the waters of the South Atlantic are far smaller, starting at 240,000lb in 1989 and peaking at 350,000lb in 2000 (Harrould-Kolieb, 2007: 8, fig. 2.2). More specifically, in 2008 321,648lb of red shrimp were landed in Florida with a value of just $627,720 compared to just 82,291lb in 1998 worth $250,331 (Table 2). This data, plus the fact that no red shrimp were landed in 1988, reflect the relatively late emergence and development of specialism on this species.

In terms of value, shrimp is the second most important fishery in the United States after the crab, with the average American consuming 1.9kg edible weight of shrimp a year. The combined landings for the US domestic shrimp fisheries have been about 140,000 tons annually in recent years, valued at a catch value of $425 million (Gillett, 2008: 1, 17, 34). Shrimp fishing is exceptional in the amount of controversy it has generated. A recent UN Fishing and Agriculture Organization study revealed that tropical shrimp trawl fisheries generally have high discard rates, which account for over 27% of total estimated discards in all the marine fisheries of the world, amounting to some 1.8 million tonnes per year. Shrimpers are continually working to improve the waste of bycatch.

The general impacts of trawl gear on sea bottoms are well known. Demersal otter trawls are the primary fishing gear that have been employed in the US shrimp industry since at least the early 1950s and are rigged with standard loop chains with a spread of 2.4 x 1.0m alongside chain doors (Watson *et al.*, 1984: 1, 5). This fishing method has the potential to reduce or degrade structural components and habitat complexity by removing or damaging epifauna, smoothing bedforms (which reduces bottom heterogeneity) and removing structure-producing organisms. Trawling may change the distribution and size of sedimentary particles, increase water column turbidity, suppress growth of primary producers and alter nutrient cycling. The magnitude of trawling disturbance is highly variable and its ecological effects depend on the site-specific characteristics of the local ecosystem, such as bottom type, water depth community type and gear type, as well as the intensity and duration of trawling and natural disturbances (Gillett, 2008: 303-304).

Fig. 115. Vermillion snapper (Rhomboplites aurorubens) *on the surface of Area A on Site BA02.*

Fig. 116. Vermillion snapper (Rhomboplites aurorubens) *on the surface of a large keg on Site BA02.*

Fig. 117. A conger eel hiding beneath the possible stem structure of Area A on Site BA02.

Fig. 118. A crushed keg located between kegs K3 and K4 in Area B.

Fig. 119. Lines of ceramics apparently cleared by trawl doors running north/south across Area G on Site BA02.

The specific impacts on wrecks located off United States as a whole, and within the nearshore and offshore fishing grounds of Florida and Georgia, are undocumented. The data from Site BA02 offer a clearer understanding of the nature of the effects such equipment may cause. The evidence of trawl impacts to Site BA02 can be summarized as including:

1. Exploitation of this area of seabed as a fishing ground for red shrimp since the early 1960s.
2. Oral testimony, combined with physical evidence in the form of snagged ceramic sherds from single fragments to an intact jar, for site impacts since 1977.
3. Site BA02's wreck formation displays a disproportionate balance of cargo across the site, which cannot be an accurate reflection of original stowage. Compared to the dense concentration of glass bottles and ceramics in Area A, cushioned on three sides from impacts, the remainder of the site has been heavily flattened, artifacts have been scattered and some kegs crushed.
4. The above point is substantiated by the presence of lines of ceramics juxtaposed alongside lines devoid of any artifacts, reflecting the geography of inflicted damage and small zones cleared between trawl doors. Smashed pots ground down into sherds and completely crushed wooden kegs characterize the southeastern quadrant of Site BA02. Anchor A1, broken along the lower shank, may have been dragged and fractured from its original context related to being lashed on the portside bow.
5. The differences in levels of artifact and structural preservation between 2003 and 2005 reflect an accelerated level of site impact.

13. Anatomy of an East Coast American Coastal Trader

The ship wrecked at Site BA02 can be solidly dated to the mid-19th century, certainly within the decade spanning 1850-60. The absence of wire rigging is indicative of a pre-Civil War timeframe anteceding 1861. This vessel was thus not a blockade runner. The lack of cannon and the presence of a large cargo of ceramics are indicative of a merchant vessel. The visible remains of the keel for 17.6m and planking across a breadth of 2.5m on the starboard side suggest a minimum keel length of 18m, while the anchor size favors a capacity of 100 tons or less, making the vessel an unlikely candidate for a transatlantic trader.

The ship was outward-bound with a mixed cargo consisting of various British ceramics stowed alongside glass bottles filled with American liquor, condiments, patent medicines and colognes, as well as with glass window panes and two types of wooden kegs, some perhaps containing musket shot, tobacco pipes and maybe leather shoes. It is realistic to assume that an additional organic cargo, now perished, originally accompanied these goods. The nature of this cargo is indicative of a modest coastal trader of North American origin originating in a port along the Northern Atlantic seaboard. Both the lead ingots and spring balance plaque bear inscriptions reflecting manufacture in New York, which best fits the profile of the Site BA02 ship's home port and final point of departure (see Section 15 below for the controlling role of New York in mid-19th century East Coast trade).

The British ceramic wares would have been shipped initially to New York before being loaded onto the Site BA02 vessel alongside local products to head to the South.

Since America pursued a protectionist policy in its coastal trading, whereby President James Monroe's Navigation Act of 1 March 1817 permanently excluded foreign vessels from participating in coastal cabotage, and which later evolved to ban foreign ships from trading between the US and its offshore possessions and territories (Forsyth, 1989: 5; Morris, 1973: 17), the American origin of the vessel lost at Site BA02 may be judged to be secure.

Rather than being rigged with a square sail suited to generating tremendous driving force for a vessel crossing oceans, the Jacksonville 'Blue China' coastal trader probably featured a fore-and-aft rig, which was far better suited to the localized varying breezes, the need for maneuverability along the shore, and perhaps amongst the islands of the Caribbean, and the necessity to sail against various inshore currents and the powerful Gulf Stream.

Henry Hall's famous *Report on the Ship-Building Industry of the United States* of 1882 confirms that fore-and-aft rigged schooners were preferred for coasting because fewer sailors were required to handle a vessel, which could be worked in and out of harbors and along rivers more easily than a square-rigged craft. Since this form of craft could sail closer into the wind, trips were generally quicker (MacGregor, 2003: 69-72). These vessels could be sailed by a skipper and just two to three crew members, resulting in low operating costs (Chapelle, 1935: 258; MacGregor, 2003: 72-73). One working rule favored the use on schooners of two men per mast, plus the captain, but often with fewer personnel on smaller vessels (Morris, 1973: 119).

By 1800 the schooner had become the basic coastal cargo carrier in America, and from around 1825 New England and New York merchants preferred schooners

Fig. 120. The 91-ton Mary Langdon *schooner built at Rockland, Maine, in 1845 and rebuilt in 1860 is probably close to the lines and origins of the Site BA02 ship. Photo: Maine Maritime Museum, Bath, Maine (Capt. W.J. Lewis Parker Photograph Collection).*

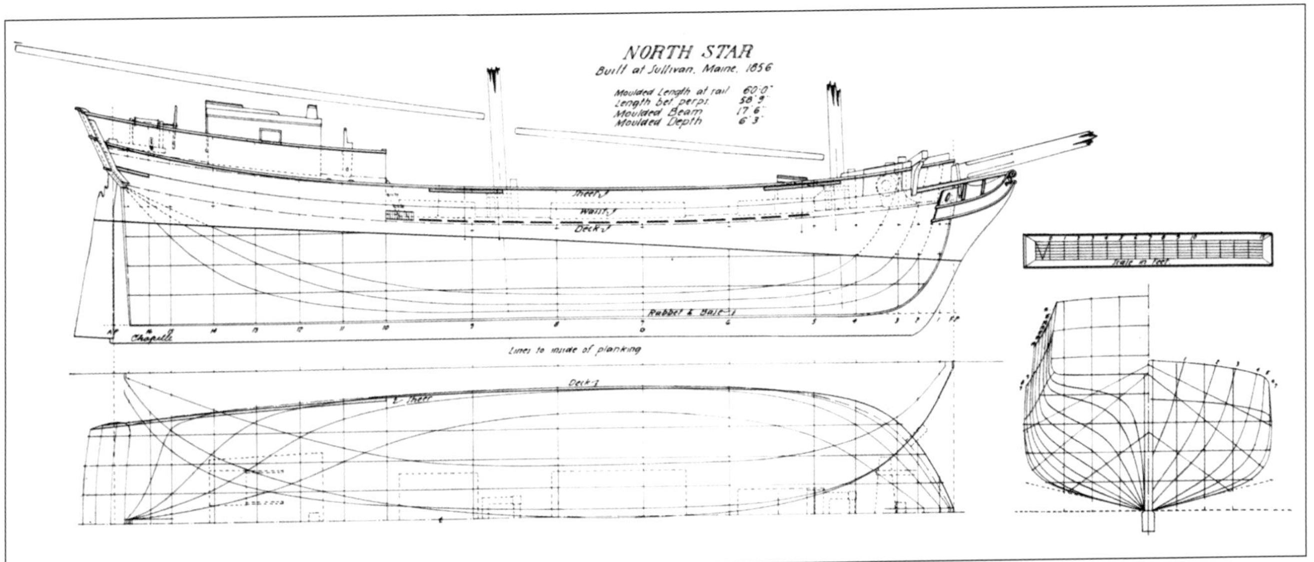

Fig. 121. Lines of the two-masted schooner North Star *built at Sullivan, Maine, in 1856 (from Chapelle, 1960: 76).*

with lengths of 50-75ft (15-22.5m) for maritime trade, although brigantines and topsail schooners were exploited to transport cotton to New York from the Southern ports and for voyages to the West Indies (Figs. 120-122). In the 1830s America's coastal trade eclipsed the country's ships involved in foreign trade. Schooners owed their popularity to the fact that they were much cheaper to build than square rigged vessels, more weatherly than square-riggers and could be handled by much smaller crews (Morris, 1973: 17, 19).

American schooners were renowned for their 'flush deck' or 'hurricane deck' construction form, a term that referred to a vessel where "the weather, or upper, deck ran unbroken from the bow to the stern" (Parker, 1960: 52). The after accommodation on such vessels consisted of a large stern deckhouse that spread across almost the entire deck width, leaving just a narrow passage on either side at the same level as the poop. Unlike British schooners, which carried the after accommodation below the main deck, this arrangement preserved valuable cargo space. The main cabin, or afterhouse, was half sunk into the deck abaft the spanker mast and foreward of the wheel. During the period of the Jacksonville 'Blue China' ship's life, crew berths were located in the bows, below deck in a forecastle. If the ship had a midship house, this would have contained the galley and carpenter's shop (MacGregor, 2003: 78-9; Morris, 1973: 65). The presence of the grindstone just northeast of Area A on Site BA02 may point towards such a structure.

A companionway would have provided access to the crew's quarters: merely bunks, benches and a table, with the sailors expected to bring their own mattresses and blankets on board. The skipper would have taken his meals in the after cabin, and in bad weather the cook would have had an acrobatic time balancing the food during his traverse from the forecastle to the stern. Fitting out the captain's after cabin would have been dependent on the tastes of the owner and master, but might be "fitted out with paneled hardwood and decorated in the style of fashionable quarters ashore. A large coal stove provided heat for the whole space, which consisted of the saloon for sitting around and for officers' meals, rooms for master, mates and cook, a bathroom of sorts, and a pantry containing the smaller items of the ship's stores and usually provided with a sink for cleaning up" (Parker, 1960: 59).

The coasting schooner as used in America up to *c.* 1850 can be typically characterized as "a rather full-ended two-master, like the packets that ran between Maine ports

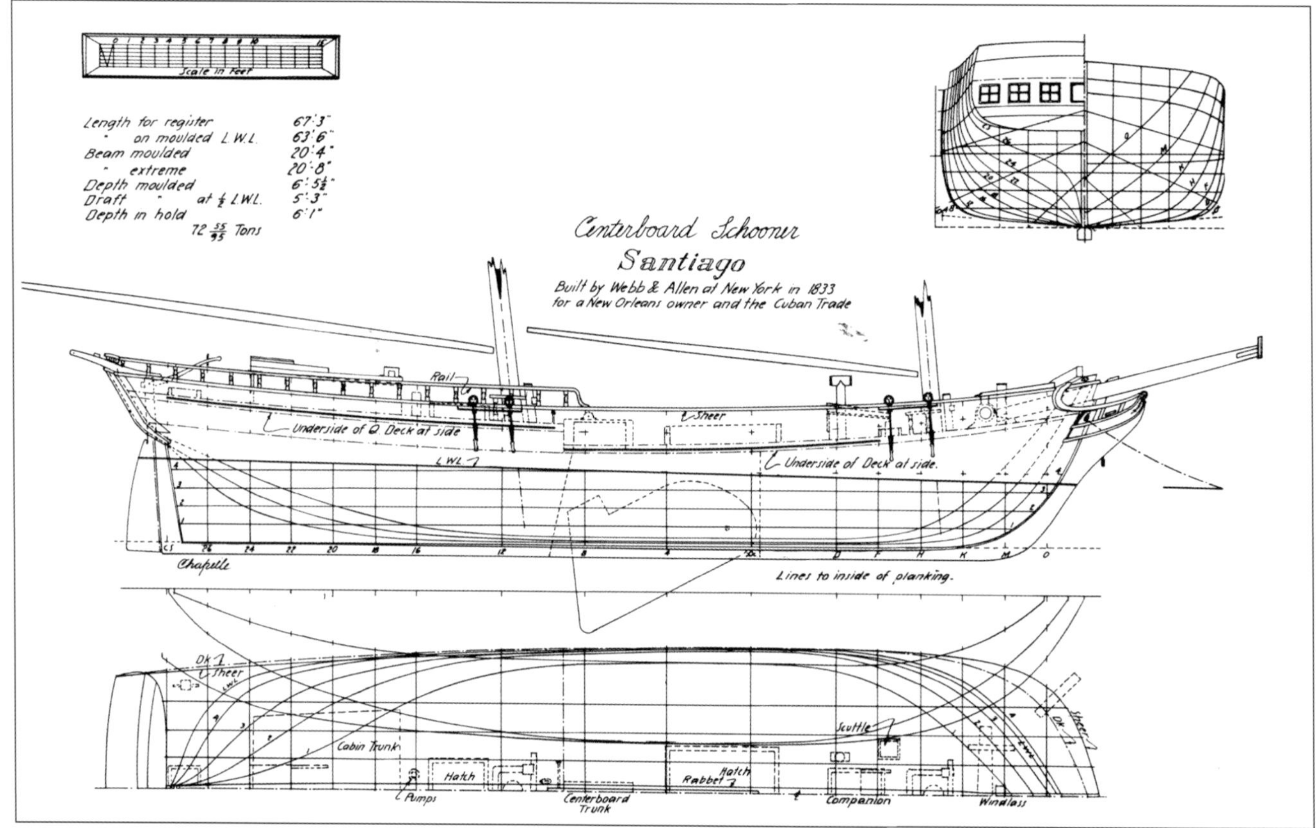

Fig. 122. Lines of the centerboard schooner Santiago *built for the Gulf and Cuban trade in 1833 (from Chapelle, 1967: pl. 82).*

and Boston. Most of them were fore-and-afters, but a great many of the Maine-built schooners were fore-topsail rigged. There were some sharp-lined coasters, particularly in the South. After 1860 the 'Essex model' became common, differing from the 'Bankers' of that particular model only in deck-plan" (Chapelle, 1935: 258). Vessels of this type frequently featured high hatch coamings and were commonly loaded until the main deck was virtually awash. Figureheads were rare and the bow was more likely to be decorated with a billet head and trailboards. The typical stern featured an old round tuck with wide upper and lower transoms, a style that gradually changed as the two-master evolved, first to a flat raking transom with a round tuck and subsequently with a short counter, a raking transom, curved athwart-ship and usually elliptical on New England vessels (Morris, 1973: 19-20).

After the War of 1812, Southern shipbuilders were more inclined to use oak and cedar, whereas oak, hatchmatack, pine and spruce was favored in the north. Hard pine was also imported northward, with the long leaf pine of Georgia and Florida considered the optimum medium. Mid-19th century schooners were most commonly built with trunnels for fastenings, which explains the absence of masses of concreted nails on Site BA02. Around 1861 a schooner cost about $70 per ton to build (Morris, 1973: 63-5).

Purely fore-and-aft schooners were rare in Britain and in much of northern Europe on commercial craft, whereas in the United States the opposite was the case after the 1850s, when square sails became a rare exception, particularly on the East Coast. The most common rig was a fore and aft foresail and a main with two headsails (the fore-staysail or jumbo and jib), with gaff topsails on the fore and main (Morris, 1973: 19). This pattern is typified by the *Mary Langdon* of 91 tons built at Rockland, Maine, in 1845 and rebuilt in 1860, which had two large deckhouses, a boat on the stern davits, a wooden balustrade as far forward as the fore rigging because the deck was level with the main rail, and 'lazy jacks' on the mainsail to prevent the sail spilling on to the deck when being lowered (Fig. 120). Such American schooners were broader in proportion to their length, the *Mary Langdon* having a length of 22m that was equal to only 3.5 breadths. This feature seems to be shared by the Site BA02 ship, for which available data reveal a keel length of some 17.6m and starboard planking across a breadth of 2.5m. A total beam of around 5.0m seems to fit the smaller variety of this class of craft (Table 3).

Based on combined historical and archaeological evidence, the following picture can be drawn for the Jacksonville 'Blue China' merchant vessel (cf. Figs. 120-122):

- Approximately 100 tons.
- A two-masted fore-and-aft schooner rig; no square topsails.
- Possibly fitted with a centerboard.
- A small boat rigged on davits across the stern.

Name	Date	Build Location	Area of Operation & Cargo	Length (ft)	Beam (ft)	Depth (ft)
Lucy (coaster)	1852	Sargentville, ME	New England coasting trade (lumber south, manufactures back north)	85 (moulded, at main rail)	23.29	7.15
Wakeag (coaster)	1855	Trenton, ME	Coastal & West Indian trade	102 (moulded, at rail)	25.29 (extreme)	8.46 (in hold)
J.W. Hale (coaster)	1855	Brooklin, ME	Coastal lumber trade; marine stores out of Florida, manufactured goods south	87 (moulded, at rail)	23.0 (moulded)	7.5 (moulded)
North Star (coaster)	1856	Sullivan, ME	Coastal lumber trade	60 (moulded, at rail)	17.5 (moulded)	6.25 (moulded)
R.B. Sumner (coaster)	1858	Newburyport, MA	General coastal freighting; packet on Boston-Newburyport route	84.25 (moulded, at rail)	21.17 (moulded)	8.33 (moulded)
Aaron (coaster)	1858	Lubec, ME	West Indian & coastal trade (incl. salt fish)	108.75 (moulded, at rail)	32.83 (moulded)	14.42 (moulded)
Charmer (packet, 116 tons)	c. 1860	Newburyport, MA	Passengers & light freight on Boston-Newburyport route	81 (moulded, at rail)	22.5 (moulded)	7.67 (moulded)
Unknown (coaster)	1860	Newburyport, MA	Possibly in coal trade	106 (moulded, at rail)	24.0 (moulded)	10 (moulded)
E. Closson (coaster, 135.37 tons)	1860	Sedgwick, ME	Coastal lumber trade	95.5 (between perpendiculars)	26.29 (extreme)	8.92 (in hold)

Table 3. A list of coastal schooners of comparable form as the Site BA02 ship (data from Chapelle, 1960: 75-9).

- Manned by a skipper and a crew of two to four.
- American registry, probably from New York.
- Not a bulk carrier.

Chapelle's *The National Watercraft Collection* (1960: 75-9) provides data from builders' half-models used to construct a number of two-masted schooners that were contemporary with the Jacksonville 'Blue China' trader and furnishes an additional understanding of its probable type (cf. Figs. 120-122). Ships with comparable lines are listed in Table 3 and indicate that lengths varied from 18-32m, widths from 5.2-7.9m and depths of 1.9-4.3m.

14. The Wreck Event & Great Storm of 1854

Historical sources dated to 1854, the midpoint of the period of interest for the Jacksonville 'Blue China' wreck, confirm that shipwrecks were common in the waters of the North Atlantic and down the East Coast of the United States all the way into the Gulf of Mexico. Approximately 90 American ocean-going sailing ships sank in the dangerous waters of the Bahamas, Cape Hatteras, Nantucket Shoals, Cape Cod, Cape Sable and Cape Race each year. Statistically, an average of one out of six American sailing packets went down during their long years of service, and these top rate vessels were judged to be safer than the regular coastal traders, which were not always well maintained and were often staffed by inexperienced mariners. The casualty rate for these vessels, particularly those engaged in the immigrant trade, was much higher. Seafaring was even more hazardous for men than ships. Sailors risked crippling injury or death as part of their daily routine, for which they typically received $12 a month (Shaw, 2002: 4, 87, 50).

Data published in the *New York Times* (26 January 1854), based on reports of marine disasters accumulated in New York, Boston, Philadelphia, Baltimore and Norfolk, reveal a more precise picture of the great hazards of East Coast shipping in the 1850s. In the year between 1 July 1850 and 1 July 1851, some 50 ships, 59 brigs, 190 schooners, 20 steamers and nine sloops were lost alongside 318 lives. These figures exclude lakes and rivers, where a further 118 vessels were wrecked with 695 lives. Some 313 (75%) of the above total craft were lost by tempest, 45 by fire, 34 by collision, 48 by snagging/beaching and two through explosions. Insurance claims reveal that the average individual value of these wrecked vessels was $9,745.

The specific reason for the loss of the Jacksonville 'Blue China' trader is unverifiable, but in the absence of any indications of fire, explosion, catastrophic hull failure or collision, it is likely that the ship was overcome by conditions of wind and wave, resulting in loss by foundering. Using software and historical information produced by the National Oceanic and Atmospheric Administration (NOAA), the major storm tracks that passed through the area of Site BA02 during the decade of interest, 1850-60, can be plotted and examined using NOAA's Historical Hurricane Tracks database.

The character of the surviving cargo on the wreck is indicative of a southern trading voyage from the vessel's home port, probably New York. In fact, the bow of the wreck points southward, but because of the confused climatic-induced gyrations that must have taken place during the ship's final minutes this may be nothing more than purely coincidental and symbolic today.

The extreme climatic episodes that struck the area of Site BA02 in the period of interest (Table 4) ranged from tropical storms (TS) through to full-blown hurricanes of categories 1, 2 and 3 (H1, H2, H3). Such storms are defined as having maximum sustained surface winds as follows:

- Tropical Storm: 34-64 knots/39-73 miles per hour inclusive.
- Category 1 Hurricane: 64-82 knots/74-95 miles per hour inclusive.
- Category 2 Hurricane: 83-95 knots/96-110 miles per hour inclusive.
- Category 3 Hurricane: 96-113 knots/111-130 miles per hour inclusive.

Between 1851 and 1860, 11 major storm and hurricane episodes are registered as having struck the area of Site BA02 (Table 4). In light of current dating criteria for the wreck, notably a transfer-printed plate bearing the maker's mark 'STONE WARE / B H & Co' (for Beech, Hancock & Co.), which was produced between 1851 and 1855, and a plaque from a Morton & Bremner spring-loaded scale, which provides a *terminus ante quem* for its manufacture before Bremner retired from business in 1854, the hurricane of 7-9 September 1854 emerges as the most plausible cause of the Site BA02's ship's loss. While the scale could easily have remained in circulation for years after this date, it would be unexpected for an old stock British product to be sold to the middle class South and its clamor for the latest and most affordable British Staffordshire wares.

1854 was renowned amongst the insurance agents of New York as the "black year" for its high record of casualties. The New York Atlantic Mutual Insurance Company's preserved 'disaster books' reveal that some of the city's largest ships took big hits. The greatest loss was the *Franklin* of the Havre Line that ran ashore on Long Island, enforcing a payout of $20,000 on the hull and $176,000

Year	Date	Wind Speed (Knots)	Category
1851	24 August	50-90	TS-H2
1852	27 August	40	TS
1852	11-13 September	50-70	TS-H1
1852	9-10 October	50-90	TS-H2
1853	19-22 October	70-90	H1-H2
1854	7-9 September	60-110 (938-950 MB Pressure)	TS-H3
1856	31 August - 1 September	50-90	TS-H2
1858	14-15 September	50-80	TS-H1
1859	18 October	40	TS
1859	28 October	70-80	H1
1860	13-14 August	40-50	TS

Table 4. A list of the principal storms that struck the area around shipwreck Site BA02 between 1851 and 1860, based on NOAA's Historical Hurricane Tracks database.

for the $472,000 cargo, part of which was salvaged. Three lost ocean-sailing packets, the Red Star Line's *Waterloo*, the London Swallowtail Line's *Prince Albert* and the Black Baller Line's *Montezuma* (lost at sea, abandoned at sea and wrecked on Long Island) were insured by the company at $7,000, $30,000 and $43,000 respectively. Altogether, the Atlantic Mutual Insurance Co. losses for 1854 totaled $4.5 million (Albion, 1970: 273-4).

The loss of these top end vessels was just the thin edge of a long list of horrors. In reality, 1854 was the culmination of appalling weather and casualties that characterized the end of the previous winter's shipping, of which the wrecking of the New York steamer the *San Francisco* on 25 December 1853 was especially dramatic. The detailed account of an anonymous female survivor in the *New York Times* of 18 January 1854, who was eventually saved by the *Kilby*, merits lengthy reproduction to provide a comparative understanding of the horrific experience that ships' passengers and crews alike experienced during the next year's even more ferocious hurricane:

> "We sailed, as you know, on the 22d December... I soon made acquaintances among the lady passengers. We sat together in the saloon and talked of Christmas, and how we should spend it... I, for one, never thought of danger in the voyage... Our ship seemed too noble, too strong for such a contingency... And even on the morning of the 24th December, when the wind throughout the night had been blowing a gale, when our engine had stopped working, and our foremast was carried away, I could not realize the danger we were in... In less than an hour afterwards, when I was in the cabin, a deafening crash, not so much like the falling of houses as the crushing them in from the roof downwards, as you might crush a pile of pill-boxes, sent the blood away from my heart, and left me so utterly petrified that I had no power even to sink upon the ground.
>
> Then I felt that our fate was decided. I heard the commencement of screams that were stifled by the choking waves, and at the same moment the water came rushing into the cabin, as if the vessel's sides had cleaved, and she had already began to sink. Then my friend, there was indeed horror on that ship. The confusion, the wailing, the praying, the groans of agony from the maimed and bruised, the shrieks from the ladies in their berths – all the tragedy, in its entirety and its details, will live in my memory forever, – is burnt into my brain, – can never perish while I have life, and "memory holds its seat." I think insanity would not obliterate it, – I think I might forget home, relatives, friends and all that is or was dear to me, – my father's and my husband's names, and the sweet faces of my children, and still retain a lively recollection of that scene.
>
> This was when the upper saloon was swept away by the force of one tremendous wave, that was afterwards described to me as literally an enormous mountain of water. Nearly one hundred and fifty human beings, mostly troops, including, as you know, COL. WASHINGTON, MAJOR TAYLOR and lady, Capt. FIELD, and Lieut. SMITH, were swept overboard. When I recovered myself after my momentary paralysis, I made an effort to reach the deck, but a sudden convulsion of the ship – I can call it by no other name, it was so like the shudder of a human being in mortal agony – threw me with violence on the floor, and left me for some minutes senseless. When my consciousness returned I was nearly covered with water that had poured in from above, and inundated the cabin.
>
> Somebody assisted to raise me up, and then I saw faces – faces only – grouped around me, as in a nightmare dream – faces so frightful from the overpowering awe that had seized

them, that I almost imagined them to be the phantom-faces of shuddering ghosts... Some of the soldiers' wives filled the ship with screams... In our part of the ship there was ejaculated prayers, sighs, half-suppressed lamentations, but no shrieks... We prayed during that night. I never knew what prayer was before. In the darkness – for we had no lights for several hours – prayers as sincere as were ever uttered by human lips or framed by human hearts, ascended to the Throne Eternal.

In the same was Christmas Day, which was also Sunday, was spent... The sunrise of that morning was splendid. The sky was unclouded, though the cold was intense, and the sea was heaving in a terrible manner. Anything more beautiful than the snowy crests of those huge waves as they shone in the sun, I cannot imagine. Our ship was lifted by them and let fall, like a dead giant. She had no longer any resemblance to a "thing of life." She was a cumbrous corpse upon the waters, without vitality or will."

The *New York Times* captures the geographic scope of this storm and its damage in graphic detail. The year opened with a report of 4 January 1854, confirming that:

"We continue to receive accounts of marine disasters in the late gale, and it is feared that further accounts, to come from Cape Cod, will show a large loss of life... A gentleman from Provincetown on Saturday says there are vessels ashore on all parts of the Cape... Parts of wrecks are all the time drifting ashore of vessels that must have been swamped in the gale, and whose crews doubtless perished. There has never been known such distress on the shores of Cape Cod."

The *New York Times* of 7 January 1854 dedicated substantial space to the subsequent outpouring of sorrow:

"The land is filled with mourning. The disasters at sea with which the papers have been crowded, and under which the telegraphic wires have staggered, for the past fortnight are fraught with more miseries than at first appear. In the centres of commerce, after the first shudder of sympathy is over, the value of the lost property is the remembered thing. But out along the sea-coast, and farther back into the country than would be supposed, are families sorrowing perpetually over the news that nestles in among our mail and marine items... Lost ships, men clinging to floating spars, dashed over by cruel waves, and uttering shrieks of despair – all are presented to the ears of the desolate, who from one brief text – a "marine disaster" – are left to deduce endless chapters of domestic and heartbreaking misery. The past month and this are likely to be remembered as epochs of fresh sorrow around thousands of firesides for many years to come."

If the fate of the *San Francisco* provides the most graphic account of the human drama felt by crew and passengers caught in the midst of an almighty storm during the period of the Site BA02's ship's loss, then an account from Newport of the *Moselle* in the *New York Times* of 5 January 1854 provides a closer image of the final hours of the same type of craft as the Jacksonville 'Blue China' ship. "An awful scene was witnessed this morning by SETH C. BATEMAN, Esq. from the shore of his farm", announced the newspaper, before continuing that "At about daylight he discovered a schooner between Brenten's Reef and the small reef, water-logged, and at the mercy of the sea, which was making a clear breach over her. The crew, four in number, were in the rigging." The schooner then heavily struck the rocks and turned over on her beam ends before she was broken into fragments by another wave, after which:

"The men were thrown into the water, and there caught at the fragments... Two others were near together on the spars, when one, losing his hold, caught by the other, who tried to disengage himself, but before he could do so they both went down. The fourth had a fearful struggle with death. He was on the spars, and was repeatedly washed off, but managed to get on again, bruised, crushed as the fragments were washed against him, and Mr. BATEMAN could hear him groan as he received blow after blow, but no aid could be extended to him, and finally his strength failed and he shared the fate of his companions. The shore is strewn with the remains of the wreck..."

February witnessed little relief from the appalling weather. A letter written from the breakwater at Philadelphia on 23 February described how "the storm of Monday night was the severest ever known, and was accompanied with terrific thunder and lightning. The beach is strewed with wrecks. Thirteen vessels are ashore within view of the Breakwater..." (*New York Times*, 24 February 1854).

Progressing to September 1854, the suggested month of the Site BA02 ship's loss, the *New York Times* was awash with reports of damage at land and sea alike. The epicenter of a great storm heavily struck Savannah, Georgia. Far out to sea off this town, on 7 September the steamer *Star of the South* battled a slow moving major hurricane for five days. One of its passengers reported later how, "As far out as the eye could see, a perfectly white mountainous sea presented itself, while the wind moaned and whistled with awful fury". The storm shredded the sails and on 8 September the waves cracked the rudder and water reached and extinguished the boilers. The steamer only reached Charleston in a "crippled condition" through the coolness and seamanship of its captain (Fraser, 2009: 121-22).

The brig *Mary Ann* capsized in the same storm far off Savannah, but another heavy sea fortunately turned her upright. Eventually the wind shredded her sails off Georgia, brought down the mainmast and again capsized the brig.

Insured for $6,000, the ship was a total write off. Caught in the same waters, the crew of the brig *Alice* described the scene as a "perfect hurricane", while the schooner *Angenett*, loaded with timber and again sailing off Savannah, was forced to cut away its masts. The nearby schooner *Edward Kidder* lost its mainsail and everything movable on deck, and the schooner *Dirigo*, again loaded with lumber, was caught by the hurricane at 5pm on 8 September, which washed the crew's food and water overboard before the masts were cut away and the hold filled with water. The dismasted schooner drifted helplessly northwards for six days before being rescued.

Off the Charleston bar another schooner, the *Mary D. Scull* of Philadelphia, loaded with merchandise for the shops of Charleston, was slammed by northeast winds on 7 September and fought the storm for 36 hours stripped of its sails, with smashed bulwarks and a holed hull (Fraser, 2009: 122, 124).

The same stories resonated across the seas of North Carolina and all the 'Low Country', where the waters were filled with wreckage and ships floating bottom up. US Navy lieutenant W.A. Bartlett of the steamer *Atlantic* would record that "Twenty-one years of trials incident to a sea life, I have not met before a gale of greater severity, and in no instance have I known the wind to blow a hurricane gale for so many consecutive hours." Captain G.P. Adams of the schooner *Aid* also survived the hurricane in the open seas and described it as "the heaviest sea ever experienced during the 25 years he has been at sea" (Fraser, 2009: 123).

The bark *Harvest* incoming from Liverpool was caught in the September hurricane as it traveled east-northeast, which at latitude 40°20' and longitude 68°30' blew away its fore and main topsails and fore-topmast staysail, as a result of which "the ship breached to, shipping a tremendous sea, sweeping the deck of water casks and everything movable, and shifting cargo. In the height of the hurricane, blew away foresail, spanker, spencer, and foretop gallant sail out of the gaskets. Thirteen steerage passengers were washed overboard..." (*New York Times*, 18 September 1854).

The coastal towns of Georgia also took the full force of the hurricane, as revealed in a report filed from Savannah on 9 September (*New York Times*, 13 September 1854):

> "...a terrific hurricane, exceeding in violence and the amount of property destroyed anything we have ever witnessed, is sweeping over Savannah from the Northeast. It is appalling to look out upon the streets and listen to the rushing, roaring, beating limbs of trees, pieces of slate and tin and boards, upon its mighty wings, as if they were lighter than chaff... Looking from the upper story of the Republican Buildings, we find that the whole of Hutchinson's Island opposite the city is submerged, and that the rice fields above and below, both on the Georgia and Carolina sides, as far as the eye can reach, are completely inundated... The loss from the destruction of the Rice and Sea Island Cotton crops, in Georgia and South Carolina, must be immense. Indeed, it can only be estimated at millions!"

On 12 September reports of a 48-hour storm were dispatched from Charleston, where all the wharves had been damaged, with estimated repair costs of $250,000 (around $5.2 million in modern value, cf. Fraser, 2009: 128), and warehouses and stores flooded. "We are called up to record one of the severest and most destructive storms that has been felt at our port for many years", wrote a local reporter in the *New York Times* (12 September 1854). "In duration, violence, and amount of damage, we can, indeed, compare the visitation which has just passed over, with nothing that has occurred since the memorable gale of 1804 – of which, by a strange coincidence, the present was the semi-centennial anniversary."

Reports suggest that the hurricane's winds varied from the southeast to northeast and northwest. Jacksonville, Florida, the closest landfall to wreck Site BA02, is reported as having just been brushed by the storm's northeastern gales before the full force of the storm made land between Brunswick and Savannah. The hurricane of September 1854 crossed the coast of Georgia at an angle as it began its slow curvature north-northeast along a track parallel to the coastline (Fraser, 2009: 131).

A combination of the above data with information from the 1831 version of Francis Beaufort's scale permits the climatic conditions deteriorating during the fateful period when the Jacksonville 'Blue China' ship was lost off the Florida/Georgia coast to be reconstructed. As the ship headed south any experienced member of the crew would have recognized from the clouds and the shifting winds the approach of foul weather. If equipped with a barometer, the falling pressure would have been further evidence of an impending storm. The crew members would have busied themselves lashing down any loose equipment, double checking that the hatches were secured and putting extra lashings on the boat or boats in the stern davits and on deck. Perhaps they would have wolfed down a last hot meal before extinguishing the stoves in the forecastle galley and the after cabin, a precaution against fire due to the pitching of the vessel that was soon to come.

The crew would have verified that the pumps were clear and functioning. With a pure fore-and-aft rig (without square topsails), as the weather deteriorated the increasing wind would have forced the crew to take in the topsails, jibs and spanker. Afterwards, the fore and mainsails would have been reefed: the heads of the sails would have been lowered and the slack material bundled up and lashed to the booms, effectively reducing the sail area. Thus, when the ship was in the troughs of the sea as the waves ran high, these sails would have gone slack as the wind was blocked. Upon rising to the crest the ship would have been exposed to the full force of the storm and the gear subjected to a sudden and heavy strain. Smaller schooners commonly carried a storm trysail, used when the mizzen was furled to aid in keeping the ship's head to the sea in stormy conditions (Parker, 1960: 57, 61).

Even under the best of conditions wooden hulls leak, working in a seaway that tends to bend and flex, causing seams between planks to open. In extreme cases the caulking washes out, causing increased water to flow into the hull through the resulting gaps. The Jacksonville 'Blue China' trader would have had no steam pumps, so the small crew would have been at the hand pumps (probably brake pumps) continuously to keep the rising water level down.

Site BA02 lies within the flow of the Gulf Stream, so a strong northerly wind would have pushed against the 2.5-knot flow of the northward-moving current. Even in isolation, such a wind of 30 knots or more would build up steep 4.5-6m high seas. As the winds reached gale force, even without the effect of the Gulf Stream, waves would have built up further to heights of 6-9m. The entire surface of the ocean would have turned a frothy white as thick streaks of foam were ripped from the waves and blown downwind. If the sails had not already been reefed, it would have been suicidal for the crew to venture onto deck in an attempt to secure them. The only distress signal available to the small ship would have been to hoist the American flag upside-down, an international signal of distress – but at this stage this would have been a final act of despair. As the wind reached speeds of 56-63 knots only the storm trysail would have held up as the waves began reaching mountainous heights of 9-13.5m. The Jacksonville 'Blue China' trader would have been completely hidden in the troughs of monster waves. In such deep waters, the presence of the anchors was meaningless. They remained strung to the bows, unused.

With the winds reaching hurricane force, the ensign on the Jacksonville 'Blue China' trader would have been shredded. The storm trysail, if still in place, would have exploded into fragments with a sound like a cannon shot. Even the furled sails might have been torn loose and whipped to pieces. The completely white sea would have been convulsed by 13m-high waves, the air so filled with foam and spray that it would have been difficult to discern the air/water interface. At this point survival on deck would have been impossible and the pumps would have been abandoned. No hope remained of controlling the direction of the ship and the only recourse would have been to run before the wind under bare poles. The master compass was probably smashed by this time, and even if not the wild gyrations of the vessel would have overcome the gimbel mechanism, making the direction impossible to read. At best the crew could have hoped of being driven to shore, which afforded at least a slim chance of survival.

By this time the ship's small boat could have been smashed to splinters in its davits, leaving only one on deck remaining if that too had not been destroyed by the pounding waves. This would have been scant comfort, however, because launching it would have been out of the question. The best that could be hoped for would have been to cut it loose as the ship went down and for the crew to cling on or lash themselves to it. At this final point in the ship's life, the men might have found themselves trapped in the gyre that, according to local folklore, characterizes this part of the ocean.

The terror that goes through a ship's crew in its final minutes can be well imagined from the above historical accounts, but these were written by fortunate survivors. The utter sadness of loss of hope is aptly laid bare in an account of August 1872 in the North Atlantic. When the schooner *Lancaster* sighted that month a dismantled derelict, the *Glenalvon*, its crew found on board several skeletons and an open Bible lying face downward in the cabin alongside a loaded revolver and a bottle, which contained a note reading "Jesus guide this to some helpers! Merciful God, don't let us perish!" (Morris, 1973: 106). As with the fate of the Jacksonville 'Blue China' ship, the Blue God had other malicious intentions.

15. Conclusion: the Port of New York

The collective data for the Jacksonville 'Blue China' shipwreck points towards the presence of a relatively modest 20m-long schooner of 100 tons or less specializing in coastal trade along the East Coast of America (cf. Figs. 120-122). The grindstone, a stoneware jug, the Morton and Bremner spring-loaded scale and McCullough lead ingots provide guiding evidence to define the vessel as originating in New York and having commenced its final voyage in or after 1851 and before 1855. This chronology coincides with the artifact dating scheme (Table 5). The vessel's New York origin is further supported by the fact that by the 1850s the bulk of Staffordshire pottery exports was handled by New York ceramic importers and dealers, who controlled the distribution network for the internal American trade.

The ship was transporting a diverse cargo of British

Artifact	Origins	Date
Grindstone	Appalachian Mountains: New York to Alabama	----
Sand's Sarsaparilla glass bottles	New York, America	1840s
Type 8 salt-glazed stoneware jug	New York/ Pennsylvania, America	1850-60
Morton & Bremner spring-loaded scale	New York, America	1851-54
McCullough lead ingots	New York, America	----
Type 2 dipped whitewares	Staffordshire, Britain	1850-60
Type 3 painted whitewares	Staffordshire, Britain	*c.* 1845-55
Type 7 transfer-printed plate	Staffordshire, Britain	1850+
Type 7 transfer-printed soup plate	Staffordshire, Britain	1851-55

Table 5. A list of the artifacts from Site BA02 with the tightest dates and reflections of the ship's origin.

ceramic dining and toilet wares, largely manufactured in Staffordshire, and which would have been exported via Liverpool, presumably to New York. In this bustling North Atlantic port they were purchased, possibly through the city's infamous dockside auctions, for trade inland and to the South. Added to the pottery shipment was a consignment of American beverages, medicinal products, condiments and cologne packaged in glass bottles, plus glass tumblers, glass lamps and building materials in the form of glass window panes and kegs holding white lead. Most ships carried some form of organic cargo, whose character in this case can only be a matter of speculation (see Table 6 for a cross-section of the most valuable New York exports of 1860). A few wooden crates of lead musket balls and tobacco pipes were slotted in amongst the overflowing merchandise as the small schooner headed towards the South, the cotton and tobacco-growing center of America.

Although the storms of late December 1853 were notoriously harsh on shipping, a small schooner is unlikely to have risked such notorious seasonal seas. Rather, the great storm of 7-9 September 1854, a category three hurricane associated with 110-knot winds (126 mph), emerges as the most likely cause of the Jacksonville 'Blue China' ship's demise. The wreck's location off the border of northern Florida and southern Georgia fits perfectly the profile of this killer storm, which hit the coast of Georgia from the east-northeast on 7 September and peaked the following day as the full force of the gale made land between Brunswick and Savannah, Georgia, and began its slow curvature north-northeast along a track parallel to the coastline.

Contemporary accounts report that Jacksonville itself largely escaped the hurricane. Brunswick is situated some 107km north of Jacksonville, which fits with the storm's southern-moving track. The steamer *Star of the South* fought the hurricane for five days and the schooner *Mary D. Scull* battled the elements for 36 hours. The Jacksonville 'Blue China' schooner, stripped of sails and masts, could easily have been propelled to the current wreck's location by the northern storm.

Alternatively, it is possible that far out to sea the hurricane was more malicious than along the shore. Although the storm peaked at Charleston and Savannah, the damage to North Carolina was also extensive and a similar trail of destruction would not be unexpected to the south. Under these circumstances, and some 70 nautical miles offshore, it would have been beyond a miracle if any of the small crew of around five people survived. Lieutenant Matthew Fontaine Maury's newly published *Wind and Current Chart of the North Atlantic* of 1847 (Laing, 1974: 199) would have been an idle tool in these climatic circumstances.

The destination of the Jacksonville 'Blue China' ship is not obvious. Both Savannah and Charleston were major cotton ports at the time and each exported respectively $4 million and $11 million worth of goods in 1854. Another candidate for the Jacksonville 'Blue China' ship's intended port of call was New Orleans in the northern Gulf of Mexico, which exported $60 million of goods in return for $14 million of imports in 1854 (Albion, 1970: 390, 402; cf. Cunningham Dobson and Gerth, 2010 for commerce in New Orleans *c.* 1865).

To what extent all three of these Southern ports were

functioning in light of the outbreak of yellow fever at the end of August 1854, which provoked widespread panic, is unclear, especially since contemporary sources described it as so highly contagious that the people of Augusta and the neighboring villages had taken to "camping it out in the open fields" according to the *New York Times*. Around 25 September 1854, 32 people died from the disease in two days in Charleston and by 29 September New Orleans had been hit by 110 deaths in three days (with 500 cases overall). Reports from 30 September listed seven dead in Savannah in a day, including the doctor (*New York Times*, 27, 29 and 30 September 1854). The extent of the social meltdown is described in a letter from Savannah published in the *New York Times* on 27 September:

> "Age nor condition afford security against the disease, and people that are acclimated are carried off by it, in common with the rest of the victims. But what shall I say of Savannah? Out of sixteen thousand people, there remains but *two thousand* – the rest have either fled or are dead. The deaths in this poor devoted city are, on an average, fifty per diem; and when you understand that bread is wanting, (the bakers have all died,) and that the Mayor of Savannah has called upon the neighboring town to send five hundred loaves of bread a day – and that the cars bring fifty coffins a day, as none can be had – you will then have some idea of affairs. In Charleston it's not quite so bad, but bad enough."

In a second scenario it would seem reasonable to question whether the Site BA02 schooner may have been sailing alternatively for the Southern ports after the 7-9 September hurricane had struck, when new window panes, white lead used for paint and to plug leaking window frames and, of course, pottery to replace damaged dining wares would have been in high demand. However, no storm episodes are listed for the second half of the month.

The emergence of a deep-sea fishing fleet off Georgia and Florida in the 1970s probably saw the wreck being impacted by bottom gear for the first time. The extent of natural deterioration caused by time and tide previously cannot be quantified. Since then pottery has been raised in fishermen's nets over the last 35-40 years. All but the southwestern quadrant of the wreck (Area A) has been heavily impacted, especially the eastern, port side of the

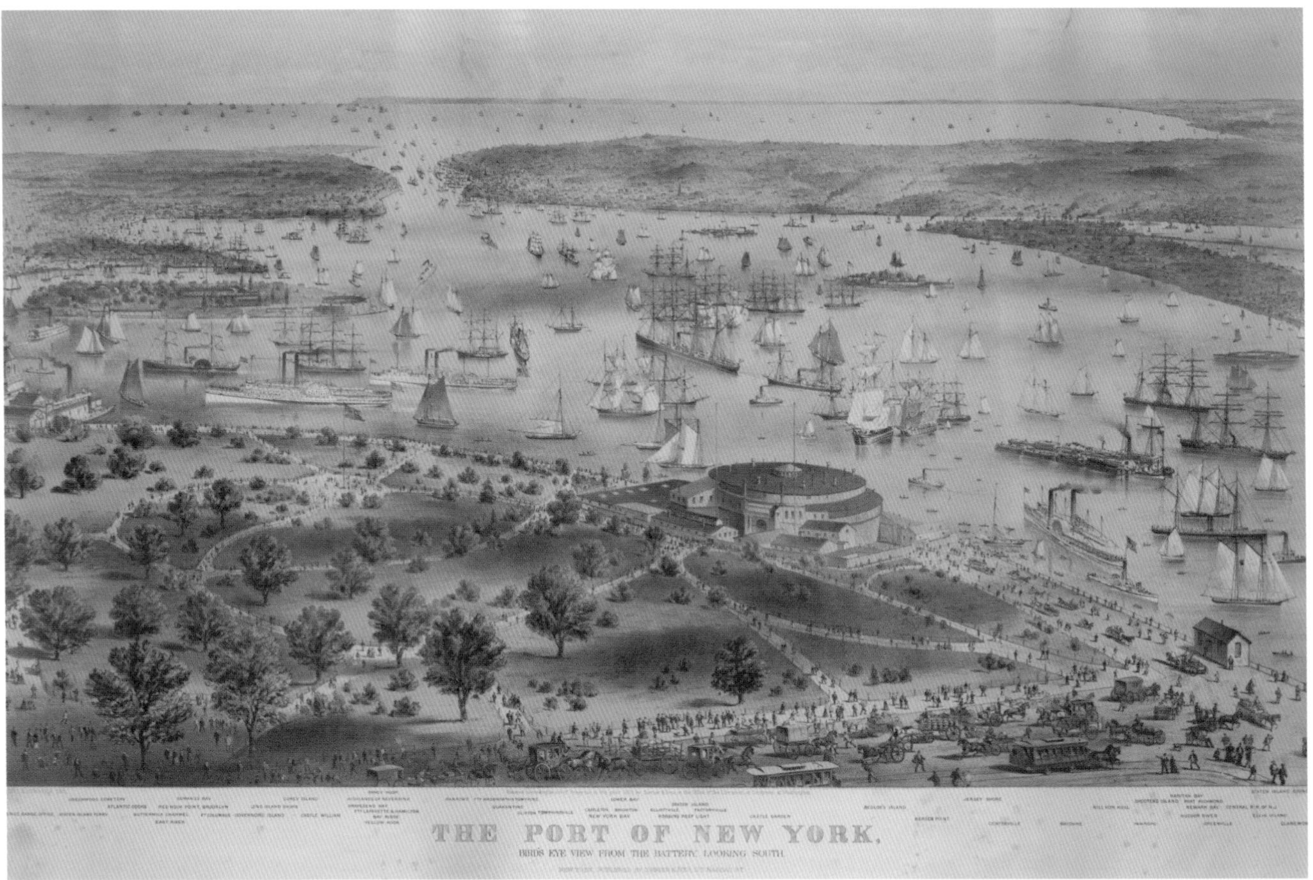

Fig. 123. A bird's eye view of the port of New York from the Battery, looking south, published by Currier & Ives, 1872. Photo: Eno Collection, Miriam and Ira D. Wallach Division of Art, Prints and Photographs, the New York Public Library, Astor, Lenox and Tilden Foundations.

ship, where the ceramic cargo is widely scattered and linear furrow lines are present.

In one sense this form of impact is synonymous with the burrowing actions of moles and rabbits on land sites that simultaneously damage, yet expose, new sites of archaeological significance for the first time. Few shipwrecks are static, but rather are subjected to varying degrees of continuous impacts from natural degradation by currents, dredging for gravel and sands and the oil and gas industry, at one extreme characterized by the 19th-century 'Mica' wreck in the Gulf of Mexico, which was unwittingly cut in half in 2001 by a 20cm-diameter ExxonMobil Corporation pipeline (Jones, 2004).

Site BA02 is a unique type of shipwreck. A wide cross-section of sea craft has been identified and recorded off the East and Gulf coasts of America, including: remains of Spanish galleons of 1559, 1622 and 1733 off Emanuel Point and the Florida Keys (Mathewson, 1986; McKinnon, 2007; Smith *et al.*, 1998); the early 18th-century wreck of the pirate ship *Queen Anne's Revenge* off Beaufort Inlet, North Carolina (Lawrence, 2007); the deep-sea SS *Republic* steamer wreck of 1865 off Georgia; the early 19th-century 'Mica' wreck schooner and possible armed 'Mardi Gras' privateer shipwreck of *c.* 1820, both in the Gulf of Mexico (Jones, 2004; Ford *et al.*, 2010: 95); and various regional early modern and modern vessels off Dog Island, northwest Florida (Meide *et al.*, 1999). More recently, the wreck of a two-masted 19th-century brig that sailed between New York and the Caribbean was recovered from the foundations of the World Trade Center in New York (Lobell, 2010).

None of these sea craft typify or reflect the most common form of coastal trade conducted by schooners between New York and the Southern ports of Savannah, Charleston and New Orleans that were the economic life force of New York. These lesser schooners that carried everything from coal cargos worth just $1,000 to consignments of tea, spices and other exotic imports insured for $200,000 have been termed a "neglected virgin subject" (Albion, 1970: 122-23). The small schooner of around 100 tons in fact was the favorite instrument for coastal trips of moderate length of about 300km: of 2,869 ship arrivals in New York in 1835, 2,521 were schooners. In 1860 New York built 372 schooners of 75-150-ton range (as well as 289 sloops and canal boats, 264 steam vessels, 141 ships, 36 brigs) that formed the rank and file of lesser coastal runs from Maine to North Carolina and on to the Caribbean and Spanish Main (Albion, 1970: 124, 305). The wreck at Site BA02 currently stands as the sole archaeological representative of this voluminous mercantile operator. It is also the only cargo of British ceramics and American glass wares found on any schooner off the United States.

Fig. 124. View along the docks of New York City, 1800s, from Harper's Weekly: A Journal of Civilization. *Photo: Picture Collection, the Branch Libraries, the New York Public Library, Astor, Lenox and Tilden Foundations.*

Following the end of the Napoleonic War in 1812, the US evolved from national adolescence to nationhood during the ensuing 50 years. The decade of peace from 1815-25 cemented New York's status as the preeminent American seaport. The city's position at the heart of US maritime trade grew rapidly through a series of social and economic developments strongly grounded in the 1820s: the appearance of packet lines, the rise of the 'cotton triangle', the opening of the Erie Canal, growth in immigration and the California Gold Rush.

The establishment of timetabled packet lines between America and Britain created the foundations of a long-term, long-distance trade mechanism. The Black Ball Line was founded in October 1817 between New York and Liverpool, which was followed in January 1822 by Byrnes, Trimble and Company's expansion of its flour trade business to set up the Red Star Line with monthly sailings between the same two destinations. Thaddeus Phelps & Company's Swallowtail Line soon expanded the healthy competition (La Guardia, 1941: 142-3, 148-9). These early packets were modest ships of around 257 tons and 28m in length (Albion, 1970: 40-41).

Once the packet line service was bedded in as a reliable

Fig. 125. View along South Street, New York, from Harper's Weekly: A Journal of Civilization, *1878. Photo: Picture Collection, the New York Public Library, Astor, Lenox and Tilden Foundations.*

and constant feature of eastern American travel, New York found itself in the perfect position to play middleman in the 'cotton triangle' (Fig. 123). Southern cotton cultivated in abundance in Charleston, Savannah and New Orleans was first shipped to New York before being loaded to England (La Guardia, 1941: 150-1). Prior to the completion of the railroad system shortly before the American Civil War, coastal craft offered merchants the only means of moving their goods in quantity between the North and South (Bauer, 1979: 44).

It has been observed that women's bell skirts with voluminous underpinnings were literally a style that launched a thousand ships. Never before had American female society demanded greater volumes of cloth. The average woman's dress in 1855 required some 30 yards of material, while petticoats and other garments underneath brought the total per woman to a staggering 100 yards (eight times the amount needed in 1800 and sufficient to clothe 14 women in the 1920s). In a rather convoluted and economically embedded manner, Southern cotton was shipped raw first to New York, exported to Britain and then imported in finished form back to America. By 1860, $85 million of the total of $125 million woolen and cotton goods imported annually into America derived from Britain and mainly Liverpool, compared to just $900,000 per annum of silk imports from China (Albion, 1970: 58).

The early autumn to late spring (October to April) cotton season made the southward sea lane from Sandy Hook past Hatteras to the cotton ports second in importance only to the Atlantic shuttle. New York's total coastwise trade in 1835 – comprising 2,869 arrivals of 302,000 tons a day, almost 10 vessels a day – almost equaled that of its two chief city rivals combined.

New York's economy received an enormous boost in 1825 with the opening of the artificial Erie Canal (the total length from Buffalo to Albany was 226km, where it fed into the Hudson River), which linked New York with Lake Erie, Lake Ontario and the fertile hinterland (Bauer, 1979: 47). The canal allowed the western counties centered on Rochester to replace the Hudson Valley as the center of the flour industry. The stimulus to New York's economy was dramatic. In the immediate wake of the canal's opening, 500

Product	Value (Million $)	Product	Value (Million $)
Specie & bullion	50.3	Staves	1.3
Cotton Cotton goods	12.4 5.9	Skins & furs	1.3
Flour	6.6	Indian corn	1.1
Iron & related products	3.2	Oil cake	1.1
Tobacco	2.6	Rice	1.0
Naval stores	2.7	Drugs/medicine	0.8
Wheat	2.3	Lumber	0.8
Lard	2.0	Manufacturers of wood	0.7
Whale oil	2.0	Butter	0.7
Beef	1.8	Furniture	0.5
Pork	1.6	Spirits	0.5
Hams & bacon	1.5	Rye/oats	0.4
Cheese	1.4	Livestock	0.3
Copper/brass	1.4	Raw hides	0.2

Table 6. A list of New York exports by value in descending order compiled from the Reports on Commerce and Navigation for 1860 (from Albion, 1970: 401).

new mercantile establishments set up business in the first few months of the year, and the April edition of the *Gazette* carried 1,115 new advertisements. By the end of 1825, 12 banks and 13 marine insurance companies representing an aggregate investment of $23 million had been established. New York shipyards were filled with more orders than they could meet and the overflow trade passed to Boston, Philadelphia, New Bedford and Gloucester (La Guardia, 1941: 151). Where 218,000 tons of goods were carried along the canal in 1825, by 1850 the amount had mushroomed to 3,076,617 tons. Vessels shipping cash crops to New York returned with myriad imports from Europe, China and Latin America, creating an explosion of small stores and consumers in the western interior (Albion, 1970: 85-91).

New York had become the center of mercantile America and once gold was discovered in California in autumn 1848, a starry-eyed multitude crowded its docks (Figs. 123-125). By March 1849 more than 150 ships carrying 11,000 passengers had left for California, with a total of 775 vessels by the end of the year. Again the shipyards of New York were overstretched, which enabled Maine, with its shipyards perched on the edge of forests, to wrench leadership in the regional ship construction industry away from New York. Whereas New York had 44,104 tons of ships in construction that year, Maine's yards had 82,256 tons in production (LaGuardia, 1941: 166-68). With New York focusing on larger craft and Maine specializing in smaller vessels, it was probably in the latter region that the Site BA02 ship was most likely constructed.

New York was also infamously the landfall of choice for any aspiring mid-19th century speculator, large or small, and of 5.4 million immigrants that arrived in the United States from 1819-60, 3.7 million entered at New York. In 1854, the peak year of movement, the city received 327,000 immigrants (including 177,000 Germans, 82,000 Irish, and 36,000 people from England, Scotland and Wales), almost three-quarters of the national total (Albion, 1970: 337-38).

By the mid-19th century, New York stood second only to London in the tonnage of shipping it handled, and New York vessels exceeded the combined tonnage of Boston, Philadelphia, Baltimore and New Orleans. The city's 1,377,000 tons of registered vessels manned by 60,000 people carried 52% of the nation's combined imports and exports and had 33% of its registered tonnage. The *Reports on Commerce and Navigation* for 1854 demonstrate that of total US exports amounting to $275 million, New York City handled $122 million. Of $304 million US imports, the city's ships carried $195 million of its value (Albion, 1970: 54-58, 95, 123, 267, 390-91, 398). The types and total values of New York imports and exports are presented in Tables 6-7.

The original source of this virtual maritime empire was New York's geographical position as an outstanding natural harbor with 481km of protected waterfront. One arm was formed by the outer shore of Long Island, stretching eastward 65km from Coney Island to Montauk Point. The opposite arm was the New Jersey coast, extending

Product	Value (Million $)	Product	Value (Million $)
Woolen goods	34	Furs	1.7
Silk goods	30.7	Glass	1.7
Cotton goods	22.6	Clothing	1.5
Sugar	20.7	Lead	1.6
Iron/steel	12.3	Molasses	1.6
Linen/flax	8.6	Hats/bonnets	1.5
Coffee	8.5	Jewelry/gems	1.5
Tea	8.3	Raw silk	1.3
Raw hides/skins	6.9	Rubber	1.3
Leather goods	4.5	Soda	1.3
Tin	4.5	Rags	1.0
Lace	3.5	Linseed	0.8
Spirits	3.4	Indigo	0.6
Tobacco	3.3	Spices	0.6
Wine	2.9	Hemp	0.5
Clocks/watches	2.6	Copper	0.4
Chinaware	2.4	Salt	0.3
Fruit	2.4	Gunny	0.2
Raw wool	2.4	Saltpetre	0.1
Specie/bullion	2.3		

Table 7. A list of New York imports by value in descending order compiled from the Reports on Commerce and Navigation for 1860 (from Albion, 1970: 401).

68km from Sandy Hook to Cape May. The main sea lane to Europe ran along the former, while the latter was skirted by shipping for the Southern and Caribbean ports (Albion, 1970: 16).

By 1840 the city possessed 60 wharves on the East River and 53 on the Hudson (Figs. 124-125). Data from a single day in spring 1836 reveal that 921 vessels were moored up East River and only 320 in the Hudson, the latter largely consisting of small schooners and sloops (Albion, 1970: 221-22). For all its mercantile wealth, port facilities for handling the increased trade were inadequate. The 1.8km-long stretch of wooden piers in lower Manhattan was rotting and sand and silt drifting into the slips between docks. In 1836 Mayor Lawrence bemoaned the "decaying timbers around our wharves and bulkheads that cause spread of disease" (La Guardia, 1941: 2, 155). The old docks in the East River at Coenties Slip, Old Slip, Coffee House Slip, Fly Market Slip, Burling Slip and Peck Slip caused a Glasgow printer to refer to New York in 1823 as an "overgrown sea-port village" (Albion, 1970: 220):

> "The slips run up a considerable way in the center of the buildings, as it were in the middle of the streets; and being built or faced up with logs of trees cut to the requisite length, allow free ingress and egress to the water, and being completely out of the current of the stream or tide, are little else than stagnant receptacles of city filth; while the top of the wharves exhibits one continuous mass of clotted nuisance, composed of dust, tea, oil, molasses, &c, where revel countless swarms of offensive flies."

In a letter to a visiting foreigner in 1824, Fenimore Cooper, the author of *The Last of the Mohicans*, had explained (Albion, 1970: 220) that:

> "The time has not yet come for the formation of permanent quays in the harbor of New York. Wood is still too cheap, and labor too dear… All the wharves of New York are of very simple construction – A frame of hewn logs is filled with loose stone, and covered with a surface of trodden earth… the whole of the seven miles of water which fronts the city, is lined with similar constructions… [forming] a succession of little basins, which are sometimes large enough to admit thirty or forty sail, though often much smaller."

The shrewd reasons for the conditions of the docks were partly a result of low mooring rates in New York, which seem to have been a deliberate strategy geared towards attracting ever-increasing shipping. In the *New York Times* of 13 January 1854 a ship and wharf owner explained the unfair criticism he received thus:

"Complaints are made by shipmasters of our bad wharves, shoal-waters, encroachments upon the harbor, &c; but they do not consider that the earnings of our Wharves in this City are so small that we cannot pay for excavating the mud and sediment constantly washing from our streets into and filling up our slips. It is well known that there is no charge here upon articles of merchandise landed upon our docks and wharves, and that a vessel of say 100 tons pays in New-York 62½ cents per day wharfage, with an addition of 12½ cents per days for every fifty tons; whereas if she takes a cargo of 500 barrels flour to Providence, or to any other Eastern or Southern seaport, and lands it upon the wharves there, she pays $15, or 3 cents per barrel. No doubt the low rates of wharfage here help to promote business; but is it necessary that our rates of wharfage should be kept so ruinously low as to compel us to let them rot and go to ruin, while our slips become shoals upon which vessels dare not venture."

By the mid-1850s most docks were 60-90m long and covered with pine planking that needed replacing every four or five years, largely due to horses hoisting cargo wearing out the wood. 'Wharfingers' estimated a normal pier to have a life span of 30 years and that new repairs cost about $15,000, a third to a quarter of the original construction's value. Many wharves were leased by the city to private individuals, who charged mooring costs of 75 cents a day for vessels of 100 tons. In 1852 the total gross rentals of the city's piers, wharves and bulkheads came to $127,000 and repairs to $37,000 (Albion, 1970: 222-23).

The scale of business derived from New York's maritime trade in the first half of the 19th century is laid bear by the fact that the city's Custom House was the principal source of revenue for the Federal Government, which collected enough duties in 1828 to cover the entire running expenses of the national government. By 1843 the Custom House had 503 members of staff with total salaries of $489,000. In downtown New York in 1852 Wall Street was already the focus of monetary operations (including marine insurance), Broadway was a promenade of beauty and fashion, and the principal shipping houses were clustered along South Street on the East River, where the counting-houses stood strikingly opposite the piers, from where ships' bowsprits stretched well across the cobbled street (Fig. 125).

Doggett's *New York Business Directory* of 1846 listed 31 "general merchants", 51 "importing and commission merchants", 138 "shipping and commission merchants" and eight "shipping and importing merchants" as based on South Street. Nearly 60 different fields of importation were listed in this directory, including more than 100 importers of dry goods and allied commodities, 89 in wines and liquors, 86 in hardware and cutlery, 69 in coffee, and 53 in china, glass and earthenware. By 1860 New York was credited as containing an astounding 21,677 resident merchants, a rather liberal definition that included country storekeepers (Albion, 1970: 224, 266, 270, 275).

Such was the bustling world of the small schooner that met its fate in the greatest hurricane of the generation. 1854 was a year of seemingly apocalyptic winds of change. Already wracked by a great outbreak of yellow fever across the entire South, the category three hurricane of 7-9 September 1854 destroyed the rice and cotton crops and left the towns with little means of economic respite. The South was also on the verge of a new revolution, the railroad, which was offering cut-price tickets to willing passengers. The great age of the East Coast schooner was on the verge of extinction. The humble remains of a small ship of this class at Site BA02, the Jacksonville 'Blue China' wreck discovered by Odyssey Marine Exploration, is a physical reminder of a time and place that made New York the great metropolis it is today.

Acknowledgements

Site BA02 was first brought to the attention of Odyssey Marine Exploration through the careful observations and interest of Savannah fisherman Woody Moore, whose wife first dubbed the term 'Blue China' wreck for the origins of the mysterious pottery snagged in her husband's nets. Odyssey offers its sincere gratitude to Mr. Moore for enabling this historical wreck to be discovered and studied.

The rescue archaeology subsequently conducted was facilitated through the decisions and vision of Greg Stemm and John Morris of Odyssey Marine Exploration. The authors express their thanks to the diligence of the 2003 and 2005 survey and excavation teams led by Tom Dettweiler and Ernie Tapanes (Project Managers) and Hawk Tolson (Director of Field Archaeology), who conducted some of the research for this report into the anchors, marine environment, site impacts, and especially mid-19th century schooners and 19th-century hurricanes. In the extensive post-excavation research we have benefited enormously from the support at Odyssey Marine Exploration of Greg Stemm, Mark Gordon, Laura Barton and especially John Oppermann and Fred Van De Walle at the Archaeology, Research & Conservation (ARC) laboratory in Tampa. Alan Bosel (photography and responsible for the identification of spring-loaded scale brass plaque BC-05-00210-ML), Chad Morris (recording) and Gerri Graca (archives) toiled endlessly to process an endless stream of requests and queries with good humor, and we offer great appreciation for their camaraderie and professionalism. Mark Mussett at Odyssey provided the names of the fish species present on Site BA02 and as ever Melissa Dolce patiently designed this report. Alice Copeland kindly helped proofread this article.

The authors are especially grateful to an elite group of scholars and professionals, who so generously offered their invaluable time and expertise regarding artifacts recovered from the Jacksonville 'Blue China' shipwreck: David Barker (archaeological consultant and specialist in post-medieval and early-modern ceramics); John Broadwater (former Chief Archaeologist, Office of National Marine Sanctuaries, NOAA); Dorothy G. Hogan-Schofield (Curator of Collections, Sandwich Glass Museum, Sandwich, MA); Robert Hunter (Editor of *Ceramics in America*); Bill Lindsey (formerly Bureau of Land Management and author of the Society for Historical Archaeology/BLM Historic Glass Bottle Identification and Information website); George Miller (historical archaeologist and ceramic specialist); David Naar (Associate Professor, Geological Oceanography, College of Marine Science, University of South Florida); Jonathan Rickard (ceramic historian); Jane Spillman (Curator of Glass, Corning Museum of Glass, New York); Barbara Perry (former Curator of Decorative Arts, the Mint Museum of Art, Charlotte, NC); Valentine Povinelli (journeyman shoemaker, Colonial Williamsburg Foundation); Jeffrey Ryan (Geology Department, University of South Florida); Byron Sudbury (clay tobacco pipe historian); Ping Wang (Department of Geology, University of South Florida); Jeanne Willoz-Egnor (Director of Collections Management, Curator of Scientific Instruments, the Mariners' Museum, Newport News, VA); Jill Yakubik (President of Earth Search, Inc., New Orleans).

A final respectful acknowledgement is offered in special memory of the former conservator Herbert Bump, whose work provided Odyssey with the foundation upon which we have built our conservation program.

Notes

1. See: http://sofia.usgs.gov/publications/maps/florida_geology/intro.html.
2. See: US Geological Survey GLORIA Mapping Program, US EEZ Atlantic Continental Margin GLORIA: http://coastalmap.marine.usgs.gov/gloria/eastcst/geology.html.

Bibliography

Albion, R.G., *The Rise of New York Port (1815-1860)* (Newton Abbot, 1970).

Barlow, R.E. and Kaiser, J.E., *The Glass Industry in Sandwich. Volume 2* (Barlow-Kaiser Publishing Company, Inc. 1989).

Bauer, K.J., 'The Golden Age'. In R.A. Kilmarx (ed.), *America's Maritime Legacy: A History of the U.S. Merchant Marine and Shipbuilding Industry Since Colonial Times* (Boulder, 1979), 27-65.

Bell, E., *Pharmaceutical Journal and Transactions Volume XVI, 1856-57* (London, 1857).

Blacker, J.F., *Nineteenth-century English Ceramic Art* (Boston, 1911).

Bock, G., 'Glass Notes', *Old House Journal* (July/August 1988), 35-43.

Bowditch, N., *Bowdich Explains How to Select, Use, and Maintain the Marine Sextant, Adapted from American Practical Navigator* (New York, 1976).

Brocket, L.P. (ed.), *Our Country's Wealth and Influence* (Hartford, 1882).

Bryant, S., *Shoe & Leather Trade of the Last Hundred Years* (Boston, 1891).

Carpentier, D. and Rickard, J., 'Slip Decoration in the Age of Industrialization'. In R. Hunter (ed.), *Ceramics in America* (Chipstone Foundation, Milwaukee, 2001), 115-34.

Chapelle, H.I., *The History of American Sailing Ships* (New York, 1935).

Chapelle, H.I., *The National Watercraft Collection* (Washington, 1960).

Chapelle, H.I., *The Search for Speed Under Sail 1700-1855* (New York, 1967).

Chipman, F.W., *The Romance of Old Sandwich Glass* (Boston, 1932).

Clark, E., *History of the Seventh Regiment of N.Y. 1806-1889* (New York, 1890).

Cotter, J.L., Roberts, D.G. and Parrington, M., *The Buried Past. An Archaeological History of Philadelphia* (University of Pennsylvania, 1993).

Cunningham Dobson, N. and Gerth, E. 'The Shipwreck of the SS *Republic* (1865). Experimental Deep-Sea Archaeology. Part 2: Cargo'. In G. Stemm and S. Kingsley (eds.), *Oceans Odyssey. Deep-Sea Shipwrecks in the English Channel, Straits of Gibraltar & Atlantic Ocean* (Oxford, 2010), 25-68.

Cunningham Dobson, N., Gerth, E. and Winckler, L., 'The Shipwreck of the SS *Republic* (1865). Experimental Deep-Sea Archaeology. Part 1: Fieldwork & Site History'. In G. Stemm and S. Kingsley (eds.), *Oceans Odyssey. Deep-Sea Shipwrecks in the English Channel, Straits of Gibraltar & Atlantic Ocean* (Oxford, 2010), 1-24.

De Bow, J.D.B., *De Bow's Review of the Southern and Western States, Vol. X* (New Orleans, 1851).

De Bow, J.D.B., *Industrial Resources, Etc, of the Southern and Western States, Vol. 2* (New Orleans, 1852).

Dodsworth, R., *Glass and Glassmaking* (Princes Risborough, 2003).

Ewins, N., *"Supplying the Present Wants of Our Yankee Cousins...". Staffordshire Ceramics and the American Market 1775-1880* (Journal of Ceramic History 15, Stoke-on-Trent City Museum and Art Gallery, 1997).

Fike, R.E., *The Bottle Book: a Comprehensive Guide to Historic, Embossed Medicine Bottles* (Salt Lake City, 1987).

Ford, B., Borgens, A. and Hitchcock, B., 'The 'Mardi Gras' Shipwreck: Results of a Deep-Water Excavation, Gulf of Mexico, USA', *International Journal of Nautical Archaeology* 39.1 (2010), 76-98.

Forsyth, C.J., *The American Merchant Seaman and his Industry: Struggle and Stigma* (London, 1989).

Gillett, R., *Global Study of Shrimp Fisheries* (Fisheries Technical Paper 475, Food & Agriculture Organization of the United Nations, Rome, 2008).

Godden, G. A., *Godden's Guide to Ironstone, Stone & Granite Wares* (Woodbridge, Suffolk, 1999).

Graham, J.T., *Scales and Balances* (Princes Risborough, 2003).

Hawley, G., *Treasure in a Cornfield* (Kansas, 1998).

Holcombe, H.W., *Patent Medicine Tax Stamps* (Lawrence, MS, 1979).

Hopkins, A.A. (ed.), *The Scientific American Cylopedia of Formulas* (New York, 1913).

Hunter, R.R. and Miller, G.L., 'English Shell-Edged Earthenware', *The Magazine Antiques* 145.3 (1994), 432-43.

Hunter, R. and Miller, G., 'Suitable for Framing: Decorated Shell-Edge Earthenware', *Early American Life* (August 2008), 8-19.

Jervis, W.P., *A Pottery Primer* (New York, 1911).

Jones, T.N., *The Mica Shipwreck: Deepwater Nautical Archaeology in the Gulf of Mexico* (MA Thesis, Texas A&M University, 2004).

Kennett, J., *Marine Geology* (Prentice Hall, 1982).

La Guardia, F.H., *A Maritime History of New York* (New York, 1941).

Laing, A., *Seafaring America* (New York, 1974).

Lawrence, R.W., *Archaeological Investigations at Beaufort Inlet: A Summary of Submerged Cultural Resource Surveys and Investigations at Beaufort Inlet, North Carolina* (Underwater Archaeology Branch, Department of Cultural Resources, State of North Carolina, 2007).

Lobell, J.A., 'The Hidden History of New York's Harbor', *Archaeology* 63.6 (2010): http://www.archaeology.org/1011/etc/wtc.html.

MacGregor, D.R., *The Schooner: its Design and Development from 1600 to the Present* (London, 2003).

Marx, R.F., *Shipwrecks of the Western Hemisphere: 1492-1825* (New York, 1975).

Mathewson, R.D., *Treasure of the Atocha* (London, 1986).

McDougall, D.P., 'The Bottles of the Hoff Store Site'. In A.G. Pastron and E.M. Hattori (eds.), *The Hoff Store Site and Gold Rush Merchandise in San Francisco, California* (Society for Historical Archaeology, Special Publication Series, No. 7, 1990).

McKearin, G.S. and McKearin, H., *American Glass* (New York, 1941).

McKearin, H. and Wilson, K., *American Bottles and Flasks and their Ancestry* (New York, 1978).

McKinnon, J., 'Creating a Shipwreck Trail: Documenting the 1733 Spanish Plate Fleet Wrecks'. In J.H. Jameson and D.A. Scott-Ireton (eds.), *Out of the Blue. Public Interpretation of Maritime Cultural Resources* (New York, 2007), 85-94.

Meide, C., McClean, J.A. and Wiser, E., *Dog Island Shipwreck Survey 1999: Report of Historical and Archaeological Investigations* (Florida State University, 1999).

Miall, A.D., Balkwill, H.R. and McCracken, J., 'The Atlantic Margin Basins of North America'. In A.D. Miall (ed.), *The Sedimentary Basins of the United States and Canada* (Oxford, 2008), 473-504.

Miller, G., 'Classification and Economic Scaling of Nineteenth-century Ceramics'. In M. Beaudry (ed.), *Documentary Archaeology in the New World* (University of Cambridge, 1988), 172-83.

Miller, G., 'A Revised Set of CC Index Values for Classification and Economic Scaling of English Ceramics from 1787 to 1880'. In D.R. Brauner (ed.), *Approaches to Material Culture Research for Historical Archaeologists* (Society for Historical Archaeology, United States, 2000), 86-110.

Morris, P.C., *American Sailing Coasters of the North Atlantic* (Chardon, 1973).

Murphy, L.E. and Jonsson, R.W., 'Environmental Factors Affecting Vessel Casualties and Site Preservation'. In L. Murphy (ed.), *Dry Tortugas National Park Submerged Cultural Resources Assessment* (National Park Service Submerged Cultural Resources Unit, Santa Fe, 1993), 96-110.

Parker, J.P., *Sails of the Maritimes* (Slough, 1960).

Potter, J.S., *The Treasure Diver's Guide* (New York, 1972).

Pratt, R.M. and Heezen, B.C., 'Topography of the Blake Plateau', *Deep Sea Research and Oceanographic Abstracts* 11.5 (1964), 721-28.

Richardson, J., *The Young Sea Officer's Sheet Anchor: Or a Key to the Leading of Rigging, and to Practical Seamanship* (unabridged reproduction of 2nd edition by Darcy Lever, New York, 1998).

Rickard, J., *Mocha and Related Dipped Wares, 1770-1939* (University Press of New England, 2006).

Shaw, D.W., *The Sea Shall Embrace Them: the Tragic Story of the Steamship Arctic* (New York, 2002).

Sheridan, R.E., 'The Passive Margin of the U.S.A.', *Episodes* 10.4 (1987), 254-58.

Smith, R.C., Bratten, J.R., Cozzi, J.C. and Plaskett, K., *The Emanuel Point Ship. Archaeological Investigations 1997-1998* (University of West Florida, 1998).

Spillman, J., 'Sunken Treasure: the SS *Republic*', *The Glass Bulletin Club of the National American Glass Club* 204 (2006), 13-17.

Stiles, M.L., Harrould-Kolieb, E., Faure, P., Ylitalo-Ward, H. and Hirshfield, M.F., *Deep Sea Trawl Fisheries of the Southeast US and Gulf of Mexico: Rock Shrimp, Royal Red Shrimp, Calico Scallops* (Oceana, 2007).

Swinton, W., *History of the Seventh Regiment, National Guard, State of New York, during the War of the Rebellion (Vol. 7)* (Memphis, 2009).

Sudbury, J.B., 'White Clay Pipes from the Old Connellsville Dump, 36 fa 140', *Historic Clay Tobacco Pipe Studies* 1 (2006), 23-28.

Thurston, G.H., *Pittsburgh and Allegheny in the Centennial Year* (Pittsburgh, 1976).

Tolson, H., Gerth, E. and Cunningham Dobson, N., 'Ceramics from the "Blue China" Wreck'. In R. Hunter (ed.), *Ceramics in America* (Chipstone Foundation, Milwaukee, 2008), 162-83.

Tomlinson, C., (ed)., *Cyclopaedia of Useful Arts, Mechanical and Chemical, Manufactures, Mining, and Engineering, in Three Volumes, Volume I* (London, 1854).

Tryckare, T., *The Lore of Ships* (New York, 1963).

Van den Bossche, W., *Antique Glass Bottles: their History and Evolution (1500-1850)* (Woodbridge, 2001).

Van Hoeson, W.H., *Crafts and Craftsmen of New Jersey* (New Jersey, 1973).

Walker, I.C., 'TD Pipes – a Preliminary Study', *Archaeological Society Quarterly Bulletin* 20.4 (1966), 86-102.

Walter, J.F., *Low Country Hurricanes. Three Centuries of Storms at Sea and Ashore* (University of Georgia Press, 2006).

Watson, J.F., *Annals of Philadelphia, and Pennsylvania in the Olden Time* (Philadelphia, 1884).

Watson, J.W., Workman, I.K., Taylor, C.W. and Serra, A.F., *Configurations and Relative Efficiencies of Shrimp Trawls Employed in Southeastern United States Waters* (NOAA Technical Report NMFS 3, 1984).

Williams, L.W., *Sandwich Glass* (Bridgeton, Connecticut, 1922).

Wilson, H., *Trow's New York City Directory for the Year Ending May 1, 1857* (New York, 1857).

Zumwalt, B., *Ketchup, Pickles, Sauces: 19th Century Food in Glass* (Fulton, 1980).

The Jacksonville 'Blue China' Shipwreck (Site BA02): the Ceramic Assemblage

Ellen Gerth

Odyssey Marine Exploration, Tampa, USA

Discovered in 2003 by Odyssey Marine Exploration and subjected to rescue archaeology in 2005, the Jacksonville 'Blue China' shipwreck (Site BA02), located 70 nautical miles off Jacksonville, Florida, at a depth of 370m, was an American coastal trader transporting a cargo of largely British ceramic imports between the eastern ports. The 318 vessels recovered comprise ten principal pottery types that date generally to between 1845 and 1860 and are largely of British manufacture, except for six individual pieces that originated in China, America and Europe.

The value of the collection lies in its contextual relationship as a large, closed single deposit of mainly Staffordshire imports that reflects the cultural tastes and consumer habits of middle class America in a very narrow timeframe. The internal ceramic evidence indicates a date between 1851 and 1860 for the ship's loss, while additional artifacts from Site BA02 point to a date of wreckage in 1854. No comparable assemblage has been found on the wreck of any other merchant vessel off America.

1. Introduction

The survey of Site BA02 recorded a minimum of 703 ceramic vessels on the surface of the wreck (Figs. 1-10). A sample of 318 examples was recovered for study. The most conspicuous artifacts on the Jacksonville 'Blue China' shipwreck are the concentration of ceramics clustered in Area A at the southern end representing the bows: circular plates, octagonal platters, bowls, tea bowls/tea cups, saucers, creamers, sugar bowls, jugs, mugs, jars, chamber pots and wash basins (Figs. 11-87). An analysis of the distribution of these different ceramic wares across the wreck site is presented elsewhere (Gerth *et al.*, 2011). The retrieved collection has led to extensive research and the identification and dating of the wares. In turn, this has enabled their function and significance within a broader historical context to be understood. The Site BA02 ceramic assemblage represents one of the few surviving intact collections of its kind and the only example from an American coaster of this era.

Except for a few examples, the Jacksonville 'Blue China' pottery assemblage covers the full range of British tea, table and toilet earthenwares most common on North American archaeological sites of the 1850s and 1860s. From as early as the late 18th century, England dominated the world market in ceramics, which was driven by a number of significant developments: the construction of canals for transporting raw materials and finished products in and out of potteries, steam power for working clay and pottery, and the astute marketing of creamware from which other product lines later evolved (Miller, 1988: 172-3).

The pottery industry now revolutionized, Great Britain's Staffordshire earthenwares and stonewares, in particular, were central to the home market and Europe, as well as becoming a major force in North America. In 1762 approximately 150 separate Staffordshire potteries employed 7,000 people (Barker, 2001: 73, 86). The subsequent opening of the Trent and Mersey Canal in 1777 provided the Staffordshire potteries with direct access to the sea, expediting shipments to foreign ports through Liverpool (Barker, 2001: 81; pers. comm. Jonathan Rickard, 6 December 2010). At this same time, while promising political change the success of the American Revolution had in fact little impact on British pottery imports. Plates and dishes would continue to pour in across the Atlantic following political independence and for a hundred years thereafter (Martin, 2001: 35).

By the close of the 18th century the global conquest of British ceramic wares was illustrated in glowing manner in an account by B. Faujas de Saint-Font of his travels to England, Scotland and the Hebrides, published in 1797 (Miller, 1988: 173):

> "Its excellent workmanship, its solidity, the advantage which it possesses of sustaining the action of fire, its fine glaze, impenetrable to acids, the beauty and convenience of its form, and the cheapness of its price, have given rise to a

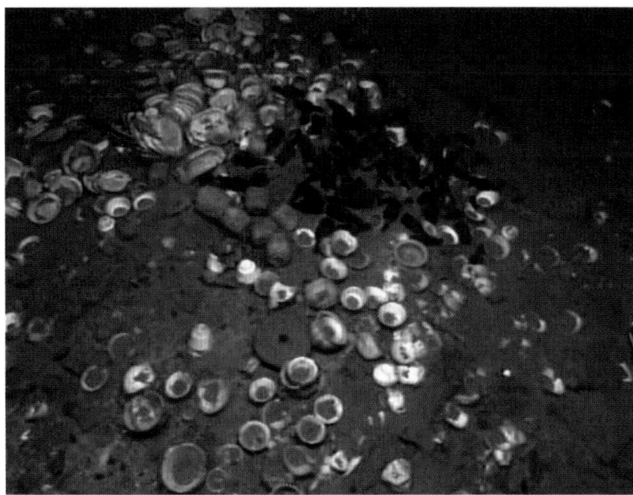

Fig. 1. Overview of the concentration of Type 1 shell-edged earthenware in Area A looking southwest across Area G.

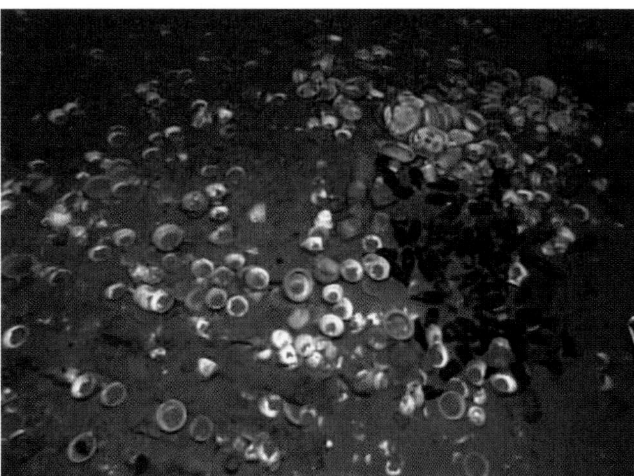

Fig. 2. Overview looking south of Type 1 shell-edged earthenware in Area A at right and trawler-impacted ceramics in Area G at left.

Fig. 3. Detail of Type 1 shell-edged earthenware and a stack of Type 4D white ironstone wash basins (foreground) in Area A.

> commerce so active and so universal that in traveling from Paris to Petersburg, from Amsterdam to the further part of Sweden, and from Dunkirk to the extremity of the south of France, one is served at every inn with English ware. Spain, Portugal and Italy are supplied, and vessels are loaded with it for the East and West Indies and the continent of America."

The continued growth in the Staffordshire pottery trade further stimulated manufacture to such an extent that by 1800 the number of workers in the industry had risen to nearly 20,000 and would continue to multiply in the 19th century (Barker, 2001: 73, 76). This increased production ultimately influenced and set the standard for manufacturing throughout much of England. With the ever-growing demand for refined earthenwares and stonewares, new pottery factories were established in many parts of the country, all of which produced Staffordshire-type wares in form, decoration and methods of manufacture. In line with these developments, by 1850 Staffordshire wares were influencing trends in consumer behavior from North America to Australia (Barker, 2001: 76, 91).

Beginning in the latter part of the 18th century, continental Europe was generally the largest export market for Staffordshire ceramics. Yet by the mid-1830s this trend had shifted to America, with its expanding population providing a fast developing market for British ceramics. Ewins's (1997) detailed study of the scale and structure of British exports has demonstrated that by 1850 the US had imported in just two decades over 30 million pieces of Staffordshire earthenware, which in 1850 totaled twice the volume of ceramics exported to Europe. Most of these wares were transported on ships loaded in the port of Liverpool, which from the 1820s was the main hub for receiving raw cotton, the largest single export from America to Great Britain. Liverpool was the most convenient port for the Lancaster textile industry and therefore attracted the greatest volume of ships carrying US cotton. This resulted in a steady surplus of vessels returning to America requiring freight for transport at competitive rates. Because of its location, Staffordshire, in particular, was able to capitalize on the port of Liverpool to a greater extent than the other British potteries. By 1857 and 1858, one-third of the pottery manufacturers in Staffordshire were allegedly involved in the American trade, increasing to one-half of the potteries in 1861 (Ewins, 1997: 5-6, 10-11, 14).

Many Staffordshire manufacturers set up pottery outlets in several US cities. As the largest port, New York boasted the greatest presence, followed by Philadelphia, Boston and Baltimore. Also essential to the transatlantic ceramics trade were the merchants, American importers and agents with whom the Staffordshire manufacturers

'Blue China' Wreck Type	Generic Type	Forms	No.	Date
Type 1A	Shell-edged ware (whiteware)	Dinner plates, British	105	1845-55
Type 1B	Shell-edged ware (whiteware)	Soup plates, British	35	1845-55
Type 1C	Shell-edged ware (whiteware)	Octagonal platters/ serving dishes, British	17	1845-55
Type 2Ai	Dipped wares (whiteware)	Bowls (London shape), slip decorated, British	35	1845-55
Type 2Aii	Dipped wares (whiteware)	Bowls (London shape), slip decorated, 'common cable' pattern, British	2*	1845-55
Type 2B	Dipped wares (whiteware)	Jugs, slip decorated, British	8	1845-55
Type 2C	Dipped wares (whiteware)	Mugs, slip decorated, British	4	1845-55
Type 3A	Underglaze painted whiteware	Saucers, British	27	1845-55
Type 3B	Underglaze painted whiteware	Teabowls (London shape), British	19	1845-55
Type 3C	Underglaze painted whiteware	Cream jugs, British	9	1845-55
Type 3D	Underglaze painted whiteware	Sugar bowls, British	4	1845-55
Type 3D	Underglaze painted whiteware	Sugar bowl lid, British	1	1845-55
Type 4A	White granite/ white ironstone china	Dinner plates, British	3	*c.* 1850-60
Type 4B	White granite/ white ironstone china	Bowls, British	17	*c.* 1850-60
Type 4C	White granite/ white ironstone china	Chamber pots, British	5	*c.* 1850-55
Type 4D	White granite/ white ironstone china	Wash basins, British	4	*c.* 1850-55
Type 4Ei	White granite/ white ironstone china	Salve jars, British	12	*c.* 1850-60
Type 4Eii	White granite/ white ironstone china	Salve jar lids, British	4	*c.* 1850-60
Type 4F	White granite/ white ironstone china	Small, fluted bowl, British	1	*c.* 1850-60
Type 5A	Dipped wares (yellow ware)	Mug, slip decorated, British	1	1850-60
Type 5Bi	Dipped wares (yellow ware)	Chamber pots, slip decorated, British	1	1850-60
Type 5Bii	Dipped wares (yellow ware)	Chamber pots, slip-decorated 'dendritic' style, British	4	1850-60
Type 6	Oriental ware (Porcelain)	Ginger jars, Canton	4	1840-60
Type 7Ai	Transfer-printed wares (whiteware)	Plate, 'Asiatic Pheasants' pattern, British	1	1850-60
Type 7Aii	Transfer-printed wares (whiteware)	Soup plate, 'Willow' pattern, British	1	1845-55
Type 7B	Transfer-printed wares (whiteware)	Sauce boat, British	1	1850-60
Type 8	Salt-glazed stoneware	Jug, New York	1	1850-60
Type 9	Salt-glazed Stoneware	Mineral Water Bottle, German	1	1850-60
Type 10	Bristol-glazed stoneware	Jar, British	1	1850-60

* Not recovered.

Table 1. Typology of ceramic wares from the Jacksonville 'Blue China' shipwreck (Site BA02).

'Blue China' Wreck Type	Generic Type	Forms	No.
Type 1A/1B	Shell-edged ware (whiteware)	Dinner & soup plates, British	118
Type 1C	Shell-edged ware (whiteware)	Octagonal platters/ serving dishes, British	17
Type 2A	Dipped wares (whiteware)	Bowls (London shape), slip decorated, British	345
Type 2B	Dipped wares (whiteware)	Jugs, slip decorated, British	12
Type 2C	Dipped wares (whiteware)	Mugs, slip decorated, British	1
Type 3A	Underglaze painted whiteware	Saucers, British	12
Type 3B	Underglaze painted whiteware	Teabowls (London shape), British	56
Type 3C	Underglaze painted whiteware	Cream jugs, British	15
Type 3D	Underglaze painted whiteware	Sugar bowls, British	4
Type 4B	White granite/ white ironstone china	Bowls, British	10
Type 4C	White granite/ white ironstone china	Chamber pots, British	18
Type 4D	White granite/ white ironstone china	Wash basins, British	4
Type 4Ei	White granite/ white ironstone china	Salve jars & lids, British	8
Type 5A	Dipped wares (yellow ware)	Mug, slip decorated, British	1
Type 5Bi/Bii	Dipped wares (yellow ware)	Chamber pots, slip decorated, British	13
Type 6	Oriental ware (Porcelain)	Ginger jars, Canton	4

Table 2. Pre-disturbance count of ceramics visible on the surface of the Jacksonville 'Blue China' shipwreck (Site BA02). In some cases counts are lower than the volume recovered due to concealment of underlying deposits subsequently exposed by excavation.

dealt. For example, the Staffordshire-based ceramic merchant John Hackett Goddard of Longton purchased ceramics from British manufacturers, while his US partners John Burgess and Robert Dale operated the American wholesale ceramic outlets from Baltimore and New York. Goddard typically toured the Staffordshire potteries to determine what wares would best suit the American market and regularly sent out samples to his American-based partners (Ewins, 1997: 88-91, 105-107, 109).

Throughout the 19th century New York was the major port for imported wares (Miller and Earls, 2008: 70), beginning largely after the war of 1812 fought between Britain and the United States. As Albion observed in *The Rise of the New York Port, 1815-1860* (Newton Abbot, 1970), the British "settled upon New York as the best port for the bulk of their "dumping" of manufactures", which English merchants had stockpiled in Liverpool, Halifax and Bermuda during the war, awaiting the eventual reopening of the American market. New York apparently was better suited for these purposes than Boston, which had not been deprived of European goods to such an extent (Miller and Earls, 2008: 76).

By the 1850s the bulk of Staffordshire exports was handled by New York ceramic importers and dealers, who controlled the distribution network for the internal American trade. Inland and Southern dealers would frequently travel to East Coast ports to make their purchases, as reported in the *New York Commercial Record* of May 1862: "a moderately active business has been done during the past week and several out-of-town buyers have been in the market." When a buying trip was not possible, regular orders from the country or the West were sent to New York. This city, however, did not hold a total monopoly, but had to compete with ceramic importers located in other East Coast ports, such as Boston, Philadelphia and Baltimore (Ewins, 1997: 58, 91). The ceramic importers Henderson & Gaines, for instance, were based at 43 Canal Street in New Orleans from 1836 to 1853 (Ewins, 1997: 58) and sold their imported Staffordshire wares to customers in the American West (see Section 2 below). The 'country trade' was especially relevant, whereby New York importers and wholesalers supplied stores in small towns and rural areas. Surviving invoices document that in 1790 the consumers serviced by these country stores represented 90% of the population and more than 40% in 1880 (Miller and Earls, 2008: 67, 70).

Over 90,000 packages of ceramics were exported from Liverpool to the United States in 1871 and the quantity continued to increase at the end of the 1870s (Ewins, 1997: 17, 66). The *London Pottery Gazette* of 1880 recorded that British ceramics shipped to the United States in 1879 comprised about 75% of the country's total imports, representing over one-third of Britain's total ceramic exports worldwide (*Reports of the United States Commissioners to the Paris Universal Exposition,* 1878, 1880: 192). Of more than 75,000 packages of British pottery sent to America in 1879, the majority arrived in the northern ports of Boston, New York, Philadelphia and Baltimore. From the previous year, British pottery imports to the United States had increased by more than 11,000 packages *(Reports of the United States Commissioners to the Paris Universal Exposition,* 1878, 1880: 193).

By this time, however, protective tariffs and duties on the importation of foreign wares and an infusion of capital were beginning to encourage increased American domestic pottery production, supported by the construction of over 30 new kilns in the year 1879 alone (*Reports of the United States Commissioners to the Paris Universal Exposition,* 1878, 1880: 194). Some 800 potteries now employed 7,000 workers.

Just 30 years prior there had been little encouragement to introduce new capital for the opening of additional clay beds or to erect more kilns, compounded by the prevailing prejudice of most people in favor of imported wares (*Reports of the United States Commissioners to the Paris Universal Exposition*, 1878: 191). In fact, throughout much of the 19th century many Americans considered English wares superior to any others available to the American market (Martin, 2001: 35). According to the US census returns of 1860, there were only 557 domestic pottery establishments nationwide, employing some 908 hands. The dismal state of the American pottery industry in the mid-19th century is effectively conveyed in the following excerpt from the *Reports of the United States Commissioners to the Paris Universal Exposition* (1878: 191):

> "Despite an abundance of the best materials for pottery lying at our very doors, with transportation by water and rail for the breadth of the State, alongside of inexhaustible beds of the finest clay, with fuel, either coal or wood, abundant and cheap, and men seeking employment, we were importing nearly all of our domestic ware from the ancient potteries of Staffordshire..."

By the 19th century the major type of ceramics available was English earthenware, which included creamware,

Fig. 4. Detail of Type 1 British shell-edged earthenware and Type 2A dipped whiteware bowls in Area A.

Fig. 5. Detail of a stack of Type 4D white ironstone wash basins in Area A.

Fig. 6. Type 1 shell-edged earthenware, Type 2A dipped whiteware bowls and Type 4D white ironstone wash basins in Area A.

Fig. 7. Scatters of largely Type 2A and 2B dipped whiteware bowls and jugs and Type 4B and 4C white ironstone bowls and chamber pots in Area G.

Fig. 8. A Type 2B dipped whiteware jug in front of a Type 6 Canton ginger jar to the northwest of Area G, surrounded by broken glass window panes spilled out of Area D.

Fig. 9. A Type 2Aii dipped whiteware bowl decorated in the 'common cable' pattern alongside two Type 5B dipped yellow ware chamber pots in Area G. Alongside are Type 2Ai dipped whiteware bowls, glass tumblers and the two parts of leather shoes.

Fig. 10. A second Type 2Aii dipped whiteware bowl decorated in the 'common cable' pattern in Area G alongside Type 4B white ironstone bowls.

pearlware, whiteware and stone china (Miller, 1988: 172). The ten different types of ceramic wares recovered from the Jacksonville 'Blue China' wreck (Table 1) are classified largely by their decoration – according to the names they were given by mid-19th century potters, merchants and consumers. The assemblage includes shell-edged earthenware, dipped wares, painted wares, white granite/white ironstone china, transfer-printed wares, Canton (porcelain) ginger jars and stoneware (Miller, 1988: 172; Miller and Earls, 2008: 71). Of the above, all are white-bodied earthenware, with the exception of the dipped yellow ware and stoneware examples, as well as the porcelain ginger jars. Apart from a few individual pieces, all of the ceramics were being shipped as cargo, and would have first arrived at one of the major American ports such as New York, Philadelphia or Boston (cf. *Reports of the United States Commissioners to the Paris Universal Exposition,* 1878, 1880: 193; Tolson *et al.*, 2008: 166).

2. Jacksonville 'Blue China' Wreck Type 1: British Shell-Edged Earthenware

The most conspicuous concentration of earthenware on Site BA02 is Type 1 British shell-edged earthenware, plates, platters and shallow soup plates produced for use on tables and recognized as "the most popular and long-lived style ever produced by the English ceramics industry" (Hunter and Miller, 1994: 433). Statistically this ware was the second most numerous class of ceramic on the wreck based on counts of surface artifacts: 134 examples or 14% of the total (Table 2; Gerth *et al.*, 2011: 25; Figs. 1-4, 11-27). Initially marketed for upper middle class families and sold as complete dinner services, British shell-edged ware very quickly became accessible to the masses, especially shell-edged pearlware, which resembled Chinese porcelain, but was far less expensive (Hunter and Miller, 1994: 441).

Contributing to its popularity was the decorative pattern itself, a molded rim frequently colored blue or green, which excelled at framing the food on the plate. While the rim design was sometimes highlighted in red, brown, black and purple on early shell-edged ware, both blue and green remained the most popular and cost-effective colors (Hume, 1969: 24; Hunter and Miller, 1994: 434, 437; 2009: 9-10; McAllister, 2001:10; Meteyard, 1875: 330).

British shell-edged earthenware was produced and exported in such large volumes between 1780 and 1860 that it appears to have been used in almost every American household (Hunter and Miller, 1994: 433). Even the most modest consumers could afford small sets of plates or dishes or a serving bowl (Miller, 1991: 6; Hunter and Miller, 2009: 9). In terms of quantity, being the least expensive English earthenware available with color decoration, shell-edged ware was in fact one of the most successful developments in ceramic production during the 18th and 19th centuries (Hunter and Miller, 1994: 443).

The use of shells as a decorative element is rooted in antiquity and was a common motif in the 18th-century Anglo-American world. The subsequent introduction of the shell-edged pattern was inspired by mid-18th century rococo design elements on Continental porcelain and earthenware, although at this time it was a minor component of more elaborate enameled decoration. By comparison, when it was introduced into English earthenware the molded shell edge served as the principal decoration (Hunter and Miller, 1994: 434; 2009: 10).

Josiah Wedgwood was the earliest documented potter to use the molded shell edge on uncolored creamware in the mid-1770s: the decoration first appeared in the company's pattern book published in 1775 and was later presented in the Leeds pattern book of 1783 (Hume, 1969: 24; Hunter and Miller, 1994: 434; 2009: 8; Miller, 1991: 5). Both blue and green shell-edged ware was apparently popular at this time, listed among the fashionable patterns and borders available (Meteyard, 1875: 330; Hunter and Miller, 1994: 434). Shell-edge proved to be so successful for the mass market that virtually all British manufacturers involved in the export trade quickly appropriated the pattern, adapting it to creamware and the blue-tinted pearlwares of the 1780s.

In the last quarter of the 18th century virtually every imaginable vessel form – from teapots to soup tureens and chamber pots – carried the distinctive shell-like molded edge. However, after the turn of the century potters began limiting the shell-edge to mostly plates and

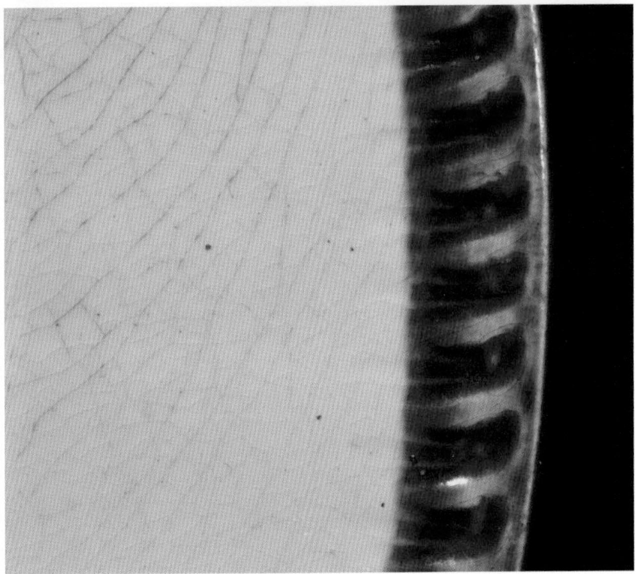

Figs. 11-12. A Type 1A British shell-edged whiteware dinner plate, Diam. 24cm (BC-05-00040-CR). (Figs. 11-87 by Alan Bosel, Odyssey Marine Exploration.)

platters. By the 1830s the shell-edged rim pattern rarely resembled shells (pers. comm. Jonathan Rickard, 6 December 2010). By the 1840s the so-called shell edge was being used on the cheaper and sturdier whitewares that had now become the standard earthenware for the British ceramic industry (Hunter and Miller, 1994: 437; 2009: 8-9; McAllister, 2001: 10, 32). More than 50 British manufacturers representing all the major Staffordshire potters have been identified as producing shell-edged ware and it was also one

Figs. 13-14. A Type 1A British shell-edged whiteware dinner plate, Diam. 23.7cm (BC-05-00233-CR).

of the standard products of potteries in Leeds, Castleford, Northumberland, Bristol and Devonshire (Hunter and Miller, 1994: 434).

The prevalence of British shell-edged ware is well documented in the archaeological record through ceramic fragments unearthed from most archaeological sites of the period, regardless of socio-economic class. In Williamsburg, Virginia, for example, these wares were present in the ruins of fine houses in the city, as well as in cabins formerly occupied by slaves on the outlying plantations (Hunter and Miller, 1994: 440; Tolson *et al.*, 2008: 167). Excavations of this former town's establishments have also yielded the same products, such as blue-rimmed examples recovered from a well behind Anthony Hay's Cabinet Shop, which date to *c.* 1800 (Hume, 1969: 25).

The excavation of British earthenware from a slave cabin at the Stafford Plantation on Cumberland Island, Georgia, further attests to the use of these wares by diverse socio-economic communities. Dating from the early-to-mid 19th century, the cabin site yielded a high frequency of blue and green shell-edged sherds. At least part of the ceramic assemblage is believed to have been used initially by the planter family before being given to the slave family when chipped or no longer considered of use or value.

The ceramic evidence from Couper Plantation, a contemporary site on St. Simon's Island, Georgia, presents a similar scenario. Interestingly, Robert Stafford was not only the major planter on Cumberland Island during the antebellum years, he was also the key exporter and importer for the island, suggesting that he possibly played a role in the import of its British earthenware, including the blue shell-edged examples discovered at the site. Coastal trading vessels, such as that present at wreck Site BA02, were probably active in this island trade.[1]

The prevalence of shell-edged wares in early American homes is further highlighted by a study of the types of dishes used in several middle class New York households dating to the early 19th century. Those recovered from privies and basements reveal that all of the households from this period possessed sets of shell-edged plates with the typical blue or green-painted decoration around their rims (Cantwell and diZerega Wall, 2001: 214). Contemporary diary entries document how middle class women were putting substantial thought into the dishes they purchased. Sherds from archaeological sites provide insights into the types of ceramics these women were choosing to grace their table – particularly relevant in a period when greater emphasis was being placed on the meaning of family meals and family life within the homes of the city's middle class (Cantwell and DiZerega, 2001: 213, 215).

Beyond the Eastern Seaboard, shell-edged wares also appealed to the inhabitants of America's Western frontier, with steamboats such as the *Arabia* transporting shipments up the Missouri River. Outward bound from St. Louis, the primary supply depot for the West, on 5 September 1856 the *Arabia* struck a submerged walnut tree, which pierced her hull, sinking the vessel and her 222 tons of cargo (Hawley, 1998: 34-37). Excavation of the steamboat, now silted 13.5m under a Kansas farmer's cornfield, uncovered a diverse cargo of trade goods still preserved in wooden barrels and crates (Cunningham Dobson and Gerth, 2010:

64-5; Hawley, 1995: 32-3). Included in this enormous shipment was a large quantity of blue shell-edged wares: plates, soup bowls, octagonal platters and casserole dishes, whose proportions and volume are very similar to those found on the Jacksonville 'Blue China' wreck (Hawley, 1998: 204; Tolson *et al.*, 2008: 183). Unlike the Site BA02 wreck assemblage, however, which bears no maker's marks, the majority of the *Arabia*'s shell-edged wares feature the mark of the Davenport pottery of Longport in Stoke-on-Trent, Staffordshire, which was in operation between 1794 and 1887 (Campbell, 2006: 304; Rickard, 2006: 4).

Fragments of shell-edged wares dating from 1810-35 have been found in an antebellum home site in Washington, Arkansas, a growing gateway community on the edge of the Western frontier. It has been suggested that these everyday pieces may have served both the family and its slave community. Beginning in the 1820s, the Southwest Trail brought explorers, merchants and families to this small outpost town, which by the middle of the century had become a major commercial center supplying the plantations and communities of southwest Arkansas. Merchants shipped in goods from New Orleans, the East Coast and Europe (Kwas, 2009: xi, 55).

Shell-edged pottery has also been found in western sites in eastern Oklahoma and Kansas, many associated with Native American groups, which resettled there from the 1820s onwards. A number of the wares are found in habitation sites affiliated with the Shawnee and Pottawatomie in Kansas and with the Creek, Choctaw, and Chickasaw in Oklahoma, suggesting that such ceramics were important high-status utilitarian items serving a similar function to the ceramics found on American sites of the same period. Especially striking, however, is the presence of shell-edged wares, plates in particular, in Native American burials. In some cases the pottery is arranged around the body and nested, suggesting a clear pattern of structured deposition. In addition to serving a domestic function, these European ceramics also apparently functioned within a religious/sacred context in these antebellum Native American cultures and, when placed in their burials, symbolized domestic usage continued in the afterlife (Lees and Majewski, 1993: 3-4). In the same light it is also likely that shell-edged wares enjoyed higher status within Native American society, presumably because these less affluent groups coveted these imports as luxuries.

Additionally, it has been suggested that the selection of edge-decorated wares in these burials, as well as other types including dipped/mocha bowls and hand-painted cups (see Section 6 below), was consistent with long-standing artistic traditions of the Native American groups in question. In terms of design and colors, the most striking comparison can be made between the British ceramics found in these sites and contemporary beadwork (Lees and Majewski, 1993: 4). Of particular interest is a shell-edged plate from a possible Native American Creek burial in Oklahoma that bears the stamp of 'Henderson Walton & Co. Importers, New Orleans, Davenport' (Lees and Majewski, 1993: 4). This highlights the role of American ceramic merchant dealers and import agents located in the major port cities, including New Orleans, many of whom established

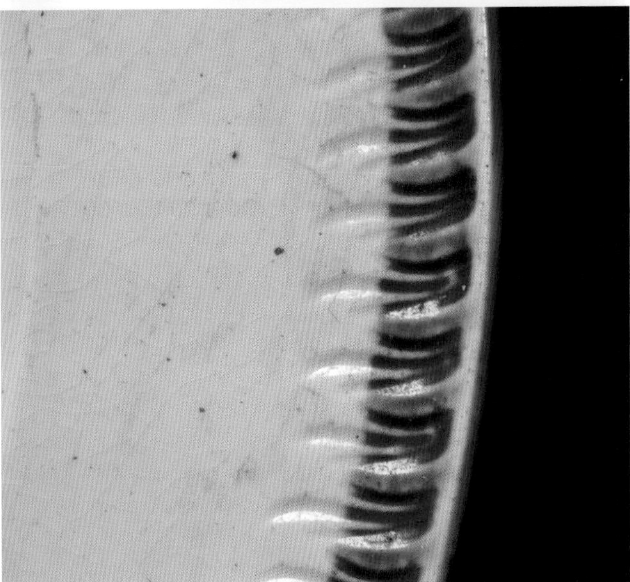

Figs. 15-16. A Type 1B British shell-edged whiteware soup plate, Diam. 26.8cm (BC-05-00102-CR).

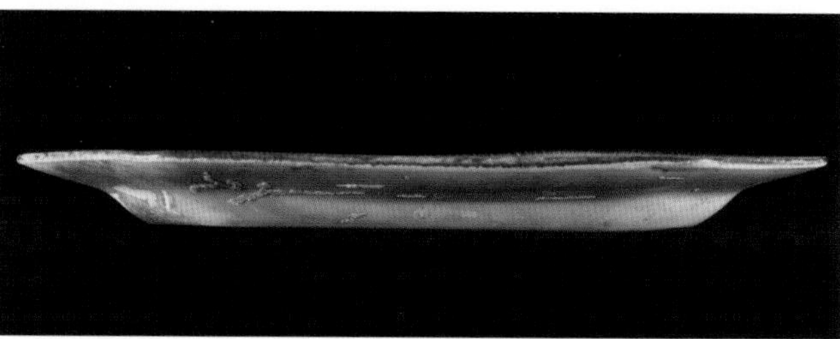

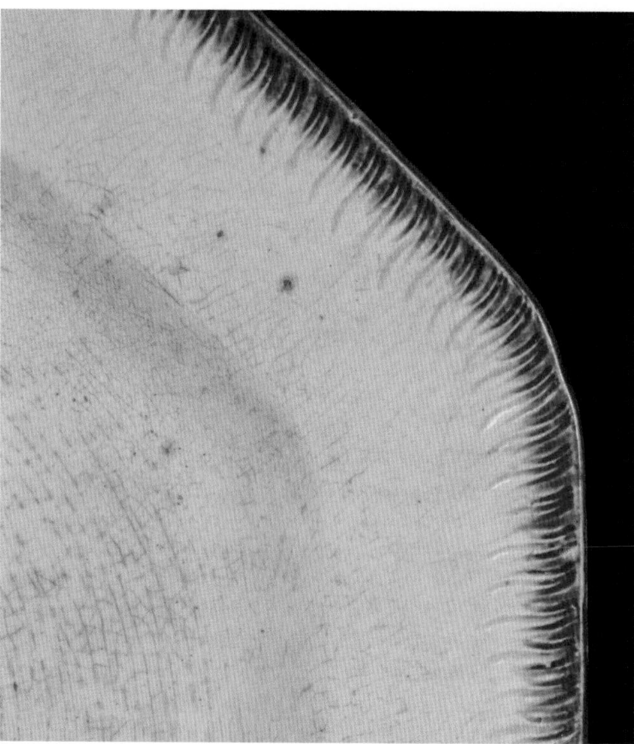

Figs. 17-19. A Type 1C large British shell-edged whiteware octagonal platter, L.39.9cm (BC-05-00323-CR).

connections with British potteries, such as Staffordshire's Davenport, and distributed their imported wares throughout the US (Barker, 2001: 82). Many of the Davenport wares associated with the Washington, Arkansas, home site bear the mark of 'Henderson & Gaines', suggesting that Henderson had a number of partners in the British pottery import business (Kwas, 2009: 55).

Supporting the archaeological evidence, records of Staffordshire potters document the vast quantities of shell-edged wares that were made both for the British market and for export (Hunter and Miller, 1994: 440-41). While shell edge was used all over the world, pottery-hungry Americans were the largest consumers. Enoch Wood's Burslem pottery works shipped 262,000 pieces in a single consignment (McAllister, 2001: 5). The surviving invoices of American merchants are especially telling: shell-edged products accounted for 40-70% of dinnerware sold in America between 1800 and the eve of the Civil War in 1861, despite the introduction of a number of more fashionable styles during this period (Hunter and Miller, 2009: 9; Hunter and Miller, 1994: 441; Tolson *et al.*, 2008: 167).

Equally revealing shipping records of the period confirm the importation of huge cargos of earthenwares into America. According to a single invoice of 1791, Liverpool exporters Rathbone & Benson shipped 5,724 shell-edged plates with many other ceramics on the vessel *Ceres* to Andrew Clow and Company in Philadelphia. Manifest records of other vessels indicate similarly large shipments (Hunter and Miller, 2009: 9). In addition to crockery, Rathbone and Benson also exported hardware and textiles, highlighting the variety of British goods transported on ships bound for America. While not all of the records of Rathbone and Benson have survived, the fact that they had 20 to 25 ships loading or unloading at Liverpool at any one time underscores the scope of their operations, of which British pottery exports to America appear to have been a major element (Wake, 1997: 28-29). Shell-edged whitewares, it would seem, were the main staple of mid-19th century tablewares used by the average American consumer household representing every economic and social strata (Martin, 2001: 34; McAllister, 2001: 5; Tolson *et al.*, 2008: 183).

The dating of shell-edged wares is based on the typological evolution of the rim shape and design. The earliest shape, fashionable between 1775 and 1880, was an asymmetrical, undulating scallop with impressed curved lines. Around 1800 the scallops of the shell edge became even and symmetrical; tablewares reflecting this style were produced largely in blue or green shell edges and were made almost exclusively of pearlware until well into the 1830s. As noted above, by the 1840s heavy whiteware replaced pearlware and, to cut costs, impressed lines typically colored blue were used instead of the scalloped rims (Hunter and Miller, 1994: 437; McAllister, 2001: 10-11; Tolson *et al.*, 2008: 168).[2] By now green shell-edge had become rare, while blue shell-edged wares remained a commonly available type listed in potters' and merchants' invoices into the 1860s (Miller, 1991: 6).

Further production changes in the second half of the century (1860s-90s) eliminated the impressed lines and, instead, simulated the blue shell-edged pattern with simple brush strokes of underglaze blue coloring (Hunter and Miller, 1994: 437; McAllister, 2001: 11). At this time the quality of manufacture declined to the point where blue shell-edge became a basic, generic, everyday utilitarian ware. Any sense of the exotic had disappeared. Although production continued into at least the 1890s, shell-edged wares are not commonly found in these later archaeological assemblages (Hunter and Miller, 1994: 437; Miller, 1991: 6; Tolson *et al.*, 2008: 168).[3]

The shell-edged products recovered from the Jacksonville 'Blue China' shipwreck are heavy whitewares featuring unscalloped, straight rims impressed with simple repetitive lines colored blue, indicative of mid-19th century production of the 1840s to 1850s (Figs. 11-21). As noted above, by the 1850s blue shell-edge had become a common, generic ware produced by virtually all of the British manufacturers involved in the pottery export trade. Thus, without identifiable maker's marks it is virtually impossible to attribute the objects to a particular manufacturer since most potteries were producing largely indistinguishable wares.

The examples on Site BA02 appear to have been made from fairly new, crisp molds, as opposed to worn molds, which make it far more difficult to see the pattern, especially when it is filled with glaze and heavy blue color (pers. comm. George Miller, 21 August 2007). Most of the shell-edged wares bear on their underside an impressed stamp in the form of an encircled floral-like design with dots or, in a few cases, a variant (Figs. 22-27). These are likely 'tally' marks, also known as 'potters batch marks', used by pottery workers to keep track of the vessels that came out of the kiln in marketable condition (Draper, 2001: 50; Tolson *et al.*, 2008: 168-69). Workers in the typical British earthenware factory were paid on a 'good-from-oven' basis on the number of pots that successfully made it through the many different manufacturing steps from the initial forming of the vessel shape through the glost firing (i.e. the process of glazing and firing ceramic ware, which had previously been fired at a higher temperature). Naturally, some pieces made it through with flaws and were sold nonetheless, but as seconds (Rickard, 2006: 106).

Fig. 20. A Type 1C medium British shell-edged whiteware octagonal platter, L.36.5cm (BC-05-00326-CR).

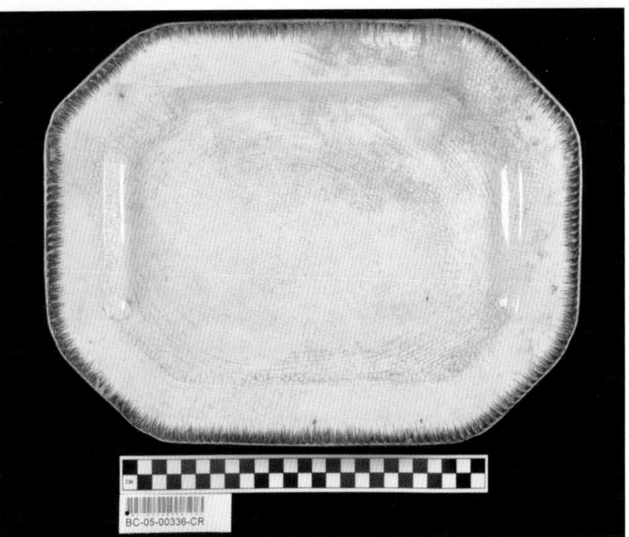

Fig. 21. A Type 1C small British shell-edged whiteware octagonal platter, Diam. L. 34.4 cm (BC-05-00336-CR).

Of the 105 Type 1A circular dinner plates from the Jacksonville 'Blue China' wreck (Diam. 23.8cm, H. 2.8cm, Th. 0.45cm, raised rim W. 3.5cm, blue edged rim band decoration W. 0.6-1.0cm, base Diam. 13.6cm), 80 bear the impressed tally mark mentioned above (Diam. 1.6cm) and 11 feature an impressed number '5'. Two general shades of blue applied over the shell-edged border were noted in the assemblage, ranging from medium blue to a very dark blue (Figs. 11-14).

Some 35 Type 1B soup plates were also recovered from the site (Diam. 26.7cm, H. 4.3cm, Th. 0.42-0.53cm, raised rim W. 3.9cm, blue edged rim band decoration W. 0.9cm but with incised striations continuing through

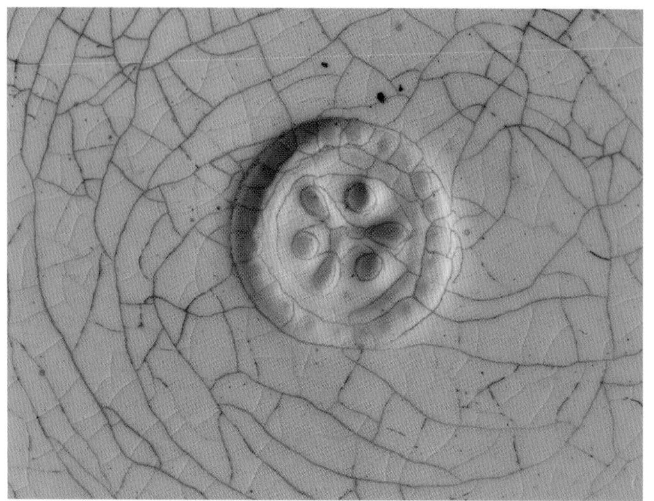

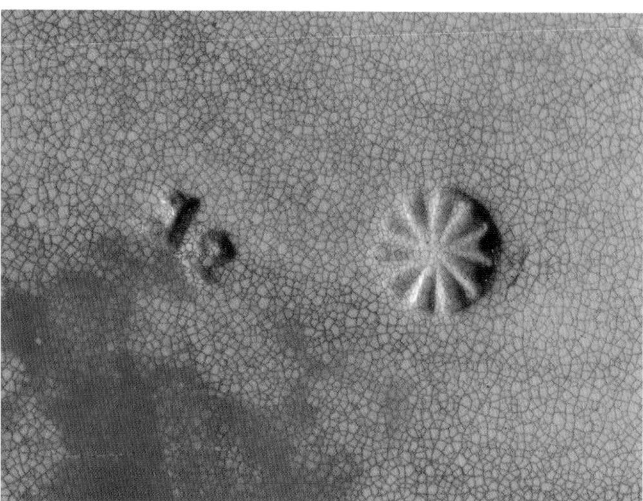

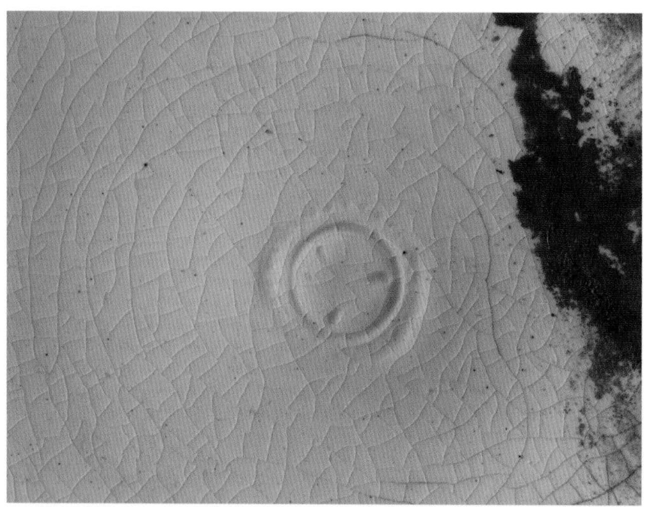

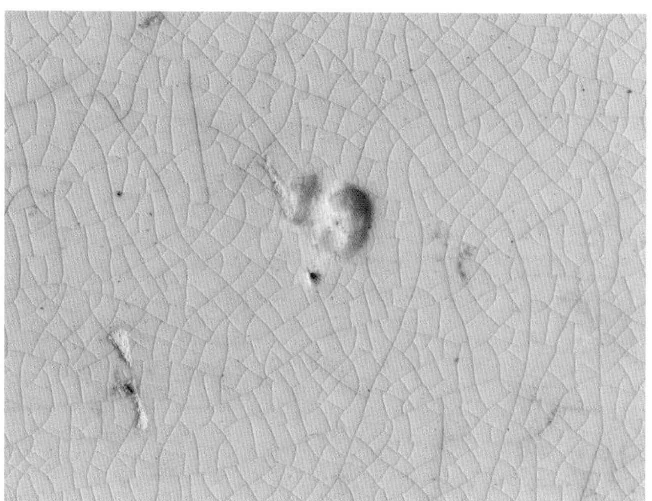

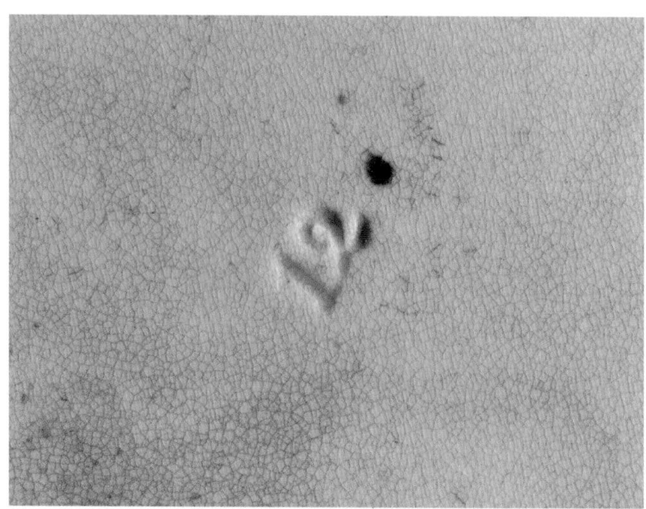

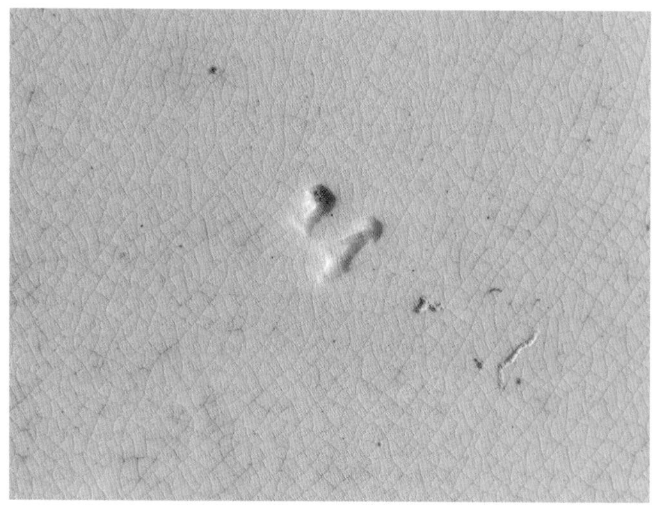

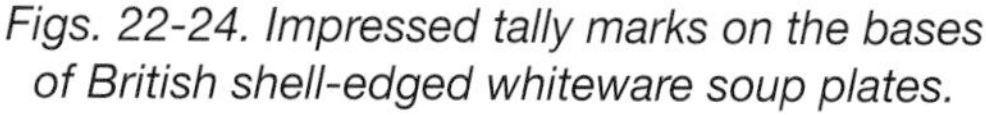

Figs. 22-24. Impressed tally marks on the bases of British shell-edged whiteware soup plates.

Figs. 25-27. Impressed tally marks on the bases of British shell-edged whiteware platters.

the white plate edge for a total L. 1.4cm, base Diam. 13.6cm), all of which incorporate the darker cobalt blue border (Figs. 15-16); 19 of these bear a tally mark on the bottom (Diam. 1.9cm), four feature a variant of the tally mark, one has a mark too illegible to identify, and one has no mark at all.

Some 17 Type 1C octagonal platters or serving dishes were recovered from the wreck in three sizes, with minimal variation: six small, five medium and six large (Figs. 17-21). All feature the dark cobalt blue rim. Most of the platters bear an impressed number on the underside: the smaller varieties exhibit a number '12', the medium a '13', and the largest the number '14' (Figs. 25-27). Such impressed numbers on plates and platters typically reflect their size, designated in inches. In this case, however, while the numbers do suggest graduated sizes, the pieces do not precisely correlate to the numbers indicated. One small and one medium platter have a tally mark in the form of a pinwheel blossom with triangular petals (Tolson *et al.*, 2008: 168-71).

The dimensions of the larger Type 1C platters are: L. 39.7cm, W. 30.6cm, H. 4.0cm, rim Th. 0.65cm, raised rim W. 4.5cm, blue edged rim band decoration W. 1.0cm but with incised striations continuing through the white plate edge for a total L. 1.5cm, base L. 27.8cm, base W. 19.2cm. The medium sized variants measure: L. 36.5cm, W. 28.4 cm, H. 3.3cm, Th. 0.53cm, raised rim W. 4.3cm, blue edged rim band decoration W. 1.0cm but with incised striations continuing through the white plate edge for a total L. 1.3cm, base L. 25.7cm, base W. 17.8cm. The dimensions of the small examples are: L. 34.8cm, W. 26.7cm, H. 3.1cm, Th. 0.6cm, raised rim W. 3.8cm, blue edged rim band decoration W. 1.2cm, base L. 25.1cm, base W. 17.6cm.

3. Jacksonville 'Blue China' Wreck Type 2: Dipped Wares

The largest category of ceramics visible on the surface of the Jacksonville 'Blue China' wreck site in Areas A and G were 358 British slip-decorated utilitarian earthenwares representing 37.3% of the total pottery (Tables 1-2; Figs. 4, 7-10). They comprise an assortment of bowls, jugs and mugs referred to in contemporary sources as 'dipped' or 'dipt' ware. A sample of 47 examples was recovered for study (Figs. 28-40). First produced in the late 18th century by Staffordshire potters on creamware and pearlware bodies, by the mid-19th century they had become generic whitewares (pers. comm. Jonathan Rickard, 6 December 2010). Along with shell-edged ware, dipped wares enjoyed a long period of popularity and were the least expensive

Fig. 28. A Type 2A British dipped whiteware bowl, 'London' shape, H. 7.8cm (BC-05-00146-CR).

Fig. 29. A Type 2A British dipped whiteware bowl, 'London' shape, H. 8.7cm (BC-05-00269-CR).

Fig. 30. A Type 2A British dipped whiteware bowl, 'London' shape, H. 8.0cm (BC-05-00384-CR).

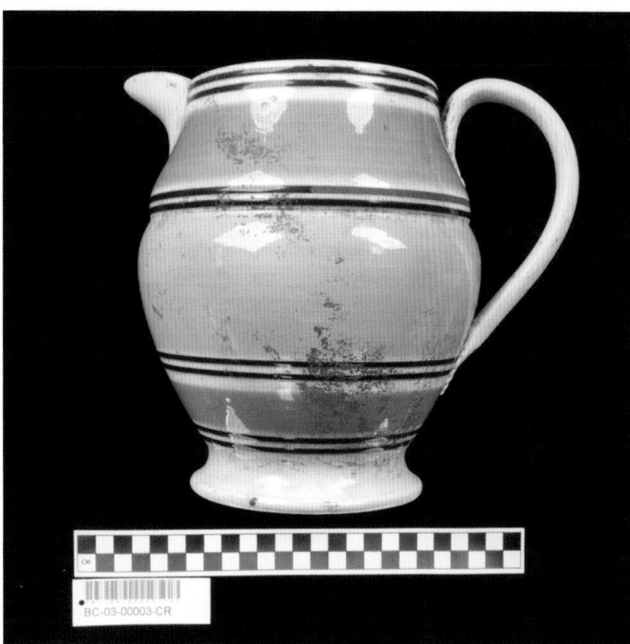

Fig. 31. A Type 2B large British dipped whiteware jug with slip-banded decoration, H. 18.6cm (BC-03-00003-CR).

Fig. 32. A Type 2B large British dipped whiteware jug with slip-banded decoration, H. 18.9 (BC-05-00019-CR).

imported decorated earthenware available to American consumers from the 1780s well into the 1850s (Carpentier and Rickard, 2001: 115, 133; Miller, 1988: 178; Tolson *et al.*, 2008: 171). Advertisements from the first half of the 19th century often used the term 'fancy' to describe these products, a concept which was applied at the time to a form of decorative arts intended to appeal to a burgeoning 'underclass' unable to afford the best imported or city goods (Rickard, 2006a: 15).

The most common slip decoration, comprising simple slip bands in one or many colors (as represented within the Site BA02 examples), was used on a wide range of utilitarian vessels throughout the nearly 170-year period of dipped ware's production. Also prevalent were wares ornamented with the fanciful 'cat's-eye' slip decoration, which is present on two of the wreck's mugs (Figs. 38-40). These wares are well represented amongst archaeological assemblages excavated in American taverns and households of the first half of the 19th century along the Eastern Seaboard. The British manufacture and export of these bold and colorful dipped wares was in fact so extensive that their sherds are found on nearly every American domestic archaeological site.

The most common form of dipped ware present in archaeological contexts is the bowl (Carpentier and Rickard, 2001: 115, 121, 128). This form is consistent with the majority presence of Type 2Ai slip-decorated bowls (35 examples) fashioned in the distinctive 'London' shape recovered from the Jacksonville 'Blue China' wreck (Figs. 28-30). Two bowls observed and left *in situ* just east of Area A, again in the 'London' shape, are more elaborately decorated and distinct from the rest of the assemblage and presumably derived from a small stack of these wares stowed in the ship's bows (Figs. 9-10). These Type 2Aii slip-decorated whiteware bowls with a gray, tan or pale yellow field feature a decorative motif known as the 'common cable' pattern (Rickard, 2006a: 63). The decoration is bracketed by two thin black lines or annular bands above and below. The 'London' shape was introduced in 1807 and by 1810 was the dominant form of earthenware production to the exclusion of former Chinese-style hemispherical bowls.

In imitation of Chinese porcelain shapes, British bowls of the last three decades of the 18th century were hemispherical, with a comparatively tall foot ring, slightly tapered in profile. The shape of these bowls, however, changed quite abruptly in the first decade of the 19th century when the porcelain industry introduced the so-called 'London' shape attributed to the Spode factory. The shape resembles an inverted truncated cone with a steeply angled shoulder directly above a high standing foot ring. Other potters referred to this shape as 'Grecian'. The 'London' or 'Grecian' shape occurs in all sizes of bowls as well as cups (Miller, 1991: 15). Earthenware manufacturers were quick to copy this popular form (Carpentier and Rickard, 2001: 121; Tolson *et al.*, 2008: 171).

By the middle of the century dipped wares had undergone a number of changes. They now had a thicker, heavier

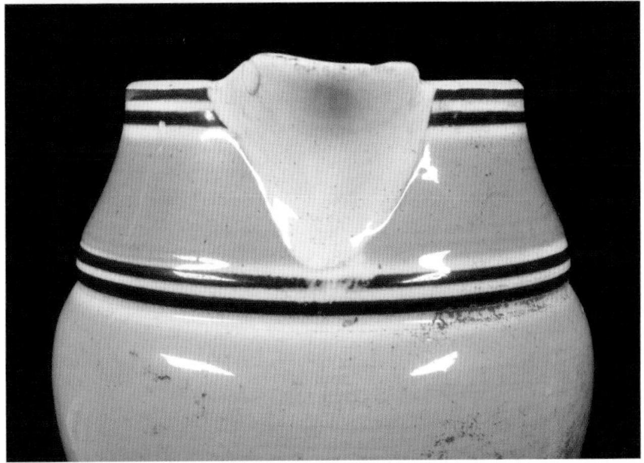

Figs. 36-37. A Type 2B small British dipped whiteware jug with slip-banded decoration, H. 15.9cm (BC-05-00356-CR).

Figs. 33-35. A Type 2B small British dipped whiteware jug with slip-banded decoration, H. 15.5cm (BC-05-00341-CR).

body resulting from a consumer need for relatively strong utilitarian wares. Yet, while technical advances created pottery that resisted breakage, the quality of the ware was compromised (Rickard, 2006b: 5). They thus presented a less elegant appearance than wares manufactured between 1790 and the 1830s and also now featured fewer decorative features. The need for faster manufacture demanded by price competition eliminated most slip decoration beyond the banded and dendritic patterns (Carpentier and Rickard, 2001: 132; Rickard, 2006b: 5; Tolson *et al.*, 2008: 171), the latter of which is described below under 'Yellow Ware' (see Section 6 below).

Fig. 38. A Type 2C British dipped whiteware mug with slip-banded decoration, H. 11.1cm (BC-05-00161-CR).

A number of features related to production changes that took place in the 19th century independently confirm the date range of 1850-60 for the dipped wares found on the Jacksonville 'Blue China' shipwreck, while additional artifacts from the site narrow its most plausible date of loss to 1854. One was a reduction in color choices. Originally slips comprised a variety of earth colorants. Iron oxide produced reds and rusts, and manganese produced black and dark browns. Cobalt oxide yielded blue, copper oxide green, and antimony and uranium yellow. The lead glaze that vitrified the objects also enhanced these earth colors. When the toxicity of many of these substances became realized, they were removed from circulation and became obsolete. As a result, the colors found on dipped wares in the second half of the 19th century are predominantly black, blue, gray and white and lack the earlier vitality (Carpentier and Rickard, 2001: 122; Rickard, 2006b: 2; Tolson *et al.*, 2008: 171). However, blue-banded ware, such as is represented by mugs and jugs on Site BA02, became the most common type of dipped ware after the 1840s and continued to be produced well into the 20th century (Miller, 1991: 6-7).

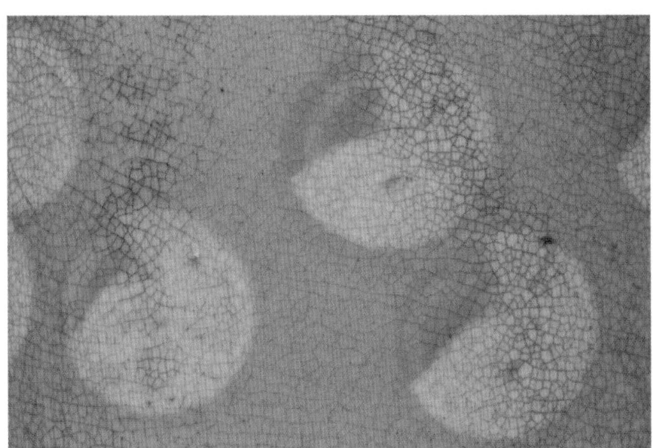

Figs. 39-40. A Type 2C British dipped whiteware mug, with 'cat's-eye' slip decoration, H. 9.2cm (BC-05-00193-CR).

Demands for even lower priced wares caused the variety of decorative techniques to diminish to the point that the market for the above imported dipped wares reduced to a trickle, seemingly in the second half of the 19th century. They were soon superseded by less expensive British white granite/white ironstone, along with yellow-bodied dipped wares produced by American pottery manufacturers now catering to the home market (Rickard, 2006b: 2).

Interestingly, no dipped wares were found on the 1856 wreck of the steamboat *Arabia*, perhaps confirming the ceramic production trends and changes in consumer preference noted above. The presence of so many dipped wares on the Jacksonville 'Blue China' wreck of 1854, compared to the *Arabia's* cargo of the much more fashionable white ironstone china, seems to reflect the changes in tastes when the latter emerged as the preferred wares used in American households (Tolson *et al.*, 2008: 183).

Of the 35 Type 2A 'London' shape bowls recovered from Site BA02 from a total visible cargo of 345 dipped bowls on the wreck's surface (96% of the total Type 2 products on the wreck), two different sizes (12 smaller sized bowls and 23 larger bowls) were recorded. Some comprise a cream ground with a tan band enclosed by double narrow brown bands raised on a foot ring. Others display a gray-tan band, and two of the bowls have a cream ground with a wide brown band enclosed by double narrow brown bands (Figs. 28-30). The largest Type 2A bowls measure H. 8.7cm, Diam. 16.9cm, rim Th. 0.34cm, base H. 0.55cm, base Diam. 8.3cm, upper band W. 1.4cm, lower band W. 1.2cm, W. between bands 3.9cm. The smaller variety measures H. 7.8-8.0cm, Diam. 14.1-14.3cm, rim Th. 0.37cm, base H. 0.55-0.6cm, base Diam. 6.7-7.0cm, upper band W. 1.1-1.4cm, lower band W. 1.0-1.4cm, W. between bands 3.3-3.8cm.

Also retrieved from the wreck site were eight Type 2B dipped jugs of baluster form with a shaped pouring lip, an extruded handle with molded foliate terminals and a turned base (from a total of 12 visible on the site's surface, representing 3.4% of all of the Type 2 dipped wares). All are unmarked and feature similar decoration (Figs. 31-37): a wide, blue-gray or tan central band flanked by two brighter light blue bands. Eight narrow brown slip lines define the boundaries of four main bands. Two principal sizes are recorded, with two sub-types evident within the larger examples: one displays an everted rim, the other a vertical rim. As in the case of the shell-edged wares, the quantity recorded leaves no doubt that these items were cargo. Especially noteworthy was the discovery that five of the jugs each contained a single clear glass tumbler stowed within; a sixth contained fragments of two pale green glass tumblers. This suggests a packing strategy that maximized all available space within the relatively small hold of this coastal schooner (Tolson *et al.*, 2008: 171-2).

The larger jugs measure: H. 18.8cm, Diam. of mouth 13.1cm (excluding pouring lip), pouring lip L. 3.8cm, max spout W. 5.4cm, handle L. 13.7cm, handle W. 2.3cm, handle Th. 1.0cm, max body W. 15.3cm, base H. 1.2cm, base Diam. 10.5cm, upper band W. 1.5cm, second band W. 1.2cm, third band W. 1.1cm, lower band W. 1.1cm. The dimensions of the small jugs are: H. 16.0cm, Diam. of mouth 10.8cm (excluding spout), spout L. 3.1cm, max spout W. 4.0cm, handle L. 11.7cm, handle W. 1.7cm, handle Th. 0.9cm, max body W. 12.9cm, base H. 1.1cm, base Diam. 9.0cm, upper band W. 1.3cm, second band W. 1.7cm, third band W. 1.3cm, lower band W. 1.2cm.

The assemblage also includes four Type 2C dipped mugs featuring an extruded handle and turned stepped base (Figs. 38-40), with measurements corresponding to one-half and one full pint capacities (H. 9.2-11.7cm, mouth Diam. 7.4-8.7cm, rim Th. 0.3-0.37cm, handle L. 7.2-9.5cm, handle W. 1.1-1.6cm, handle Th. 0.65-0.76cm and base W. 7.4-9.3cm). Two of the mugs are decorated with combinations of wide blue and/or gray bands plus six or eight brown stripes. No maker's marks have been detected. One of the mugs has a cream ground with blue bands and is decorated with a 'cat's-eye' pattern below a blue and cream band separated by six narrow brown bands. Another features the 'cat's-eye' decoration enclosed by double narrow brown bands (Tolson *et al.*, 2008: 172). Although stylistically similar to the jugs referenced above, these wares were typically not sold as sets (pers. comm. Jonathan Rickard, 21 August 2006).

4. Jacksonville 'Blue China' Wreck Type 3: Painted Teawares

The sample of 60 Type 3 underglaze painted whitewares recovered from the 87 examples recorded on the surface of the Jacksonville 'Blue China' wreck (9.1% of the total wreck pottery count: Tables 1-2) incorporate three different variations of a floral motif (Figs. 41-58). Based on the quantity found, these British products of *c.* 1845-55 were also a component of the vessel's cargo. They have been identified as elements of a tea set, and include tea bowls (cups in the 'London' shape), saucers, creamers and sugar bowls. No teapots were recovered or observed, although one would certainly expect these items to have been included in such shipments (Tolson *et al.*, 2008: 175, 183).

Blue-painted teawares with floral motifs became popular in the 1820s and a decade later witnessed the introduction of new colors that included red, black and lighter shades of green and blue. Further stylistic changes occurred in the floral painting, which included the introduction of sprig-painted wares bearing simple stylized floral motifs – isolated flowers, sprays and leaves – such as those represented by the Site BA02 examples (Miller, 1988: 174; 1991: 8). These new painted teawares, called 'sprig' or 'sprigged' patterns in advertisements and invoices of the period, were common from around 1835 to the beginning of the Civil War in 1861. An advertisement of 10 September 1831 of

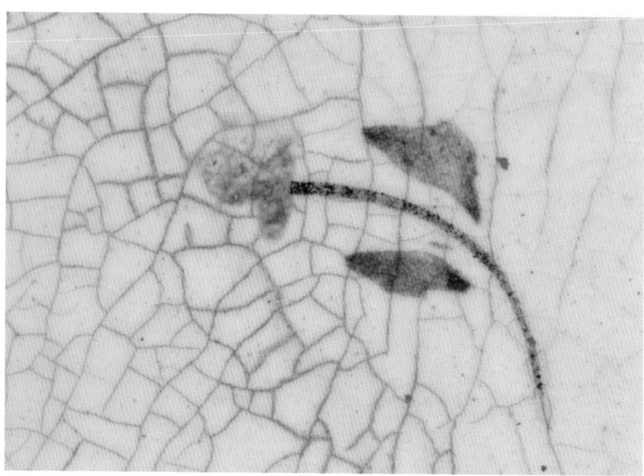

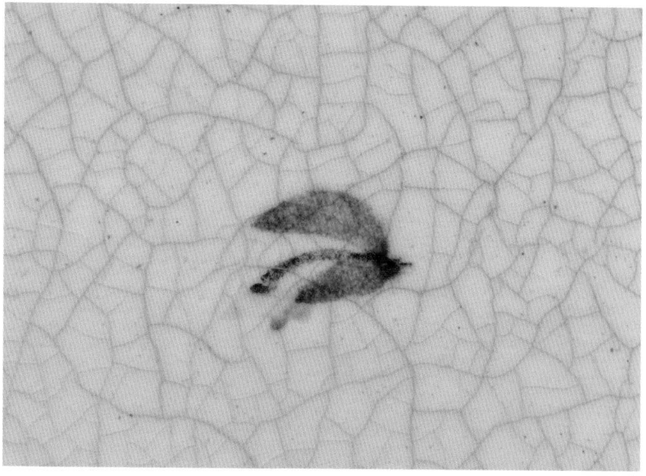

Figs. 41-44. A Type 3A British underglaze painted whiteware teabowl saucer, with details of floral (small sprig) motifs, Diam. 14.9cm (BC-05-00313-CR).

R. Wright of Washington, listing "printed and sprigged tea china", is the earliest known reference to sprig teawares, which may initially have appeared on porcelain. A later invoice dated to 14 April 1841 from New York importer-Joseph Cheeman and Son again listed "Sprig Teas" (Miller and Earls, 2008: 95).

These hand-painted wares required much less color, very few brush strokes and thus just needed artisans with minimal skill to duplicate patterns. Sets of matched pieces could be assembled faster than any of the previous floral patterns (Miller and Earls, 2008: 95). Painted decoration at this simple level, used largely on utilitarian tea, table and toilet wares, created products that were typically more costly than the shell-edge and dipped wares of the period; and yet they were relatively cheap compared to the much higher quality painted wares produced by more skilled artisans that ranked amongst the most expensive wares available. These painted wares are amongst the less expensive wares of this class and are commonly found on North American sites after the late 1840s (Miller, 1988: 174; Miller and Earls, 2000: 93).

Some 27 Type 3A saucers with six floral motifs on the edges and a seventh at the center (H. 3.2cm, Diam. 14.9cm, Th. 0.36cm, base Diam. 7.1cm) and 19 Type 3B 'London'-shaped teabowls with four floral motifs painted onto the exterior and three within the interior (H. 6.4cm, Diam. 10.5cm, rim Th. 0.34cm, base H. 0.5cm, base Diam. 5.4cm) were recovered from the wreck site (Figs. 41-55). At least two different floral decorations are present: roses in full bloom with green leaves, and sprays in cobalt blue, green and red. Four different impressed marks characterize the tea bowls and saucers, and are probably tally or workmen's marks to pay for piece work. Workers' wages were frequently based on the number of vessels that came out of the kiln in good shape. However, it should also be born in mind that merchants not only bought seconds, but also thirds (Shaw, 1900: 207). "Send the best thirds", an 18th-century Portsmouth merchant of New Hampshire wrote in a letter to a 'Liverpoole' supplier of earthenware (Rickard, 2006b: 8). These tally marks unfortunately do not help identify a particular manufacturer because similar marks were used at a number of different factories (Tolson *et al.*, 2008: 175).

The painted wares also include nine Type 3C cream jugs in two sizes (Figs. 56-57) with six floral motifs running across mid-body and a black wavy-line extending down the center of the handle (H. 11.4-11.7cm, mouth Diam. 8.0cm, spout L. 3.0cm, spout W. 3.6cm, rim Th. 0.39cm, handle L. 8.5-9.5cm, handle W. 1.4cm, handle Th. 0.8cm, max body W. 9.7-10.2cm, base H. 0.6cm, base Diam. 6.0-6.8cm); four Type 3D sugar bowls with four floral motifs mid-body and three more adorning the rim (H. 8.4cm, mouth Diam. 11.2cm, rim Th. 0.38cm, max body W. 10.9cm, base H. 1.2cm, base Diam. 8.0cm); as well as one sugar bowl lid bearing a single floral motif (H. 2.8cm, Diam. 8.3cm, rim Th. 0.27cm, handle Diam. 1.2cm; Fig. 58). The jugs feature two different painted designs: red berries and green leaves, with a painted black symmetrical stripe on the ear-shaped handle; on the other example green leaves and a blue tulip with a painted black symmetrical stripe on the simple extruded loop handle. The four painted sugar bowls were found in two different sizes.

The Site BA02 floral wares feature many stylistic characteristics in common with teacups and saucers bearing the impressed mark 'ADAMS'. The Adams family opened potteries in Staffordshire as early as 1650. At that date two brothers, William and Thomas, ran separate ventures in Burslem. In the latter part of the 18th century, and continuing into the 19th, three William Adams, all of whom were cousins, operated their own large potteries independent of one another and, with one exception, were succeeded by sons bearing the same given name. At various stages the potteries were located in Tunstall, Burslem, Cobridge and Stoke-upon-Trent, all in Staffordshire. The Adams company survived into the 20th century (Jervis, 1911: 98; Rickard, 2006b: 4).[4]

Similar hand-painted wares have been recovered by Earth Search, Inc. from an archaeological context of *c.* 1850 in downtown New Orleans. These also bore the maker's mark (which remained in use until 1864) of the Adams Pottery (pers. comm. Jill Yakubik, 2006). The 1856 wreck of the steamboat *Arabia* also yielded similar unmarked floral teaware, largely 20 cups, five saucers and a single teapot (Hawley, 1998: 205; Tolson *et al.*, 2008: 183).

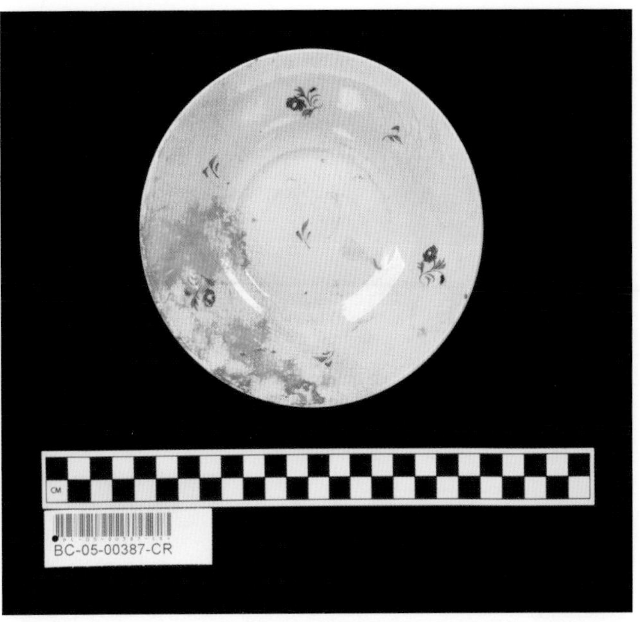

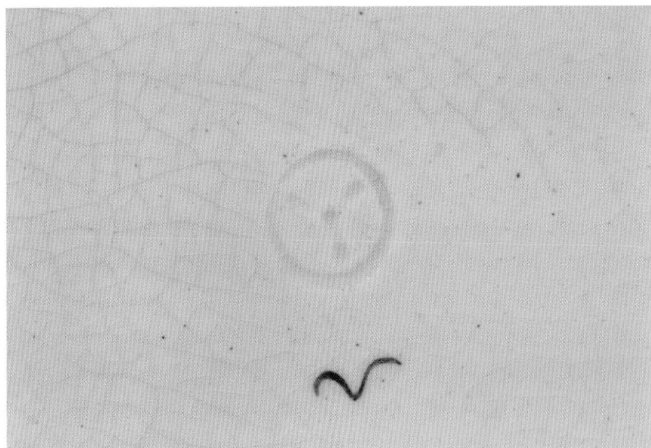

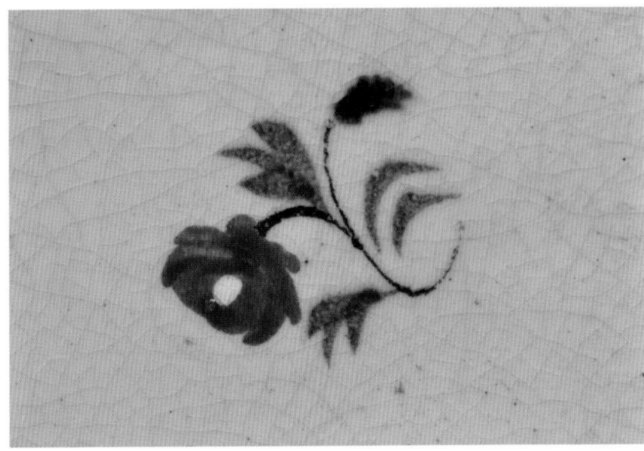

Figs. 45-47. A Type 3A British underglaze painted whiteware teabowl saucer, with detail of floral (small sprig) motif and a tally/workman's mark, Diam. 14.9cm (BC-05-00387-CR).

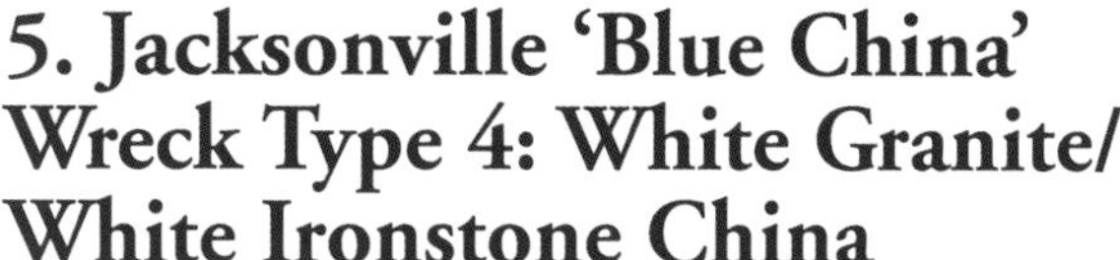

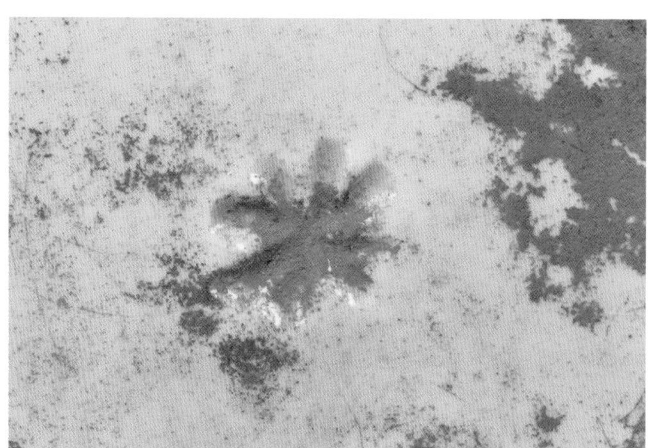

Figs. 48-51. A Type 3B British underglaze painted whiteware teabowl, 'London' shape, with details of floral (small sprigs) motifs and a tally/workman's mark, H. 6.4cm (BC-05-00390-CR).

5. Jacksonville 'Blue China' Wreck Type 4: White Granite/ White Ironstone China

Six different forms of Type 4 British undecorated ironstone china (originally known as white granite) were recovered from Site BA02: three molded dinner plates, 17 flared bowls, one fluted bowl, five chamber pots, four wash basins and 12 salve jars with four lids (Figs. 3, 5-7, 59-67). None of the examples bear identifiable tally or maker's marks.

White ironstone is a heavy, thick-bodied utilitarian ceramic ware that was mass-produced primarily for the American market by England's Staffordshire potters (Blacker, 1911: 177; Godden, 1999: 160-62). By the mid-19th century this ware had become quite popular with both commercial and domestic consumers across the country and was the least expensive ceramic product of the period (Miller, 1988: 175).[5] The Staffordshire district, in particular, home to hundreds of large and small potteries, produced thousands of tons of white ironstone wares (Godden, 1999: 160). Staffordshire offered proximity to the major seaports of Liverpool and Hull from where the majority of these wares were exported to North America and northern Europe respectively (pers. comm. David Barker, 11 November 2010; pers comm. Jonathan Rickard, 6 December 2010; Wedgwood, 1913: 92). The potteries of Staffordshire monopolized the vast and ever-growing American market with its white ironstone pottery, which, as noted by an American authority writing about British ironstone in the 1850s, was "the English export *par excellence*" (Godden, 1999: 162). Although clay was

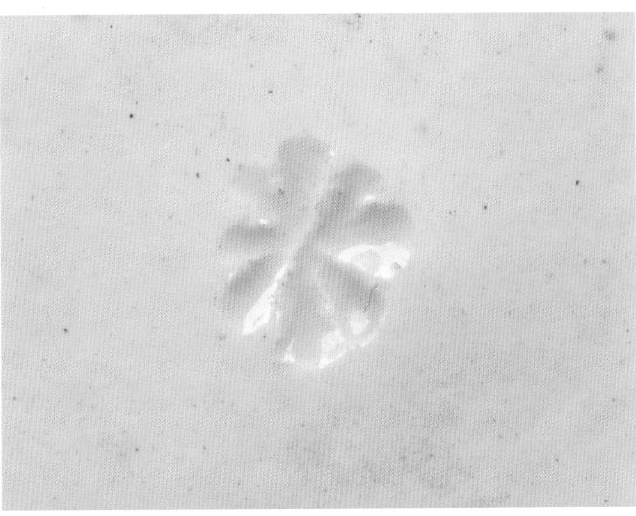

Figs. 52-55. A Type 3B British underglaze painted whiteware teabowl, 'London' shape, with details of floral (small sprigs) motifs and a tally/workman's mark, H. 6.4cm (BC-05-00396-CR).

plentiful in areas of the United States, most dinner and toilet wares, including chamber pots and wash basins, were imported until the late 19th century (*Reports of the United States Commissioners to the Paris Universal Exposition*, 1878: 191). American clay was reserved for making bricks, tiles and other practical utensils, such as crocks and jugs (Cunningham Dobson and Gerth, 2010: 49).

Also known as English porcelain, opaque porcelain, stone china, and white granite, ironstone china was first introduced by Staffordshire potters in the early 19th century, in large part to emulate the popular Chinese-style porcelain dinner services, yet without the cost of these finer wares and with the added advantage of great strength and durability. William Turner of the Lane End potteries at Longton, Stoke-upon-Trent, is said to have achieved the first successful manufacture of stone china and obtained a patent in 1800. Others soon followed, including Josiah Spode's stone china introduced *c.* 1813, who also called his bluish gray wares 'new stone', as well as the stone china produced by John Davenport's Longport pottery *c.* 1815 or slightly earlier. However, the more common term 'ironstone' applied to these hard white stonewares derived from the products that Charles James Mason marketed as 'Mason's Patent Ironstone China' from 1813 (Blacker, 1911: 190; Coutts, 2001: 214; Godden, 1999: 160, 226; Miller, 1991: 9; Orser, 2002: 336).

The early ironstone china produced by these potters was seemingly originally intended to replace the Chinese

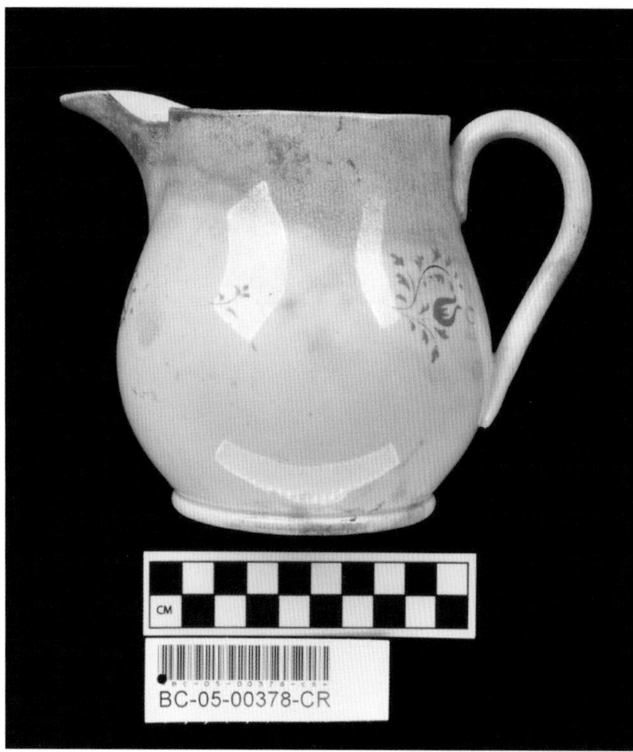

Fig. 56. A Type 3C British underglaze painted whiteware cream jug, H. 11.4cm (BC-05-00378-CR).

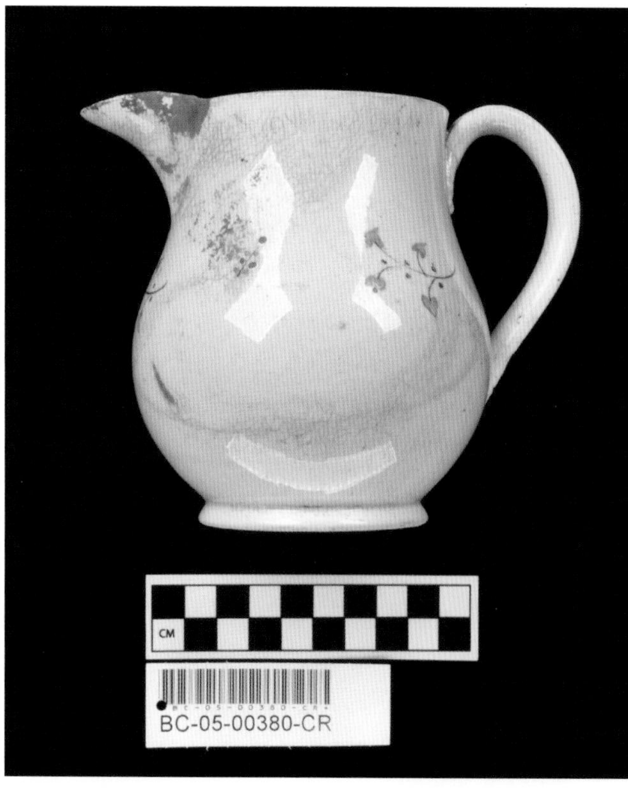

Fig. 57. A Type 3C British underglaze painted whiteware cream jug, H. 11.7cm (BC-05-00380-CR).

Fig. 58. A Type 3D British underglaze painted whiteware sugar bowl, H. 8.4cm (BC-05-00365-CR).

porcelain that the British East India Company stopped importing in 1791. By 1799 a customs duty of over 100% was placed on the import of Chinese porcelain into England, providing the incentive and opportunity to successfully introduce the cheaper stonewares, including 'Mason's Patent Ironstone China'. Most of the English stone china and the ironstone-type wares manufactured prior to the 1830s in fact were heavily decorated, often in a Chinese style and were produced to imitate the popular Chinese export-market porcelains in both design and shape (Godden, 1999: 60-62; Miller, 1991: 10).

The later ironstone and granite wares introduced after 1830 were denser, more thickly potted, often relief-molded or undecorated utilitarian vessels mass produced by a host of Staffordshire manufacturers in large part for the export markets (Godden, 1999: 160). Invoices of earthenware shipped to Philadelphia show that by the early 1840s America had started receiving steady shipments of undecorated ironstone china and 'white granite' (Miller, 1991: 10). English potters had discovered that the inhabitants of the 'colonies' greatly preferred this modestly priced, plain and durable earthenware to more expensive, exotic wares. The name ironstone china, in particular, was especially fitting because it was immediately identifiable, implied high quality, and yet was dense, hard and very durable (Cunningham Dobson and Gerth, 2010: 49; Godden, 1999: 160).[6]

Ironstone china's mass appeal was also explicable because of its physical similarity to white porcelain, yet economically it undercut the popular white French porcelains produced by Haviland and other Limoges and Paris makers (Godden, 1999: 160, 162). White granite, in effect, was a cheap substitute for French china. It offered a similarity that "could be consumed by a section of American society that, whilst unable to aspire to owning French china still sought to imitate trends identified with the more affluent" (Ewins, 1997: 47). Innovative crockery dealers placed advertisements that promoted a visual resemblance between English white granite and French china. The success of this marketing strategy is highlighted in the 1857 obituary of the Dale Hall manufacturer James Edwards, who was noted as bringing "to its present state of perfection the "granite body" which competes so successfully in the markets of the States with French China" (Ewins, 1997: 47-49).

By the 1850s these British white wares were dominant in the American market. In 1852 a ten-piece fine white granite toilet set could be purchased in Baltimore for as little as $2.25, while a 133-piece white ironstone dinner set sold for $25.00. At the same time New York importers of Staffordshire pottery were selling 44-piece white granite teawares for a highly competitive $2.63. By contrast, in the 1860s a New York crockery dealer offered fancy French 44-piece tea sets for $20.00 to $25.00 per piece (Ewins, 1997: 48-9).

While its porcelain-like appearance was certainly a key selling point, other ceramic dealers focused on the durable advantages of Staffordshire white ironstone and began expanding their market to include services used by large steamship companies, clubs, taverns, colleges and hotels, advertising in city newspapers and via popular trade cards (Blacker, 1911: 194).[7] This is exemplified by the case of a Philadelphia crockery dealer in 1848, who promoted the virtues of Francis Morley's white ironstone china with the advertising phrase "suitable for Hotel and Steamboat services" (Ewins, 1997: 47).

As documented in the archaeological record, 'public houses' on the Eastern Seaboard, including eating and drinking establishments such as Trenton, New Jersey's Eagle Tavern, relied heavily on ironstone china to serve its growing clientele. From the mid-1840s onward the tavern flourished with the founding of iron rolling mills and wire mills at two nearby sites (which research suggests specialized in the production of iron and steel rails for the American railroads, structural I-beams for building construction and telegraph wire, bridge wire and wire fencing, respectively). In addition to catering to the many factory workers settling in the neighborhood, the tavern likely provided meals to teamsters hauling coal to the ironworks. The sherds of ironstone china recovered from the site comprise much of the domestic and tavern-related ceramic assemblage dating to the mid-to-late 19th century (White *et al.*, 2005).

Further afield, based on an early advertisement the trade in white ironstone china appears to have reached the

Fig. 59. A Type 4A British white ironstone dinner plate, Diam. 22.7cm (SC-04-00003-CR).

Fig. 60. A Type 4B large British white ironstone bowl (flaring 'London' shape), Diam. 16.2cm (BC-05-00277-CR).

Western frontier by 1839, supplied in large part by a network of wholesalers working in St. Louis, who had strong ties with large-scale wholesalers and importers in Philadelphia and New York. It was not uncommon to see St. Louis storefront displays showcasing ironstone china alongside the more costly French white porcelain that they imitated. By the 1850s the St. Louis wharf was the major entrepôt for steamboats supplying the burgeoning American frontier. As the primary depot for goods needed to colonize the westernmost regions, the St. Louis wholesalers supplied

Fig. 61. A Type 4B non-flaring small British white ironstone bowl, Diam. 12cm (BC-05-00298-CR).

Fig. 62. A Type 4B medium British white ironstone bowl (flaring 'London' shape), Diam. 14.2cm (BC-05-00280-CR).

numerous small-scale retail merchants with essential necessities, such as ironstone table and toilet wares that were then further transported to some of the more remote frontier settlements (Hawley, 1995: 4).[8]

Extensive urban salvage excavations in the city of St. Louis have exposed a large collection of ironstone wares bearing both regional and non-local importers' marks. While local consumption was no doubt very great, the Mississippi Valley and the territory west of St. Louis formed an extensive further market for these goods, supported in large part by the growth of the river trade. As Western settlements grew and trade flourished, the Missouri River in fact became a major commercial highway supporting hundreds of tons of cargo at any one time. By the 1850s river traffic had reached its peak (Hawley, 1995: 5).[9]

The steamboat *Arabia*, laden with 222 tons of frontier-bound cargo, is an example of one such vessel involved in this profitable ceramics trade. Lost in the Missouri River in September 1856, excavations over a century later uncovered crates of ironstone china, including bowls, plates, dishes, casseroles, cups and saucers, as well as water pitchers, wash basins and one odd chamber pot, most marked with the names of Staffordshire potters. Over a hundred unmarked examples were also present (Cunningham Dobson and Gerth, 2010: 64-5; Hawley, 1998: 203-204; Tolson *et al.*, 2008: 183).

While shipping records are sadly lacking, the importance of the ironstone china trade in mid-19th century America is especially apparent from the discovery of the side-wheel steamer the SS *Republic*, which sank in a fierce hurricane off the eastern coast of the United States in October 1865 (Cunningham Dobson *et al.*, 2010). Bound for New Orleans, the steamship's enormous cargo of ironstone table and toilet wares, from which a sample of nearly 3,000 individual pieces was recovered, many bearing the mark of well-known Staffordshire potters, may very possibly have been destined for further trans-shipment up the Mississippi River (Cunningham Dobson and Gerth, 2010: 25).

Upon arrival in the port of New Orleans the *Republic*'s ironstone shipment would likely have been received by agents or wholesale merchants established by the pottery manufacturers or perhaps even commission merchants, the latter of whom played an important role in the city's trade through their handling of incoming (and outgoing) goods. Commission merchants in New Orleans were quite common at this time, particularly for the cotton export industry. Commission merchants were the planter's agent, serving as the intermediary between the planter and the mercantile world (Reinders, 1998: 40). Similarly, the commission merchants of San Francisco had strong international ties to maritime trade and were integral in the development of the Gold Rush frontier through the trans-shipment of goods. Many of these West Coast commission merchants were no strangers to the process, having in fact been instrumental in developing the Mississippi frontier before the California Gold Rush (Delgado, 2009: 8-9).

While the mainstay of the ceramics trade in the first half of the 19th century had been the thousands of crates of imported shell-edged, slip-decorated, painted and printed earthenware, similar to the ceramic examples highlighted above, by the middle of the century a steady stream of strong and attractive table and utilitarian ware – the equivalent of thousands of tons – served the American consumer (Godden, 1999: 160-62). Its popularity is further confirmed by the invoices, receipts and export documents of the mid-1850s, which began listing large quantities of undecorated white ironstone china in ceramic marketing records. At this time undecorated ironstone china appears to have moved into a position of status comparable to transfer-printed wares, which they soon even replaced in popularity, at least temporarily before printed wares made a comeback after 1870 (Miller, 1988: 175; Miller and Earls, 2008: 87). Now more commonly referred to as white granite ('W.G'.), perhaps to avoid confusion with the highly decorated stoneware or earlier ironstones, these wares had become the dominant type in use and would remain so through the Civil War and into the 1880s (Godden, 1999: 162; Miller, 1991: 10; Miller and Earls, 2008: 84).

As noted above, 19th-century ironstone china was largely of British Staffordshire manufacture, yet the influence of Staffordshire potters in America is witnessed by the development of early industries producing white granite ware in potteries in East Liverpool, Ohio, and Trenton, New Jersey, amongst others, whose workers in many cases had in fact originated in Staffordshire and were competing directly with the home-produced British products (Barker, 2001: 82). By the mid-19th century, even the American South produced some high-fired ironstone wares after the establishment of the Southern Porcelain Company in 1856 by potters and businessmen associated with the US Pottery Company in Bennington, Vermont. The factory continued in operation until 1864 when it was destroyed by fire (Steen, 2001: 226).

The ironstone china discovered on the Jacksonville 'Blue China' wreck, although unmarked, is believed to be of British production and was clearly cargo because the wares were found alongside the bulk of the ceramics at the bow end of the site in Area A and scattered across Area G to the southwest. The undecorated ironstone found on Site BA02 includes the following:

Fig. 63. A Type 4C British white ironstone chamber pot, H. 12.5cm (BC-05-00134-CR).

Fig. 64. A Type 4D British white ironstone wash basin, H. 9.9cm (BC-05-00292-CR).

A. Three molded Type 4A dinner plates (H. 3.0cm, Diam. 22.7cm, rim Th. 0.64cm, base H. 0.25cm, base Diam. 12.9cm) with no identifiable maker's marks (Fig. 59).
B. 17 Type 4B 'London' shape fluted bowls featuring flared sides and resting on a pronounced foot ring in three sizes, 10 large, five medium and one small bowl (Figs. 60-62): small bowl H. 7.0cm, Diam. 12.2cm, rim Th. 0.28cm, base H. 0.6cm, base Diam. 6.0cm, tally mark Diam. 0.68cm; medium bowl H. 8.4cm, Diam. 14.7, rim Th. 0.32cm, base H. 0.6cm base Diam. 6.7cm; large bowl H. 9.2cm, Diam. 16.2cm, rim Th. 0.35cm, base H. 0.75cm, base Diam. 6.9cm. Some 13 of the 16 bowls bear no tally or maker's marks; one has a possible mark, although it is too illegible to be certain, and one displays a rudimentary gouge. Two of the bowls bear the number 18, which possibly represents a size designation typically used to denote a potter's dozen products (Tolson *et al.*, 2008: 177).
C. Five undecorated Type 4C chamber pots differing slightly in size: H. 12.3-12.8cm, Diam. 20.5cm, rim Th. 0.52-0.56cm, rim W. 2.2-2.4cm, handle L. 8.9-9.1cm, handle W. 2.0cm, handle Th. 0.99-1.1cm, base H.0.6cm and base Diam. 10.6-11.2cm. Each has an extruded handle with a leaf terminal and standing foot

Figs. 65-66. A Type 4E British white ironstone salve jar, closed and with the lid opened, H. 3.1cm, Diam. 8.3cm (BC-05-00204-CR).

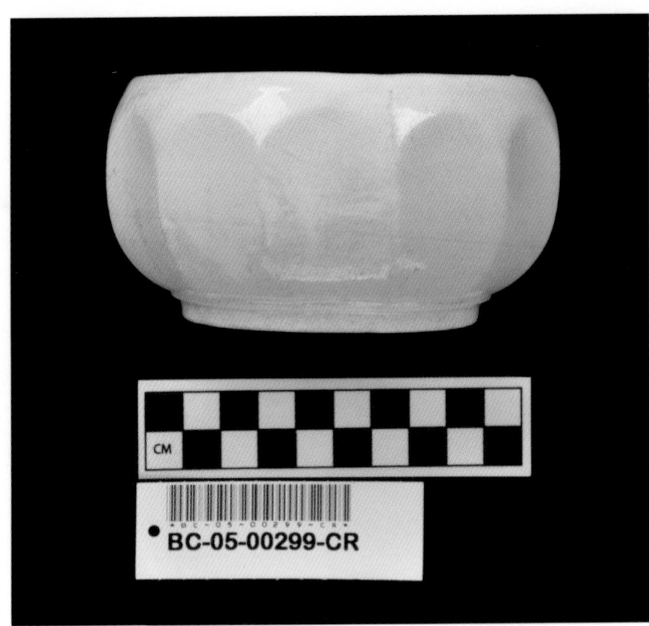

Fig. 67. A Type 4F British white ironstone small fluted bowl, H. 5.7cm (BC-05-00299-CR).

ring. No tally or maker's marks are visible on any of the chamber pots (Fig. 63).

D. Four Type 4D wash basins with no visible tally or maker's marks. All measure H. 9.9cm, Diam. 27.1cm, rim W. 2.3cm, rim Th. 0.46cm, base H. 1.55cm and base Diam. 12.4cm (Fig. 64).

E. 12 Type 4Ei salve jars and four Type 4Eii lids (Figs. 65-66): jar H. 3.1cm, Diam. 8.3cm, rim Th. 0.23cm, body Th. 0.66cm; lid H. 1.3cm, Diam. 8.4cm, Th. 0.34cm. Three of the jars contain a salve or grease-like substance, possibly cosmetic or medicinal in nature (Tolson *et al.*, 2008: 177-79).

F. One Type 4F sturdy small ironstone bowl with a gently incurved rim and vertical fluted sides consisting of 12 concave zones: H. 5.7cm, mouth Diam. 9.4cm, rim Th. 0.46cm, max body Diam. 10.5cm, base H. 0.55cm, base Diam. 6.9cm (Fig. 67).

6. Jacksonville 'Blue China' Wreck Type 5: Yellow Dipped Ware

Two types of artifacts made of yellow earthenware were recovered from Site BA02, a mug and five chamber pots, all of which bear a slip decoration (Figs. 9, 68-71). A total of 14 examples of Type 5 ceramics (all but one, chamber pots) were counted on the surface of the wreck and account for 1.5% of its total ceramic assemblage. The yellow bodies resemble American-made yellow wares produced by British immigrant potters, who established a number of potteries in the United States in the 1830s. Much of the yellow ware produced at this time was decorated in the British tradition with slip predominating. US pottery manufacture locations included Bennington, Vermont; Trenton, New Jersey; East Liverpool and Cincinnati, Ohio; Troy, Indiana; and Louisville and Covington, Kentucky. Since no commercially viable white-firing clay sources were found in America until later in the 19th-century, yellow ochre bodies predominated.

North American dipped wares of the period are not easy to distinguish from the yellow-bodied wares produced in potting centers in Great Britain. However, given the predominance of British ceramics identified on the Jacksonville 'Blue China' shipwreck, the yellow wares are also very probably of English manufacture, most likely from the south Derbyshire region renowned for its yellow-bodied wares (Rickard, 2006b: 2; Tolson *et al.*, 2008: 179). Bristol, the northeast and Scottish potteries were also engaged in its manufacture (pers. comm. David Barker, 9 November 2010).

The slip decoration on the one Type 5A yellow ware mug recovered from the wreck (H. 7.8cm, mouth Diam. 6.7cm, rim Th. 0.32cm, handle L. 6.3cm, handle W. 1.2cm, handle Th. 0.64cm and base W. 7.4cm), with a light buff discolorisation, consists of four thin brown stripes, two at the top and two at the bottom (Fig. 68). The handle has broken off and no tally or maker's mark is present. Interestingly, while similar to the slip-decorated whiteware mugs referenced above (see Section 3), this yellow ware mug is the only example recovered from the ceramic assemblage.

Of the five yellow earthenware chamber pots recovered (Fig. 69), one features Type 5Bi slip decoration (H. 12.6cm, mouth Diam. 22.1cm, rim Th. 0.57cm, rim W. 2.1cm, handle L. 8.7cm, handle W. 2.2cm, handle Th. 0.94cm, max body W. 19.1cm, base H. 0.8cm, base Diam. 13.4cm, upper band W. 0.95cm). It is unadorned except for a series of thin, slip-trailed blue lines encircling the body and rim of the vessel. All five of the pots incorporate an extruded handle and are raised on a foot ring. The handle on one of the pots has broken off. No tally or maker's marks are apparent on any of the examples.

The other four Type 5Bii chamber pots (H. 13.0cm, mouth Diam. 21.9cm, rim Th. 0.64cm, rim W. 2.2cm, handle L. 8.5cm, handle W. 2.2cm, handle Th. 0.93cm, max body W. 18.6cm, base H. 0.65cm, base Diam. 13.2cm) are decorated with thin blue lines framing a wide white band (H. 5.7cm), over which is a blue 'dentritic' tree-like decoration (Tolson *et al.*, 2008: 181; Figs. 70-71). The clay core is merely a light buff discolorisation. Such surface-decorated slip-glazed ceramics are known as

Fig. 68. A Type 5A British dipped yellow ware mug, with slip-trailed lines surrounding the body and rim, H. 7.8cm (BC-05-00168-CR).

Fig. 69. A Type 5Bi British dipped yellow ware chamberpot, with slip-trailed lines surrounding the body and rim, H. 12.6cm (BC-05-00322-CR).

mocha ware, which of all the different types of slip-decorated wares seem to have been considered especially attractive.

Mocha ware developed in late 18th-century Staffordshire, where the earliest written reference to this pottery form is associated with Lakin and Poole factory invoices dating to 1792-96, which mention 'mocoa tumblers' (Rickard, 2006a: 46, 54). This distinctive pottery type was named after the Yemeni port city of Al Mukah, called 'Mocha' in the 18th and 19th centuries by the English-speaking world. Famous for its export of coffee, this Red Sea port city was also renowned for the large quantities of Arabian moss agate or 'mocha stone' it shipped to London in the latter part of the 18th century. Characterized by delicate and beautiful fern or tree-like (dendritic) striations, this semi-precious gemstone was imported by London merchants for setting in fashionable gold and silver women's jewelry (Carpentier and Rickard, 2001: 122; Rickard, 2006a: 46).

The popularity of moss agate seems to have inspired the production of slip-decorated white or cream earthenware, decorated with patterns simulating the stone's dendritic visual effect, and was typically featured on common utilitarian wares such as jugs, mugs, chamber pots and bowls (Rickard, 2006a: 46). The resulting name for this distinctive new pottery was 'Mocoa'. While some surviving documentary evidence points to Staffordshire's Lakin and Poole as its earliest producer, other sources alternatively identify even earlier mocha production by William Adams soon after he established his Tunstall factory, again in Staffordshire, in 1787. This colorful domestic pottery ware was sold at a moderate price and is said to have helped bring Adams' work into eminence (Turner, 1904: 37). The following decade the potter's cousin, another William Adams, was also making mocha at his Cobridge factory. By 1820 mocha ware was being produced by several additional Staffordshire potteries (Rickard, 2006a: 137).

The original process for creating the tree and branch-like pattern unique to mocha ware involved producing an acidic solution potters called 'mocha tea' (often also referred to as a 'tobacco tea'), which was then applied to an alkaline slip. The resulting chemical and physical reaction between the 'tea' and wet slip would quickly and randomly produce the underglaze's arboreal patterns. In 1833 an observer of the process described it as follows (Carpentier and Rickard, 2001: 122, 125):

> "The 'Moco' pattern on the outside of the basons makes them appear as if delicate branches of seaweed have been laid upon their surfaces... The fluid employed is a preparation of tobacco-water; and in applying it the effect is brought out with little waste of either time or labour. A camel's hair pencil full of the decoction is taken in the hand, and with the point of it the surface of the bason is dotted with two or three dots where the pattern is intended to be. The fluid instantly spreads and runs into these ramifications."

Most potters however, seem to have developed their own formulas for the mocha solution, which, as described in surviving formulas of the period, called for the inclusion of printers ink, hops, tansy, urine and, in at least one case, spirits of turpentine (Carpentier and Rickard, 2001: 125). Two different types of dendritic decoration are found: the more recognizable bearing a resemblance to trees and the other reproducing a branching, seaweed effect (Figs. 70-71). Both entailed slightly different techniques, yet were clearly the result of a dynamic process between the two liquids, the acidic tea and the alkaline slip, with the element of chance playing a key role in the final production (Rickard, 2006a: 46, 49). Of the four mocha-patterned chamber pots recovered from the Jacksonville 'Blue China' wreck, three are adorned with the vertical tree-like decoration and one with the branching seaweed design. The handle of this latter vessel is broken off.

The widespread popularity of mocha wares amongst North American consumers is well documented in early 19th-century records. This testimony, however, is likely to refer to mocha on cream and pearlwares and not to the importation of yellow wares, for which there is apparently little documentary evidence (pers. comm. David Barker, 9 November 2010). Advertisements cite the shipment of mocha to a number of eastern port cities, including New York and Boston. An 1815 entry from the *Boston Daily Advertiser* lists "53 dozen Moco Bowls" for sale. Another advertisement of 2 August 1823 presents the name of the potter as Andrew Stevenson, who was offering "30 crates Mocho...for sale by package from Liverpool. Manufacturers of goods they bring to market." Stevenson was operating out of Cobridge, Staffordshire, between about 1816-30. Like a number of British potters, it would appear that he also maintained an office or pottery outlet in New York on 58 Broadway to serve what at the time was quite likely the Staffordshire Potteries' most important export trade (Rickard, 2006a: 52).

An even earlier invoice of 2 June 1797 lists "5 doz [jugs]...Mocoa" shipped to Boston "on the Account and Risque of Wood and Caldwell of Boston", which also operated a pottery in Burslem between 1790 and 1818. Of the 80 crates of British earthenware mentioned in this invoice, a significant 19% was mocha. A further 56% of the shipment represented additional dipped wares. This consignment of mocha and other dipped wares combined represented 75% of the pottery shipment, which when compared with data from other records for this period supports the contention that these wares were amongst the cheapest British decorated hollow-wares available to the American market (Carpentier and Rickard, 2001: 115; Rickard, 2006a: 52).

Mocha was most popular during the period 1795-1835, as documented on American sites (Miller, 1991: 6). However, by the middle of the 19th century the US market for British utilitarian slipwares, including dendritic-decorated 'mocha' ware, was on the decline, supplanted in large part by American potteries populated by British workmen producing similar slip decorations on yellow bodied pots. Dendritic decoration continued to be produced for the domestic market for use in pubs and markets until 1939, spanning nearly 150 years. At this time T.G. Green, the last British company known to have produced mocha commercially, halted manufacture to concentrate on supporting the war effort (Carpentier and Rickard, 2001:125; Rickard 2006a: 56).

Fig. 70. A Type 5Bii British dipped yellow ware chamber pot, slip-decorated 'dendritic' pattern (vertical tree-like decoration), H. 13.0cm (BC-05-00320-CR).

Fig. 71. A Type 5Bii British dipped yellow ware chamber pot, slip-decorated 'dendritic' pattern (branching seaweed design), H. 13.0cm (BC-05-00405-CR).

7. Jacksonville 'Blue China' Wreck Type 6: Canton Ginger Jars

Asian (Canton) ginger jars were popular exports to both America and Britain for much of the mid-19th century. The name 'ginger jar' derives from the fact that similar containers were used for the export of large quantities of crystallized ginger (as well as other pickled food items) from China.

Four intact Type 6 ginger jars, all the same height (H. 15.4cm, mouth Diam. 7.0cm, rim H. 0.65cm, rim Th. 0.5cm, max. body Diam. 15.3cm, base Diam. 12.9cm), were recovered from the northwest flank of Area A on the Jacksonville 'Blue China' wreck site, possibly representing a small consignment of higher value exotic ceramics aboard the vessel (Figs. 8, 72-78). All four are missing their lids and no maker's marks are present. The hand painted blue-underglaze decoration features a house by the water, a man fishing and a sailing boat. The outline of the embellishment is drawn in light and heavy blue lines and the color is washed to lighter shades to contrast with the white porcelain (Tolson *et al.*, 2008: 181). Dated generally to the period 1840-60, the proposed date of 1854 for the loss of the Site BA02 coastal schooner helps further pinpoint the period of this style's circulation.

Americans' taste for fine china developed during the Colonial era, when Chinese goods first arrived in the New World in British hulls. After the American Revolution, merchants were freed from the embargos and monopoly restrictions formerly imposed on the colonies. The Orient, long a monopoly of the British East India Company, was now accessible to American shipping. Direct trade between the United States and China began in 1784 with the famous *Empress of China*, which sailed from New York to Canton, the only Chinese port open to Western nations (Swift *et al.*, 1939: 24). By the 1790s American trade with China had surpassed that of all other nations except for Great Britain (Layton, 1997: 24). Five American ships arrived in Canton between 1786 and 1787, a figure which increased tenfold to 59 ships from 1832-33 (Yong, 2000: 23-24).

The China trade had, in fact, become especially important to America as a prolific source of revenue to both merchants and the government and for the essential 'necessities' it provided the American consumer – tea, silks and porcelain, in particular – the importance of which was somewhat absurdly deemed "almost equivalent to that of bread" in one early 19th century account. While Chinese porcelain was largely employed by the upper and middle classes, even poorer families could boast at least a limited proportion of chinaware on their mantelpieces (Mudge, 1981: 145-46).

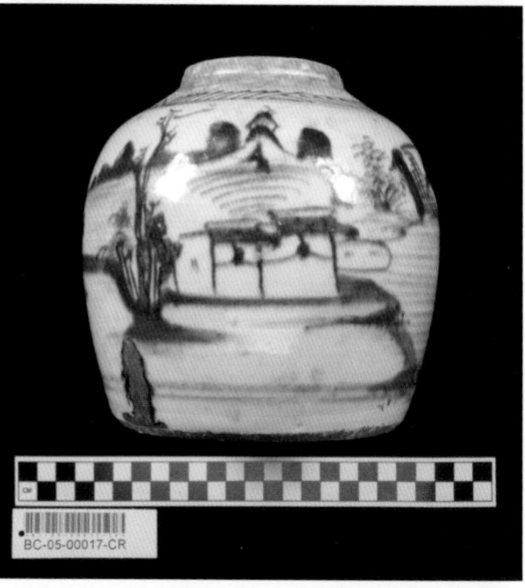

Figs. 72-74. A Type 6 porcelain Canton ginger jar, H. 15.4cm (BC-05-00017-CR).

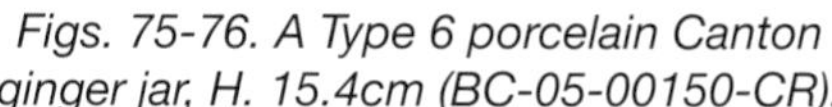

Figs. 75-76. A Type 6 porcelain Canton ginger jar, H. 15.4cm (BC-05-00150-CR).

Figs. 77-78. A Type 6 porcelain Canton ginger jar, H. 15.4cm (BC-05-00151-CR).

By as early as the 1830s America's interest in Chinese porcelain appeared to be on the wane and incoming cargos diminished. In the 1833-34 shipping season, only 1,322 boxes of china wares left Canton, a quantity easily handled by a mere four or five ships. As often was the case this trend seems to have reflected a pattern established by the British, whose East India Company stopped importing porcelain in 1801, partly due to an overstocked market, as well as an apparent decrease in consumers' interest in all things Chinese. Also relevant, of course, were the increased activities of the English ceramic industry and the imposition of high import tariffs to protect them (Mudge, 1981: 147). By the mid-1850s, as the ceramic composition of the Jacksonville 'Blue China' shipwreck verifies, Chinese porcelain was greatly surpassed by British earthenware and was no longer considered to be an obligatory necessity for the majority of fashionable American households.

Figs. 79-81. A Type 7Ai British transfer-printed whiteware plate, 'Asiatic Pheasants' pattern, with details of decoration and pottery dealer/agent stamp on the base; Diam. 23.8cm (SC-04-00001-CR).

8. Jacksonville 'Blue China' Wreck Type 7: Transfer-Printed Wares

Only three individual examples of transfer-printed wares (two circular plates and a sauce boat) were recovered from Site BA02 (Figs. 79-85). These few examples may hint at the presence of a larger consignment of decorated cargo wares not identified during the limited on-site recovery of surface material or loss through bottom trawling impacts. It is perhaps hard to imagine the crew using a relatively fancy sauce boat at sea.

The technique of transfer printing designs under the glaze on ceramics represents one of the great 18th-century English innovations that revolutionized the Staffordshire ceramic industry, enabling the application of complex decoration both quickly and relatively inexpensively. It also permitted uniformity of design between vessels that had previously not been possible (Samford, 2000: 56). Significantly, transfer printing developed at a time when businesses were searching for ways to produce more economic goods by mechanical processes. Until then, the only methods known to potters for decorating their wares was painting, which was not only labor intensive but also costly. Only the most affluent English could afford complete sets of dinnerware since every dish had to be carefully painted by an artisan. Transfer printing in effect allowed hundreds of sets of dinnerware to be produced at a fraction of the time painting took and for a fraction of the cost, thus making such table wares more readily accessible to middle class families.[10]

Transfer printing is the process by which a pattern or design is first engraved on a copper plate. The plate is then inked with a metallic oxide pigment and the pattern printed onto a special tissue; the inked tissue is used to transfer the design onto a biscuit-fired ceramic object. The object is then glazed and fired again, which vitrifies the glaze and transforms the metallic oxide pigment to the desired color.

Of all the economically accessible ceramic products available during the period of interest, transfer-printed products were still amongst the most expensive decorated earthenware available to the US market until the mid-19th century. By the 1790s transfer printing had become a common method of decorating ceramics in the Staffordshire potteries and its products were three to five time more expensive than undecorated plain whiteware vessels (Miller, 1988: 174). Most North American archaeological assemblages dating to the first half of the 19th century contain few wares whose cost exceeded that of transfer-printed wares (the major exception is porcelain, for which there are minimal pricing records). Gradually however, the price differential between transfer-printed wares decreased to less than two times the cost of undecorated whiteware, and as they became cheaper consumption naturally increased. While the prices of all ceramics were falling, as documented by Staffordshire invoices for ceramics exported to America from 1809-44, the prices for printed wares fell most sharply. By the 1850s the cost of printed plates was only slightly higher than of shell-edged plates (Miller and Earls, 2008: 97, 98).

This trend is readily documented on sites dating after the War of 1812 (Miller, 1988: 174). Following this war, despite a complex set of tariffs, English wares still continued to flood the American market (Martin, 2001: 34). The increase in the consumption of printed wares at this time, as indicated by New York invoices for pottery, was probably the result of a major decline in ceramic prices. Almost 43% of the plates and soup plates ordered by New York merchants between 1838 and 1840 were transfer-printed wares. While formerly a luxury of the upper classes, by 1842 a group of New York pottery dealers considered these Staffordshire wares sufficiently inexpensive to have penetrated the poorest households (Samford, 2000: 58-9).

Staffordshire potters manufactured thousands of printed earthenware designs in a variety of colors and patterns, which gained immediate acceptance from both the British and American markets, many of which remained immensely popular until the mid-19th century. While the production span of most patterns was short-lived and often limited to one potter, designs such as 'Asiatic Pheasants' and 'Willow', both of which are individually represented amongst the Jacksonville 'Blue China' examples, were extremely popular and were manufactured by a number of potters (Samford, 2000: 56).

One of the two transfer-printed plates recovered from Site BA02 (H. 2.8cm, Diam. 23.7cm, rim Th. 0.48cm, base H. 0.8cm, base Diam. 13.4cm) is decorated in brown with an elaborate bird-and-flower motif known as 'Asiatic Pheasants' (Type 7Ai; Figs. 79-81), which was one of the most popular dinnerware patterns of the Victorian era and is still produced in Staffordshire today. Podmore Walker & Co., which opened for business in Well Street, Tunstall, in 1834 is generally acknowledged as being the first producer of the 'Asiatic Pheasants' pattern (although who actually originated the pattern remains unsubstantiated). The company was joined by Enoch Wedgwood in 1854 and became Wedgwood & Co. in 1860.[11] Well before this partnership, the pattern was used by a number of other manufacturers and not always under license. However, co-operation between pottery firms was not unusual, patterns were frequently loaned, and when large orders arrived they were often sub-contracted to other firms, even competitors, to meet demand.

Fig. 82-83. A Type 7Aii British transfer-printed whiteware soup plate, 'Willow' pattern, with pottery dealer/agent stamp on the base, Diam. 23.8cm (BC-05-00348-CR).

The town most associated with the 'Asiatic Pheasants' Pattern is Tunstall, where from *c.* 1838-1939 it was in continuous production by a number of different pottery firms, including the Well Street, Swan Bank, Unicorn, and Pinnox works (Jewitt, 1883: 563; Tolson *et al.*, 2008: 176). The pattern was also copied by several potteries along the Clyde in Scotland, the Tyne and Tees in Northumberland, in Yorkshire, London, Devon and South Wales (Bebb, 2004: 38; Tolson *et al.*, 2008: 176). The 'Asiatic Pheasants' pattern was so well-received, in fact, that it was considered one of the standard patterns of Great Britain and the colonies (Jewitt, 1878: 425; 1883: 563).

The reverse of this plate bears the large printed mark 'F. PRIMAVESI/& SONS/CARDIFF' measuring 4.0 x 3.3cm (Fig. 81). Fedele Primavesi's firm, located in Cardiff and Swansea, Wales, specialized in the re-sale of Welsh and

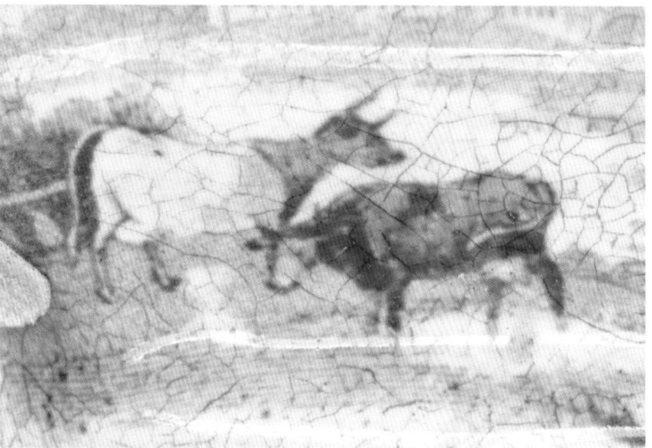

Figs. 84-85. A Type 7B British transfer-printed whiteware sauceboat and detail of decoration, L. 14.3cm (BC-05-00347-CR).

Staffordshire pottery wares. The company was active from 1850-1915. Pottery agents or dealers such as Fedele Primavesi served as middlemen between the potteries and the china retailers or warehouses. In this case, the Primavesi mark was applied by the manufacturing pottery.

A second transfer-printed plate recovered from Site BA02 (Type 7Aii: H. 3.8cm, Diam. 23.8cm, rim W. 3.4cm, rim Th. 0.51cm, base Diam. 12.3cm, base stamp 4.8 x 1.2cm) is a soup plate decorated in the standard 'Willow' pattern, perhaps the best known design on early 19th-century pottery and which, by 1814, was the cheapest transfer-printed pattern available in the potters' price fixing lists (Figs. 82-83). It apparently retained that position throughout the 19th century (Miller, 1988: 8).

The standard 'Willow' pattern, produced after 1810, was developed by Josiah Spode in his Staffordshire Stoke-upon-Trent pottery and derived from an original Chinese pattern called Mandarin. However, apparently no Chinese pattern contained all of the features of the standard 'Willow' pattern created by Spode. Spode may have produced an earlier version of the 'Willow' pattern *c.* 1790 and a second 'Willow' pattern engraved from copper plates about the same period, but of a finer quality. His third version became what is now known as the true 'Willow' pattern. The design is based on oriental temple landscape patterns and consists of the following principal features: a bridge with three people crossing it, the willow tree, the boat, the main tea house, two birds and a fence across the foreground of the garden (Copeland, 1980: 33-5). The dainty little design instantly became popular and for nearly two centuries thereafter remained the stock-pattern of virtually every British pottery manufacturer and amongst potters in other countries as well (Miller, 1991: 8).[12]

The Type 7Aii Jacksonville 'Blue China' soup plate decorated in this transfer-printed style bears a maker's mark containing the words 'STONE WARE / B H & Co.' (Fig. 83). This mark has been identified as deriving from Beech, Hancock & Co., a Staffordshire pottery workshop that began production at the Swan Bank Works in Burslem. Research indicates that this mark was used between 1851 and 1855 (Tolson *et al.*, 2008: 177).[13] The excavation of the 1865 wreck of the SS *Republic* yielded only one 'Willow' patterned item: a large platter without any visible maker's mark.

The third transfer-printed ware from Site BA02 is an earthenware sauce boat with a broken handle, printed with a light blue design on a white ground depicting cows in a country setting (Jacksonville 'Blue China' wreck Type 7B: H. 9.5cm, total L. 14.3cm, Diam. 7.8cm, spout L. 4.3cm, spout W. 5.0cm, spout Th. 0.36cm, body Th. 0.48cm max, max body W. 8.4cm, handle W. 1.1cm, handle Th. 0.47cm, base H. 1.1cm, base Diam. 7.8 x 4.9cm, base Th. 0.62cm max; Figs. 84-85). The discolored clay fabric core is reddish yellow, 5YR 7/6. The original name of this pattern has yet to be identified, but it is similar to the pastoral genre produced during this era. While the early transfer-printed wares typically featured popular oriental themes, historical events and pastoral settings depicting scenes from rural life with farming, cattle and others animals soon became fashionable as well. No tally or maker's mark is visible.

9. Jacksonville 'Blue China' Wreck Type 8: Stoneware

Stoneware vessels were an integral part of daily life in North America from the time of European settlement and were deposited on domestic archaeological sites throughout the 17th and 18th centuries (Skerry and Hood, 2009).

By the mid-19th century Americans continued to maintain a strong preference for stoneware pottery, primarily due to its remarkable durability.

Most stoneware was originally salt-glazed, creating a distinctive pitted texture on the surface, which is more evident on brown and gray than on white wares. This rough-surfaced glaze was produced by throwing common salt directly on the fire as the heat of the kiln approached its maximum temperature. The intense heat vaporized the salt, which settled in a fine mist on the pottery, giving it a transparent and exceedingly hard finish (Barber, 1907: 5; Skerry and Hood, 2009: 1). These stoneware vessels were considered safe to use, presumably because they were not made with a toxic lead-based glaze, were relatively inexpensive and especially sturdy. Impervious to the harmful effects of highly saline or acidic solutions, stoneware was also particularly well suited for use in preparing and storing a wide range of liquids and foodstuffs (Skerry and Hood, 2009: 1-2). Ralph Russell, an early Pennsylvania potter, used poetic license to describe his hardy wares. "Genuine stoneware", stated Russell, "will never sour, rust, or rot in the shape of a churn, jar, or pot." If properly cared for they would outlast their users by many generations.[14]

Stoneware was first produced in the West during the Middle Ages in modern Germany, with salt-glazed wares manufactured extensively from the early 16th century (Barber, 1907: 5; Greer, 1981: 180; Skerry and Hood, 2009: 1). The Rhineland region produced the first brownware to arrive on American shores, largely in the form of storage jugs for liquids, and some mugs, both of which would serve as essential objects for everyday American life over the course of the 17th century (Skerry and Hood, 2009: 7).

The oldest English salt-glazed stoneware was apparently a close imitation of the German brownware, which was being produced in quantity by English Staffordshire potters by the last quarter of the 17th century, and soon supplanted German imports. As documented in advertisements in this period, the presence of German brown stoneware in England and the American colonies declined as English salt-glazed wares became more readily available to fulfill the demands of a burgeoning market (Skerry and Hood, 2009: 66-7, 205; Weatherill, 1971: 9).

The export of large quantities of both German and English salt-glazed stoneware to America discouraged local production during the Colonial period. A further major deterrent was the lack of high-firing clay suitable for manufacturing stoneware. Most of the clay used to make early American stoneware came from the Raritan Formation in New Jersey, New York and Pennsylvania (Skerry and Hood, 2009: 185). Salt-glazed stoneware production in North America was thus originally centered around New York and New Jersey because of their close proximity to stoneware clay beds and their ready access to the coastal trade, which marketed their product widely (Baldwin, 1993: 14).

Fig. 86. A Type 8 American salt-glazed stoneware jug, New York, H. 34.2cm (BC-03-00005-BE).

The development of early American stoneware was largely inspired by European imports and was frequently produced by immigrant craftsmen trained in Germany or England. Stoneware production in the colonies, like so much of American history, began in Yorktown, Virginia, around 1720. The first salt-glazed stoneware objects produced in William Rogers' manufactory were close imitations of British brown stoneware, which is found in large quantities on 18th-century American archaeological sites (Skerry and Hood, 2009: 185-87).

Shortly thereafter, a domestic salt-glazed stoneware industry emerged in the northeast on Manhattan Island, favorably situated between two large deposits of stoneware clay. Production began with the migration of two German stoneware potters, first Johan Willem Crolius in 1718, and in 1731 Johannes Remmi (later known as John Remmey). Both potters originated in the Westerwald, the center of 18th-century German stoneware production, and would

Fig. 87. A Type 9 salt-glazed German stoneware bottle, H. 26.9cm (BC-03-00002-BE).

later become related by marriage, linking their American potteries (Barber, 1907: 24-5; Skerry and Hood, 2009: 192-3).[15]

With the discovery of stoneware deposits (originally called 'fireclay') in Western Pennsylvania in the early 1800s, Pennsylvania too became a prolific producer. While New York's Erie Canal system supported more factories, Pennsylvania's industry had greater longevity. Her immigrant population increased dramatically mid-century, and with it an increase in the number of people who depended on stoneware crockery for a variety of needs.[16] With its early start in Virginia, the mid-Atlantic region and the South would also support a thriving stoneware industry (Baldwin, 1993: 14; Barber, 1907: 24-26; Burrison, 2007: 119; Skerry and Hood, 2009).

Of the three stoneware vessels recovered from the Jacksonville 'Blue China' shipwreck, Type 8 is a heavy-bodied salt-glazed stoneware jug of American production dating to 1850-60, the core fabric of which is discolored today but was typically brown or gray-bodied (Fig. 86). The interior of this vessel emits a strong smell of oil or tar (H. 34.2cm, external mouth Diam. 5.4cm, rim H. 1.9cm, rim Th. 1.3cm, handle W. 3.2cm, handle Th. 2.5cm, max body W. 21.3cm, base Diam. 17.0cm). The upper rim/handle junction has a strip of burning across it and a reddish brown pitch-like residue occurs on the interior and exterior of the rim and down the outer neck. A thumb imprint impressed into the clay of the lower handle lug measures 2.2 x 1.1cm. This vessel represents the only identifiable American ceramic object found on the wreck site (Tolson *et al.*, 2008: 181). The elongated, ovoid-shaped vessel with a bifurcated handle is devoid of decoration with the exception of cobalt highlights at the handle terminal. This feature stylistically imitates jugs of Germanic tradition that often display cobalt blue brushed within an incised design around handle terminals (Burrison, 2007: 119; Skerry and Hood, 2009: 196-7).

The Type 8 style of jug was typically used to bulk store any number of liquids, such as water, wine, rum, vinegar and oil. Such vessels were produced in large quantities in the northeastern United States in New York and Pennsylvania in particular, either of which may have been the origin of the Jacksonville 'Blue China' example, although New York is most probable, as observed by ceramic historian Robert Hunter and documented for similar wares (Skerry and Hood, 2009: 197; Tolson *et al.*, 2008: 182). A similar, although slightly less ovoid-shaped, one-gallon salt-glazed jug with a large cobalt floral spray brushed on the front, bears the impressed company name 'PFALTZENGRAF & CO./York Pennsylvania' and dates to the second half of the 19th century (Greer, 1989: 165). The longevity of the form is reflected by a similar two-gallon salt-glazed jug dated to *c.* 1805-1810 and attributed to Frederick Carpenter of Charleston, 'Boston', with the capacity numeral impressed on the front of the vessel just below the mouth ring (Greer, 1981: 165). The form was also recovered from the 'Mardi Gras' shipwreck in the Gulf of Mexico, decorated down its body with an incised floral motif, and dated to between 1808 and *c.* 1820 (Ford *et al.*, 2008: fig. 5.17; Ford *et al.*, 2010: 93).

A second stoneware vessel recovered from the shipwreck (Type 9; Fig. 87), also apparently salt-glazed, is a tall cylindrical dark red (2.5YR 4/8) bottle (H. 26.8cm, external mouth Diam. 3.0cm, rim Th. 0.63cm, neck H. 2.4cm, handle L. 5.4cm, handle W. 1.7cm, handle Th. 1.3cm, max body W. 9.2cm, base Diam. 8.7cm). Seemingly originating as a form in mid-18th century Germany with a more ovoid body (Gaimster, 1997: 271, pl. 135), this unmarked vessel is similar to stamped examples of the latter half of the 19th century that held various fluids better suited to storage in dark, cool environments: mineral water, sarsparilla, wine, beer, vinegar cider, oil, molasses and even ink. While the origin of this jug is Rhenish, the bottle style is similar to stoneware jugs that bear foreign pottery or company marks, most frequently from Denmark, England, Germany and Sweden (pers. comm. Byron Dille, 2006; Tolson *et al.*, 2008: 181).

The sole Site BA02 Type 9 example appears to be similar to 12 bottles of Amsterdam ale packaged in tall, wheel-turned reddish-brown unglazed stoneware bottles recovered from the hull of the steamboat *Bertrand*, which sank in Portage La Force near De Soto Landing in Nebraska Territory in 1865. The cork stoppers sealing the *Bertrand* bottles are covered with thick embossed foil caps that extend onto the necks, suggesting the manner in which the Jacksonville 'Blue China' bottle was once sealed. The relief-stamped cap features the words 'WYNAND FOCKINK/AMSTERDAM.' The words 'AMSTERDAMSCHE' and 'AMSTERDAM' also appear on the bottles (Switzer, 1974: 13, 15).

A single unmarked individual jug of this type was also recovered from the 1865 wreck of the *Republic*, which carried a large cargo of stamped British salt-glazed stoneware master ink bottles as well as a few unmarked examples. An almost identical example was also recovered from the deep-sea Ormen Lange shipwreck off Norway, from which recovered coins post-date 1802 (Bryn *et al.*, 2007: 142, 159).

The third stoneware vessel recovered from the site, a Type 10 English jar with a so-called Bristol glaze (Fig. 88), is the original artifact recovered in a fisherman's net that ultimately led to the discovery of the shipwreck (this artifact resides with a fisherman, so dimensions are unavailable). It bears the incised stamp of 'Pearson & Co., Whittington Moor Potteries, near Chesterfield'. Chesterfield in Derbyshire was renowned for its many potteries and James Pearson established a pottery at Whittington Moor around 1810, which continued to operate well into the 20th century (Blacker, 1911: 312; Jewitt, 1883: 354).[17]

The jar's form of glaze was developed in Bristol, England, in 1835, and was adopted by American stoneware potters in the late 1800s (Burrison, 2007: 116), soon replacing much of the brown salt-glazed stoneware used for utilitarian wares (Greer, 1981: 210; Sweezy, 1994: 57, 94; Tolson *et al.*, 2008: 181). The 'Bristol' glaze also supplanted the earlier British lead-glazed wares when the poisonous nature of raw lead compounds was recognized as a health hazard in the growing pottery industry in the 19th century.

Fig. 88. A Type 10 British stoneware jar, Bristol-glazed (BC-03-00002-BE).

Bristol glaze historically used zinc oxide as a substitute for lead (Greer, 1981: 212; Rhodes, 2000: 206).

To create the two-toned effect, vessels were typically dipped vertically, with a creamy-white color more often present on the bottom half and a rich yellow ochre on the top. As a result, the Bristol glaze is sometimes called 'double glazed' (Jewitt, 1883: 94; 1878: 142). Bristol-glazed wares are most commonly reported in bottle forms from American archaeological sites, yet the glaze is also found on stoneware crocks, jars and other utilitarian items (Tolson *et al.*, 2008: 181).

All three stonewares on Site BA02 occur as single examples and were recovered from the northwest end of the wreck, which represents the stern where the ship's galley and crew's belongings would have been stowed. This depositional pattern, coupled with the small size of this assemblage, suggests use as domestic assemblage by the small crew of four to five people, rather than identification as remains of cargo.

10. Conclusion

The ceramics recovered from the Jacksonville 'Blue China' shipwreck present a unique opportunity to study the composition of a largely British-made ceramic cargo carried by an American coastal trader in the mid-19th century. As a single assemblage the ceramic evidence is indicative of a date between 1851 (the earliest date of the transfer-printed plate bearing the maker's mark 'STONE WARE / B H

& Co.') and 1860 at the latest, which is consistent with the evidence from other artifacts recovered from the site. Additional artifacts from the wreck point to its most plausible loss in 1854, perhaps during the great hurricane of 7-9 September, which inflicted the greatest damage to the vicinity of Charleston and Savannah in Georgia (cf. Gerth *et al.*, 2011: 206-10).

The diversity of ceramic wares present amongst the wreck's cargo accurately reflects the range of relatively cheap table, tea and toilet wares accessible to the North American market at a time when the British ceramic industry retained a cultural dominance over US pottery consumption and strove to meet the demands of a burgeoning working and middle class by developing popular styles intended to imitate more expensive wares. The success, in fact, of the British manufacturers and Staffordshire potters in particular "was largely due to the appeal of their products by the mass-consuming lower, lower-middle and middle class markets for whom price was as significant a factor as quality" (Barker, 2001: 81).

By the mid-19th century American trade was so important that many British factories were entirely devoted to this market, with larger manufacturers retaining outlets or relying on agents in the main American ports, while the smaller firms depended more heavily on the American dealers, whose role became increasingly more important (Barker, 2001: 82). With the growth in river travel, North American importers and wholesale merchants relied on an effective network for the distribution of these British wares from the Eastern Seaboard into the American frontier, which included the channeling of goods via land, canal, and ocean transportation, with coastal vessels typified by the Jacksonville 'Blue China' wreck playing an active role in this commerce.

Moreover, the cargo on Site BA02 provides direct archaeological evidence of mid-19th-century purchasing and manufacturing patterns, whereby ceramics were segregated into categories of tea ware, tableware and kitchenware. While some of these functional products were available both undecorated and transfer-printed, the decorative types were almost always limited to wares of a particular function. For example, shell-edged wares were tableware; painted wares were primarily teaware; and dipped wares were limited to hollow wares such as bowls, mugs, jugs and chamber pots. The existence of such cargos is merely hinted at in contemporary shipping records, but very few of these assemblages have survived intact, making the discovery of the Jacksonville 'Blue China' wreck off southeastern America especially significant.

The recovery of this ceramic assemblage, albeit merely representing a minor sample of the total cargo associated with the wreck (since it is impossible to determine how many artifacts were dragged off-site by trawlers), facilitates comparisons with the assemblage excavated from the steamboat *Arabia* dated to 1856, both of which provide insights into the composition of ceramic cargos of the period. Further, the archaeological data derived from the Site BA02, combined with primary historical documents such as shipping records, potters' invoices, and trade catalogs, have contributed to a greater understanding of the variety, availability and marketing of ceramics in North America, while at the same time highlighting the production and consumer trends that influenced and shaped the American household during the mid-1800s. The ultimate research value of the ceramic cargo from the Jacksonville 'Blue China' wreck – a single-phase closed archaeological deposit – is its rare primary data that reveal the specific types, status and relationships of products that circulated contemporaneously throughout much of mid-19th century America.

Acknowledgements

In addition to sincerely thanking Odyssey's directors, management and offshore survey and excavation teams, and archaeology research and conservation personnel as listed in *OME Papers* 19, the author is especially grateful to the specialist group of scholars and professionals who so generously offered their invaluable time and expertise to comment on the ceramic artifacts recovered from the Jacksonville 'Blue China' shipwreck: Gavin Ashworth (Gavin Ashworth Photography); David Barker (archaeological consultant and specialist in post-medieval and early-modern ceramics); Byron Dille' (bottle collector and historian); Robert Hunter (historical archaeologist, ceramic specialist and editor of *Ceramics in America*); Barbara Perry (former Curator of Decorative Arts, the Mint Museum of Art, Charlotte, NC); Jonathan Rickard (ceramic historian); Jane Spillman (Curator of Glass, Corning Museum of Glass, New York); Jill Yakubik (President of Earth Search, Inc., New Orleans).

A final respectful acknowledgement is offered in special memory of the former Odyssey conservator Herbert Bump, whose work provided Odyssey with the foundation upon which we have built our conservation program.

Notes

1. See: www.nps.gov/seac/archy79.htm and Ehrenhard, J.E. and Bullard, M.R., *History and Archeology at the Robert Stafford Plantation, Cumberland Island* (SEAC report, 1981).
2. See also *Diagnostics Artifacts in Maryland* (Maryland

Archaeological Conservation Lab): http://www.jefpat.org/diagnostic/PostColonial%20Ceramics/Shell%20Edged%20Wares/Shell%20Edged%20Wares%20Main.htm.
3. See *Diagnostic Cultural Materials*, C-2 to C- 3: http://www.ncdot.org/doh/preconstruct/pe/ohe/Archaeology/craven/DiagnosticCulturalMaterials.pdf.
4. See also: http://www.thepotteries.org/potters/adams.htm.
5. See also: http://virtual.parkland.edu/lstelle1/len/archguide/documents/arcguide.htm.
6. See also: http://www.thepotteries.org/types/ironstone.htm.
7. See also, *White Ironstone China Importers and Retailers Saint Louis Mo 1829-1860*: 4, 28, 71, http://members-only.whiteironstonechina.com/import.pdf.
8. See also, *White Ironstone China Importers and Retailers Saint Louis Mo 1829-1860*: 3, 70. Web link as in Note 7.
9. See also, *White Ironstone China Importers and Retailers Saint Louis Mo 1829-1860*: 51, 60. Web link as in Note 7.
10. See: http://www.thepotteries.org/types/transfer_ware.htm and http://www.antiqueweb.com/articles/antiquepottery.html.
11. See: http://www.thepotteries.org/patterns/asiatic_p.html.
12. See: http://www.thepotteries.org/patterns/willow.html.
13. See: http://www.asiaticpheasants.co.uk/Makers/Beech%20Partnerships.html.
14. See, Phil Schaltenbrand, *Western Pennsylvania's Stoneware Potters:* http://www.tfaoi.com/aa/7aa/7aa782.htm. The data in this section is also derived from an essay published in *Resource Library,* 28 June 2007, relating to an exhibit entitled *Made in Pennsylvania: A Folk Art Tradition* at the Westmoreland Museum of American Art from 23 June to 14 October 2007.
15. See: *New York State Museum 59th Annual Report* (1905: 26).
16. See Note 14.
17. See also: http://www.oldminer.co.uk/Chesterfield/Chesterfield_Potteries.htm.

Bibliography

Baldwin, C.K., *Great and Noble Jar. Traditional Stoneware of South Carolina* (University of Georgia Press, 1993).

Barber, E.A., *Salt-glazed Stoneware - Germany Flanders, England and the United States* (New York, 1907).

Bebb, L., *Welsh Pottery* (Aylesbury, 2004).

Barker, D., '"The Usual Classes of Useful Articles": Staffordshire Ceramics Reconsidered'. In R. Hunter (ed.), *Ceramics in America* (Chipstone Foundation, Milwaukee, 2001), 73-93.

Blacker, J.F., *Nineteenth-Century English Ceramic Art* (Boston, 1911).

Bryn, P., Jasinski, M.E. and Soreide, F., *Ormen Lange. Pipelines and Shipwrecks* (Oslo, 2007).

Burrison, J.A., *Roots of a Region* (University Press of Mississippi, 2007).

Campbell, G., (ed.), *The Grove Encyclopedia of Decorative Arts* (Oxford University Press, 2006).

Cantwell, A-M. and diZerega Wall, D., *Unearthing Gotham: The Archaeology of New York City* (Yale University Press, 2001).

Carpentier, D. and Rickard, J., 'Slip Decoration in the Age of Industrialization'. In R. Hunter (ed.), *Ceramics in America* (Chipstone Foundation, Milwaukee, 2001), 115-34.

Copeland, R., *Spode's Willow Pattern & Other Designs after the Chinese* (New York, 1980).

Coutts, H., *The Art of Ceramics: European Ceramic Design 1500-1830* (Yale University Press, 2001).

Cunningham Dobson, N. and Gerth, E., 'The Shipwreck of the SS *Republic* (1865). Experimental Deep-Sea Archaeology. Part 2: Cargo'. In G. Stemm and S. Kingsley, (eds.), *Oceans Odyssey. Deep-Sea Shipwrecks in the English Channel, Straits of Gibraltar & Atlantic Ocean* (Oxford, 2010), 25-68.

Cunningham Dobson, N., Gerth, E. and Winckler, L., 'The Shipwreck of the SS *Republic* (1865). Experimental Deep-Sea Archaeology. Part 1: Fieldwork & Site History'. In G. Stemm and S. Kingsley (eds.), *Oceans Odyssey. Deep-Sea Shipwrecks in the English Channel, Straits of Gibraltar & Atlantic Ocean* (Oxford, 2010), 1-24.

Delgado, J.P., *Gold Rush Port: The Maritime Archaeology of San Francisco's Waterfront* (University of California Press, 2009).

Draper, J., *Post-Medieval Pottery: 1650-1800* (Aylesbury, 2001).

Ewins, N., *"Supplying the Present Wants of Our Yankee Cousins..." Staffordshire Ceramics and the American Market 1775-1880* (Journal of Ceramic History 15, Stoke-on-Trent City Museum & Art Gallery, 1997).

Ford, B., Borgens, A., Bryant, W., Marshall, D., Hitchcock, P., Arias, C. and Hamilton, D., *Archaeological Excavation of the Mardi Gras Shipwreck (16GM01), Gulf of Mexico Continental Slope* (US Department of the Interior, Minerals Management Service, Gulf of Mexico OCS Region, New Orleans, LA. OCS Report MMS, 2008).

Ford, B., Borgens, A. and Hitchcock, P., 'The 'Mardi Gras' Shipwreck: Results of a Deep-Water Excavation, Gulf of Mexico, USA', *International Journal of Nautical Archaeology* 39.1 (2010), 76-98.

Gaimster, D., *German Stoneware 1200-1900. Archaeology and Cultural History* (London, 1997).

Gerth, E., Cunningham Dobson, N. and Kingsley, S., 'The Jacksonville 'Blue China' Shipwreck (Site BA02): An American Coastal Schooner off Florida'. In G. Stemm and S. Kingsley (eds.), *Oceans Odyssey 2. Underwater Heritage Management & Deep-Sea Shipwrecks in the English Channel & Atlantic Ocean* (Oxford, 2011), 143-220.

Greer, G., *American Stonewares: the Art and Craft of Utilitarian Potters* (Atglen, 1981).

Godden, G.A., *Godden's Guide to Ironstone, Stone & Granite Wares* (Woodbridge, 1999).

Hawley, D., *Treasures of the Steamboat Arabia* (Kansas, 1995).

Hawley, G., *Treasure in a Cornfield* (Kansas, 1998).

Hume, I.N., *Pottery and Porcelain in Colonial Williamsburg's Archaeological Collections* (Colonial Williamsburg Foundation, 1969).

Hunter, R.R. and Miller, G.L., 'English Shell-Edged Earthenware', *The Magazine Antiques* 145.3 (1994), 432-43.

Hunter, R. and Miller, G., 'Suitable for Framing: Decorated Shell-Edge Earthenware', *Early American Life* (August 2009), 8-19.

Jervis, W. P., *A Pottery Primer* (New York, 1911).

Jewitt, L., *The Ceramic Art of Great Britain. Volume 1* (London, 1878).

Jewitt, L., *The Ceramic Art of Great Britain. Volume 2* (London, 1883).

Kwas, M.L., *Digging for History at Old Washington* (University of Arkansas Press, 2009).

Layton, T. N., *The Voyage of the Frolic. New England Merchants and the Opium Trade* (Stanford University Press, 1997).

Lees, W.B. and Majewski, T., 'Ceramic Choices West of the Mississippi: Considering Factors of Supply and Ethnicity'. In *Proceedings of the 1993 Conference on Historical and Underwater Archaeology, Kansas City, Missouri*: http://uwf.edu/wlees/CERAMICS.pdf.

Martin, A.S., 'Magical, Mythical, Practical and Sublime: the Meanings and Use of Ceramics in America.' In R. Hunter (ed.), *Ceramics in America* (Chipstone Foundation, Milwaukee, 2001) 29-46.

McAllister, L.S., *Collector's Guide to Feather Edge Ware* (Paducah, 2001).

Meteyard, E., *The Wedgwood Handbook. A Manual for Collectors* (London, 1875).

Miller, G.L., 'A Revised Set of CC Index Values for Classification and Economic Scaling of English Ceramics from 1787 to 1880', *Historical Archaeology* 25.1 (1991), 1-25.

Miller, G., 'Classification and Economic Scaling of Nineteenth-century Ceramics'. In M. Beaudry (ed.), *Documentary Archaeology in the New World* (University of Cambridge, 1988), 172-83.

Miller, G.L. and Earls, A.C., 'War and Pots: the Impact of Economics and Politics on Ceramic Consumption Patterns'. In R. Hunter (ed.), *Ceramics in America* (Chipstone Foundation, Milwaukee, 2008), 67-108.

Mudge, J.M., *Chinese Export Porcelain for the American Trade: 1785-1835* (Associated University Presses, Inc., London, 1981).

New York State Museum 59th Annual Report. Volume I. Report of the Director, 1905 (New York State Education Department, 1905).

Orser, C.E., *Encyclopedia of Historical Archaeology* (New York, 2002).

Reinders, R.C., *The End of an Era. New Orleans, 1850-1860* (Gretna, 1998).

Reports of the United States Commissioners to the Paris Universal Exposition, 1878. Volume III (Government Printing Office, Washington, 1880).

Rhodes, D., *Clay and Glazes for the Potter* (Iola, 2000).

Rickard, J., *Mocha and Related Dipped Wares, 1770-1939* (University Press of New England, 2006a).

Rickard, J., *Blue China Ceramics* (Unpublished Report, July 2006b).

Samford, P.M. 'Response to a Market: Dating English Underglaze Transfer-Printed Wares'. In D.R. Brauner (ed.), *Approaches to Material Culture Research for Historical Archaeologists* (Society for Historical Archaeology, 2000), 56-85.

Shaw, S., *History of the Staffordshire Potteries and the Rise and Process of the Manufacture of Pottery and Porcelain - With Preferences to Genuine Specimens and Notices of Eminent Potters* (London, 1900).

Skerry, J.E. and Hood, S.F., *Salt-glazed Stoneware in Early America* (Colonial Williamsburg Foundation, University Press of New England, 2009).

Steen, C., 'Industrial Pottery in the Old Edgefield District'. In R. Hunter (ed.), *Ceramics in America* (Chipstone Foundation, Milwaukee, 2001), 226-29.

Sweezy, N., *Raised in Clay: the Southern Pottery Tradition* (University of North Carolina Press, 1994).

Swift, J.W., Hodgkinson, P. and Woodhouse, S.W., 'The Voyage of the Empress of China', *Pennsylvania Magazine of History and Biography* 63.1 (1939), 24-36.

Switzer, R.R., *The Betrand Bottles. A Study of 19th-century Glass and Ceramic Containers* (National Park Service U.S. Department of the Interior, Washington, 1974).

Tolson, H., Gerth, E. and Cunningham Dobson, N., 'Ceramics from the "Blue China" Wreck'. In R. Hunter (ed.), *Ceramics in America* (Chipstone Foundation, Milwaukee, 2008), 162-83.

Turner, W., (ed.), *William Adams, an Old English Potter* (London, 1904).

Wake, J., *Kleinwort Benson. The History of Two Families in Banking* (Oxford University Press, 1997).

Weatherill, L., *The Pottery Trade and North Staffordshire, 1660-1760* (Manchester University Press, 1971).

Wedgwood, J.C., *Staffordshire Pottery and its History* (New York, 1913).

White, R., Sergejeff, N., Lieberknecht, W. and Hunter, R., *A Historical Account and Archaeological Analysis of the Eagle Tavern City of Trenton Mercer County, New Jersey* (Trenton Historical Society. New Jersey Historical Commission, 2005).

Yong, C., *Chinese San Francisco: 1850-1943* (Stanford University Press, 2000).

The Jacksonville 'Blue China' Shipwreck (Site BA02): Clay Tobacco Pipes

J. Byron Sudbury
J.S. Enterprises, Ponca City, Oklahoma, USA
(jschemistry@hotmail.com)

Ellen Gerth
Odyssey Marine Exploration, Tampa, USA

A rescue excavation conducted by Odyssey Marine Exploration in 2005 on the deep-sea Jacksonville 'Blue China' shipwreck (Site BA02) recorded 63 intact and fragmentary clay tobacco pipes of two major types. This New York based East Coast schooner was apparently transporting a minor consignment of pipes to a Southern port when it was lost in the mid-19th century, possibly September 1854.

Visual analysis of a sample of 16 tobacco pipes recovered, featuring a ribbed bowl (Type 1) and the letters 'TD' embossed on an otherwise undecorated bowl (Type 2), combined with a study of mid-19th century clay pipe production across Europe and America, has not identified specific manufacturing origins. While some of the examples are most characteristic of English and German manufacture, Scottish and American provenances cannot be excluded. The Site BA02 cargo of tobacco pipes is the first discovered on the wreck of a schooner off America and is one of the larger pipe assemblages found at sea off the USA. The wreck's relatively well-established date helps secure the chronology of these common styles of an important artifact within both American and European archaeological contexts.

1. Introduction

Amongst a primary cargo of British ceramics and American glass bottles, window panes and other glassware, the Jacksonville 'Blue China' shipwreck discovered by Odyssey Marine Exploration at a depth of 370m, 70 nautical miles off Jacksonville, Florida, contained a comparatively small consignment of clay tobacco pipes, 63 examples of which were recorded across the site. The assemblage is clearly cargo and was scattered across the wreck in a wide zone extending from the northernmost flank in Area E, through Areas B, F and G (Fig. 1).

Two main clusters occur to the north. Area B contains 39 pipes (33 within the confined limits of Area B1, 3.0 x 2.2m), which are associated with deposits of dark glass liquor/spirits bottles (Fig. 2). An additional 11 pipes were present in Area E: six in Area E3 to the southwest of storage keg K7 and another six were scattered around the north and east ends of keg K5 (Figs. 3-6). A seventh example concreted to the upper surface of keg K6 may reflect the original form of the pipes' stowage within wooden kegs reinforced with iron hoops (Fig. 7). Finally, a cluster of eight pipes along the keel line at the center of Area G may denote the presence of a further decomposed container of these wares. In total, this pattern of deposition perhaps points towards the presence of a relatively minor consignment of cargo within two or three batches restricted to the stern half of the ship.

Recovery of 16 examples from this assemblage has led to the identification of two different pipe styles. The 13 Type 1 ribbed examples (also referred to as fluted or cockled) measure 18.2-21.4cm in length and feature 16 4.4cm-long raised vertical lines (excluding the pipe seam) set 0.2cm apart that encircle the entire pipe bowl, beginning at the stem bowl juncture and rising to within a few millimeters just below the pipe rim (Figs. 9, 11-23). The three Type 2 pipes are characterized by the attribute of the letters 'TD' (H. 0.4-0.6cm and W. 0.5-0.6cm) embossed in relief on the back of the pipe bowl facing the smoker and set on either side of the mold seam; the bowls are otherwise undecorated (Figs. 10, 24-28). Of these three examples, only one is nearly intact, measuring 14cm in length. All of the pipes visible on the wreck site photomosaic are of Type 1, which seems to have been the predominant form being shipped.

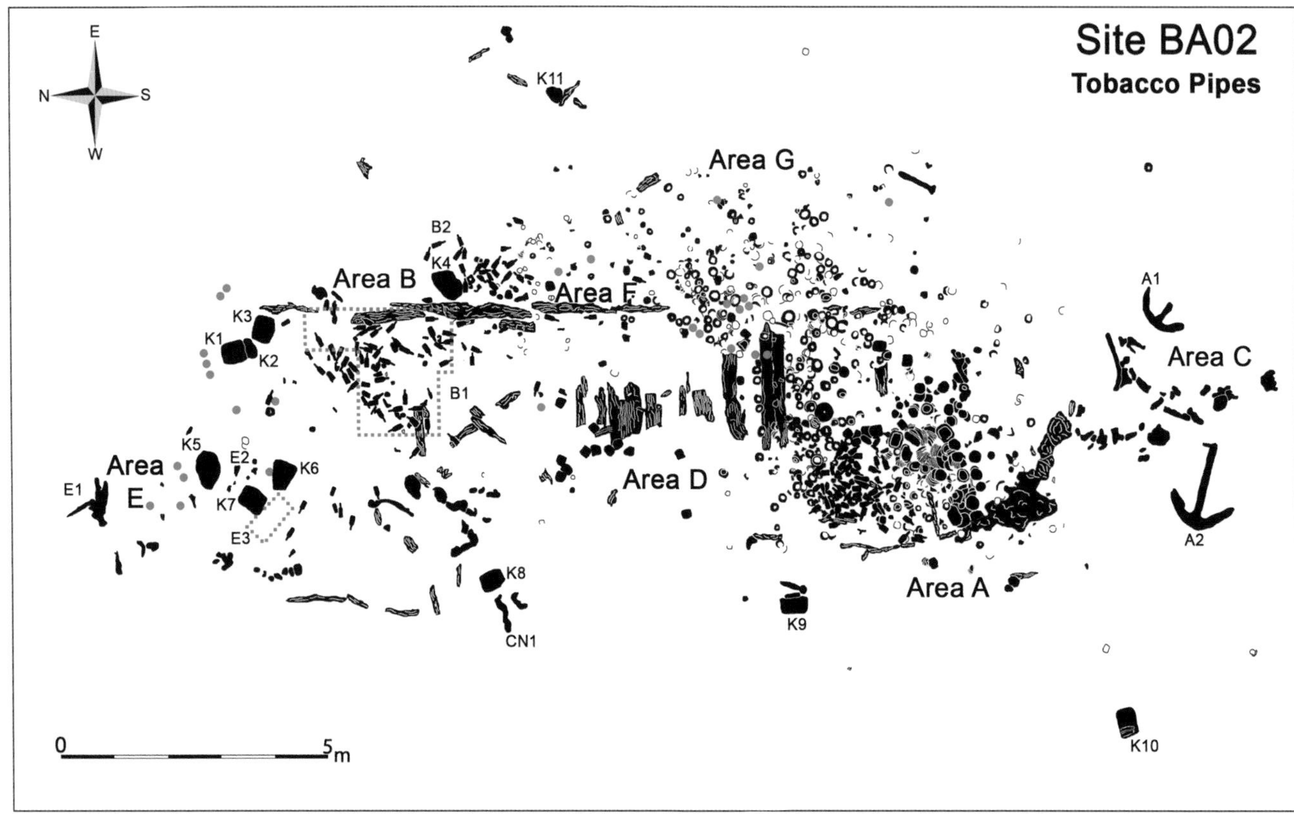

Fig. 1. The distribution of tobacco pipes on the Jacksonville 'Blue China' shipwreck (Site BA02).

All of these white clay pipes were manufactured as single pieces in two-part molds. Slight variations in the ribbing within the Type 1 assemblage indicate that production of the assemblage was executed using different pipe molds of identical style. The 'TD' pipe letter detail also displays minor discrepancies that similarly reflect manufacture using different molds. Thus, the variation within both forms suggests production by one of the larger 19th-century factories using multiple molds of one style to fill an order. Both pipe styles feature peg spurs at the juncture of the bottom of the bowl and stem. Unlike pointed spurs, the peg variant has a flat end, although the spurs are slightly tapered.

The pipes recovered from Site BA02 vary in levels of preservation from largely intact bowls and stems to fragmentary examples consisting of just a surviving bowl (sometimes broken) with very little of the original stem extant. Several of the pipes are heavily stained by what appears to be iron oxide. This may be due to alterations of the clay from the saltwater environment or perhaps caused by contamination from adjacent artifacts or ship structures. None of the pipes display any evidence of having been smoked in the form of use-wear marks, including teeth impressions on pipe stems, evidence of reworking of the pipe bowls or charring, thus supporting the conclusion that the assemblage comprised ship's cargo.

2. An Overview of Mid-19th Century Pipe Production

Pipe making technology remained substantially unchanged from the 17th century onwards. A sausage or tadpole-shaped piece of clay was rolled to the right length and thickness and a wire was then inserted the length of the stem to form the bore. The clay with inserted wire was then placed in an open two- or three-part metal mold, which when closed formed the final shape. A plunger was used to make the bowl cavity and the wire to connect the stem bore to the bowl. Once removed from the mold, the pipe was cleaned and stamps for additional decoration or maker's marks could be applied.

By the mid-19th century, most decoration was imparted by the mold, so that a new mold was required for each style of pipe. Some pipe makers did equip their molds with changeable inserts so that individual names or motifs could be molded onto a pipe upon request. Once removed from the molds, the pipes were dried, placed in a kiln, fired and after cooling packed in shipping containers cushioned with straw or wood shavings for transport. A skilled pipe maker working by hand could produce about 500 long-stemmed pipes a day. Production could be increased by breaking down the process into separate tasks or by using steam-driven machines for steps in the process (Gojak and Stuart, 1999: 38). Use of barrels for shipping pipes was documented *c.* 1830 (Stradling and Stradling, 2001: 183), whereas by 1864 wooden boxes were in use (Pfeiffer, 2006: 101-2, 106-7).

3. The Site BA02 Pipe Typology

None of the Site BA02 pipes incorporate any company names, maker's initials or symbols on the pipe bowls or stems, an exclusion which the results of land-based excavation indicates was not uncommon in the mid-19th century. Nonetheless, this complicates attempts to identify the original pipe makers (Brassey, 1991: 27). To make matters more obscure, literally hundreds of 19th-century pipe manufacturers existed in a number of countries using thousands of molds, many of which were virtually identical because the craftsmen copied the most popular styles in production. A specific example of this phenomenon are the 'TD'-embossed pipes on the Jacksonville 'Blue China' shipwreck, which are not indicative of an individual maker or a particular company, but instead represent a 'trademark' used by many different pipe makers of the era (Walker, 1966: 86).

Artifact Reg. No. & Type	Pipe L. (cm)	Bowl H. (cm) **	Max Bowl W. (cm) ***	External Mouth Dia. (cm)	Spur W. (cm)	Th. at Spur/Stem Junction (cm)
BC-05-00010-CP (Type 1) *	13.4 (broken)	4.35	2.78 x 2.48	2.67 x 2.47	0.68 x 0.52	0.89
BC-05-00011-CP (Type 1)	18.2 (intact)	4.21	------	2.67	0.65 x 0.49	0.98
BC-05-00012-CP (Type 1) *	10.8 (broken)	4.28	2.86 x 2.44	2.68	0.62 x 0.46	0.93
BC-05-00013-CP (Type 1) *	6.7 (broken)	4.19	2.89 x 2.44	2.65 x 2.42	0.65 x 0.43	0.97
BC-05-00014-CP (Type 1) *	13.0 (broken)	4.21	2.73 x 2.36	2.48	0.62 x 0.46	0.94
BC-05-00015-CP (Type 1) *	6.2 (broken)	4.27	2.72 x 2.47	2.62 x 2.41	0.61 x 0.45	0.98
BC-05-00016-CP (Type 2)	14.0 (broken)	3.70	2.50	2.10	0.50	0.90
BC-05-00220-CP (Type 1) *	21.4 (intact)	4.30	2.49 x 2.81	2.68 x 2.48	0.66 x 0.51	0.86
BC-05-00221-CP (Type 1) *	19.6 (broken)	4.28	2.85 x 2.82	2.68 x 2.54	0.62 x 0.52	0.96
BC-05-00222-CP (Type 1)	20.4 (intact)	4.35	2.90	2.30	0.60	0.80
BC-05-00223-CP (Type 1)	19.1 (intact)	4.30	2.80	2.30	0.60	0.80
BC-05-00224-CP (Type 1) *	10.5 (broken)	4.36	2.84 x 2.84	2.77 x 2.50	0.68 x 0.52	0.89
BC-05-00225-CP (Type 2)	11.7 (broken)	4.1	2.20	2.00	0.50	0.90
BC-05-00226-CP (Type 1)	5.2 (broken)	4.37	2.76 x 2.51	2.66 x 2.41	0.65 x 0.54	0.97
BC-05-00227-CP (Type 2) *	10.5 (broken)	3.95	2.35 x 2.19	2.29	0.50 x 0.44	0.98
BC-05-00228-CP (Type 1)	11.3 (broken)	4.32	2.58 x 2.82	2.77 x 2.50	0.69 x 0.52	0.88

* Spur displays a prominent elevated clay mold seam line on proximal edge.

** Measured from directly in front of spur.

*** Measured at mid height up the bowl.

Table 1. Relative dimensions of Type 1 and Type 2 tobacco pipes from Site BA02.

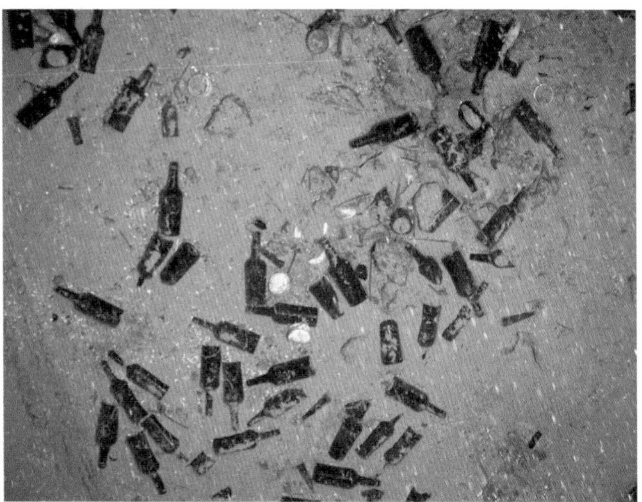

Fig. 2. A cluster of ribbed Type 1 tobacco pipes in situ *in Area B1 in association with black glass liquor/spirits bottles.*

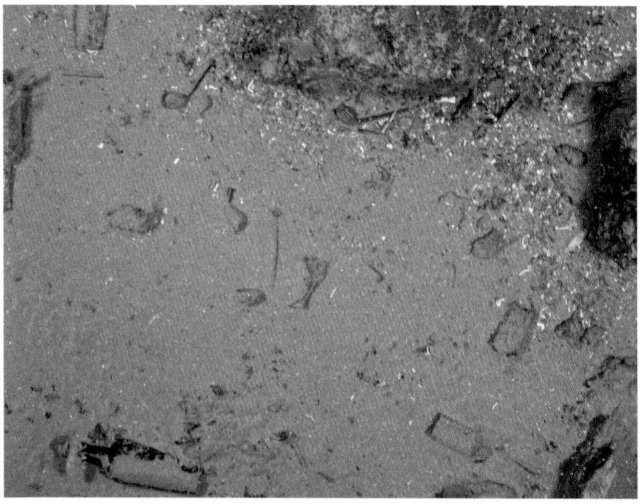

Figs. 3-4. Type 1 tobacco pipes in Area E3 to the southwest of transport keg K7.

Fig. 5. Type 1 tobacco pipes on the eastern flank of Area E with the outline of the keel running north/south and a shattered transport keg at left.

Clay pipe fragments are extremely durable, survive in vast quantities on terrestrial sites and have been discovered underwater as shipwrecked cargos and domestic assemblages, while individual broken examples were deliberately thrown into harbors at the end of their useful lives. The clay tobacco pipe has become a very valuable archaeological clue for dating and interpreting historical sites. In most cases, pipes were manufactured, imported, smoked and discarded within a relatively short period of time, often less than two years. This factor, combined with a recognizable evolutionary change in the pipe bowl from before the start of the 17th century into the 19th century, permits individual styles to be identified and traced to specific periods of production (Higgins, 1995: 47, 50; Hume, 1974: 296).

Research, including analysis of dimensions, suggests that the two styles of tobacco pipe on the Jacksonville 'Blue China' wreck are indicative of examples produced between the years 1840 and 1860. The probable date of September 1854 for the loss of the schooner wrecked at Site BA02, based on a combination of artifactual and historical evidence (Gerth *et al.*, 2011), contributes to the fine-tuning of these pipe types' chronology.

A representative sample of four pipes from the Jacksonville 'Blue China' pipe cargo, which typify the assemblage as a whole, was examined in detail: two ribbed examples (BC-05-00010 and BC-05-00224; Figs. 16-17) and two 'TD'-embossed variants (BC-05-00225 and BC-05-00227; Figs. 25-26). This analysis confirmed that each of the four pipes was produced in a different two-part mold. The pipes appear to be lightly varnished, although glazing or varnishing is quite uncommon in this period. All four pipes are made of white clay, which is also apparently the case for the other 12 pipes recovered from the wreck.

The ribbed pipes BC-05-00010 and BC-05-00224 are

distinct from each other. Even though both examples are essentially typologically comparable, they were produced in two different molds, albeit most probably in the same workshop. Use of multiple molds in a single factory to fulfil orders for popular styles was not uncommon for the larger pipe manufacturers. A number of the other ribbed pipes, as well as the 'TD' examples, also feature slight variations and measurement discrepancies suggestive of production using different molds (Table 1).

Based on these minor differences in dimensions, many of the 16 pipes seem to be attributable to different molds (Table 1). Thus, the heights of the Type 1 ribbed pipe bowls vary from 4.19-4.37cm and their maximum bowl widths range from 2.49-2.89 x 2.36-2.84cm. The external diameter of the Type 1 mouths display an amplitude of 2.62-2.77 x 2.30-2.54cm; their spur widths range from 0.61 x 0.45cm to 0.69 x 0.52cm wide, while the clay thickness at the spur/stem junction varies from 0.80-0.98cm.

The three 'TD'-embossed Type 2 tobacco pipes display comparable minor discrepancies in their dimensions. Their bowl heights each measure 3.7cm, 3.95cm and 4.1cm, while their maximum bowl widths are 2.2cm, 2.5cm and 2.35 x 2.19cm. The external diameters of the mouths range from 2.0cm to 2.1cm and 2.29, while spur widths are all 0.5cm wide and the thickness of the clay at the spur/stem junction is also close at 0.90cm for two pipes and 0.98cm for the third (Table 1).

Analysis suggests that three of the examined pipes (BC-05-00224, BC-05-00010 and BC-05-00225), two ribbed and one 'TD'-embossed respectively, appear to be stylistically similar in production technology. While two of the three examples are stylistically different, in terms of manufacture they incorporate common overall traits evidenced in the cutting stroke used to trim the rim of the pipe bowl.

In terms of origins, the flat trimmed rim of pipe bowl BC-05-00227 suggests that this 'TD'-embossed Type 2 pipe appears to be British-made and crafted of white ball clay, deposits of which are indigenous to Dorset and Devonshire in southwest England. Ball clay was largely restricted to use in England, which was a major exporter of products made from this clay in the mid-19th century. Although kaolin clay was available in Britain, with notable sources near Glasgow in Scotland, it was typically reserved for better quality products, while ball clay was more commonly used in pipe manufacture (Sudbury, 1980b: 27).

The origins of pipes BC-05-00224, BC-05-00010 and BC-05-00225 remain unverified. They may be exports from the European continent, possibly of Dutch or more likely German manufacture, the latter of whose products were the predominant pipe imported into the United States

Fig. 6. A Type 1 tobacco pipe in Area E2 in situ in association with a glass salt cellar.

Fig. 7. The bowl of a Type 1 tobacco pipe concreted to the top edge of transport keg K6, perhaps reflecting the original stowage method of these wares within such containers.

Fig. 8. A Type 1 tobacco pipe being recovered by the ROV Zeus' limpet suction device from Area E3.

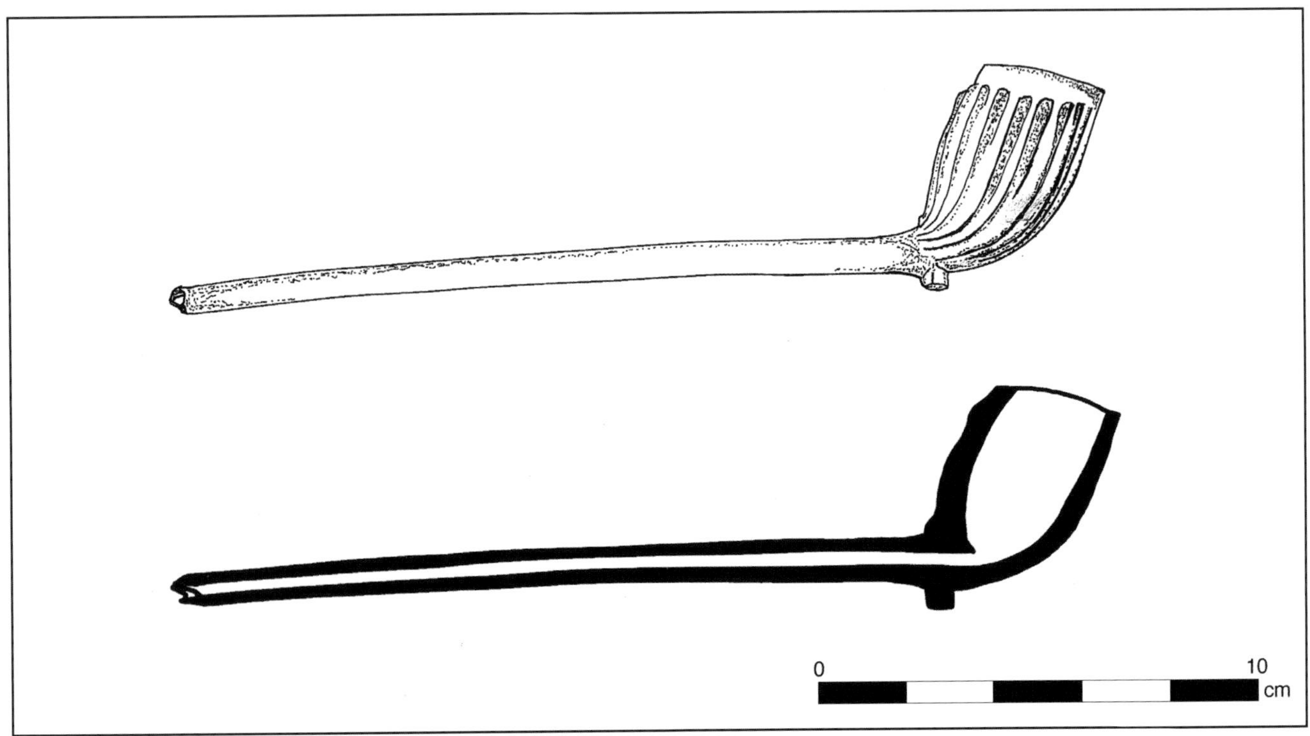

Fig. 9. Drawing of Type 1 ribbed tobacco pipe BC-05-00221-CP (L. 19.6cm). Drawing: Chad Morris, Odyssey Marine Exploration.

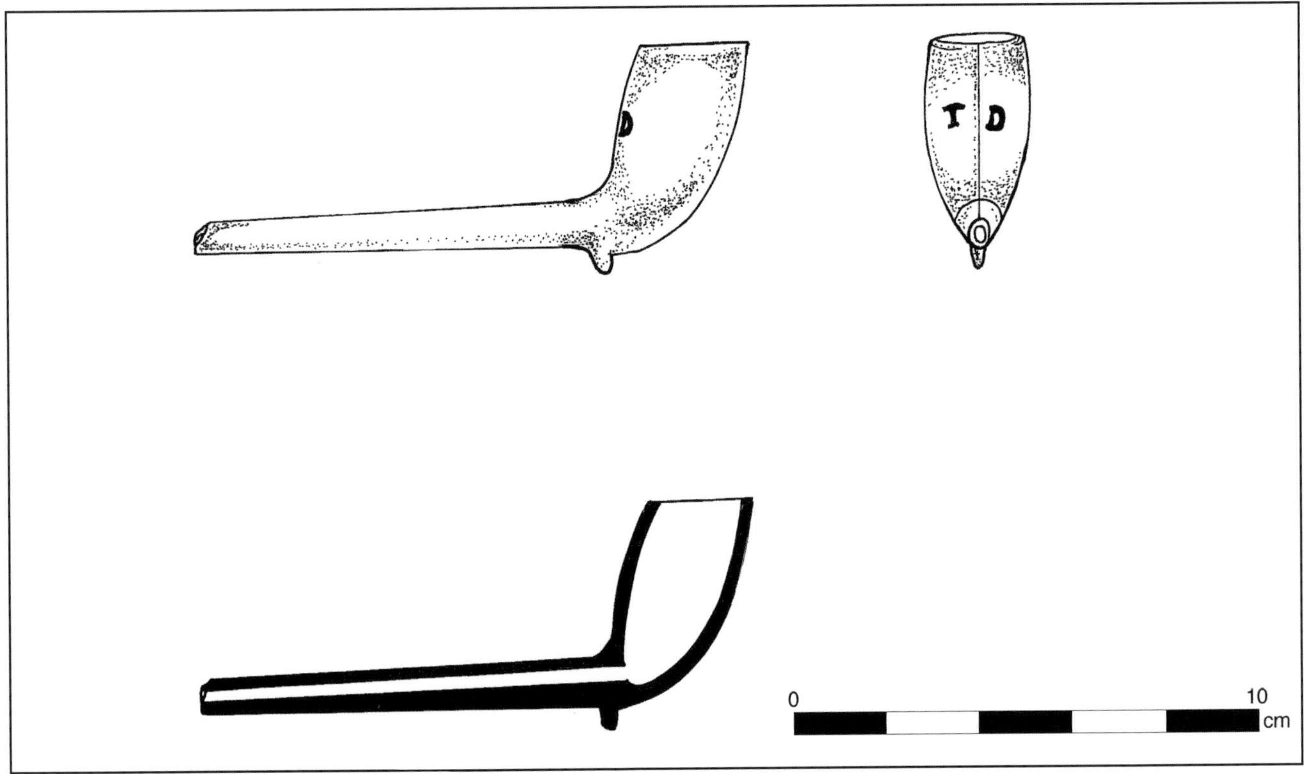

Fig. 10. Drawing of Type 2 'TD'-embossed tobacco pipe BC-05-00225-CP (L. 11.7cm). Drawing: Chad Morris, Odyssey Marine Exploration.

for several decades following 1845. European tobacco pipes were largely manufactured from kaolin clay because ball clay deposits were not present on the continent. Like ball clay, kaolin clay (also called china or porcelain clay) was white or near-white and caused little shrinkage when fired.[1] Potentially, but less likely, some of the Site BA02 tobacco pipes may have been produced in North America, either Canada or America. Increased American pipe manufacture was a feature of the post-1850 era and was possibly the result of improved efficiencies in manufacturing and distribution, as well as of new protective tariffs (Gartley, 2009: 215-16; Sudbury, 2009: 106-7).

Both Site BA02 pipe Types 1 and 2 incorporate design elements similar to styles excavated at the Fort Union Trading Post on the Upper Missouri River in North Dakota (see Section 10 below). The post's long occupation from 1829-67, and extensive trade activity, resulted in the deposition of an extensive and varied pipe assemblage attributed largely to suppliers in Germany, England and the United States. The Jacksonville 'Blue China' wreck examples closely resemble Fort Union's white clay pipes attributed to German manufacture, which prior to the study of the Fort Union Trading Post collection were generally identified as English or possibly American products (Sudbury, 2009: 104, 168). The problems of assigning provenances to pipes found in America are discussed in greater detail in Section 8.

Assessment of the origins of the Site BA02 tobacco pipes rests on typological attributes and ultimately on the nature of the clay fabric. Potters often exploited multiple clay sources that resulted in conspicuously different pipe finishes, but relying on fired ceramic clay colors to identify provenance is a problematic science. Divergences in clay color can occur during firing via exposure to thermal and atmospheric differences caused by the wares' location in the kiln and variations in the interior atmosphere. Thus, the visual appearance of red or yellow-fired clays is often not a manifestation of the clay source exploited, but rather caused by the state of oxidation of the iron within the clay (the oxidizing or reducing atmosphere). The presence of darker colors in pipe fabrics may thus not reliably reflect origins, but may be explained as the effects of overheating or reactions of or between different minerals.

The red stain on a number of the Site BA02 pipes – the ribbed versions, in particular – may be reactions induced by proximity to adjacent materials, notably ferrous materials, or by changes in levels of oxidation within the submerged anaerobic environment. The ribbed Site BA02 clay pipes notably display greater evidence of extensive red staining than the 'TD'-embossed types. This may be a direct consequence of mineral deposits in the clay, perhaps was the result of firing in the kiln or was caused by a combination of both of these factors, possibly further influenced by the sea floor environment and contamination from nearby artifacts.

4. 'TD'-Embossed Pipes: Historical Background

According to some historical accounts, white clay pipes incorporating the initials 'TD' on the bowl originate with the London pipe maker Thomas Dormer, who manufactured pipes between the mid-1750s and about 1780 along with his sons. The 'TD' insignia has also been credited to two other British mid-to-late 18th-century pipe makers, Thomas Duggan of London and Thomas Dennis of Bristol, thus making a definitive attribution inconclusive. In addition, an origin for the 'TD' pipes in the early 1700s has been argued (Sudbury, 1980b: 34).

An even earlier timeframe is provided by a clay pipe assemblage excavated from London's Bear Wharf at Bankside, London, which dates from 1660-80, where a number of the pipes are stamped on the base of the heel with the letters 'TD' in a heart-shaped frame above a Tudor rose. Towards the latter part of the 16th century, clay tobacco pipes had become an important part of everyday London life and many city pipe makers marked their products with their personal initials or symbols, very likely the case for the Bear Wharf examples.[2]

From about the time of the American Revolution, 'TD' pipes became synonymous with a style commonly found in North America. The design became so popular that by the early 19th century numerous pipe manufacturers had copied or modified the earlier form, so that a multitude of variations were in circulation. For example, at least 37 different types of 'TD' pipes were listed as in production amongst a number of firms operating out of Glasgow, Scotland, alone as late as 1900 (Cotter *et al.*, 1993: 422; Walker, 1996: 86, 88). Exported wares possibly made by both Duggan, Dennis and/or Dormer may have been imported through Hudson Bay and other large provincial ports and are found in numerous Colonial contexts, including urban and rural sites in Virginia, Maryland, Pennsylvania and New York, as well as in Western contexts (Hardesty, 1997: 106; Pfeiffer, 2006: 12).[3]

Eventually 'TD' pipes came to stand for a generic style of pipe and not for the actual pipe maker. The initials themselves became a 'trademark' used by numerous pipe makers to denote a certain style of pipe and not to publicize a manufacturer possessing the actual 'TD' initials (Cotter *et al.*, 1993: 422; Walker, 1996: 86). Today they represent a major recognizable decorative motif. Thousands of

Fig. 11. Type 1 ribbed tobacco pipe BC-05-00220-CP, L. 21.4cm.
Photos in Figs. 11-28 by Alan Bosel, Odyssey Marine Exploration.

Fig. 12. Type 1 ribbed tobacco pipe BC-05-00222-CP, L. 20.4cm.

Fig. 13. Type 1 ribbed tobacco pipe BC-05-00221-CP, L. 19.6cm.

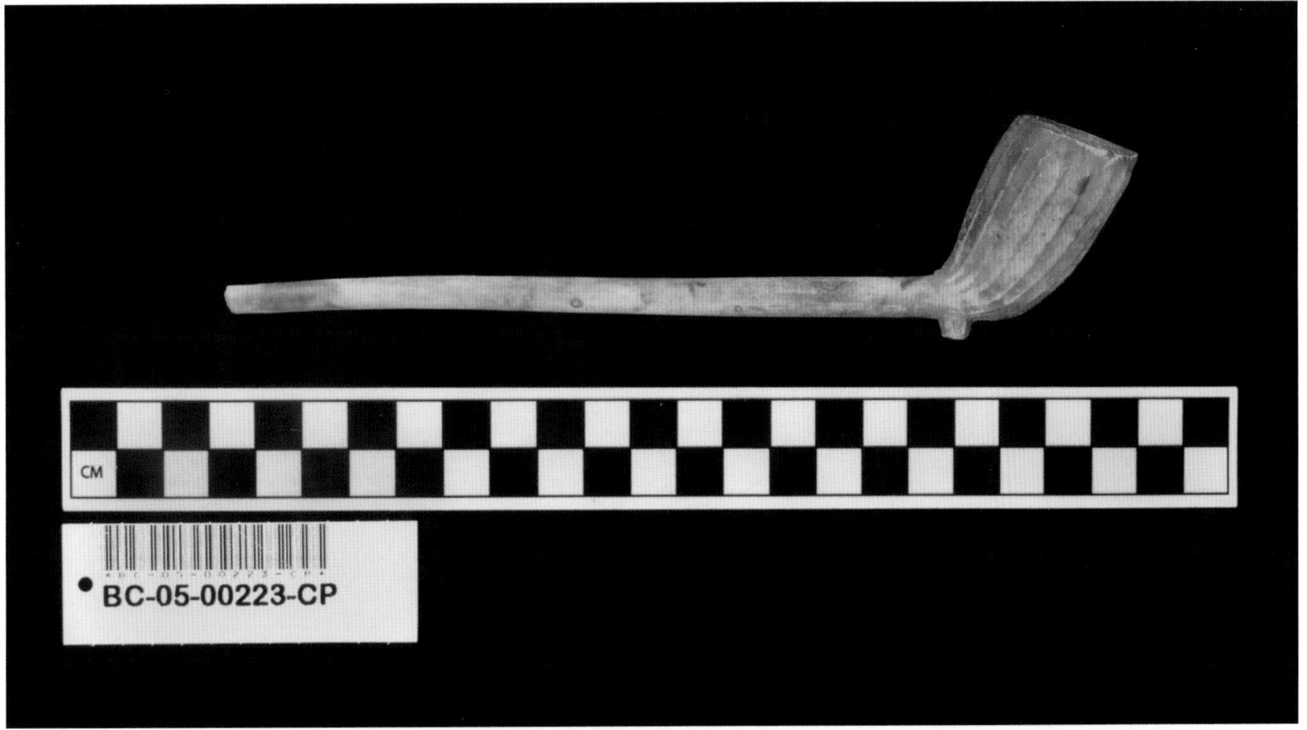

Fig. 14. Type 1 ribbed tobacco pipe BC-05-00223-CP, L.19.1cm.

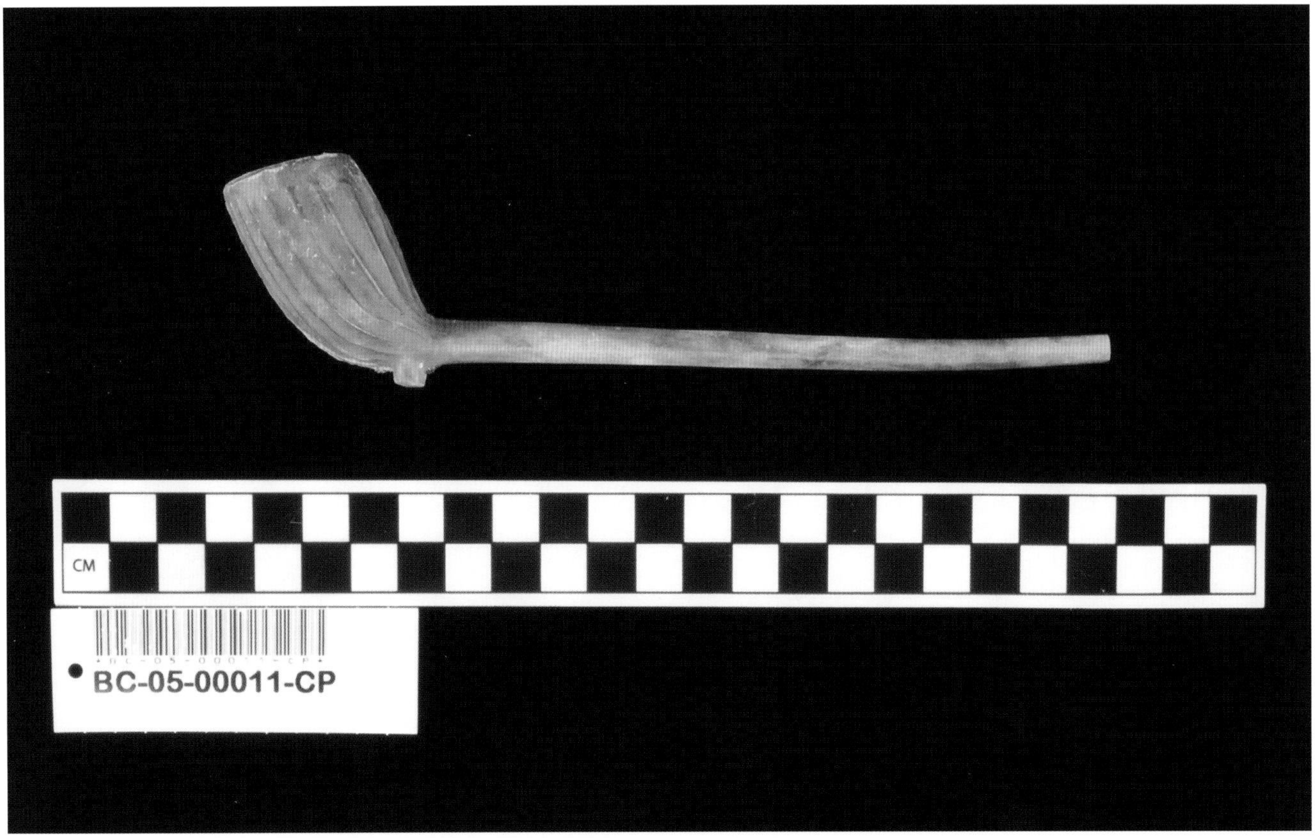

Fig. 15. Type 1 ribbed tobacco pipe BC-05-00011-CP, L. 18.2cm.

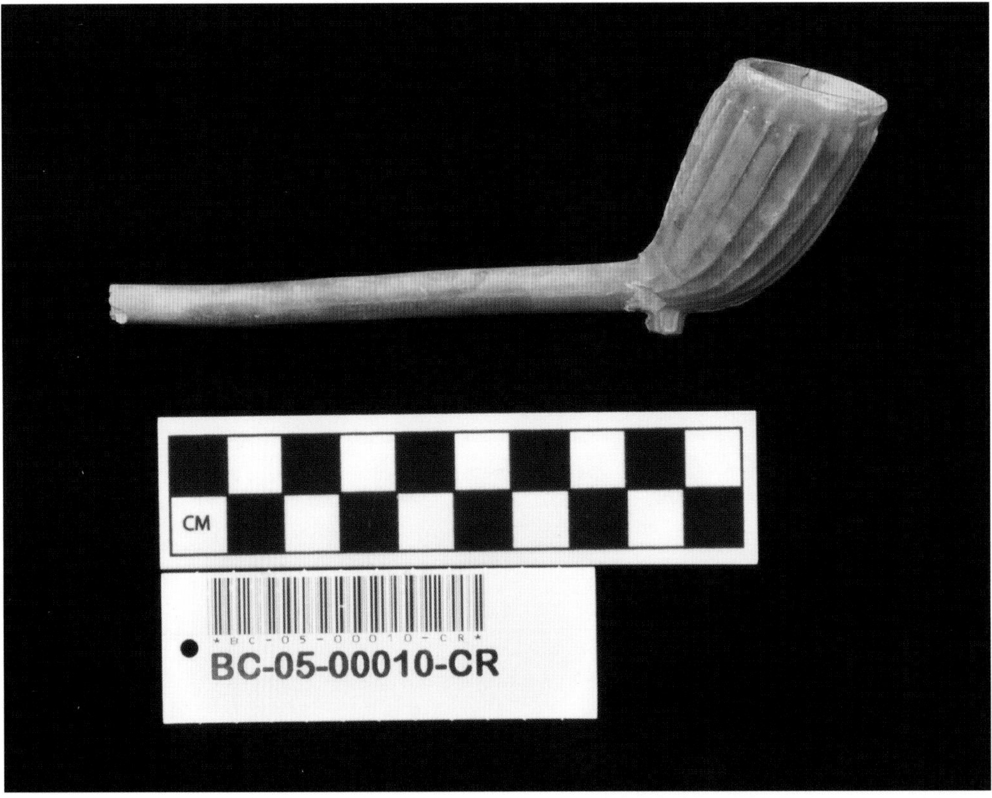

Fig. 16. Type 1 ribbed tobacco pipe BC-05-00010-CP, L. 13.4cm.

examples have been excavated from archaeological contexts across the United States dating from the mid-18th century into the early 20th century.

5. English White Ball Pipe Clay

Of Site BA02's four white clay pipes analyzed in detail, at least one is clearly of British production and was thus very likely manufactured from the white ball clay favored by pipe makers from at least the early 17th century until the cessation of the industry in the 20th century. Production close to the coast was favored due to extensive clay deposits present in Dorset and Devonshire in southwest England, followed by subsequent distribution around the coast in two main networks: one supplying the west and the other the south and east. Inland, other sources of clay were utilized, but probably only for intra-regional pipe use (Vince and Peacey, 2006: 17).

White ball clay had been exploited in Britain since the Roman period for pottery production. However, the introduction of tobacco into England in the 16th century, and the requirement for suitable clay for pipe manufacture, was a major catalyst for the start of the ball clay trade in the United Kingdom.[4] Consequently, with relatively few deposits available worldwide British ball clays became so highly-prized for tobacco pipes, and were judged to be so valuable, that exports to foreign countries were prohibited in 1662 by an Act of Parliament introduced under King Charles II. The Act was not repealed until nearly 200 years later in 1853, which triggered a thriving British ball clay export trade (Bristow *et al.*, 2002: 26).[5]

Ball clay was not discovered in the United States until the later 19th century and only then in the East, Midwest and South. A pit of ball clay was opened in Jefferson County, Missouri, in 1880, which became an important source of material for the East Liverpool potters of Ohio and other potting centers. Later developments in 1890 saw the exploitation of ball clay deposits in Florida, followed by the discovery of deposits in Tennessee, Kentucky and New Jersey. Many potters, however, did not consider the latter to be a true ball clay because it was not deemed to be as good in color or capable of vitrifying as easily as the English clay (Ries and Leighton, 1909: 59-61).

Prior to the emergence of the American ball clay industry, nearly all of the clay supply for American potters came from the Devonshire district of England. Unlike kaolin clay, which was more frequently used for porcelain and other fine china, English ball clay was typically used for producing disposable ceramic goods. Ball clays consist of ultra fine particles with chemical properties that give them special plasticity and resistance to breakage due to shrinkage as well as the capability to be easily shaped when damp.

Fig. 17. Type 1 ribbed tobacco pipe BC-05-00224-CP, L. 10.5cm.

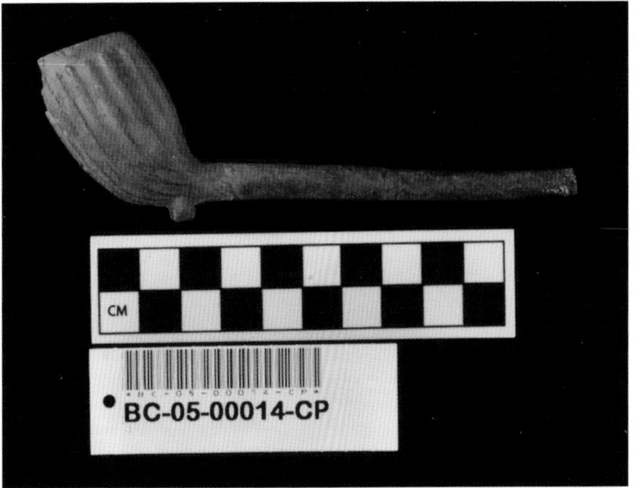

Fig. 18. Type 1 ribbed tobacco pipe BC-05-00014-CP, L. 13.0cm.

The name of the clay derived from the original method of production, which consisted of cutting out the clay in open pits into cubes, the sides of which measured approximately 22-25cm and individually weighed 14-16kg. Due to the clay's high plasticity the cubes adhered together, and after being handled several times the corners rounded off and the cubes turned into balls. As a result, this white firing plastic clay was known to potters as 'ball clay'.[6]

6. The British Clay Pipe Industry

By the end of the 16th century the custom of smoking in public places had become widespread, as witnessed by a visitor to England in 1598, who noted that "The English have

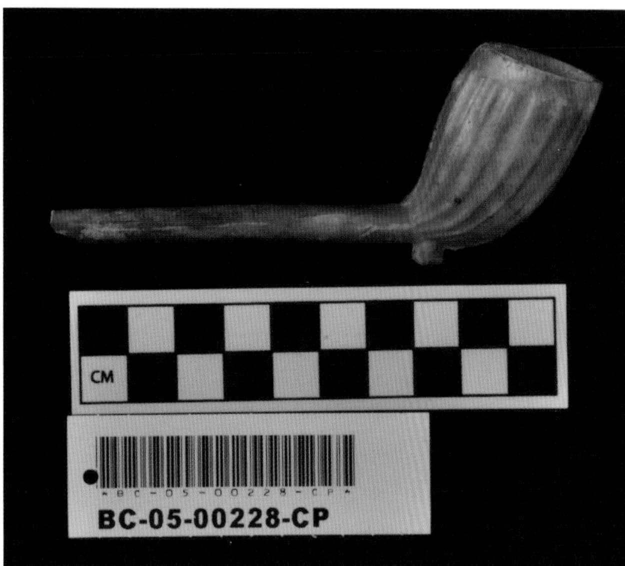

Fig. 19. Type 1 ribbed tobacco pipe BC-05-00228-CP, L. 11.3cm.

Fig. 20. Type 1 ribbed tobacco pipe BC-05-00012-CP, L. 10.8cm.

pipes on purpose made of clay into the farther end of which they put the herb, and putting fire to it draw the smoak into their mouthe" (Vince and Peacey, 2006: 13). At this time pipe makers established in England exclusively used white clay and two-piece molds to produce their wares in enormous quantities (Higgins, 1995: 47; Vince and Peacey, 2006: 13). Relatively quick and easy to manufacture, pipes were cheap to make and thus "could be bought for as little as one to two shillings per gross" (Higgins, 1995: 47). By the 17th century pipes were readily available commodities and the clay pipe trade had extended to colonies all around the world. The Darien Company of Scotland, for example, commissioned the manufacture of over a quarter of a million pipes between the years 1696 and 1699 for its Central American venture (Higgins, 1995: 47).[7]

Supplied with ball clay exclusively from Poole and the Isle of Wight (Vince and Peacey, 2006: 16), London was the center of the tobacco pipe-making industry during the first half of the 17th century, dictated in large part by a 1624 Act that demanded imported tobacco pass only through London (Oswald, 1960: 42-3). However, within less than a century pipes were being produced in a network of centers across the whole country, including major cities, small market towns and rural settlements (Vince and Peacey, 2006: 11). The size of workshops varied from a single pipe maker to large export firms in Scotland, which employed several hundred workers (Gojak and Stuart, 1999: 39). Bristol, in particular, is the most thoroughly documented English pipe export hub for the period covering the 1600s to the mid-19th century (Walker, 1977). Beginning in 1639 with the royal recognition of this city as an outport for tobacco, Virginia tobacco was sent to England in Bristol ships, which returned to Virginia laden with commodities. During the 18th century ball clay extraction from the Bovey Basin in Devon fuelled the growing demand for high-quality ceramic clay. Increasing use was made of the local port at Teignmouth to ship the clay to the ports of London and Liverpool (Bristow *et al.*, 2002: 26).

Bristol soon developed into an important center for the retail tobacco trade with a flourishing pipe making industry, which in fact became the model for the English pipe-making trade (Mitchell, 1983: 5-6; Sudbury, 2009: 109). Export records for the Bristol Ring pipe firm document that shipments to North America in the post-1850 period tended to enter the continent through New York, whereas earlier shipments more often arrived at Canadian destinations. By this time most Bristol pipes tended to be unmarked, making the identification of manufacturers problematic (Sudbury, 2009: 109, 113).

Based on parallel evidence from the vast pipe assemblage excavated from the Fort Union Trading Post in North Dakota (see Section 10 below), the one examined 'TD'-embossed Jacksonville 'Blue China' pipe (BC-05-00227) attributed to British manufacture may very well be a product of Bristol, England, which was a major supplier to the Post until 1850 (Sudbury, 2009: 1) and continued to export to America in the post-1850 era. It seems reasonable to suspect that some of the other 'TD' pipes recovered from Site BA02 may also be British and have originated in the workshops of Bristol.

In addition to England, by the early decades of the 17th century large quantities of white clay pipes were made in Scotland, which was largely influenced by the fashion of the London court, where smoking had become en vogue. From its earliest known pipe manufacturer in 1618, the Scottish pipe-making industry witnessed an expansion in the 1660s encouraged in part by a tax that imposed heavy duties on imports (Gallagher and Harrison, 1995: 1131). By the middle of the 19th century the largest single exporter of pipes worldwide was Duncan McDougall of Glasgow. Founded in 1846, the Scottish company produced pipes until its close in 1967 (Pfeiffer, 2006: 12, 83; Walker and Walker, 1969: 132-33). Large quantities of its pipe fragments have been recorded on terrestrial sites around the world, including the 'TD'-embossed variety of which McDougall was a major 19th-century producer (Dixon, 2005: 114).

Contemporary with McDougall, other Scottish pipe manufacturers located in Glasgow were also mass exporters and distributors of white clay pipes to the United States. These included Alexander Coghill (1826-1904), William Murray (1830-61) and William White (1805-1955) (Pfeiffer, 2006: 12), who began in 1824 to manufacture pipes at Glasgow's Bain Street under the name of W. White & Son, before expanding with new buildings in 1867-77 (Smith, 2001: 393). As noted in a company catalogue, by 1900 William White had produced 606 separate varieties of pipes (Gojak and Stuart, 1999: 39). While it was common for pipe makers to stamp their names, initials and/or various symbols either on the stem or the bowl of their pipes, thus making it possible to associate specific makers with excavated examples today, many pipe manufacturers simply left their wares plain, as was the case with the Jacksonville 'Blue China' examples. Hence, the product of dozens of pipe makers remains anonymous.

By the second half of the 19th century the clay pipe industry began its demise, struggling with competition first from the meerschaum pipe and then from the much more affordable and durable briar. The number of English pipe makers eventually fell from over 600 to less than 150, with most firms ceasing manufacture by 1870 (Oswald, 1960: 47).

7. Continental White Clay Pipe Production

By the late 16th century the manufacture of white clay pipes had spread rapidly across northern Europe, first to the Netherlands, then into the Germanic states and central Europe and later into France. By the mid-1600s thousands of pipe manufacturers were operating across Europe

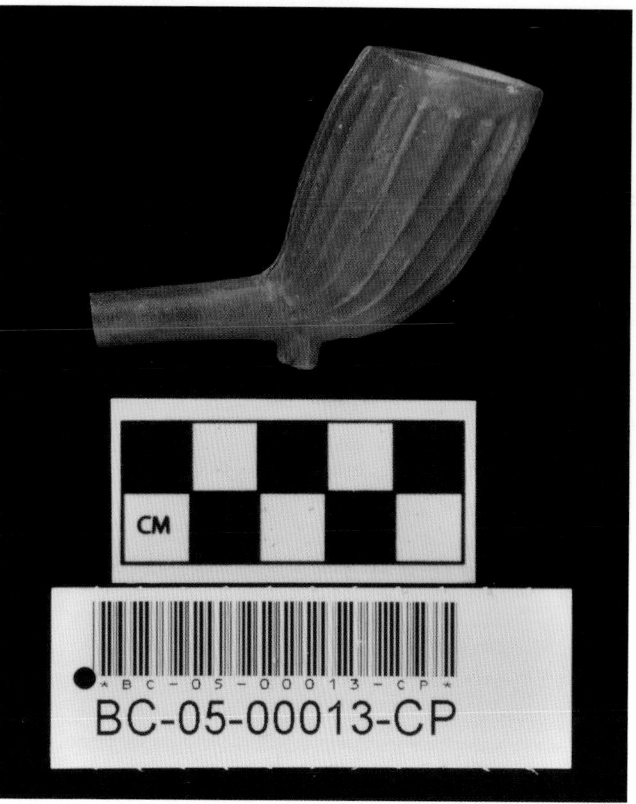

Fig. 21. Type 1 ribbed tobacco pipe BC-05-00013-CP, L. 6.7cm.

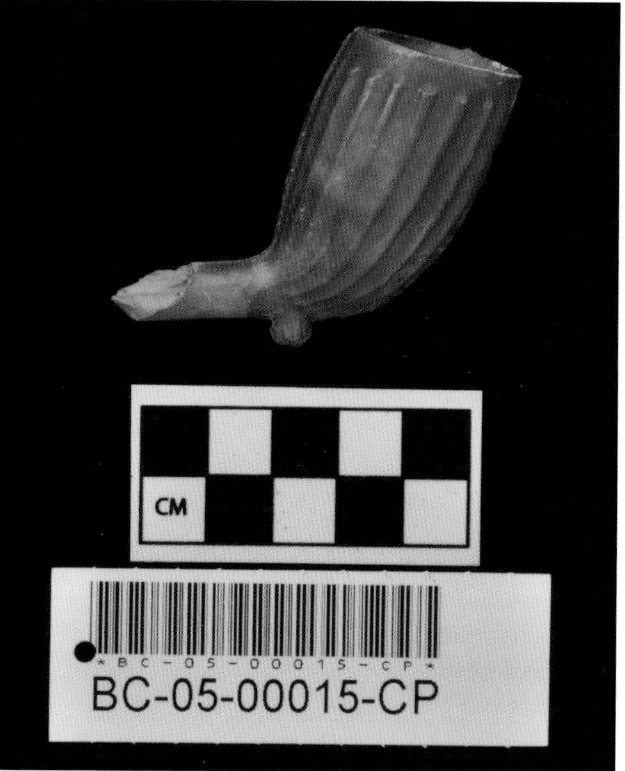

Fig. 22. Type 1 ribbed tobacco pipe BC-05-00015-CP, L. 6.2cm.

Fig. 23. Type 1 ribbed tobacco pipe BC-05-00226-CP, L. 5.2cm.

(Trubowitz, 2005: 146). Local manufacturing centers throughout the continent produced distinctive regional forms presenting a wide range of decorative styles that evolved over time. From the late 17th century onwards, clay pipes conformed to a basic shape: a hemispherical or egg-shaped bowl on top of a tapering stem (Gojak and Stuart, 1999: 38).

Until the mid-19th century, British pipes predominated amongst American white clay pipe imports. But other countries also manufactured and shipped pipes worldwide, including Holland and Germany, both of which were major exporters (Sudbury, 2009: 106, 170). White clay pipes were exported from France, Belgium, Canada, and other countries to a lesser degree, many of which entered the American pipe market after the Revolutionary War (1775-83), when some English products lost favor with the American public (pers. comm. Michael Pfeiffer, October, 2006).[8]

In the early period of manufacture, Dutch law prohibited German pipe makers from using ports in the Netherlands, which essentially landlocked and barred the Germans from participating in the overseas pipe trade (Stam, 2009: 116). By the end of the 18th century, however, the export of German pipes from Ulsar to Holland was underway and the export of German white clay pipes to the US began in the 1830s. A decade later, German pipes had become especially abundant in the United States, as documented on archaeological sites and in export records. In 1845 an enormous 4.5 million pipes were exported to America from Ulsar (Gartley, 2009: 206; Sudbury, 2009: 106).

A large number of German products have been recorded on US historical sites, in particular at the Fort Union Trading Post (1828-67) in North Dakota (see Section 10 below). Most German pipes arrived mainly via the major ports of New York, Baltimore and New Orleans and were then distributed nationwide. By the mid-19th century, companies such as the Heye Brothers of New York were advertising the sale of both imported Dutch and German pipes (Sudbury, 2009: 106, 170-71).[9]

In one year alone the German manufacturing town of Grosselmerode exported more than 13.5 million pipes to the United States (Stephan, 1993: 56; Pfeiffer *et al.*, 2006: 12). In 1866, the peak year in German pipe exports, 95% of seven Grosselmerode pipe manufacturers' products were being shipped to the US. Three of the four Site BA02 white clay pipes (both of the ribbed and 'TD'-embossed variety) could quite feasibly be attributed to German manufacture based largely on comparisons with similar contemporary German pipes from the Fort Union Trading Post. This could also be the case for the other 12 pipes recovered from the Jacksonville 'Blue China' wreck site. In the absence of chemical analysis or positive identification by comparison to identical reference collections of known origin, this supposition must remain a matter of conjecture.

8. North American White Clay Pipes

Compared to Great Britain, whose extensive pipe data have been carefully documented and published for decades, the study of historic clay tobacco pipes in the United States and Canada is still in its infancy (Sudbury, 1979: 152). While the commercial manufacture of clay pipes was initially based in Great Britain and Continental Europe, following the political aftermath of the Revolutionary War and the War of 1812 some British products, including pipes, appear to have become less appealing to the American populace or were less easily accessible. However, this was a short-lived 'boycott'. After 1812, commerce with England re-commenced and a flood of other British products, such as cloth and pottery offered at reduced prices, in many cases actually drove American manufacturers out of business (Martin, 2001: 35; Wait, 1999: 282). A total of 19 US pipe makers have been identified as active in North America between 1776 and 1840, although there were undoubtedly many other domestic specialists active during this period, as yet unrecorded. The mid-19th century continued to witness an increase in the number of known American pipe makers, which may be the result of superior documentation for these decades but is probably also due to improved mechanization, which no doubt contributed to the growth of the US industry.[10]

Canadian pipe makers also made their mark at this time with the emergence of the early Montreal pipe industry, which evolved from a single pipe maker recorded in 1847 to 18 in 1875, supported by a workforce comprised largely of Irish immigrants who had fled Ireland's potato blight. Of particular relevance to the Jacksonville 'Blue China' 'TD'-embossed pipes are similar wares produced by Montreal pipe makers such as Henderson and Bannerman. The recent excavations of a Henderson pipe wasters' dump in Montreal, used from 1847-72, revealed that the predominant style represented was the 'TD' form, which also had 'Henderson' marked on the stem (Roy, 2007: 47-51). Robert Bannerman, who also originated from a Glasgow pipe-making family, began his Canadian production line in 1854. By 1858, he had his own Montreal pipe factory, which remained active until 1888 (Sudbury, 1979: 175-6; 1980a: 4; 2009: 66).

In 1875 Robert Bannerman established the Eagle Tobacco Pipe Manufactory in Rouses Point, New York, apparently to meet the growing US demand and to avoid high export duties on his finished products (Sudbury, 1979: 175-76; 2009: 66). Output per employee during the first year of the New York operation was approximately 600 to 750 pipes per day (Sudbury, 1980a: 9, 11). Bannerman's US factory continued to remain under Montreal ownership and its pipe production line, including 'TD' examples, probably reflects a style consistent with pipes simultaneously manufactured by his Canadian company, part of whose wares were produced contemporary with the Jacksonville 'Blue China' ship's lifetime.

Importantly for the issue of determining the origins of the Site BA02 products, the white clay used in Bannerman's workshops was reportedly imported from Devonshire, England, because no US ball clay sources were available prior to 1880. Nearly all of the American supply also came from this distant location (Ries and Leighton, 1909: 59). Shipments arrived first in Montreal and were then transported to the Eagle Tobacco Pipe Manufactory at Rouses Point, New York (Sudbury, 1980a: 11).

On at least one documented Rouses Point 'TD'-marked pipe fragment, Bannerman's company name was stamped onto the stem (Sudbury, 1979: 51, 53, pl. 6.2), thus confirming the style's availability in New York. No doubt the type's production would not have been restricted to Robert Bannerman's two factories (Sudbury, 1980a: 5). 'TD' pipes were still being manufactured in Detroit in the 1880s-90s (Sudbury 1979: 166-67, pl. 6.11), Philadelphia in 1892 (Jung, 1989: 8) and in Brooklyn, New York, in the early 1900s (Jung, 1988: 16). The availability of long-stemmed clay tobacco pipes is known from New York State due to advertisements published as early as 1735. The excavation of a 19th-century Long Island pipe kiln has uncovered fragments of long-stemmed white clay ribbed pipes, as well as a ribbed version of the 'TD'-embossed pipe (Sudbury, 1979: 175). Although this site, active from 1870-1920, post-dates the Jacksonville 'Blue China' wreck by around 15 years, it is quite plausible that earlier New York clay tobacco pipe factories will be uncovered in the future (Sudbury, 1980a: 6), whose wares may have included pipes similar to those found at Site BA02.

9. The Socio-Economics of the Tobacco Pipe Trade

In the absence of a cargo manifest or the remains of stamped shipping containers, it is impossible to determine to whom the Jacksonville 'Blue China' wreck's tobacco pipes were being shipped. Since Colonial days clay tobacco pipes were extremely inexpensive. The excavation of mid-19th century sites in America indicates that they were readily available across the socio-economic divide (Hume, 1974: 296). Of particular relevance are similar white clay pipes excavated in Virginia City, Nevada, which was founded in 1859 after the discovery of the Comstock Lode, the richest silver deposit in America. Virginia City became the most important town between Chicago and the Pacific and at its peak was populated by nearly 25,000 residents (Goldman, 1981: 13). Amongst its early 1860s inhabitants was the journalist and author Mark Twain (born Samuel Clemens), who was a reporter for the city's most influential daily paper.

Excavations conducted since 1993 have uncovered four Virginia City saloons yielding over 300,000 artifacts. The majority of the numerous tobacco pipe bowls and pipe stem fragments are of undecorated white clay – an especially telling factor since all four drinking establishments catered to town patrons of distinctly different social classes and ethnicities ranging from the wealthy to the poor and African-Americans to Irish (Dixon, 2005: 113). Some of the Virginia City finds include 'TD'-monogrammed pipe bowls recovered from Piper's Old Corner Bar and the Boston Saloon, which served Irish and African-American customers respectively, two clearly disparate populations within the broader Virginia City community (Dixon, 2005: 114). In light of this data, the pipes from the

Jacksonville 'Blue China' wreck could have been intended for use by any strata of Southern American society.

10. The Fort Union Trading Post White Clay Pipes

Numerous mid-19th century American terrestrial sites have yielded both ribbed and 'TD'-embossed or stamped white clay pipes featuring a number of different variations. Of particular relevance is the Fort Union Trading Post due to its extensive occupation and the enormous quantity of white clay pipe fragments recovered. The most important fur trading post on the Upper Missouri River, Fort Union was occupied from 1828 to 1867 under a series of different company affiliations and served as the chief establishment where the Assiniboine, Crow, Cree, Blackfeet, Métis and other Indian tribes from both sides of the American-Canadian border traded buffalo robes and other furs in return for various goods, including beads, guns, blankets, cloth and tobacco pipes (Pfeiffer, 2006: 113; Sudbury, 2009: 1-2).[11]

Since its acquisition by the National Park Service in 1965, subsequent large-scale excavations at the Fort Union Trading Post between 1968-72 and 1985-88 uncovered over 500,000 artifacts, including 11,777 intact and fragmentary tobacco pipes (Pfeiffer, 2006: 113; Sudbury, 2009: 1, 7). Over 10,000 of these were produced of white clay and many feature pipe bowls with similar patterns to the two styles found on the Jacksonville 'Blue China' wreck. Significantly, these have been largely attributed to German manufacture (Pfeiffer, 2006: 114; Sudbury, 2009: 1, 7, 168, 170).[12]

Unlike the Site BA02 collection, however, the majority of pipe bowls in the Fort Union collection show evidence of having been smoked, suggesting that few if any of the pipes excavated were broken discards from shipping crates (Pfeiffer, 2006: 114). The Fort Union 'TD' pipe assemblage comprises dozens of different variations of the monogram, including a number of decorated varieties with stars, circles, braided ovals and radiating rays, as well as four different types of otherwise plain 'TD' motifs classified according to differences in letter heights and orientations (large angled letters, large letters, medium letters and small letters). Within these broader 'TD' categories are a number of different sub-types derived from further variations in the positioning of the letters (Pfeiffer, 2006: 118-19; Sudbury, 2009: 31, 46, 50-1).

While typologically very close to the Fort Union pipe variety designated 'Medium Plain TD' (Pfeiffer, 2006: 118; Sudbury, 2009: 48-54), the Site BA02 'TD' letter measurements are nonetheless not a perfect match. Further differences, albeit slight, also occur in some of the pipe dimensions, including bowl depth and diameter and stem bore diameters. In some cases discrepancies amongst pipe component sizes presumably made from the same or similar molds may be due to changes in the water content of the clay: in effect, two different sized pipes can be made from the same mold as a result of differences in clay shrinkage (variations in original moisture content or clay type). Over the years, molds also wore down and may have been rebuilt or modified, further impacting measurement disparities.

The Jacksonville 'Blue China' wreck's ribbed pipes, each of which feature 16 raised flutes encircling the pipe bowl (with some minor variations), are also similar to a few of the Fort Union white clay ribbed or cockled pipe varieties, yet again are not exactly identical.

11. Mid-19th Century Shipwrecks

Excavations of early to mid-19th century American shipwrecks contemporary with Site BA02 have produced surprisingly few long-stemmed white clay tobacco pipe finds. Of the examples discovered, none appear to be the same as those recovered from the Jacksonville 'Blue China' wreck. The following overview discusses pipes associated with the steamboats *Heroine* (1838), *Arabia* (1856) and *Bertrand* (1865), as well as the sidewheel steamers *Maple Leaf* (1864) and SS *Republic* (1865).

The earliest example of the celebrated 'Western river steamboat' is the wreck of what historical research suggests is the steamboat *Heroine*, a 42.7m-long, 160-ton single centerline mounted engine vessel, which sank on the Red River in May 1838 while transporting military provisions and stores to the US army garrison at Fort Towson in Oklahoma. The wreck remained visible for five years before a major flood in 1843 shifted the river channel and buried the ship, which was not re-exposed until 1991 (Crisman, 2005: 220-21).[13]

The initial fieldwork on the Red River Project was conducted by the Oklahoma Historical Society in the late 1990s. Subsequently, in partnership with the Institute of Nautical Archaeology (INA) at Texas A&M University, the excavation was continued from 2003-2008 and yielded dozens of artifacts, including cargo, personal items, tools and equipment, as well as sections of the ship itself. Tobacco pipes proved to be highly limited and to date only one white clay pipe stem has been recovered. Some etching appears at the end of stem, but no maker's mark is apparent. The stem was clearly intended for use with a

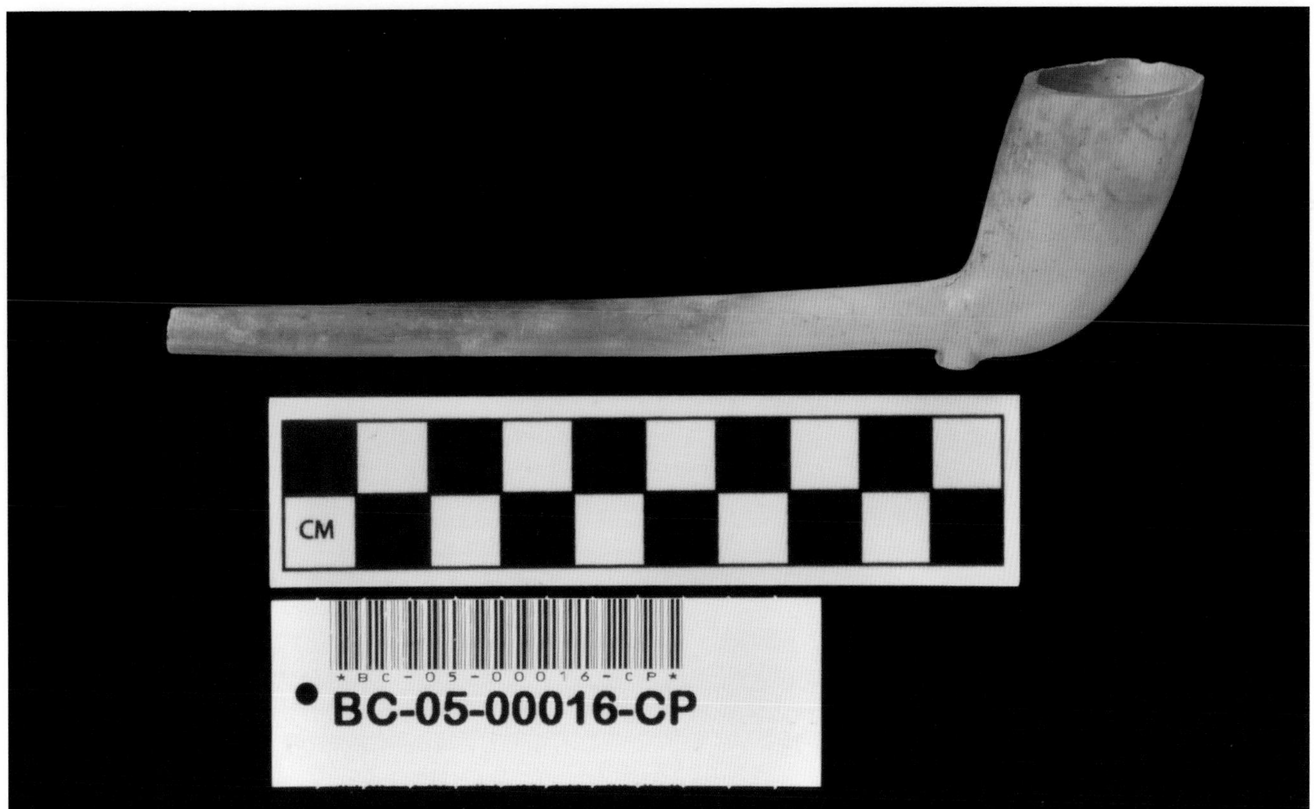

Fig. 24. Type 2 'TD'-embossed tobacco pipe BC-05-00016-CP, L. 14.0cm.

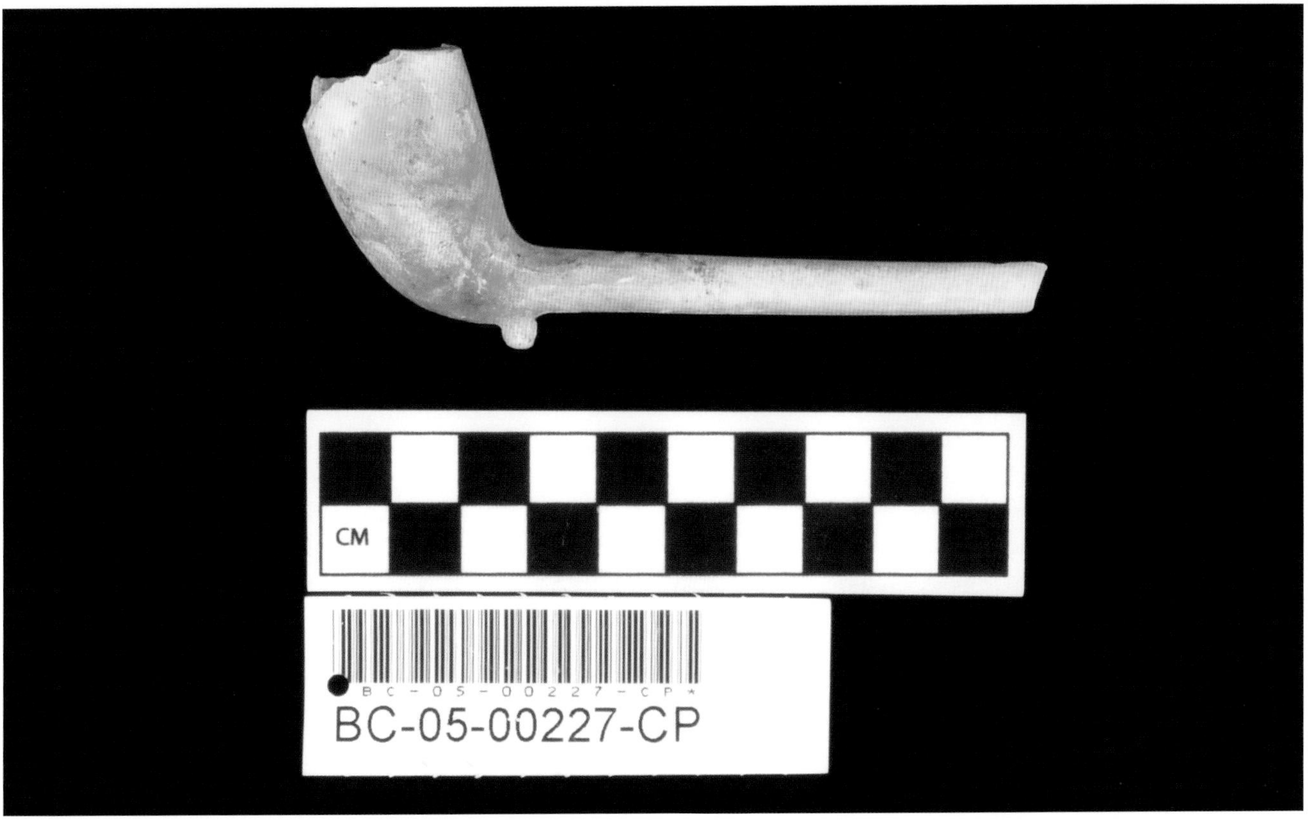

Fig. 25. Type 2 'TD'-embossed tobacco pipe BC-05-00227-CP, L. 10.5cm.

Fig. 26. Type 2 'TD'-embossed tobacco pipe BC-05-00225-CP, L. 11.7cm.

separate pipe bowl and does not bear any resemblance to the integral long-stemmed Site BA02 examples.

The discovery of only one tobacco pipe is quite unusual considering the size of the vessel and the fact that the ship carried a crew of around 20 people (pers. comm. Kevin Crisman, 5 November, 2009). Since the wreck was heavily salvaged in the years after its loss and the original crew survived the disaster, the absence of material culture is not unexpected. Materials lost with the ship may also have been swept away by the river's fairly strong current. While sedimentation probably filled in the hull rather quickly, any items not secured, weighted or trapped in the hull are likely to have been eroded by the current and transported off site (pers. comm. Heather Jones, 6 November 2009).

More closely dated to the era of the Jacksonville 'Blue China' ship was the 51.3m-long *Arabia*, a wooden river steamboat built in 1853 by John Snyder Pringle in Brownsville, Pennsylvania. Heavily laden with 222 tons of cargo bound for frontier merchants, on 5 September 1856 the *Arabia* struck a submerged walnut tree, piercing the vessel's thick oak hull. Within minutes much of the ship and virtually all of the cargo sank into the Missouri River (Hawley, 1995: 12, 17). Over the decades the river changed its course, so that when the wreck was discovered in 1988 it was located 13.5m under a Kansas farmer's cornfield and over 800m away from the riverbank (Hawley, 1995: 20). The salvage operation produced thousands of artifacts, including around 100 clay pipe bowls and some 100 bamboo pipe stems (Hawley, 1998: 210).

Unlike the white clay pipes with their integral stem, these elbow-style, short-shanked clay pipes had the advantage of incorporating easily replaceable stems. By contrast, the former had to be discarded when the stem broke (Pfeiffer, 2006: 105) or may have been salvaged, modified and/or reworked to permit additional use (Sudbury, 2009: 118-21). The flexible reed stem clay pipe was a more durable design – especially in a working environment – than the all-clay pipe because its removable reed stem was much less susceptible to breakage. Reed stem pipes became the style of choice carried by soldiers during the

American Civil War of 1861-65; oral history suggests that pipe molds were at times available in Civil War camps, enabling itinerant pipe manufacture.[14]

The Civil War US army transport the *Maple Leaf* was sunk on 1 April 1864 when the sidewheel steamer struck a Confederate enemy torpedo (or a mine in modern terminology) in the St. Johns River, just 24km from Jacksonville, Florida (Gaines, 2008: 42). Four crew members were lost as well as 400 tons of military equipment, including the goods of 'sutlers' (army camp peddlers), tents, garrison equipment and the personal gear of three regiments. In 1984 the Jacksonville-based St. Johns Archaeological Expeditions, Inc. (SJAEI) confirmed the presence of the *Maple Leaf*'s remains at a depth of over 6m of water and under 2m of mud. The ship's hull and contents were preserved virtually intact in the muddy anaerobic environment (McCarthy, 1992: 66; Smith, 2002: 152-3).[15]

Excavation conducted by SJAEI in tandem with East Carolina University exposed thousands of artifacts with an equivalent weight of 1,100lb (Gaines, 2008: 42; McCarthy, 1992: 66). The personal effects recovered included around a dozen pipes, including both wood and vulcanite pipe stems and bowls, some of which feature ornately carved and molded decoration. A few hand-painted porcelain pipe bowls were also discovered, as well as at least one fragment of a long-stemmed clay pipe with the letter 'D' impressed in the bowl, probably indicative of the common 'TD'-stamped pipe. The pipe stem features the maker's name of H. White of Glasgow. This is the only example from the *Maple Leaf* that bears a resemblance to the Jacksonville 'Blue China' 'TD'-embossed pipes (pers. comm. Keith Holland, 8 December 2008; pers comm. Marie Prentice, 9 December, 2009).[16] However, further excavations may produce additional pipe finds since only part of the 400-ton cargo has been recovered.

In addition to the *Arabia*, the steamer *Bertrand*, built in Wheeling, West Virginia, in 1864, also fell foul of the Missouri River. This 48.3m-long, low draft vessel sank less than a year later on 1 April 1865, when the steamer struck a submerged snag near De Soto Landing in Nebraska Territory carrying at least 10 passengers and over 250 tons of agricultural and mining supplies, household paraphernalia, munitions and clothing, as well as canned and bottled foodstuffs, wines and bitters. Also onboard was an estimated 35,000lb of mercury, probably intended to help extract gold through the amalgamation process. Two contemporary attempts to salvage the cargo were largely unsuccessful, other than apparently recovering most of the mercury (Switzer, 1974: 1).

After being preserved for over a century in deep mud and silt, the *Bertrand* was discovered with its enormous

Fig. 27. Detail of a Type 2 tobacco pipe with the letters 'TD' embossed on either side of the mold seam on the face of the bowl.

Fig. 28. Detail of the letters 'TD' embossed on the bowl of Type 2 tobacco pipe BC-05-00016-CP.

cargo largely intact. In 1968 and 1969 a recovery project supervised by archaeologists from the National Park Service and personnel from the Bureau of Sports Fisheries and Wildlife excavated the ship's voluminous shipment of frontier-bound trade goods – a collection of over two million artifacts (Corbin, 2002a: 14; 2002b: 201; Switzer, 1974: 1). The finds included a large quantity of diverse pipe stems and bowls, including two distinct types of the American-made Pamplin elbow-style short-shanked pipe bowl (see Sudbury, 2009: 87).[17] A quantity of reed or willow pipes of unknown origin was also found packed alongside the Pamplin pipes (Pfeiffer, 2006: 102-103).

The wreck of the *Bertrand* was also associated with 212 wooden pipes, 182 of which represent several varieties of briar; the remaining 30 are of a wood species that remains unidentified (Pfeiffer, 2006: 103). The absence of any evidence for white ball clay pipes from the *Bertrand*'s large cargo is particularly noteworthy, reflecting the changing tastes of American smokers at the time. Another contributing factor, no doubt, was the mounting customs duties that impacted on British, French and Dutch white clay pipes imported into the United States. In combination, these factors probably played a role in stimulating the rise of the American clay pipe industry and influenced the shift towards the use of American tobacco paraphernalia (Pfeiffer, 2006: 102, 105; Sudbury, 2009: 107). While large numbers of European pipes continued to be imported into the United States, arriving in major ports and then distributed nationwide – often by waterways – by the late 1850s domestic output was beginning to supplant imports.[18]

Surprisingly, the excavation of the SS *Republic*, a side-wheel steamer en route from New York to New Orleans when it sank 150km off the southeastern coast of the United States in October 1865, did not yield any tobacco pipes, intact or fragmentary, despite the fact that the thorough excavation recovered artifacts as small as porcelain buttons, individual coins, fragile gaming pieces and toothbrushes. The archaeological excavation conducted by Odyssey Marine Exploration between October 2003 and February 2005 yielded over 14,000 artifacts and more than 51,000 gold and silver coins, a vast assemblage of material goods representative of daily life in post-Civil War America (Cunningham Dobson *et al.*, 2010; Cunningham Dobson and Gerth, 2010).

In an era when tobacco use was rampant (Martin, 1942: 81-82), one would have expected the excavation to have produced some clay tobacco pipes, especially since New York and New Orleans were major ports for the shipment of imported clay pipes. The lack of such wares from the *Republic* is intriguing and may reflect a preference for chewing tobacco, which in 1860 was used by at least half of the tobacco consuming populace (Martin, 1942: 81-2). The vessel's cargo may have included the lighter, more durable briar wood pipe, examples of which would not be expected to have survived within this particular marine environment. By the late 1860s briar pipes would become prevalent as industries in France, England and the United States "greatly increased the number of pipe smokers" (Pfeiffer, 2006: 102-3).

12. Conclusion

The predominant significance of the Site BA02 clay pipe assemblage is as one example of the vast inter-regional trade once conducted along the East Coast of America by a small schooner probably based in New York. Perhaps stowed in two or three shipping containers in the stern half of the ship, the pipes were essentially low volume, low cost space fillers shipped to maximize the profits attainable from trade with the cotton ports of the South or frontier outposts. Most plausibly dated to 1854, the Jacksonville 'Blue China' shipwreck provides a new chronological context for these two common tobacco pipe styles.

The origins of this assemblage are obscured by an interlocking web of commercial, historical and political complexities. One Type 2 'TD'-embossed pipe has been identified as a British product manufactured from white ball clay, which most logically suggests comparable British origins for the remainder of this type from the Jacksonville 'Blue China' wreck. In this model the flourishing pipe industry in Bristol emerges as a credible source for the Type 2 collection, especially given similarities between the wreck material and 'TD' examples from Bristol excavated in the Fort Union Trading Post, North Dakota, and the fact that products from the Bristol Ring company entered America via New York, the Site BA02 ship's proposed home port.

However, identifications of British white clay pipe fabrics on mid-19th century American sites are not watertight proof of British origins: before the development of the American ball clay industry in 1880, almost all clay supplies for US white clay pipe makers were imported as raw material from the Devonshire district of England. Nonetheless, Henderson's products of this period appear to have all been marked, whereas Bannerman's Montreal 'TD' pipe output started in 1854 and his Eagle Tobacco Pipe Manufactory at Rouses Point, New York, opened in 1875. Both of the Bannerman production sources emerged too late to have served the markets with which the Jacksonville 'Blue China' schooner traded. A British provenance for some of the Type 2 tobacco pipes thus seems highly probable.

Analysis of three of the four Site BA02 pipes – both of the Type 1 ribbed and Type 2 'TD' variety – are more suggestive of German manufacture. Such an interpretation is tempting in light of the notion that some British products allegedly lost popularity in America after the War of 1812 in tandem with the sharp rise in Germanic pipe imports starting in the 1830s. Nevertheless, the sheer presence of abundant ceramic wares from Staffordshire, England, on the Jacksonville 'Blue China' shipwreck of 1854 demonstrates archaeologically that perhaps too much has been read into this anti-British cultural bias. More detailed historical analysis actually demonstrates that British ceramics came to be preferred again over American products, partly due to reduced prices (Gerth, 2011).

Taking into account the large volume of the exclusively British ceramic cargo shipped aboard the Site BA02 vessel, the internal evidence favors a British origin for its tobacco pipes. If accurate, the Jacksonville 'Blue China' wreck assemblage can be interpreted as a microcosm of the final years of a traditional trade that was in decline, as was the age of the traditional small-scale schooner itself. By the late 1850s American-made tobacco pipes began to supplant European imports, and by 1860 a significant population of consumers had turned to tobacco chewing rather than pipe smoking. If the wreck of the *Bertrand* is typical of prevailing trends, then by 1864 wooden pipes may have found favor over clay by this date too. The introduction of the vulcanized rubber bit provided impetus for use of other materials in pipe manufacture.

However, objectively literally hundreds of pipe makers co-existed in the mid-19th century in five to ten different countries, each copying prevalent styles. In the absence of additional reference materials from the US, and despite the weight of evidence pointing to Britain, the origins of the Jacksonville 'Blue China' tobacco pipes currently remains unidentified.

Acknowledgements

The authors express their sincere gratitude to all of the directors, managers, and marine operations, archaeological and technical staff at Odyssey Marine Exploration as presented in the Acknowledgements cited at the end of *OME Papers* 19. In addition, the authors extend a special thank to a select group of scholars and professionals who very kindly offered valuable information relevant to the Jacksonville 'Blue China' wreck clay pipe analysis: Kevin Crisman (Associate Professor, Nautical Archaeology Program Director, Center for Maritime Archaeology and Conservation, Texas A&M University); Keith Holland (the Maple Leaf Shipwreck Project); Heather Jones (the Heroine/Red River Steamboat Project); Michael Pfeiffer (archaeologist and clay tobacco pipe historian); and Marie Prentice (the Maple Leaf Shipwreck Project).

The pipe dimensions for this report were catalogued and tabulated by Sean Kingsley (Wreck Watch Int., London) and Chad Morris (Odyssey Marine Exploration, Tampa). The photographs in Figs. 11-28 were taken by Alan Bosel (Odyssey Marine Exploration, Tampa). The pipe line drawings in Figs. 9-10 were made by Chad Morris (Odyssey Marine Exploration, Tampa). This report was edited by Sean Kingsley (Wreck Watch Int., London), proofread by Greg Stemm and Alice Copeland and designed by Melissa Dolce (Odyssey Marine Exploration, Tampa).

Notes

1. See Hitchcock, J.A., *Clay Pipes - Then and Now*: http://computeme.tripod.com/claypipe.html.
2. See: http://www.museumoflondon.org.uk/claypipes/pages/mark.asp?mark_name=TD.
3. See *Archaeological Excavations at Stenton:* http://www.stenton.org/research/excavations.cfm.
4. See the White Ball Clay Heritage Society: http://www.clayheritage.org/pages/wideuses.htm.
5. See the White Ball Clay Heritage Society: http://www.clayheritage.org/pages/wideuses.htm and *A Potted History of the Devon Ball Clay Industry*: http://savikivi.blogspot.com/2009/07/potted-history-of-south-devon-ball-clay.html.
6. See Note 4 above.
7. See: http://ashadocs.org/aha/17/17_04_Gojak.pdf.
8. See *Politics of the Fur Trade: Clay Tobacco Pipes at Fort Union, North Dakota* (National Park Service, US Department of the Interior): http://www.nps.gov/archeology/sites/npSites/fortUnion.htm.
9. See Note 8 above.
10. See Note 8 above.
11. See Note 8 above.
12. See Note 8 above.
13. See the Red River Project: http://inadiscover.com/redriver/history/ship.html and http://inadiscover.com/redriver/index.htm.
14. See *Point Pleasant Pottery, 1838-1890:* http://www.flickr.com/photos/42613470@N00/sets/72157602945863364/.
15. See *Maple Leaf Shipwreck Site - National Park Service:* http://www.nps.gov/history/Nr/travel/flshipwrecks/map.htm.
16. See *Significance of the Artifacts Recovered from the Maple Leaf*: http://www.mapleleafshipwreck.com/Book/other/contents.htm.

17. See *Pamplin Clay Tobacco Pipes*, Museum of Anthropology, College of Arts and Sciences, University of Missouri: http://anthromuseum.missouri.edu /minigalleries/pamplinpipes/pamplinpipes.shtml.
18. See Note 8 above.

Bibliography

Brassy, R., 'Clay Tobacco Pipes from the Site of the Victoria Hotel Auckland, New Zealand', *Australian Historical Archaeology* 9 (1991), 27-30.

Bristow, C. M., Palmer, Q., Witte, G.J., Bowditch, I., Howe, J.H., 'The Ball Clay and China Clay Industries in Southwest England in 2000'. In P.W. Scott and C.M. Bristow (eds.), *Industrial Minerals and Extractive Industry Geology* (Geological Society Publishing House, 2002), 17-42.

Corbin, A., *The Material Culture of Steamboat Passengers. Archaeological Evidence from the Missouri River* (New York, 2002a).

Corbin, A., 'Steamboat Archaeology on the Missouri River'. In C. Ruppé and J. Barstad (eds.), *International Handbook of Underwater Archaeology* (New York, 2002b), 193-206.

Cotter, J.L., Roberts, D.G. and Parrington, M., *The Buried Past. An Archaeological History of Philadelphia* (University of Pennsylvania, 1993).

Crisman, K., 'The Sidewheel Steamer *Heroine*: Red River, Oklahoma'. In G.F. Bass (ed.), *Beneath the Seven Seas* (London, 2005), 220-21.

Cunningham Dobson, N. and Gerth, E. 'The Shipwreck of the SS *Republic* (1865). Experimental Deep-Sea Archaeology. Part 2: Cargo'. In G. Stemm and S. Kingsley (eds.), *Oceans Odyssey. Deep-Sea Shipwrecks in the English Channel, Straits of Gibraltar & Atlantic Ocean* (Oxford, 2010), 25-68.

Cunningham Dobson, N., Gerth, E. and Winckler, L., 'The Shipwreck of the SS *Republic* (1865). Experimental Deep-Sea Archaeology. Part 1: Fieldwork & Site History'. In G. Stemm and S. Kingsley (eds.), *Oceans Odyssey. Deep-Sea Shipwrecks in the English Channel, Straits of Gibraltar & Atlantic Ocean* (Oxford, 2010), 1-24.

Dixon, K.J., *Boomtown Saloons: Archaeology and History in Virginia City* (University of Nevada Press, 2005).

Gaines, W.C., *Encyclopedia of Civil War Shipwrecks* (Louisiana State University Press, 2008).

Gallagher, D.B. and Harrison, J., 'Tobacco Pipemakers in 17th Century Stirling', *Proceedings of the Society of Antiquaries of Scotland* 125 (1995), 1131-42.

Gartley, R.T., 'German 'Stummelpfeifen' from Excavations in the USA'. In *Politics of the Fur Trade: Clay Tobacco Pipes at Fort Union Trading Post* (Clay Pipes Press, Ponca City, 2009), 205-17.

Gerth, E., 'The Jacksonville 'Blue China' Shipwreck (Site BA02): the Ceramic Assemblage'. In G. Stemm and S. Kingsley (eds.), *Oceans Odyssey 2. Underwater Heritage Management & Deep-Sea Shipwrecks in the English Channel & Atlantic Ocean* (Oxford, 2011), 221-62.

Gerth, E., Cunningham Dobson, N. and Kingsley, S., 'The Jacksonville 'Blue China' Shipwreck (Site BA02): An American Coastal Schooner off Florida'. In G. Stemm and S. Kingsley (eds.), *Oceans Odyssey 2. Underwater Heritage Management & Deep-Sea Shipwrecks in the English Channel & Atlantic Ocean* (Oxford, 2011), 143-220.

Gojak, D. and Stuart, I., 'The Potential for Archaeological Study of Clay Tobacco Pipes from Australian Sites', *Australasian Historical Archaeology* 17 (1999), 38-49.

Goldman, M.S., *Gold Diggers and Silver Miners. Prostitution and Social Life on the Comstock Lode* (University of Michigan Press, 1981).

Hardesty, D.L., *The Archaeology of the Donner Party* (University of Nevada Press, 1997).

Hawley, D., *Treasures of the Arabia* (Kansas, 1995).

Hawley, G., *Treasure in a Cornfield: the Discovery and Excavation of the Steamboat Arabia* (Kansas, 1998).

Higgins, D., 'Clay Tobacco Pipes: a Valuable Commodity', *International Journal of Nautical Archaeology* 24.1 (1995), 41-52.

Hume, I.N., *A Guide to Artifacts of Colonial America* (New York, 1974).

Jung, S.P., *American Clay Pipe Works, Inc., c. 1915-1920, Brooklyn, New York* (Joppa, 1988).

Jung, S.P., *George Zorn & Co. Fifth Edition Catalogue of Pipes and Smoker Articles, c. 1892* (Joppa, 1989).

Martin, E.W., *The Standard of Living in 1860 – American Consumption Levels on the Eve of the Civil War* (University of Chicago Press, 1942).

Martin, A.S., 'Magical, Mythical Practical and Sublime: the Meanings and Use of Ceramics in America.' In R. Hunter (ed.), *Ceramics in America* (Chipstone Foundation, Milwaukee, 2001), 29-46.

McCarthy, K., *Thirty Florida Shipwrecks* (Sarasota, 1992).

Mitchell, V., 'The History of Nominy Plantation with Emphasis on the Clay Tobacco Pipes'. In B. Sudbury (ed.), *Historic Clay Tobacco Pipe Studies* 2 (1983), 1-38.

Oswald, A.H., 'The Archaeology and Economic History of English Clay Tobacco Pipes', *Journal of the British Archaeological Association* 23 (1960), 40-102.

Pfeiffer, M.A., *Clay Tobacco Pipes and the Fur Trade of the Pacific Northwest and Northern Plains* (Historic Clay Tobacco Clay Pipe Studies Research Monograph 1, Phytolith Press, Ponca City, OK, 2006).

Pfeiffer, M.A., Gartley, R.T., and Sudbury, J.B., 'President Pipes: Origin and Distribution', *Wyoming Archaeologist* 50.1 (2006), 15-36.

Ries, H. and Leighton, H., *History of the Clay Working Industry in the United States* (New York, 1909).

Roy, C., 'Premiers regards sur le dépotoir de la fabrique de pipes à fumer Henderson, 1847-1876', *Archéologiques* 20 (2007), 38-54.

Smith, R., *The Making of Scotland* (Edinburgh, 2001).

Smith, R.C., 'Florida Frontiers: from Ice Age to New Age'. In C. Ruppé and J. Barstad (eds.), *International Handbook of Underwater Archaeology* (New York, 2002), 143-68.

Stam, R.D., 'Tonpfeifen-Export aus dem Westerwald über Holländische Häfen im 19. Jahrhundert', *Knasterkopf* 20 (2009), 116-18.

Stradling, D. and Stradling, J.G., 'American Queensware–The Louisville Experience, 1829-1837'. In R. Hunter (ed.), *Ceramics in America* (Chipstone Foundation, Milwaukee, 2001), 162-85.

Sudbury, B., 'Historic Clay Tobacco Pipemakers in the United States of America'. In P. Davey (ed.), *The Archaeology of the Clay Tobacco Pipe II. America I* (BAR Int. Series 60, Oxford, 1979), 151-341.

Sudbury, B., 'A Preliminary Report on the R. Bannerman Eagle Tobacco Pipe Manufactory, Rouses Point, New York', *Historic Clay Tobacco Pipe Studies* 1 (1980a), 3-22.

Sudbury, B., 'White Clay Pipes from the Old Connellsville Dump, 36 Fa 140', *Historic Clay Tobacco Pipe Studies* 1 (1980b), 23-46.

Sudbury, J.B., *Politics of the Fur Trade: Clay Tobacco Pipes at Fort Union Trading Post* (Historic Clay Tobacco Pipe Studies Research Monograph 2, Clay Pipes Press, 2009).

Switzer, R., *The Betrand Bottles: A Study of 19th Century Glass and Ceramic Containers* (National Park Service Department of the Interior, 1974).

Trubowitz, N.L., 'Smoking Pipes: An Archaeology Measure of Native American Cultural Stability and Survival in Eastern North America, A.D. 1500-1850'. In S.M. Rafferty and R. Mann (eds.), *The Culture of Smoking: The Archaeology of Tobacco Pipes in Eastern North America* (University of Tennessee Press, 2005), 143-64.

Vince, A. and Peacey, A., 'Pipemakers and their Workshops: the Use of Geochemical Analysis in the Study of the Clay Tobacco Pipe Industry'. In S.N. Archer and K.M. Bartoy (eds.), *Between Dirt and Discussion: Methods, Methodology and Interpretation in Historical Archaeology* (New York, 2006), 11-31.

Walker, I.C., 'TD Pipes – a Preliminary Study', *Archaeological Society Quarterly Bulletin* 20.4 (1966), 86-102.

Walker, I.C., *Clay Tobacco Pipes, with Particular Reference to the Bristol Industry* (History and Archaeology, No. 11, National Historic Parks and Sites Branch, Parks Canada, Ottawa, 1977).

Walker, I.C. and Walker, L. de S., 'McDougall's Clay Pipe Factory, Glasgow', *Industrial Archaeology* 6.2 (1969), 132-46.

Wait, E.M., *America and the War of 1812* (New York, 1999).

The Jacksonville 'Blue China' Shipwreck (Site BA02): the Glass Assemblage

Ellen Gerth
Odyssey Marine Exploration, Tampa, USA

Bill Lindsey *
Klamath Falls, Oregon

Odyssey Marine Exploration's survey and excavation in 2005 of the Jacksonville 'Blue China' shipwreck identified two main forms of cargo at a depth of 370m, 70 nautical miles off Jacksonville, Florida. Unlike the British ceramic table, tea and toilet wares, a consignment of glassware proved to be of entirely American origin. Alongside rectangular glass window panes, the ship was transporting an eclectic mix of spirits, mineral water, condiments, colognes and medicinal products packaged in glass bottles of diverse shape and color. In addition to the bottle assemblage were limited glass lamp components and glass bar tumblers, as well as tableware typified by a singular salt cellar.

Of 261 glasswares recorded on the surface of Site BA02, a sample of 52 was recovered for analysis. This article examines the variety of types found on the wreck, their dimensions, origins, manufacture and use. As with the site's ceramic assemblage and clay tobacco pipes, the suggested internal dating evidence of September 1854 for this East Coast schooner's sinking provides a tightened chronological marker for these classes of artifact. The glass cargo reflects the wide range of affordable goods readily available to the average American middle class consumer and provides insights into the social, cultural and economic trends of the period.

1. Introduction

Odyssey Marine Exploration's survey and rescue excavation of the Jacksonville 'Blue China' shipwreck in 2005 identified conspicuous spreads of glass cargo wares across the site, predominantly bottles in various shapes, colors and sizes, all without their cork stoppers and devoid of their original contents (Fig. 19). Less numerous products included lamp components, glass bar tumblers and tableware (Fig. 20). In stark contrast to the exclusive British origins of the ceramic assemblage (Gerth, 2011), the glasswares are all of American manufacture and were probably loaded onto the Site BA02 East Coast schooner at New York, the ship's proposed home port. The ship was also transporting a significant consignment of window glass panes, which are discussed elsewhere (Gerth *et al.*, 2011: 10, 41-44).

A total of 261 glasswares (excluding the window panes) from four classes of artifacts – bottles, bar wares, tableware, and lamps – were recorded on the surface of Site BA02, representing 27.0% of the total artifacts present:

- Black glass spirits/liquor bottles: 193.
- Tumblers: 44.
- Various bottles: 18.
- Lamp globes: 2.
- Lamp bases/fonts: 2.
- Salt cellar: 1.
- Inkstand: 1.

The most extensive concentration of bottles defines the northern, stern section of the wreck in Area B, where 115 Type 1 black glass liquor bottles cover an area of 5.7 x 3.9m

* Bill Lindsey, formerly of the Bureau of Land Management (BLM), is the author and manager of the *Historic Glass Bottle Identification & Information Website* published online through the Society for Historical Archaeology: http://www.sha.org/bottle/index.htm.

Fig. 1. A consignment of Type 1 black glass liquor bottles in Area A on the Jacksonville 'Blue China' shipwreck.

Fig. 2. Overview of Area A showing a consignment of Type 1 black glass liquor bottles north of a large concentration of British ceramics.

Fig. 3. Detail of Type 1 black glass liquor bottles in Area A.

on both the eastern and western side of the keel (Figs. 6-10). Two Type 4 Sands's Sarsaparilla medicine bottles lie on the western edge of keg K1 and two glass oil lamp globes and two lamp fonts with bases were recorded 1.5m to its northwest.

The second most extensive concentration of glass bottles occurs in Area A, the starboard bow, immediately north of a dense cluster of British ceramic cargo wares (Figs. 1-4). Some 65 Type 1 black glass spirits/liquor bottles, three transparent glass tumblers and two Type 3 transparent long-necked sauce/utilitarian bottles cover an area of 2.0 x 1.9m. One Type 6 green glass cologne bottle is present on the southern flank of the main ceramics cluster.

Immediately north of the large keg K6 in Area E2 is a rich deposit of small finds, including a glass salt cellar (Fig. 18), a glass inkstand and two light aqua Type 3 sauce/utilitarian glass bottles on the northwestern side of keg K7. These wares are associated with part of a brass and glass sextant and a brass hinge, which may denote the position of the stern galley remains. An additional Type 8 cobalt blue 12-paneled cologne bottle juxtaposed with a lead ingot and a series of at least six degraded wooden kegs is present in Area D (Fig. 11).

Area G contains the scattered remains of cargo ceramics and glasswares within an area of 6.7 x 3.0m, which has seemingly been heavily impacted by fishing trawlers' bottom gear. A 7.2m-long and 0.7m-wide narrow band extending down the northwestern side of this zone, terminating at the northern end of Area A, contains 25 scattered glass tumblers (Figs. 15-16, 20). Area G merges with Area F on the eastern, port side of the wreck, where a further seven tumblers were recorded. Two more tumblers are present in Area A, one in Area B, four in Area D, four in Area E and one next to concretion CN1. The tumblers in Areas F and G are contextualized with a spread of glass window panes on either side of the keel covering a 1.8 x 1.3m section of wreckage in the northern end of Area D and parallel to a second 1.8 x 1.2m cluster in Area F (Figs. 12, 17, 19).

The glassware assemblage, from which a small sample of 52 artifacts was recovered for study (Table 1), seems to comprise remains of a larger cargo that no longer survives, having been severely impacted or dragged by bottom trawlers (select excavation encountered insufficient stratigraphy to conceal significant additional cargo). The glasswares are all American products indicative generally of production in the decades 1840-60, when glassmaking was becoming one of the largest and most important industries in the country. Having undergone severe fluctuations in successes and failures over the decades, by the latter part of the century America's glass production was identified as being the US's most highly developed industry (Henderson, 1893: 434).

Class	No. Recovered	Height (cm)	Date Range	Content
Type 1 bottle	6	26.5	*c.* 1850s to *c.* 1860	Spirits/liquor
Type 2 bottle	1	18.2	1820s to *c.* 1860	Mineral water
Type 3 bottle	2	21.4	1830s to *c.* 1860	Sauce/utilitarian
Type 4 bottle	4	15.3	1839 to *c.* 1860	'Sands's Sarsaparilla' medicine
Type 5 bottle	7	13.5	*c.* 1840-1860	Medicine
Type 6 bottle	2	19.1	*c.* 1830s-1860	Cologne
Type 7 bottle	1	13.0	1820s to 1860s	Cologne
Type 8 bottle	1	18.8	1830s to late 1850s	Cologne/ toilet water
Type 9A bottle Type 9B bottle	9 total	16.5 11.8	Late 1840s to *c.* 1860	Spices/condiments
Smooth-sided tumbler	5	8.9	*c.* 1845-75	----
Fluted tumbler	10	9.0	*c.* 1845-75	----
Oil lamp font & base	1	21.2	*c.* 1840-1870	----
Oil lamp globe (semi-opaque glass)	1	16.2	1850s to 1880s	----
Oil lamp globe (ruby red)	1	19.8	1850s to 1880	----
Salt cellar	1	5.0	*c.* 1835 and 1860	----

Table 1. Classes of glasswares recovered from the Jacksonville 'Blue China' shipwreck (Site BA02).

The small sample of glass bottles recovered during the rescue excavation of the Jacksonville 'Blue China' shipwreck comprised:

- Six Type 1 long-necked black glass spirits/liquor bottles (Figs. 29-31).
- One Type 2 dark olive green black glass mineral water bottle (Figs. 33-36).
- Two Type 3 long-necked aquamarine sauce/utilitarian bottles (Figs. 38-41).
- Four Type 4 rectangular aquamarine 'Sands's Sarsaparilla' patent medicine bottles (Figs 42-47).
- Seven Type 5 cylindrical, tapered vial-like aquamarine medicine bottles (Figs. 49-53).
- Two Type 6 transparent olive green glass cologne bottles (Figs. 54-56).
- One Type 7 colorless glass figural cologne bottle (Figs. 57-62).
- One Type 8 12-paneled cobalt blue glass cologne/toilet water bottle (Figs. 63-66).
- Nine Type 9 rectangular aquamarine spice or condiment bottles (two different sizes/varieties) (Figs. 67-74).

None of their paper and/or foil labels has survived intact and only one bottle type has an embossment defining the company and product name. The wooden packing crates that would have typically carried the stenciled names of the company and bottled product, or possibly the merchant consignee to whom the goods were being shipped, were also no longer preserved. In their absence, attributing the Jacksonville 'Blue China' glassware to particular glass factories is largely impossible, with the exception of a few pattern glass artifacts that exhibit distinctive features. As with Site BA02's ceramic wares, the glassware cargo was probably intended for delivery to a coastal port along the southeastern United States or perhaps in the Gulf of Mexico (such as New Orleans, from where some of these goods may been shipped up the Mississippi to the Western frontier or south to Central and South America).

2. Mid-19th Century US Glassworks

The growth of the bottle industry throughout the 19th century hinged on a combination of factors. Urbanization and a rising standard of living increased the markets for products that had formerly been produced in the home, such as liquor and preserved food, and for other products like carbonated beverages and medicines that had previously been consumed in limited quantities. The greater demand for packaged goods boosted the use of sealed glass containers, guaranteeing consumers that the contents were untainted and sanitary. Packaging also permitted customers to bring home and store products for later use. Further developments in road and canal communications, as well as steamboats and railroads, necessitated the production of

Fig. 4. Detail of Type 1 black glass liquor bottles on the west flank of Area A.

Fig. 5. A Type 9A large glass condiment bottle alongside a Canton porcelain ginger jar northwest of Area A.

Fig. 6. Overview of a second consignment of Type 1 black glass liquor bottles in Area B, east and west of the keel.

more bottles and other glassware to protect and preserve goods during shipment. Customer confidence was also reassured by the application of brand names in the form of company labels and/or embossments (Busch, 2000: 176).

The diversity of the Jacksonville 'Blue China's glass cargo provides a unique window into America's thriving glass industry *c.* 1854, the most likely date of the ship's loss based on available data analyzed. By the mid-19th century, factories, firms, and workers were increasingly specializing in various branches of glassmaking, including the manufacture of flat glass (plate and window glass), tableware and bottles, the latter of which were particularly vital to US merchants and druggists, who relied on vast volumes to conduct their business – a burgeoning industry that just 50 years previously was still in its infancy, eclipsed by more expensive imported bottles (Busch, 2000: 175).

Whereas only a verified eight (and no more than 11 or 12) glassworks are known to have been operating across America in 1800 (Davis, 1949: 28; McKearin and Wilson, 1978: 68), within two decades at least 33 glasshouses were in existence. Of the 71 such factories operational by 1832, over half produced glass bottles as either their main output or as a sideline. The industry continued to grow and 50 years later 169 glasshouses were manufacturing annually over 70 times the number of bottles produced in 1820 (Busch, 2000: 176; McKearin and Wilson, 1978: 68-70). Virtually all of the US glassworks were located in three major geographical regions: New England, the Middle Atlantic States and the Midwest (McKearin and Wilson, 1978: 68-70).

Most of these opened in the wake of the 1824 protective tariff designed to safeguard American industry, including glass production and trade, from cheaper imported British commodities (Busch, 2000: 176; McKearin and Wilson, 1978: 69, 70). The US had recently witnessed a period of technological innovation in the bottle manufacturing industry that increased productivity. The adoption of full-size multi-section molds around 1810, for instance, facilitated uniformity and speed. The subsequent growth in manufacturing was naturally accompanied by a decrease in bottle prices. By the latter part of the 19th century, beer, soda and whiskey bottles were valued at $3.75 per gross, which was roughly half their cost earlier in the century. This was still relatively expensive compared to other products, such as basic provisions like pork, which in 1853 sold in San Antonio, Texas, for 11 cents per pound and coffee from Rio for 12.5 cents per pound (*Southwestern Historical Quarterly*, October 1947: 170). The skilled labor required for blowing glass kept bottle prices high. Demand for bottles continued to grow, nevertheless, so much so that it still exceeded supply (Busch, 2000: 176-7).

Fig. 7. Mixed glass bottles to the southwest of Area B on either side of the keel: Type 1 liquor bottles in the background and a Type 4 Sands's Sarsaparilla bottle and a Type 5 tapered medicine bottle in the foreground.

Fig. 8. Type 1 black glass liquor bottles alongside keg K4 and the keel in Area B.

Fig. 9. Type 1 black glass liquor bottles and Type 5 cylindrical medicine bottles in Area B intermixed with clay tobacco pipes.

Fig. 10. Type 1 black glass liquor bottles and two Type 5 cylindrical medicine bottles in Area B intermixed with clay tobacco pipes.

Fig. 11. A Type 8 cobalt blue glass cologne bottle alongside small wooden kegs, glass window panes and a lead ingot in Area D.

Fig. 12. A Type 9B small glass condiment bottle in Area F, with glass window panes on either side of the keel. Mixed pottery is visible in the background.

Fig. 13. A Type 6 olive green glass cologne bottle on the southeastern edge of Area G.

Fig. 14. Type 3 glass sauce/utilitarian bottles scattered around concreted keg K7 in Area E3 in association with clay tobacco pipes.

Fig. 15. Fluted glass bar tumblers in situ *in Area G.*

Fig. 16. Fluted glass bar tumblers in situ *in Area G.*

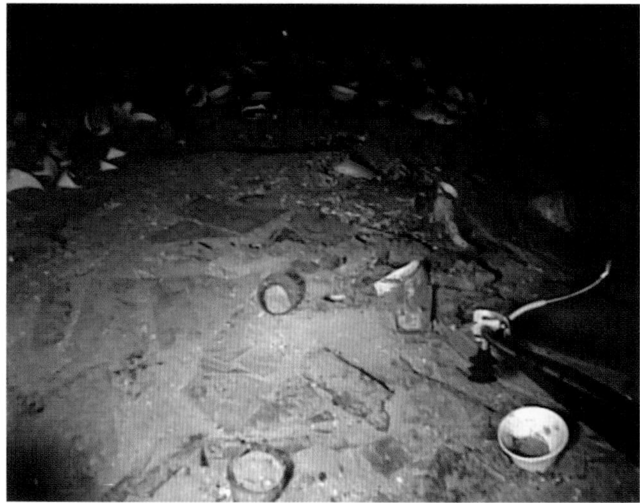

Fig. 17. Glass tumblers in Area D2 in association with glass window panes.

Fig. 18. A glass salt cellar in situ *next to keg K6 in Area E2.*

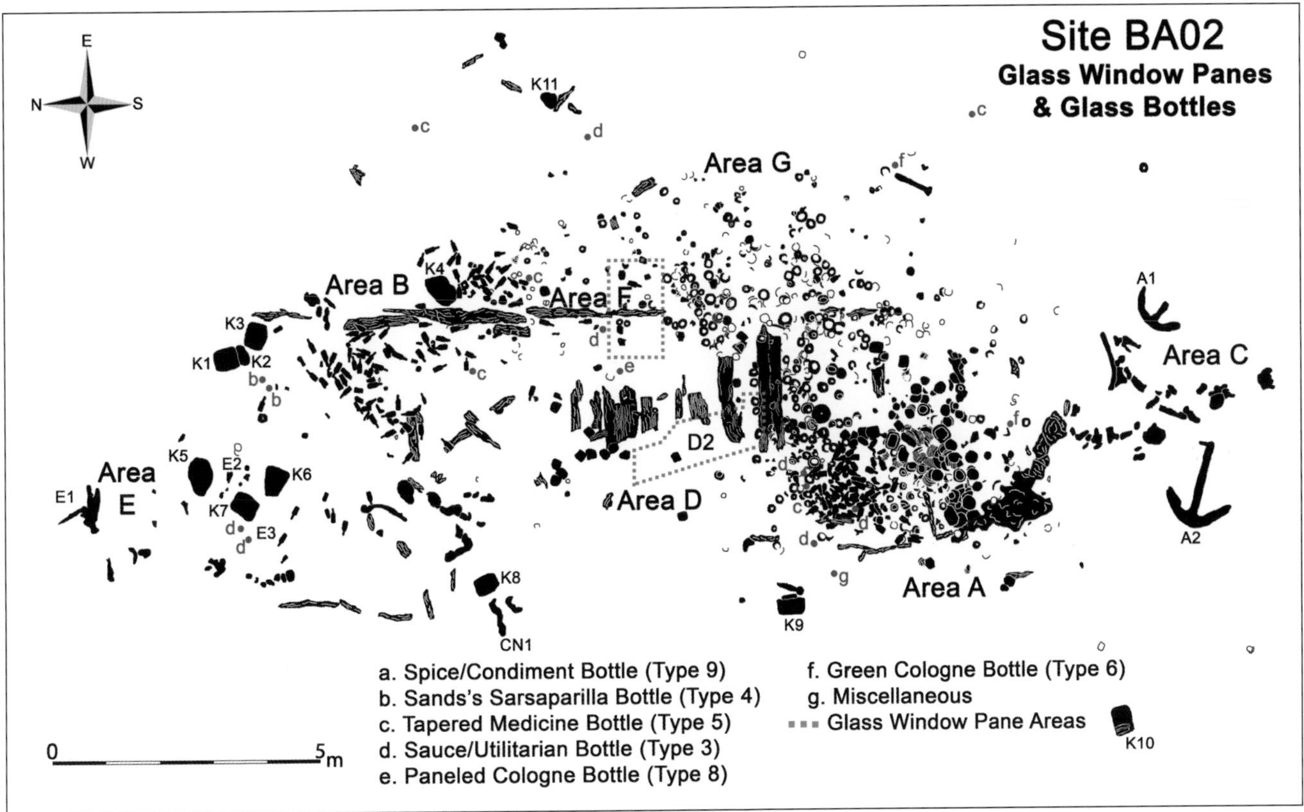

Fig. 19. The distribution of American Type 3-9 glass bottles and window panes on Site BA02.

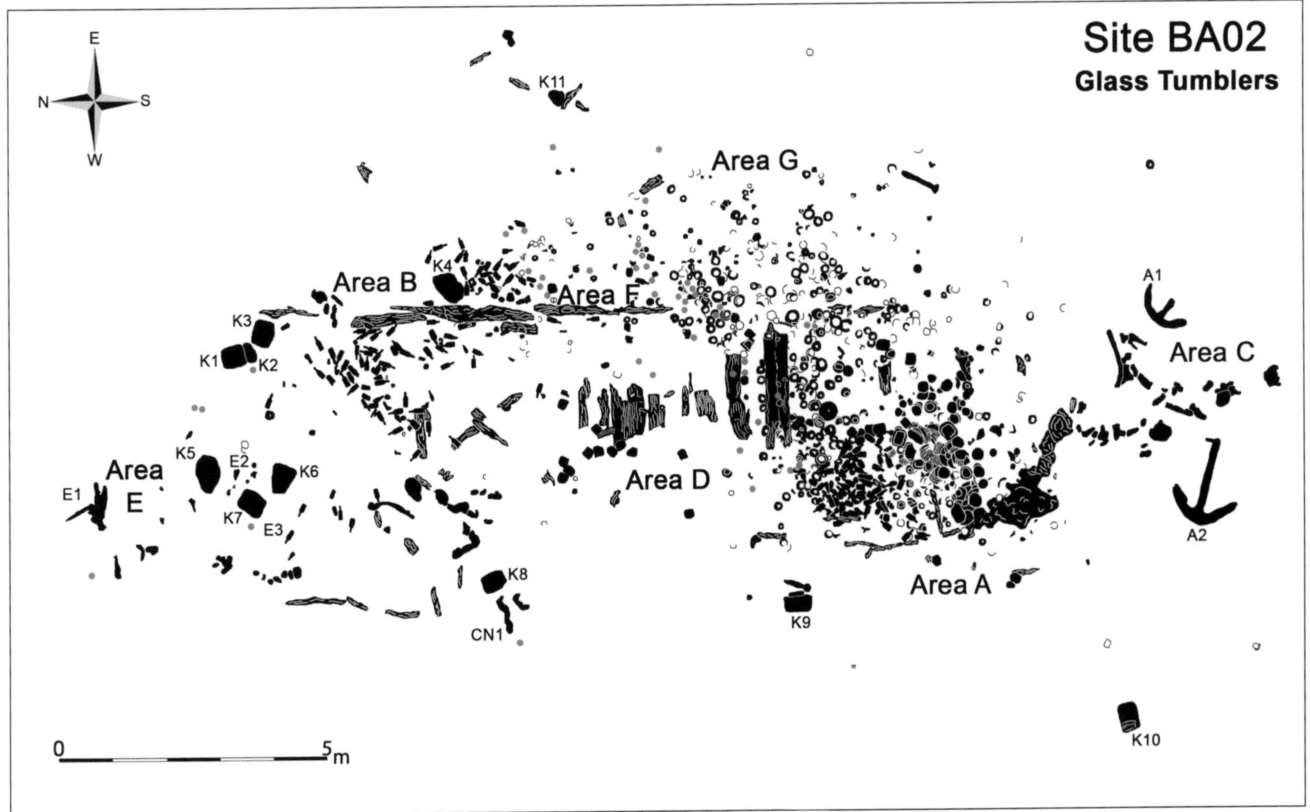

Fig. 20. The distribution of American glass tumblers on Site BA02.

Fig. 21. A trade card issued by the Liebig Company of New York for the European market featuring late 19th-century glassblowers at work next to a glass furnace. Photo: courtesy of SHA/BLM Historic Glass Bottle Identification & Information Website.

Fig. 22. A glass blower and mold boy in a glass factory at Grafton, Virginia, in October 1908. Photo: courtesy of the US Library of Congress.

Fig. 23. Workmen washing, filling and crowning mineral water bottles in November 1918 in a plant run by the New York State Conservation Commission in the New York State Reservation, now Saratoga Spa State Park, near Saratoga Springs. Photo: New York State Archives, 14297-87, SARA No.375.

While a comprehensive overview of the US glassworks operating in the mid-1800s is beyond the scope of this paper, this brief outline offers insights into some of the regional firms located within reasonable transportation distances from New York City, the suggested port of origin for the Jacksonville 'Blue China' vessel. These produced glasswares contemporary with the ship's lifespan and their output included the manufacture of bottles and vials. For most glasshouses in the region under discussion, as well as across the country, bottles were unmarked (not embossed with proprietary information relative to the glass maker or user of the bottle) (McKearin and Wilson, 1978: 89). This fact is confirmed by the anonymity of the recovered Site BA02 bottle assemblage.

Of particular relevance is the southern area of New Jersey, which in the first three decades of the 19th century became a regional center of glass manufacture that continues today. Most of the factories were located in the flat, wooded part of southern New Jersey, where suitable sand for glass was abundant, as was wood for furnace firing, potash and building materials. Like most glassworks of this era, the majority of 'South Jersey' firms were built on or near waterways, railroads and turnpikes, providing easy access to city markets, and in particular, to Philadelphia, where companies had established agents and outlets (McKearin and Wilson, 1978: 89). While most were window glasshouses, a number of manufactories specialized in bottles.

One such example was Glassboro's Harmony Glass Works (1813), which, like many such companies, experienced multiple ownership changes, later becoming

Whitney Brothers (1839-87) and finally the Whitney Glass Works (1887-1918) (Toulouse, 1971: 519-24). This long-lived factory apparently turned out a large variety of vials, bottles and druggist wares of every description, as well as wines, porters (a dark colored beer similar to stout) and Dutch gin bottles "equal to the best in Europe", as an 1857 circular recognized (McKearin and Wilson, 1978: 92). Other 'South Jersey' factories that may have contributed to the Site BA02 cargo included the Waterford Glass Works (1822-80), whose output regularly consisted of window glass, bottles and flasks; the Washington Glass Works (1839-1917; called the Williamston Glass Works by the 1850s) located in Williamstown, Camden County (McKearin and McKearin, 1941: 603); and the Millville Glass Works and its later manifestations (1844-1938) (McKearin and Wilson, 1978: 90-95).

Closer to New York City, Philadelphia's Union Glass Works opened in 1826 and, following a fire in the 1840s, was reopened in 1847 by the firm of Hartell and Lancaster, primarily for the production of bottles. An 1858 advertisement for this company lists an assortment of bottles being sold, including druggist glass, wine, porter and mineral water bottles (McKearin and Wilson, 1978: 88-9). Another high probability Philadelphia bottle-producing company conducting significant business in the region was the Dyottville Glass Works, which underwent various ownerships and renaming from its founding about 1816 to its demise in 1923. This company produced "vast quantities of various kinds of bottles and flasks" during the mid-19th century (McKearin and Wilson, 1978: 79-88; Toulouse, 1971: 171).

Further west, the plethora of glass factories in the Pittsburgh area, as well as neighboring Ohio and West Virginia, could well have been a source of some of the Jacksonville 'Blue China' vessel's bottle cargo given the efficiency and regional expansion of railroad transportation by the 1850s. Strong possibilities include the larger producers of bottles (known as 'hollowware'), such as the Pittsburgh firms of Ihmsen & Sons (1836-68 onwards), Samuel McKee & Co. (1834-86), A. & D.H. Chambers (1841-88), Cunningham & Co. (1845-1930), William McCully & Co. (1841-86) and possibly other smaller concerns in Ravenna and Zanesville, Ohio. Additional firms included glasshouses in Wheeling and Wellsburg, West Virginia (McKearin and Wilson, 1978: 153-69).

Finally, New York State itself possessed a number of bottle-producing glasshouses operating in the 1850s, which could have contributed some of the bottles discovered on Site BA02. These included the upstate factories of the Lockport Glass Works (1843-80s) and the Mount

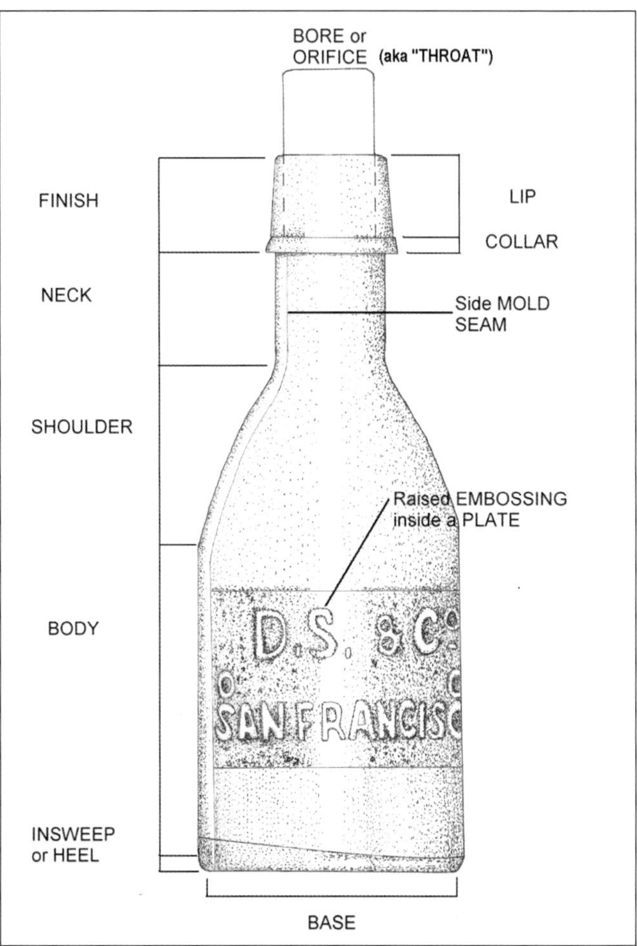

Fig. 24. A stylized 19th-century mineral water bottle with the standard morphological components located and named, as used in this paper for descriptive purposes. Drawing: Peggy Corson. Photo: courtesy SHA/BLM 'Historic Glass Bottle Identification & Information' website.

Vernon Glass Works in Mt. Pleasant (1844-90), both of which were known producers of the 'Saratoga' style of bottles corresponding to the Site BA02 Type 2 discussed below (McKearin and Wilson, 1978: 137-42, 234-35; Tucker, 1986: xii-xiii). In addition, as noted below in the discussion of the Type 1 spirits/liquor bottles, both the Brooklyn Glass Works (1831-76) and the Ellenville Glass Works (1836-96) northwest of New York City are viable candidates for the production of this bottle type in particular.

The assorted Site BA02 glass cargo reflects the manufacturing developments that characterized the United States during the seven decades following its independence, indicative of an emerging economy still reliant on British ceramic imports, but increasingly becoming self-sufficient through a booming domestic market in American glasswares. Significantly, this combined cargo exemplifies the wide range of affordable goods readily available to the average American consumer and provides insights into the social, cultural and economic trends of the period.

3. 19th-Century Glass Bottles: Limits of Interpretation

The dating and classification of the Site BA02 glass bottles is based largely on their shape, mode of manufacture and to a lesser extent on their color, which together provide a general production timeframe of 1840-60. This is consistent with the independent dating of the Jacksonville 'Blue China' wreck to around 1854. The interpretation of the Site BA02 bottles also benefits from comparative analysis with examples recovered from contemporary marine and terrestrial sites, particularly well-preserved examples retaining their company labels and/or remains of contents.

Similar assemblages derived from far-flung historic sites also contribute to a better understanding of the extensive trade networks that developed in the mid-19th century and supplied American consumers east and west. The coastal schooner represented by the Jacksonville 'Blue China' wreck played a role in the country's early maritime commerce along the Eastern Seaboard and reflects the variety of products traded and transported from the crowded docks of New York at the time.

The majority of American bottles produced from the early 1820s until after the turn of the 20th century, which witnessed the development of semi-automatic and automatic bottle machines, were largely mouth-blown examples (blown by human lungs) manufactured in multi-section molds typically made of cast iron and brass, although ceramic and wooden molds were not uncommon. When forming the shape of the bottle, molds leave behind diagnostic physical features reflecting the manufacturing techniques used, which helps to determine not only production methods but is also a useful index of chronology.[1]

Consistent with these production trends, the Site BA02 assemblage represents mostly mold-blown examples, with the exception of two bottle forms (Type 3 and Type 6) that appear to have been free-blown, possibly with the aid of a one-piece dip mold (a tool used to assist in free-blown production to gain uniformity and consistency in the shaping of the body and sometimes the base) (Griffenhagen and Bogard, 1999: 103; Lawrence, 2006: 372; McKearin and Wilson, 1978: 14; Walbridge, 1920: 67-9). Free-blown bottles were typically produced without a mold, instead being formed and shaped by the skills of the glassblower using manipulation of the blowpipe and various hand tools. Bottles formed without a mold will generally not be symmetrical in body, shoulder, neck or

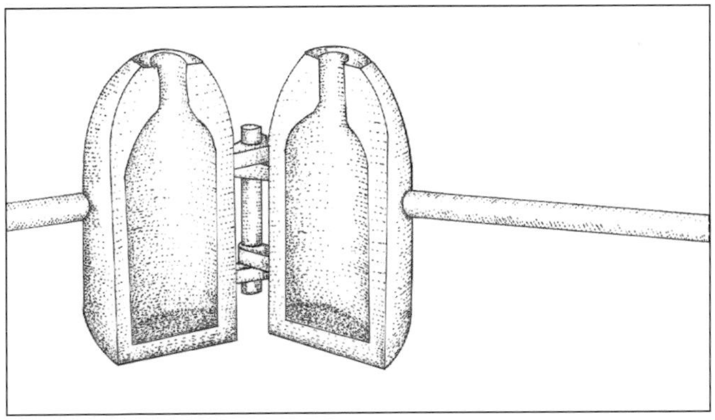

Fig. 25. A true two-piece, side-hinged bottle mold. Drawing: Peggy Corson. Photo: courtesy SHA/BLM 'Historic Glass Bottle Identification & Information' website.

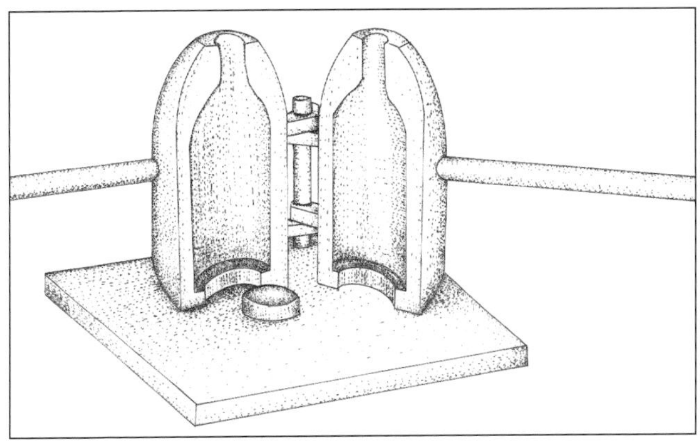

Fig. 26. A side-hinged, two-piece bottle mold with a separate post-style base plate ('post-bottom' or 'post-base' mold). Drawing: Peggy Corson. Photo: courtesy SHA/BLM 'Historic Glass Bottle Identification & Information' website.

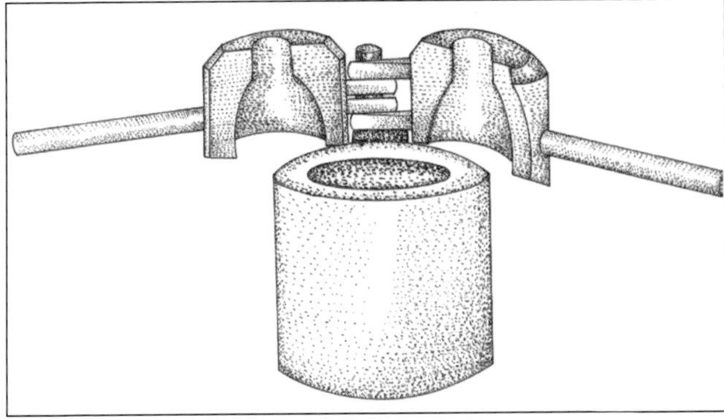

Fig. 27. A three-piece mold comprised of a one-piece body/base mold part ('dip mold') surmounted by a two-part, side-hinged shoulder/neck forming mold. Drawing: Peggy Corson. Photo: courtesy SHA/BLM 'Historic Glass Bottle Identification & Information' website.

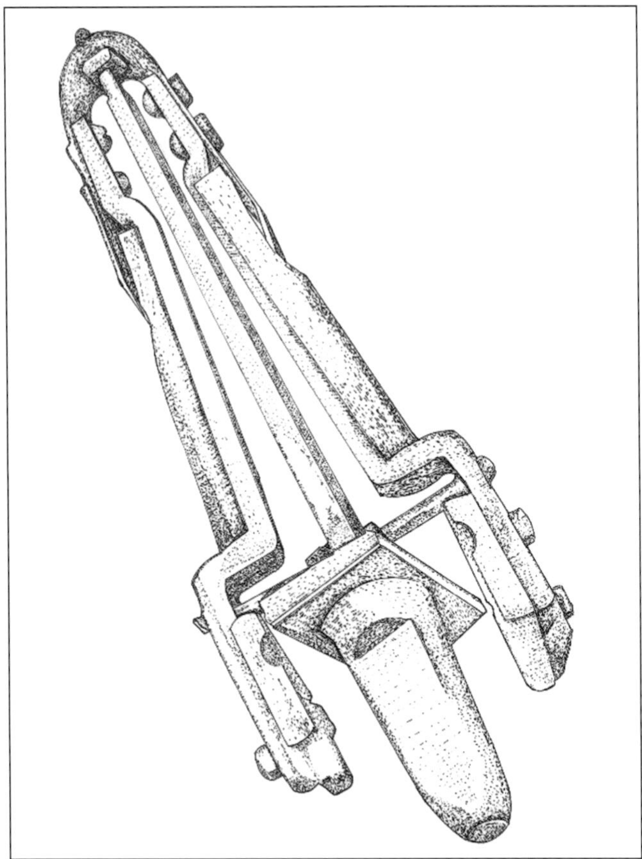

Fig. 28. A finishing or lipping tool used to form ('finish') the conformation of a bottle lip (the 'finish'). The tool's central plug fitted inside the bottle bore, so that when the tool was rotated the opposing pads on the caliper ends formed the outside of the finish while the glass was still hot and pliable. Drawing: Peggy Corson. Photo: courtesy SHA/BLM 'Historic Glass Bottle Identification & Information' website.

base shape and will not incorporate mold seams, embossing or molded decoration. Although less common, bottles produced by free-blown manufacture were still available up until about the American Civil War of 1861-65.

The bases of early to mid 19th-century bottles – both free-blown and mold-blown – usually feature some type of pontil mark or scar derived from the long iron pontil rod usually fixed to the base of the bottle with a small glob of glass to enable a worker to hold the bottle to complete the 'finishing' of the mouth and lip (cf. Fig. 24 for bottle terms used in this paper). Typically a ring or strip of hot glass was added to the neck of the bottle at the point where the blowpipe was removed and was subsequently shaped to form a smooth rim that took a cork stopper. The finish was formed while the bottle was rotated by another glassworker holding it by the base with the pontil rod. When the bottle was finished, the rod was snapped off, frequently leaving a patch of roughened glass or a pontil scar on the base (Jones, 2000: 156; Lawrence, 2006: 372). The different empontilling techniques included the plain glass-tipped pontil, the sand glass-tipped pontil, the blowpipe as pontil and the bare iron pontil, each of which left a characteristic mark or scar (Jones, 2000: 156). The Site BA02 bottles exhibit evidence of the sand, glass-tipped or blowpipe pontil scars. No bare iron pontil marks were apparent.

In the 1840s, a new method of holding bottles during finishing was developed, which is a useful chronological marker, whereby a 'snap case' or an iron cradle held the post-mold hot bottle by the base and/or body while the finish was being completed. The snap case gradually replaced the various types of pontil rods and empontilling techniques and was one of the most significant inventions that facilitated more efficient production during the mid-19th century. Unlike the pontil rod, the snap case left little, if any, marks or other physical evidence on the bottle (Lawrence, 2006: 372; McKearin and Wilson, 1978: 14). Examples with pontil scars largely disappeared by the late 1860s as various 'snap case' tools replaced the use of the pontil rod to grasp the hot bottle for finishing the lip. Significantly for our understanding of the transition between these techniques, this 'new' technology is absent from the Site BA02 glass bottle assemblage, which clearly looks back rather than forward in time in terms of tradition.

In effect, the presence or absence of pontil marks or scars, and the specific type of mark derived from different empontiling techniques, is a very useful tool for dating 19th-century bottles. The presence of distinctive pontil scars on all of the Site BA02 bottles establishes a general end date of 1860 for their production. However, the transition from the use of the pontil rod to the snap case occurred over a period of many years and at different times and contexts dependent on the adoption of the newer technology by a specific factory and its craftsmen.

Only one bottle type amongst the Jacksonville 'Blue China' assemblage features an embossed company name useful in dating and identifying the bottled product (the Type 4 Sands's Sarsaparilla medicine bottle, see Section 7 below). The other bottle types, however, can largely be identified and dated by shapes closely associated with distinct products, such as liquor, medicine, mineral water, condiments and cologne/perfume (Fike, 1987: 13), although this is far from an exact science.

It is important to bear in mind that bottle reuse was common in the 19th century and even earlier, when supply in America could not meet the growing demand. Archaeological excavations have demonstrated that bottles could be retained for decades and reused multiple times before being discarded. For example, wine bottles excavated from the John Curtis house in Williamsburg, Virginia, were at least 20 years old when they were deposited. Other 18th-century sites present a similar scenario (Busch, 2000: 176).

Customers habitually returned their empty bottles directly to merchants and druggists in return for cash (McKearin and Wilson, 1978: 229-30) or took their own bottles to druggists to be refilled. Thus, even medicine bottles might contain a different product to what they originally held (Busch, 2000: 177). Old bottles had both trade and property value. It was not unusual to offer customers three shillings or more a dozen for returns. Entrepreneurs, including brewers, snuff manufacturers and druggists, who needed bottles to market their products, offered cash or goods for both new and old bottles. Merchants strove to sustain supplies by offering reduced prices for returns. For example, in May 1774 a New York brewer sold a dozen new bottles of beer for 10 shillings, but for seven shillings if the bottles were returns (Busch, 2000: 175). In a similar vein, a dealer from Hartford, Connecticut, offered a dozen bottles of porter for 16 shillings, two pence or at the discounted price of 12 shillings if the bottles were returns (McKearin and Wilson, 1978: 230).

Bottle reuse was also customary in bars and saloons, where whisky was purchased in barrels and then served to customers in bottles. Each morning bartenders refilled empties from the night before. Firms devoted entirely to the trade in used bottles emerged as big business, with middlemen facilitating their transfer between manufacturers, merchants and consumers. The first such company allegedly opened in New York City in the late 1840s. By the end of the century the second-hand bottle business was thriving throughout America's cities (Busch, 2000: 177).

Although color is generally of limited use in classifying a bottle's age or content type, it offers some insights into chronology. The Jacksonville 'Blue China' assemblage consists largely of pale or light aquamarine examples, which are indicative of production in the 1850s and later. Medicine, sarsaparilla and utilitarian bottles made during the period 1830-40 were typically a darker colored glass – ambers, greens and deeper shades of aquamarine.

Analysis of the recovered bottles from Site BA02, based largely on the above factors of production, has permitted the following descriptive identifications and dating to be proposed. This study includes an overview of the bottles in both an historical and archaeological context in light of the social, economic and cultural trends prevalent in mid-19th century America.

4. Type 1 Spirits/Liquor Bottles

As with all of the bottles recovered from Site BA02, the six Type 1 spirits/liquor bottles were found empty (Figs. 1-4, 6-10, 29-31). They would have been sealed originally with cork stoppers, which either imploded during the schooner's sinking as a result of pressure or degraded over the decades within the corrosive marine environment. The half dozen liquor bottles retrieved represent a small fraction of the 193 cargo bottles of this type recorded on the wreck.

Type 1 spirits/liquor bottles are tall, moderate width cylinder 'fifth' capacity containers (approximately one-fifth of a gallon) with a combined body and shoulder height that is greater than 1.5 times (but less than 1.8 times) the combined height of the straight-sided neck and finish. The base is composed of a flat exterior ring with a moderately domed bell-shaped center plate, which exhibits a sand pontil scar typical of the period. The base diameter is slightly less than one-third the height of the entire bottle. The applied finish is of the 'mineral' style that was common on pre-Civil War American liquor bottles in many forms (plus many other bottles). Type 1 exhibits a horizontal mold seam at the base of the gently rounded shoulder and two opposite and perpendicular (to the shoulder seam) vertical shoulder/neck seams typical of bottles produced in a three-piece mold (known as a Ricketts' patent mold style in the 19th century; Fig. 27).

The Type 1 bottles display the following dimensions: H. 26.5cm; W. mid-body 8.1cm; max. W. of shoulder 8.2cm; neck H. 7.2cm; total finish H. 1.8cm; collar H. 0.6cm; collar W. 3.0cm; lip H. 1.2cm; neck W. 4.0cm; bore Diam. 1.8cm; rim Th. 0.3cm; body H. 14.8cm; shoulder H. 2.8cm; base Diam. 7.9cm; weight: 583gr.

Liquor of all types – bourbon, rye, gin, cognac and scotch – was bottled in a wide variety of shapes and sizes in mid-19th century America, ranging from small flasks holding a few ounces to larger bulk containers, such as demijohns and carboys that stored gallons. Although the diversity of 19th-century liquor bottles is enormous, distinct forms and shapes permit specific examples to be correlated to particular contents.

The Jacksonville 'Blue China' wreck examples are representative of a common spirits/liquor bottle type with bodies that are moderately slender in cross-section with a long, tapering narrow neck, a form that evolved from the wider and squatter late 17th/early 18th-century English cylindrical 'onion' bottle made of dark green glass and typifying some of the earliest types found in North America. Like its predecessor, the Type 1 bottles are typically associated with any number of liquors from rum to whiskey and brandy and frequently even contained wine. This popular three-piece molded cylinder bottle, commonly referred to as a 'patent style cylindrical fifth' (one-fifth of a gallon), was manufactured by numerous eastern American glasshouses from 1844 until about 1880, with production

Fig. 29. Type 1 black glass spirits/liquor bottle BC-05-00002-BE, H. 26.5cm.

concentrated in the decades between the 1850s and 1870s (Jones, 1986: 29; McKearin and Wilson, 1978: 207, 219).

Although the Site BA02 Type 1 examples are all unmarked – not uncommon for the time – similar bottles of the period are embossed on their bases with the names of the major, largely East Coast, glassworks active during the height of this bottle types' popularity. Identified embossments include the Dyottsville Glass Works of Philadelphia, Pennsylvania, a company that was in business from 1833 to 1923; Weeks & Gilson of South Stoddard, New Hampshire (1853-73); Whitney Glass Works (Harmony Glass Works until 1835) of Glassboro, New Jersey (1813-1918) (Griffenhagen and Bogard, 1999: 105); Willington Glass Works of West Willington, Connecticut (1814/5-72); Ellenville Glass Works of Ellenville, New York (1836-96); Bushwick Glass Works of Brooklyn, New York (1865-90s); Cunningham & Ihmsen of Pittsburgh, Pennsylvania (1857-78) and W. McCully & Co., also of Pittsburgh, Pennsylvania (1841 to late 1860s), amongst others (McKearin and Wilson, 1978: 220-21).

The three-piece molds relied on to make cylinder liquor bottles, as exemplified by the Site BA02 Type 1 bottles, were often referred to as a Ricketts mold, one of the United States' earliest multi-section mold types (Fig. 27). This technology utilized one large body piece from base to shoulder and two shoulder sections that folded out to allow the bottle to be removed after blowing. It also permitted the name of the glassworks or company and the address to be molded onto the outer rim of the base. First used in England *c.* 1814, the mold was later patented in 1821 or 1822 by Henry Ricketts of Bristol, England, and then adopted by many US glassworks by the 1830s, making its presence in archaeological contexts a good index of chronology (Jones, 2000: 154; McKearin and Wilson, 1978: 216; Sutton and Arkush, 1996: 177).

The Ricketts mold standardized the size of most categories of spirits (and wine bottles) in the first half of the 19th century. It also enabled an interchangeable 'slug' plate to be added to the bottom of the mold, which could be used to emboss a company name. Production in a three-piece mold leaves a diagnostic horizontal mold seam around the bottle at the junction of the body and shoulder. The Jacksonville 'Blue China' Type 1 examples are indicative of the classic three-piece Ricketts mold type spirits bottle of American manufacture (unlike the true Ricketts' bottles that were of English manufacture).

The Site BA02 'cylindrical fifths' feature an applied 'mineral' finish, a common lip form seen on this bottle type. A sand pontil scar present on the base of the bottle is of a form that was popular on English dark green glass wine bottles from the 18th century onwards and similar American-made bottles of the first half of the 19th century (Jones, 2000: 156). This particular mark derives from a common method of empontilling a bottle so that it could be securely held for finishing. The pontil scar was formed when the hot glass on the ball-shaped tip of an iron pontil rod was dipped in sand (or small glass chips) prior to application to the bottle base. The sand or glass chips were apparently intended to keep the pontil rod from adhering too closely to the bottle, facilitating easier removal. This form of sand pontil conformed better than other pontil types to molded base shapes without causing distortion (Jones, 2000: 156; Van den Bosche, 2001: 64).

The Type 1 bottles' round bodies, an inherently strong shape, were made of thick glass to survive extensive post-bottling handling, which was essential because this bottle type was typically reused many times. These liquor bottles are of a dark olive green glass often referred to as 'black glass': it is typically so dense that the color appears visually to be black. Other much less common 'black glass' colors include dark ambers, deep reddish purple and other more rare hues. The dark color was produced by combining many proportions of substances and impurities, most usually high concentrations of iron, but also carbon derived from ashes or copper with iron and magnesia. These raw materials produced a strong and resilient glass whose dense color best protected the contents from the effects of sunlight, thus preventing spoilage (McKearin and Wilson, 1978: 9-10).

The process for making black glass, one of the oldest bottle colors, was commonly employed by glass blowers in Britain in the 17th century, although the term apparently was not adopted until the following century, when advertisements in American newspapers of the 1740s offered for sale 'black-glass-bottles' (Jones, 1986: 11; McKearin, 1978: 10). By this time it would appear that the production of black glass was known to glass makers in the 'colonies', where it was being produced in some quantity. Most black glass bottles were intended to contain liquor, wine and ale for which protection against light was an important quality. Between the 1840s and 1880s, in particular, they were mass-produced as a cheap container in a thousand shapes and sizes. Black glass bottles and fragments are ubiquitous on historic sites pre-dating the last quarter of the 19th century.

Of particular interest for the period under discussion and the Jacksonville 'Blue China' Type 1 wares are the comparable black glass liquor bottles recovered from the Hoff Store site, which collapsed into San Francisco Bay during the 'Fifth Great Fire' that ravaged the city on 3-4 May 1851. Situated along the south side of Howison's Pier, hundreds of W.C. Hoff's bottles containing preserved foods, medicines, toiletries, alcoholic beverages and various other contents for retail purchase were deposited into the muddy waters and many were excavated with their sealed contents intact (McDougall, 1990: 58).

The largest class of bottles represented by the Hoff Store assemblage was alcoholic beverages (49.5% of the total) of which two types were recovered: black glass, many of which are seemingly identical to the Jacksonville 'Blue China' liquor bottles, and other bottles reserved for wine and champagne. Black glass bottles blown from both dark olive green and amber glass predominate, totaling 258 examples (64.6% of the alcoholic beverage class). Some

Figs. 30-31. Detail of the finish and base of Type 1 black glass spirits/liquor bottle BC-05-00002-BE.

80 bottles exhibit morphological characteristics that are thought to reflect contents of brandy (cylindrical liquor bottles similar to the Site BA02 examples), with four intact examples retaining their liquor content. Some of the Hoff Store bottles exhibit embossed bases advertising an original content of ale (McDougall, 1990: 58-61). By the time they were lost, many of the examples may have been recycled and used for other products, which, of course, cannot be discounted for the Site BA02 cargo. The wreck's Type 1

Fig. 32. 'Patent' style bottles from the wreck of the SS Republic *(1865), similar in shape to and the descendants of Site BA02 Type 1. There was extensive overlap in the making of these two forms concurrently in the 1850s and 1860s.*

glass bottles very likely contained any number of liquid substances within the broad category of liquors or wine.

All but two of the Hoff store bottles were formed within molds, and 77% of the mold-blown bottles (198 bottles) exhibit sand pontil scars similar to those on the Jacksonville 'Blue China' examples. Unlike the shipwreck's 'cylindrical fifths', however, a handful of the San Francisco bottles are embossed with company names – both proprietors and glass makers – including a Baltimore, Maryland, retail and wholesale grocer and a glass manufactory in Bristol, England (McDougall, 1990: 59-60). Until the 1860s there were no glass companies producing bottles on the West Coast, so all of the Hoff store bottles were either of Eastern US origin or possibly imported.

The Hoff store liquor bottles and others within the assemblage reflect the global nature of the city's maritime trade network. Around the mid-19th century, the port of San Francisco functioned as the primary commercial emporium and depot of the Gold Rush and relied on ship-borne consumer goods from eastern US cities, as well as British and other imports, many of which were competing with American manufacturers, including apparently some of the Hoff Store liquor bottles (Delgado, 2009: 130-31).

By the 1850s, spirit bottles similar to the Site BA02 Type 1 examples, both embossed and unembossed, were evidently still imported from Britain to some degree. However, with the growth of American glass companies, dozens of US glassworks were now manufacturing this product style and selling it to various liquor companies to such an extent that imports were diminishing. This development is confirmed, in part, by the other distinctly American bottles recovered from the Jacksonville 'Blue China' wreck, as well as by similar bottles excavated from other contemporary sites (discussed below).

Excavations of other mid-19th century American shipwrecks have yielded similar black glass cylinder liquor bottles shipped as cargo, further attesting to their mass production, distribution and appeal. The form was present on the 1865 wreck of the SS *Republic*, located 150km off the coast of Georgia at a depth of 500m, not far from Site BA02 and within a similar shipping lane (Fig. 32). En route from New York to New Orleans, the steamship sank in a ferocious hurricane transporting an enormous cargo of goods. Amongst the 8,429 glass and stoneware bottles recovered by Odyssey Marine Exploration in 2003-2005 (Cunningham Dobson and Gerth, 2010: 43) were two dozen black glass 'cylindrical fifths', largely dark amber in color. The majority of the recovered spirits/liquor bottles, like the Jacksonville 'Blue China' examples, are unembossed, except for a few bearing the names of New York glassworks, including the Ellenville Glass Works established in 1836 (McDougall, 1990: 65) and the Brooklyn Glass Bottle Works operative from 1831 to 1876 (McKearin and Wilson, 1978: 134). With dozens of contemporary glassworks producing similar bottles, determining the manufacturer of the Site BA02 Type 1 'cylindrical fifths' is virtually impossible. However, given the proposed New York point of departure for the Site BA02 vessel, a glass company such as the Brooklyn firm or the Ellenville glasshouse in Ulster County, 90 miles northwest of New York City, seems a viable candidate.

The excavation of the steamboat *Bertrand*, lost in the Missouri River in April 1865 – just six months prior to sinking of the *Republic* – yielded a similarly voluminous cargo of bottled goods well preserved in deep mud and silt (Corbin, 2002a: 14; 2002b: 201; Cunningham Dobson and Gerth, 2010: 65; Switzer, 1974: 1). Of more than 6,000 bottles retrieved from the *Bertrand*, most still packed in their original wooden shipping crates and with their paper labels intact, two cases yielded 12 bottles each of 25% alcohol bourbon whiskey. These 25 and 21.5-ounce amber and dark green bottles, all made from three-piece molds, bear the embossed name of a few American companies, including the Ellenville Glass Works of New York (Switzer, 1974: vii, 29, 31). The recovery of these cylindrical liquor bottles, and their surviving packing crates bearing the names of company consignees receiving the goods, provides direct evidence of the packing methods that are likely to have been used on the Jacksonville 'Blue China' ship.

As a cost-effective measure, Type 1 spirits/liquor bottles were rarely embossed with the liquor or wine company names that ordered them (as was the case for most bottles). Embossing was not a common practice until the mid-19th century, and even then most companies chose not to do so (Fike, 1987: 4). Most firms selling their beverages did not want to incur the expensive cost of the production of private or proprietary molds, which were cost prohibitive for the majority of businesses. Thus, the far more affordably manufactured non-embossed bottles prevailed and companies found it more cost effective to simply apply their own paper label to glass containers.

According to one reliable source, in 1890 at least 60% of bottles were not embossed and prior to this date there were even fewer (Fike, 1987: 4). While plate molds (with interchangeable embossing plates) made the production of proprietary bottles cheaper, companies nonetheless still had to incur the cost of the plate and its engraving. This was still substantially less than the cost of producing a complete mold for their bottles (McKearin and Wilson, 1978: 89).

To summarize, by the mid-19th century the Type 1 spirits/liquor bottle was a generic shape, but one that is readily identifiable and associated with certain products, largely a wide variety of high-percentage alcohol liquors, including bourbon, rye, gin, cognac, scotch and even wine. As today, the consumption of such libations was enjoyed by a broad cross-section of society. The allure of numerous straight liquors was enhanced by the belief that they possessed therapeutic value. They were thus often touted as remedies for various ailments: gin for the kidneys, rum for bronchitis, and 'Rock and Rye' for the symptoms of the common cold (Powers, 1998: 77, 86-7). Whiskey was even often labeled "For Medicinal Purposes Only" (Wilson and Wilson, 1968: 67, 84, 115, 121), while Duffy's Malt Whiskey was proclaimed by the company to be "a medicine for all mankind." Advertisements and testimonials of the 1880s cited the efficacy of Duffy's Pure Malt Whiskey in curing a host of ailments including pneumonia, dyspepsia and heart trouble (Hoolihan, 2008: 209-10).

Without a company embossment the origins of the Site BA02 liquor bottles cannot be definitively identified. Comparable embossed examples recovered from mid-19th century coastal contexts, including San Francisco's Hoff Store site and the 1865 wreck of the SS *Republic*, as well as the riverine steamboat *Bertrand*, suggest that the Jacksonville 'Blue China' examples were East Coast products, quite plausibly manufactured by a New York glassworks. This hypothesis is supported by additional artifactual evidence pointing to New York as the final port of departure for the Site BA02 vessel's southbound voyage.

5. Type 2 Mineral Water Bottles

One dark olive green mineral water bottle was recovered from the Jacksonville 'Blue China' wreck, which, as with the other forms, almost certainly comprised part of a once larger cargo (Figs. 33-36). The bottle's relatively heavy and squat body (characterized by a far shorter neck than in the Type 1 wares) typifies mineral water bottles designed to survive the rigors of the high-pressure bottling process as well as extensive post-bottling handling and multiple reuse. The Type 2 bottle, as in the case of the majority of mineral water bottles, is round in cross-section because a cylindrical bottle is inherently stronger than other shapes and thus able to withstand the gaseous pressure of the product itself. Bottles made to endure internal carbonation pressure were known as 'pressure ware' in the bottle making industry.

The Type 2 mineral water bottle has a relatively short and squat body with a short neck. The body and shoulder height is about 3.5 times the combined height of the neck and finish. The base is largely flat with a slight central indentation and the presence of a sand pontil scar. The base diameter is about half the height of the body and shoulder length combined, lending the overall design a 'squat'

Fig. 33. Type 2 black glass mineral water bottle BC-05-00194-BE, H. 18.2cm.

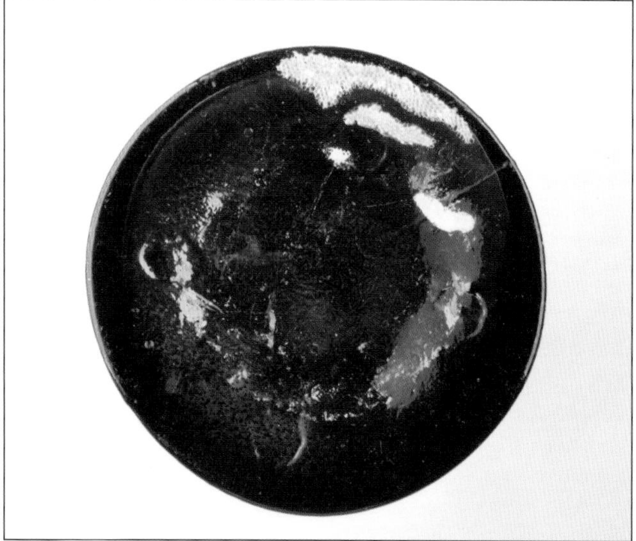

Figs. 34-36. Detail of the finish and base of Type 2 black glass mineral water bottle BC-05-00194-BE.

appearance. The applied finish is of the 'mineral' style, which typified such bottles produced between the 1830s and the 1890s. The bottle was produced in a two-piece mold (two side mold halves) with a separate base plate (Fig. 26).

The Type 2 bottle displays the following dimensions: H. 18.2cm; W. mid-body 8.2cm; max. W. of shoulder 7.8cm; neck H. 2.2cm; total finish H. 2.4cm; collar H. 0.8cm; collar W. 3.0cm; lip H. 1.6cm; neck W. 3.4cm; bore Diam. 1.8cm; rim Th. 0.4cm; body H. 10.8cm; shoulder H. 2.8cm; base Diam. 8.4cm; weight 1,188gr.

As in the case of the Type 1 cylinder liquor wares, the Site BA02 Type 2 bottle is also made of 'black glass,' which was especially functional in reducing exposure to heat and light to better preserve contents. The bottle is characterized by particularly thick glass, again similar to that of the Type 1 bottles, a feature intended to reduce breakage and increase safety during shipping (Gerth, 2006: 59; McKearin and Wilson, 1978: 9).

The Type 2 glass bottle form was blown in a post-base mold, a typically three-part mold where the middle part of the base was formed by a separate small plate or post, while the neck, shoulder, body, heel and outside edges of the base were formed by two-part mold sections of equal size and conformation (Fig. 27). The date or origin of this mold style is unknown, although it was in use in the US at least as early as the 1820s. Like the Site BA02 Type 1 'cylindrical fifths', this bottle form similarly exhibits a sand pontil scar on its base and a 'mineral' or 'double oil' finish, also known by a variety of other names, including a double long tapered collar, tapered collar with ring, long tapered collar with ring and short brandy with ring (Fike, 1987: 8).

Often referred to as a 'Saratoga' bottle, this distinctive style was used by hundreds of different 19th-century companies to bottle mineral water, including a large number operating out of Saratoga Springs, New York. The demand for this bottle type led to an especially profitable line produced in several glassworks in various parts of the country. It continued in use from the earliest products made in the 1820s and 1830s until the end of the 19th century (McKearin, 1978: 238). This possible source contributes to the plausible conclusion that the Jacksonville 'Blue China' ship was based in New York (cf. Gerth *et al.*, 2011).

Saratoga was renowned for its therapeutic mineral waters present in 122 natural springs and was a major source of bottled water during the 19th century (LaMoreaux, 2001: 135). While these mineral waters were the first to be bottled and marketed in the US, and are believed to represent the source of the majority of mid-19th century spring-water bottles, Saratoga's mineral waters were so popular that they inspired many 'knock-off' bottles and contents. Other US springs thus also served the industry, including waters in Pennsylvania, Connecticut, Vermont, Virginia, Maine and Missouri. Even the far western state of California produced a product named after Saratoga's famous 'Congress Spring' (Mc Kearin and Wilson, 1987: 235-36).

By the mid-19th century, the bottling of mineral water had become such an established American industry that these contents not only provided water for table use, but were also used for medicinal purposes because the combination of gases and dissolved salts was widely regarded to have curative qualities (Fike, 1987: 17; LaMoreaux, 2000: 135). Several springs, in reality long known to the Native American Indians to contain medicinal properties, were 'discovered' in the 18th century, including one in Boston "recommended by the most Eminent Physicians for their efficacy in a great Variety of Disorders" (McKearin and Wilson, 1978: 233).

As early as the 1830s the popular consumption of mineral water, and flavored soda waters derived from mixing syrups of various flavors with mineral waters, seems to have been so great that it even challenged sales of hard liquor. Advertisements of the period refer to establishments in Boston offering a combination liquor bar and soda stand. The passion for these non-alcoholic beverages increased further as the burgeoning 19th-century Temperance Movement became more effective (McKearin and Wilson, 1978: 238).

Although primarily an eastern American bottle style, similar mineral water bottles have been found widely across the US from the south to the far west. The 'Saratoga' style was produced in two distinctive sizes, universally referred to as a pint and a quart. Like so many bottles of the day, these varieties were 'scant' sizes in that they did not hold the full measure capacity of the actual bottle size. The pint typically held at least 12 ounces and the quart around 25-30 ounces. 'Saratoga' bottle colors were shades of aquamarine, green and blue, as well as dark glass (olive ambers and olive greens), the latter of which is represented by the Site BA02 example.

While some 'Saratoga' bottles feature the name of the user and/or bottlers in an attempt to encourage as many as possible of these expensive products to be returned to the original manufacturer or merchant for reuse (McKearin and Wilson, 1978: 240-41), unembossed examples are common on historic American sites, making it virtually impossible to identify makers or users of these bottles. Well over half of the bottles produced in the mid and latter part of the 19th century lacked an embossment identifying the company and product (Fike, 1987: 4). Non-embossed 'Saratoga' mineral water bottles were common amongst consumers of all socio-economic classes.

Fig. 37. A mineral water bottle from the wreck of the SS Republic *(1865) of the same style as Site BA02 Type 2, but embossed with 'Clarke & White' and 'New York' of Saratoga Springs.*

Although dated later than Site BA02 to 1865, two bottles recovered from the wreck of the SS *Republic* bear the embossed name of Saratoga's 'Clarke & White' of 'New York' (Fig. 37). These bottles are very similar typologically to the Jacksonville 'Blue China' unembossed example. The 'Clarke & White' bottles are the most common Saratoga products found today. Originally owned by Lynch & Clarke, Dr. John Clarke purchased the 'spring farm' on which the Columbia and Congress Springs were located and commenced bottling Congress Waters for export and sale. Following Clarke's death in 1846, his heir formed Clarke & Company. Around 1852, William White acquired an interest in the company and the firm became Clarke & White (McKearin and Wilson, 1978: 234; Pollard, 1871: 280).

As in the case of the Clarke & White firm, a number of glasshouses producing mineral water bottles were based in Saratoga Springs, but also elsewhere at the time when the Jacksonville 'Blue China' vessel sailed. The South Stoddard Glass Works of New Hampshire opened in 1850 and was particularly renowned as a producer of spring water bottles for Saratoga's Star Spring Company and High Rock

Congress (McKearin and Wilson, 1978: 235). The upstate New York Lockport Glass Works (1843-80s) and the Mount Vernon Glass Works in Mt. Pleasant, New York (1844-90), were also both known producers of the 'Saratoga' style bottle (McKearin and Wilson, 1978: 137-42, 234-35; Tucker, 1986: xii-xiii). Without a company embossment, any number of the bustling mid-19th century glasshouses striving to meet the consumer demands of this especially profitable product line could have produced the 'Saratoga' style bottle recovered from the wreck site.

6. Type 3 Sauce/ Utilitarian Bottles

Two Type 3 sauce or condiment bottles, light aquamarine in color, were recovered from Site BA02 in two slightly different sizes (Figs. 14, 19, 38-41). This bottle is also often referred to as a utilitarian bottle because it was frequently used for varied products, particularly patent medicines. Utilitarian containers make up the bulk of bottles produced during the 19th and first half of the 20th centuries. Like Site BA02's Type 1 and 2 bottles, these too were reused during the pre-Civil War era. As free-blown examples, they were of a much lighter and less durable glass than the former and thus were not subject to extensive reuse as were the thicker and heavier black glass bottles.

Without embossments or paper labels, identifying the contents is again virtually impossible. However, long-necked, narrow-mouthed bottles are commonly associated with liquid food products, including oils, sauces and other non-solid condiments manufactured by a host of mid-19th century companies (Zumwalt, 1980: 247, 252). The form's shape facilitated the efficient pouring of fluid contents and minimized spillage. The long neck and narrow mouth bore were also useful in retaining seasoning and flavor.

The Type 3 sauce or utility bottles have a relatively tall and narrow profile, with the neck and finish in combination equaling about two-thirds of the total height of the body and shoulder. The base features a distinctive push-up formed by the application and pushing of the blowpipe type pontil rod against the hot, pliable base glass, which also resulted in a distinctly circular blowpipe type of pontil scar. The base diameter is just over one-third the height of the body and shoulder combined. The applied finish is of the common 'oil' style. The bottle appears to have been produced by either free-blowing or more likely given the symmetrical conformation of the bottle in a simple dip mold.

The Type 3 bottles display the following dimensions: H. 21.4cm; W. mid-body 6cm; max. W. of shoulder 6.0cm; neck H. 6.5cm; total finish H. 1.4cm; lip W. 2.2cm; lip H. 1.4cm; neck W. 2.7cm; bore Diam. 1.4cm; rim Th. 0.2cm; body H. 11.7cm; shoulder H. 1.6cm; base Diam. 5.1cm; heel H. 0.3cm; weight 156gr.

Fig. 38. Type 3 sauce/utilitarian glass bottle BC-05-00003-BE, H. 21.4cm.

The free-blown (or dip molded) form with a blowpipe pontil scar present on the Jacksonville 'Blue China' Type 3 bottles is found on examples dating from as early as the 17th century. The steep rise or pushed-up section of the base enhanced bottle strength and stability because the process helped form an even base so that the bottle could sit upright without wobbling. The steep heel indentation also reduced the interior volume of the bottle and may have been useful in trapping content sedimentation in the groove around the outside edge of the base. This may have allowed the liquid content to be poured with minimal sediment delivery (Jones, 2000: 150; Van den Bossche, 2001: 395). Modern home brewing activities confirm that sediment trapping occurs within bottles featuring steep 'push-ups' such as the Type 3 examples.

The Type 3 bottles feature an 'oil' or 'ring' finish, one of the most commonly used finishes encountered on a wide

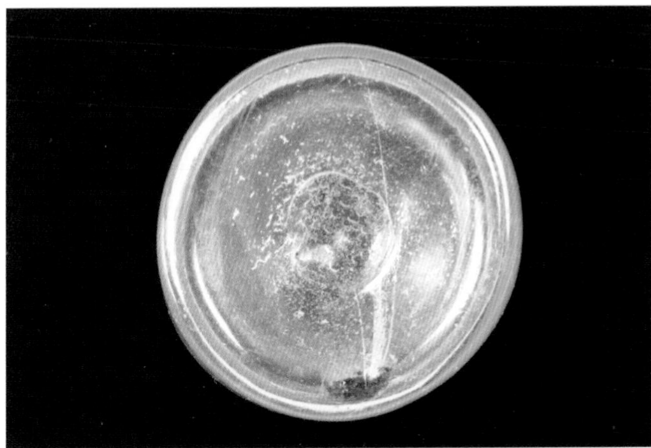

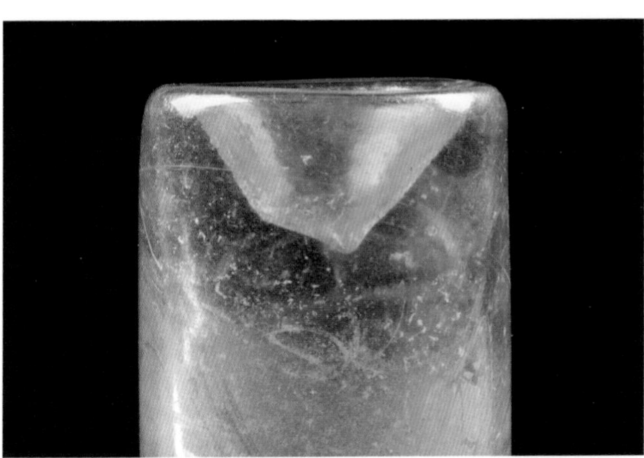

Figs. 39-41. Detail of the finish and base of Type 3 sauce/utilitarian glass bottle BC-05-00003-BE.

array of bottle forms dated between the 1830s and 1920s. This finish is frequently seen on all types of proprietary and patent medicines, such as bitters, tonics, cures and balsams, as well as a number of liquid sauce food bottle types (Fike, 1987: 8). The finish was used on many different bottle types and is related to a single function: it is a simple, but stout finish for securely corking and has sufficient lower rim space to wire down the cork securely or to seat a capsule-type foil seal.

Prior to 20th-century advances in preservation and cold storage, food was often excessively bland, of dubious freshness and frequently tainted due to a lack of refrigeration, all of which necessitated the use of table sauces and condiments to mask or improve unpleasant tastes (Gerth, 2006: 65-70). Condiments had been available to Americans since Colonial times to enhance or alter unsatisfying foods. The various products available to the 19th-century consumer included mustard, Worcestershire Sauce, pepper sauces and even ketchup, the latter of which was bottled in relatively small quantities until after the Civil War in 1865, when commercial production rapidly increased (Allen and Albala, 2007: 93-4).

Given the importance of sauces, oils and condiments to 19th-century America, bottles associated with these products are very common on historical sites of the period, epitomized by the prevalence of Lea & Perrins Worcestershire Sauce, which was recovered in large quantities from the wrecks of the *Republic* and *Bertrand*, both lost in 1865 while transporting a huge cargo of essential bottled foods to American consumers (Cunningham Dobson and Gerth, 2010: 42, 65). The Type 3 bottle may have also once contained some zesty condiment or sauce designed to spice up consumers' plates or possibly olive oil essential for cooking.

7. Type 4 Sands's Sarsaparilla Medicine Bottles

Four rectangular, aquamarine-colored patent medicine bottles embossed with the company and product name 'SANDS'S SARSAPARILLA NEW YORK' were recovered from amongst the Jacksonville 'Blue China' cargo (Figs. 42-47). These wares are significant representations of the probable earliest variant of the Sands's Sarsaparilla bottle, which first came onto the US market in the 1840s. Illustrations depicted in advertisements of 1848 and later feature a slightly modified version with embossed lettering that reads 'SANDS'S SARSAPARILLA // GENUINE // NEW YORK' (Fike, 198: 220; *Gazette of the Union*, 1849: 83). Both embossed variants were possibly manufactured simultaneously and overlapped for a period of time.

Fig. 42. Type 4 Sands's Sarsaparilla glass medicine bottle BC-05-00191-BE, H. 15.3cm.

The Type 4 bottles are typical of many patent medicine bottles of the era and characterized by their basically rectangular cross-section with widely beveled corners, making the bottle essentially eight sided with two wider flat sides. The front wide and flat side bears the embossed lettering 'SARSAPARILLA' and the two adjacent narrow sides feature separately the embossment 'NEW YORK' and 'SANDS'S'. The body/shoulder combination is almost three times the height of the neck/finish height. The base is mildly indented from the pushing action of the pontil rod on the hot, pliable glass (pushing inwards was done in an attempt to ensure that the residual blowpipe pontil scar did not inhibit the bottle from standing upright). The applied finish is a variation of the 'oil' finish seen in the Type 3 bottle. The bottle was blown in a true two-piece mold with no separate base plate (Fig. 25).

The Type 4 bottle displays the following dimensions: H. 15.3cm; W. mid-body 5.4cm; maximum W. of shoulder 5.2cm; neck H. 2.5cm; total finish H. 1.0cm; lip W. 2.1cm; lip H. 1.0cm; neck W. 2.1cm; bore Diam. 1.3cm; rim Th. 0.3cm; embossed lettering frame 8.6 x 0.9cm; body H. 10.3cm; shoulder H. 1.5cm; base Diam. 5.4cm; insweep range 0.3-0.9cm; weight 184gr.

The Type 4 bottle blowpipe pontil scar, also called a ring pontil, was formed when a hollow blowpipe was used as the pontil rod (Jones, 2000: 156-8), probably employed to cut costs by limiting the number of tools used by the glass blower and to save time. The 'oil' finish was a popular style on a number of different bottle types, particularly between 1850 and 1910, and was most common on a wide array of patent medicines, sauce bottles and other narrow-necked food bottles. Its popularity was most probably the result of a combination of factors, including corking strength, relative ease of manufacturing and perhaps even aesthetics to capture the consumer's attention.

Sands's Sarsaparilla was one of the many 19th-century products known as 'patent medicines' sold during an era when snake oil, worm pills, invigorators and elixirs emerged on the market as 'sure' cures for any and all afflictions. The 'Patent Medicine Era' – often referred to as 'the Age of Quackery' – was represented by a host of products, many laced with harmful narcotics and readily available to the consumer without revealing their contents or requiring a prescription. They were especially popular at a time when most people relied on home cures for medical problems and when a doctor was only called upon when death was feared. Shrewd entrepreneurs such as A.B. & D. Sands were among the many bold 19th-century businessmen who amassed large fortunes from their wholesale drug business, including enormous earnings from the sale of their prized Sarsaparilla (Fike, 1987: 3-4; Cunningham Dobson and Gerth, 2010: 39-41; Gerth, 2006: 23; Shimko, 1969: 153-55; Wood, 1904: 41).

Abraham B. and David Sands established their business in New York City in 1836 (Holcombe, 1979: 450). An 1842 advertisement listed their retail and wholesale druggist operation as based at several locations under a number of family names: A.B. & D. Sands Druggists, David Sands & Co., and A.B. Sands & Co. The first two companies apparently served as retail outlets, the latter for the company's wholesale/retail and export business. By 1863, the separate companies had merged as A.B. Sands & Co. before the business was sold to W.H. Schieffelin & Co. in March 1875 (Fike, 1987: 179; Odell, 2000: 211).

The Sands's Sarsaparilla product was first produced around 1839, as documented in the *Sands Family Recipe & Medical Almanac* published in 1853, which stated that the product "has now borne the test of over fourteen years' experience" (Fike, 1987: 220). Early advertisements dating to 1844 touted the many virtues of the product, which claimed to cure "All diseases arising from an impure state of the blood or habit of the system." The compound was alleged to differ "entirely in its character from the various preparations of sarsaparilla... offered to the public."

Fig. 43-44. Detail of the 'SANDS'S SARSAPARILLA NEW YORK' embossment on glass medicine bottle BC-05-00191-BE.

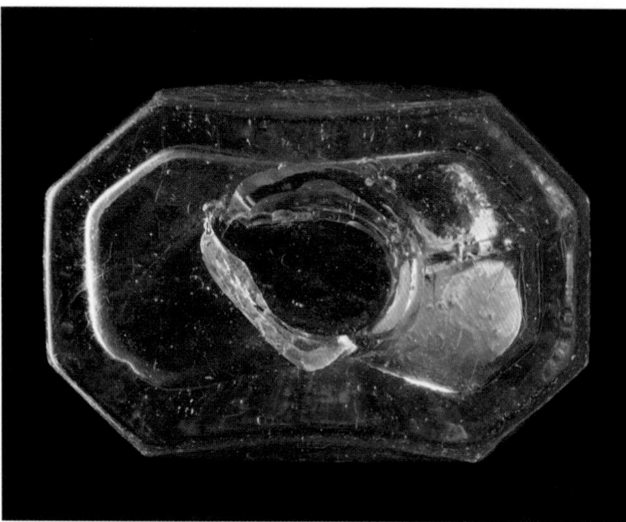

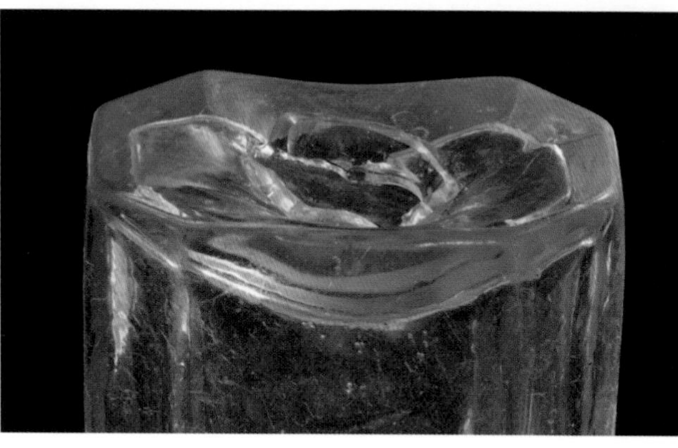

Figs. 45-47. Detail of the finish and base of Type 4 Sands's Sarsaparilla bottle BC-05-00191-BE.

Also touted was its "powerful healing effect", which Sands described as "entirely harmless so that it cannot injure the most delicate constitution" (*Sheldon & Co.'s Business or Advertising Directory*, 1845: 55).

The Sands's were one of the US's most ambitious glass bottle promoters and advertisements for their sarsaparilla ran continuously in newspapers throughout the country (Odell, 2000: 212). As was the case amongst other patent medicine men of the era, their advertising ploys often relied on testimonials from respected members of the community advocating the use of a particular product that miraculously cured them. One grateful user of Sands's Sarsaparilla, formerly suffering from breast cancer, claimed the product cured her when nothing else could. Following years of enduring untreatable leg sores, a Justice of the Peace too found no relief until he reached for Sands's famous product (*Sheldon & Co.'s Business or Advertising Directory*, 1845: 55).

In addition to selling its sarsaparilla, Sands offered an eclectic assortment of 'Druggist and Manufacturers Articles', ranging in diversity from East Indian, Mediterranean and European drugs to perfumery, fancy soaps and surgical equipment. They also sold patent medicines of every description, paints, oils and even 'Saratoga' mineral waters (*Sheldon & Co.'s Business and Advertising Directory*, 1845: 55). The one 'Sarsaparilla' bottle recovered from the Jacksonville 'Blue China' wreck may have originated from a larger cargo originally shipped aboard the vessel.

While the mid-19th century was touted the 'sarsaparilla era' due to the host of sarsaparilla products flooding the US markets in the 1830s and 1840s, its popularity for medicinal use began to wane in the latter part of the century. At this time, however, the consumption of sarsaparilla-based beverages increased, very likely enhanced by its earlier remedial application (Shimko, 1969: 11; *Transactions for the Illinois State Historical Society*, 1906: 240).

8. Type 5 Cylindrical, Tapered Patent Medicine Bottles

The Site BA02 glassware cargo includes seven Type 5 cylindrical, tapered vial-like bottles, aquamarine in color (Figs. 7, 9-10, 19, 49-53). Each exhibits a 'rolled' lip finish and a blowpipe pontil scar similar to a number of the other bottles recovered from the wreck. Again, they were retrieved empty, having been originally sealed with cork stoppers, some of which were found preserved inside the bottles (Fig. 51).

The Type 5 bottles are small cylindrical and conical shaped medicine vials distinctly narrower at the shoulder than the base. The base incorporates a blowpipe pontil scar

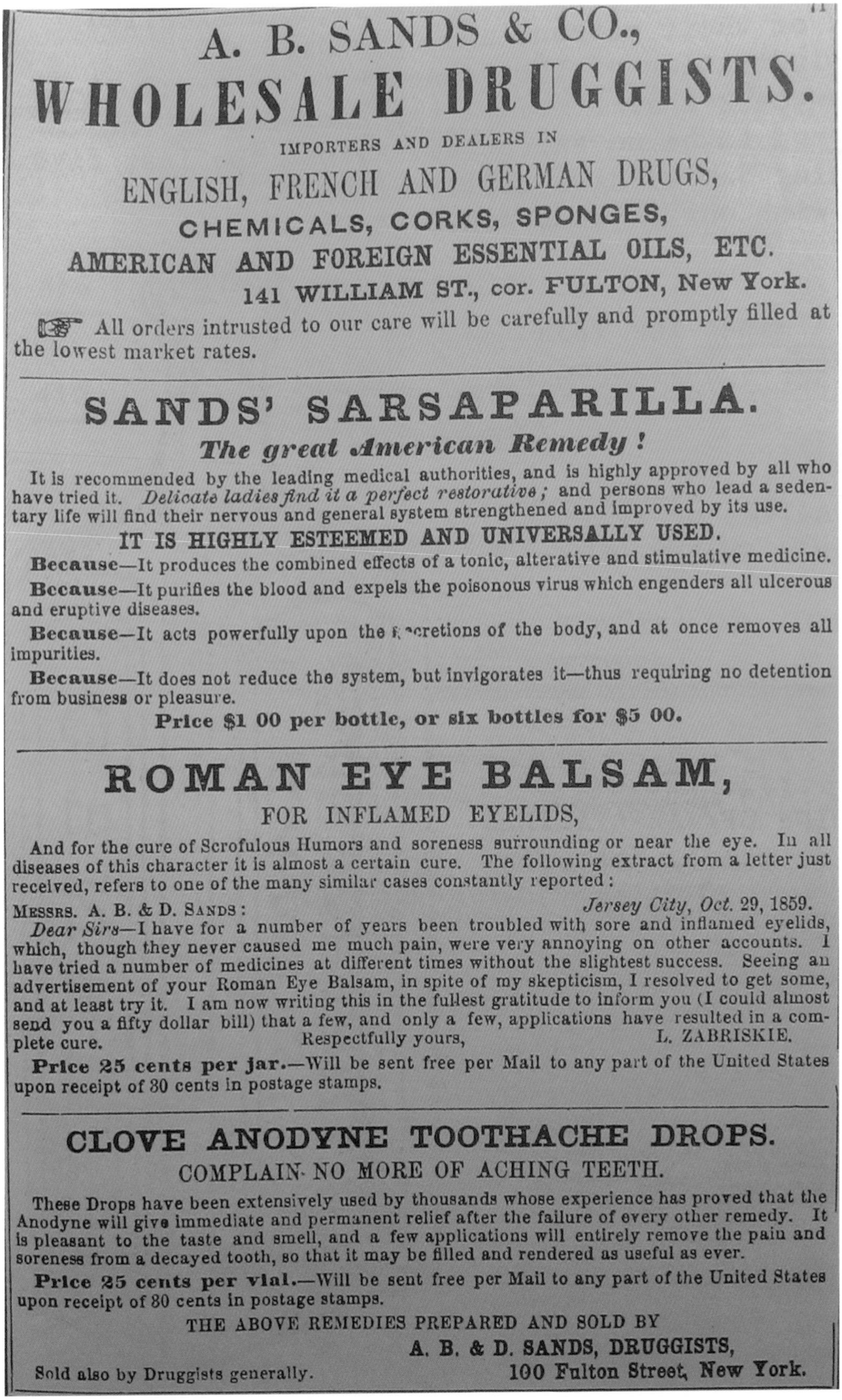

A. B. SANDS & CO.,

WHOLESALE DRUGGISTS.

IMPORTERS AND DEALERS IN

ENGLISH, FRENCH AND GERMAN DRUGS,

CHEMICALS, CORKS, SPONGES,

AMERICAN AND FOREIGN ESSENTIAL OILS, ETC.

141 WILLIAM ST., cor. FULTON, New York.

☞ All orders intrusted to our care will be carefully and promptly filled at the lowest market rates.

SANDS' SARSAPARILLA.

The great American Remedy!

It is recommended by the leading medical authorities, and is highly approved by all who have tried it. *Delicate ladies find it a perfect restorative;* and persons who lead a sedentary life will find their nervous and general system strengthened and improved by its use.

IT IS HIGHLY ESTEEMED AND UNIVERSALLY USED.

Because—It produces the combined effects of a tonic, alterative and stimulative medicine.

Because—It purifies the blood and expels the poisonous virus which engenders all ulcerous and eruptive diseases.

Because—It acts powerfully upon the secretions of the body, and at once removes all impurities.

Because—It does not reduce the system, but invigorates it—thus requiring no detention from business or pleasure.

Price $1 00 per bottle, or six bottles for $5 00.

ROMAN EYE BALSAM,

FOR INFLAMED EYELIDS,

And for the cure of Scrofulous Humors and soreness surrounding or near the eye. In all diseases of this character it is almost a certain cure. The following extract from a letter just received, refers to one of the many similar cases constantly reported:

MESSRS. A. B. & D. SANDS: *Jersey City, Oct.* 29, 1859.

Dear Sirs—I have for a number of years been troubled with sore and inflamed eyelids, which, though they never caused me much pain, were very annoying on other accounts. I have tried a number of medicines at different times without the slightest success. Seeing an advertisement of your Roman Eye Balsam, in spite of my skepticism, I resolved to get some, and at least try it. I am now writing this in the fullest gratitude to inform you (I could almost send you a fifty dollar bill) that a few, and only a few, applications have resulted in a complete cure. Respectfully yours, L. ZABRISKIE.

Price 25 cents per jar.—Will be sent free per Mail to any part of the United States upon receipt of 30 cents in postage stamps.

CLOVE ANODYNE TOOTHACHE DROPS.

COMPLAIN NO MORE OF ACHING TEETH.

These Drops have been extensively used by thousands whose experience has proved that the Anodyne will give immediate and permanent relief after the failure of every other remedy. It is pleasant to the taste and smell, and a few applications will entirely remove the pain and soreness from a decayed tooth, so that it may be filled and rendered as useful as ever.

Price 25 cents per vial.—Will be sent free per Mail to any part of the United States upon receipt of 30 cents in postage stamps.

THE ABOVE REMEDIES PREPARED AND SOLD BY

A. B. & D. SANDS, DRUGGISTS,

Sold also by Druggists generally. **100 Fulton Street, New York.**

Fig. 48. 'The Great American Remedy!' touts an advertisement for Sands's Sarsaparilla published in an 1860 issue of the New York Daily Tribune. *Photo: courtesy SHA/BLM Historic Glass Bottle Identification & Information Website.*

Fig. 49. Type 5 cylindrical and tapered glass medicine bottle BC-05-00350-BE, H. 13.5cm.

Figs. 50-51. Detail of the finish of Type 5 cylindrical and tapered glass medicine bottle BC-05-00350-BE, with remains of its cork stopper preserved.

with some minor indenting caused by the action of the pontil rod. The base diameter is between one-quarter and one-fifth the height of the bottle to the cursory shoulder. The short neck is topped with a 'rolled' finish – an early and indistinct style that essentially involved just rolling the hot glass back on itself to form a narrow, slightly bulging finish or lip. This bottle was produced in a true two-piece mold, which lacked a base plate, with the lower sides of the two-mold halves forming the two halves of the base (Fig. 25).

The Type 5 bottle displays the following dimensions: H. 13.5cm; W. mid-body 2.9cm; max. W. of shoulder 2.0cm; neck H. 1.0cm; total finish H. 0.3cm; lip W. 1.9cm; lip H. 0.3cm; neck W. 1.6cm; bore Diam. 1.2cm; rim Th. 0.3cm; body H. 11.7cm; shoulder H. 0.4cm; base Diam. 3.7cm; insweep range 0.2-0.5cm; weight 57gr.

The distinctive Type 5 bottle shape with its narrow neck and mouth was ideal for the pouring of liquid contents and was possibly an American 'knock-off' imitation of the enormously popular 'Dalby's Carminative' and 'Godfrey's Cordial'. While both were of British origins, the latter were never embossed and the product was eventually also bottled in American-manufactured vessels. First advertised in 1721, 'Godfrey's Cordial' was still available over 200 years later in 1931 (Fike, 1987: 14). These soothing syrups were touted as remedies for various ailments afflicting infants and young children. By the mid 19th-century the products of both Dalby and Godfrey and their many imitators, including those discovered on the Jacksonville 'Blue China' wreck, were readily available in the US, where they were listed among the countless patent medicines that actually contained harmful opiates.

The children's market was especially profitable at a time when limited health care and high infant mortality were

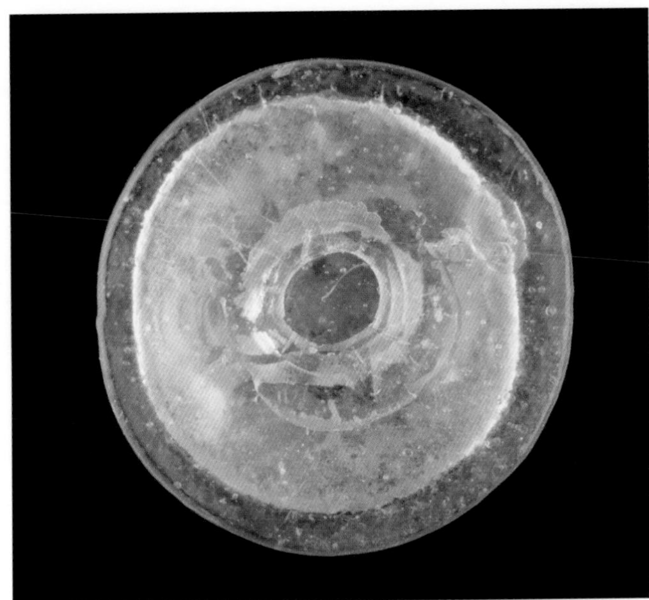

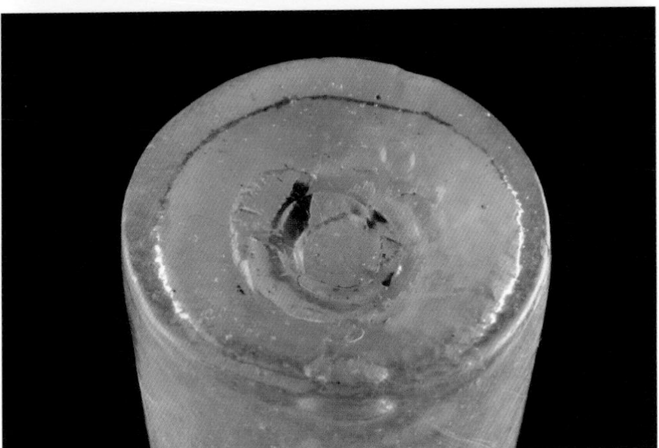

Figs. 52-53. Detail of the base of Type 5 cylindrical glass medicine bottle BC-05-00350-BE.

pervasive and hope for a suffering child frequently lay solely in the purchase of a small bottle containing "syrup of poppies" (Beck, 1864: 16; Gerth, 2006: 26; Jordan, 1987: 95). As history has sadly demonstrated, such products sometimes proved fatal because they were typically offered without prescription, a common practice of the era. In one documented case, "forty drops of Dalby's Carminative destroyed an infant" (Beck, 1864: 16). In reality, doses as small as even half a teaspoon could also be lethal.

Nonetheless, the production of such dangerous nostrums did not cease. A survey of 10,000 prescriptions filled by 35 Boston drugstores in 1888 revealed that 1,481 contained opiates. Among prescriptions refilled three or more times, 78% contained opiates. Such dangerous 'medicine' was not restricted to the US. In 19th-century Coventry in Britain, ten gallons of Godfrey's Cordial (a happy mixture of opium, molasses and sassafras instilled for flavoring), enough for 12,000 doses, was sold weekly and was administered to 3,000 infants under two years old.[2]

By the turn of the 19th century, and perhaps earlier, glass factories such as the Illinois Glass Company advertised in their company catalog generic patent medicine vials sold as 'Godfrey's Cordial', confirming that these distinctively shaped, tapered cylindrical bottles had in fact become a common medicine bottle style (*Illinois Glass Company Catalog*, 1908: 102-3). An 1822-23 catalog for the Obear-Nester Glass Company, featuring the 'Godfrey's Cordial' vial among other patent medicine bottle types, attests to the ongoing use of this century-old medicinal bottle style (*Obear-Nester Glass Company Catalog*, 1922-3: 32). At the time when the Jacksonville 'Blue China' ship was lost around 1854, its cargo of small aquamarine vials was clearly in its heyday amongst a host of opiate-laced patent medicines catering to a hugely receptive market.

9. Type 6 Cologne Bottles

Two Type 6 transparent green unembossed bottles with their neck tops broken off were recovered from the Jacksonville 'Blue China' wreck (Figs. 13, 19, 54-56). Both were seemingly free-blown, with possibly some dip molding to rough out the basic body shape. The bottles feature a glass-tipped pontil scar, which was formed by the use of a solid iron rod dipped in molten glass and then applied and fused to the base of the bottle. When the rod was broken free of the bottle, a generally round but fragmented scar was left behind on the base (Jones, 2000: 155).

The Type 6 bottles are distinctively very narrow and tall, resulting in a form that is almost impossible to stand upright. The neck and finish (as known from intact examples elsewhere) are very narrow and typically about one-half the height of the body/shoulder. The base is slightly indented with a glass-tipped pontil scar, a distinct but formless 'rough area' covering most of the base. The finish on intact examples consists of a simple cracked-off or sheared opening, often flared slightly to make corking easier. These bottles are free-blown or possibly partly body formed in a dip mold.

The Type 6 bottle displays the following dimensions: H. 19.1cm; W. mid-body 3.0cm; max. W. of shoulder 3.4cm; surviving neck H. 1.6cm; neck W. 1.9cm; bore Diam. 0.1cm; rim Th. 0.2cm; body H. 16.5cm; shoulder H. 0.7cm; base Diam. 2.3cm; insweep/heel H. range 0.4-0.8cm; weight: 83gr.

Type 6 bottles are identical to examples discovered in a foundation trench in New Orleans' French Quarter, whose material culture dates between 1830 and 1850 (as identified by Bill Lindsey). A much later molded example

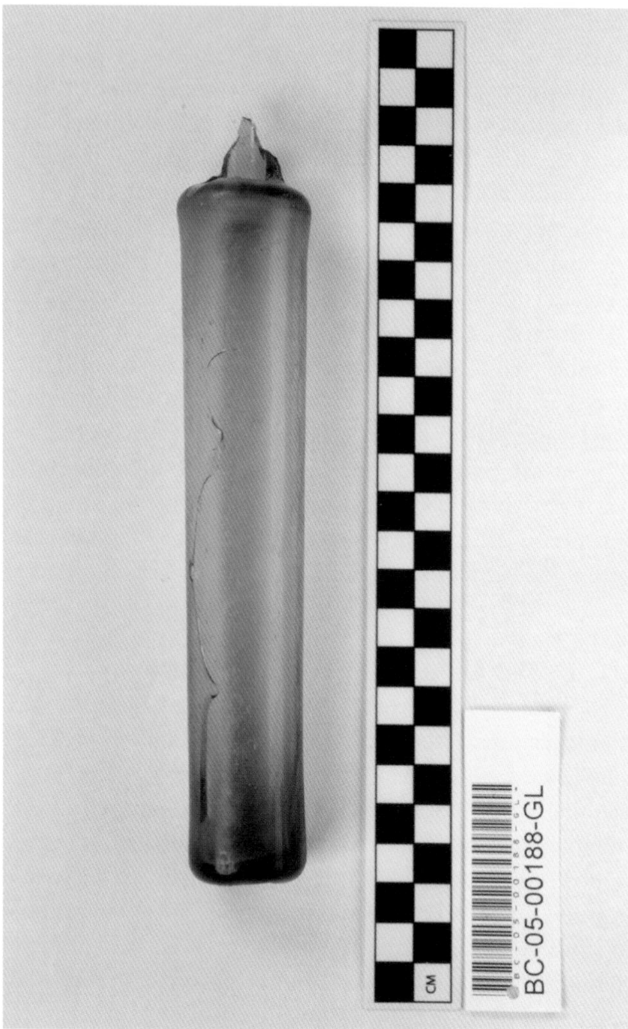

Fig. 54. Type 6 green glass cologne bottle BC-05-00188-GL, H. 19.1cm.

(1880s-90s), acquired from a collector in New Orleans, bears the embossed name 'Lundborg', who was a prominent 19th-century American perfumer with an establishment on Barclay Street in New York City (*The Cosmopolitan,* February 1887; *Current Literature*, September 1890: 179; *Illustrated New York*, 1888: 177). An 1886 advertisement claimed that Lundborg's perfume bottles were "very tastefully put up in little boxes, and are suitable offerings to give to any lady" (*The Brooklyn Magazine*, April 1886: xix).

A similarly-shaped bottle, with a wider, flared mouth, was recovered from the 1857 wreck of the sidewheel steamer *Central America*, which sank 2,200m off Cape Fear, North Carolina, en route to New York from the California gold fields. This wreck's bottle has probably been incorrectly identified as a "wine-tester bottle" (Herdendorf, 1995: 172), which has openings at both ends and thus is not a bottle in the true sense. However, the similarity of the Jacksonville 'Blue China' wreck Type 6 bottles to the New Orleans finds strongly suggests that they too probably contained cologne. This theory is supported by six intact and virtually pristine bottles dating to approximately 1840, which still survive today and represent products marketed by the French Perfumer L.T. Piver of Paris. These wares remain packaged in their original box with fancy labels identifying the product as 'EXTRAIT D'EAU COLOGNE de Jean Maria Farina – Fournisseur de plusieurs Cours à COLOGNE s/R' (Van den Bossche, 2001: 220, 362).

Jean Maria Farina was a descendant of Giovanni Maria Farina (1685-1766), an Italian perfume maker whose cologne formula derived from the recipe of his uncle, Gian Paolo Feminis. In 1709, Feminis traveled to Germany to market his distilled herbal 'water', which had been in use among Italian families for centuries (Stamelman, 2006: 53). The scent, which Feminis later enhanced, was so well received that he called upon his nephew, Giovanni Maria Farina, to join him in Cologne. In 1732, the younger partner took over the business and, 25 years later during the Seven Years War, French troops stationed in the city carried the scent back to France, where it was named after the city where it was first discovered. In 1809 Farina's grandson, Jean-Marie, moved to Paris to open a shop at 331 rue Saint-Honore, which catered to distinguished patrons, including Emperor Napoleon (Stamelman, 2006: 54). This product proved so successful that it prompted countless other businessmen to sell their own fragrances under the same name, many claiming to be descendants of Feminis.

In 1819, the official gazette of Cologne reported the existence of 60 manufactories of Eau de Cologne, most flatteringly, but inaccurately, launched under the Farina name. Only three were linked to the original founding family and the vast majority was apparently fraudulent (*The Ladies' Companion and Monthly Magazine*, 1856: 324). Farina, in fact, took to court a host of imposters, passionately defending his family's legal claim to the scent. To reassure his faithful customers that they were purchasing the genuine cologne, Farina had his signature, accompanied by an image of an imperial eagle and the coats of arms of the French and German courts, stamped in green wax on the cases of his products. Nevertheless, by 1865 well over 30 establishments are said to have still falsely carried the name Farina, deemed to be the "scent sensation of the age" (Stamelman, 2006: 54).

The popular knock-off cologne also found favor across Europe and America (McKearin, 1978: 383). Quite possibly even L.T. Piver, a prominent French perfumer in his own right, with company branches around the world, also pirated the Farina name. Piver's beauty products were readily available in the US by at least the mid-1860s and most

Figs. 55-56. Detail of the lower neck and base of Type 6 green glass cologne bottle BC-05-00188-GL.

likely earlier, as indicated by the shipment of Piver cosmetic pots and perfume bottles recovered from the 1865 wreck of the SS *Republic* (Cunningham Dobson and Gerth, 2010: 43, 48). American publications of the 19th century advertised L.T. Piver's perfumes and toilet articles as "demanded by a large class of select consumers" and obtained from jobbers or direct from the sole agent for the United States located in New York City (Parsons, 1896: 729). If a Piver product, the Type 6 perfume bottles recovered from Site BA02 may have originated from the company's factory in New York City.

The attractiveness of Eau de Cologne is perhaps best understood in the context of changing Western trends. Historically, European perfumes were common for both men and women and identical fragrances were used by both genders. During the 19th century, however, when cleansing became more habitual, men started to use little or no perfume, turning instead to toilet soap, scented oils for the hair and lighter fragrances such as Eau de Cologne (Jones, 2000: 24). Use of genuine Jean Marie Farina, applied to the "temples, wrists and behind one's ears", even spread in Victorian America to the Western frontier, where a shortage of bathing water apparently demanded large quantities of Farina's Eau de Cologne (Sala, 1886: 423).

While it would be reasonable to assume that the Jacksonville 'Blue China' wreck's Type 6 bottles once contained a fashionable cologne, perhaps even Farina's original famous French fragrance or a similar version sold by L.T. Piver, this bottle was apparently also used for less celebrated products, including balsam, oil, medicines and liqueur such as the Italian Rosolio (Van den Bossche, 2001: 220). Thus, its original contents remain a matter of speculation.

10. Type 7 Figured Cologne Bottle with Plume Pattern

The Jacksonville 'Blue China' wreck's cologne bottles included one mold-blown, colorless glass example, possibly made from a higher quality flint (lead) glass (Mc Kearin and Wilson, 1987: 388; pers. comm. Dorothy Hogan-Schofield, 11 February 2011). The bottle's long neck exhibits a 'wide prescription' finish, also termed a 'flared', 'flat top' or 'flanged' finish (Figs. 57-62). It features an especially thin version of this particular style, which is commonly found on medicinal and druggist types of bottles and vials dating between 1800 and 1870. This finish is also observed on early to mid-19th century liquor decanters and utilitarian ink bottles.

The Type 7 cologne bottle is rectangular in cross-section with heavily embossed, molded sides exhibiting a central bold plume-like decorative composition on the front side and similar, but narrower, plumes on the two narrow sides. The reverse features elements of the plume design running along its periphery. The neck of the bottle is relatively long (about three-quarters the height of the body), with a pronounced medial, bulging rib (known as a 'ball neck') and an early flared tooled finish. The base exhibits a typical blowpipe pontil scar with some indentation deliberately crafted to enable the bottle to stand upright. The bottle was produced in a true two-piece mold, as evidenced by the seam dissecting the base (Fig. 25).

The Type 7 bottle displays the following dimensions: H. 13.0cm; W. mid-body 5.3cm; max. W. of shoulder 5.1cm; neck H. 4.1cm; total finish H. 0.3cm; ring H. 1.0cm; ring W. 2.8cm; lip W. 2.7cm; lip H. 0.3cm; neck W. 3.0cm; bore Diam. 1.4cm; rim Th. 0.2cm; body H. 8.0cm; shoulder H. 0.3cm; base Diam. 5.2cm; insweep range 0.1-0.6cm; weight 120gr.

The Jacksonville 'Blue China' wreck's Type 7 bottle's central plume motif is typical of figured cologne bottles dating from the 1830s to 1860s, examples of which were also produced in blues and aquamarine (McKearin and

Figs. 57-59. Type 7 figured glass cologne bottle BC-05-00147-BE, H. 13.0cm.

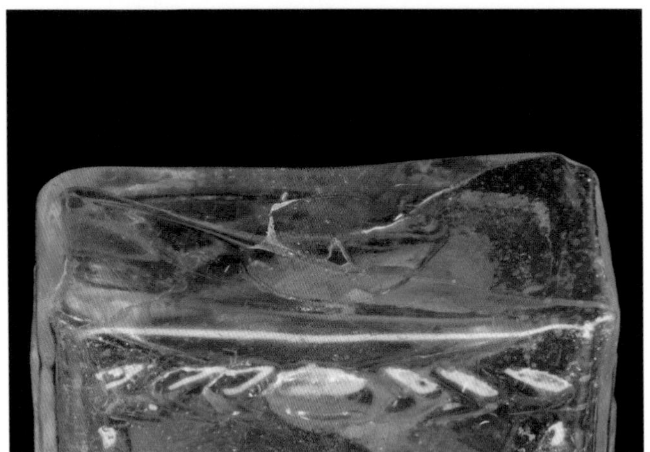

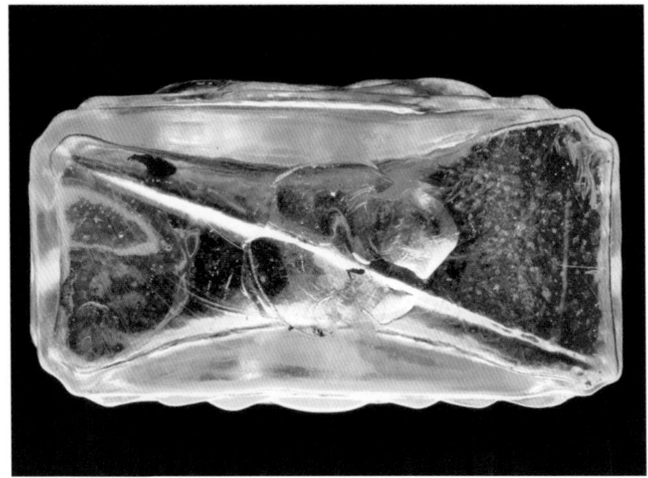

Figs. 60-62. Detail of the finish and base of Type 7 figured glass cologne bottle BC-05-00147-BE.

Wilson, 1978: 396-7, 400-401). Like most commercial cologne products, this bottle originally would have been sealed with a simple cork stopper. A fancy label may have been adhered to the top of the cork. Some ornamental perfume bottles featured a decorative glass stopper.

As noted above, Eau de Cologne was first manufactured commercially in the early 18th century and soon became a major success. By the following century, it had become such an important staple of daily life that no perfumer and very few apothecaries did not attempt to reproduce it. This was especially true in the United States, where each manufacturer strove to improve upon the original formula, creating in effect a diversity of sweet-smelling toilet waters for the American consumer, all generically called 'cologne' (*Appleton's Journal of Literature, Science and Art*, 24 February 1872: 210).

A number of American glass firms manufactured and sold a wide variety of fancy cologne bottles during this period, exemplified by an advertisement published in the 2 July 1832 issue of *The New York Commercial Advertiser* that stated, "Cologne Water – Put up in a variety of bottles comprising about 30 different designs, 30 different kinds…" (McKearin and Wilson, 1978: 386). The growing popularity of cologne, perfume and sweet water of all types is apparent from the increasing number of advertisements offering these products, especially in the second quarter of the mid-19th century, supported by a host of glass US companies devoted to the manufacture of fancy cologne bottles catering to ladies' tastes (McKearin and Wilson, 1978: 383, 389).

By the 1840s and especially after 1850, decorative bottles were frequently produced of finer quality flint glass by numerous firms specializing in perfume and cologne containers. One well-known firm was the Brooklyn Flint Glass Works located in Brooklyn, New York, between Atlantic and State Streets, near the Atlantic Ferry. An 1851 advertisement in the *Brooklyn Evening Star* announced that "Every description of staple and fancy Flint Glass Ware is made in this establishment" (McKearin and Wilson, 1978: 388).

The manufacturer of the single Site BA02 example recovered is unknown, but research suggests that the bottle may have been produced in South Boston by one of three glasshouses: the Suffolk Glass Company (1850-59), Perry, Wynn & Company established in 1851, and the American Glass Company (1847-57). The Jacksonville 'Blue China' wreck bottle style is especially similar to decorated commercial cologne bottle fragments retrieved from the site of the latter company (pers. comm. Dorothy Hogan-Schofield, 9 February 2011; Kaiser, 2009: 190).

11. Type 8 Paneled Cologne Bottle

A stunning 12-paneled blue cobalt glass bottle of a style typically associated again with cologne or toilet water was recovered from Area D on the Jacksonville 'Blue China' shipwreck (Figs. 11, 19, 63-66). The form was in circulation between approximately the 1830s and the late 1850s, a date range confirmed by the pontiled base. Like the Type 7 cologne ware, the bottle also features a flanged or flared lip finish produced using a simple tool to manipulate the hot glass at the end of the neck, creating a relatively thin finish that projects away from the top of the bottle mouth or bore at an angle of about 90° (McKearin and Wilson, 1978: 518-19). Originally sealed with a cork stopper, the bottle was recovered empty and may have represented a small collection of select cologne containers carried on the Site BA02 schooner.

The Type 8 bottle features a long and somewhat cylindrical body, a rounded sloping shoulder and a long

Fig. 63. Type 8 12-paneled cobalt blue glass cologne/toilet water bottle BC-05-00018-BE, H. 18.8cm.

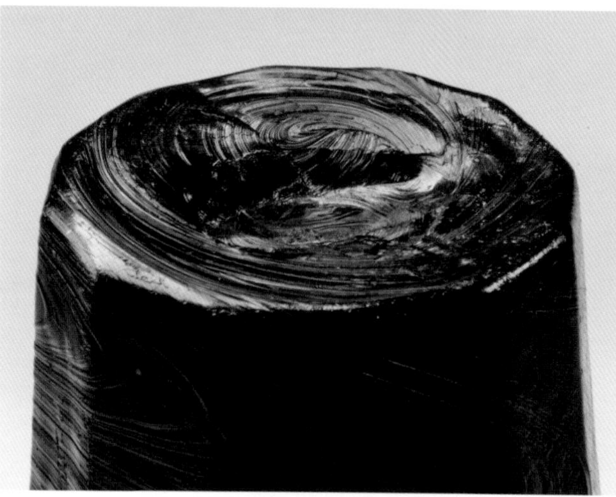

Figs. 64-66. Detail of the finish and base of Type 8 12-paneled cobalt blue glass cologne/toilet water bottle BC-05-00018-BE.

cylindrical neck with a narrow 'bead' finish with an abrupt lower edge. This crude 'bead' finish was formed by the same process used to produce a 'rolled' finish and is considered one of the more simple methods used for finishing bottle lips. While the bottle was held on the pontil rod, the blowpipe was cracked off and the rough end re-heated. The flap of the glass was then folded back on itself with a simple tool such as an iron nail. Decorative or speciality bottles such as the Type 8 example were typically finished with more refinement than usual. Consequently, the craftsman finishing the bottle spent more time flaring the finish out slightly to add more structure to it and to make it more aesthetically pleasing, rather than simply and crudely rolling the flap of glass back onto the upper neck, which would have been the case for more cheaply produced bottles.

The base exhibits a glass-tipped pontil scar with some deliberate indenting from the pontil rod to facilitate standing upright. It appears to have been blown in a true two-piece mold (Fig. 25), although some examples were made with a three-piece leaf mold that would have formed three vertical seams on the bottle's neck (a feature that is often difficult to recognize).

The Type 8 bottle displays the following dimensions: H. 18.8cm; W. mid-body 5.7cm; max. W. of shoulder 6.3cm; neck H. 5.7cm; total finish H. 0.8cm; lip W. 3.0cm; lip H. 0.8cm; neck W. 2.9cm; bore Diam. 1.7cm; rim Th. 0.4cm; body H. 9.0cm; shoulder H. 3.2cm; base Diam. 5.0cm; weight 237gr.

While the wearing of perfume, cologne, rosewater and other scented concoctions played a major role amongst both ladies and gentlemen of the era, their use was seemingly not restricted to the more cosmopolitan middle and upper classes. As noted above, by the mid-19th century widespread advertisements for cologne and sweet waters of all kinds had increased dramatically, often published in small-town local gazettes as well as in larger urban newspapers. The sale of colognes and other scented waters targeted the general public in its broadest definition (McKearin and Wilson, 1978: 382-84).

By the last quarter of the 18th century a number of perfumery manufactories had been established in America, with small quantities of fragrant waters and colognes frequently put into square or long, flat bottles. These relatively simple vessels were soon joined by fancier cologne bottles, which had become very popular in America and abroad, especially in France, by the late 1820s (Griffenhagen and Bogard, 1999: 60; McKearin and Wilson, 1978: 382). One of the earlier advertisements offering for sale "Cologne Water; in rich fancy bottles, of various qualities", available at N. Prentiss' Perfume Manufactory, was published in the *New York Commercial Advertiser* of August 1829. An advertisement for cologne water in "panell bottles" appeared in the same newspaper as early as 1832 (McKearin and Wilson, 1978: 386).

'Panelled' bottles, as they were descriptively called even in the 19th century, were in vogue from the early 1830s and remained popular until late in the century (McKearin and Wilson, 1978: 406). They were produced in a variety of colors representing virtually the full spectrum of the palette from milk glass to black, pinks and greens, as well as purples and blues. Bottles of this type are usually attributed to the Boston & Sandwich Glass Company, although a number of glass factories produced paneled colognes, and many companies used them for their products, including the New York wholesale perfumer and importers Snyder & Company, which advertised a diversity of styles in 1832. The Williamstown Glass Works (1840-54) also offered these distinctive paneled bottles in a variety of sizes ranging from 3-18 ounces, with corresponding prices from $0.50 to $1.50 a dozen. As an agent for the company, New York City wholesale druggist William Burger, published an 1851 price list featuring a host of fancy perfume bottles, including the 'panelled' type (Griffenhagen and Bogard, 1999: 60).

Fig. 67. Type 9A large spice/condiment glass bottle BC-05-00182-BE, H. 16.5cm.

12. Type 9 Spice or Condiment Bottles

The Jacksonville 'Blue China' wreck contained a number of aquamarine glass bottles in two different sizes. The five large Type 9A (Figs. 5, 67-70) and four small Type 9B examples (Figs. 12, 71-74) recovered represent the dominant style used for various spices as well as other condiments in the mid to late 19th century. This unusual eight-sided bottle appears to have originated in the 1850s or possibly late 1840s. The original design that was subsequently copied is believed to have been the work of the J.L. Hunnewell Co. of Boston, Massachusetts (Zumwalt, 1980: 253). Mid-19th century Boston directories list the druggists as located at 8 Commercial Wharf (*The Boston Directory*, 1848: 161; 1852: 135). By 1856, and perhaps earlier, the firm had changed its name to J.W. Hunnewell & Co. (*Boston Board of Trade* 1856: 163). In addition to medicinal products, its line apparently included the manufacture of paints, oils and condiments, such as mustard and relish packaged in bottles similar to the larger Jacksonville 'Blue China' wreck Type 9A examples (Zumwalt, 1980: 253). By 1905, the company was still in existence and its primary product line was apparently paint (*The Era Druggists Directory*, 1905: 252).

The Type 9A and B spice bottles feature wide, concave front and back panels with flat narrow side panels bound together by relatively wide, concavely beveled corners. They exhibit blowpipe pontil scars on the bases with enough pontil rod push-up on the Type 9B variants to limit pontil scar protrusion, so that the bottle could stand upright. Bottle Type 9A was molded to include an indentation to eliminate pontil scar protrusion. The Type 9A finish is a typical 'rolled' finish utilizing no applied glass and only minimal tooling. The Type 9B finish is a short applied 'oil' finish, with its lip formed from applied glass from molten material taken from near the blowpipe removal point, along with a little reheating to make the glass more pliable. Both bottles were produced in true two-piece molds, which did not include a separate base plate (Fig. 25).

The large Type 9A bottle form displays the following dimensions: H. 16.5cm; W. mid-body 6.9cm; max. W. of shoulder 6.8cm; neck H. 0.9cm; total finish H. 0.5cm; lip W. 3.6cm; lip H. 0.5cm; neck W. 3.4cm; bore Diam. 2.4cm; rim Th. 0.3cm; body H. 10.2cm; shoulder H. 4.7cm; base Diam. 6.1cm; insweep/heel H. range 0.1-0.8cm; weight 236gr. The small Type 9B bottle form displays the following dimensions: H. 11.8cm;

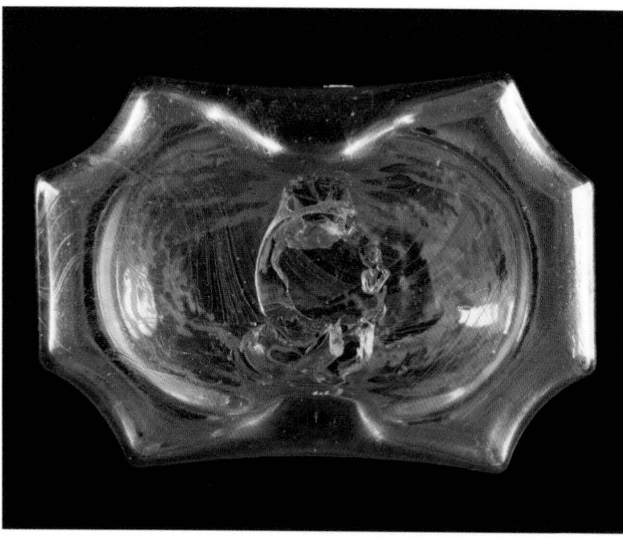

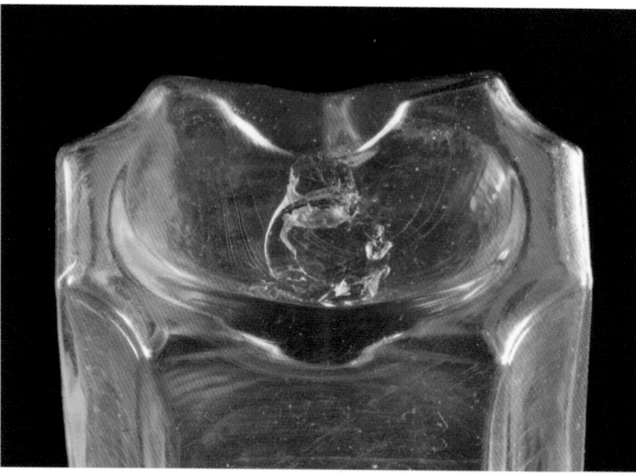

Figs. 68-70. Detail of the finish and base of Type 9A large spice/condiment glass bottle BC-05-00182-BE.

W. mid-body 4.8cm; max. W. of shoulder 4.8cm; neck H. 1.7cm; total finish H. 0.8cm; lip W. 2.1cm; lip H. 0.8cm; neck W. 2.1cm; bore Diam. 1.4cm; rim Th. 0.2cm; body H. 8.0cm; shoulder H. 0.9cm; base Diam. 4.2cm; insweep/heel H. range 0.1-0.7cm; weight 55gr.

The bottle type's moderately wide mouth or bore allowed for easier access during packing in crates and for extraction by the consumer. As was the case with all of the bottles recovered from Site BA02, these wares' original paper labels are not preserved, making identification of their contents particularly difficult, in this case especially so given the diversity of spices and condiments distributed in this bottle style.

Both the larger and smaller varieties feature a blowpipe pontil, often produced from the same blowpipe used to blow the bottle. In this case the glass blower used the residual glass left after the bottle was cracked off the blowpipe. To detach and then finish the bottle, it had to be laid on a marver (a metal or wooden table or slab) or on a cradle, which permitted the blower to move to the other end of the bottle to finish the lip (Jones, 2000: 155-7). The larger bottles' 'rolled' lip finish provides strong dating criteria because it was not significantly used after about 1870. To form the lip, while hot the sheared top was folded inward or outward (the latter method in the case of the Site BA02 Type 9 bottles). This lip finish added strength and/or gave a more refined and smooth appearance.

Various shades of aquamarine, often referred to as blue aqua, green or greenish aqua or pale blue aqua, are very common for all types of bottles, including culinary/food bottles such as the Type 9 style, and were particularly common between the 1850s and 1880s. Natural aqua glass derives from sand that is relatively low in concentrations of iron. High levels of iron produce darker greens, black glass and even amber. Sand deposits with very low iron content were highly valued commodities and although good quality sand was plentiful in the eastern United States, some was still imported from Belgium as late as the 1940s for Western American glass factories. By the early 20th century, aqua bottles were largely replaced by colorless glass, preferred by bottle users wishing their product to be more visible to the buyer.

Some condiment/spice bottles virtually identical to the Site BA02 Type 9 examples feature labels identifying the diversity of different spices these bottles contained, including pepper, thyme, cloves, cinnamon, marjoram, as well as mustard condiment. San Francisco's Hoff Store site assemblage is again useful in interpreting the Jacksonville 'Blue China' wreck wares. The most numerous type of culinary container found was a minimum of 122 similar condiment bottles (46.6% of the total assemblage) like the Site BA02

Fig. 71. Type 9B small spice/condiment glass bottle BC-05-00004-BE, H. 11.8cm.

assemblage recovered in two different sizes. All examples exhibit pontil scarred bases, with the majority displaying the same kind of blowpipe pontil scar present on the Site BA02 examples. One of the Hoff Store site bottles retained black pepper, a decisive discovery in determining these specific bottles' function (McDougall, 1990: 63), which is arguably relevant to the contents of the Jacksonville 'Blue China' wreck examples. In addition to salt, black pepper was the most common condiment in 19th-century America and was largely imported into cities across the United States by small traders like the Jacksonville 'Blue China' schooner (cf. Allen and Albala, 2007: 94).

A number of the Hoff Store condiment bottles preserved a lead foil cap covering the cork, collar and uppermost section of the neck, illustrating the method of sealing that was probably originally used for the Site BA02 wares. The proprietors identified by these lead foil caps are 'WELLS, MILLER & PROVOST 217/FRONT/ST/NEW YORK' (McDougall, 1990: 63). During the mid-19th century, John B. Wells, Ebenezer Miller and Stephen H. Provost, located on New York's Front Street from 1844 to 1852, were one of the leading manufacturers and wholesale distributors of preserved foods and condiments (McDougall, 1990: 64; Zumwalt, 1980: 428,

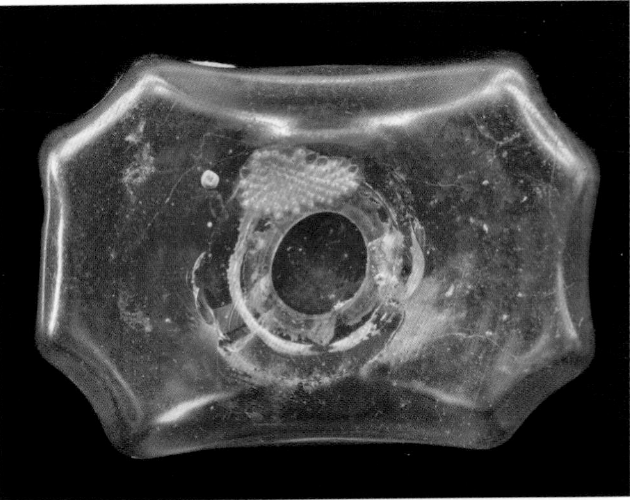

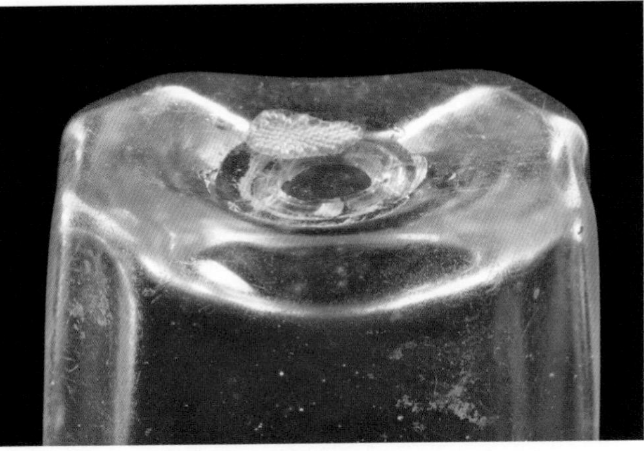

Figs. 72-74. Detail of the finish and base of Type 9B small spice/condiment glass bottle BC-05-00004-BE.

431). An 1850 advertisement listing the wide assortment of goods offered at the company warehouse noted that the products were either manufactured by the proprietors themselves or imported direct from responsible houses (Tremayne, 1850: 28). Miller soon left the partnership and the Wells & Provost firm relocated to 215 Front Street in 1861 (Wilson, 1861: 904). Having later moved again to Yonkers, New York, they became one of the most successful bottlers of the era (Smith, 1996: 39). The Site BA02 Type 9 bottles may quite plausibly have held comparable black pepper attributable to this same New York company, providing further evidence pointing to New York as the vessel's final port of departure.

Well-preserved examples of this distinctive bottle type were retrieved from the wreck of the Steamship *Bertrand* that sank down the Missouri River in April 1865. The original intact labels and packing crates indicate that the *Bertrand* bottles, significantly like those from the Hoff Store site, contained both ground pepper and other spices that the company made and probably also stored in this same bottle style, such as cinnamon, mace and white pepper (Switzer, 1974: 60-1). The excavation of the 1865 shipwreck of the sidewheel steamer *Republic*, which sank six months after the *Bertrand*, produced over 90 examples of this common eight-sided condiment/spice bottle – unembossed and devoid of paper labels – from a collection of over 1,500 food/culinary bottles.

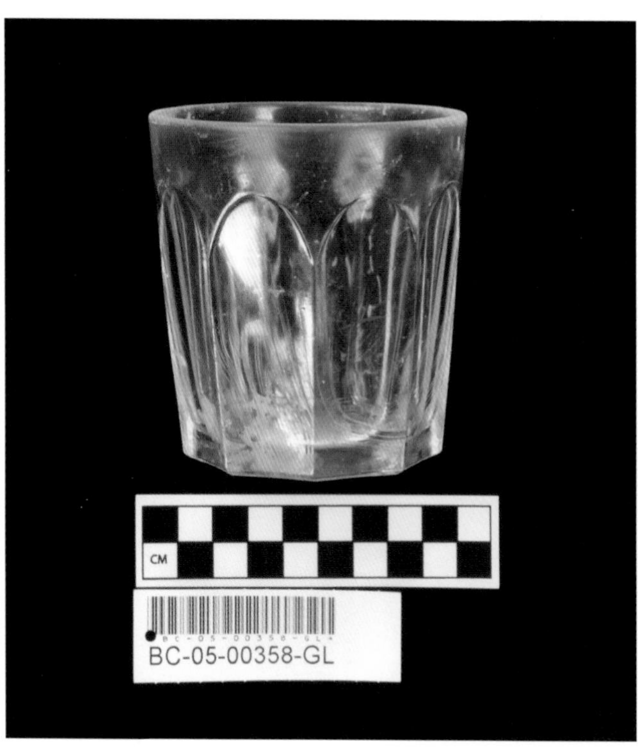

Fig. 75. Fluted glass bar tumbler BC-05-00358-GL, H. 9.0cm.

13. Glass Tumblers

The additional glassware recovered from the Jacksonville 'Blue China' wreck (excluding the window panes: cf. Gerth *et al.*, 2011: 41-4) included pressed glass tableware, pressed and mold-blown (and possibly free-blown) bar wares and individual lamp parts. Two types of short glass bar tumbler are represented among the recovered cargo: ten colorless fluted/paneled examples and five smooth-sided, pale green forms (Figs. 15-17, 20, 75-77).

The sample of short, colorless fluted/paneled bar tumblers represents the more common pressed glasswares produced in great quantities in the 19th century and is almost identical visually to today's common 'rock' glass.

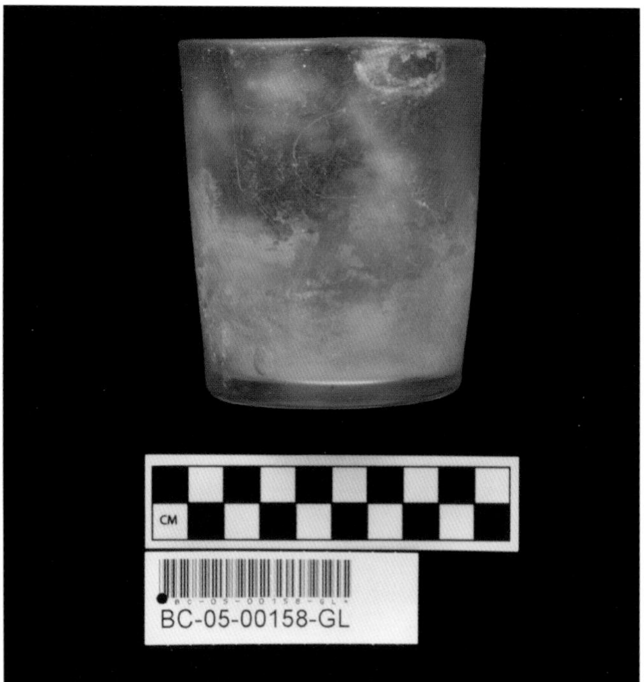

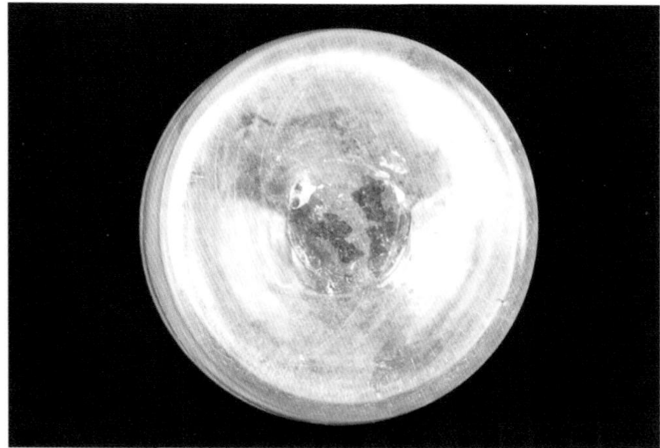

Figs. 76-77. Pale green, smooth-sided glass bar tumbler BC-05-00158-GL, H. 8.9cm, and detail of its base.

The fluted or paneled pattern was produced in a number of varied styles, which correspond to different factory designations, such as French flute, reverse flute, gill flute, pillar flute, column and edge flute (Chipman, 1932: 155). The Site BA02 examples are relatively squat and taper gradually outward from the base of the glass towards the top. These fluted bar tumblers display the following dimensions: H. 9.0cm; external Diam. of mouth 8.4cm; rim Th. 0.3cm; base Diam. 6.9cm; weight 326gr.

The Jacksonville 'Blue China' wreck fluted/paneled glass tumblers considerably post-date 1827, when Deming Jarves, using an iron mold, allegedly produced the first pressed glass water tumbler at the Boston & Sandwich Glass Company in Massachusetts, which he founded in 1826 (*The Glass Industry*, 1917: 16). The process of pressing molten glass by mechanical means was perfected in the United States between 1825 and 1826. However, as Jarves acknowledged, the introduction and development of glass manufacture by pressing, although once alleged to have been an American innovation, actually originated in Europe. Metallic molds for crudely pressing candlesticks and other glasswares were in use in both Holland and England by 1815 and perhaps earlier (Davis, 1949: 82). Around 1827, the full-size press machine requiring two men to operate was invented and the Boston & Sandwich Glass Company in Massachusetts was quick to exploit its potential. The company's founder would later receive several patents for improvements in pressing techniques and mold designs (Davis, 1949: 83).[3]

Soon, pressed glass was being manufactured by other glass factories, including many centered in Pittsburgh, Pennsylvania. From 1830-45 the pressed glass industry made slow progress, marked by experimentation and competition between both domestic and foreign blown glassware (Davis, 1949: 83). By the mid-19th century, however, American glass companies were profiting as never before as pressed glass wares threatened to take control of the market away from the more costly cut and engraved wares. Many of the new designs imitated English and Irish cut glass patterns, but were more easily made and required less skilled labor. Efficiency created products that were cheaper and more readily accessible to the modest American consumer. For the first time, the average household could afford glassware to grace the family table.[4]

Site BA02's five smooth-sided, pale green bar tumblers were probably either free-blown or mold-blown because they exhibit a blowpipe pontil mark on their bases, indicating not only differences in manufacture from the pressed glass fluted/paneled examples, but quite possibly production at different glassworks. Both free-blown and mold-blown examples represent a technique involving blowing by human lungs, the latter blown directly into a mold, the former without a mold. Their production date overlaps with the wreck's fluted bar tumblers, even though by the mid-1850s pressing glass into a mold was more common than mold-blown glassware. The smooth-sided, pale green bar tumblers display the following dimensions: H. 8.9cm; external Diam. of mouth 7.9cm; rim Th. 0.1cm; base Diam. 6.7cm; weight 122gr.

Site BA02's particular style of glass tumbler broadly dates from 1845-75 and could have been manufactured in any number of American glass factories producing bar and table wares. Especially likely candidates are one of the New England glass factories, quite possibly the Boston & Sandwich Glass Company or its competitor, the New England Glass Company (Spillman, 2006: 16). A handful of identical glass fluted tumblers was recovered from the later dated 1865 shipwreck of the SS *Republic*, testament to the longevity of this paneled pattern form.

The identification of the Site BA02 glass tumblers as cargo is based on their significant volume, widespread distribution and the discovery of five paneled examples inside five British dipped whiteware ceramic jugs into which they seem to have been packed to maximize space efficiency during shipping (Tolson *et al.*, 2008: 172). Further fragments of two green glass tumblers were found inside a sixth dipped whiteware ceramic jug. This nested stowage method may suggest that at least some of the ceramics and glasswares were being delivered to a single consignee.

14. Oil Lamp Fonts

The excavation of Site BA02 identified four parts of oil lamps in the northeastern, stern section of the wreck: two globes and two fonts with bases, with the exception of one base all of which were recovered. These wares were located 1.5m to the northwest of keg K1 to the north of Area B. Although the schooner's stern would have contained the crew's galley structure, these lighting devices probably did not illuminate the cabin because a shipboard lamp would have been gimbaled and rigidly mounted. In addition, no burners or chimneys were found on the site and lamp stems and brass joint connectors were conspicuously absent. This leads to the conclusion that the ship was transporting separate glass lamp components as cargo, a common trend at a time when factories specialized in the production of individual glass parts (globes, fonts and bases) for the lamp industry (Barlow and Kaiser, 1989: 155; Gerth *et al.*, 2011: 41).

The heavy colorless glass lamp font and base from Site BA02 (BC-05-00024-GL; Fig. 78) is pressed in the 'Circle and Ellipse' pattern, with a hexagonal base and dates

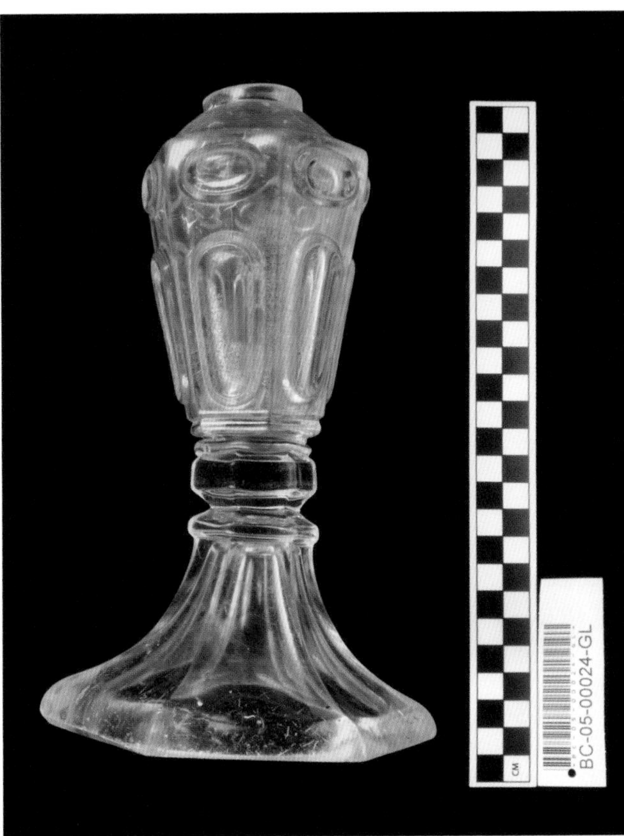

Fig. 78. Oil lamp font BC-05-00024-GL pressed in the 'Circle and Ellipse' pattern, with a hexagonal base, H. 21.2cm.

generically to 1840-70 (Barlow and Kaiser, 1989: 43). Its distinctive design is also seen on vases produced in the eastern United States (McKearin and McKearin, 1941: 388, 392; Wilson, 1994: 457). An identical second font and base was recorded alongside the former and left *in situ*.

The top section of the lamp is an oval-shaped font comprised of six panels, each of which feature a repeating pattern consisting of a circle on top and an elongated oval form on the bottom. The top of the font ends in a relatively small opening with a narrow rim, which would have held the lamp burner. Below the font is a small, thick wafer of glass, which connects into a hexagonal base with a flared foot. The BC-05-00024-GL oil lamp font displays the following dimensions: H. 21.2cm; H. of body (from bottom of lowest flange above base to top of artifact) 14.6cm; Diam. of bore 2.7cm; max. Diam. of upper body 8.0cm; H. of base (up to first flange) 6.4cm; base Diam. (up to first flange) 13.5cm; weight 884grs.

Lamp fonts of this style were manufactured by the Boston & Sandwich Glass Company and the McKee and Brother Glass Works of Pittsburgh, Pennsylvania. The latter featured the lamp in its 1859-60 catalog, which stated that a dozen could be purchased with a whale oil burner for $4.00 and with a fluid burner at $4.66 per dozen (Barlow and Kaiser, 1989: 90). A number of other companies specialized in similar patterned glass lamps.

The advent of the pressing machine in the late 1820s revolutionized the manufacture of glassware and facilitated the production of vast quantities of pressed glass in hundreds of different patterns. While mold-blown glass necessitated the muscle and lung technique of glass blowers, by contrast pressed glass consisted of molten glass mechanically pressed into a mold by a metal plunger affixed to a long lever-like handle (Berry, 2001: 47, 48). This new technique permitted the mass production of glassware, lowered manufacturing costs and consequently retail prices (McKearin and McKearin, 1948: 332, 377-8). Once thousands of identical items could be readily produced, glassware was no longer a luxury for the wealthy, but rather a commodity that could be afforded by all, and demand soared accordingly.

By the 1840s, companies such as the Boston & Sandwich Glass Company realized that in order to remain competitive, they needed to introduce major stylistic changes to their products. They invested heavily in the purchase of molds to make glass fonts in the knowledge that it required far less time to teach a glassworker how much glass to drop into a pressing mold than it did to train a glassblower to make free-blown fonts or blow the correct size bubble into a patterned mold (Barlow and Kaiser, 1989: 43). Pressing glass transformed the glass industry from one that relied almost exclusively on artisans to one that was augmented by molds. Deming Jarves, founder of the Boston & Sandwich Glass Company, estimated that by the mid-1850s glass companies were spending more than $2 million dollars on pressing machinery and molds alone (Berry, 2001: 47, 48; Davis, 1949: 83).

The Jacksonville 'Blue China' wreck lamp font does not appear to be a companion to either of the glass lamp globes recovered from the site because the opening at the bottom of the globes are too large to fit the smaller lamp stem. The lamp font and base appear to have been pressed in a multi-section metal mold of either brass or iron. Such lamps produced at the Boston & Sandwich Glass Company were pressed in two-part molds. The pressed 'Circle and Ellipse' patterned font was attached to the pressed base using a wafer construction, whereby a circular glass merese inserted between the two pieces interconnected them while the glass was still extremely hot. The Site BA02 lamp font and base was seemingly produced by this same process. However, if it was pressed in one piece, then it could have been manufactured by the New England Glass Company of Massachusetts.

The American Flint Glass Company of South Boston, Massachusetts, also manufactured such mold-blown lamps (pers. comm. Dorothy Hogan-Schofield, 8 February 2010).

The Site BA02 lamp font – one of two on the wreck – is likely to have been part of a small cargo because, as mentioned above, a shipboard lamp would have been gimbaled and rigidly mounted. The recovery of two other non-related glass lamp globes suggests that the ship was carrying a minor consignment of lamp parts. Lamp components were frequently produced separately and their varied glass and brass pieces often derived from different manufacturers that were later assembled by employees of the lamp industry (pers. comm. Jane Spillman, 2006; Barlow and Kaiser, 1989: 155).

Fig. 79. Semi-opaque oil lamp globe BC-05-00021-GL, H. 16.2cm.

15. Oil Lamp Globes

Two spherical lamp globes recovered from the northeast flank of Site BA02, corresponding to the ship's stern, typify mid-19th century products. Both globes were apparently mold blown. Despite the introduction of the more cost-effective pressing machine, the earlier mold-blown technology remained the preferred method of production for larger glasswares, such as lamp globes. If pressed, the center of the globe would be cylindrical with very thick sides, thus allowing the plunger to enter and escape. The end product would have been too heavy and thick for a lamp globe intended to shed light. Period lamp globes produced by the Boston & Sandwich Glass Company were virtually all mold blown, further confirmed by examples featured in the Company's catalogs of the 1860s to 1880s (pers. comm. Dorothy Hogan-Schofield, 3 and 4 February 2011).

By the mid-1800s the number of glass companies in the US had increased substantially compared to the turn of the century, and by 1867 most glass factories in the United States were involved in the manufacture of glass lighting devices (Berry, 2001: 47). The business had become so immense that many glasshouses were entirely devoted to pressing lamp globes, while others concentrated solely on lamp shades and yet more only produced chimneys (pers. comm. Dorothy Hogan-Schofield, 8 February 2010; Barlow and Kaiser, 1989: 153-54, 156).

Lamps produced in the mid-1850s used whale oil, burning fluid and newly introduced kerosene. When the price of whale oil began climbing precipitously, 'burning fluid' became especially popular throughout North America. First patented in 1830, its use spread quickly in the following decade. Derived from high-proof alcohol and redistilled turpentine, it was cheap and produced a white, smokeless flame. Further, the lamps that burned it were relatively simple to make and operate. Nevertheless, it was

Fig. 80. Ruby red oil lamp globe SC-04-00006-GL, H. 19.8cm.

still one of the most dangerous fuels ever to gain widespread use. By 1857, over a million gallons of 'burning fluid' were manufactured in Philadelphia alone and sold for about 60 cents a gallon (Russell, 1968: 93-4).

Kerosene burning fuel was also readily available in the United States by the 1850s, when companies such as the Boston & Sandwich Glass Company started kerosene lamp manufacture. The introduction of this liquid is credited to the Canadian geologist Abraham Gesner, who in 1846 discovered how to produce crude lamp oil from coal. The product (later known as kerosene) was first introduced into the English lighting industry by James Young of Glasgow, Scotland (Barlow and Kaiser, 1989: 43), through a patent he obtained in 1850. His United States patent was issued in 1852 and two years later 8,000 gallons of kerosene were being sold weekly across the country under Young's patent by the Kerosene Oil Company of Long Island, New York. Safe to use in glass lamps, kerosene had become a household word (Barlow and Kaiser, 1989: 153). Given the purported 1854 date for Site BA02, it is quite plausible that the Jacksonville 'Blue China' lamp globes were intended for kerosene lighting.

The wreck's two glass globes, one semi-opaque (BC-05-00021-GL; Fig. 79) and the other ruby red (BC-04-00006-GL; Fig. 80), were sufficiently common to have been intended for use in relatively modest homes of the period. They could have been crafted by any number of glasshouses that specialized in lighting accessories, including the Boston & Sandwich Glass Company, which by 1844 had constructed a furnace specifically for the manufacture of colored glass, which facilitated the increased production of lamps and other glassware in a variety of beautiful colors (Barlow and Kaiser, 1898: 43).

Both of the Site BA02's lamp globes are undecorated and spherical in shape, but slightly dissimilar in style. The ruby red example is rounder and squatter than the semi-opaque globe. Both feature a circular opening at each end of the globe, the semi-opaque one being smaller in diameter than the ruby red example. The semi-opaque globe features a rim around the opening that is relatively thin and tapers slightly outward, while the rim around the opening of the ruby red example is thicker, rounded and slightly curved. The semi-opaque lamp has a small chip on the rim of the lower opening and exhibits what appears to be iron oxide staining.

The BC-05-00021-GL semi-opaque glass oil lamp globe displays the following dimensions: H. 16.2cm; max. body W. 16.0cm; external Diam. of top opening 9.8cm; external Diam. of lower opening 9.9cm; rim Th. of top opening 0.4cm; rim Th. of bottom opening 0.4cm; weight 1.708kg. The BC-04-00006-GL ruby red oil lamp globe displays the following dimensions: H. 19.8cm; max. body W. 14.5cm; external Diam. of top opening 12.3cm; external Diam. of lower opening 11.4cm; rim Th. of top opening 0.6cm; rim Th. of bottom opening 0.7cm; weight 7.1kg.

16. Pressed Salt Cellar

A single opalescent pale blue pressed glass salt cellar in the 'Bee Hive' pattern (BC-05-00007-GL; Fig. 81) was recovered from the Jacksonville 'Blue China' shipwreck, some 2.9m northeast of the large keg K6 in Area E2. Its context included a glass inkstand, part of a brass and glass sextant and a brass hinge. Although found in the original general area of the ship's stern cabin, it is hard to envisage practical sailors taking the time to 'pass the salt' during meals at sea. Instead, this was possibly another part of a small-scale bespoke consignment of glasswares.

The salt cellar is rectangular in shape, with sides tapering outwards from the base to the top of the vessel. The base consists of a series of five projecting curves or ridges that form an uneven exterior. The exterior perimeter of the container is comprised of alternating projecting curved rows. The top rim of the vessel again is uneven, consisting of alternating small ridges. The interior of the vessel is relatively shallow. The appearance of the glass varies from a milky pale blue semi-opaque color to an almost transparent colorless glass. The BC-05-00007-GL glass salt cellar displays the following dimensions: H. 5.0cm; max. Diam. 7.8cm x 5.3cm; rim Th. 0.8cm; top flange W. 7.8cm; lower flange W. 6.8cm; base Diam. 5.3cm x 3.0cm; weight 287gr.

This particular style of salt cellar style was in circulation between *c.* 1835 and 1860 and is attributed to the Boston & Sandwich Glass Company, where identical fragments have been unearthed from the former factory site. Also called a 'salt' by the Sandwich glassworks, this is one of the earliest forms pressed by the company, the original mold pattern having been designed in the 1820s. Its heavy horizontal ribs and curved rim typify the forms of blown molded salt cellars and sugar bowls of the period. Its early use is highlighted by the ten dozen 'Bee Hive' salts shipped to New Orleans in 1827 (pers. comm. Dorothy Hogan-Schofield, 8 February 2010; Barlow and Kaiser, 1985: 278; Wilson, 1994: 455).

While the New England Glass Company also produced a similar salt cellar patterned form, the Boston & Sandwich Glass Company is believed to have been an important – if not the leading – manufacturer of the 'Bee Hive' pressed salt cellar (Barlow and Kaiser, 1985: 278; Spillman, 1981: 242). Salt cellars of various design and decoration were produced in many other establishments equipped to work with molten glass and iron molds, including factories

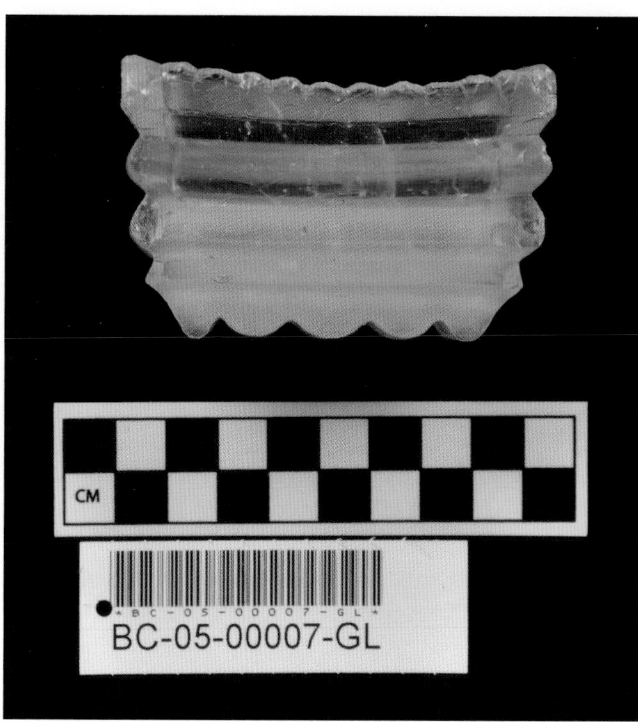

Fig. 81. Glass salt cellar BC-05-00007-GL, H. 5.0cm.

that copied their competitors' popular designs. Typically unmarked, it is impossible to state categorically just which exact American glass factory manufactured this small table piece.

Salt making is believed to have been a very early American industry. In 1620, the colonists at Jamestown, Virginia, established salt works at Cape Charles and in 1633 began to send salt to the Massachusetts Puritans (Greeley, 1872: 124). By 1689, salt was being made in South Carolina. Early American settlers, however, imported most of their salt, but the British blockade imposed during the Revolutionary War made the receipt of imports virtually impossible and unaffordable due to high tariffs (Barlow and Kaiser, 1985: 275). The American market so long dependent on foreign manufacturers was compelled to rely on its own resources.

In the late 18th century, commercial salt works were established in coastal communities along the Atlantic coast, where salt was especially needed for curing fish. The leading manufactories were located in Virginia, Delaware, New Jersey, Massachusetts and Maine (Greeley, 1872: 124) and could produce one bushel of salt from 350 gallons of water. By the late 1830s, coastal towns such as Cape Cod, Massachusetts, were supporting a thriving salt industry. The town of Dennis boosted 114 salt works in 1837. Even Deming Jarves, the founder of Sandwich's glass company, outlined a plan to build a salt-making facility on the grounds of the Sandwich factory in 1838. The operation relied on iron pipes to convey the heat beneath trays filled with salt water and reportedly produced ten bushels of salt per day, which at the time brought $6 to $8 per bushel (Barlow and Kaiser, 1985: 275).

Further inland, the Kentucky salt springs were in use before 1790. The first salt manufacture began in Ohio in 1798 and in Pennsylvania in 1812. More important sources existed in New York, West Virginia and Ohio, with New York ultimately generating more than half of the entire domestic supply of America. The state's leading salt works were situated in Syracuse, where the Onondaga Salt Springs was a major producer (Greeley, 1872: 125).[5] Systematic production began in 1797, when state legislature designated a one mile-wide strip of land around the southern half of the lake as the Onondaga Salt Springs Reservation. Laws regulating the method of production (boiling or solar evaporation), as well as the storage and sale of salt, were implemented along with a collection duty for every bushel of salt produced on the Reservation. The rapid development of the salt industry in the 18th and 19th century led to Syracuse becoming known as 'The Salt City'. Between 1797 and 1917, the Reservation produced more than 11.5 million tons of salt. The expansion of the United States into areas that had natural salt brines and rock salt mines resulted in the decline of coastal salt evaporating facilities (Barlow and Kaiser, 1985: 275).

Whether derived from land or sea, coarsely milled salt frequently absorbed moisture and had a tendency to lump and, as a result, salt was placed on the table in an open container. Although the glass container held only a limited supply of salt, the term cellar was in common use at the time and meant a place of storage. The popular use of such glassware was supported in large part by a population that consumed an enormous amount of salt, which was delivered to the table in an open salt cellar throughout the 19th century (Barlow and Kaiser, 1985: 275-6).

17. Conclusion

Despite numerous trials and errors, the War of 1812 and British competition, American glass production increased steadily throughout the 1800s to become a booming industry in the second half of the century. A number of factors influenced this trend, including urbanization driven by developing industrialization. At the start of this period, only 5% of America's population lived in urban areas, whereas by 1850 the figure had increased to nearly 20% (Machor, 1987: 121), a growth that in large part was triggered by a flood of foreign immigrants and economic expansion (Selcer, 2006: 272). Initially only five cities exceeded 5,000 residents. However, by the middle of the century over 60 cities could boast this population size and six cities catered to populations in excess of 100,000. The Northeast experienced the most substantial growth, with its four leading cities, Baltimore, Boston, Philadelphia and New York (including Brooklyn) sustaining a combined 1.3 million inhabitants (Machor, 1987: 120-21). During the three decades from 1830 onwards, these four major Atlantic seaports grew at a rate of 25% or more per decade (Selcer, 2006: 272). All of these cities were home to the burgeoning glass industry.

With increased urbanization, the development of better roads, canals, steamboats and railroads and a rising standard of living, America's population became increasingly reliant on glass containers to package products that had formerly been manufactured and consumed domestically. Bulk packaging in ceramic and wooden containers was the norm during the 18th century, glass bottles being relatively expensive to manufacture and domestic production being hampered by shortages of capital, competent labor and adequate transportation. Most bottles at this time were imported, and supply could not meet the growing demand (Busch, 2000: 175). Hand in hand with the phenomenon of expanding US cities were technological innovations, an infusion of skilled craftsmen and an increased consumer population, which, amongst other factors, by 1850 supported a thriving domestic glass industry. The industry, in turn, fed into a host of merchants, druggists and shopkeepers, whose retail and wholesale businesses depended on providing bottled goods and household glassware to customers across the country.

While many glass companies produced finer wares catering to a wealthier clientele, the Site BA02 glassware cargo confirms that US glassworks mass-produced a diversity of affordable items intended for the modest American consumer, including glass lamps, table and bar wares, as well as various bottle forms essential to the merchant trade and domestic life in the mid-19th century United States. Most of the US glassworks were built on or near waterways, railroads and turnpikes, providing efficient access to city markets and consumers. Improved transportation systems naturally facilitated increased trade networks. Ships typified by the Jacksonville 'Blue China' schooner, very likely based in and having departed from New York City on its final voyage, played a central role in the distribution of glasswares and bottled goods well beyond the major industrial centers.

The Site BA02 bottle assemblage is not unusual for the mid-1800s. Except for the more decorative cologne bottles (Type 7 and Type 8), the representative glass bottles recovered from the shipwreck typify 1850s US domestic refuse assemblages often found broken in privies and dumps. The Jacksonville 'Blue China' bottle assemblage provides a clear snapshot of the diversity of bottled products (medicines, liquor, mineral water, condiments and cologne) present in mid-19th century households and stores and relied on by the American consumer.

All of the bottles from Site BA02 are seemingly of domestic American production. Given the relatively firm dating of the wreck to the mid-1850s, the bottle assemblage confirms and conforms to several previously established trends in US bottle manufacturing. First and most significantly, the use of pontil rods was at this time still by far the dominant method of holding the bottle for the final finishing (forming of the lip). All of the bottle types featured in the Jacksonville 'Blue China' assemblage exhibit pontil scars evocative of a method of manufacture that had largely ended by the late 1850s, replaced by the use of the snap case that left no mark on the bottom of the bottle. However, as is the case with most technological innovations, the new snap case device was adopted at varying rates by different factories over a period of time. Bottles exhibiting pontil scars indicative of the older technology continued in use until the end of the American Civil War of 1861-65.

Secondly, the Site BA02 bottles reveal that the finishing techniques of the 1850s were dominated by crudely applied finishes formed by the prevalence of the earlier, more basic tools. Thin 'flared' and 'rolled' finishes, formed without the use of a specifically designed finishing tool, were still a common method of forming the lip of the bottle at this time.

Thirdly, in light of the prevailing study of glass bottle production technology, the various methods applied in the production of the Site BA02 bottles clearly reflect the period of technological flux in American glass-making that occurred during the 1850s, whereby some of the methods employed reflected much older methods and others represented newer Industrial Age innovations. The bottle forming methods represented amongst the Jacksonville 'Blue China' assemblage range from the traditional age-old method of free-blowing and/or dip molding (Types 3 and 6) to the period-typical true two-piece molds with no separate base plate (Type 4, 5, 7 and possibly 8 and 9A). Also evident is the use of the Ricketts' style three-piece mold relied on to produce the Type 1 bottle and earlier versions of the relatively modern (for the period) post-base molds seen in the Type 2 and 9B examples. This latter mold type would subsequently become a dominant form for at least another three decades.

The non-bottle glass forms recovered from Site BA02 represent a sample of the modestly priced American products readily accessible to the average mid-19th century US consumer. While the prevalence of these wares was not uncommon, a number of the glass cargo items uniquely reflect the technological trends and transitions that characterized the glass industry in the 1850s. The two different bar tumblers – the pale green example and the colorless fluted variety – exhibit co-existent production methods. While the fluted tumblers were pressed in a mold, the pale green samples were likely free-blown or mold-blown because they exhibit a blowpipe pontil mark on their bases. In the final analysis, as a microcosm of the early Victorian United States, the Jacksonville 'Blue China' shipwreck's glass cargo and the recovered sample symbolize the success of the country's industrial and mercantile revolution and, in particular, its burgeoning glassware industry, which proved resistant to failure and would help propel the country into the future.

Acknowledgements

The authors wish to extend their sincere gratitude to the entire survey, excavation, conservation and management teams at Odyssey Marine Exploration that made the recording of the Jacksonville 'Blue China' wreck and the recovery of a sample of its artifacts possible, the names of whom are fully listed in the acknowledgements in *OME Papers* 19.

Particular gratitude is extended to Dorothy Hogan-Schofield, curator of the Sandwich Glass Museum and Jane Spillman, curator of the Corning Museum of Glass. In addition, special thanks at Odyssey to Alan Bosel, who took the photographs of the Site BA02 glassware artifacts, and to Chad Morris, who provided their measurements.

Notes

1. The bottle identifications, technology, and history presented in this paper rely heavily on data published in the Historic Glass Bottle Identification and Information website (US Department of the Interior Bureau of Land Management/Society for Historical Archaeology): http://www.sha.org/bottle/typing.htm.
2. See Brecher, *The Consumers Union Report on Licit and Illicit Drugs* (1972): http://www.druglibrary.org/schaffer/Library/studies/cu/cumenu.htm.
3. See: http://www.sandwichglassmuseum.org/about_us/history.
4. See Note 3 above.
5. Section 16 draws extensively on *Salt Production in Syracuse. 'The Salt City' and the Hydrogeology of the Onondage Creek Valley:* http://ny.water.usgs.gov/pubs/fs/fs13900/FS139-00.pdf.

Bibliography

Allen, G. and Albala, K., (eds.), *The Business of Food. Encyclopedia of the Food and Drink Industries* (Connecticut, 2007).

Appleton's Journal of Literature, Science and Art. Volume Seven, January 6 to June 29 1872 (New York, 1872).

Barlow, R.E. and Kaiser, J.E., *The Glass Industry in Sandwich. Volume 1* (New Hampshire, 1985).

Barlow, R.E. and Kaiser, J.E., *The Glass Industry in Sandwich. Volume 2* (New Hampshire, 1989).

Beck, J.B., *Essays on Infant Therapeutics* (New York, 1864).

Berry, N.E., 'Lasting Impressions', *Old House Journal* (Nov/December 2001), 47-51.

Boston Board of Trade 1856. Second Annual Report of the Government Presented to the Board at the Annual Meeting, on the 16th of January 1856 (Boston, 1856).

Busch, J., 'Second Time Around: A Look at Bottle Reuse'. In D.R. Brauner (ed.), *Approaches to Material Culture Research for Historical Archaeologists* (California University of Pennsylvania, 2000), 175-88.

Chipman, F.W., *The Romance of Old Sandwich Glass* (Boston, 1932).

Current Literature. A Magazine of Record and Review 5 (July-December 1890), 179-83.

Davis, P., *The Development of the American Glass Industry* (Harvard University of Press, 1949).

Delgado, J.P., *Gold Rush Port. The Maritime Archaeology of San Francisco's Waterfront* (University of California Press, 2009).

Ebert, E.A., 'Early History of the Drug Trade of Chicago', *Transactions for the Illinois State Historical Society* (1906), 237-60.

Fike, R.E., *The Bottle Book. A Comprehensive Guide to Historic, Embossed Medicine Bottles* (Salt Lake City, 1987).

Gerth, E., 'The Jacksonville 'Blue China' Shipwreck (Site BA02): the Ceramic Assemblage'. In G. Stemm and S. Kingsley (eds.), *Oceans Odyssey 2. Underwater Heritage Management & Deep-Sea Shipwrecks in the English Channel & Atlantic Ocean* (Oxford, 2011), 221-62.

Gerth, E., Cunningham Dobson, N. and Kingsley, S., 'The Jacksonville 'Blue China' Shipwreck (Site BA02): An American Coastal Schooner off Florida'. In G. Stemm and S. Kingsley (eds.), *Oceans Odyssey 2. Underwater Heritage Management & Deep-Sea Shipwrecks in the English Channel & Atlantic Ocean* (Oxford, 2011), 143-220.

Greeley, H., *The Great Industries of the United States* (Chicago and Cincinnati, 1972).

Griffenhagen, G. and Bogard, M., *History of Drug Containers and their Labels* (Madison, 1999).

Hart, E., (ed.), *The British Medical Journal. Vol. II, July-December 1881* (London, 1881).

Henderson, H.C., 'The Glass Industry', *Popular Science Monthly* (February 1893), 433-44.

Herdendorf, C.E. (ed.), 'Science on a Deep-Ocean Shipwreck', *Ohio Journal of Science* 95.1 (1995), 4-224.

Holcombe, H.W., *Patent Medicine Tax Stamps* (Lawrence, Mississippi, 1979).

Hoolihan, C., *An Annotated Catalogue of the Edward C. Atwater Collection of American Popular Medicine and Health Reform, Vol. III, Supplement: A-Z* (University of Rochester Press, 2008).

Illustrated New York. The Metropolis of To-Day (New York, 1888).

Jones, G., *Beauty Imagined: a History of the Global Beauty Industry* (Oxford University Press, 2000).

Jones, O., 'Glass Bottle Push-Ups and Pontil Marks'. In D.R. Brauner (ed.), *Approaches to Material Culture Research for Historical Archaeologists* (California University of Pennsylvania, 2000), 149-60.

Jones, O.R., *Cylindrical English Wine and Beer Bottles, 1735-1850* (National Historic Parks and Sites Branch, Parks Canada, Ontario, 1986).

Jordan, T.E., *Victorian Childhood* (State University of New York Press, 1987).

Kaiser, J., *The Glass Industry in South Boston* (University of New England Press, 2009).

LaMoreaux, P.E., 'Famous Springs and Bottled Water'. In P.E. LaMoreaux and J.T. Tanner (eds.), *Springs and Bottled Waters of the World* (Berlin, 2001), 133-37.

Lawrence, S., 'Artifacts of the Modern World'. In J. Balme and A. Paterson (eds.), *Archaeological Practices. A Student Guide to Archaeological Analyses* (Oxford, 2006), 362-85.

Machor, J.L., *Urban Ideals and the Symbolic Landscape of America* (University of Wisconsin Press, 1987).

McDougall, D.P., 'The Bottles of the Hoff Store Site'. In A.G. Pastron and E.M. Hattori (eds.), *The Hoff Store Site and Gold Rush Merchandise in San Francisco, California* (Society for Historical Archaeology, Special Publication Series, No. 7, 1990).

McKearin, G.S., and McKearin, H., *American Glass* (New York, 1941).

McKearin, H. and Wilson, K., *American Bottles and Flasks and their Ancestry* (New York, 1978).

Odell, J., *Digger Odell's Pontil Medicine Encyclopedia: a Look at America's Pre-Civil War Medicine Bottles* (Digger Odell Publications, 2000).

Parsons, C.W. (ed.), *The Pharmaceutical Era. Volume XV, January-June 1896* (New York, 1896).

Pollard, E.A., *The Virginia Tourist Sketches of the Springs and Mountains of Virginia* (Philadelphia, 1871).

Powers, M., *Faces along the Bar: Lore and Order in the Workingman's Saloon, 1870-1920* (University of Chicago Press, 1998).

Russell, L.S., *A Heritage of Light. Lamps and Lighting in the Early Canadian Home* (University of Toronto Press, 1968).

Sala, G.A., *From the Bay of New York to the Gulf of Mexico* (London, 1886).

Selcer, R.F., *Civil War America 1850-1875* (New York, 2006).

Sheldon & Co.'s Business and Advertising Directory (John F. Trow & Company, 1945).

Shimko, P., *Sarsaparilla Bottle Encyclopedia* (Privately Published, 1969).

Smith, A.F., *Pure Ketchup: A History of America's National Condiment* (University of South Carolina, 1996).

Spillman, J.S., *American and European Pressed Glass in the Corning Museum of Glass* (New York, 1981).

Spillman, J.S., 'Sunken Treasure: the SS *Republic*', *The Glass Bulletin Club of the National American Glass Club* 204 (2006), 13-17.

Stamelman, R., *Perfume. A Cultural History of Fragrance from 1750 to the Present* (New York, 2006).

Sutton, M.Q. and Arkush, B.S. (eds.), *Archaeological Laboratory Methods. An Introduction* (Dubuque, Iowa, 1996).

Switzer, R.R., *The Bertrand Bottles. A Study of 19th Century Glass and Ceramic Containers* (National Park Service, US Department of the Interior, 1974).

The Boston Directory: Containing the City Record, a General Directory of the Citizens and a Special Directory of Trades, Professions, &c. 1848-9 (Boston, 1848).

The Boston Directory for the Year 1852, Embracing the City Record, a General Directory of the Citizens and a Business Directory, with an Almanac, for July 1852 to July 1853 (Boston, 1852).

The Era Druggists Directory (New York, 1905).

The Gazette of the Union. Volume XI. July – December 1849 (New York, 1849).

The Glass Industry. Report on the Cost of Production of Glass in the United States (Washington, 1917).

The Ladies' Companion and Monthly Magazine (London, 1856).

Tolson, H., Gerth, E. and Cunningham Dobson, N., 'Ceramics from the Blue China Wreck'. In R. Hunter (ed.), *Ceramics in America* (Chipstone Foundation, Milwaukee, 2008), 162-83.

Tremayne, E., *Tremayne's Table of the Post-Offices in the United States* (New York, 1850).

Van den Bossche, W., *Antique Glass Bottles: their History and Evolution (1500-1850)* (Woodbridge, 2001).

Walbridge, W.S., *American Bottles Old and New. A Story of the Industry in the United States* (Toledo, 1920).

Wilson, H., *Trow's New York City Directory* (New York, 1861).

Wilson, K.M., *The Toledo Museum of Art American Glass 1760-1930. Volume 1* (New York, 1994).

Wilson, B. and Wilson, B., *Western Bitters* (Santa Rosa, 1969).

Wood, W.H.S., *Friends of the City of New York in the Nineteenth Century* (New York, 1904).

The 'Atlas' Survey Zone: Deep-Sea Archaeology & U-boat Loss Reassessments

Axel Niestlé
Dabendorf, Germany

Between June 1944 and May 1945 the waters of the English Channel witnessed intense naval operations during the final phase of the German U-boat campaign against allied shipping. Operating close to shore and also the along the cross-Channel convoy supply lanes, German schnorkel-equipped U-boats suffered grievous losses with only moderate success. The majority was sunk with all hands while submerged. Official post-war loss lists were largely based on incomplete wartime signal intelligence derived from intercepted and decoded Axis radio communications. In the heat of battle, this historical documentation was often incomplete.

In July 2008 Odyssey Marine Exploration mounted an expedition designed to determine the formerly unknown or vague identities of six World War II German U-boat wrecks located in the Western English Channel and along the northern coast of Cornwall. The survey was conducted using the ROV Zeus launched from the *Odyssey Explorer*. Authoritative new evidence obtained during the survey has led to the definitive identification of the former German U-boats U 325, U 400, U 650, U 1021 and U 1208. Consequently, previous errors in the operational history of the German U-boat campaign in the Western English Channel have been corrected. The project serves as a positive example of how deep-sea wreck archaeology, working in tandem with historians, can access fresh data and rewrite major naval history.

1. Introduction

In the heat of battle, historical documentation often remains necessarily incomplete. With naval history usually based on information found in official documents or oral recordings filed in archives or museums, the precision in the accounts of naval actions or operations decrease markedly in cases where contemporary records are lacking or incomplete. This lack of information has led sometimes to dreadful distortions in the true narrative of how historical events unfolded. The operational history of the German U-boat campaign during both world wars of the 20th century offers splendid examples of this deficiency. A high percentage of U-boats lost in combat went down with all hands under circumstances that even remain obscure today. Documentation of the German role in operations often remains fragmentary.

Modern deep-sea marine archaeology offers a completely new dimension for historians to investigate and reconstruct operational events in naval conflicts of the last centuries. Thanks to advanced manned or unmanned underwater vessels equipped with powerful lights and the latest sensors and cameras, numerous wrecks of sunken ships, formerly hidden in the darkness of the deep sea, can now be located and examined to learn more about their features and final fate. Some 60 years after the last war, many of the wartime wrecks are still preserved in surprisingly good condition. Exploration and detailed documentation by experienced archaeologists and expert historians can result in successful wreck identification and a more precise understanding of events otherwise left obscured by the shadows of history. The search and detailed inspection of the famous German World War II battleship *Bismarck*, for instance (Ballard and Archbold, 1990; Garzke and Dulin, 1991), offer an excellent example of a collaborative effort by marine archaeologists and historians to rewrite history.

During the last two decades the wrecks of several formerly unrecorded World War II German U-boats were discovered off the south-west coast of Britain in locations where no wartime losses were recorded in the official list of German U-boat losses compiled during the war and published jointly by the British Admiralty and the US Chief of Naval Operations (CNO) in 1946.[1] Further, several of these U-boat wreck sites are substantially distant from known positions of allied anti-submarine attacks made during the war. Hence, these losses were probably caused by some other means, such as mining, marine accidents or malfunction.

The discovery of unexplained U-boat losses in this part of Britain's coastal waters did not come as a surprise. Between June 1944 and May 1945 the waters of the English Channel saw intense operations during the final phase of the German U-boat campaign against allied shipping. Operating close to the coastline and along the cross-Channel convoy supply lanes, German schnorkel-equipped U-boats suffered grievous losses in exchange for moderate success. The majority was sunk with all hands while submerged, and evidence for their destruction was often limited to oil and debris observed rising from the depths. It is now known that official post-war loss lists were mainly based on incomplete wartime signal intelligence derived from intercepted and decoded Axis radio communications (Niestlé, 2008). The rapid disbanding of allied naval departments related to the assessment of German wartime U-boat losses after May 1945 left no opportunity for a thorough check of results with the help of German military records, which fell into allied hands at the end of the war. In September 1945 it was estimated that the translation and detailed analysis of every German U-boat log, together with correlation of all attacks reported therein with corresponding Allied attacks, would require the services of a significant-sized staff for the better part of a year.[2] With this work never initiated, the degree of error in the 1946 publication of the Admiralty and the US Chief of Naval Operations is evident from the fact that until today more than 150 losses have been re-assessed.

In July 2008 Odyssey Marine Exploration initiated an expedition to survey hitherto unidentified or vague German World War II U-boat wreck sites in the Western English Channel and the north Cornish coast as part of its Atlas Shipwreck Survey Project (Fig. 1). The author was given the opportunity to join the expedition team as expert historian responsible for actual wreck identifications. A total of six dive target sites were selected, to be examined using the Remotely-Operated Vehicle Zeus based on the *Odyssey Explorer* research vessel. In the hands of experienced operators this multi-purpose vehicle offers optimum conditions for wreck surveys. The ambitious purpose of the expedition was to collect maximum information to form objective assessments about the identity of each wreck. As a precondition of success, close cooperation between the onboard Project Manager and the expert historian in planning every dive operation ensured that all sections and details of the wrecks helpful in the identification process were fully investigated and documented by high-definition video supported by the digital photography. While many wreck details were identified live during the underwater surveys, others only became apparent following numerous repeat viewings of the video footage.

In the following sections, the results of the individual wreck surveys are presented in combination with the 'forensic' interpretation of the available information in order to reveal the identity of the wrecks.

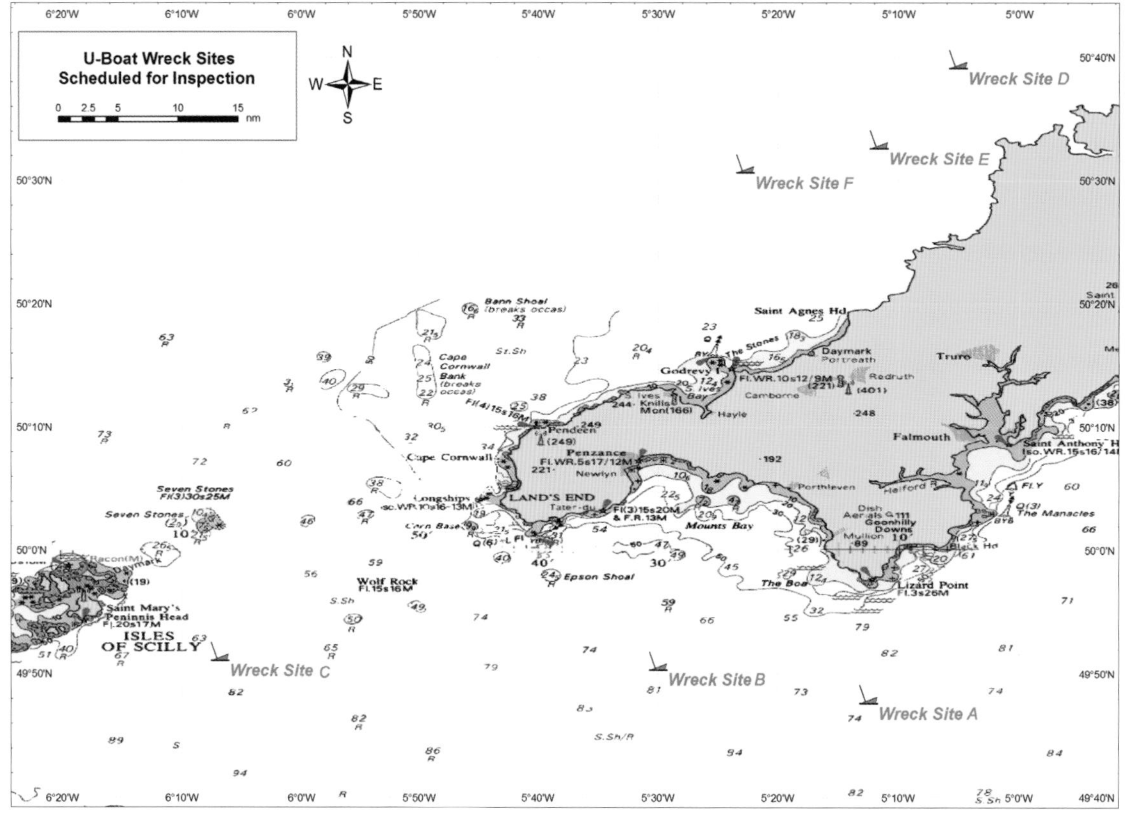

Fig. 1. Map of Odyssey's 2008 U-boat expedition area, denoting the locations of wreck sites visited.

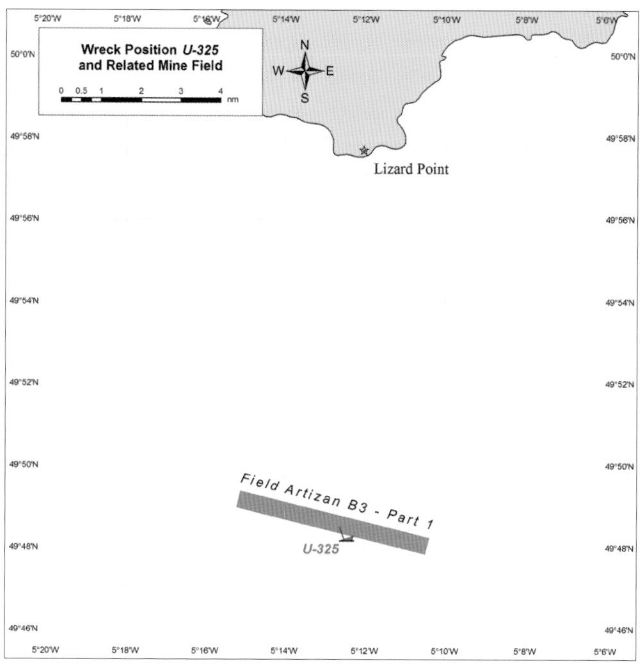

Fig. 2. Map showing wreck site U 325 alongside the English 1945 minefield location south of the Lizard.

2. Wreck Site A – U 325

In 2007 the wreck of a German World War II Type VIIC U-boat was discovered by Scuba divers off Lizard Point in the English Channel at coordinates 49°48.283N, 05°12.383W. No German wartime U-boat loss has been documented as existing in this position (Niestlé, 1998). Similarly, no anti-U-boat attack was ever recorded at or close to the present wreck location. Examination of all German U-boat losses in the general area revealed that U 399 and U 1018 lay closest to the wreck's position. However, although both boats were sunk, survivors picked up afterwards created a trail of positional data. Their wrecks have since been discovered by Scuba divers close to the recorded historical loss position of these boats (McCartney, 2003: 28-30).

On 17 July 2008 wreck site A was located at a depth of 84m, listing 80° to portside. Most of the former upper deck structure above the pressure hull, which had previously formed the outer lines of the vessel above the water line, is no longer intact. All pressure hull hatches are closed with both periscopes down. Forward hydroplanes show a 5° tilt upwards, while the aft hydroplanes are in a neutral position. The outer hatches of forward torpedo tubes Nos. II, III and IV are closed, while that of tube I is half open with a loaded torpedo still inside. At the extreme stern of the boat the forward part of a heavily crushed torpedo, formerly loaded in the aft torpedo tube (No. V), is sticking out of the remaining part of the tube, bent down towards port. The presence of live ordnance indicates a formerly unidentified wartime loss.

Visible battle damage to the wreck, apart from destruction caused by corrosion and obvious extensive post-war fishing activity, is limited to a semi-circular destruction area aft at the extreme end of the pressure hull, including a large hole in the pressure hull itself on the starboard side in front of the stern bulkhead (Fig. 3). The outer hull of the extreme stern with the two rudders attached is completely separated from the rest of the hull, lying just astern on the sea bottom. Battle damage on the wreck offers sufficient evidence to suggest that mining was the most plausible explanation of this submarine's loss.

In fact the British Royal Navy laid down various minefields in the general area during 1945. To counter the increasing number of schnorkel-fitted U-boats in UK coastal waters, on 15 January 1945 the First Sea Lord ordered a heavy anti-U-boat mining program to be undertaken in the Western Approaches, Plymouth and Portsmouth Commands. Three days later the Commander in Charge at Portsmouth and Commander in Charge at Plymouth were requested to prepare an agreed program for the laying of deep minefields in the English Channel on the assumption that 10,000 mines were available for the task. On 9 February 1945, the Plymouth's naval Commander-in-Charge forwarded to the Admiralty a plan for deep minefields in his Command, which would necessitate the expenditure of 3,600 mines. Mines were to be laid at a depth of 60ft in two parallel dog-legged lines, 5 and 7 miles seaward of the coastal convoy route and in conformity with it. Fields were to be completed first off Wolf Rock (Serial 'A': 800 mines), followed by the area off Lizard Head (Serial 'B': 1,400 mines) and finally off Start Point (Serial 'C': 1,400 mines). On 26 February 1945 the Admiralty approved the plan.

With priority given to the laying of the new fields in the Portsmouth Command, work on fields in the Plymouth Command, code-named operation 'Artizan', only started on 3 April 1945. Contrary to the initial plan, mine laying started with the fields of Serial 'B' off Lizard Head. Up to 30 April 1945, nine different fields (Serial B1, part 1 to 4, Serial B2, part 1 to 4, and Serial B3, part 1), comprising 900 mines, were laid. On 6 May 1945, following the German surrender, operations on the remaining fields was suspended.[3]

Comparison between the exact coordinates of the individual mine fields with the nautical position of the U-boat surveyed by Odyssey in 2008 revealed that the wreck's position is a near perfect match to field B3, part 1 (Fig. 2). This field was laid by the coastal minelayer HMS *Plover* escorted by the minesweepers HMS *Ilfracombe* and HMS *Shippigan*. After leaving Portsmouth at 16.12hrs on 29 April 1945, the mines were laid at a depth of 60ft between 08.14 and 08.42 the next day using 100 Mk XVII/XVII(8) units, along a line extending for 3.3 miles in a direction 283½° from position 49°48'03"N, 05°10'26"W. At 22.26hrs on the same day the ships returned to Portsmouth.[4] From the evidence reported above it is beyond all doubt that the U-boat in question was in fact lost to the secretly laid allied minefield, which remained unknown to German U-boat Command for the duration of the war.

With the minefield laid as late as 30 April 1945, only four German U-boats then designated for operations in the Channel area, and recorded as lost during the final days of the war, emerge as likely candidates for the wreck. The four boats in question are U 325, U 398, U 1017 and U 1055, all belonging to the famous Type VIIC, which was modified in 1944 with schnorkel equipment for continuous underwater operations (Niestlé, 1998: 228, footnote 46; 234, footnotes 110 and 115).

The survey of technical features on this first submarine wreck revealed the fitting of a Type 2 folding schnorkel installation in combination with a ring-float schnorkel valve and 'Jaumann'-type anti-radar coating above the exhaust outlet (Köhl and Niestlé, 1989: 35-6; Niestlé, 1994: 444-46; Figs. 4-5). In the area of the former upper deck in front of the conning tower only two compressed air bottles, fitted onto the pressure hull, were found. Pressure-tight containers holding five-men life-saving rubber dinghies, formerly fitted in the upper deck on the fore ship, were discovered on the sea bottom close to their former position. A Type LM42U mount of the 3.7cm anti-aircraft gun, originally located on the lower anti-aircraft gun bandstand aft of the conning tower, is clearly visible among the residual pile of debris from the former bridge construction on the port side of the wreck (Fig. 6). The outer hull at the forward end of the keel was not modified for the late-war balcony array of the multi-unit listening gear.

Although no direct identifying marks were found on the wreck, comparison of individual features with available information on the contemporary fittings of the four likely U-boats eventually led to the conclusion that the wreck must be U 325. Each of the other three boats in question could be positively excluded from the list on account of the wreck features described above. U 325 is known to have been fitted with the same schnorkel installation, including schnorkel valve and a type of anti-radar coating, as was found on the wreck.[5] The other wreck features are also identical to those present on U 325.

U 325 (Oberleutnant zur See Erwin Dohrn: Senior Lieutenant, U-boat commanding officer) left Trondheim in Norway on 20 March 1945 for its second war patrol in British inshore waters. On 29 March 1945 U-boat Command ordered the boat to occupy naval grid square

Fig. 3. Mine damage at the after end of the pressure hull, just forward of the stern bulkhead on the wreck of U 325, with a bent-up starboard propeller shaft underneath. The shape of the stern torpedo tube is faintly visible in the upper left corner.

Fig. 4. Schnorkel head lying on the deck of wreck of U 325, with the cylindrical part covered with Jaumann-type anti-radar camouflage.

Fig. 5. View of the ring-float schnorkel head installed on U 637 taken post-war at Lisahally, Northern Ireland, displaying a Jaumann anti-radar absorber used to camouflage the schnorkel head against radar detection, comparable to that installed on U 325. The layered absorber measured about 7cm in thickness. On top of the schnorkel head the 'Bali I' -detector antenna, used against metric radar sets, can be seen, which, however, were hardly in use any more in 1945.

Fig. 6. A Type LM42U gun mount, complete with 3.7cm M42U AA-gun, lying on the seabed beside the wreck of U 325. The gun mount is upside down with both sides of the hinged protection shield folded back. The circular object on the right is the bottom of a pressure-tight ready-ammunition container formerly fitted to the gun platform.

BE 3531 (50°03'N, 13°25'W) with an operational radius of 30 nautical miles. This order was however cancelled the next day and on 31 March 1945 the boat was advised to continue its southward passage west of Ireland as far as the latitude of naval grid square BE 31 (50°33'N). On 7 April 1945 U 325 sent a routine passage report from naval grid square AL 61 (55°47'N, 19°45'W), indicating that the boat had hauled far to the west on its outbound route. Three days later U-boat Command ordered U 325 to operate on the coastal convoy route on both sides of Lands End from Bull Point to Lizard Head. At the time of the cessation of hostilities, U-boat Command considered U 325 to be still operational. When U 325 thereafter failed to enter base or to show up at one of the Allied assembly points, its loss became apparent. No information about the cause of its loss was then available to U-boat Command.[6]

After the war the allied anti-submarine assessment committee attributed the loss of U 325 to a series of depth charge attacks by the destroyers HMS *Hesperus* and HMS *Havelock* on 30 April 1945 in position 53°42'N, 04°53'W. When fresh information on U 325's actual operational area became known from German records during the 1950s, the Naval Historical Branch of the British Ministry of Defense revised the original assessment. Now allocating the destruction of U 242 to the action on 30 April 1945, U 325 was then considered to have been lost to an unknown cause in the absence of any specific explanation.

Following the discovery of three hitherto unknown German World War II U-boat wrecks off the Cornish Coast between 1990 and 2001, the author believed that U 325 could be one of them, based on the fact that the position of the wrecks was situated well within its operational area. However, insufficient information on individual wreck features then available allowed any definitive interpretation (Niestlé, 2004). In light of the new information obtained during the 2008 Odyssey survey and presented above, previous conclusions about the likely wreck location of U 325 can no longer be retained.

From the fact that U 325 passed a transit report from the area west of Ireland and the absence of any promising Anti-Submarine attacks along its expected route or in its assigned operational area, it is most likely that U 325 arrived in its assigned operational area on or around 17 April 1945. Equipped with fuel and provisions for a patrol length of at least ten weeks, theoretically U 325 should have left its operational area for return to base no later than about 9 May 1945. Nothing is known about the final movements of U 325, but the wreck's position is within its assigned operational area, although at its eastern limit. German U-boats still at sea around Britain at the time of the German surrender started to surface from 9 May 1945 onwards in accordance with radio orders, with U 249, then also operating in the Channel, being the first German U-boat to surrender to allied forces on the same day. It is therefore reasonable to assume that U 325 would have acted accordingly or at least would have finally left its operational area at that time in order to commence return to base. Hence, it is assumed that U 325 was sunk with all hands between 30 April 1945 and 9 May 1945 by mining on the British field 'Artizan B3, part 1' in position 49°48.283'N, 05°12.383'W.

3. Wreck Site B – U 650

In 1976 the Risdon Beazley salvage company reported the discovery of a submarine wreck at coordinates 49°51.25'N, 05°29.86'W, which was confirmed in 1997 by a local Scuba diver. The presence of ferrous propellers pointed to the presence of a late World War II U-boat (McCartney, 2003: 27). On 17 July 2008, Odyssey surveyed the wreck of a German Type VIIC U-boat at a depth of 79m at position 49°51.061'N, 05°29.971W. The hull is heavily corroded and lies with a 75° list to port side on a flat, sandy bottom.

Almost all of the superstructure has disintegrated, with just piping and compressed air bottles left undisturbed. Periscopes and a Type 1 schnorkel mast with a ball float head are in a lowered position. The 3.7cm model LM42U anti-aircraft gun mount has fallen off its foundation and is lying on the seabed. The conning tower hatch is shut, while the forward torpedo hatch and galley hatch aft are open. Torpedo tubes II and V were found empty, the condition of tube IV remains unclear, and tubes I and III are inaccessible owing to accumulations of debris. Four life-saving rubber dinghy containers were found on the sea bottom below the fore ship. A modified ('Atlantic') bow is fitted without a towing eye conversion for underwater refueling. However,

Fig. 7. The massive gun mount for the 8.8cm deck gun features prominently on the wreck of U 650. Beneath is the lower part of the schnorkel mast lying on the deck. The circular opening of the pressure flange connecting to the fresh air intake tube, characteristic of the older Type 1 schnorkel installation, is partly obscured by the rectangular wooden deck cover of the former 8.8cm ready ammunition store located just behind the gun mount.

Fig. 8. Bow view of U 53 during building at Kiel, with the massive deck gun mount clearly visible on top of the pressure hull in front of the conning tower behind, which was technologically similar to U 650.

the most interesting and unusual feature of the wreck is the presence of the original 8.8cm deck gun platform in front of the conning tower (Figs. 7-8).

Battle damage to the wreck is apparently limited to a small breach in the pressure hull on the starboard side of the forward torpedo room (Fig. 9). From the interpretation of the wreck details it is evident that the U-boat was cruising submerged or had bottomed on the seabed when an explosion ruptured the pressure hull. The damage appears consistent with the destruction caused by a direct hit from a contact-fused hedgehog projectile, carrying a 35lb Torpex explosive charge. From the relative position of the damage it can be expected that large amounts of air must have escaped from inside the boat through the hole in the pressure hull. However, as no fuel oil tanks were located near the damage area, the submarine is expected to have only discharged small amounts of oil, if any at all. As a result of the structural damage, all compartments forward of the control room are likely to have been flooded instantly, making any attempts to surface the vessel impossible. The open hatches may implicate a possible attempt by surviving crew members to escape from the boat. Post-war, the upper structure disintegrated, probably by a combination of corrosion and fishing impacts.

From all German schnorkel-equipped U-boats directed to operate in the English Channel during the period June 1944 to May 1945, and presently recorded as missing or whose fate remains open to question, only U 650 fits the reported wreck details. The crucial wreck features underlying this conclusion was the installation of the original 8.8cm deck gun platform in front of the conning tower in combination with the presence of dinghy containers on the fore ship. None of the other U-boats presumed lost in the English Channel carried this fitting. With the wreck identified as U 650 without doubt, the reason for its loss still remains open to question.

U 650 (Oberleutnant zur See z.V. Rudolf Zorn: Senior Lieutenant, U-boat commanding officer) left Bergen/Norway on 9 December 1944 to continue its sixth patrol. Having initially sailed from Bergen on 26 November, the patrol had to be aborted north of the Shetlands owing to technical failures, returning to Bergen for repairs on 3 December. Shortly before midnight on 9 December 1944, U 650 was released by its escort V 5116 near the small island of Hellisoey at the northern end of the Fedjefjord. According to the daily log of U-boats on patrol kept at U-boat Command, the boat was instructed to travel through the Shetland-Faroe passage into the Atlantic, heading for a preliminary steering area west of Ireland. On the outbound trip U 650 kept strict radio silence in accordance with standing orders during November/December 1944, which instructed outbound boats to report positions only upon direct request. When U-boat Command assumed that the boat must have almost reached its preliminary steering area, U 650 was directed on 20 December 1944 to continue into the English Channel as its operational area, concentrating on attacking cross-Channel shipping off Cherbourg and Seine Bay. Together with U 325 and U 905, the boat was intended to be a replacement for U 322, U 485, U 486 and U 680, then operating in the Channel. On 30 December 1944 U-boat Command informed U 650 that its arrival in the allocated operational area was expected on or after 31 December 1944.

In the following weeks U-boat Command believed that the boat would continue to operate within its assigned area until the exhaustion of fuel and provisions forced it to commence the return voyage to Norway. When no status report was received by 5 February 1945, U-boat Command sent a reminder signal on the same day. In a

Owing to unexpected changes to the expeditions time schedule, eventually only two dives could be realized. Site D was first dived on 19 July 2008 and the U-boat hull was discovered in excellent visibility at a depth of 50.2m on a flat, sandy bottom. With the general condition of the wreck surprisingly good, much of the upper superstructure aft and forward of the conning tower is still in place. Battle damage caused by the explosion of the mine on contact at starboard in the area of the Petty Officer's living quarters, aft of the control room, is clearly apparent but localized. The force of the explosion formed a semi-circular destruction area measuring about 10m in diameter and caused a massive breach in the pressure hull. The complete superstructure in that area is now lying to starboard next to the hull on the sea bottom.

Among the debris a late-war Type LM43U gun mount with part of its 3.7cm M42U anti-aircraft gun still attached was discovered (Fig. 15). The boat is fitted with the old Type 1 folding schnorkel installation, which was installed up to autumn 1944, with a half-height pressure flange connection to the diesel air intake tube along the port side of the conning tower casing, in combination with a ring-float schnorkel valve with 'Wesch'-type anti-radar coating on the circular stem tube between the exhaust outlet and the ring-float head (Figs. 16-17). No anti-radar coating was found on the drum-shaped ring-float head. A circular grating in place of the deck gun platform in front of the conning is clearly visible (Figs. 18, 20). The extreme bow superstructure has collapsed and the towing eye is visible on the seabed. A balcony array for the multi-unit listening gear is fitted at the forward end of the keel (Fig. 19).

Site E was dived next on the same day. The wreck is sitting upright on a hard, flat sea bottom at a depth of 52.3m. Aft of the conning tower the complete hull and its superstructure remain in place, except for the wooden planking. This includes the hydroplanes, rudders, shafts, propellers and aft torpedo tube V at the extreme stern. The rudders and planes are in a neutral position. The after torpedo hatch and galley hatch are both shut. The hatch cover to the conning tower is missing, lying to one side on the sea bottom. Both periscopes are down. The former bridge structure has collapsed and slid down onto the seabed with a Type LM43U gun mount for the 3.7cm anti-aircraft gun lying inverted alongside the hull. Forward of the conning tower a 'Marcks' liferaft container has been fitted in place of the deck gun plate (Figs. 21-22), together with the old Type 1 schnorkel installation with a ball-float schnorkel valve and a 'Wesch'-type anti-radar coating on the schnorkel head. Battle damage is obvious just for-

Fig. 22. U 400 during its commissioning ceremony at the building yard of Howaltswerke Kiel on 18 March 1944. The Marcks-container positioned in front of the conning tower is clearly visible.

ward of the schnorkel head. The forward torpedo hatch is dislodged, with a large crack in the pressure hull running diagonally along its perimeter. The forward bow section with torpedo tubes has been completely separated from the rest of the hull by the force of the mine's explosion. Four pressure-proof dinghy containers formerly located on the forward deck now lie on the seabed.

The identification of U-boat wrecks depends to a high degree on finding key identification marks on hulls, which may lead to identification when compared with fitting features known to have been carried during the war on individual boats. Although U 400 is known to have carried one of the first Type LM43U anti-aircraft gun mounts for frontline testing, this item offers no help because this type of gun mount is present on both wrecks sites. Instead, other features proved to be the crucial factors. Site D is characterised by a circular grating in place of the deck gun plate in front of the conning tower, while site F had a 'Marcks' liferaft container fitted at that location.

By comparing war-time photographs it was observed that the circular grating plate, whose appearance on previous, low power lighted video footage had resembled that of a deck gun plate (Figs. 18, 20), was never fitted onto U 400 and her late-war sister boats built at the yard at Howaldtswerke Kiel. Instead, these boats did carry the 'Marcks' liferaft container in that location, which was moved to that position in order to free its original place for the cut in the upper deck required to insert a schnorkel. Correspondingly, U 1021 was fitted with a grating plate and very probably also with a modified balcony array for the multi-unit listening gear at the forward end of the keel present at wreck site.

Based on the available evidence it is now proposed to amend the historical records so that we can conclude that U 400 was mined on field 'HW A3' (site E). According to U-boat Command's daily plot, U 400 was expected to arrive in its operational area on or shortly after 14 December 1944. Thus, it is entirely plausible that U 400 met its fate only days after the new anti-submarine minefield was laid.

U 1021 was lost in field 'HY A1' (site D). This U-boat is expected to have arrived in its operational area on or about 10 March 1945. That appears to coincide with the sighting of a suspected periscope on the afternoon of 10 March 1945 by the minesweeping trawlers HMS *Concertator* and HMS *Lorraine* at position 50°36'N, 05°15'W. The trawlers carried out an attack, expending their full outfit of eight depth charges, without result. On the afternoon of 14 March 1945 the north-bound British steamer *Rolfsborg*, a straggler from convoy TBC-95, heard a heavy explosion when at a location 294° and 4 miles off Trevose Head, which converts to approximately 50°34'N, 05°07'W. Patches of oil were later observed on the surface of the sea. At the time of the incident there were no other surface vessels in the area. In light of this evidence it is possible that U 1021 met its end on that day.

It is most regretful that there was no opportunity to inspect the third U-boat wreck in position 50°32'24"N, 05°23'12"W (site F), previously misidentified as U 325, but with its identity now again open to question following the confirmed discovery of that U-boat off Lizard Head. This mystery will be solved hopefully by choosing the site as a dive target during a future expedition.

6. Conclusion

In 2008 Odyssey Marine Exploration mounted an expedition to determine the hitherto unknown or vague identities of World War II U-boat wrecks in the Western English Channel and north coast of Cornwall. The five wreck sites visited showed different levels of preservation due to wartime damage, natural degradation and the detrimental impact of bottom fishing trawling. Visual site reconnaissance was achieved using the Remotely-Operated Vehicle Zeus on board the research vessel *Odyssey Explorer*. Close cooperation between various specialists both before and during the dive operations ensured that key wreck features essential for successful forensic wreck examination were pre-selected.

Based on authoritative evidence obtained during the ROV surveys, the wrecks were eventually identified as the former German U-boats U 325, U 400, U 650, U 1021 and U 1208 (Fig. 23). Of these, U 325 and U 650 had been recorded as missing on patrol without any further information about their fate being available since the end of World War II. Offering fresh information on the boats' final patrols and fates, the 2008 Odyssey expedition results have now corrected previous errors in the operational history of the German U-boat campaign in the Western English Channel during the final phase of the war. The survey project stands out as a fine example of successful teamwork between marine archaeologists and historians rewriting naval history. Further expeditions could lift the secrets of the fate of many more known, but as yet unidentified U-boat wrecks strewn across the seabed around Great Britain and Atlantic waters.

Apart from the historical results achieved by the expedition, and the realization that high-tech ROV techniques in marine archaeology offer great potential for future survey options, it should not be forgotten that the wrecks visited during the expedition are the final resting place of 241 German submariners, who paid the ultimate price in loyal service for their country. Even after more than 60 years having passed since the fateful days of World War II, those killed on board are not forgotten by their families and relatives. There are no roses on a sailor's grave, but remembrance to those killed has now at least become a clear focal point in an underwater space. Odyssey Marine Exploration and the whole expedition team take special pride in this achievement of the expedition.

Acknowledgements

Results presented in this report would have been impossible without the initiative and support of Odyssey Marine Exploration. Special thanks go to Tom Dettweiler and Mark Martin as on-site Project Managers, Neil Cunningham Dobson and Hawk Tolson as Directors of Field Archaeology, and to the whole expedition team on board the *Odyssey Explorer.* John Oppermann helped greatly with support and encouragement. Gerhard Seiffert deserves special credit for producing the wreck site maps. Sean Kingsley, the Director of Wreck Watch International, kindly edited the manuscript for publication. This project would have been impossible without the support of Jason Williams, JWM Productions and the Discovery Channel, to whom I am extremely grateful for permission to produce some images used in this report. Last but not least, I would like to add to the credit numerous Scuba divers, especially my fellow researcher Innes McCartney, for their long-term help and courage shown in the past during their innumerable deep dives in the waters around Britain to uncover the secrets of German U-boat wrecks hidden in the darkness of the sea.

Notes

1. *British Admiralty. German, Italian, and Japanese U-boat Casualties during the War* (HMSO, London, 1946).
2. 'German U-boat Records, Memorandum by Commander Kenneth A. Knowles, 7 September 1945'. In: D. Syrett (ed.), *The Battle of the Atlantic and Signals Intelligence: U-boat Tracking Paper, 1941-1947* (Ashgate, 2002), 346-50.
3. *British Mining Operations, 1939-1945, Naval Staff History, BR 1736(56), Vol. I* (London, 1973), 250-52
4. Supra Note 3, 262-63. Times are given as Central European Time (GMT+1).
5. TNA DEFE 3/743, Teleprinted Translations of Decrypted German U-boat Traffic, December 1942-May 1945, ZTPGU 38115.
6. TNA, DEFE 3/742, ZT GU 37736, 37758, 37736, and 37795, DEFE 3/743, ZTPGU 38024; National

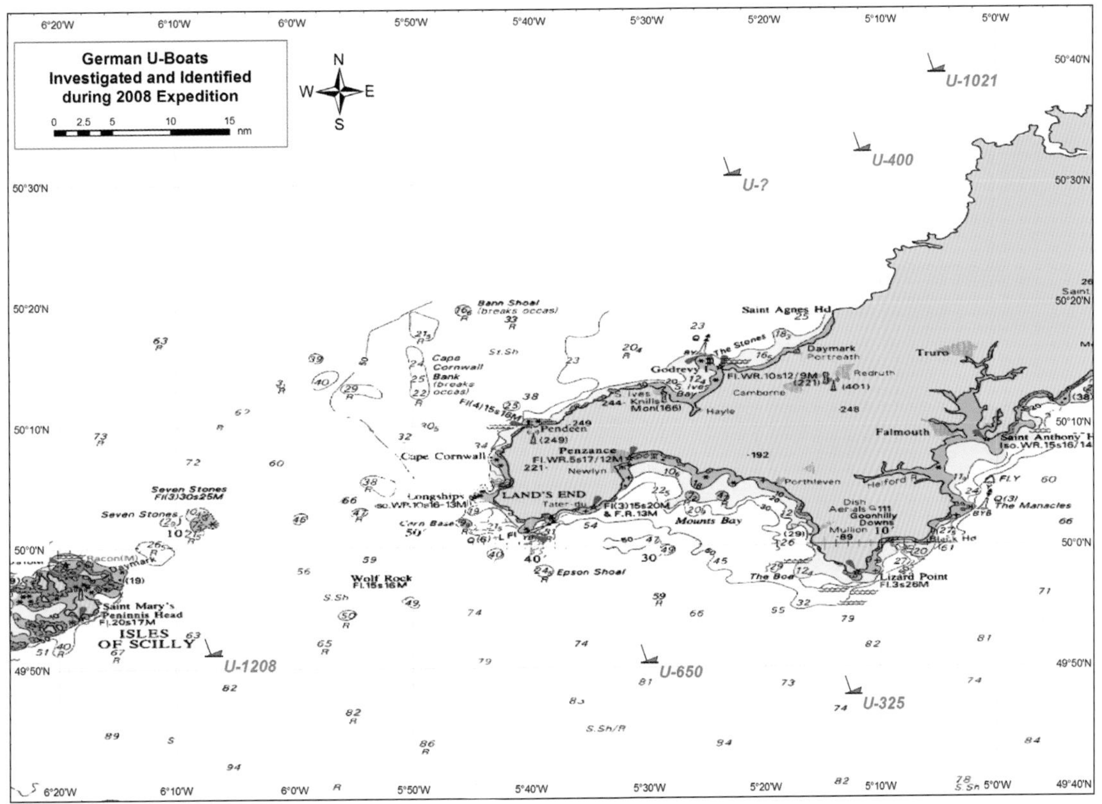

Fig. 23. Map of Odyssey's 2008 U-boat expedition area, correlating the locations of wreck sites with reassessed U-boat losses.

Archives and Records Administration, College Park, Maryland (hereafter NARA II), Microfilm Publication T1022, roll 4082, RG 242, record item PG 31798c, Befehlshaberder Unterseeboote (BdU) Situation Report #823, 10.04.45, ComNavEu Confidential Report 1178 of 14 June 1945, Enclosure (A), Part G: German Naval High Command, Location of Operational U/boats at Time of Surrender , record item PG 13953 NID.

7. TNA, DEFE 3/742, ZTPGU 33807, 34559, 34910, 34923, 36028, 36099; NARA II, T1022, rolls 4066 & 3981, RG 242, record item PG 30359 – PG 30362, *Kriegstagebuch des Befehlshabers der Unterseeboote* (hereafter KTB/BdU), 26.11.44 – 15.01.1945.
8. ComNavEu Confidential Report 1178 of 14 June 1945, Enclosure (A), record item PG 13953 NID.
9. National Defence Headquarters, Directory of History and Heritage, Document 81-520-8440, Box 304, File 3, Report of Proceedings 9th Escort Group 29 Dec 1944 to 25 Jan 1945, p.3.
10. See Note 9, attachment list of wrecks and non-submarine contacts.
11. TNA, ADM 199/1442, Plymouth Command: War Diaries 1945.
12. TNA, ADM 199/603, T.B.C. and B.T.C. convoys: 1944/1945.
13. NARA II, RG 457, SRH 236, submarine warfare message reports, Admiralty to Cominch 24 May 1942 to 12 June 1945, Serials 1551 and 1597.
14. NARA II, T1022, roll 4066, RG 242, record item PG 30362 KTB/BdU, entries for 14.01.45 – 15.01.1945; TNA, DEFE 3/740, ZTPGU 35766, 35889, 35931; DEFE 3/741 ZTPGU 36058.
15. TNA, DEFE 3/737, ZTPGU 32950, 32987, DEFE 3/738, ZTPGU 33437, 33529, 33681, 33883, 3905.
16. *British Mining Operations, 1939-1945, Naval Staff History, BR 1736(56), Vol. I* (London, 1973), 207-211.

Bibliography

Ballard, R.D. and Archbold, R., *The Discovery of the Bismarck* (London, 1990).

Garzke, W.H., Jr. and Dulin, R.O., Jr., 'Who Sank the Bismarck?', *Naval Institute Proceedings* (June 1991), 48-57.

Köhl, F. and Niestlé, A., *U-Boottyp VIIC* (Koblenz, 1989).

McCartney, I., *Lost Patrol – Submarine Wrecks in the English Channel* (Penzance, 2003).

Niestlé, A., 'German Technical and Electronic Development'. In S. Howarth and D. Law (ed.), *The Battle of the Atlantic 1939-1945, the 50th Anniversary International Naval Conference* (London 1994).

Niestlé, A., *German U-boat Losses during World War II* (Naval Institute Press, Annapolis, 1998).

Niestlé, A., *The Loss of U 325, U 400 and U 1021* (2004): http://uboat.net/articles/index.html?article=69.

Niestlé, A., 'The Role of Ultra in the Assessment of German U-boat Losses', *World War II Quarterly* 5.3 (2008), 40-45.

Whitby, M. (ed.), *Commanding Canadians: The Second World War Diaries of A.F.C. Layard* (UBC Press, Vancouver, 2005).

Young, R. and Armstrong, P., *Silent Warriors, Submarine Wrecks of the United Kingdom, Vol. 2* (Stroud, 2009).

further signal on 9 February 1945 the boat was ordered to head for the port of Stavanger in Norway. In the absence of any report from U 650 after its departure from Bergen on 9 December 1944, and its failure to reach a German base, U-boat Command eventually posted U 650 as missing in the English Channel with effect from 7 January 1945. The given date for its loss was necessarily somewhat arbitrary in the absence of any clue about its loss, but clearly indicates that U-boat Command assumed that the boat reached its assigned operational area before disappearing.[7]

From Ultra signal intelligence the British U-boat tracking room at the Admiralty Operational Intelligence Centre was aware that U 650 had ceased patrols, although the exact date of the boat's departure could not be established. Also U-boat Commands operational order of 20 December was duly intercepted, but could not be read owing to the newly introduced special one-time pad cipher system in German U-boat radio traffic. Only from U-boat Commands signal of 30 December 1944 did it became known that U 650 was bound for operations in the Channel. However, similar to the situation on the German side, the tracking room had no clue about the whereabouts of U 650 in the following months, except for the fact that it did not return to base. On 5 March 1945 the boat was eventually recorded as lost to unknown causes sometime during January 1945. After the war the allied assessment committee similarly felt unable to attribute the loss of U 650 to any known anti-submarine attack carried out along its outbound route or in the English Channel during the given period when the boat supposedly disappeared. Therefore, the loss of U 650 remained unexplained and the boat was recorded as 'lost to unknown cause' in the joint official list on the assessment of German U-boat losses during World War II.[8]

Following the daily plot kept by U-Boat Command, it is reasonable to assume that its loss must have taken place sometime during January 1945. No anti-U-boat attack took place during the war at the present wreck location. A detailed examination of all anti-submarine attacks during January 1945 in the general area of the wreck site revealed two anti-submarine incidents in the general area (Fig. 10):

- On 15 January 1945 by the frigates HMCS *Saint John* and HMCS *Port Colborne* in position 49°54'N/05°40'W.
- On 21 January 1945 by the corvette HMS *Dahlia* in position 49°56'N/ 05°35'W.

Both attacks were apparently not examined by the U-boat assessment committee because no report could be located in the official archives. The Report of Proceedings of

Fig. 9. Battle damage on the wreck of U 650, displaying a dent in the forward part of the pressure hull level at the after end of the forward torpedo room. The size of the opening compares to the open rectangular battery-loading hatch, measuring 70 x 45.6cm. Battle damage is consistent with the destruction expected by a direct hit from a contact-fused projectile fired from a Mk 10 Hedgehog A/S mortar used during World War II.

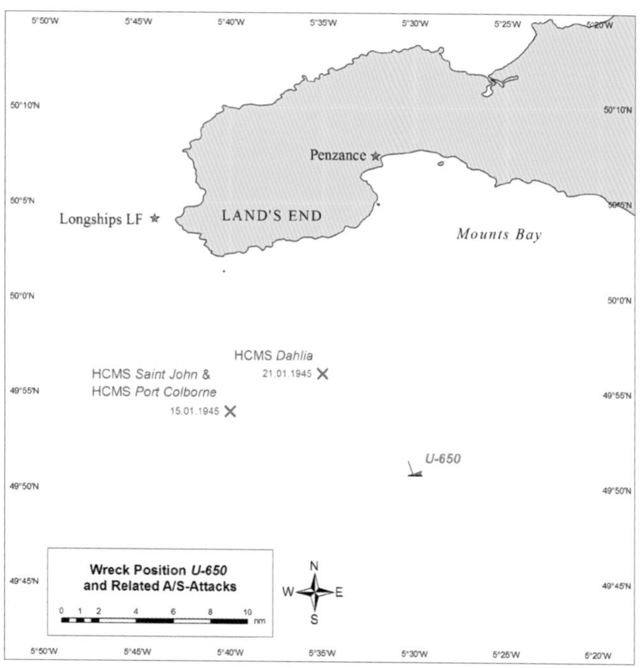

Fig. 10. Map showing wreck site U 650 in the Western English Channel in relation to known Allied anti-submarine attack positions.

Escort Group 9 for the period between 29 December 1944 and 25 January 1945 merely mentions that on 15 January 1945 several Anti-Submarine contacts were investigated and attacked in the vicinity of Wolf Rock, which were all finally classified as wrecks or non-subs.[9] More substantial information is documented in the diaries of the commanding officer of HMCS *Saint John* (Whitby, 2005: 268):

> "Monday, January 15 – At Sea
> A quiet fairly undisturbed night. We arrived back off the Lizard at about 0800 and turned round to the W. once more. As soon as it was properly light I turned to 310° to sweep up to the E. of the Wolfe. At about 1030 [GMT] P.C. [*Port Colborne*] got contact and we had to go and investigate it. A bottom contact of indefinite proportions and not previously plotted and so I decided to attack. It was difficult to hold and after 2 H/H [Hedgehog] attacks we lost it and spent some time bumming round. P.C. then got off on yet another echo while we at last regained the first one and attacked it again twice. Nothing but fish and a wisp of oil and so classified it wreck."

From the description in the diary the result of the attacks was inconclusive. Although the damage on the wreck of U 650 could well have resulted from a hedgehog projectile exploding on the deck casing, the apparent absence of any air bubbles coming to the surface indicates that the target attacked on 15 January 1945 was probably one of the non-submarine objects located frequently by the ships of Escort Group 9 during their patrol in January 1945. Moreover, a list of all new non-submarine contacts obtained by ships of Escort Group 9 between 29 December 1944 and 25 January 1945, appended to the Report of Proceedings, records no position at or close to the reported wreck position.[10]

The attack by HMS *Dahlia* on 21 January 1945 took place nearest to the wreck. The present site location is about 7 nautical miles bearing 130° true away from *Dahlia*'s historical attack position. Unfortunately, no report of her attack could be found among allied records. Therefore, information remains somewhat enigmatic. What is clear is that while escorting the eastbound nine-ship coastal convoy BTC-44, the corvette obtained a submerged contact on her asdic. The war diary of Plymouth Command contains the following entry for 21 January 1945:[11]

> "At 0859 this morning HMCS [sic] *Dahlia*, escorting convoy BTC 44, attacked a firm contact in position 140 deg Longships 10 miles; *Icarus* and *Duncan* of the 14th Escort Group, were despatched to take over from *Dahlia* but at 1000 the latter decided her target to be non-sub and proceeded to rejoin her convoy."

The report of the Convoy Commodore for BTC-44 mentioned the incident in a single sentence (but without disclosing the identity of the escort): "Escort dropped D/Cs [Depth Charges] off Bute Head. No results observed."[12] It should be noted that the reported nautical coordinates for the attack place it in a position about 13 nautical miles bearing 130° from Longships, which slightly differs from the information recorded in the war diary of Plymouth Command cited above. Moreover, with the actual wreck position about 21 nautical miles bearing 130° from Longships, its bearing is identical to that calculated for *Dahlia*'s attack. No information is available to assess the navigational accuracy in the positioning of the attack under the prevailing conditions. HMS *Dahlia*, like other Flower-class corvettes in 1945, was fitted with depth charge throwers and a Mk 10 hedgehog mortar. Therefore, it is possible that hedgehog projectiles were fired in the attack. It is regrettable that no other information on the action of HMS *Dahlia* on 21 January 1945 appears to have been preserved. In the absence of data it is impossible to reach a final conclusion about the identity of the contact and the result of her attack on this date.

Based on the information given above a final decision about the cause of U 650's loss is considered impossible at present. Nevertheless, it is proposed to correct the record of how U 650 was lost during January 1945 with the conclusion that its demise was caused by a hedgehog attack by an as yet unidentified allied vessel in the position 49°51.061'N, 05°29.971'W.

4. Wreck Site C – U 1208

On 24 February 1945 a German U-boat was sunk in a series of attacks by the frigates HMS *Duckworth* and HMS *Rowley* of the British Escort Group 3 south-west of Lands End at position 49°55'N, 06°08'W. Following the torpedoing of the British freighter *Oriskany* in convoy BTC.78 early on the morning of 24 February 1945, the ships of Escort Groups 3 and 15 started to search for the attacker. After six hours *Rowley* made an asdic contact at 10.20hrs on a U-boat contact steering south-west and just under the surface of the sea. Following several unsuccessful attacks, oil was observed on the water's surface after a hedgehog attack carried out by *Duckworth* at 12.25hrs. Further attacks against the now bottomed contact resulted in conclusive evidence for the destruction of a U-boat. At the time the action was assessed as "U-boat probably sunk" (Young and Armstrong, 2009: 334-8).

On 27 March 1945 the British U-boat tracking room at the Admiralty Operational Intelligence Centre tentatively identified U 480 as the attacked and sunk boat, probably based on pieces of very thin synthetic rubber picked up from the scene afterwards. U 480 was known to have been covered with rubber sheets (codenamed 'Alberich') as a counter measure against allied sonar detection.[13] After the war the allied assessment committee felt no reason to question the wartime tracking room allocation.

However, in 1997 the wreck of a German Type VII C U-boat with an 'Alberich' rubber anti-sonar coating was found by Scuba divers in the English Channel to the south-west of Portsmouth at position 50°22'04"N, 01°44'10"W. With U 480 known to have been the only 'Alberich'-coated U-boat lost in the Channel area, the identity of this wreck must in fact be U 480. Hence, the identity of the U-boat sunk by the frigates of Escort Group 3 on 24 February 1945 off Lands End became again open to question (McCartney, 2003: 99-100).

On 18 July 2008 ROV Zeus located the wreck of a German Type VII C U-boat in 81m of water at position 49°51.783'N, 006°06.750'W (site C, Fig.1). The hull is heavily corroded and lying with a 45° list to portside on a flat, sandy bottom. The wreck displays widespread battle damage, especially forward of the conning tower, where large sections of the pressure hull are missing or stove in (Fig. 11). Almost all of the superstructure has disintegrated, only with piping and air flasks undisturbed. The periscopes are in a lowered position. Most of the schnorkel installation is missing owing to battle damage forward. No anti-aircraft guns were observed, partly due to heavy fishing netting across the port mid-ship section of the hull, which made ROV inspection impossible. The modified 'Atlantic' bow is fitted with a towing eye conversion for underwater refueling (Figs. 12-13). No balcony array for the multi-unit listening gear was observed at the forward end of the keel. The extensive wartime damage is evidently the result of numerous 'tin-opener' depth charge attacks, which were carried out by various allied escort vessels in the days after the sinking in an effort to secure evidence from inside the hull leading to a positive identification of the sunken U-boat.

According to operational orders signaled from U-boat Command to boats on frontline patrol up to 24 February 1945, a total of six German U-boats may have been operating in the English Channel on that date. Of these, only U 1004 and U 1203 returned from patrol while U 927, U 1018, U 1208 and U 1279 went missing. From those lost on patrol, only U 1018 is now recorded as known sunk on 27 February 1945 by ships from Escort Group 2 in position 49.56'N, 05.20'W, with two survivors being picked up from the sea. No conclusive information about the fate of the other three boats has been obtained so far. Already during the war the British U-boat tracking room at the Admiralty Operational Intelligence Centre became aware of their loss from Ultra signal intelligence. However, similar to the situation on the German side, the tracking room had no exact clue as to the whereabouts of these three boats in the following months, except the fact that they never returned to base. Based on available information about allied anti-submarine attacks along their outbound track, or within the assigned operational areas, eventually their losses were tentatively allocated to the following attacks:

- U 927: air attack by Warwick 'V' of RAF Squadron 179 on 24 February 1945 in the Channel at position 59°54'N, 04°43'W.
- U 1208: depth charge attack by the sloop HMS *Amethyst* on 20 February 1945 south of Ireland at position 51°48'N, 07°07'W.
- U 1279: depth charge attack by the frigates HMS *Bayntun*, HMS *Braithwaite* and HMS *Loch Eck* on 3 February 1945 north-west of Bergen in position 61.21'N, 02.00'E.

A new investigation by the British MoD/NHB-FDS in 1991 revealed that the U-boat sunk by HMS *Amethyst* was in fact U 1276, based on a name label of a crew member from U 1276 attached to articles of clothes picked up after the attack. Hence, the fate of U 1208 again became open to question.

U 1208 (Korvettenkapitän Georg Hagene) left Kristiansand on 14 January 1945 for its first patrol. At 20.13hrs on 31 January 1945 the boat sent a routine passage report from naval grid square AM 4855 (54°09'N, 13°45'W). In return, U-boat Command directed the

Fig. 11. An example of the massive, widespread battle damage visible on the forward part of U 1208's pressure hull, caused by numerous depth charges dropped on the bottomed wreck ('tin-opener' attacks) after its sinking in order to obtain evidence for the boat's identity from paperwork and other material that would hopefully float to the surface.

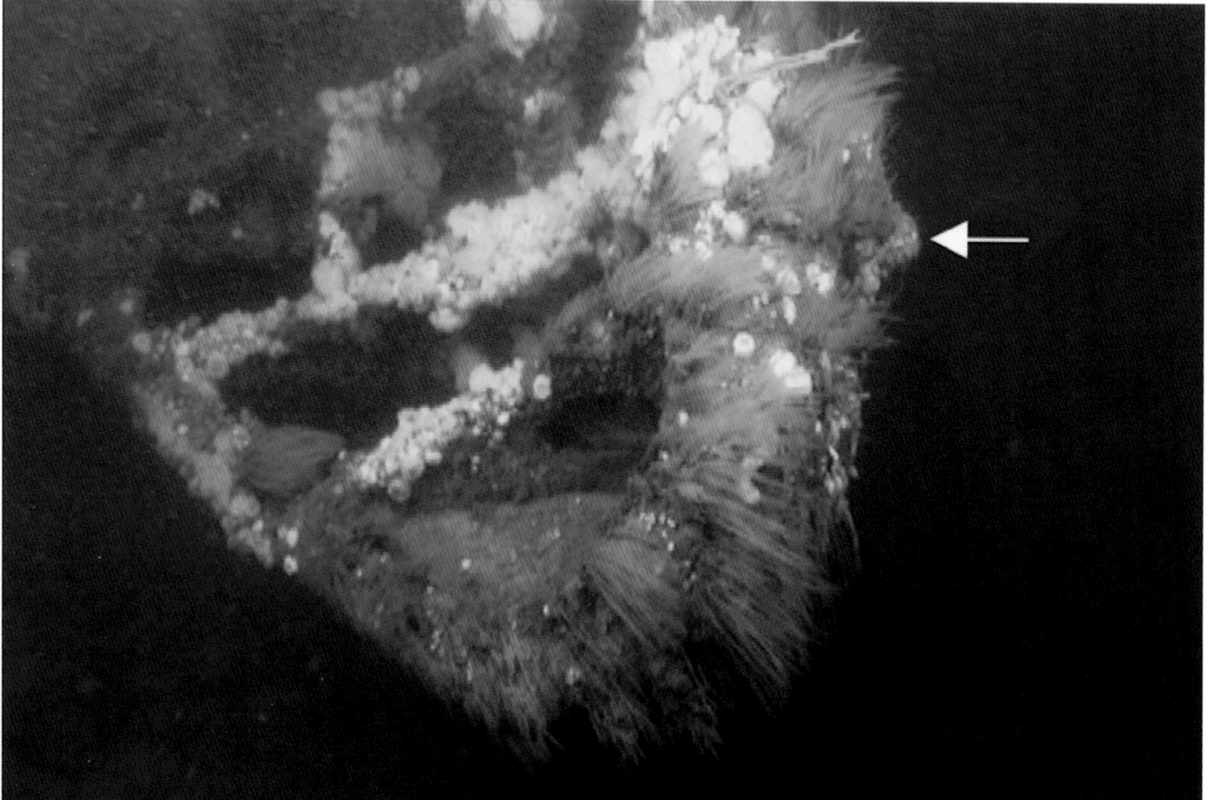

Fig. 12. The bow of U 1208's wreck, with an arrow pointing to the fastener for the antenna cable. Its sister ship, U 1206, was the first boat of the building yard Danziger Werft to be completed with this new design.

Fig. 13. U 1056 during its launching ceremony in April 1944 at the building yard of Germaniawerft AG Kiel, showing the enlarged Atlantic bow of U 1208 type and towing eye conversion for underwater refuelling. The radio antenna cable is fixed to a fastener visible on the right side of the towing eye. A number of different designs to fix antenna cables were used by U-boat building yards or on individual batches of newly built U-boats.

boat on 1 February 1945 to patrol against shipping at the western exit of the English Channel. On 5 February U-boat Command granted freedom to all boats then operating in the Channel to leave their assigned operational area towards the middle of the Channel or towards the coastal convoy route under the British coast between Brighton and Lands End in case no traffic was encountered in the erstwhile area. U 1208 should have arrived at the western exit of the Channel on or about 8 February. Having acquainted itself with the conditions inside this area, it is perfectly plausible that U 1208 closed the traffic focal point at Lands End. No further message was received from the boat after its last signal on 31 January 1945. When the boat later failed to return to Bergen, U-boat Command posted it as missing in its operational area effective from 5 March 1945.[14]

Comparison of the individual wreck features found during Odyssey's 2008 survey of the wreck, and a subsequent examination of available video footage, produced sufficient evidence to define its identity. Crucial features leading to the identification were the absence of the balcony array for the multi-unit listening gear and the presence of the 'Atlantic' bow with towing eye conversion for underwater refueling. These observations thus excluded U 927 and U 1279 from the list of likely candidates, leaving U 1208 as the only other possible alternative for this particular U-boat wreck. The identity of the U-boat sunk on 24 February 1945 by the two frigates of Escort Group 3 has thus been established without doubt as U 1208, which was lost with all 49 men on board.

5. Wreck Sites D, E & F – U 1021 & U 400

Between the years 1990 and 2001 Scuba divers discovered three wartime wrecks of German World War II Type VIIC U-boats off the Cornish coast (sites D, E and F). Previously, no German U-boats at all had been recorded as wartime losses in these waters. A thorough examination of all German U-boat losses in historical records revealed that all boats recorded as lost up to the end of November 1944, having been directed to operate off Cornwall, are known to have sunk in other areas. After November 1944 several more Type VIIC boats received explicit orders to operate in the general area off the Cornish coast between Lands End and Milford Haven. Of these, U 400, U 1021 and U 325 never returned. Thus, it was assumed that these three U-boats had to be identical to the three wrecks in question. Based on somewhat incomplete wreck information obtained during former Scuba dives, a first guess about their individual identities was made in 2004 (Niestlé, 2004).

Previous research had also established that all three U-boats were lost to mining on secretly laid allied minefields, which remained unknown to German U-boat Command for the duration of the war. At the end of October 1944 intercepted 'Ultra' intelligence exposed the German intention for a probable renewal of U-Boat operations between Lands End and the Bristol Channel from Norwegian bases. On 29 October 1944 U-boat Command radioed a situation report for the Bristol Channel area to all boats at sea, which was to be kept permanently by the boats in their situation report files. Accordingly, it clarified that the limits of Britain's declared mine area were as follows: 52°10'N, 06°15'W and 52°00'N, 07°35'W through 51°35'N, 06°15'W and 51°00'N, 07°15'W to 51°01'N, 04°31'W and 50°33'N, 05°01'W. Noting that British authorities last mentioned the area in relation to naval warfare at the beginning of 1943, the boats were informed that otherwise no evidence was available that mines were still there. It was assumed that the minefields had not been renewed, so there would no longer be any danger to the boats.

The German situation report further provided the coordinates of the English convoy route along the Channel as operating at 51°05N, 04°43'W as far as 51°02N, 04°32'W to 50°33'N, and 05°02'W as far as 50°35'N, 05°15'W. Boats were informed to expect around three convoys steaming for the Channel ports daily from and to the Bristol Channel, passing Lands End at night, as well as war and merchant vessels sailing singly. On 18 November 1944 the Bristol Channel situation report was amended so that it now assumed the presence of minefields inside the declared area, to which the U-boats were reminded to pay attention. However, U-boat Command gave assurances that English convoy shipping routes radioed in were mine-free. Four days later U 680, which had left Bergen on 13 November 1944 for a patrol in British coastal waters, was directed to become the first boat to occupy the area cited in the Bristol Channel situation report as an attacking area. However, following a promising situation report from the English Channel area by U 978, U 680 was redirected to the latter area on 2 December 1944. Only two days latter U 400 received the order to patrol off the Cornish coast as a replacement for U 680.[15]

Through Ultra decrypts the British Admiralty was well and timely informed about all of the above-mentioned German situation reports and operational intentions. On 15 November 1944 the Admiralty issued a policy signal to the Commander in Charge of the Western Approaches, stating that:

> "...further consideration has been given to the relative importance of anti-U-boat minefields in the NW and SW Approaches. Routing of ocean convoys south of Ireland not only renders this the more attractive area but U-boats' course of action can to some extent be anticipated. In the NW Approaches, mine-laying operations must follow rather than anticipate U-boat activities... Consider therefore as a matter of policy that mine-laying operations should be concentrated in the SW Approaches."

In pursuance of their stated policy, and to meet the expected concentration of U-boats in the southwestern Approaches, the Admiralty ordered by signal on 25 November 1944 that the minelayer HMS *Apollo* should lay three lines of deep mines off Trevose Head before cleaning boilers and making good defects at Plymouth. Operation 'HW' was to be conducted by the Commander in Charge of Plymouth and it was anticipated that the minelayer HMS

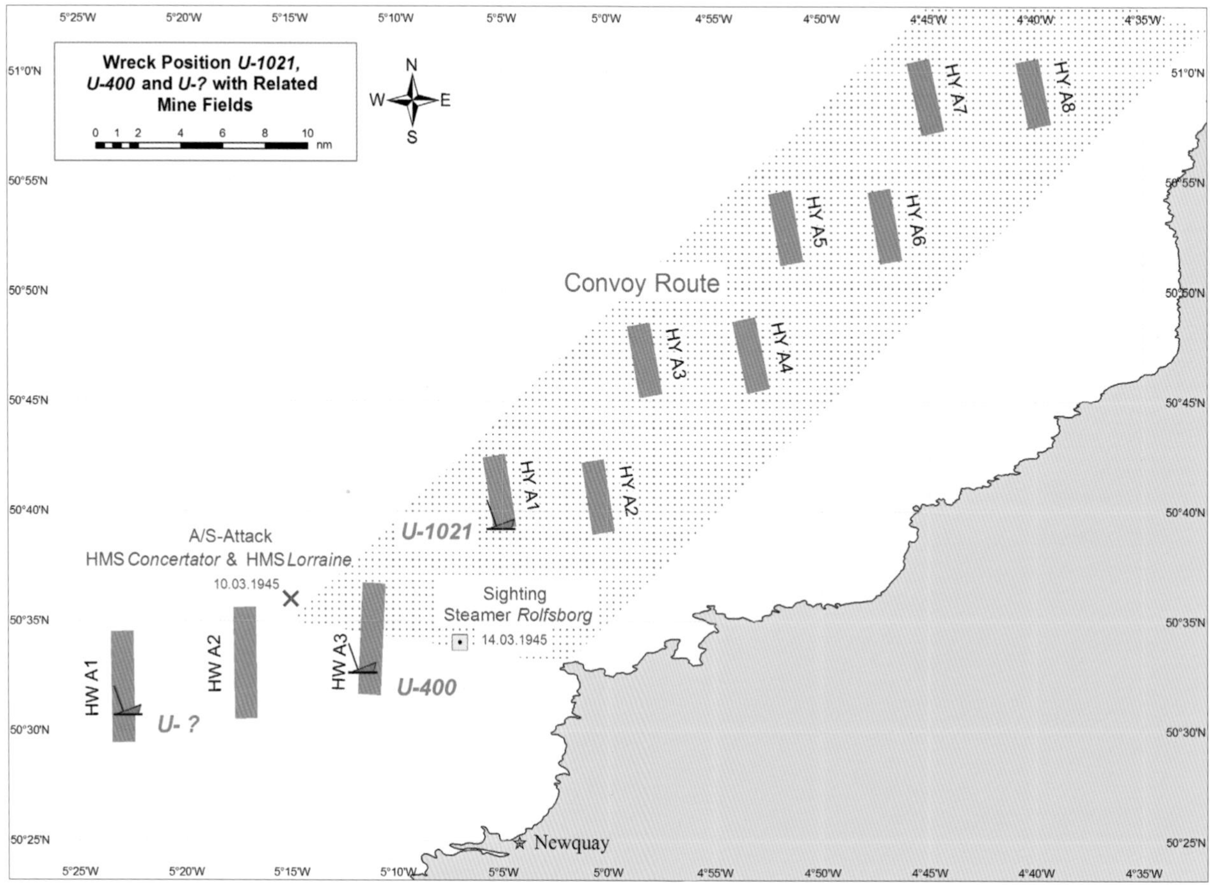

Fig. 14. Map showing the locations of wreck sites off the Cornish coast in relation to British mine field positions.

Plover would be available at the beginning of December to continue establishing these fields along the swept channel between Trevose Head and Hartland point in operation 'HY'. Between 29 November 1944 and 3 January 1945 the two minelayers laid over 1,200 Mk XVII moored mines in 11 'deep fields' across the coastal convoy route along the north coast of Cornwall.[16] Moored mines were used because ground mines sensitive enough to catch slow-moving U-boats would also have posed a threat to Allied surface ships. It should be noted that these mines were placed exactly within the area U-boat Command had explicitly declared mine-free in its amendment to the Bristol Channel situation report of 18 November 1944. Being aware of this advice, the British Admiralty set a well placed mine trap.

Comparison of the exact geographical coordinates of the individual minefields with the nautical positions of the three German U-boat wrecks revealed that each of the wreck positions is a near-perfect match with one of the above-mentioned minefields at sites D, E and F (Fig. 14):

- Site D (50°39'48"N, 05°05'04"W) rests in the southern half of field 'HY A1' laid by *Plover* on 12 December 1944. Consisting of 100 Mk XVII (39)/XVII units, it spread along a line extending for 3.3 miles in direction 171° from position 50°42.5'N, 05°05.4'W at a depth of 70ft. Two surface failures were reported during laying.

- Site E (50°33'16"N, 05°11'37"W) is situated in the southern half of field 'HW A3', laid by *Apollo* between 01.31 and 01.56hrs on 3 December 1944. Consisting of 156 Mk XVII (39)/XVII units, it spread along a line extending for 5 miles in direction 182.5° from position 50°36.7'N, 05°11.1'W at a depth of 70ft. One possible failure was observed during laying.

- Site F (50°32'24"N, 05°23'12"W) lays at the southern end of field 'HW A1', laid by Apollo between 01.31 and 01.56hrs on 29 November 1944. Consisting of 156 Mk XVII (39)/XVII units, it spread along a line extending for 5 miles in direction 179° from position 50°34.5'N, 05°23.0'W at a depth of 70ft.

Initially Odyssey anticipated surveying all three U-boat wrecks in the area to obtain new and comparative information.

Fig. 15. A late-war Type LM43U gun mount, complete with a 3.7cm M42U AA-gun lying on the seabed besides the wreck of U 1021 (site D). The gun mount is inverted with the gun breech present just above the sandy sea bottom. The crew protection shield has already fallen off.

Fig. 16. The schnorkel top on U 1021 and its ring float valve. Contrary to the same installation shown in Figs. 4-5, this example is covered with Wesch-type anti-radar camouflage, displaying a thin plastic layer with a waffle-like surface. Normally only applied to the curved structure of ball-float schnorkel heads, it was occasionally also fitted to other head types. Incidentally, the supporting ring at the lower end of the head valve, designed to back the more bulky Jaumann-type absorber, is clearly visible on U 1021's schnorkel head.

Fig. 17. The ring-float schnorkel head installed on U 826 (similar to U 1021), taken post-war at Lisahally, Northern Ireland, displaying a Wesch-type anti-radar absorber to camouflage the schnorkel head against radar detection. Like the Jaumann-type absorber, it was glued onto the metal surface of the head valve and the smaller stem tube below, above the exhaust outlet to the right. The latter should be submerged when the U-boat proceeded at correct schnorkel diving depth.